2012
CyberArts

ARS ELECTRONICA

HATJE
CANTZ

PRIX ARS ELECTRONICA 2012

Damien Hirst, Spot Painting and Ars Electronica 2012

Hannes Leopoldseder

What do Damien Hirst, spot painting and Ars Electronica 2012 have to do with each other? At first glance, nothing. However, when I began thinking about the Festival's theme—THE BIG PICTURE—, Damien Hirst's "spot paintings", which are currently showing at the Tate Gallery in London, came to my mind. Damien Hirst entitled one of these 1994 pictures *Anthraquinone-1-Diazonium Chloride*. And he wrote about the process: ... "to create that structure, to do those colors, and do nothing. I suddenly got what I wanted. It was just a way of pinning down the joy of color."[1]

THE BIG PICTURE—this means the big frame within which the digital revolution is happening: everything is changing, in our lives, in the economy, in culture, in education, in politics—I could list as many different areas as there are spots in Hirst's paintings.

Though here I'll just concentrate on two of them: politics and education, two areas in which unexpected upheaval is imminent.

The speed at which different areas of our lives are being digitized is accelerating constantly. Everywhere. And with Occupy, Anonymous, WikiLeaks and the Pirates—the Internet has finally entered the political arena.

In early 2006, a Swede named Rickard Falkvinge founded the Pirate Party. Its point of departure was the fight for free software and the right to ignore copyright laws. The Pirates did not, interestingly enough, give the party its name, but the traditional media, which wanted to protect copyrights and, by calling them "Pirates", hoped to give them a negative image. Yet instead, these copyright objectors not only accepted the name, but saw in it a positive concept of freedom, one going back to the freebooters of the sea.

It is an irony of history: a new party could not have been given a better name.

Already in the pioneering years of filmmaking, in *The Black Pirate* from 1926, actor Douglas Fairbanks creates a pirate-like character who seeks revenge on the pirates responsible for his father's

Was haben Damien Hirst, Spot Painting und Ars Electronica 2012 miteinander zu tun? Auf den ersten Blick nichts. Beim Nachdenken über das Festivalthema THE BIG PICTURE erinnerte ich mich jedoch an die „Spot Paintings" von Damien Hirst, zurzeit in der Tate Gallery in London zu sehen. *Anthraquinone-1-Diazonium Chloride*, so betitelt Damien Hirst eines dieser Bilder aus dem Jahr 1994. Er schreibt dazu: „To create that structure, to do those colours, and do nothing. I suddenly got what I wanted. It was just a way of pinning down the joy of colour".[1]

THE BIG PICTURE – das bedeutet den großen Rahmen, innerhalb dessen sich der digitale Umbruch vollzieht: Alles wird anders, im Leben, in der Wirtschaft, in der Kultur, in der Bildung, in der Politik – man könnte so viele Punkte aufzählen, wie es Spots in Hirsts Bildern gibt.

Ich konzentriere mich im Weiteren auf die Spots Politik und Bildung, zwei Bereiche, in denen ein unvermuteter Umbruch bevorstehen wird.

Die Geschwindigkeit der Digitalisierung unserer Lebensbereiche hat um einen deutlichen Schub bekommen. Überall. Mit Occupy, Anonymous, WikiLeaks und den Piraten ist das Internet schließlich definitiv in die politische Arena eingetreten.

Zu Jahresbeginn 2006 gründete der Schwede Rickard Falkvinge die erste Piratenpartei. Ausgangspunkt war der Kampf um Freie Software, um die Nicht-Anerkennung des Urheberrechts. Den Parteinamen gaben sich die Piraten zunächst interessanterweise nicht selbst, sondern die traditionelle Medienindustrie, die das Urheberrecht verteidigte, wollte ihnen mit der Bezeichnung „Piraten" einen negativen Anstrich verpassen. Die Copyright-Gegner akzeptierten den Namen nicht nur, sondern sahen in ihm einen positiven Freiheitsbegriff, ausgehend von den Freibeutern der Meere. Es ist eine Ironie der Geschichte: Eine neue Partei hätte keinen besseren Namen erhalten können.

Bereits in den Pionierjahren des Films prägt der Schauspieler Douglas Fairbanks 1926 in *Der schwarze Pirat* den Typus des Piraten, der sich an Seeräubern rächt, die den Tod seines Vaters auf dem Gewissen haben. Der Pirat tritt in der Filmgeschichte mehrfach als Einzelner auf, als Rächer und Verbrecher, aber er steht auch als Sympathieträger, wie Jack Sparrow, fabelhaft gespielt von Johnny Depp, in den vier Folgen *Fluch der Karibik*. Selbst der vierte Teil hielt in den Kinocharts der USA am ersten Wochenende den Spitzenplatz. Zu den Klassikern des Piratenfilms zählt *Der Herr der Sieben Meere* (*The Sea Hawk*) mit Errol Flynn als Sir Francis Drake (1940). Francis Drake mutiert vom englischen Admiral zum Piraten. Es gelingt ihm, im Auftrag von Königin Elisabeth I. im Jahr 1580 das Kap der Guten Hoffnung an der Südspitze Afrikas zu umsegeln und damit eine der ersten Weltumseglungen für die Englische Krone zu verbuchen.

432 Jahre nach Sir Francis Drake segeln wieder Piraten um die Welt – nicht auf den Weltmeeren, sondern im globalen Datenmeer. Keine andere Partei hat sich in den letzten Jahren so rasant weltweit ausgebreitet wie die Piraten. Warum es für die traditionellen Parteien so schwierig ist, mit der neuen Bewegung umzugehen, liegt unter anderem darin, dass die jungen Menschen, die mit dem Computer aufgewachsen sind, anders denken.

Wenn aus dem Chaos die Welt entstanden ist, ist es denkbar, dass aus einer „Chaostruppe", als die die Piraten vielfach bezeichnet werden, eine Partei entsteht, die mit dem digitalen Alphabet unserer Zeit aufgewachsen ist.

„Das Erfolgsrezept der Piraten ist ihr Anderssein", schreibt die Journalistin Merlind Theile, selbst in Facebook und Twitter vernetzt, treffend in *Der Spiegel* und fährt fort: „Sie wollen keine Hinterzimmerpolitik, keinen Personenkult und keine Polit-Karrieristen. Ihr Mantra heißt Transparenz, ihr politischer Held ist der Amateur, die Macht soll beim Schwarm bleiben. All das birgt ein Versprechen auf eine bessere Politik, auf Bürgernähe und selbstlose Volksvertreter."[2]

In der Zwischenzeit haben sich in den meisten europäischen Ländern, aber auch in den USA, in Russland, in Neuseeland Piratenparteien gegründet. In Österreich erfolgte die Gründung 2006. Einen ersten Erfolg erzielte die österreichische Partei in Innsbruck bei der Gemeinderatswahl 2012 mit 3,8 Prozent der Stimmen und konnte sich mit einem Mandat den Einzug in den Gemeinderat sichern.

Während für die Piraten die Freie Software als Triebkraft ihrer Entstehung fungierte, ist es für *WikiLeaks* der freie Zugang zu geheimer Information in öffentlichen Bereichen, insbesondere in der Politik. Der Ursprung bzw. die tatsächliche Gründung liegt nach wie vor im

death. Through the history of film, pirates have appeared as lone wolves, avengers and villains, but also as likeable figures, such as Jack Sparrow, so brilliantly played by Johnny Depp in the four episodes of *Pirates of the Caribbean*. Even the fourth episode went right to the top of the movie charts on its first weekend in the USA. Another early pirate classic is *The Sea Hawk* with Errol Flynn as Sir Francis Drake (1940). Francis Drake mutates from English admiral to pirate. On commission from Queen Elisabeth I, he rounds the Cape of Good Hope, Africa's southern tip, in 1580, allowing the English Crown to take credit for one of the first successful circumnavigations of the world.

432 years after Sir Francis Drake, pirates are now circumnavigating the world again—not on the earth's oceans but on a global sea of data. In recent years, no other party has spread so swiftly around the world as the Pirates have. And one reason it has turned out to be so difficult for traditional parties to deal with this new movement is the fact that young people, who have been raised on computers, think differently.

If the world was born out of chaos, then it is also conceivable that a party might be born out of a "bunch of chaotic nerds"—as the Pirates are often called—who have grown up using the digital alphabet of our times.

"The Pirates' recipe for success is that they are different", journalist Merlind Theile, who herself uses Facebook and Twitter to network, quite fittingly writes in *Der Spiegel*. She then goes on to say: "They don't want politics happening in back rooms, nor do they want personality cults or political careerists. The Pirates' mantra is transparency, their political hero is the amateur, (...) and power should belong to the swarm. All this brings promise of better policies, a closeness to the people and selfless representatives."[2]

In the meantime, Pirate Parties have been founded in most European countries, as well as in the USA, Russia and New Zealand. In Austria, the Pirates were established in 2006 and scored their first success at municipal elections in Innsbruck in 2012: with 3.8 percent of the votes, they secured one seat on the municipal council.

While free software was the initial motivating force behind the rise of the Pirates, for *WikiLeaks* it was a question of open access to secret information in public spheres, especially in politics. Its beginnings or rather its actual establishment is still unclear, but then Julian Assange stepped forward as the driving force behind it (though he was not its founder). After *WikiLeaks* activists carried out some spectacular actions, and with greater frequency as of 2009, Julian Assange was finally arrested on the controversial charge of rape und sexual assault in London on December 7, 2012; he applied for asylum to Ecuador on June 21, 2012. *WikiLeaks* activities have declined since Assange's arrest.

Meanwhile, Daniel Domscheit-Berg, a one-time close ally of Assange, has switched sides. Along with his wife Anke, a committed Internet activist and advisor, he has joined the Pirates. Literature critic and journalist at *Zeit Online*, Ijoma Mangold (who was, by the way, also on the jury for the Ingeborg Bachmann Prize in 2007) describes his visit to the "political couple of our digital era" in the print edition of *Die Zeit's* feuilleton: "With Anke and Daniel Domscheit-Berg, the digital world now, for the first time, has a model couple, too."[3] Mangold sees a number of the tendencies of our time prototypically united in this couple: "A union of web avant-garde and social engagement. The belief that the world has become a different one through technological progress and that this goes hand in hand with the promise of socio-political change."[4]

Anke and Daniel are convinced: the Internet is changing the world. Whether in the form of a revolution or social process, nothing is as it was before, everything will be otherwise. With reason, the two cite the inventor of the WorldWideWeb: Tim Berners-Lee. He believed that the Internet was not so much a technical revolution, but a social one. As leading medium, it brings about a new democratic

Dunkeln, als treibende Kraft, aber nicht als Gründer trat Julian Assange in den Vordergrund. Nach spektakulären Aktionen von *WikiLeaks*-Aktivisten, vermehrt ab 2009, wurde Julian Assange schließlich am 7. Dezember 2012 in London wegen nach wie vor umstrittenen Vorwürfen von Vergewaltigung und Nötigung verhaftet und hat in Ecuador um Asyl angesucht (21. 6. 2012). Die Aktivitäten von *WikiLeaks* haben seit der Verhaftung von Assange abgenommen.

In der Zwischenzeit hat Daniel Domscheit-Berg, ein enger Verbündeter von Assange, die Seiten gewechselt. Er ist zusammen mit seiner Frau Anke, einer engagierten Internet-Aktivistin und Internet-Beraterin, den Piraten beigetreten. Der Literaturkritiker und Journalist von *Zeit Online*, Ijoma Mangold, der 2007 auch Mitglied der Jury des Ingeborg-Bachmann-Preises war, zeichnet im Print-Feuilleton von *Die Zeit* ein Bild von seinem Besuch beim „Politpaar unserer digitalen Zeit": „Mit Anke und Daniel Domscheit-Berg hat jetzt auch die digitale Welt erstmals ihr exemplarisches Paar."[3] Dabei sieht Mangold in diesem Paar mehrere Tendenzen unserer Zeit prototypisch vereint: „Die Verbindung von Netzavantgarde und gesellschaftspolitischem Engagement. Der Glaube, dass die Welt durch den technologischen Fortschritt eine andere geworden ist und dass damit auch ein gesellschaftspolitisches Versprechen einhergeht."[4]

Anke und Daniel sind überzeugt: Das Internet verändert die Welt. Ob als Revolution oder als sozialer Prozess, nichts ist mehr wie zuvor, alles wird anders. Mit Recht zitieren die beiden den Erfinder des WorldWideWeb, Tim Berners-Lee: Das Internet sei weniger eine technische als eine soziale Revolution. Das Internet als Leitmedium führt zu einem neuen demokratischen Verständnis, zu neuen Modellen der Demokratie, denn nur so wird es möglich, die Politikverdrossenheit, insbesondere der jungen Menschen, zu überwinden.

Mitte Juni 2012 präsentierte das Österreichische Institut für Jugendkulturforschung eine länderübergreifende Repräsentativumfrage unter JungwählerInnen (16- bis 29-Jährige). Das Ergebnis ließ in den Parteizentralen mehr als aufhorchen. Wäre am 17. Juni 2012 Wahltag in Österreich gewesen, hätte das Ergebnis so aussehen können: Die Piraten wären in Österreich von 12 Prozent

und in Deutschland von 23 Prozent der JungwählerInnen gewählt worden. Vor ihnen liegen in Österreich mit 17,4 Prozent die Freiheitlichen und die Grünen mit 12,9 Prozent, weit abgeschlagen sind die beiden „Großparteien" ÖVP mit 8,9 Prozent bzw. die SPÖ mit 8,5 Prozent.[5]

Zusammenfassendes Resultat der Umfrage: „16- bis 29-Jährige sehen die Piraten als Jugend-, Internet-, Transparenz- und Mitbestimmungspartei. Darüber hinaus ist die Piratenpartei bei JungwählerInnen als ‚junge Bürgerrechtsbewegung' positioniert. Ihre Kernkompetenz ist der Schutz des Individuums vor staatlichen Zugriffen und Einschränkungen. Als neue Diskurspartei steht sie für das Angebot, Argumente auszutauschen und den Dingen auf den Grund zu gehen".[6]

Wie immer sich die Piratenparteien entwickeln werden: Das Internet hat mit den vor allem von jungen Menschen getragenen Aufständen, Protesten und Revolutionen, im arabischen Frühling, aber auch in anderen Ländern, mit einer Parteigründung die politische Bühne betreten. Wer das revolutionäre Potenzial des neuen Mediums nicht begreift oder nicht nutzt, wird in den Mahlstrom der dramatischen Zeitenwende geraten.

Von der Politik zur Bildung. Auch hier zeichnet sich durch das Vordringen der digitalen Medien ein Umbruch ab: Die traditionelle Bildungspolitik hat die im Gang befindliche Revolution im Bildungsbereich nur vereinzelt erfasst. Doch hier entscheidet sich für die junge Generation, mit welchen Kompetenzen sie für ihr Leben in der Zukunft ausgestattet wird, um in der neuen Arbeitswelt konkurrenzfähig zu sein.

Wo immer auch die Ursachen liegen mögen, Schulen und Bildungseinrichten haben ein großes Beharrungsvermögen, in manchen Ländern mehr, in manchen weniger. Trotz bemerkenswerter Bestrebungen einzelner hat das österreichische Schulsystem ein besonderes Beharrungsvermögen, sowohl was die Zeitgemäßheit der Lerninhalte als auch was deren Vermittlung betrifft. Am Bildungsbereich gehen die neuen Medien keineswegs spurlos vorbei. Die Bildungsangebote im Internet nehmen ständig zu und präsentieren sich mit steigender Professionalität. Gerade das Jahr 2012 könnte sich als Schlüsseljahr für die Internet-Revolution im Bildungsbereich erweisen, wie Projekte aus den USA

awareness and new models of democracy—and this is the only way for young people in particular to overcome their disenchantment with politics.

In mid June 2012, the *Österreichische Institut für Jugendkulturforschung* (Austrian Institute for the Study of Youth Culture) presented a representative transnational survey conducted among young voters (16- to 29-year-olds). The results caused many in party headquarters to do more than just prick up their ears. If elections had been held in Austria on June 17, 2012, the outcome might have been as follows: 12 percent of young voters in Austria for the Pirates; 23 percent, in Germany. In Austria, the Freedom Party (FPÖ) would have gotten 17.4 percent, and the Greens, 12.9 percent, and so would have done better than the Pirates. Whereas the two "big parties", the Austrian's People's Party (ÖVP), with 8.9 percent, and the Socialist Party of Austria (SPÖ), with 8.5 percent, would have done worse.[5]

To sum up the results of the survey: "16- to 29-year-olds see the Pirates as a young people's party that is pro-Internet, -transparency and -citizen participation. In fact, the Pirate Party has established itself among young voters as a "new civil rights movement". Its core competence is to protect the individual from state intervention and restrictions. As a new party of discourse, it stands for the chance to debate ideas and get to the bottom of things."

No matter how the Pirate Party develops: with the uprisings, protests and revolutions largely carried out by young people in Arab Spring nations, but also with the establishment of this new party in other countries, the Internet has now entered the political arena. All those who do not recognize and exploit the revolutionary potential of the new medium will be pulled down into the maelstrom of this dramatic turning point in history.

Let's now move on from politics to education. Here, too, upheaval is imminent due to the advance of digital media: so far the current revolution has only affected traditional educational policies in

isolated instances. Yet for the young generation, it is here that the decisions will be made that will determine the skills they will acquire in their future lives, skills they will need to compete in the new world of work.

No matter what the causes might be, schools and educational facilities often lapse into inertia, though more so in some countries than in others. Despite the remarkable efforts of individuals, the Austrian school system is particularly prone to inertia, and this affects both the actuality of its teaching and learning contents, and how they are taught. Yet, by no means have the new media left the field of education untouched. Online educational programs are steadily increasing and presenting themselves with ever greater professionalism. 2012 may turn out to be a key year for the Internet revolution in the educational sector, as projects from the USA that are unlike any in Europe demonstrate—for once again this is an innovation from the USA and not from Europe: in 2012, three prominent American universities have launched online study courses: Stanford, Harvard and the Massachusetts Institute of Technology (MIT). All three universities agree: the time is ripe—online study programs are to open up lecture halls and national borders; a global study course with hundreds of thousand of students is the goal. Stanford President John Hennessy sums it up: "There is a tsunami coming." He believes that, like the print media or music industry, universities are going to have to radically change.

By experimenting with his own lectures series, Professor Andrew Ng, computer scientist at Stanford, became an online university pioneer. Usually about 400 students attend his lectures, but last semester he had 100,000 students in an online course: "To reach that many students before, I would have had to teach my normal Stanford class for 250 years."[8]

In May 2012, enrolment for online courses at Stanford crossed the one-million line. The online study program which offers MOOCs (Massive

zeigen, denen Europa nichts Vergleichbares entgegenzusetzen hat – wieder eine Innovation, die aus den USA und nicht aus Europa kommt: 2012 steigen drei prominente amerikanische Universitäten in das Online-Studium ein: Stanford, Harvard und das Massachusetts Institute of Technology (MIT). Alle drei Universitäten sind sich einig: Die Zeit ist reif, das Online-Studium öffnet die Grenzen der Hörsäle, die Grenzen der Länder, das globale Studium mit hunderttausenden Studentinnen und Studenten ist das Ziel. Stanford Präsident John Hennessy bringt es auf den Punkt: „There is a tsunami coming."[7] Wie die Printmedien oder Musikindustrie werden sich, so Hennessy, auch die Universitäten radikal ändern müssen.

Professor Andrew Ng, Computerwissenschafter in Stanford, wurde durch ein Experiment mit seiner Vorlesung zu einem Vorkämpfer der Online-Universität. Im Durchschnitt hat er 400 Studenten bei seiner Vorlesung, aber letztes Semester hatte er 100.000 Studenten in einem Online-Kurs: „To reach that many students before, I would have had to teach my normal Stanford class for 250 years".[8]

Im Mai 2012 haben in Stanford die Inskriptionen zu Online-Kursen die Millionengrenze erreicht. Das Online-Studium „Courses", jetzt MOOC (Massive Online Open Classroom via *Coursera*) genannt, wurde in Stanford von Andrew Ng und Daphne Koller ins Leben gerufen, weitere Universitäten haben sich in der Zwischenzeit angeschlossen. Ein Drittel der StudentInnen kommen aus den USA, zwei Drittel aus der internationalen Universitätsszene.

Einen radikalen Aufbruch im universitären Leben will auch die Online-Plattform *Udacity*, ein Kunstwort aus „university" und „audacity" erreichen, eine Initiative des Stanford-Professors und Google Fellow Sebastian Thrun. Seine Kurse sind jetzt noch kostenlos. Die Gründungsidee kam für Thrun aus einem persönlichen Erlebnis: Er stellte eine seiner best besuchten Vorlesungen über Künstliche Intelligenz ins Internet und erhielt 160.000 Anmeldungen aus fast allen Ländern der Welt. 23.000 davon schlossen die Prüfung positiv ab. Sebastian Thrun:„ Wenn wir es schaffen, Leuten in jeder Phase ihres Lebens und überall auf der Welt eine gute Ausbildung zukommen zu lassen, dann bin ich zufrieden." Das erklärte Ziel von *Udacity* ist es, Bildung weltweit zu verändern.[9]

Die Harvard University und das Massachusetts Institute of Technology (MIT) starteten ebenfalls im Mai 2012 ein bahnbrechendes Unternehmen: einen gemeinsamen universitären Online-Unterricht. Das Ziel setzen die beiden Eliteuniversitäten extrem hoch an: eine Idee, zwei Universitäten – MIT und Harvard; Online-Education via der gemeinsamen Plattform *http://www.edxonline.org* (*edX*); und eine Milliarde StudentInnen. Professor Anant Agarwal, Präsident von *edX*, sprach bei der feierlichen Eröffnung am 2. Mai 2012 von einer Bildungsrevolution: „There is a revolution dawning in Boston and beyond. This revolution has to do with the pen and the mouse. Online education – it is revolutionary, online education will change the world. In the prototype course the number of students that participate is insane. 120.000 students from around the world – from Tunisia, Pakistan, India, New Zealand, Australia, Columbia, Canada, USA and some other countries. Online technology truly has the potential to change the world."[10] Sowohl MIT als auch Harvard zielen auf eine Demokratisierung des Lernens, auf ein Auflösen des Klassenzimmers, auf einen Entwicklungsschritt, der mit der Erfindung des Buchdrucks vergleichbar ist. Agarwal wörtlich: „This is the single biggest change in education since the printing press."

Noch ein weiteres Beispiel aus den USA ist anzuführen, das ebenfalls eine weltweite Dimension anstrebt. Die Khan Academy (*http://www.khanacademy.org*): „Sal Khan commands a worldwide classroom. What began as a labor of love is sparking a revolution in online education". Das war die Headline einer zweiseitigen Reportage in *USA Today* am 30. Mai 2012 über Salman Khan, den Gründer der Khan Academy.[11] Salman Khan, mit drei Abschlüssen am MIT und einem MBA der Harvard Business School, gab zunächst seiner Cousine Nachhilfe in Mathematik, dann kamen immer mehr Freundinnen und Freunde dazu, und er entschloss sich, seine „Nachhilfestunden" auf YouTube zu stellen. Am 16. November 2006 ging das erste Video online. Es war staubtrocken: Salman erklärte das kleinste gemeinsame Vielfache. Als die Nachfrage immer größer und größer wurde, hängte Khan seinen Job als Hedgefond-Manager an den Nagel und gründete die Khan Academy. Dort sind an die 3.100 Videos über YouTube *http://www.youtube.com.*

Open Online Courses) via "Coursera", was started at Stanford by Andrew Ng and Daphne Koller; in the meantime, other universities have joined in. A third of the students are form the USA, two thirds are from the international university world.

The online platform *Udacity*, a name made up from the words "university" and "audacity", also hopes to instigate a radical departure in university life. It is an initiative of Stanford Professor and Google Fellow Sebastian Thrun. At present, his courses are still free of charge. The idea was Thrun's and it stemmed from a personal experience: he had put one of his most popular lecture courses on artificial intelligence on the Internet and received 160,000 applications from almost every country on earth. 23,000 completed the course and passed the final exam. Sebastian Thrun: "If we succeed in making a good education available to people in each phase of their lives and everywhere in the world, then I'll be content." The goal of *Udacity* is to change education worldwide.[9]

Harvard University and the Massachusetts Institute of Technology (MIT) also started a groundbreaking enterprise in May 2012: they are offering university classes together online. The two elite university have set a very high goal—one idea: two universities—MIT and Harvard; online education via a joint platform called *http://www.edxonline.org* (*edX*); and with a billion students. Professor Anant Agarwal, president of *edX*, spoke of an educational revolution at the opening ceremony on May 2, 2012: "There is a revolution dawning in Boston and beyond. This revolution has to do with the pen and the mouse. Online education—it is revolutionary, online education will change the world. In the prototype course the number of students that participate is insane. 120,000 students from around the world—from Tunisia, Pakistan, India, New Zealand, Australia, Columbia, Canada, USA and some other countries. Online technology truly has the potential to change the world."[10] Both MIT and Harvard aim at democratizing learning, eliminating the classroom and taking a step in

development that is comparable to the invention of movable type. Agarwal literally claims: "This is the single biggest change in education since the printing press."
Another example from the USA warrants mentioning as it is also striving to achieve global dimensions. The Khan Academy *(http://www.khanacademy.org/)*: "Sal Khan commands a worldwide classroom. What began as a labor of love is sparking a revolution in online education". This was the headline of a two-page report in *USA Today* on May 30, 2012, about Salman Khan, the founder of the Khan Academy. Salman Khan, who holds three degrees from MIT and an MBA from the Harvard Business School, first tutored his younger cousin in math. Soon more and more friends and relatives were seeking his help, and he decided to put his "tutorials" on YouTube. On November 16, 2006, his first video went online. And it was as dry as can be: in it Salman explains the least common multiple. As the demand got greater and greater, Khan quit his job as hedge-fund manager and launched the Khan Academy. There are now some 3,100 videos available on YouTube, at *http://www.youtube.com.khanacademy*, on almost every school subject—math, history, biology, geography, chemistry, economy, finance, and so on.
The Khan Academy is a non-profit organization and runs on donations, for example, from the Bill and Melinda Gates Foundation. As Bill Gates says: "At 3,000 lessons online, Sal's personal ability as a teacher is remarkable."[12] And with a budget of two million dollars, Google finances translations into the world's most common languages. Salman Kahn is convinced that technology is about to bring about a similar revolution in education as it has in industry and economics. In one year, the Academy gets some 50 to 70 million (!) visitors.
What did Damien Hirst say about the "spot painting" I mentioned earlier, the one he named after an organic compound? That it is about structure and color—and both of these are going to be decisive for politics and education in the digital age.

khanacademy abrufbar, aus nahezu allen Schulgegenständen, Mathematik, Geschichte, Biologie, Geografie, Chemie, Wirtschaft, Finanzen u. a.
Die Khan Academy ist eine Non-Profit-Organisation und lebt von Spenden, u. a. von der Bill and Melinda Gates Foundation. Bill Gates: „At 3,000 lessons online, Sal's personal ability as a teacher is remarkable."[12] Google finanziert mit zwei Millionen Dollar Übersetzungen in die am weitesten verbreiteten Sprachen. Salman Kahn ist überzeugt, dass die Technologie dabei ist, in der Bildung den gleichen Umbruch zu bewirken, wie es in Industrie und Wirtschaft bereits geschehen ist. In einem Jahr erreicht die Khan Academy im Internet 50 bis 70 Millionen (!) BesucherInnen.
Was sagt Damien Hirst zu seinem zitierten „Spot", der nach einer organischen Verbindung benannt ist? Es geht um Struktur, um Farbe – beides wird entscheidend sein für Politik und Bildung im digitalen Zeitalter.
Ich konnte nur zwei Punkte von Damien Hirsts 550 Spots ansprechen. Sowohl die diesjährigen PreisträgerInnen des Prix Ars Electronica als auch die zahlreichen Wissenschaftler und Künstler werden beim Festival Ars Electronica 2012 noch viele „Spots" beitragen, sodass ein BIG PICTURE entsteht, voll von „joy of colour", um noch einmal Hirst zu zitieren.

1 Damien Hirst zitiert nach: Damien Hirst and Gordon Bum: *On the Way to Work*, Faber and Faber, 2001, S. 119
2 *Der Spiegel* Nr.23, 31. Mai 2012, S. 43ff
3 Ebenda
4 Ebenda, S. 44
5 *http:// www.jugendkultur.at*, „Wer sind die Piraten und was wollen sie?"
6 Ebenda
7 *http:// www.zeit.de/studium/hochschule/2012-05/princeton-uni-online*
8 *http://nytimes.com/2012/05/16/opinion/friedman-com-the-revolution*
9 Catharina Koller: *Hal sagt, wie's geht. Wie lässt sich der Uni-Betrieb neu erfinden?*, in: *Die Zeit* Nr. 20, 10. Mai 2012, S. 68
10 *http://www.edxonline.org*
11 *USA Today*, 05. 30. 2012, S. 2D
12 *http://www.youtube.com.khanacademy*

I have only been able to address two of the 550 "spots" on Damien Hirst's painting. This year's Prix Ars Electronica winners, as well as the innumerable experts and artists at the 2012 Ars Electronica Festival will surely contribute many more "spots", and so create a BIG PICTURE that is—to quote Hirst once more—full of the "joy of color".

1 Damien Hirst and Gordon Bum, *On the Way to Work*, Faber and Faber, 2001, p. 119

2 Merlind Theile, "Das Ende der Amateure", in: *Der Spiegel*, 12/2012, p. 26

3 Ijoma Mangold, "Die Domscheit-Bergs", in: *Die Zeit*, 23/2012, p. 43

4 Ibid, p. 44

5 "Wer sind die Piraten und was wollen sie?", at: *http://www.jugendkultur.at*

6 Ibid.

7 Ute Mehnert, "Der Princeton-Prof im Wohnzimmer": *Zeit-Online*, May 31, 2012

8 Thomas L. Friedman, "Come the Revolution", in: *The New York Times*, May 15, 2012

9 Catharina Koller, "Hal sagt, wie's geht. Wie lässt sich der Uni-Betrieb neu erfinden?", in: *Die Zeit*, 20/2012, p. 68

10 See: *http://www.edxonline.org/*

11 Marco R. della Cava, "Sal Khan's 'Academy' sparks a tech revolution in education", in *USA Today*, May 30, 2012, p. 2D

12 See: *http://www.youtube.com/khanacademy*

Prix Ars Electronica 2012

Christine Schöpf

With its 2012 edition, the Prix Ars Electronica is embarking upon its second quarter of a century. The "Competition for Computer Art"—as it was first called—was launched by ORF's Upper Austrian Regional Studio in 1987. Meanwhile, this "International Competition for CyberArts" has become a platform for computer activists worldwide.

In the competition's 26th year, more than 3,500 participants from 74 countries, with projects in the most diverse fields of computer art, make the Prix Ars Electronica a platform unlike any other in the world. Over the years, it has brought together artists and scientists from very different countries and cultures, from east and west, and north and south—creative individuals from a great variety of fields: engineer-artists who work on new interfaces, artist-scientists who explore the bio-sciences with their strategies, filmmakers who go beyond the bounds they once set for themselves, activists who reinterpret and reinvent social networks, and sound artists who introduce us to new listening experiences with their incredible sound constructions.

This year a jury also selected the first recipient of the Prix Ars Electronica Collide@CERN Residency Award, the new artist-in-residence program established by CERN and Ars Electronica. The aim of this award is to expand the dimensions of digital creativity by letting the minds of scientists "collide" with the imaginations of artists. In this way, we seek to accelerate innovation across cultures in the 21st century—creating new dimensions in the digital arts, inspired by the ideas, engineering and knowledge generated at CERN, and produced by the winning artist in collaboration with the transdisciplinary expertise of Ars Electronica's FutureLab team.

This new prize marks a three-year cultural partnership between science and art, as well as a creative collaboration between CERN and Ars Electronica, one that began with CERN cooperation during "Origin"—the Ars Electronica Festival in 2011.

The Prix Ars Electronica has thus become a meeting place for all those who demonstrate with the help of technology how our lives, modes of communication, lifestyles and financial situations are changing constantly, indeed, almost daily. The cultural or political backdrops against which these changes occur have become secondary. Be it censorship in China, demonstration tactics in the former French colonies in North Africa, or the anti-Wall Street movement in the United States, and then

Mit der Ausgabe 2012 geht der Prix Ars Electronica in sein zweites Vierteljahrhundert. Der 1987 vom ORF Oberösterreich gestartete Wettbewerb für Computerkünste – so hieß er damals noch – ist mittlerweile als Competition für Cyberarts zum weltweiten Bewerb für Computeraktivisten geworden.

Mehr als 3.500 Aktive aus 74 Ländern machen in den unterschiedlichsten Bereichen der Computerkreation im 26. Wettbewerbsjahr den Prix Ars Electronica zu einem international unvergleichlichen Netzwerk. Denn er vereint in den Jahren seines Bestehens mittlerweile Künstler und Wissenschaftler unterschiedlichster Länder und Kulturen von West und Ost, Nord und Süd – Kreative in den verschiedensten Bereichen: Ingenieurskünstler, die an neuen Interfaces arbeiten, Künstler-Wissenschaftler, die den Bereich der Biowissenschaften mit ihren Strategien ergründen, Filmemacher, die über ihre bislang gesetzten Grenzen gehen, Aktivisten, die soziale Netzwerke neu interpretieren, Sound-Künstler, die uns mit ihren unglaublichen Klangkonstrukten in neue Hörerlebnisse einführen.

Darüber hinaus wurde in diesem Jahr erstmals der Prix Ars Electronica Collide@CERN Residency Award vergeben, das neue von CERN und Ars Electronica ins Leben gerufene Artist-in-Residence Programm. Ziel des Prix Ars Electronica Collide@CERN Residency Award ist es, eine neue Dimension der Kreativität im Bereich der digitalen Kunst zu ermöglichen, indem wir das Denken von Wissenschaftlern mit der Fantasie von Künstlern „kollidieren" lassen. Wir versuchen damit, Innovation im 21. Jahrhundert über alle kulturellen Grenzen hinweg zu beschleunigen – indem wir neue Dimensionen in den digitalen Künsten eröffnen, die von den Ideen, Technologien und wissenschaftlichen Erkenntnissen, die im CERN entstehen, inspiriert sind und vom prämierten Künstler in Zusammenarbeit mit dem transdisziplinären Team des Ars Electronica Futurelab produziert werden.

Dieser Preis ist der Beginn einer dreijährigen Partnerschaft zwischen Kunst und Wissenschaft - eine kreative Kollaboration zwischen CERN und Ars Electronica, die bereits 2011 anlässlich des Ars Electronica Festivals ORIGIN begonnen hat.

Der Prix Ars Electronica ist somit zu einem Treffpunkt für all jene geworden, die mit Hilfe der Technologie demonstrieren, wie sich unser Leben, unsere Kommunikation, unser Lifestyle, unsere Finanzen kontinuierlich und nahezu täglich verändern. Es ist zweitrangig geworden, vor welchen kulturellen oder politischen Hintergründen diese Veränderungen stattfinden. Seien es die chinesische Zensur, die Demonstrationsstrategien in den vormaligen französischen Kolonien in Nordafrika

oder die Anti-Wall-Street-Bewegung in den Vereinigten Staaten und in der Folge in Europa, die politischen Verschiebungen durch die Piratenparteien: Überall hat die Entwicklung der Computertechnologie nicht nur ihre Spuren hinterlassen, sondern auch neue Strategien möglich gemacht.
Diesen Entwicklungen geht der Prix Ars Electronica nach und versucht alljährlich eine Positionsanalyse zu treffen. Es geht nicht darum, stringente Entscheidungen und Urteile zu treffen, sondern vielmehr um das verantwortungsvolle Ausloten der aktuellen Lage in der Medienkultur.
40 international anerkannte Expertinnen und Experten helfen uns als Juroren bei dieser Aufgabe. Ihnen sei an dieser Stelle unser großer Dank für ihre Kooperation ausgesprochen. Ohne sie könnte der Prix Ars Electronica nicht standhalten und sich nicht weiterentwickeln.
Die Ergebnisse des Prix Ars Electronica werden alljährlich in Ausstellungen, Symposien, dem Ars Electronica Festival, dem vorliegenden Buch und der DVD im Anschluss an das Festival im September über den aktuellen Anlass hinaus in internationalen Ausstellungen gezeigt, dokumentiert und somit weitergeführt. Mit diesen Medien lebt der Prix Ars Electronica über seinen jährlichen Anlass hinaus.
Im 26. Jahr seines Bestehens sei einmal mehr denjenigen gedankt, die den Fortbestand des Prix Ars Electronica seit 1987 durch ihre finanzielle Unterstützung absichern und damit Künstlern eine verlässliche Basis bieten. Es sind vor allem Einrichtungen der öffentlichen Hand, die das Unternehmen Prix Ars Electronica sichern.
Unser besonderer Dank gilt der Stadt Linz, die seit 1979 ohne Unterbrechung das Ars Electronica Festival, den Wettbewerb Prix Ars Electronica sowie das Ars Electronica Center mit dem Futurelab fördert. Ebenso danken wir dem Land Oberösterreich für die langjährige kontinuierliche Unterstützung.
Seitens der Wirtschaft danken wir an dieser Stelle vor allem der voestalpine nicht nur für die langjährige Unterstützung der Ars Electronica, sondern für die seit 2004 ermöglichte Installierung der Wettbewerbskategorie [the next idea] voestalpine Art and Technology Grant, mit Hilfe dessen alljährlich spannende neue Positionen in der Computerkultur erprobt werden können und den Prix Ars Electronica als eine zukunftsorientierte Teststation international positionieren.
Weiters danken wir Casinos Austria, Pöstlingberg Schlössl, Cubus, KulturKontakt Austria, Sony DAC und Linz AG für die langjährige Unterstützung und Kooperation.

the political shift embodied by the Pirate Party in Europe—the development of computer technology has not only left its mark everywhere, but has also created opportunities for new strategies.
Each year the Prix Ars Electronica investigates these developments and tries to analyze new positions. The competition is not about making firm decisions and severe judgments, but rather about responsibly assessing the current state of media culture.
Forty internationally recognized experts serve on our juries and help us carry out this task each year. We would like to express our deep appreciation for their assistance. Without them the Prix Ars would not be able to maintain its position and continue to develop as it has.
Each year the results of the Prix Ars Electronica are showcased in exhibitions, symposiums, the Ars Electronica Animation Festival, as well as in this book and DVD. Following the Festival and the events in September, winning projects are presented, documented and pursued further at international exhibitions. Through these presentations, the Prix Ars Electronica lives on even after its annual events.
In the 26th year of its existence, we would again like to thank all those who with their financial support have made the Prix Ars Electronica possible since 1987 and so provided artists with a reliable platform. Funding from public facilities and institutions has played a key role in guaranteeing the existence of the Prix Ars Electronica.
Our special thanks go to the City of Linz, which has backed the Ars Electronica Festival, the Prix Ars Electronica as well as the Ars Electronica Center with its FutureLab continuously since 1979. We would also like to express our gratitude to the Province of Upper Austria for its unflagging support over the decades.
With regards to the industry, we especially want to thank voest-alpine: not only for supporting the Ars Electronica all these years, but also for making it possible to set up [the next idea] competition in 2004. In this category, exciting new positions in computer culture may be explored each year and so contribute to establishing the Prix Ars internationally as a test station for the future.
Last but not least, our thanks go to Casinos Austria, Pöstlingberg Schlössl, Cubus, KulturKontakt Austria, Sony DAC and Linz AG for their years of support and cooperation.

COMPUTER ANIMATION / FILM / VFX

Virtual Recreation, Graphic Storytelling, and Virtual Performance

Virtuelle Neuadaption, grafisches Erzählen und virtuelle Performance

Paul Debevec, Isaac V. Kerlow, JP Lewis, Lorie Loeb, Boo Wong

The first morning of the jury we were thrilled to be in Linz, and we shared the feeling of excitement and curiosity. Our job for the next three days was to review and judge some of the best computer animation/film/VFX projects produced roughly in the last couple of years. After almost three decades of active engagement with digital creativity and innovation, the Prix Ars Electronica competition continues to provide a unique environment where the artistry, the craft and the industry of moving digital images coexist with one another.
The first round of selection presented us with slightly over 200 works (206) that had made it though the pre-selection process. This first round was useful for us jurors to calibrate our points of view and varied professional backgrounds. It also helped us to focus on the wide variety of work submitted, including individual artistic works, collective creations, student projects, and effects work for a few commercials and feature films. For each entry we considered the areas of originality, creativity, technique, storytelling, concept and craft. We each cast individual Yes or No votes for each entry. Unanimous rejections were eliminated and borderline entries with a single vote were discussed. Most of the works eliminated showed a significant weakness in one of the major areas. We spent a considerable amount of time discussing the qualities of entries that had a split vote, and these discussions helped us develop a collective point of view. In order to avoid conflicts of interest we agreed to disclose any relation to any of the

Die erste Zusammenkunft der Jury war von der Begeisterung, in Linz zu sein, und der Neugier auf die Einreichungen geprägt. Unsere Aufgabe für die nächsten drei Tage war es, einige der besten Computeranimations-, Film- und VFX-Projekte, die in den letzten Jahren produziert wurden, zu sichten und zu beurteilen. Auch nach fast drei Jahrzehnten aktiver Auseinandersetzung mit digitaler Kreativität und Innovation bietet der Prix Ars Electronica nach wie vor ein Umfeld, das auf einzigartige Weise ein produktives Miteinander von Kunst, Technik und Industrie der digitalen Bewegtbilder fördert.
In der ersten Auswahlrunde wurden uns mehr als zweihundert Arbeiten (206) vorgelegt, die es durch das Vorauswahlverfahren geschafft hatten. Diese erste Runde diente auch dazu, dass wir Juroren unsere unterschiedlichen Standpunkte und beruflichen Hintergründe kennenlernen konnten. Darüber hinaus konnten wir uns auf die große Bandbreite der eingereichten Arbeiten einstellen, die von Einzelarbeiten über Gemeinschaftsproduktionen bis hin zu Studentenprojekten und visuellen Effekten für Werbe- und Spielfilme reichte. Jeder Beitrag wurde nach den Kriterien Originalität, Kreativität, Technik, Narration, Konzept und Handwerk bewertet. Alle Juroren stimmten über jeden einzelnen Beitrag mit Ja oder Nein ab. Projekte, die einstimmig abgelehnt wurden, wurden ausgeschlossen und Grenzfälle, die nur eine Stimme bekamen, diskutiert. Die meisten der ausgeschiedenen Arbeiten zeigten eine signifikante Schwäche hinsichtlich einer der maßgeblichen Kriterien. Wir verbrachten viel Zeit damit, die Qualitäten der Beiträge zu diskutieren, die unterschiedlich bewertet wurden, wobei diese Diskussionen uns auch halfen, einen gemeinsamen Standpunkt

zu entwickeln. Um Interessenskonflikte zu vermeiden, einigten wir uns darauf, jede besondere Beziehung zu einer der Einreichungen offenzulegen. Juroren, die auch nur ansatzweise eine Beziehung zu einem bestimmten Beitrag hatten, verließen während der Diskussionen den Raum und enthielten sich der Stimme. Wir beendeten die erste Runde mit einer Auswahl von knapp achtzig Beiträgen (79).

In der zweiten Runde standen zahlreiche optisch überaus faszinierende Beiträge von insgesamt hohem technischem Niveau zur Auswahl. Wir waren uns bewusst, dass wir die Messlatte in dieser Phase des Auswahlverfahrens sehr hoch legen mussten, und einigten uns darauf, dass ein Beitrag ein einstimmiges Votum oder ein Mehrheitsvotum erhalten musste, um in die nächste Runde aufgenommen zu werden. Wir haben die Auswahl auf 37 Beiträge eingeschränkt, wobei uns bewusst war, dass wir uns bereits in den der nächsten Runde auf die Finalisten einigen mussten.

Zu Beginn der dritten Auswahlrunde beschlossen wir, die Beiträge in Subkategorien zu unterteilen, um sicherzugehen, dass die Endauswahl repräsentativ für das breite Spektrum der eingereichten Arbeiten sein würde. Die Kategorien reichten von Spielfilmen bis zu Studentenprojekten und beinhalteten auch Charakteranimation, nicht-narrative Animation, Kunst, Werbefilme und Game Cinematics. Jede einzelne der ausgewählten Einreichungen war in mehr als einer Hinsicht ungewöhnlich und bemerkenswert, doch mussten wir die Liste verkleinern und 60 Prozent der Beiträge ausschließen. Bei der Stimmvergabe kam es auch zu ersten Diskussionen über die Kandidaten für die Goldene Nica und die zwei

entries. Jurors who had even a slight relation to a specific entry left the jury room during deliberations and did not vote. We finished the first round with slightly under 80 selections (79).

The second round of selection included many visually striking entries and the overall technical level was high. We realized that we would have to be demanding in order to get through this stage of the selection process. We also agreed to require a unanimous or a majority vote for any entry to go through to the next round. We narrowed the field down to 37 entries, knowing that we would have to make our final selections in the next round.

At the beginning of the third round we decided to group the entries by sub-categories to ensure that the final selection would be representative of the range of work submitted. The categories ranged from feature films to student projects and also included character animation, non-narrative animation, artworks, commercials and game cinematics. Every single one of these selections was special in more than one way, but we had to narrow down the list and eliminate 60 percent of the entries. As we voted we also initiated our discussions regarding the candidates for the Golden Nica and the two Awards of Distinction. Each juror was allowed a Yes or a No vote per entry, and the competition administrators recorded the votes. The differences or similarities of opinion and preferences of the jurors became apparent during this stage. We also revisited the issues of originality, creativity, technique, storytelling and concept and

craft for many of the remaining entries. Those with a significant weakness saw their chances diminished in spite of the ardent advocacy of one juror or another. The final selections provide a snapshot of the best work being done today in the areas of computer animation/film/VFX projects.
The Golden Nica went to *Rear Window*, a three-projector installation inspired by Alfred Hitchcock's classic 1950s movie. Over the course of six weeks its creator appropriated and recycled footage from Hitchcock's film, and the unexpected result is nothing but captivating. The winning project can be enjoyed on one level as a recreation of the classic film with heightened realism in a virtual three-dimensional space, or it can also be enjoyed for its display of outstanding skill and creativity in bridging the gap between two-dimensional historical footage and virtual realities.
An Award of Distinction went to *Caldera*, a narrative character animation with flawless storytelling and an original story about a girl who struggles with mental illness. Rendered in a style reminiscent of graphic novels, this inspiring short gets interesting when the protagonist decides to confront her condition and face her fears. Another Award of Distinction also went to the visual effects of *Rise of the Planet of the Apes* by Weta Digital. This live-action movie is notable for featuring an entirely digital main character. The movie's hero, an intelligent ape called Caesar, is acted by Andy Serkis, who had previously also provided the motion-capture performances for Gollum and

Auszeichnungen. Jeder Juror durfte pro Einreichung ein Ja oder Nein vergeben, die Stimmen wurden von den Organisatoren des Wettbewerbs aufgezeichnet. Meinungsdifferenzen oder übereinstimmende Positionen sowie Vorlieben der Juroren wurden nun evident. In dieser Phase wurden erneut die Kriterien Originalität, Kreativität, Technik, Narration, Konzept und Handwerk in Zusammenhang mit vielen der verbleibenden Beiträge erörtert. Die Chancen von Beiträgen, die einen signifikanten Schwachpunkt aufwiesen, sanken trotz des einen oder anderen vehementen Verfechters in der Jury. Die Beiträge der Finalisten bieten schließlich eine Momentaufnahme der aktuellen digitalen Kunstproduktion und der besten Arbeiten, die heute in den Bereichen Computeranimation, Film und VFX-Projekte gemacht wurden.
Die Goldene Nica ging an *Rear Window*, eine visuelle Installation für drei Projektoren, die von Alfred Hitchcocks Filmklassiker *Fenster zum Hof* aus den 1950er Jahren inspiriert ist. Der Künstler appropriierte und montierte sechs Wochen lang Filmmaterial aus Hitchcocks Film – das überraschende Ergebnis ist schlichtweg faszinierend. Das Gewinnerprojekt überzeugt einerseits als Neuadaptation mit – im Vergleich zur Vorlage – gesteigertem Realismus in einem virtuellen dreidimensionalen Raum und andererseits aufgrund der Souveränität und Kreativität, mit der ein Brückenschlag zwischen zweidimensionalem historischen Filmmaterial und virtuellen Realitäten gelang.
Eine Auszeichnung wurde *Caldera* ausgesprochen, einer narrativen Charakteranimation, die in bester Erzählmanier die originelle Geschichte eines Mädchens erzählt, das mit einer psychischen Erkrankung zu kämpfen hat. Dieser inspirierende Kurzfilm, der stilistisch an Graphic

Novels erinnert, zieht in seinen Bann, sobald die Protagonistin beschließt, sich ihrem Zustand zu stellen und ihren Ängsten ins Auge zu sehen. Eine weitere Auszeichnung ging an das Animationsstudio Weta Digital für die visuellen Effekte in *Planet der Affen: Prevolution*. Dieser Actionfilm zeichnet sich durch eine digitale Hauptfigur aus. Der Held des Films, ein intelligenter Affe namens Caesar, wird von Andy Serkis gespielt, der auch die Motion-Capture-Rollen für Gollum und King Kong spielte. Für *Prevolution* wurde die Erfassung von Gesichtsmimik noch verfeinert und ein mobiles Motion-Capture-System an den realen Filmsets statt auf speziellen abgeschlossenen Studiobühnen verwendet. Wir fanden die Darstellung der Affen äußerst gelungen, nicht nur in Hinblick auf Lichteffekte und Spiegelung, sondern auch auf ihre emotionale Glaubwürdigkeit und Nuanciertheit. Die bewegenden Aufnahmen von realen Schauspielern und ihren virtuellen Kollegen, die von Angesicht zu Angesicht und Hand in Hand spielten, haben neue Maßstäbe im Bereich des Performance Capturing gesetzt.

Von den zwölf Anerkennungen ging ein hoher Prozentsatz (30 Prozent) wenig überraschend an Studentenarbeiten. Die Kurzfilme der Studenten nehmen es in technischer, handwerklicher und narrativer Hinsicht mit jeder professionellen Produktion auf. Dies ist sowohl ein Indiz für ihr Talent als auch für einen Trend, der bereits vor einem Jahrzehnt einsetzte. Weitere 40 Prozent der Anerkennungen gingen an nicht-narrative und künstlerische Projekte, die sich durch großen Ideenreichtum, Schönheit und/oder die kreative Verwendung digitaler Technologie auszeichneten. Auch Game Cinematics und VFX-Projekte wurden in dieser Kategorie ausgezeichnet.

King Kong. For this film, the fidelity of the facial motion capture was increased and the motion-capture systems were moved onto the film's physical sets instead of dedicated technical stages. We found the rendering of the ape characters to be entirely believable, not just in terms of the lighting and reflectance but in the emotional believability and subtlety of their performances. The moving shots with virtual and real actors face-to-face and hand-in-hand set a new high bar for digital actor performances.

Of the twelve Honorary Mentions, not surprisingly a significant 30 percent went to student works. The technical, craft and narrative accomplishments of these student shorts rivals any professional production. This fact is both an indication of the creators' talent as well as a trend that started about a decade ago. Another 40 percent of the Honorary Mentions went to non-narrative and artistic projects that showcased great inventiveness, beauty and/or creative use of digital technology. Game cinematics and visual effects projects were also recognized in this category.

Rear Window Loop

Jeff Desom

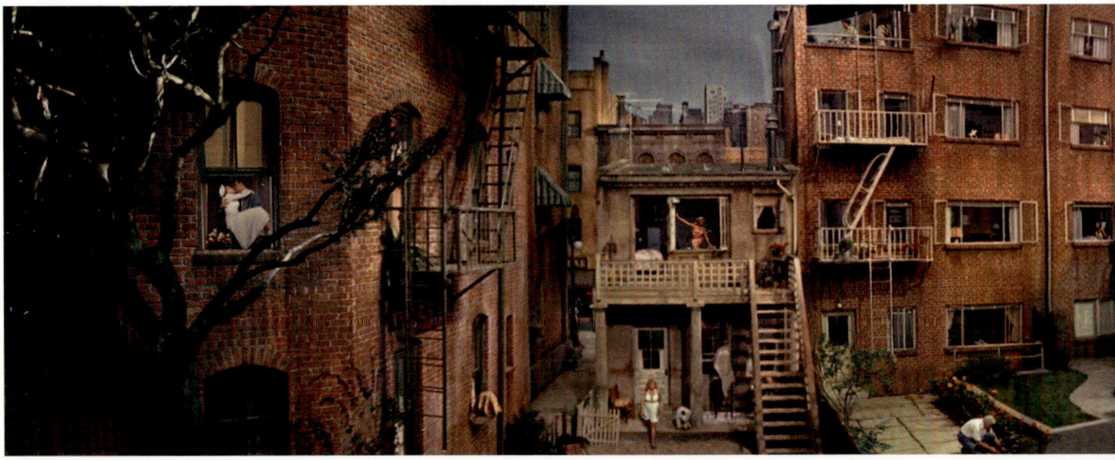

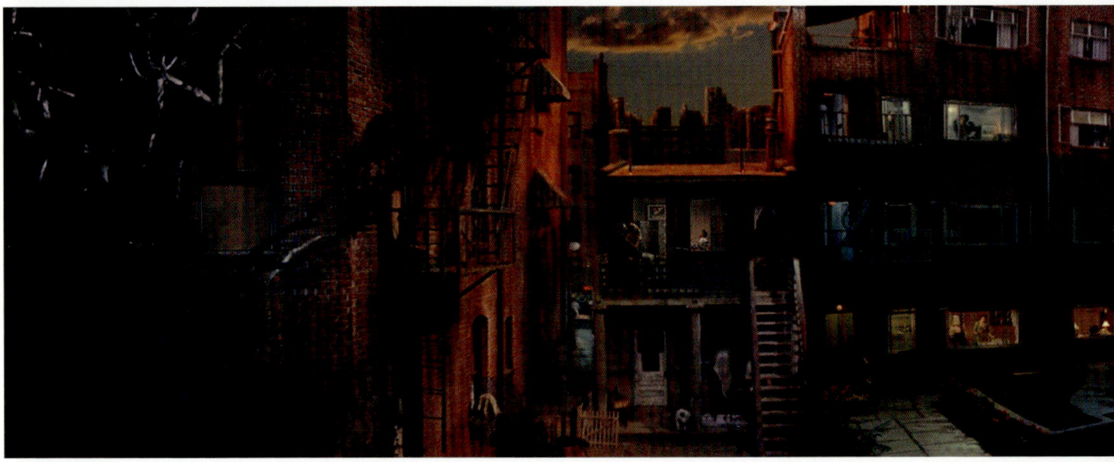

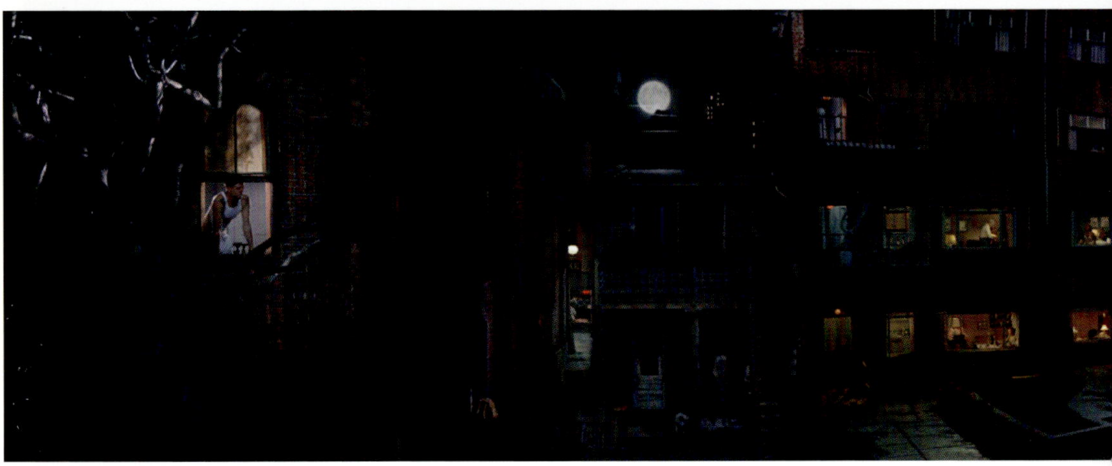

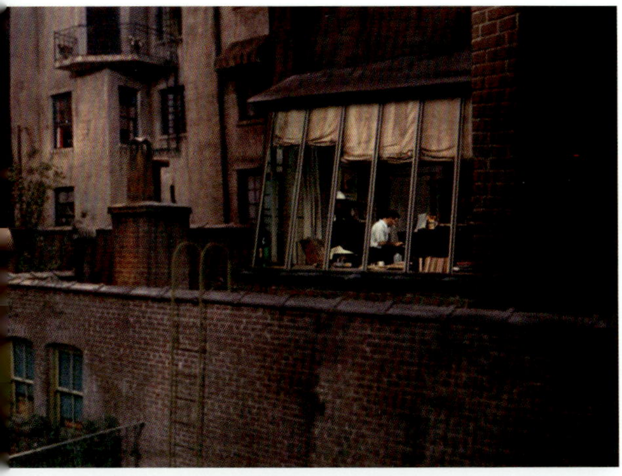

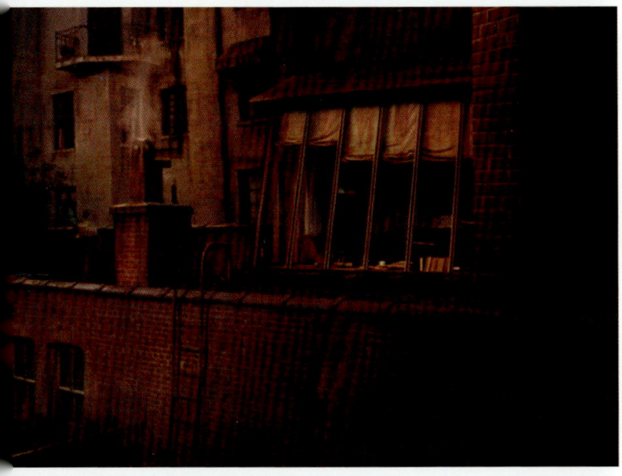

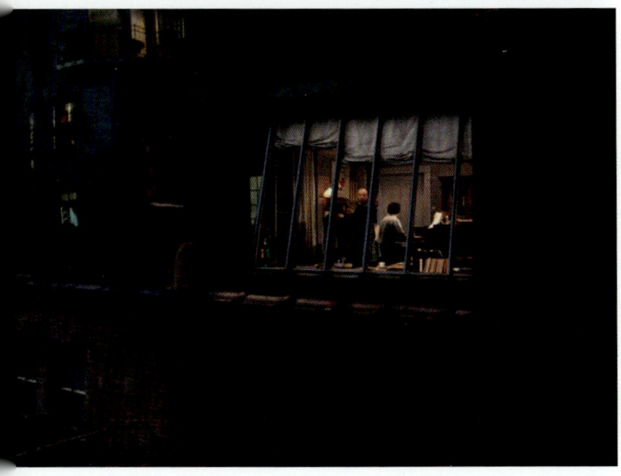

By most accounts, Alfred Hitchcock's 1954 classic *Rear Window* is as perfectly constructed a film as any the medium has ever produced. It is a "purely cinematic film," as Hitchcock later described it, whose obvious spatial handicaps both exploited and negated one of the camera's pre-eminent virtues, its effortless ability to navigate between the proximal and distal. The plot is well-known: world-weary photographer, wheelchair-bound Jeff (Jimmy Stewart) is confined to recuperative leave in his Greenwich Village apartment with only (or mostly) a panorama of the encompassing tenement complex beyond as his company. But as Jean-Luc Godard commented, one never recalls the particulars of any of Hitchcock's narratives but, rather, only the shots that framed them. In the case of *Rear Window*, however, neither specific scenes nor shots prove more memorable than the architecture and spatial configuration of the famed courtyard set. These have been analyzed to the point of exhaustion, with the chief exegetic

Alfred Hitchcocks Klassiker aus dem Jahr 1953 *Das Fenster zum Hof* ist nach Meinung vieler einer der besten Filme, die das Medium hervorgebracht hat. Es ist ein „durch und durch cinematischer Film", wie Hitchcock später meinte, in dem er durch die Besonderheit der räumlichen Enge einen der wesentlichen Vorzüge der Kamera – die Fähigkeit, mühelos zwischen Nähe und Ferne umschalten zu können – zugleich ausnützen und ignorieren konnte. Der Plot ist bekannt: Jeff (Jimmy Stewart), ein gelangweilter Fotojournalist, der auf einen Rollstuhl angewiesen ist, kann sein Apartment in Greenwich Village nicht verlassen und hat als (nahezu) einzige Ablenkung den Blick aus dem Fenster auf die Apartmentanlage gegenüber. Doch wie Jean-Luc Godard anmerkte, erinnert man sich nie an die Einzelheiten von Hitchcocks Handlungen, sondern nur an die Kameraeinstellungen, in denen sie abgebildet werden. Im Falle von *Fenster zum Hof* haben sich jedoch weder bestimmte Szenen noch Kameraeinstellungen so in das Gedächtnis gebrannt wie die Architektur und die räumliche Anlage des berühmten Hinterhofs. Diese wurden bis zum Überdruss analysiert,

jeder Filmstudent ist mit den Eckpunkten dieser Analyse vertraut, doch nie zuvor waren sie in einem Zeitraffervideo zu sehen.
Das Video, das von Jeff Desom akribisch montiert und lediglich mit After Effects und Photoshop bearbeitet wurde, verdichtet Hitchcocks Meisterwerk zu drei atemberaubenden Minuten, in denen das gesamte Filmgeschehen – ohne die dramatischen persönlichen Szenen zwischen den Protagonisten – vor Jeffs Augen ablaufen. Desoms Collage basiert zur Gänze auf Filmmaterial des Hitchcock-Klassikers, wobei die berühmte Panorama-Ansicht mit diversen Effekten (Tilt-Shift, Stabilisierung, Regeneffekt) maßgetreu nachgebastelt und vergrößert wurde, um eine täuschende Ähnlichkeit mit dem Original zu erreichen und die Veränderungen des Umfelds zu rekonstruieren, die die Erzählung vorantreiben. „Da alles aus so ziemlich demselben Winkel aufgenommen wurde, konnte ich die einzelnen Einstellungen ohne große Verzerrrungen in ein einziges Panorama des gesamten Hinterhofs einpassen", meint Desom zu seiner Arbeit.
(Text: Samuel Medina)

points being well familiar to any casual student of cinema, but never have they been seen before like this video time-lapse.
Meticulously assembled by Jeff Desom, using just After-Effects and Photoshop, the video condenses Hitchcock's masterwork into three breathtaking minutes in which the entirety of the film's events—sans the dramatic, personal scenes between the protagonists—play out before Jeff's gaze. Desom's collage is completely comprised of footage from the film, with the iconic window panorama being neatly tailored and augmented with various photographic effects (tilt-shift, stabilization, "rain") so as to achieve verisimilitude with the original and to re-create the environmental changes that propel the narrative along. "Since everything was filmed from pretty much the same angle," Desom writes, "I was able to match them into a single panoramic view of the entire backyard without any greater distortions."
(Text: Samuel Medina)

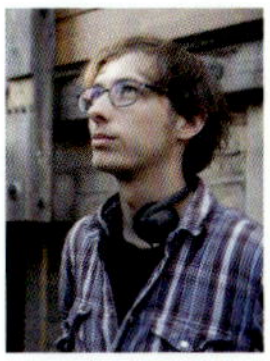

Jeff Desom (LU) is a director, animator and visual artist. His work combines live-action, found footage and digital effects. The experimental pianist Hauschka is his most frequent collaborator. Together they have produced a range of works, including short films, an audiovisual live show and a number of award-winning music videos. **Jeff Desom** (LU) ist Regisseur, Trickfilm-Künstler und bildender Künstler. Er kombiniert in seinen Arbeiten Realfilm, Found Footage (vorgefundenes und angeeignetes Filmmaterial) und digitale Effekte. Meist arbeitet er mit dem experimentellen Pianisten Hauschka zusammen, mit dem er eine Reihe von Arbeiten, darunter Kurzfilme, eine audiovisuelle Live-Show und mehrere preisgekrönte Musikvideos, produziert hat.

Caldera

Evan Viera / Orchid Animation

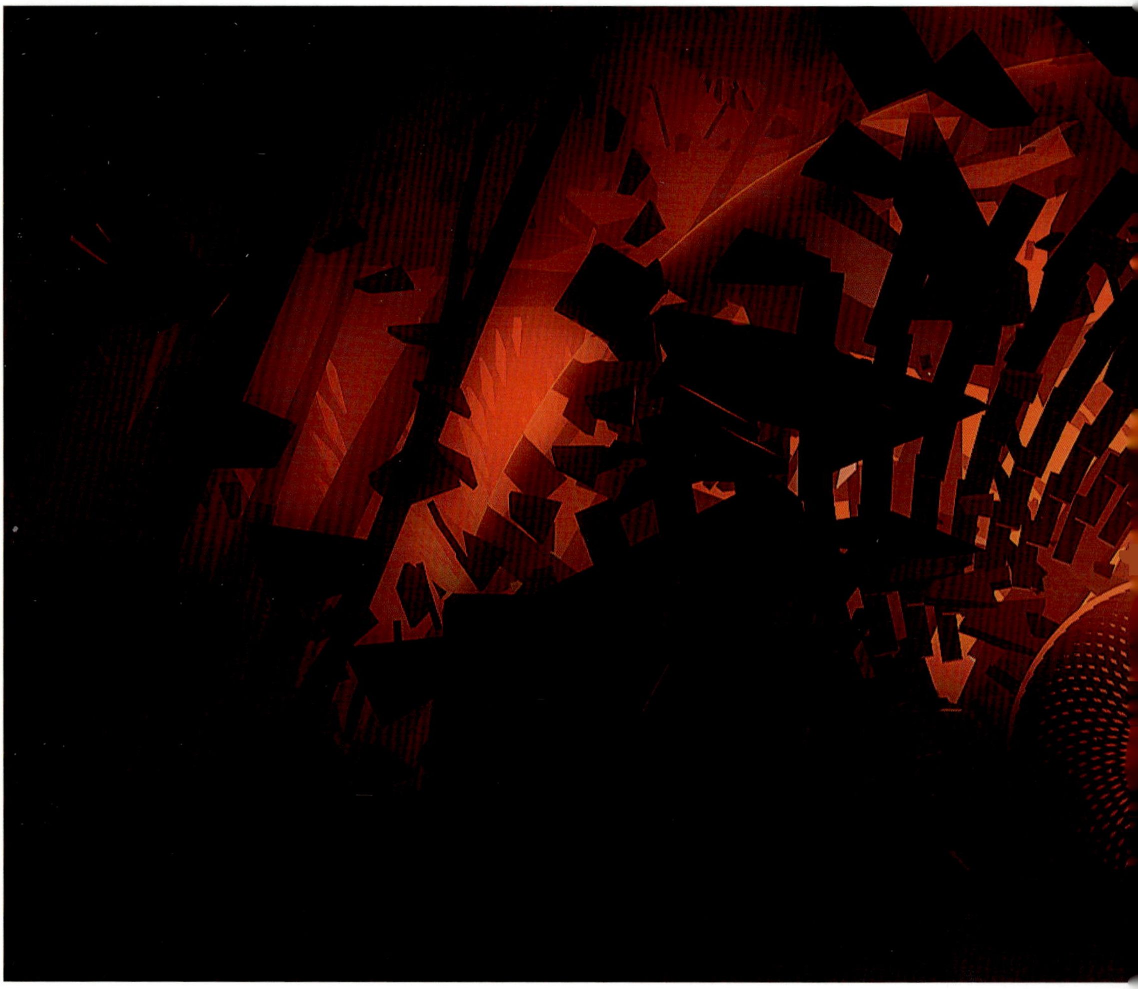

Caldera is an animated short film inspired by individuals struggling with psychotic disorders, and it venerates the brilliant minds forged in the haunted depths of psychosis. The story follows a young girl, a victim of a similar fate, who goes off her medication and leaves a bleak metropolis to immerse herself in a vibrant oceanic cove. Ultimately, the story is about the young girl's impossible predicament, where she cannot live

Inspiriert von Menschen, die an einer psychischen Erkrankung leiden, ist der Animationskurzfilm *Caldera* eine Hommage an die geniale Gedankenwelt, die sich in den quälenden Abgründen der Psychose entfaltet. Die Geschichte handelt von einem psychisch kranken jungen Mädchen, das seine Medikamente absetzt und eine trostlose Großstadt verlässt, um in einer mystischen Bucht in ein ozeanisches Lebensgefühl einzutauchen. Letztlich handelt der Film von dem unlösbaren Dilemma des

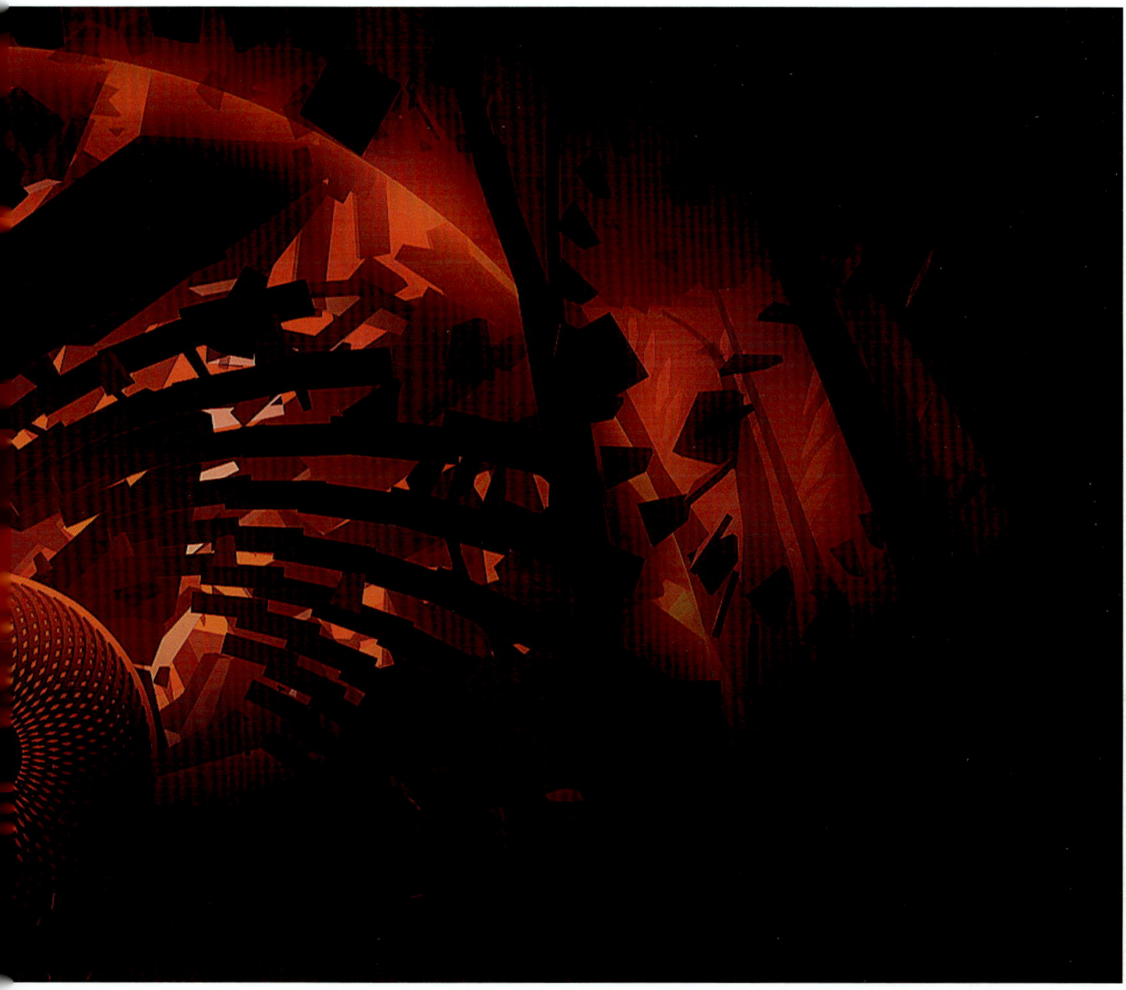

Mädchens, das weder in der fantastischen und bedrohlichen Welt der Psychose noch in der Gesellschaft, die Menschen wie sie ausgrenzt oder mit Medikamenten ruhigstellt, leben kann.
Caldera wurde 2009 als einer der ersten Filme im Rahmen des Computer Graphics Incubator Program am Hampshire College produziert. Der Film entstand während einer dreijährigen Residency in Hamsphire und hatte im März 2012 bei SXSW Weltpremiere.

in either the fantastical and haunting world of psychosis or in the marginalizing society that mandates her medication.
Caldera was invited to be made at Hampshire College in 2009 and was one of the first films to be a part of the Computer Graphics Incubator Program. The film was made during its three-year residence at Hampshire and had its world premiere at SXSW in March of 2012.

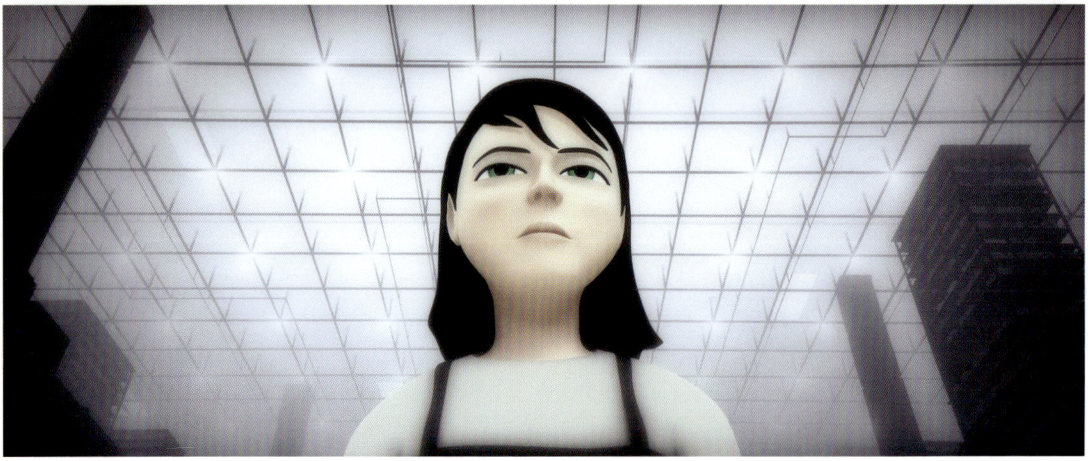

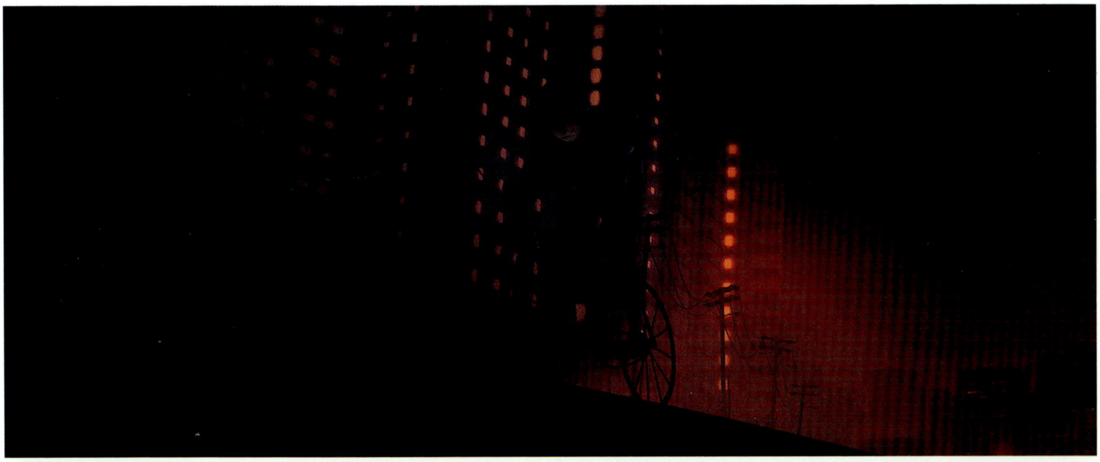

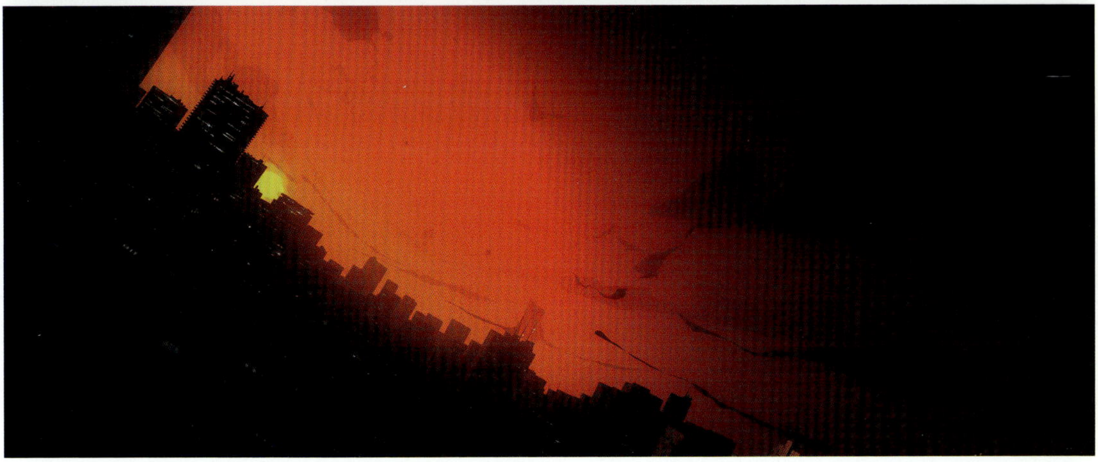

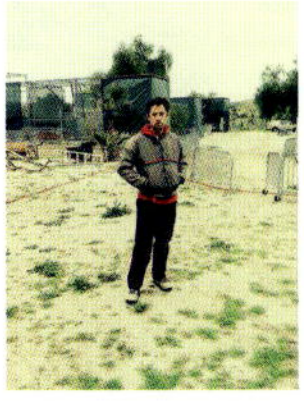

Evan Viera (US) is a filmmaker and composer. He has worked on several short films as sound designer, composer and visual artist. Evan graduated from Hampshire College in 2006 with a short animated senior thesis entitled *Sycamore Eve* that won Best Animated Film in the Scene First student film festival. *Sycamore* had an exciting festival life, screening internationally and showing at the notable Visionfest in 2007.

Evan Viera (US) ist Filmemacher und Komponist. Er wirkte bei mehreren Kurzfilmen als Sound Designer, Komponist und bildender Künstler mit. 2006 beendete er sein Studium am Hampshire College mit dem Animationskurzfilm *Sycamore Eve* als Abschlussarbeit, der als Best Animated Film beim Scene First Student Film Festival ausgezeichnet wurde. *Sycamore Eve* machte Furore auf Festivals, wurde international gezeigt, u. a. beim renommierten Visionfest.

Rise of the Planet of the Apes

Weta Digital / Twentieth Century Fox

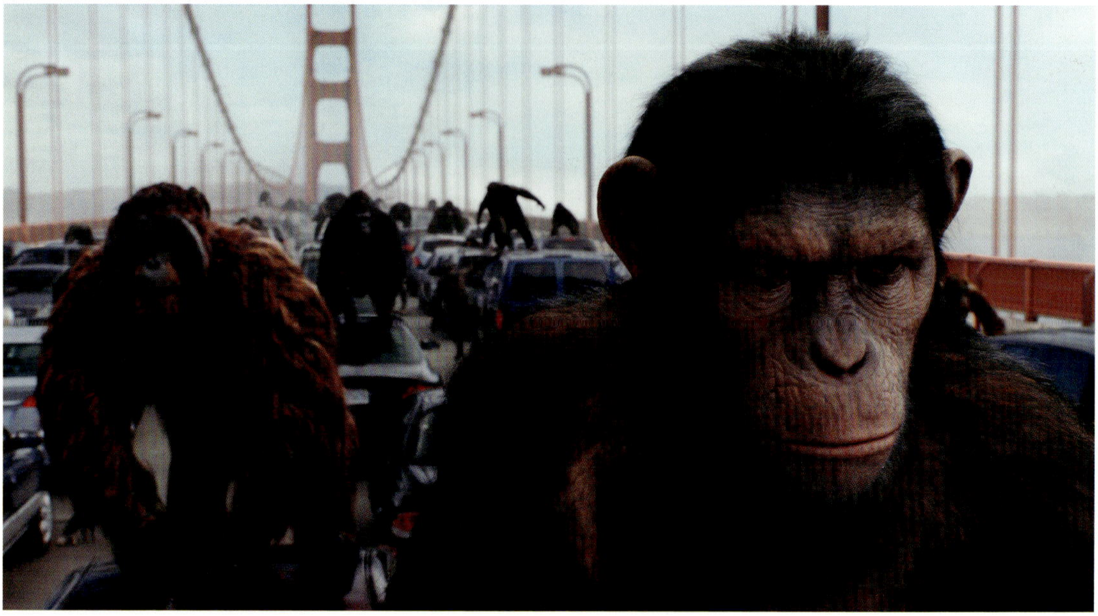

The story of *Rise of the Planet of the Apes* is built around the character of Caesar as he moves from childhood to young adult and undergoes a transformation that gives him supra-human intelligence. This was the first film in the *Planet of the Apes* franchise to move away from makeup and prosthetics to create the apes digitally. Because the apes needed to look like present-day apes, we could not be constrained by a human's size, proportions and posture. Also the apes needed to be every bit as emotionally engaging and nuanced in their performances as the humans in the film.

Enhancements we made to our performance-capture setup made it more durable, portable and able to be used outside. This meant that the ape performers were able to participate on set with their human counterparts both physically and emotionally.

Performance capture served as the foundation for the ape movements as the actors' performances. Retargeting and adjusting for the scale difference between the actor and Caesar required subtle adjustments. Broader action sequences that were physically impossible for humans to perform were accomplished with keyframe animation using a video reference library of chimp movements as a guide.

Der Film *Planet der Affen: Prevolution* handelt von einem superintelligenten Schimpansen namens Caesar, der im Zuge seines Heranwachsens außergewöhnliche Fähigkeiten entwickelt. Dies ist der erste Film aus der *Planet der Affen*-Filmreihe, in dem die Affen nicht mit Make-up und prothetischen Hilfsmitteln, sondern digital erzeugt wurden. Da sie wie Affen von heute aussehen mussten, wollten wir uns nicht auf die Größe, Proportionen und Posen von Menschen beschränken lassen. Außerdem sollten die Affen genauso emotional überzeugend sein und nuanciert agieren wie menschliche Darsteller.

Verbesserungen, die wir im Performance-Capture-Verfahren erzielten, waren die Voraussetzung dafür, dass mit dieser Technik erstmals an einem richtigen Außenset gedreht werden konnte. Daher konnten die Affendarsteller am Set mit ihren menschlichen Gegenspielern interagieren und kommunizieren. Das Performance-Capture-Verfahren ermöglicht, dass die Darstellung eines Schauspielers vor der Kamera zu einem überzeugenden Affen auf der Leinwand wird. Die Ausgleichung des Größenunterschieds zwischen Schauspieler und Caesar erforderte subtile Anpassungen. Längere Actionszenen, die physisch für Menschen undurchführbar waren, wurden mit Keyframe-Animation gemacht, wobei eine Bibliothek von Videoaufnahmen von Schimpansenbewegungen als Referenz herangezogen wurde.

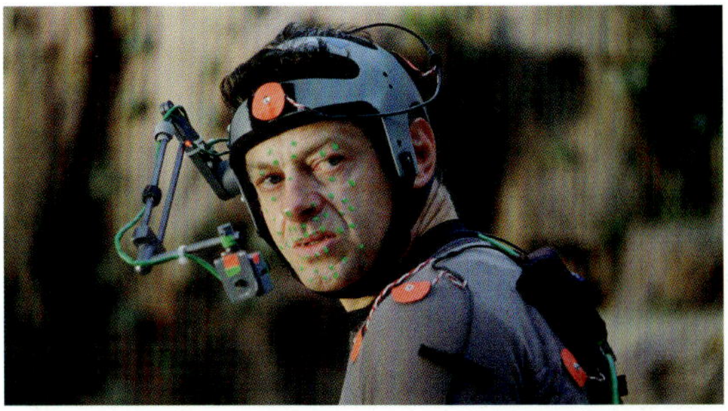

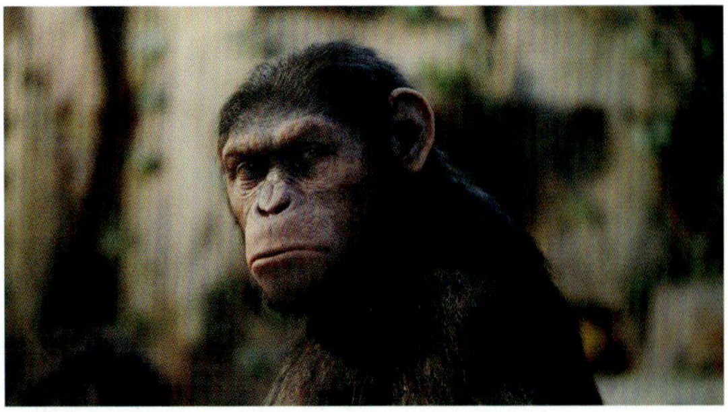

Die Animation des Schimpansen Caesar verlangte eine sensible Kombination von schimpansenartigem Verhalten und menschlichen Gesten und Bewegungen. Für die schauspielerische Leistung des Darstellers waren ein Verständnis sowohl von menschlicher als auch von tierischer Mimik und der sich darin äußernden Emotionen erforderlich.

Auch Caesars Haut musste sich mit dem Heranwachsen des Schimpansen verändern. Spezifische Texturen, kombiniert mit Schattierungen und Aufteilungen der Farbflächen, kamen zum Einsatz, um die allmähliche Veränderung der Haut wiederzugeben und das gewünschte Aussehen zu erreichen. Caesars Fell wurde mit Barbershop, einem während der Dreharbeiten eigens entwickelten Tool, bearbeitet, seine unzähligen Fellsträhnen konnten mit üblichen Hairstyling-Geräten in Form gebracht werden.

Caesar's animation required a delicate balance of chimp-like behavior and human gestures and movements. Matching the actor's performance required an understanding of both human and chimp facial actions and the corresponding emotion being expressed by each.

The quality of Caesar's skin had to evolve as the character grew from infant to adult. Custom texture treatments combined with specific shader and scattering properties reflecting the evolutionary steps of skin were used to create the final looks. Caesar's fur was modeled with a proprietary tool called Barbershop, which was developed during the film. Caesar had hundreds of thousands of strands of fur that could be groomed by an artist using tools similar to real-world hairstyling.

Joe Letteri, Senior Visual Effects Supervisor; Dan Lemmon, Visual Effects Supervisor; R. Christopher White, Visual Effects Supervisor; Erik Winquist, Visual Effects Supervisor; Daniel Barrett, Animation Supervisor; Cyndi Ochs, Visual Effects Producer

Weta Digital (NZ) is one of the world's premier visual effects companies. Led by Senior Visual Effects Supervisor Joe Letteri, Weta Digital is known for uncompromising creativity and commitment to developing innovative technology. From groundbreaking digital characters such as Gollum and Kong, to the revolutionary virtual-stage workflow on *The Adventures of Tintin* and *Avatar* and the performance-capture advancements on *Rise of the Planet of the Apes*, they continue to break down barriers between live action and computer graphics and expand what is possible in film. Weta Digital established its reputation for cutting-edge visual effects with work on blockbusters such as *The Lord of the Rings* trilogy and *King Kong*. The company began work in 1993 on co-founder Peter Jackson's film *Heavenly Creatures* and is based in Wellington, New Zealand. **Weta Digital** (NZ) ist eines der renommiertesten Unternehmen für visuelle Effekte weltweit. Es wird von Senior Visual Effects Supervisor Joe Letteri geleitet und ist bekannt für kompromisslose Kreativität und großes Engagement bei der Entwicklung innovativer Technologien. Von den spektakulären digitalen Figuren wie Gollum und King Kong über die revolutionären virtuellen Sets und Verbesserungen im Workflow in *Die Abenteuer von Tim und Struppi* and *Avatar* bis hin zur Verbesserung des Performance-Capture-Verfahrens in *Planet der Affen: Prevolution* – durch die Überwindung der Schranken zwischen Realhandlung und computergenierten Szenen erweitert das Unternehmen immer wieder die Möglichkeiten des Films. Weta Digital etablierte sich mit innovativen visuellen Effekten für Blockbuster wie der Trilogie *Herr der Ringe* und *King Kong*. Das Unternehmen aus Wellington, Neuseeland, nahm seine Tätigkeit 1993 für den Film *Heavenly Creatures* von Mitbegründer Peter Jackson auf.

Aalterate

Christobal de Oliveira / Sabotage Studio

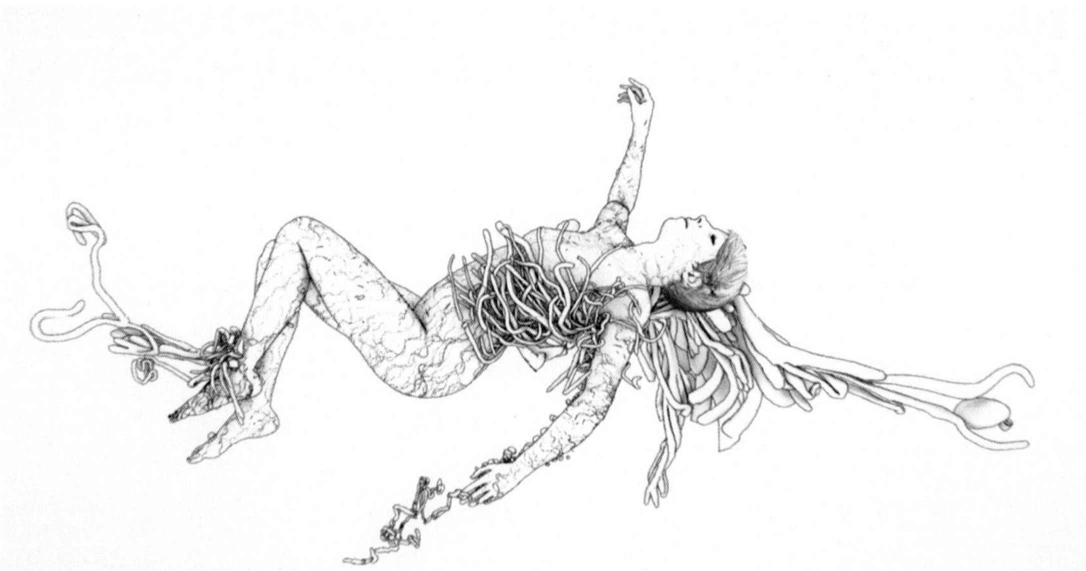

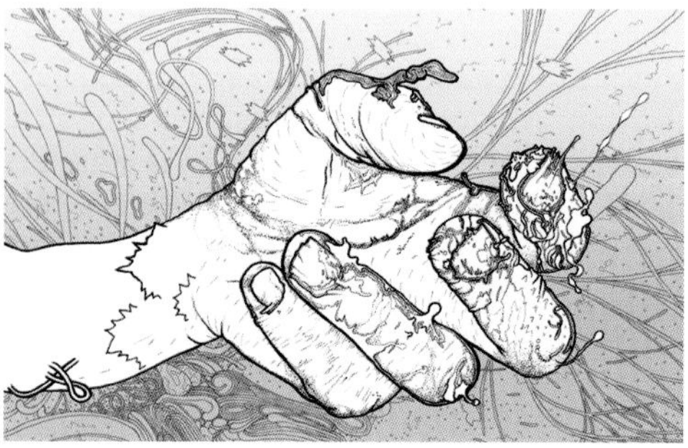

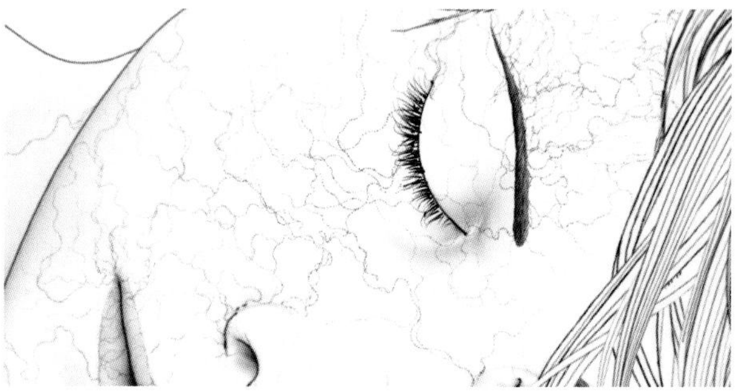

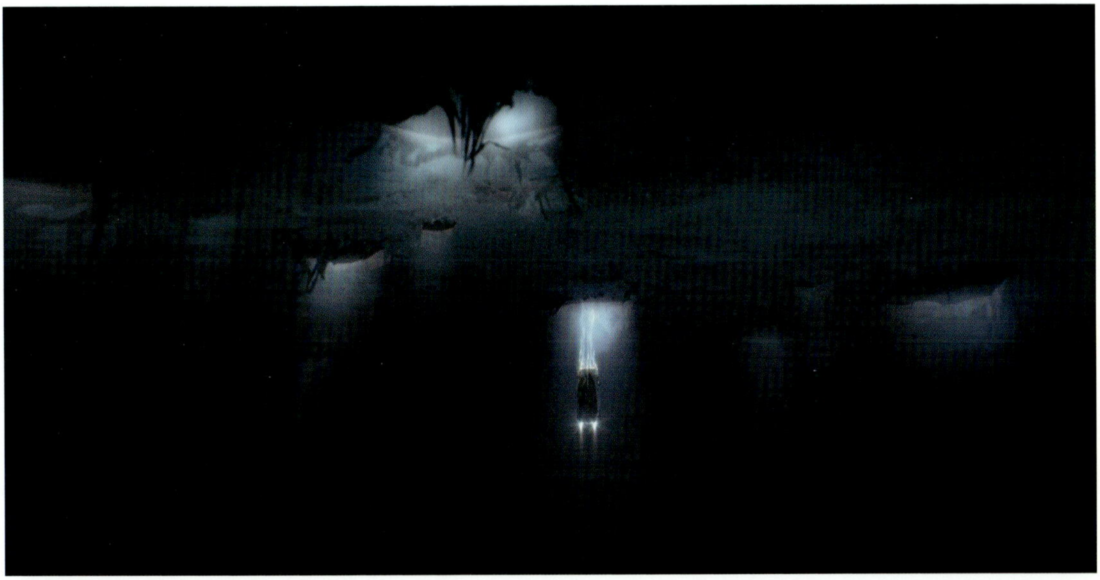

Eine Frau im Koma versucht die Ursache für ihre Bewusstlosigkeit herauszufinden. Sie steht unter extremer innerer Anspannung – ihr Körper beginnt sich zu verändern, die Konturen lösen sich auf, dringen sukzessive in den sie umgebenden weißen Raum vor, bis sie diesen zur Gänze ausfüllen. *Aalterate* ist ein Versuch, das Auftauchen der Erinnerung, die ihrem Wesen nach flüchtig ist, auf konkrete, physiologische Weise darzustellen. Durch permanente Verwandlungen, elektrische Nervenimpulse, die Ereignisse der Vergangenheit zum Vorschein bringen, organische Formen, die sich zu Erinnerungen verdichten, materialisiert sich in diesem Film das Denken körperlich. Statt Ereignisse in einer linearen Erzählstruktur zu beschreiben und frontal zu vermitteln, setzt *Aalterate* auf eine suggestive Bildsprache, die die Erzählstränge eindringlich evoziert und dem Zuseher die Freiheit gibt, andere Lesarten zuzulassen.

Diving into a coma, a woman tries to find the cause of her unconsciousness. She experiences extreme inner tension as its mutating silhouette gradually invades an empty canvas to a point of complete saturation. *Aalterate* is an attempt to represent the emergence of memory, intangible by nature, in a concrete, physiological way. By permanent transformations, electric nervous impulses which draw past events and organic forms which compose the elements of memory, in this film the body becomes the visible material of thought.
Rather than describing the events in a linear and frontal narrative, *Aalterate* promotes seductive evocation so that narrative threads weave into the mind of the audience and find the freedom to stray to other possible readings.

Direction, editor: Christobal de Oliveira
Producer: Autour de Minuit / Valk Production (FR / NL)

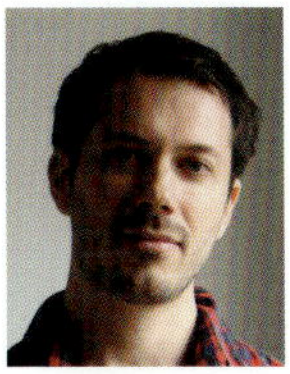

Christobal de Oliveira (FR) has been working on his own projects since 2008 at the meeting point of drawing, painting, film direction and art installations. A polymorphous creation, influenced by his Brazilian and Argentinian origins and by Japanese cinema (*Dark Water*, *Cure*), Larry Clark or Harmony Korine. **Christobal de Oliveira** (FR) arbeitet seit 2008 an eigenen Projekten, die an den Schnittpunkten von Zeichnung, Malerei, Regie und Kunstinstallation anzusiedeln sind. Sein polymorphes Werk ist beeinflusst von seinen brasilianischen und argentinischen Wurzeln und dem japanischen Filmschaffen (*Dark Water*, *Cure* ...), Larry Clark und Harmony Korine.

Assassin's Creed Revelations
Digic Pictures

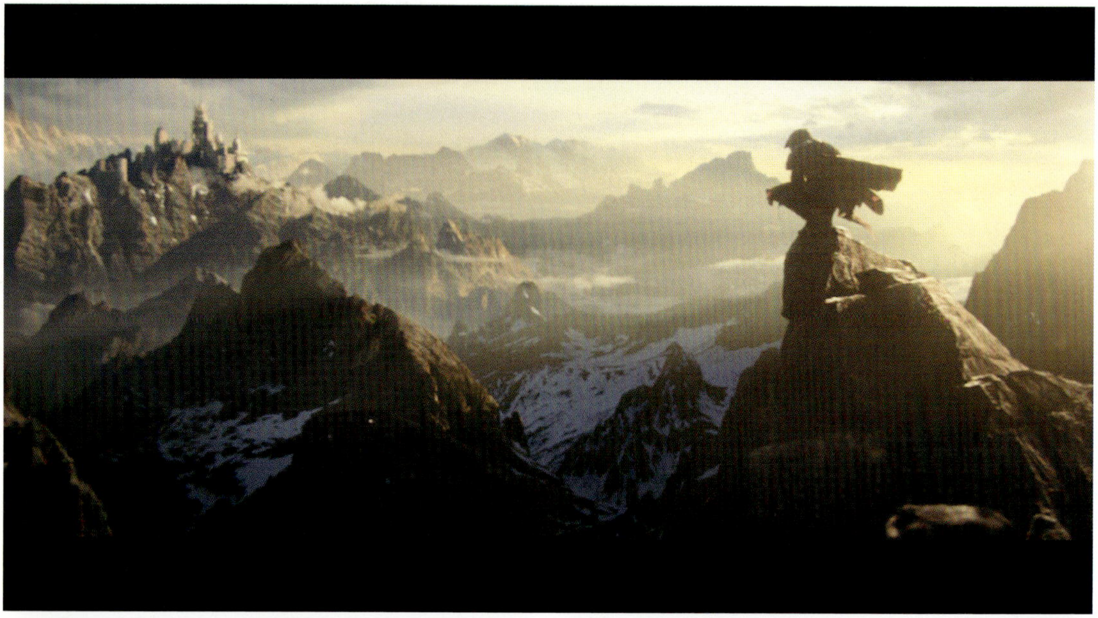

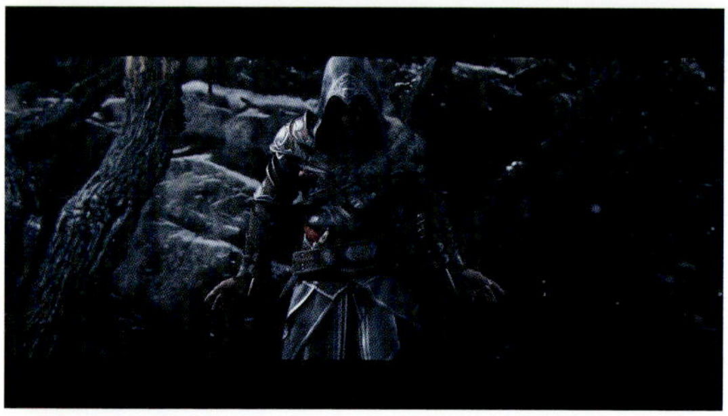

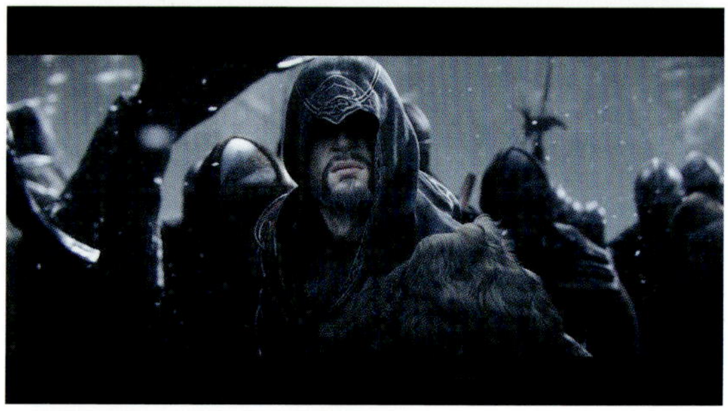

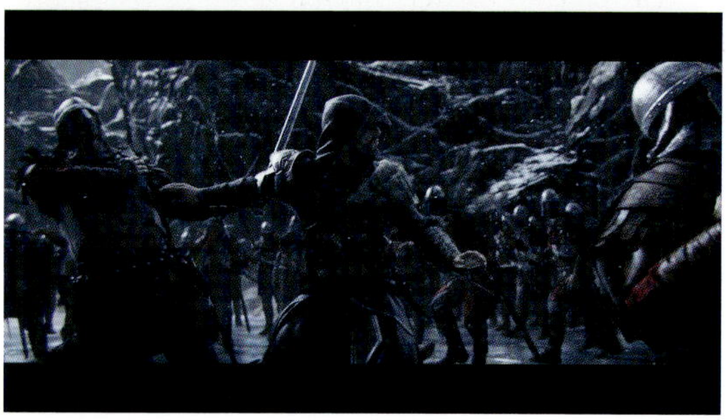

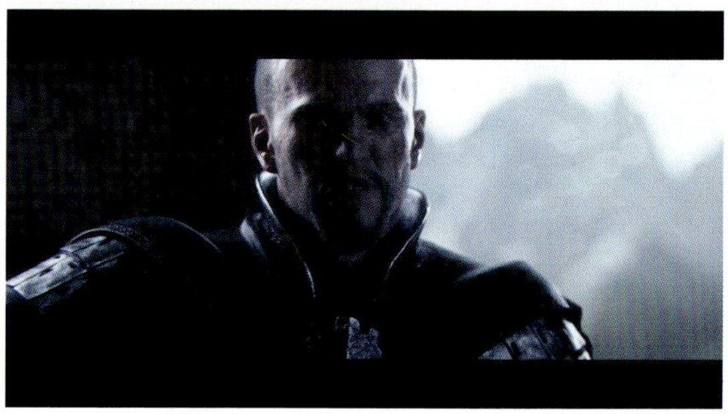

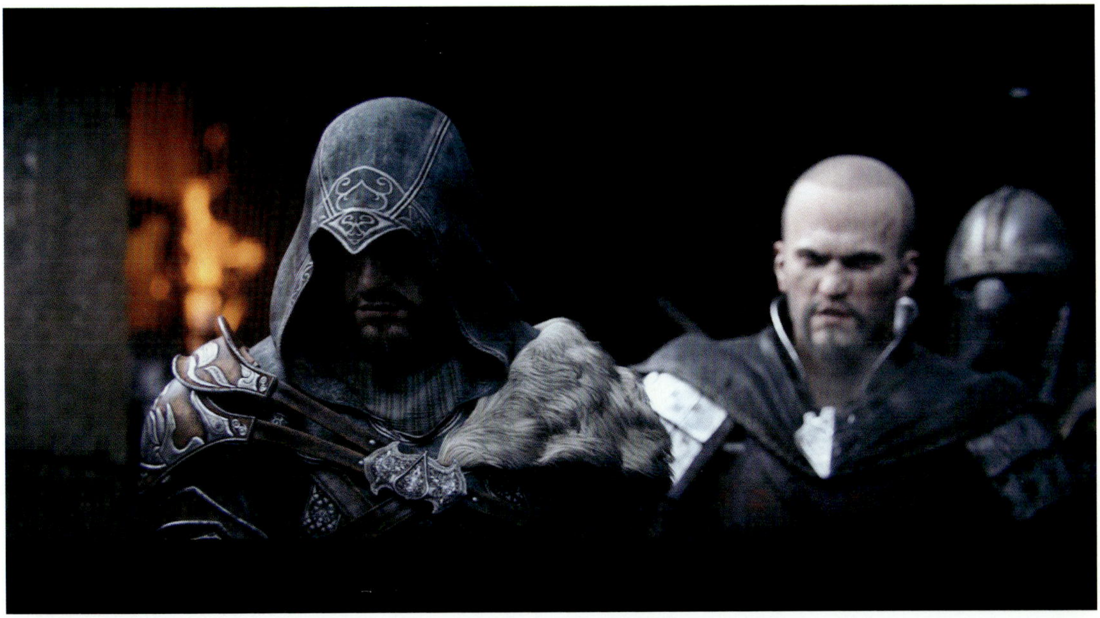

In *Assassin's Creed: Revelations* (Die Offenbarung) tritt Meister-Assassine Ezio Auditore in die Fußstapfen seines legendären Mentors Altaïr und begibt sich auf eine Reise, um fünf antike Siegel aufzuspüren, die eine Schlüsselrolle für die Zukunft der Bruderschaft der Assassinen spielen. Es ist eine gefährliche Reise, die Ezio nach Konstantinopel, in das Zentrum des Ottomanischen Reiches führt, wo eine wachsende Armee von Templern die Region zu destabilisieren droht.
Der vierte Titel der bekannten Serie wurde am 6. Juni 2011 bei der Ubisoft-Pressekonferenz auf der E3 vorgestellt und von der Redaktion und den Zusehern von gamespot.com, gametrailers.com und 1up.com als „Bester Trailer der E3 2011" ausgezeichnet.

Assassin's Creed Revelations follows master assassin Ezio Auditore as he walks in the footsteps of his legendary mentor, Altaïr, on a journey to recover five ancient seals that hold the keys to the future of the Assassins brotherhood. It is a perilous path—one that will take Ezio to Constantinople, the heart of the Ottoman Empire, where a growing army of Templars threatens to destabilize the region.
The fourth title from the renowned series debuted on June 6, 2011; at Ubisoft's E3 press conference and earned Digic the recognition for Best Trailer of E3 2011 by the editors and viewers of gamespot.com, gametrailers.com and 1up.com.

Digic Pictures (HU) is a computer-animation film studio that produces full 3D animated shorts and visual effects in association with video games, feature films or commercial advertisements. Digic's productions have earned the studio global recognition with game trailers and intro movies that were screened at the Siggraph CAF Electronic Theater or awarded Siggraph prizes. In June 2011 Digic's *Assassin's Creed Revelations* trailer became the most viewed video on top gamer community portals. Digic also provides motion-capture services at its own mocap studio, Digic Motion. **Digic Pictures** (HU) ist ein Animationsfilmstudio, das auf 3D-Animationskurzfilme und visuelle Effekte für Videospiele, Spielfilme oder Werbung spezialisiert ist. Die Produktionen brachten dem Studio weltweit Anerkennung für Spiele-Trailer und Filmintros ein, die im Siggraph CAF Electronic Theater gezeigt und mit Preisen auf der Siggraph ausgezeichnet wurden. Im Juni 2011 war *Assassin's Creed: Revelations* das meistgesehene Video auf den renommiertesten Spieleportalen. Digic Pictures bietet auch Motion Capture Services, Verfahren zur Bewegungserfassung, im eigenen Motion Capture Studio Digic Motion an.

Christmas Card to Friends

Stephen Fitzgerald, Nathan Deceasar / Group Hug

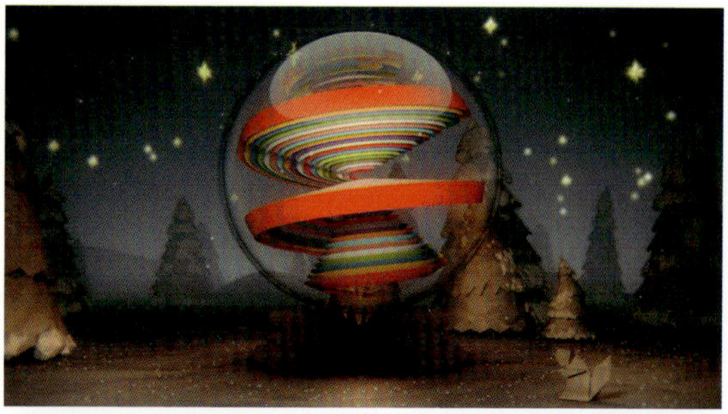

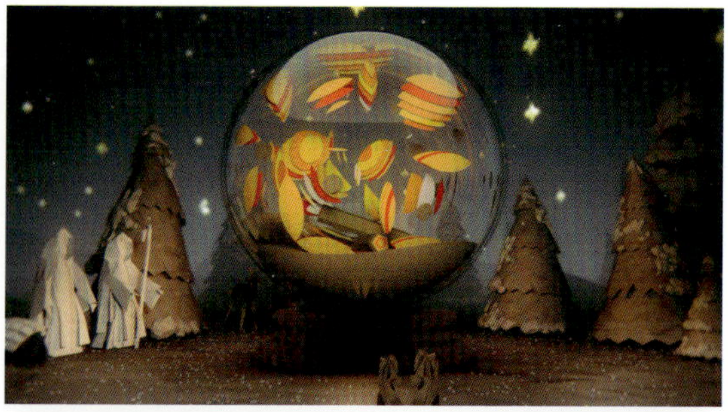

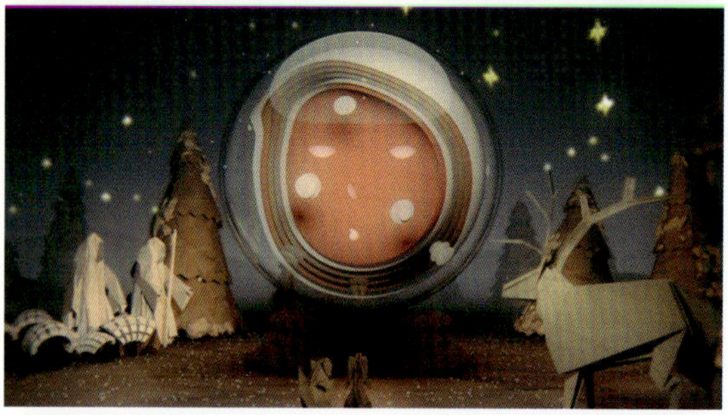

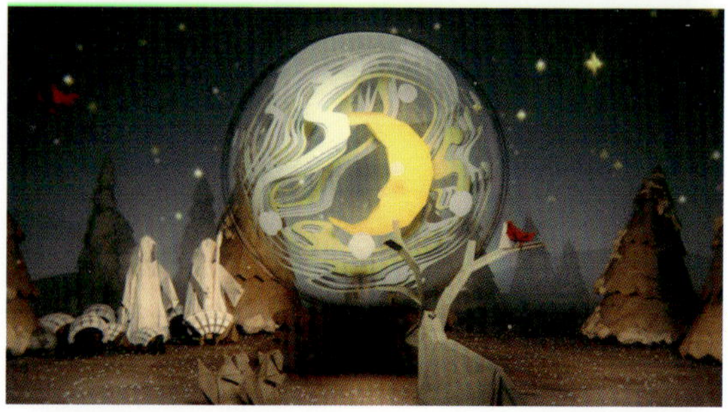

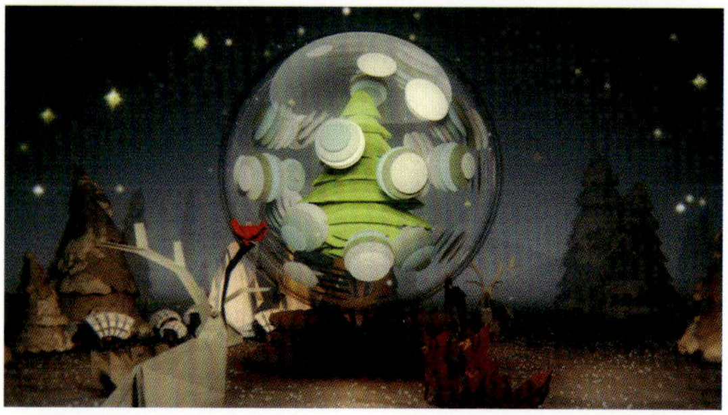

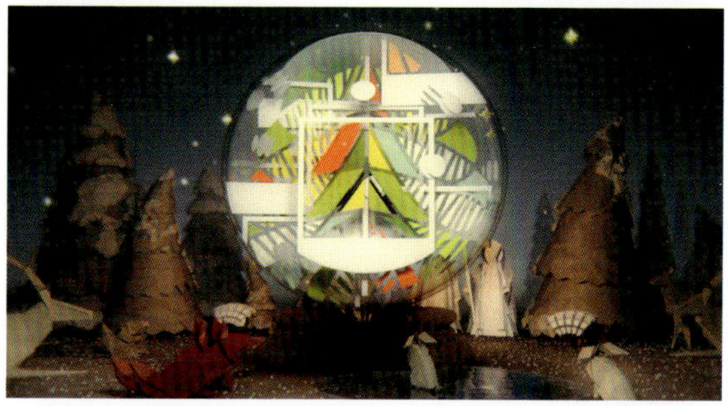

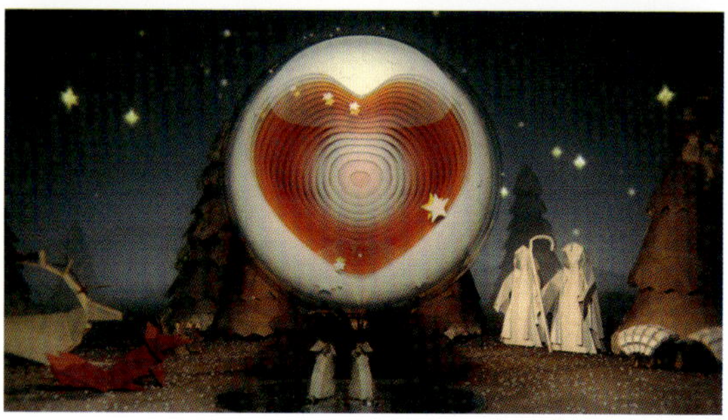

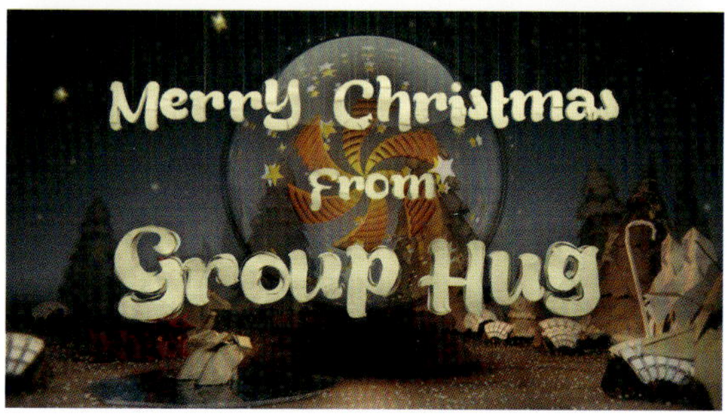

Einer meiner Freunde, Grant Harold, hat mir einen Song geschickt, den er dieses Jahr für Weihnachten geschrieben hat, dessen einfache Botschaft mir gefiel. Also rief ich meinen Freund Nathan Deceasar an und fragte ihn, ob er Lust hätte, mit mir aus dem Song eine Weihnachtskarte für Freunde zu machen. Wir nennen unser kleines Trio, das aus Grant, Nathan und mir besteht, „Group Hug". (Text: Stephen Fitzgerald)

A friend of mine, Grant Harold, sent me a song he wrote for Christmas this year, and I liked its simple message. So I rang my friend Nathan Deceasar and asked if he wanted to join me in turning it into a card for friends. Grant and Nathan and I call our little trio "Group Hug".
(Text: Stephen Fitzgerald)

Direction: Stephen Fitzgerald; music: Grant Harold; design: Stephen Fitzgerald, Nathan Deceasar; Animation: Stephen Fitzgerald, Nathan Deceasar

Group Hug (US) is a loose association of friends collaborating on projects in various audio and animation mediums. **Group Hug** (US) ist eine lose Gruppe von Freunden, die gemeinsam an Projekten in diversen Audio- und Animationsmedien zusammenarbeitet.

Countdown

Céline Desrumeaux / Passion Pictures

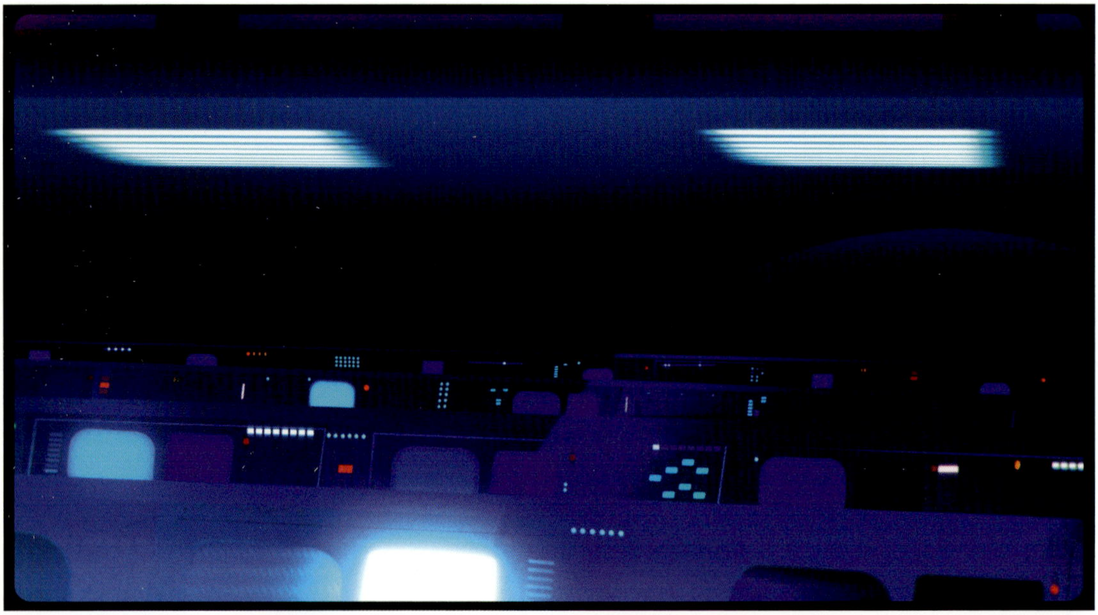

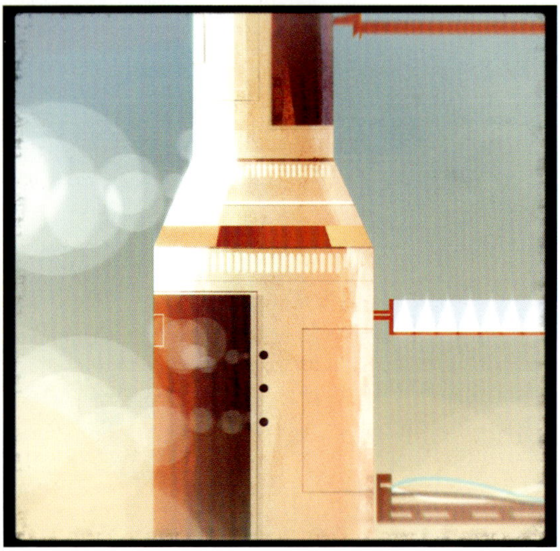

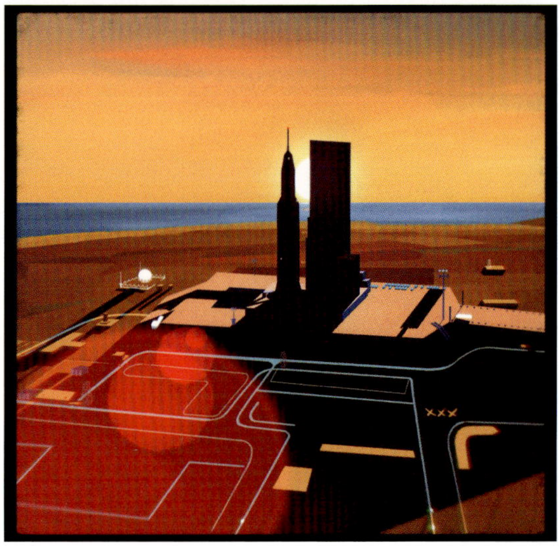

I little over two years ago, I began drawing pictures with rockets in them. I do not know why, but one evening I wanted to do an exercise for myself with some constraints, which were: using colors I do not usually use; using a square format (in tribute to the old 8mm format); sometimes it could be abstract, and everything was to be about a rocket. A couple of weeks later I discovered the music of

Vor etwas mehr als zwei Jahren begann ich, Raketen zu zeichnen. Eines Abends, ich weiß nicht mehr warum, wollte ich eine Übung für mich selbst machen, mir Einschränkungen auferlegen, zum Beispiel Farben verwenden, die ich gewöhnlich nicht nehme, und ein bestimmtes Format (eine Hommage an das alte 8-mm-Format); die Zeichnung durfte durchaus auch abstrakt sein, jedenfalls sollte sie mit einer Rakete zu tun haben.

Dann, ein paar Wochen später, entdeckte ich die Musik von Apparat und die Nummer *Granular Bastard*. Ich war fasziniert von der Idee, eine dreieinhalbminütige Animation über den Start einer Rakete zu machen.
Ich wollte einen „Stimmungsfilm" machen, nicht unbedingt eine tiefgehende Geschichte erzählen, es ging mir vielmehr um schöne Farben, eine gute Komposition und eine Rakete in der „Hauptrolle". An Godfrey Reggios Film *Koyaanisqatsi* gefällt mir, dass die Erde und das Leben die Hauptrolle spielen. Das entspricht nicht unseren Sehgewohnheiten und ist daher schön. Ich habe sogar ein Drehbuch geschrieben (verrückt für ein Musikvideo, ich weiß).
Ich habe im Sommer 2009 mit der Animation begonnen. Zunächst habe ich mir die Musik immer wieder angehört und in verschiedene Segmente zerlegt, um eine Vorstellung davon zu bekommen, welche Sequenz ich mit welcher Musik unterlegen möchte. Es beginnt mit dem Erwachen der Computer, die Maschinen beginnen zu laufen, die Astronauten steigen in die Rakete, alles steigert sich zu einem Finale, Stille – und Abflug. Ich habe alle Bilder für die Animation (bis auf zwei) in Farbe gezeichnet.
Das Bild des Rauches war wirklich wichtig für die Stilisierung des Rauches und des Feuers. Ich wollte diese Kreispartikel unbedingt für die Darstellung des Rauchs verwenden.
Die Animation wurde eigentlich nicht mehr verändert. Ich habe sie ganz am Anfang gemacht und versucht, möglichst dabei zu bleiben. Die Grafik hat sich entwickelt, aber nicht der Filmschnitt. Es war von Anfang an die Art von Schnitt, die ich wollte.
Der Beginn des Films war etwas heikel (weil ich am Beginn wirklich etwas sehr Abstraktes wollte, das Aufleuchten der Schaltflächen und Einschalten der Computer). Das lässt sich in der Animation schwer machen, man kann einen „Platzhalter" dafür einsetzen, aber im Grunde genommen entsteht das von selbst während der Arbeit.
Als Referenzen wären zu nennen: Chris Ware, Hans Richter, Len Lye, Stanley Kubrick und Godfrey Reggios Qatsi-Trilogie.

Apparat and the track *Granular Bastard*. I thought it would be amazing to do a three-and-a-half-minute animation of a rocket taking off.
I really wanted an "atmospheric movie", not necessarily a deep story but just beautiful colors, good composition and a rocket as a main character. It is what I like in Godfrey Reggio's film *Koyaanisqatsi*, the earth and life is the main character. It is not something we are used to seeing, and that is why it is beautiful. I have even written a script (which I know is crazy for a music video).
I began the animation in summer 2009. I listened to the music repeatedly and first cut the music into different parts, to get an idea of which sequence to put with which part of the music. First there are the computers waking up, then everything starts working, the astronauts enter in the rocket, everything warms up, silence, and finally take off. With one or two exceptions, I drew all the images for the animation in color.
The image of the smoke was really important for the stylization of the smoke and fire. I really wanted to keep these circle particles to represent the smoke.
I did not really change the animation. I did it at the very beginning and tried as far as possible to stick to it. The graphics evolved but not the editing. From the beginning to the end this was the kind of editing I wanted.
The beginning of the movie was a tricky part (because at the beginning I really wanted something very abstract in the way of the buttons and computers switching on). It is not something you can do in animation; you can do a rough "placeholder" but it is something that builds by itself while you are doing it.
From beginning to end, Chris Ware, Hans Richter, Len Lye, Stanley Kubrick and Godfrey Reggio's *Qatsi* trilogy were huge references.

Story, director, design, animation, compositing: Céline Desrumeaux; character animation: Florent Remize; music: "Granular bastard" from Apparat

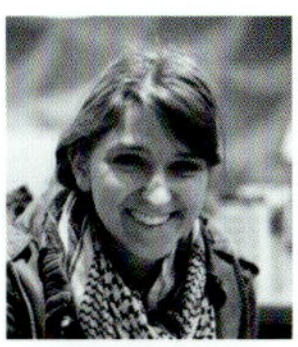

Céline Desrumeaux (FR) studied at the Supinfocom computer graphics school. She graduated with the award-winning short film *Yankee Gal* before moving to London, where she lives and works with Yann Benedi as duo directors at Passion Pictures. **Céline Desrumeaux** (FR) studierte an der Supinfocom. Sie graduierte mit dem preisgekrönten Kurzfilm „Yankee Gal" und ging dann nach London, wo sie gemeinsam mit Yann Benedi für Passion Pictures arbeitet.

Crossover

Fabian Grodde

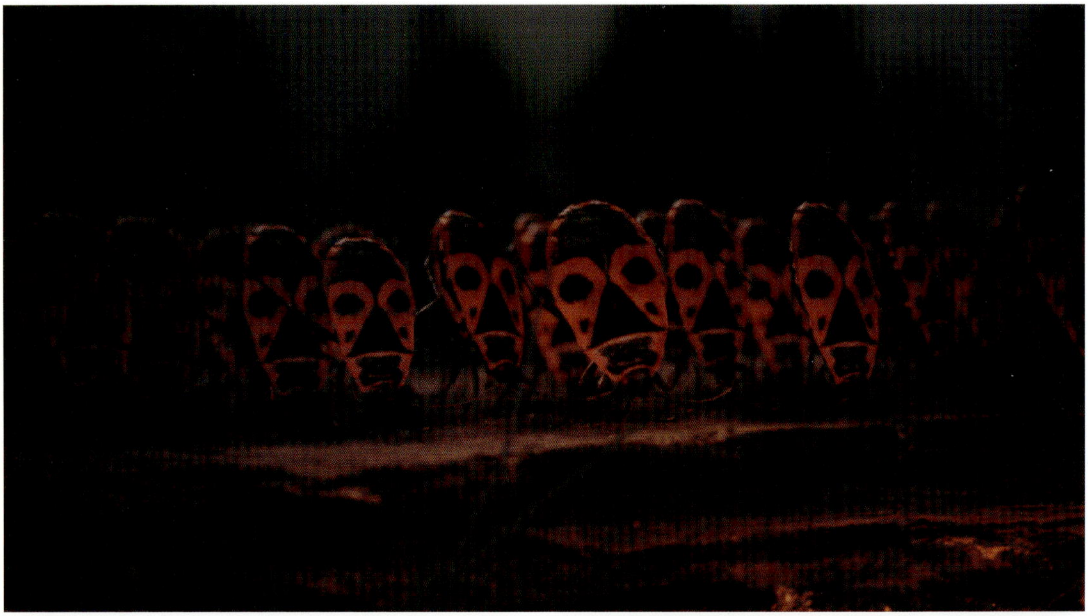

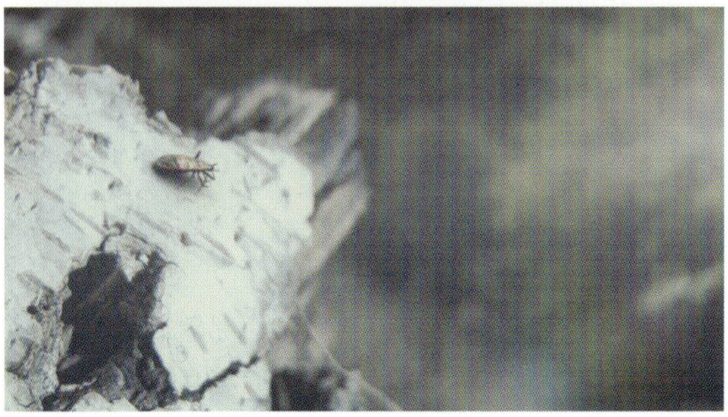

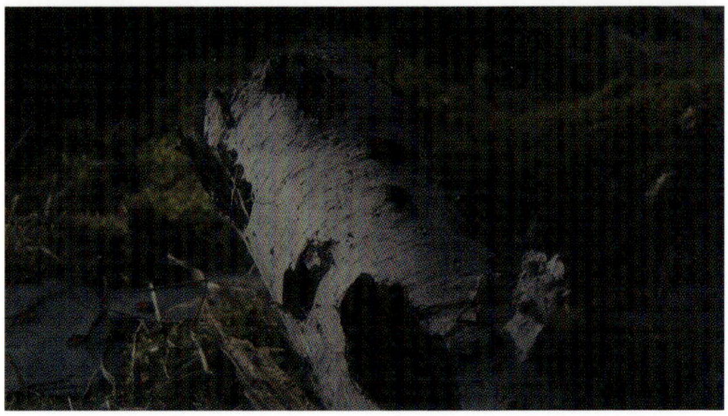

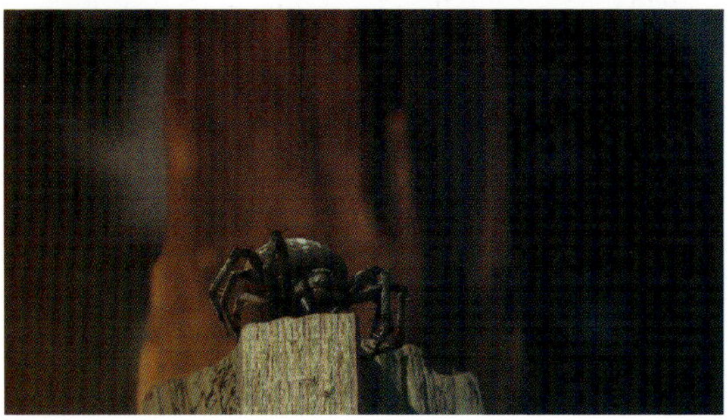

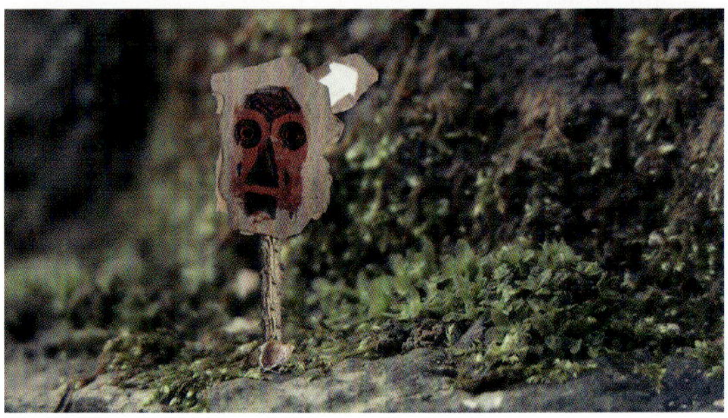

Director / Producer / Compositing: Fabian Grodde; 3D VFX Supervisor: Alexander Schumann; 3D Artists: Christian Brinkmann, Stephan Hempel; director of photography: Raphael Köhler; camera assistant, camera stage: Christian Brinkmann; 3D VFX Set Supervisor, Continuity: Stephan Hempel; line producer: Martin Goldschmidt; set photography: Nora Ströbel, Nina Röder; catering: Jennifer Haase

Mir ist alle Macht im Himmel und auf der Erde gegeben. Darum geht zu allen Völkern und macht die Menschen zu meinen Jüngern; tauft sie auf den Namen des Vaters, des Sohnes und des heiligen Geistes und lehrt sie, alles zu befolgen, was ich euch geboten habe. (Der Missionsbefehl nach Mt 28,18-20)

Mit der sogenannten Reconquista, also der Rückeroberung der iberischen Halbinsel durch das Christentum vom Islam, begann eine neue europäischen Kolonialpolitik. Neben dem Streben nach Gold gab es einen weiteren Grund für die Expansion: die Verbreitung des christlichen Glaubens. Mit den ersten Kolonien auf dem schwarzen Kontinent im 15. Jahrhundert kamen neben den Händlern und Arbeitern auch Vertreter der Kirche in die noch weitestgehend unbekannten Regionen. Im Laufe der Zeit begann man Einfluss zu nehmen auf die Bevölkerung.

Mit dem Kurzfilm *Crossover* werfe ich Fragen zu Religion und Identität auf. Im Fokus dieser Auseinandersetzung stehen Missionierung und Konvertierung fremder Kulturen durch Vertreter des Christentums. Diese komplexe Thematik wird jedoch nicht sachbezogen analysiert, vielmehr findet eine Auseinandersetzung auf der filmisch-symbolischen Ebene statt. In meinem Kurzfilm wird die christliche Missionierung hierzu ins Tierreich des Waldes transferiert. Das wilde und ursprüngliche Volk, vertreten durch Feuerwanzen, wird einer Kreuzspinne gegenübergestellt, welche mit einer List anstrebt, die Insekten zu bekehren.

Im Grunde genommen leisten Religionen für den Menschen Orientierungsangebote, welche es ihm ermöglichen, durch eine von Kultur und Konvention kreierte Welt zu navigieren. Werte und Normen, Ziele und Zwecke des Daseins generieren sich aus einer vom Glauben geprägten Weltanschauung und bilden somit Sinnsysteme, die wiederum Orientierung ermöglichen und ihrerseits Lesarten und Lebensweisen vorgeben. Jedwede Religionsgemeinschaft definiert sich vor allem auch durch eine Reihe ikonografischer Allegorien, die sie adressierbar und nach außen hin unverwechselbar macht. In *Crossover* mündet eine von Wegweisern künstlich arrangierte Wallfahrt, die als Spiegelbild der Feuerwanze durch den Wald führt, im Kreuz, dem Hauptsymbol des Okzidents.

All authority in heaven and on earth has been given to me. Therefore go and make disciples of all nations, baptizing them in the name of the Father and of the Son and of the Holy Spirit, and teaching them to obey everything I have commanded you. And surely I am with you always, to the very end of the age. (The Great Commission, Matthew 28:18-20)

A new European colonial policy began with what is called the Reconquista, when Christians recaptured the Muslim-controlled areas of the Iberian Peninsula. And there was another reason for colonial expansion besides seeking gold: to spread the Christian faith. With the first colonies on the Dark Continent in the 15th century, not only traders and workers arrived in these still largely unknown regions, but also representatives of the church. As time passed, their influence on the populations there grew.

In the short film *Crossover*, I pose questions about religion and identity. Missionary work and the conversion of foreign cultures by representatives of the church are at the heart of this investigation. And yet this complex topic is not analyzed in a factual manner but explored on a more cinematic, symbolic level. In my short film, Christian missionary activity has been transferred to the animal kingdom in the forest. Indigenous populations are represented by fire bugs and set against a garden spider (with a cross-shaped mark on its back) that tricks the insects into converting.

Essentially, religions give orientation and enable people to navigate a world shaped by culture and conventions. A world view that has been formed by religious faith generates values and norms, objectives and purposes, and these form systems of meanings that, in turn, give orientation and so provide specific readings and modes of living. Every religious community defines itself by a number of iconographic allegories and these make it addressable and outwardly unmistakable. In *Crossover*, a pilgrimage—arranged artfully along signposts with the firebug's image—leads through the forest and ends at the cross, the central symbol of the Occident.

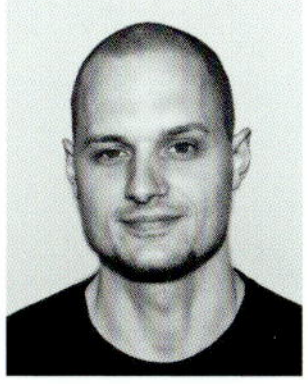

Fabian Grodde (DE), born in 1983. In 2005, he began studying media design at the Bauhaus-Universität Weimar. He received his Bachelor of Fine Arts in 2010. Since 2010, Fabian has been a junior compositor at Parasol Island. **Fabian Grodde** (DE), geb. 1983. 2005 Studium Mediengestaltung an der Bauhaus-Universität Weimar, 2010 Bachelor of Fine Arts. Seit 2010 ist Fabian Junior Compositor bei Parasol Island.

Fat

Gary Fouchy, Yohann Auroux Bernard, Sebastien de Oliveira Bispo / Supinfocom Arles

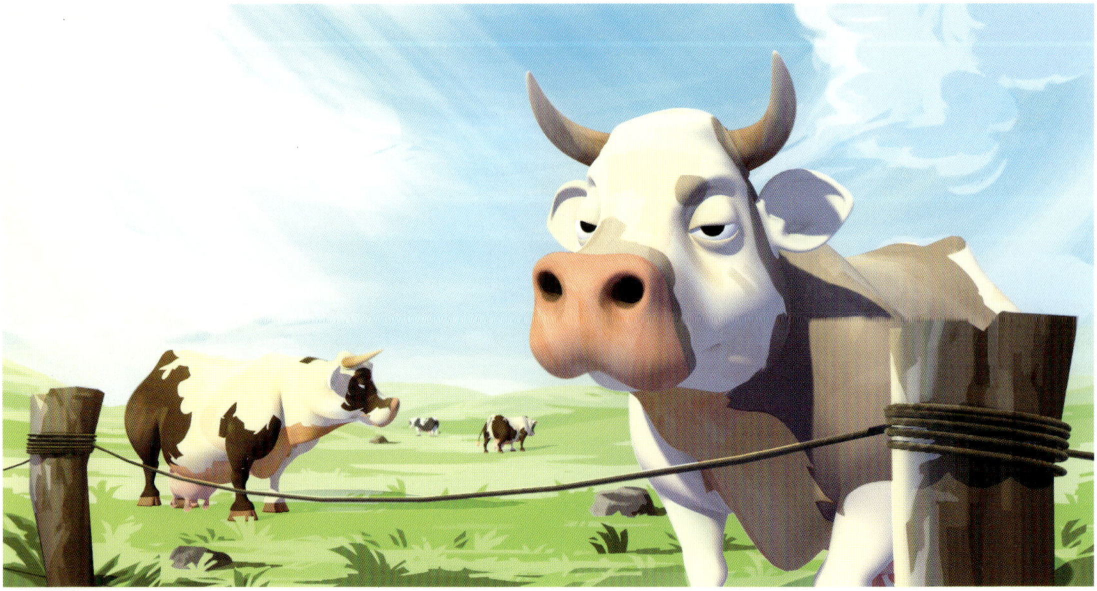

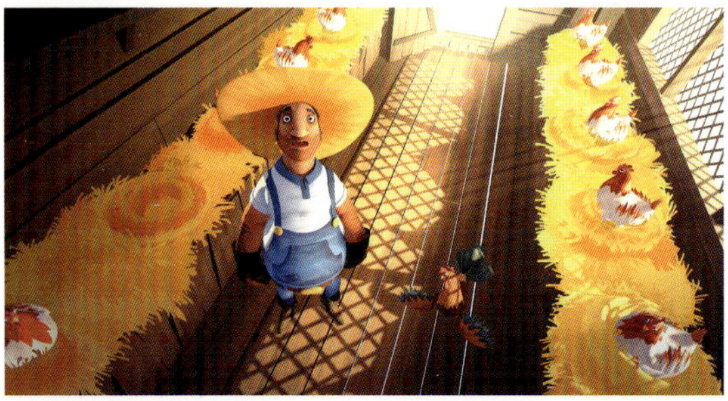

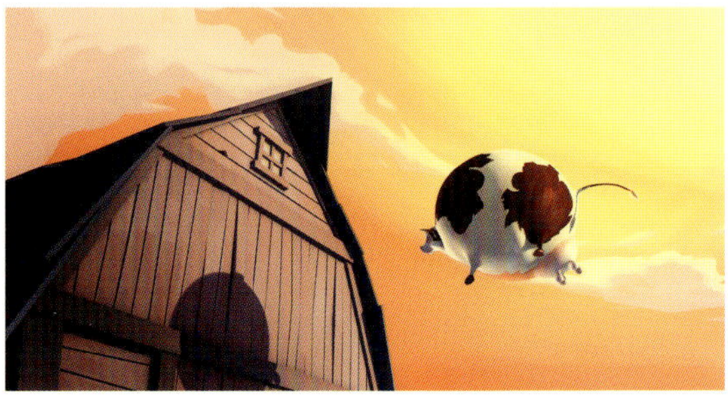

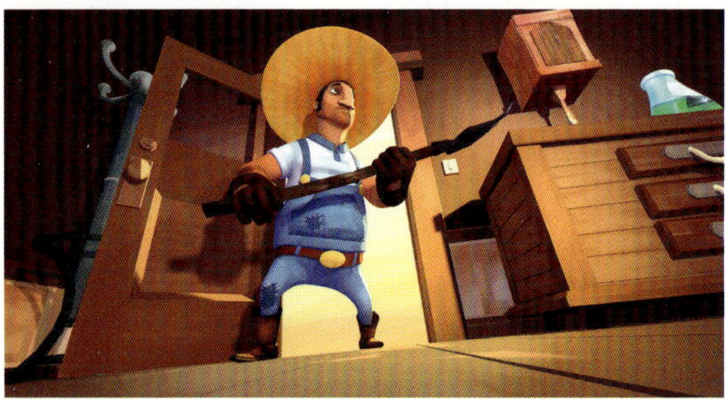

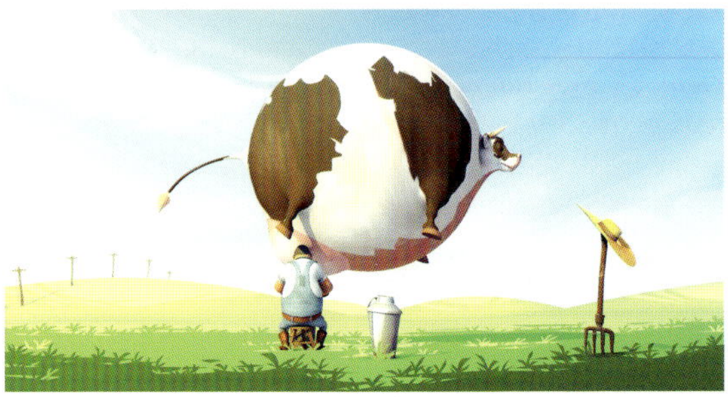

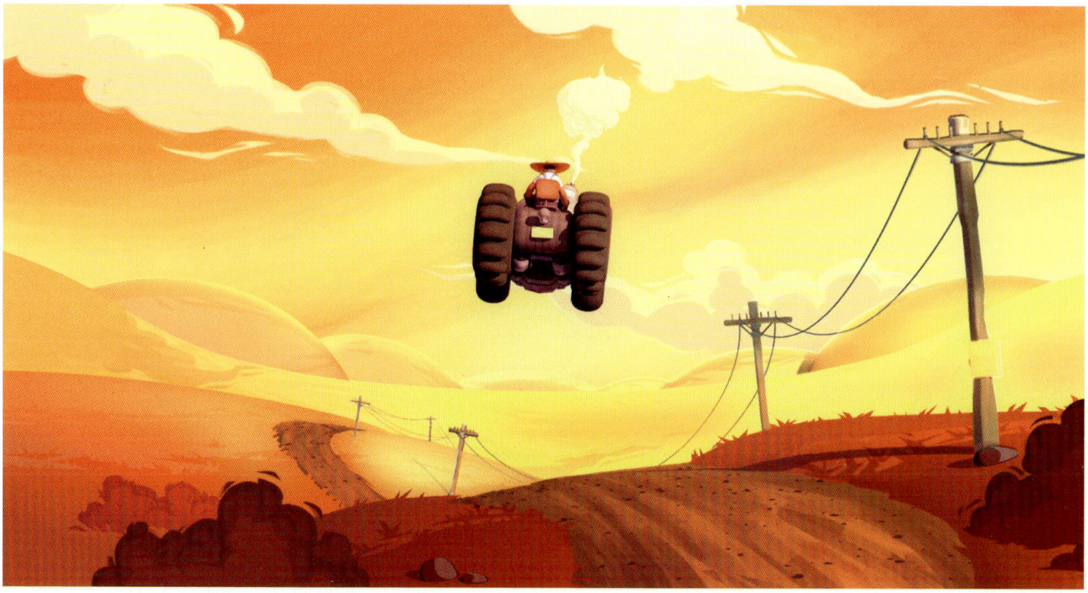

Auf einer kleinen Farm in ländlicher Abgeschiedenheit geht alles seinen gemächlichen, geordneten Gang, bis der Farmer eines Morgens entdeckt, dass ein höchst seltsames Phänomen um sich greift und eines seiner Tiere nach dem anderen befällt. Er muss sich auf die neue Situation, die ihn mit vielen seltsamen und rätselhaften Vorfällen konfrontiert, einstellen und versuchen, den Betrieb trotzdem am Laufen zu halten.
Dieser Kurzfilm, dessen zentrale Themen Verwandlung und Veränderung sind, ist eine gelungene Mischung aus Komödie und poetischer Erzählung, die in einer überschaubaren kleinen Welt angesiedelt ist. Intention des für alle Altersgruppen geeigneten Films ist es, die Zuseher zu unterhalten und vielleicht auch zum Nachdenken anzuregen, wie wir mit Veränderungen umgehen, die sich in unserem Alltag ergeben.

Lost in the middle of nowhere, a quiet little farm lives at the rhythm of its daily routine. One morning, the farmer discovers that a very strange phenomenon is spreading around him, hitting one animal after another. He has to adapt to this new environment full of strange and quirky situations and try to keep things going.
Based on the theme of metamorphosis and change, this short aims to be a well-balanced blend of comedy and poetry set in a simple, pretty little world. Suitable for all ages, it was made for enjoyment, to have fun and maybe think about how we deal with the transformations that happen in our everyday lives.

Gary Foucher (FR) has always had a deep passion for animated films. He likes to tell strange and funny stories using his imagination, and loves to use this media because of the freedom it allows. **Yohann Auroux Bernard** (FR) has enjoyed creating and drawing new characters since he was a child; now landscapes and storyboard also complete his desires. **Sebastien de Oliveira Bispo** (FR), born in the Caribbean, has been exposed to cartoons and animated films since his early childhood. Now it has become a real passion to tell a story by creating a graphic universe. **Gary Fouchy** (FR) hat seit jeher eine große Leidenschaft für Zeichentrickfilme. Er erzählt gerne merkwürdige lustige Geschichten, die der Fantasie Raum geben, und bevorzugt den Animationsfilm, weil er dem Filmemacher große Freiheiten bietet. **Yohann Auroux Bernard** (FR) erfindet und zeichnet seit seiner Kindheit mit Begeisterung neue Charaktere, mittlerweile erstreckt sich diese Begeisterung auch auf die Darstellung von Landschaften und Storyboards. **Sebastien de Oliveira Bispo** (FR) hat karibische Wurzeln und interessiert sich seit seiner Kindheit für Cartoons und Zeichentrickfilme. Geschichten durch Entwurf eines grafischen Universums zu erzählen, wurde zu seinem Lebensinhalt.

L'ère bête

Thomas Caudron, Ingrid Menet, Laurent Mériaux, Clément Tissier / Supinfocom Valenciennes

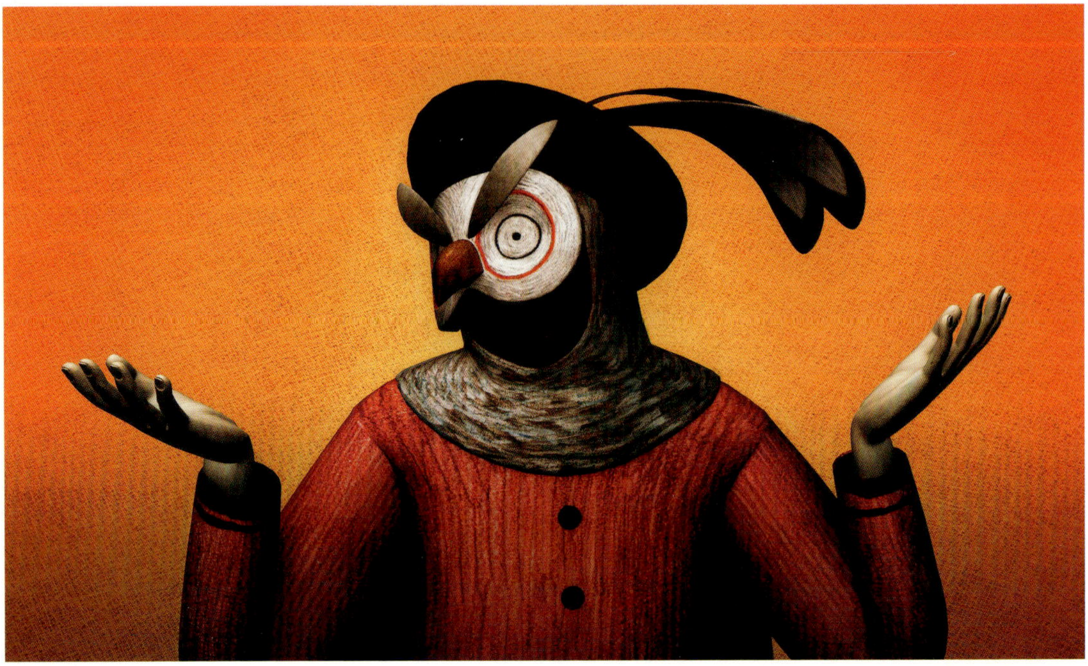

L'ère bête is a medieval farce dealing with the notions of humanity and bestiality.
In the Middle Ages, a sow and a beggar are invited to a carnival where a crowd of masked men have fun in judging and torturing animals as if they were human beings. Our heroes are arrested and judged in their turn.
The film shows an archaic pagan carnival inspired by Flemish painting as well as surrealism. We follow the two heroes in a universe with its own internal logic that we cannot completely understand and where humanity and bestiality turn out to be intimately related. The illustrative look as well as the original music on ancient instruments contribute to making this crazy vision of ancient times real.

L'ère bête ist eine Farce auf das Mittelalter, die sich mit Menschlichkeit und Verrohung auseinandersetzt.
Ein Schwein und ein Bettler werden zu einem Karneval eingeladen, wo sich eine Gruppe maskierter Männer damit vergnügt, Tieren den Prozess zu machen, als ob sie Menschen wären, und sie zu foltern. Auch unsere beiden Helden werden festgenommen ...
Der Film zeigt einen archaischen heidnischen Karneval, der sowohl von der flämischen Malerei als auch vom Surrealismus inspiriert ist. Wir folgen den Protagonisten in eine absurde Welt mit eigener Logik, die nicht wirklich nachvollziehbar ist, und in der Menschlichkeit und Brutalität sich als eng miteinander verbunden erweisen. Die überzeugende Bildsprache und die auf originalen historischen Instrumenten gespielte mittelalterliche Musik tragen dazu bei, dieser absurden Vision der Vergangenheit einen Anschein von Realität zu verleihen.

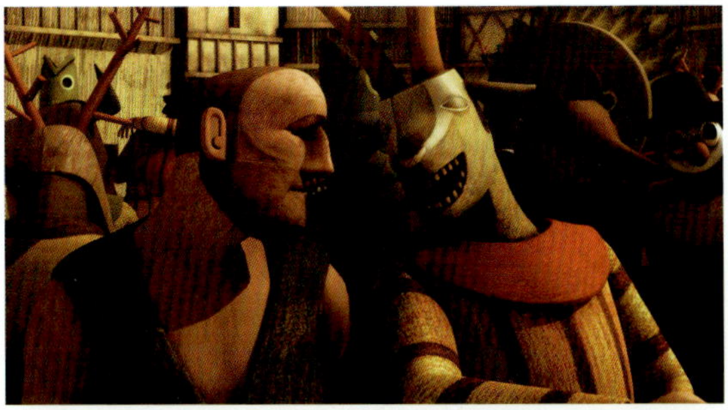

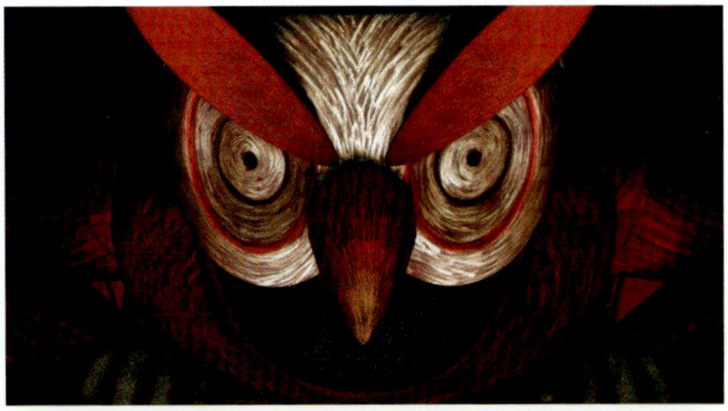

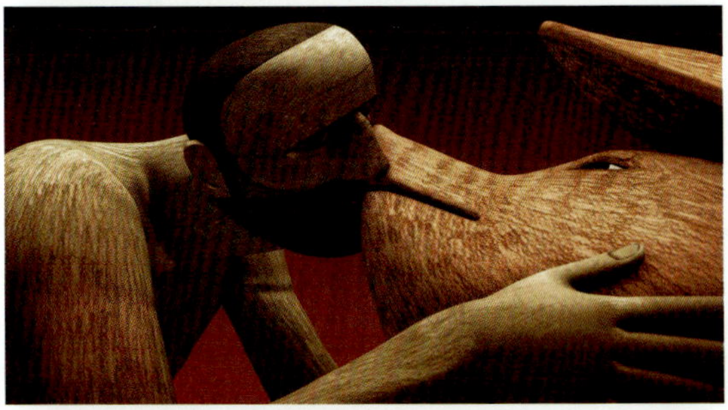

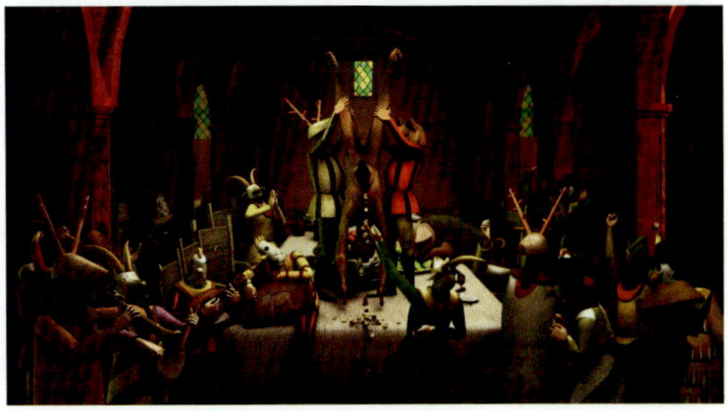

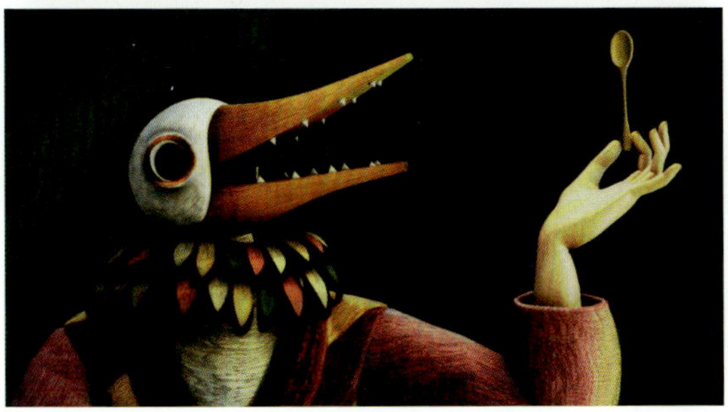

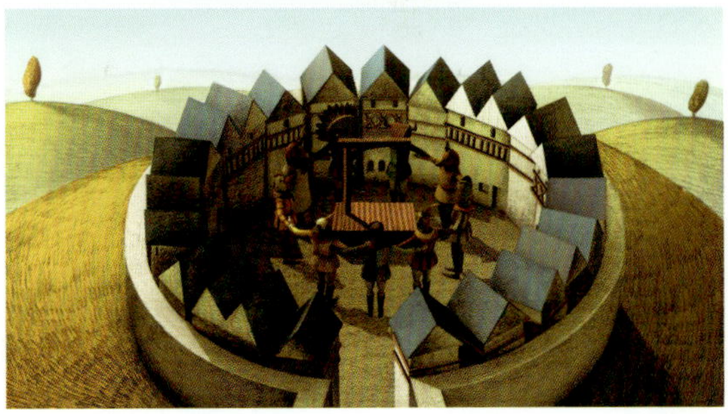

Before joining the Supinfocom school, **Thomas Caudron** (FR) studied humanities and political science for two years focusing on history. **Laurent Mériaux** (FR) graduated in graphic design, **Ingrid Menet** (FR) studied fine arts at the Valenciennes University and **Clément Tissier** (FR) studied computer graphics at Saint-Luc School in Brussels. *L'ere bête* is our graduation film from Supinfocom Valenciennes, a computer graphics and animation school in the north of France, where we met. Bevor sich die vier Künstler an der Supinfocom Valenciennes kennenlernten, studierte **Thomas Caudron** (FR) zwei Jahre lang Geisteswissenschaften und Politikwissenschaft mit Hauptfach Geschichte, **Laurent Mériaux** (FR) absolvierte ein Grafikdesignstudium, **Ingrid Menet** (FR) studierte bildende Kunst an der Universität Valenciennes und **Clément Tissier** (FR) Computergrafik an der École Supérieure des Arts Saint-Luc in Brüssel. *L'ère bête* ist die Abschlussarbeit der Gruppe an der Supinfocom Valenciennes, einer Computergrafik- und Animationsschule im Norden Frankreichs.

The Visual Effects and Animation of Rango

Industrial Light & Magic

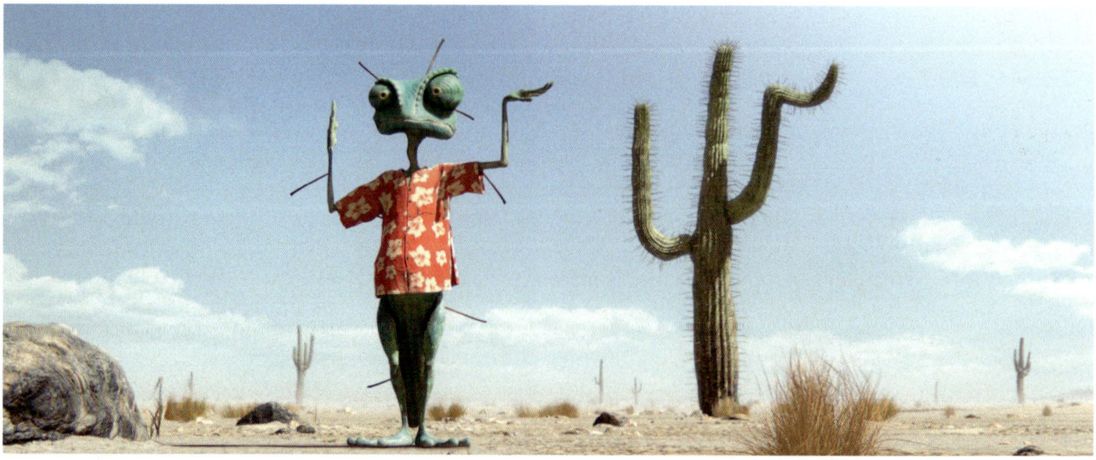

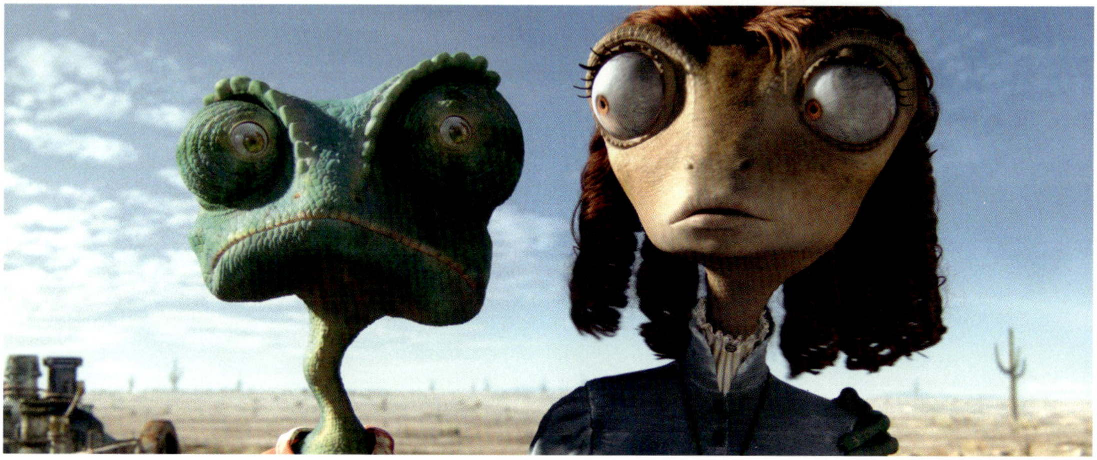

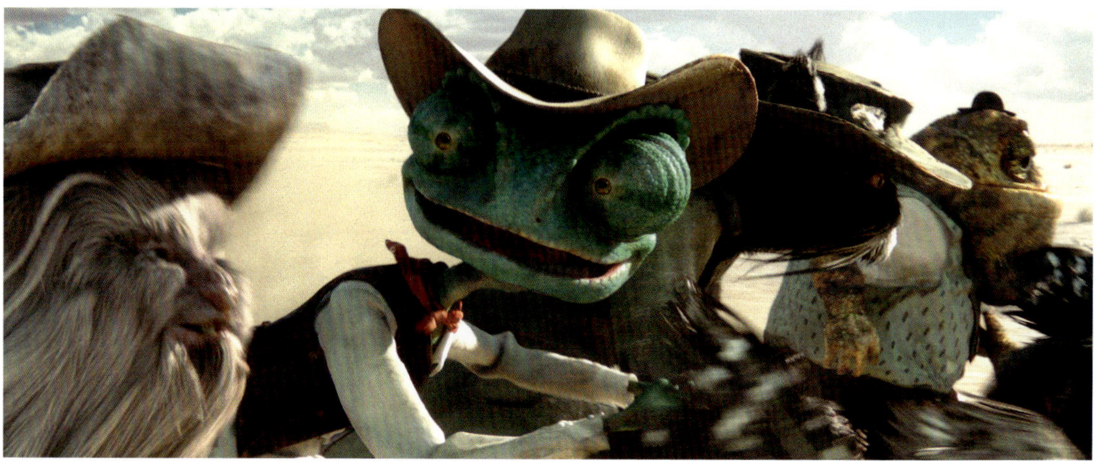

Rango ist eine originelle animierte Abenteuerkomödie, die Kinobesucher auf einen aberwitzigen, dabei aber emotional berührenden Trip in den Wilden Westen entführt. Die Geschichte folgt der kuriosen Reise des Chamäleons Rango (Johnny Depp), das zunächst ein gewöhnliches Haustierdasein fristet und eine tiefe Identitätskrise durchmacht. Als Rango entkommt und zufällig in Dirt landet, einem gesetzlosen Wüstenkaff, in dem die gerissensten und skurrilsten Kreaturen der Wildnis sich als Revolverhelden gerieren – wird die eigentlich ängstliche Echse unvermutet zum Helden. Als lange erwarteter Retter und letzte Hoffnung willkommen geheißen, ist der zum Sheriff ernannte Rango gezwungen, seine neue Rolle bis zum bitteren Ende zu spielen ... bis er in einem Showdown voller actiongeladener Szenen und Begegnungen mit ungeheuerlichen Charakteren zu dem Helden wird, der er zu sein vorgab.
Rango (Regie: Gore Verbinski) gewann 2012 den Oscar in der Kategorie bester Animationsfilm.

Rango is an original animated comedy adventure that takes moviegoers for a hilarious and heartfelt walk in the Wild West. The story follows the comical, transformative journey of Rango (Johnny Depp), a sheltered chameleon living as an ordinary family pet while facing a major identity crisis. When Rango accidentally winds up in the gritty, gun-slinging town of Dirt—a lawless outpost populated by the desert's most wily and whimsical creatures—the less-than-courageous lizard suddenly finds he stands out. Welcomed as the last hope the town has been waiting for, new Sheriff Rango is forced to play his new role to the hilt ... until, in a blaze of action-packed situations and encounters with outrageous characters, Rango starts to become the hero he once only pretended to be.
Rango, directed by Gore Verbinski, won the Oscar for Best Animated Film in 2012.

Industrial Light & Magic (US), with locations in San Francisco and Singapore, is a Lucasfilm Ltd. company serving the digital needs of the entertainment industry for visual effects. Founded in 1975 by George Lucas, ILM has created visual effects for nearly 300 feature films, and has been awarded 15 Academy Awards for Best Visual Effects and received 24 Scientific and Technical Achievement Awards. **Industrial Light & Magic** (US), mit Niederlassungen in San Francisco und Singapur, ist eine Abteilung der Lucasfilm Ltd. und auf visuelle Effekte für die Unterhaltungsindustrie spezialisiert. ILM wurde 1975 von George Lucas gegründet und entwickelte die visuellen Spezialeffekte für nahezu 300 Spielfilme. Das Unternehmen erhielt 15 Oscars für die besten visuellen Effekte sowie 24 Auszeichnungen für technische und wissenschaftliche Leistungen.

The City, Five Years Older

Dirk Koy / Equipo

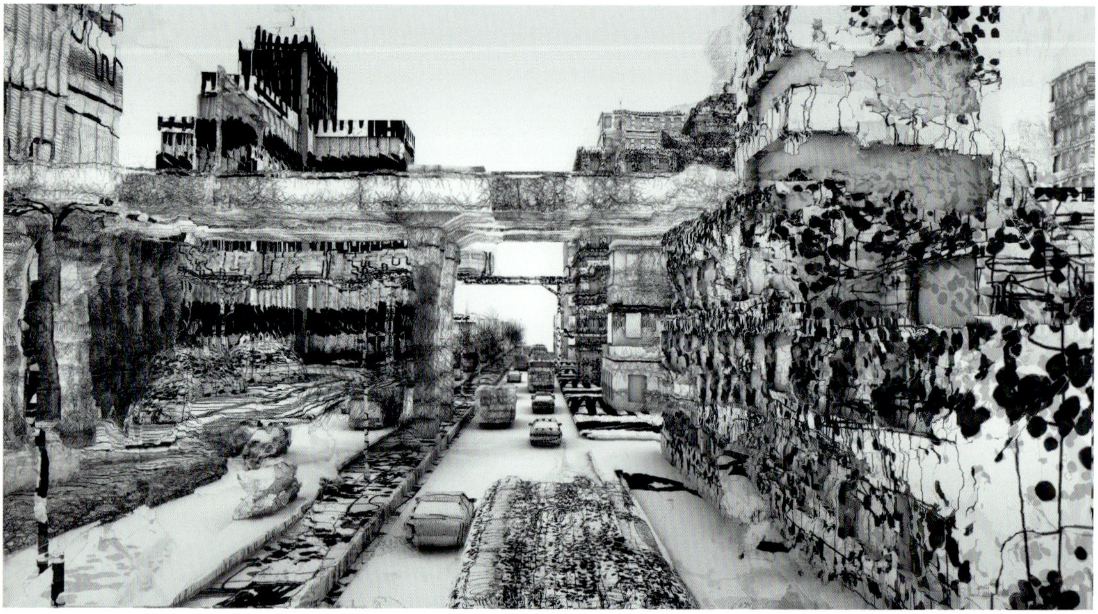

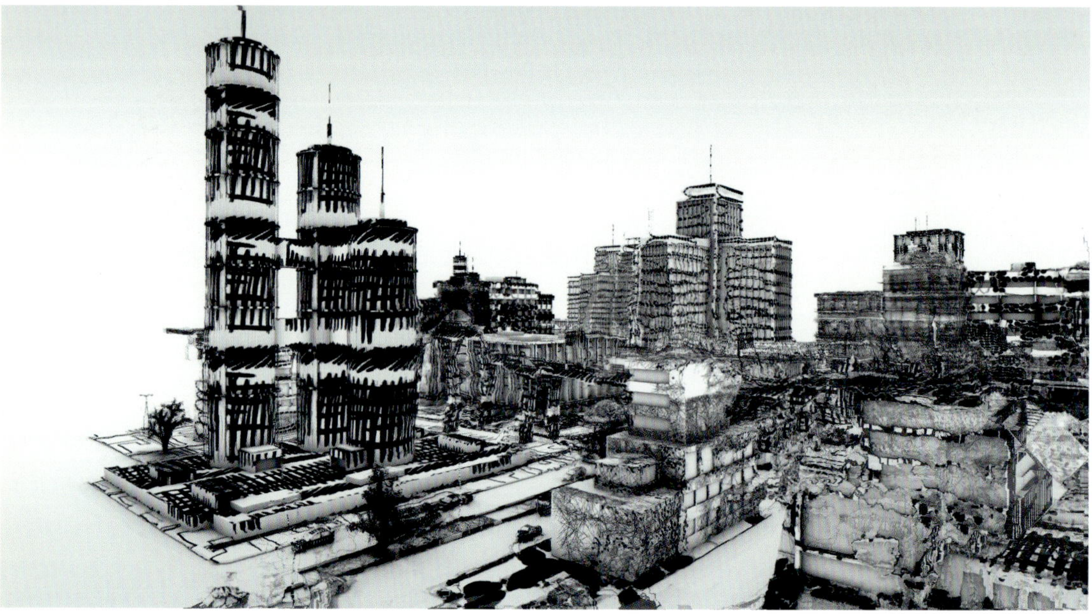

The song *The City* by the Swiss electro-pop band Five Years Older describes the process of a commuter becoming acquainted with an unknown city, adapting to its rhythm, until he is completely absorbed by it. The video clip combines

Der Song *The City* der Schweizer Electropop-Band Five Years Older beschreibt, wie ein Pendler in eine ihm unbekannte Stadt kommt, sich Schritt für Schritt mit ihr vertraut macht und ihrem Rhythmus anpasst, bis er und die neue Umgebung miteinander verschmelzen und

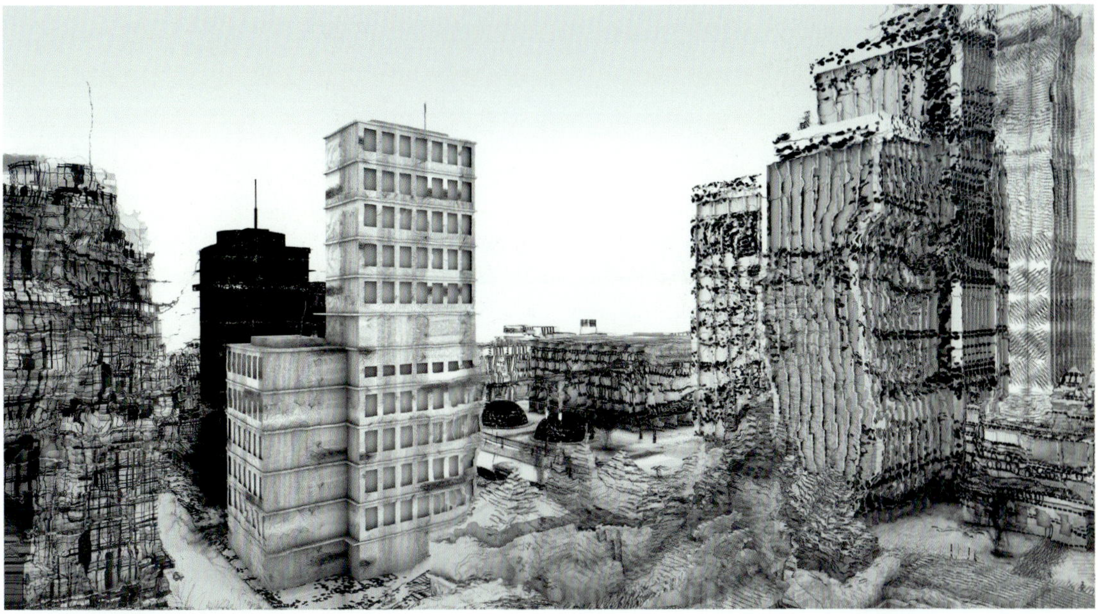

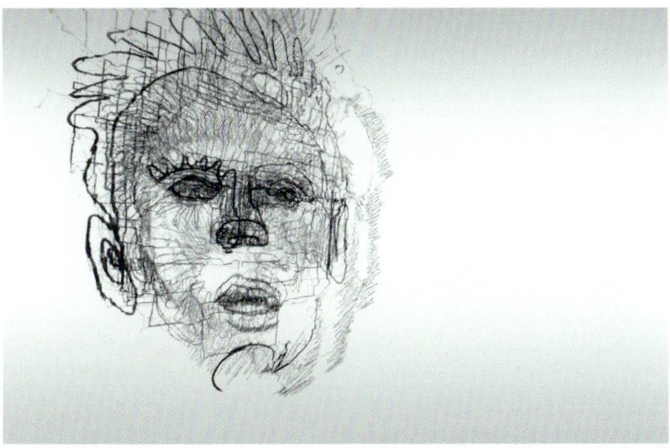

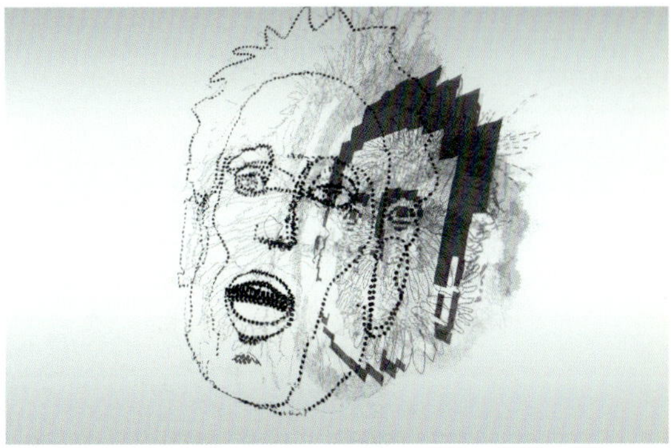

er Teil der Stadt wird. Das Musikvideo, eine Kombination von Handzeichnungen und 3D-Computeranimationen, visualisiert die Verflechtung von Mensch und Stadt.

hand drawings with 3D computer animations and ultimately visualizes the fusion of the human with the city.

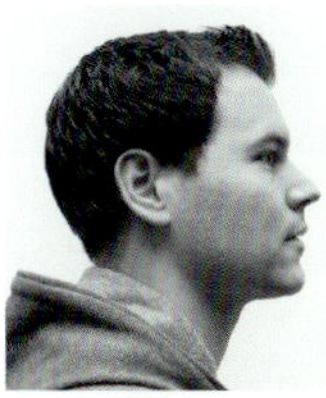

Dirk Koy (DE), born in 1977, studied visual communication at the Basel Academy of Art and Design. In 2007 he founded Equipo, an office for visual communication. Since 2011 he has been teaching time-based media at the Basel Academy of Art and Design. **Dirk Koy** (DE), geboren 1977, studierte von 1999 bis 2002 Visuelle Kommunikation an der Hochschule für Gestaltung und Kunst Basel. 2007 gründet er das Büro für visuelle Kommunikation Equipo. Seit 2011 ist er Dozent für Time Based Media an der Hochschule für Gestaltung und Kunst Basel.

The Fantastic Flying Books of Mr. Morris Lessmore

William Joyce, Brandon Oldenburg / Moonbot Studios

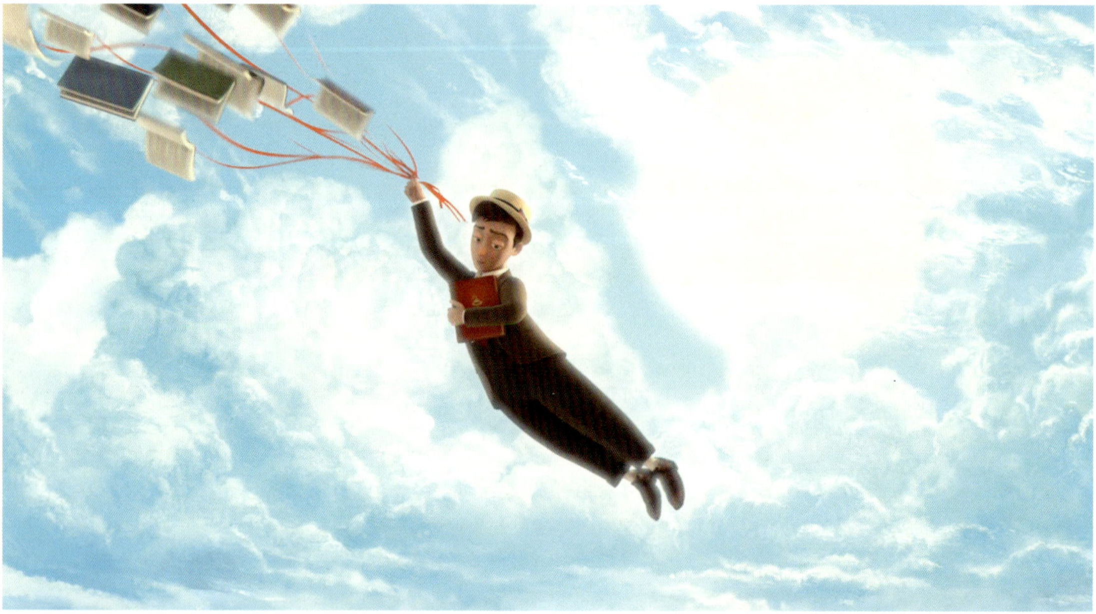

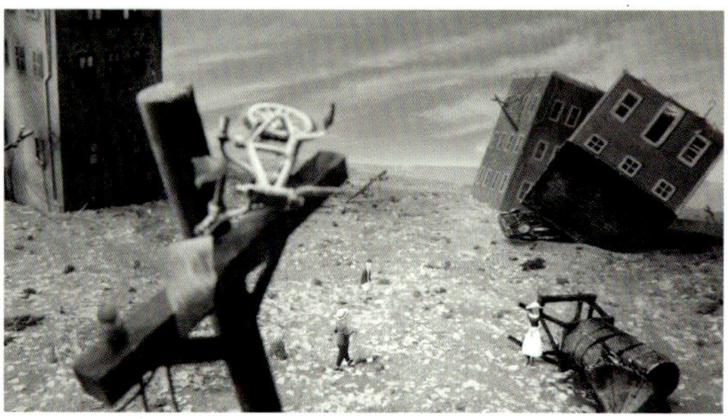

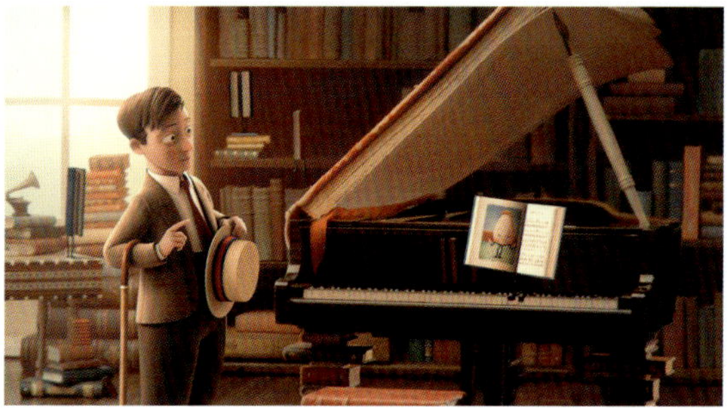

Inspired in equal measure by Hurricane Katrina, Buster Keaton, *The Wizard of Oz* and a love for books, *The Fantastic Flying Books of Mr. Morris Lessmore* is a story of people who devote their lives to books and books that return the favor. *Morris Lessmore* is a poignant, humorous allegory about the curative powers of story. Using a variety of techniques (miniatures, computer animation, 2D animation), award-winning author/illustrator William Joyce and co-director Brandon Oldenburg present a hybrid style of animation that harks back to silent films and MGM Technicolor musicals. *Morris Lessmore* is old-fashioned and cutting-edge at the same time.

The Fantastic Flying Books of Mr. Morris Lessmore, gleichermaßen inspiriert von Buster Keaton, dem Zauberer von Oz, Hurrikan Katrina und der Liebe zu Büchern, ist eine Geschichte über Menschen, die ihr Leben Büchern verschrieben haben, und von Büchern, die sich dafür erkenntlich zeigen. Der Film ist eine ergreifende, humorvolle Allegorie auf die heilsame Kraft von Geschichten. Verschiedenste Techniken (Miniaturen, Computeranimation, 2D-Animation) einsetzend, spielen der preisgekrönte Autor/Illustrator William Joyce und Koregisseur Brandon Oldenburg mit verschiedenen Genres und Animationsstilen, die bis zu Stummfilmen und MGM-Technicolor-Musicals zurückreichen. *Morris Lessmore* ist altmodisch und topaktuell zugleich.

Directed by: William Joyce, Brandon Oldenburg; written by: William Joyce; produced by: Alissa M. Kantrow, Lampton Enochs, Trish Farnsworth-Smith

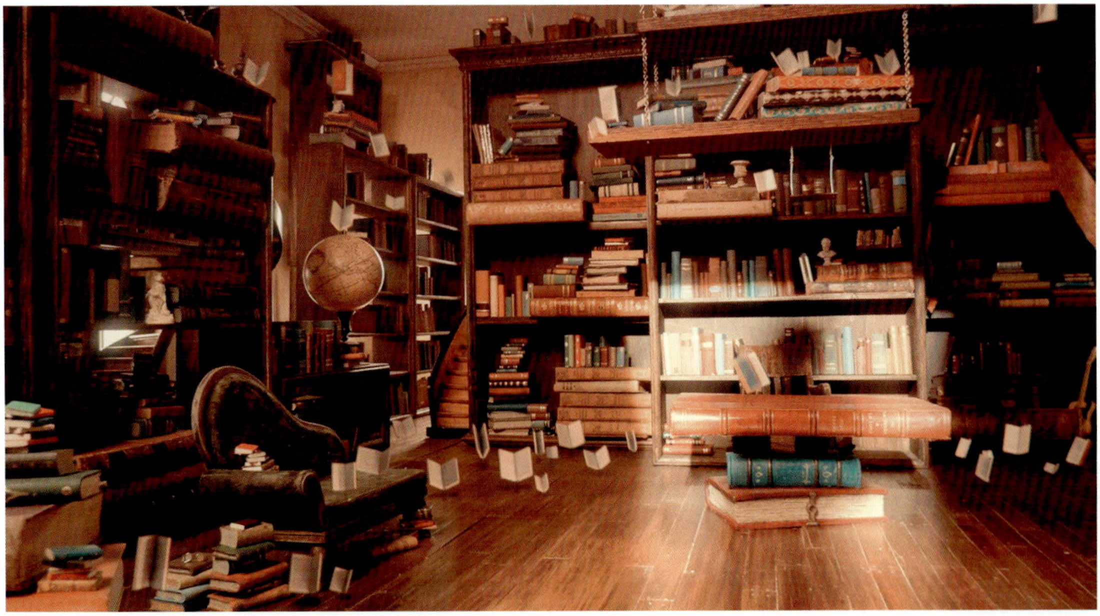

The Fantastic Flying Books of Mr. Morris Lessmore erhielt bei den 84. Academy Awards den Oscar für den „besten animierten Kurzfilm".

The Fantastic Flying Books of Mr. Morris Lessmore was awarded the Oscar for Best Animated Short Film in the 84th Academy Awards.

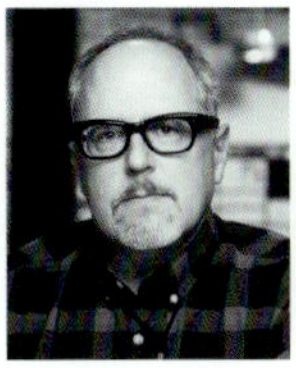

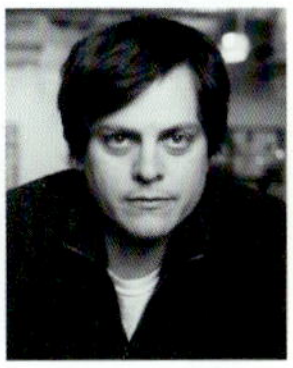

William Joyce (US) has achieved world-wide recognition as an author, illustrator and leader in the digital animation industry. He was named by *Newsweek* as one of the 100 people to watch in the new millennium and recognized as the Louisiana Author of the Year in 2008. Joyce has been heavily involved in the world of digital animation since its full-scale inception at Pixar Animation. Joyce is currently co-directing *The Guardians of Childhood*, an animated feature for DreamWorks. He is also the writer, producer and production designer on the Fox Studios feature film based on his book *The Leaf Men*. **Brandon Oldenburg** (US) was a co-founding member of Reel FX Creative Studios (1995), doing a combination of design and special effects for television and film. Serving as senior creative director for 15 years, he worked with such clients as Troublemaker Studios, Pixar, Disney, DreamWorks and Blue Sky Studios. From 1998 to 2009 Oldenburg oversaw a joint venture with William Joyce and Reel FX. Oldenburg and Joyce's other collaborations include Halloween decor for Martha Stewart, parade floats for Disney and title design for feature films. Their most recent story is now in production at DreamWorks called *The Guardians of Childhood*. **William Joyce** (US) ist international als Autor und Illustrator bekannt und einer der renommiertesten Künstler der Animationsbranche. Er wurde vom *Newsweek Magazine* in die Liste der 100 Personen aufgenommen, die im neuen Millennium eine bedeutende Rolle spielen werden, und 2008 zum Louisiana Author of the Year gewählt. Joyce hat sich mit der Welt der digitalen Animation seit deren Anfängen bei Pixar Animation intensiv beschäftigt. Derzeit wirkt er als Koregisseur bei *The Guardians of Childhood*, einem Animationsfilm für Dream Works, mit. Er ist Autor, Produzent und Art Designer des Spielfilms *The Leaf Men*, der von den Fox Studios realisiert wird und auf seinem gleichnamigen Buch basiert. **Brandon Oldenburg** (US) war Gründungsmitglied der Reel FX Creative Studios (1995), die auf Design- und Spezialeffekte für Film und Fernsehen spezialisiert sind. Als Senior Creative Director des Unternehmens arbeitete er 15 Jahre lang für Kunden wie Troublemaker Studios, Pixar, Disney, DreamWorks und Blue Sky Studios. Von 1998 bis 2009 betreute Oldenburg ein Joint Venture mit William Joyce und Reel FX. Oldenburgs and Joyces Zusammenarbeit erstreckte sich darüber hinaus auch auf Halloween-Dekor für Martha Stewart, Umzugswägen für Disney und Titelentwürfe für diverse Spielfilme. Ihre neueste Geschichte, *The Guardians of Childhood*, wird derzeit von DreamWorks produziert.

unnamed soundsculpture

Daniel Franke, Cedric Kiefer

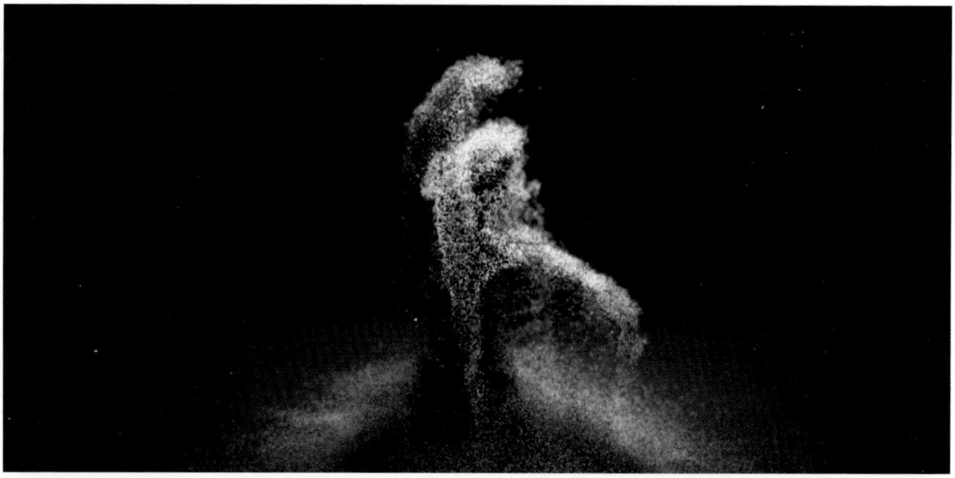

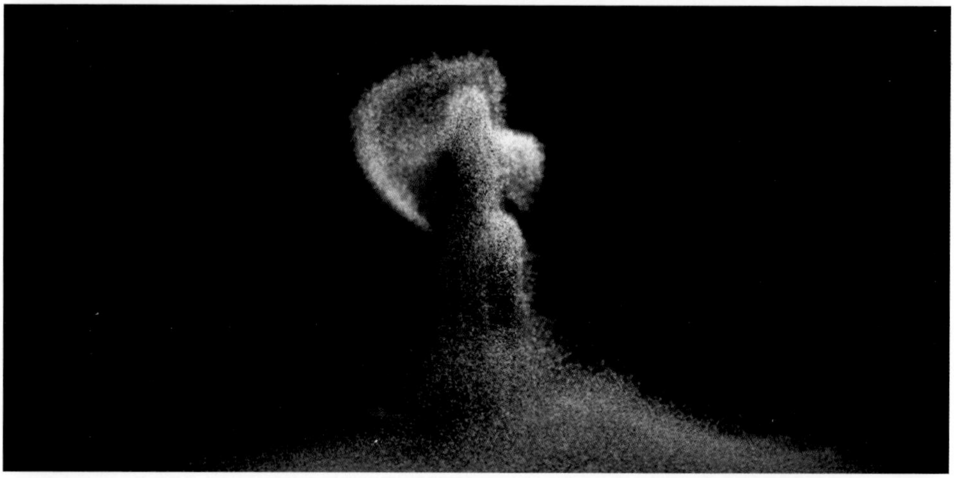

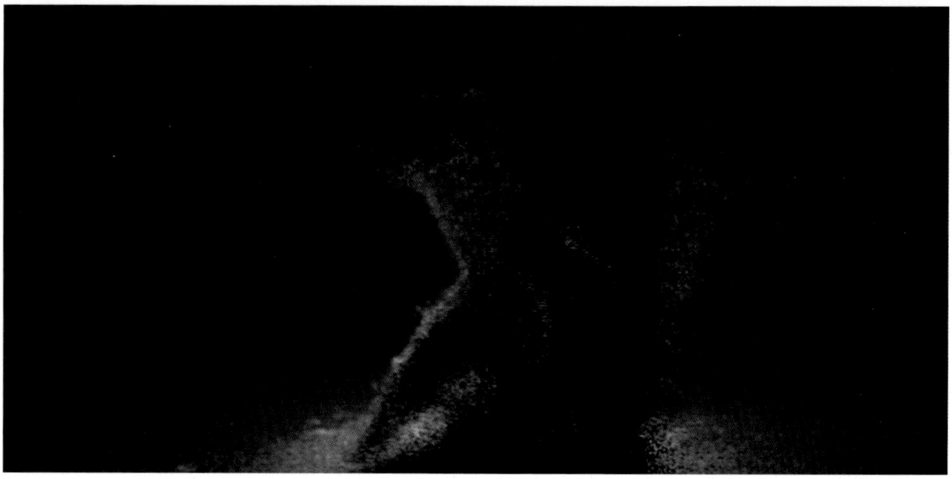

Das Projekt *unnamed soundsculpture* basiert auf der Idee, aus der Aufzeichnung von Bewegungsdaten einer realen Person eine sich bewegende Klangskulptur zu schaffen. Wir ersuchten die in Berlin lebende Tänzerin Laura Keil ein Musikstück – *Kreukeltape* von Machinefabriek – mit Bewegungen ihres Körpers möglichst exakt zu interpretieren. Sie wurde dabei von drei Tiefenkameras (Kinect) aufgenommen, die Schnittmenge der drei Aufnahmen wurde später wieder zu einem dreidimensionalen Körper (3D-Punktwolke) zusammengefügt. Diese Vorgangsweise ermöglichte uns, die gewonnenen Daten während des gesamten weiteren Prozesses zu verwenden. Das dreidimensionale Bild erlaubte eine völlig freie Kameraführung ohne jede Einschränkung in Hinblick auf die Perspektive. Die Kamera reagiert auch auf den Klang und unterstützt die tänzerische Interpretation des Musikstücks durch die Performerin. Sie bewegt sich in einem Klangfeld, in dem eine einfache Änderung des Anfangswerts für den Zufallsgenerator immer wieder neue Versionen des Videos mit einem anderen Arrangement der aufgezeichneten Performance hervorbringen kann. Die Mehrdimensionalität der Klangskulptur ist bereits in jeder Bewegung der Tänzerin enthalten, da die Kameraaufzeichnungen jede vorstellbare Perspektive zulassen.

The basic idea of the project is built upon the consideration of creating a moving sound sculpture from the recorded motion data of a real person. For our work we asked a Laura Keil, a Berlin-based dancer, to interpret a musical piece—*Kreukeltape* by Machinefabriek—as closely as possible with the movement of her own body. She was recorded by three depth cameras (Kinect), in which the intersection of the images was later put together to a three-dimensional volume (3D point cloud), which made it possible to use the collected data throughout the rest of the process. The three-dimensional image allowed us a completely free handling of the digital camera, without limitations on the perspective. The camera also reacts to the sound and supports the physical imitation of the musical piece by the performer. She moves to a noise field where a simple modification of the random seed can constantly create new versions of the video, each offering a different composition of the recorded performance. The multi-dimensionality of the sound sculpture is already contained in every movement of the dancer, as the camera footage allows any imaginable perspective.

Dancer: Laura Keil; music: Machinefabriek *Kreukeltape*

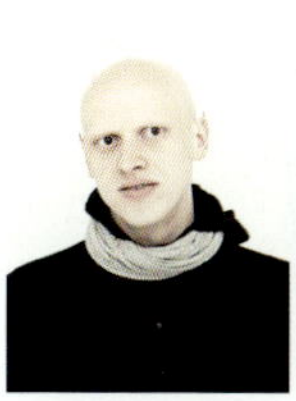

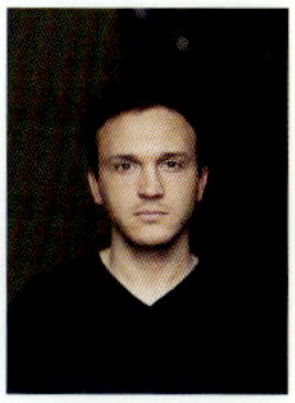

Daniel Franke (DE) works as an artist, designer and music video director. His works challenge the restrictions of conventional spatial frameworks and concepts: digital simulations should no longer be limited to an on-screen-display; instead the digital might be imagined as transferable into real space and thus extend perceptions of "the real". As a graduate of the Berlin University of the Arts he is currently preparing his main NaFoeG (Junior Scholars Support Program) work with Prof. Alberto de Campo. He is also member of the artist collective ChopChop. **Cedric Kiefer** (DE) studies in communication design at the University of Karlsruhe and Potsdam University of Applied Arts. He teaches generative design and processing at the Hildesheim University of Applied Sciences and Arts, Wiesbaden University of Applied Arts and Mainz University of Applied Arts. He is an author for *Weave* magazine. **Daniel Franke** (DE) ist Künstler, Designer und Musikvideoregisseur. Seine Arbeiten hinterfragen die Beschränkungen konventioneller räumlicher Parameter und Konzepte: Digitale Simulationen sollten nicht länger auf eine Bildschirmdarstellung beschränkt sein; sondern als in den realen Raum übertragbar gedacht werden und in der Folge Wahrnehmungen „des Realen" erweitern. Daniel Franke absolvierte ein Kunststudium, erhielt 2011 ein NaFoeG-Stipendium und ist Mitglied des Künstlerkollektivs ChopChop. **Cedric Kiefer** (DE) studierte Kommunikationsdesign an der Hochschule für Gestaltung in Karlsruhe und an der FH Potsdam. Er unterrichtet Generative Gestaltung und Processing an der HAWK Hochschule Hildesheim, an der FH Wiesbaden und an der FH Mainz und schreibt nebenbei Artikel für das Magazin *Weave*.

Zing

Kyra Buschor, Cynthia Collins

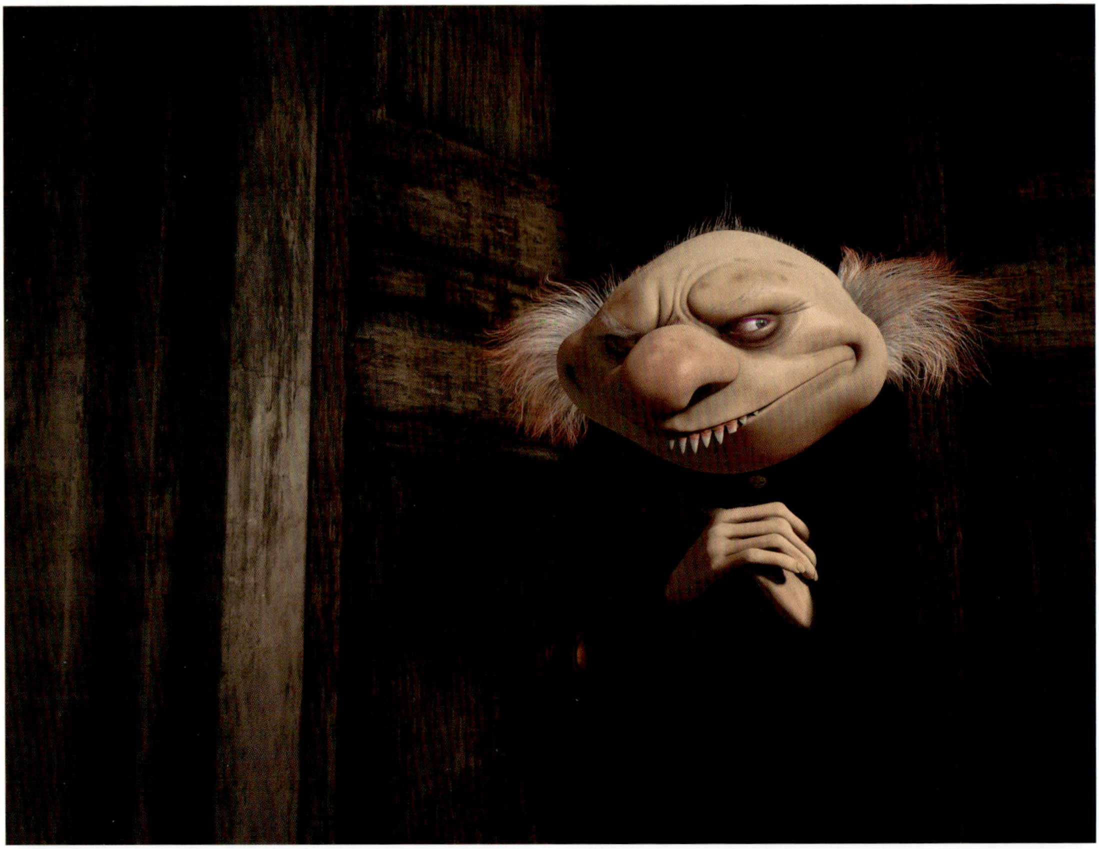

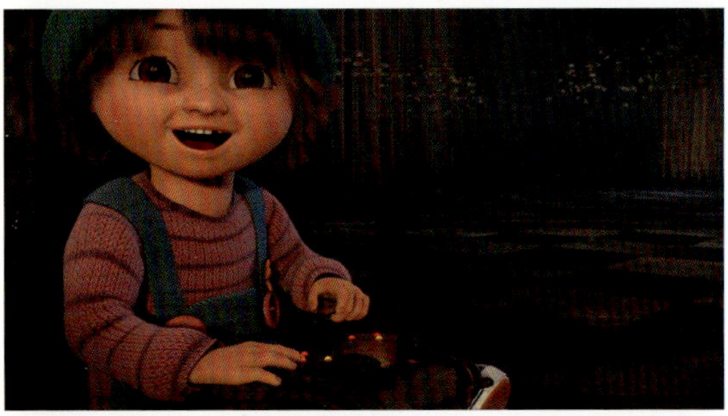

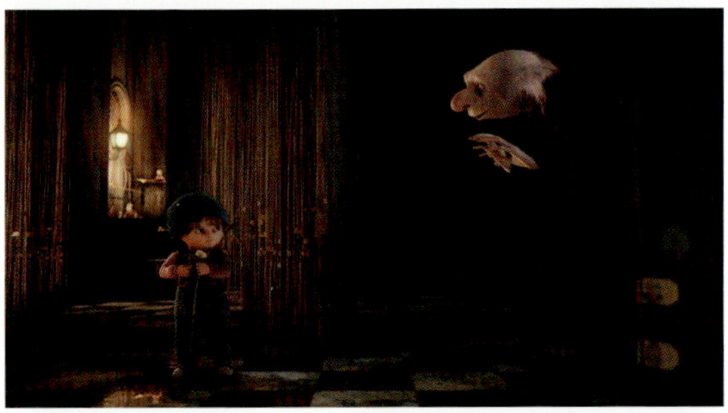

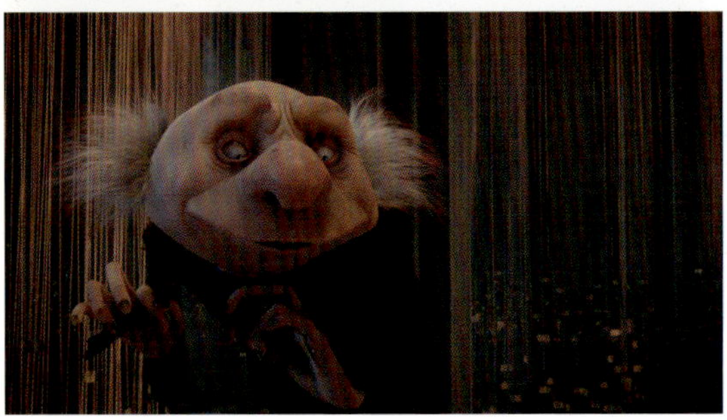

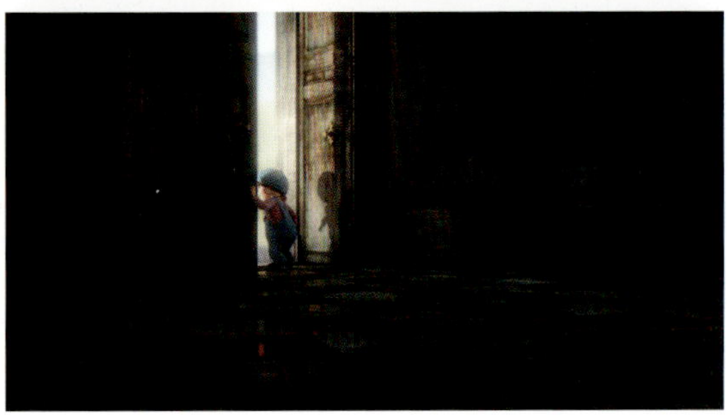

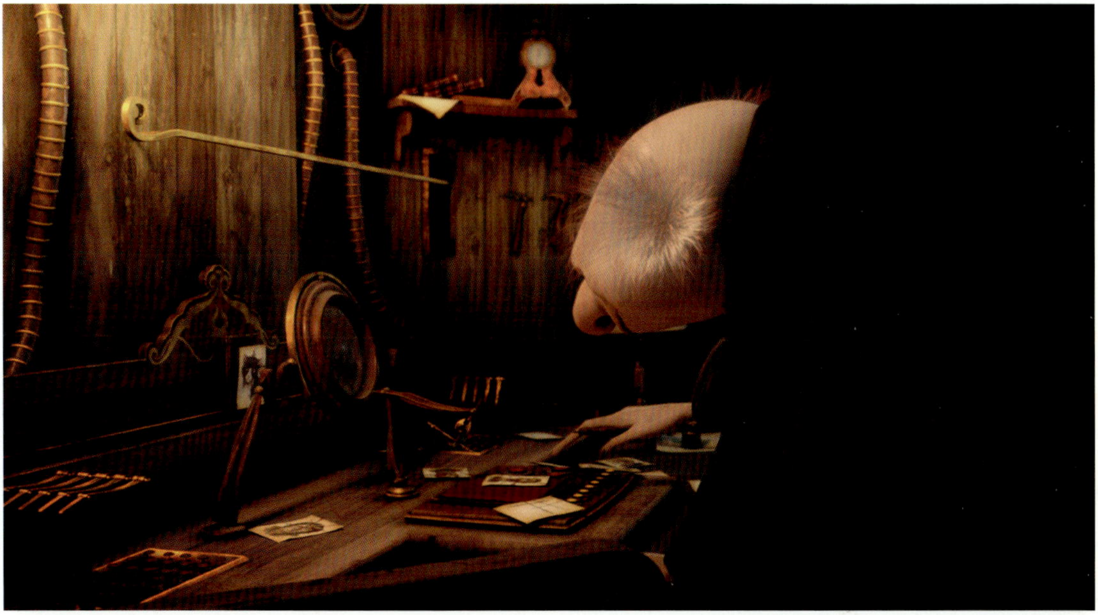

Als Sensenmann ist Mr. Grimm den ganzen Tag damit beschäftigt, den Menschen das Leben zu nehmen. Doch eines Tages klingelt es an seiner Tür, und ein kleines Mädchen steht vor ihm. Sie sucht ihre Katze. Doch was sie nicht weiß: Sie ist eigentlich sein nächstes Opfer ...

Mr. Grimm is the Reaper and busy all day taking people's lives. But then one day the doorbell rings. He opens the door and sees a little girl. She is looking for her cat. Little does she know that she is to be his next victim...

Producers: Philipp Wolf, D. Cramer-Clausbruch

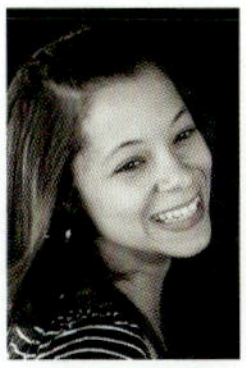

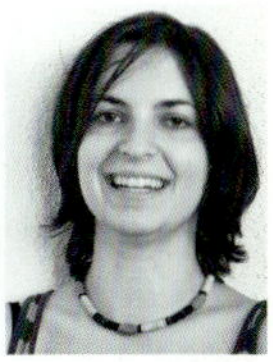

Cynthia Collins (DE), born in 1987, became interested in the arts at a very early age, in particular painting. She was also very young when she realized she wanted to study animation at the Filmakademie Baden-Württemberg. So after graduating from a college preparatory school, she completed two internships in the fields of film/media and animation; one was at Film Bilder in Stuttgart. Since autumn 2009, she has been studying animation at the Filmakademie Baden-Württemberg. **Kyra Buschor** (CH), born in 1987, has also been interested in film and art since an early age. After finishing secondary school, she attended the Liceo Artistico, a German-Italian college preparatory school with an emphasis on art. After graduating, she completed two internships in the field of 3D-animation at Los Banditos and at Digital Frame Studio, both in Stuttgart. Since autumn 2009 she has been studying at the Filmakademie Baden-Württemberg. **Cynthia Collins** (DE), geb. 1987, beschäftigte sich schon sehr früh mit Kunst, vor allem mit Malerei. Sehr früh wusste sie dann auch, dass sie an der Filmakademie Baden-Württemberg Animation studieren wollte. Also absolvierte sie nach ihrem Abitur zwei Praktika im Bereich Film / Medien und Animation, eines bei „Film Bilder" in Stuttgart. Seit Herbst 2009 studiert sie Animation an der Filmakademie Baden-Württemberg. **Kyra Buschor** (CH), geb. 1987, interessierte sich früh für Film und Kunst. Nach Abschluss der Sekundarschule ging sie auf das Liceo Artistico, ein deutsch-italienisches Sprachgymnasium mit Schwerpunkt Kunst. Nach dem Abitur absolvierte sie zwei Praktika im Bereich 3D-Animation bei Los Banditos und Digital-Frame-Studio in Stuttgart. Seit Herbst 2009 studiert sie Animation an der Filmakademie Baden-Württemberg.

DIGITAL MUSICS & SOUND ART

Excellence and Context

AGF, Christina Kubisch, Phil Mossman, Martin Supper, Dajuin Yao

2012 saw 834 submissions in the Digital Musics category, of which 708 were accepted, plus 39 nominations. The criteria that the members of the jury were collectively seeking were innovative use of technology, compelling execution, sonic quality, compositional excellence and context. After three days of careful deliberations, the jury unanimously found a winner of the Golden Nica Award as well as two Awards of Distinction and twelve Honorary Mentions.

GOLDEN NICA

Crystal Sounds of a Synchrotron

Jo Thomas

Jo Thomas is an accomplished electronic music composer from London who has gained recognition for her computer compositions and multichannel pieces. Thomas also lectures in sound design and composition at the University of East London.

Thomas's 38-minute multichannel composition *Crystal Sounds of a Synchrotron* was inspired by sounds generated at the UK's national synchrotron science facility, Diamond Light Source. *Crystal's* acoustic source is a combination of frequencies generated by the particle accelerator and binaural recordings of the large, circular and extremely reverberative environment.

In her own words, Thomas explains, "My intention was to write a piece which reflected the actual content of the spectrum, the space and the metaphorical content of the sounds."

The jury viewed the 5:1-channel composition as giving a sense of an acoustic space in continuous movement. The transformation from almost inaudible source material into complex structures with a full spectrum of sound colors is representative of the phenomena of light itself. The sounds are never overly intrusive, yet they have an intense presence and are composed with great sensitivity to create spatial work sourced from a technical environment.

2012 gab es 834 Einreichungen in der Kategorie Digital Musics, wovon 708 akzeptiert wurden, sowie 39 Nominierungen. Die Kriterien, nach denen die Jurymitglieder die Projekte bewerteten, waren: innovativer Einsatz von Technologie, überzeugende Umsetzung, klangkünstlerische Qualität, herausragende kompositorische Kompetenz und Kontext. Nach drei Tagen eingehender Beratungen entschied sich die Jury einstimmig für den Gewinner der Goldenen Nica sowie die Vergabe von zwei Auszeichnungen und zwölf Anerkennungen.

GOLDENE NICA

Crystal Sounds of a Synchrotron

Jo Thomas

Jo Thomas ist eine renommierte Komponistin elektronischer Musik aus London, die sich mit Computerkompositionen und Mehrkanalstücken profilierte. Sie unterrichtet Sound Design und Komposition an der University of East London.

Thomas' 38-minütige Mehrkanalkomposition *Crystal Sounds of a Synchrotron* ist inspiriert von Klängen, die an der staatlichen Synchrotronstrahlungsquelle Großbritanniens „Diamond Light Source" erzeugt werden. *Crystal* wurde aus Frequenzen des Teilchenbeschleunigers und binauralen Tonaufnahmen in der weitläufigen, kreisförmigen Anlage mit extremem Nachhall arrangiert.

Thomas erklärt ihr Stück wie folgt: „Meine Ambition war es, ein Stück zu komponieren, das sowohl das gesamte tatsächliche Spektrum des Raums als auch den metaphorischen Gehalt der Klänge reflektiert."

Die Jury hebt in ihrem Statement hervor, dass die 5.1-Kanal-Komposition einen Eindruck von einem akustischen Raum in konstanter Bewegung vermittelt. Die Verwandlung des nahezu unhörbaren Ausgangsmaterials in komplexe Strukturen mit einem vollen Klangspektrum zeigt Parallelen zu Lichtphänomenen. Die Klänge sind nie aufdringlich, entfalten aber dennoch eine intensive Präsenz und sind mit großem Feingefühl zu einem räumlichen Klangfeld verwoben, das aus einem technischen Umfeld kommt.

AUSZEICHNUNGEN

Scape-Sequencer

Xu Cheng

Xu Cheng stammt aus Shanghai und ist Gründungsmitglied der renommierten und erfolgreichen Harsh-Noise-Gruppe „Torturing Nurse“. Chengs Werk, das in seiner Heimat China bereits Anerkennung fand und verdientermaßen zunehmend auch internationale Aufmerksamkeit erweckt, bietet einen Einblick in die rasante Entwicklung der Klangkunst und Performance mit Neuen Medien.

Scape-Sequencer ist eine audiovisuelle Live-Performance, bei der Aufnahmen von Sinneseindrücken aus der Stadt Shanghai als Ausgangsmaterial dienen. Durch Bearbeitung der Klänge und Bilder der Stadt schafft Cheng ein chaotisches und gefühlsgeladenes Stück, das den Genius loci und die Energie von Shanghai plastischer evoziert als eine Dokumentation.

#tweetscapes

Tarik Barri, Anselm Venezian Nehls

Tarik Barri and Anselm Venezian Nehls, auch bekannt als „Heavy Listening“, sind ein in Berlin ansässiges Klangkünstlerduo.

#tweetscapes ist eine Echtzeit-Sonifikation der Vorgänge in der deutschen Twitter-Szene, die auch als Verwandlung abstrakter Daten in Klangkunst beschrieben werden kann. Die Performer des Stücks waren deutsche Twitter-User, die sich ihrer Teilnahme bewusst waren oder auch nicht, weshalb die Grenzen zwischen Performer und Publikum hier verschwimmen. *#tweetscapes* möchte einen bestimmten Zeitpunkt im Internet, das ansonsten eher ein visuelles Medium ist, klanglich erfassen. Die Intention der Künstler war es, der Entwicklung von Diskussionsthemen und dem Rhythmus des Online-Dialogs eine sinnliche Komponente hinzuzufügen. Durch Festlegung eines Regelwerks und indem den Themen und dem Trending bestimmte Klänge zugeordnet wurden, kann der Zuhörer die Gesamtstimmung des Multilogs der Twitterszene akustisch erfahren und die „Konversation einer Nation“ mitverfolgen.

#tweetscapes wurde ursprünglich 2011 im Auftrag von Deutschlandradio Kultur entwickelt und regelmäßig gesendet, wodurch deutschen Twitter-Usern ermöglicht wurde, das Kunstwerk live im Radio mitzugestalten. 2012 wurde das Projekt auf *http://tweetscapes.de* zu einem audiovisuellen Livestream erweitert.

AWARDS OF DISTINCTION

Scape-Sequencer

Xu Cheng

Xu Cheng is a native of Shanghai and a founding member of the highly acclaimed and prolific harsh-noise group *Torturing Nurse*. Cheng's work introduces us to a lively world of sound art and new media performance that has gained recognition in his homeland, China, and is deservingly attracting wider international attention.

Scape-Sequencer is an audiovisual live performance that takes everyday sensory data from the city of Shanghai as its source material. By manipulating the sounds and images of the city, Cheng creates a chaotic and emotive piece that is strangely more evocative of the spirit and energy of Shanghai than simply documentary.

#tweetscapes

Tarik Barri, Anselm Venezian Nehls

Tarik Barri and Anselm Venezian Nehls, also known as Heavy Listening, are a sonic-art duo based in Berlin.

#tweetscapes is a real-time sonification of the German twitter-sphere that can also be described as a transformation of abstract data into an audible art form. The performers of this piece were German Twitter users, either conscious of their participation or not, therefore blurring the lines between performer and audience. *#tweetscapes* sets out to give a sonic glimpse at a moment in time of the Internet, which is otherwise a more visual medium. Barri and Venezian Nehls' aim for this piece was to add a sensual element to the development of discussion topics and the rhythm of the online dialog. By implementing a fixed set of rules and assigning sounds according to topics of conversation and trending, the listener can perceive the overall mood of the twitter-sphere's multilogue audibly and sensually experience a nation in conversation.

#tweetscapes was originally developed on behalf of Deutschlandradio Kultur in 2011 and broadcast on their program regularly, allowing German Twitter users to interact with the artwork live on the radio. In 2012 the project expanded into an audiovisual live stream at *http://tweetscapes.de*.

HONORARY MENTIONS

BETWEEN | YOU | AND | ME

Anke Eckardt

Anke Eckardt is a German sound artist whose work strives to construct a bridge between music and visual art and between acoustic research and composition.

Eckardt's *BETWEEN | YOU | AND | ME* is set in a dark room with a permeable barrier of light that when breached, unleashes a euphony of broken glass sounds. The intention of the piece is to sharpen the senses and challenge the viewer to question the parameters of perception.

I am thinking in a room, different from the one you are hearing in now

Samson Young

Samson Young is a Hong-Kong-based artist who though trained in composition has expanded into the multi-disciplinary world of sound installation, video and performance.

I am thinking in a room, different from the one you are hearing in now is a non-performance realized through sound. The actors in this work are entirely immobile while brainwave sensors are monitoring their focus levels. Connected to the sensors are several solenoid motors, which are activated when focus levels are above a certain threshold. This level is pre-determined and scored into musical notation, which the actors attempt to influence through focus and distraction.

There is tension between the performance setting and the conditions of a "successful performance," which paradoxically rely on the actors' ability to ignore the presence of an audience. The constant struggle between focus and failure-to-focus, virtuosity and the loss of control is amplified through sound. The work questions the idea of a "successful" performance and the pressure to function in a certain predetermined way. It puts the actors' failure on display and thus makes a statement against the pressure to be "perfect."

Terra Prosodia

Antje Vowinckel

Antje Vowinckel is a Berlin-based composer who studied music and literature as well as being an accomplished flutist in classical orchestras and

ANERKENNUNGEN

BETWEEN | YOU | AND | ME

Anke Eckardt

Anke Eckardt ist eine deutsche Klangkünstlerin, die in ihrem Werk einen Brückenschlag zwischen Musik und bildender Kunst sowie akustischer Forschung und Komposition anstrebt.

Eckardts Performance *BETWEEN | YOU | AND | ME* ist in einem verdunkelten Raum mit einer durchlässigen Barriere aus Licht situiert, die bei Durchdringung eine Euphonie aus Klängen zerbrechenden Glases freisetzt. Intention des Stücks ist es, eine Schärfung der Sinne zu bewirken und den Betrachter anzuregen, seine Wahrnehmungsparameter zu hinterfragen.

I am thinking in a room, different from the one you are hearing in now

Samson Young

Der in Hongkong lebende Künstler Samson Young studiert Komposition, bewegt sich aber in der multidisziplinären Welt von Soundinstallation, Video und Performance.

I am thinking in a room, different from the one you are hearing in now ist eine mithilfe perkussiver Klänge realisierte Non-Performance. Die Akteure verharren völlig reglos, während Gehirnwellensensoren ihren Konzentrationspegel überwachen. Mit diesen Sensoren sind mehrere Solenoidmotoren verbunden, die aktiviert werden, wenn der Konzentrationspegel eine bestimmte Schwelle überschreitet. Der Konzentrationspegel ist vorgegeben und wird in eine Notenschrift übertragen, die die Akteure mittels Konzentration und Unkonzentriertheit zu beeinflussen versuchen.

Es besteht eine Spannung zwischen dem performativen Setting dieser Arbeit und den Voraussetzungen einer „erfolgreichen Performance", die paradoxerweise auf der Fähigkeit der Akteure beruht, die Präsenz des Publikums zu ignorieren. Der ständige Kampf zwischen Fokussierung der Aufmerksamkeit und scheiternder Fokussierung, Virtuosität und Kontrollverlust wird mithilfe perkussiver Klänge verstärkt. Das Werk hinterfragt die Vorstellung einer „erfolgreichen" Performance und den Druck, der auf einem lastet, wenn man auf eine bestimmte festgelegte Weise funktionieren soll. Das Stück stellt das Scheitern der Akteure zur Schau und bezieht damit Stellung gegen den Perfektionszwang.

Terra Prosodia

Antje Vowinckel

Die in Berlin lebende Komponistin Antje Vowinckel studierte Musik und Literatur, spielte Flöte in klassischen Orchestern und war Musikerin in Jazzbands. Als Komponistin sensibilisiert Vowinckel für die Musikalität des gesprochenen Worts, indem sie die Melodien von Dialekten und automatischem Sprechen in den Fokus rückt. Für eine Reihe ihrer Arbeiten verwendet sie Fragmente dokumentarischen Erzählens, die in musikalische Strukturen transponiert werden.

Terra Prosodia ist eine Komposition, die auf sechs vom Verschwinden bedrohten europäischen Sprachen basiert. Vowinckel nahm Einheimische auf, die ihre Umgebung in ihrem jeweiligen Dialekt beschrieben und verwandelte diese Aufnahmen mit Hilfe einer Software namens „Melodyne", die die Transienten im Redefluss erkennt und in Musiknoten übersetzt. Vowinckel interessiert sich weniger für die Bearbeitung des Materials als dafür, uns interessante und überraschende Sprachmelodien entdecken zu lassen und auf eine bestimmte Sprechweise aufmerksam zu machen, die uns, obwohl wir sie nicht verstehen, etwas weit über die Bedeutung des gesprochenen Worts Hinausgehendes vermittelt: die Bedeutung des Zuhörens.

Years

Bartholomäus Traubeck

Bartholomäus Traubeck, geboren 1987 in München, Deutschland, lebt und arbeitet als Medienkünstler in Rotterdam und Linz.

Years ist eine Medienkunst-Installation und besteht aus einem modifizierten Plattenspieler, der Holzscheiben abspielt und die Jahresringe eines Baumes in Klaviertöne überträgt. Eine Kamera analysiert die Jahresringe hinsichtlich Stärke, Dicke und Struktur. Diese Daten dienen als Grundlage für ein generatives Verfahren, das Klaviermusik erklingen lässt, und werden auf einer Skala abgebildet, die wiederum von der äußeren Erscheinung des Holzes (die von dunkler zu heller und von starker zu schwacher Maserung variiert) definiert wird. Grundlage der Musik ist zwar das festgelegte Regelwerk von Programmierung und Hardware-Konfiguration, durch die Variationen der von jedem Baum gewonnenen Daten kommt es jedoch zu sehr unterschiedlichen Interpretationen. *Years* spielt mit der Idee, etwas Physisches in Musik zu verwandeln und ihm eine neue klangliche Identität zu verleihen.

jazz bands. As a composer, Vowinckel draws attention to the musicality of the spoken word through focusing on dialect melodies and automatic speaking. A number of Vowinckel's works employ fragments of documentary speech that are transposed into musical structures.

Terra Prosodia is a composition based on six European languages that are in danger of dying out. Vowinckel recorded locals describing their surroundings in their native dialects and transformed these recordings using the Melodyne program, which is usually used to tune and manipulate audio signals, typically a singer's vocals. Vowinckel is less interested in processing the material than in getting us to discover the interesting, surprising and beautiful "melodies" of the languages and focusing our attention on a way of speaking that, although we may not understand, communicates something far more fundamental about the importance of the spoken word: listening.

Years

Bartholomäus Traubeck

Bartholomäus Traubeck is a media artist who was born in Munich in 1987 and currently divides his time between Rotterdam and Linz, where he lives and studies.

Years is a media-art piece that utilizes a modified record player that reads a tree's rings and outputs piano music. The tree rings are analyzed by a camera for their strength, thickness and rate of growth. The accumulated data serves as the basis for a generative process that outputs piano music and is mapped to a scale defined by the overall appearance of the wood (ranging from dark to light and from strong texture to light texture). The foundation for the music is certainly found in the defined rule-set of programming and the hardware setup, but the data from every tree interprets this rule-set very differently. *Years* plays with the idea of turning something physical into music, creating a new sonic identity.

untitled #275

Francisco López

Francisco López is one of the main figures on the stage of sound-art and experimental music. His experience in the field of sound creation and work with environmental recordings spans a 30-year

period, during which time he has developed an impressive sound universe that is completely personal, iconoclastic and based on profound listening of the world.
untitled #275 is a sound work based on a paradigmatic instrument of the 19th century, with manipulations of the 20th century, and realized with the technology and aesthetic of the 21st century. The unorthodox piano composition is in two parts:
(i) Movement 1 for mechanically prepared piano, performed by pianist Reinier van Houdt,
(ii) Evolutionary studio transformation of Movement 1 for immersive multichannel sound system, performed by Francisco López.

Organ of Corti
Liminal
Liminal is a partnership between architect Frances Crow and sound artist/composer David Prior.
Organ of Corti by Liminal is an experimental instrument that recycles noise from the environment; it does not make any sound of its own but rather attempts to draw our attention to the sounds already present by framing them in a new way. Named after the organ of hearing in the inner ear, *Organ of Corti* uses the acoustic technology of sonic crystals to accentuate and attenuate frequencies within the broad range of sound present in road traffic or falling water.
In a world saturated with sounds, *Organ of Corti* questions whether we need any more noise and instead offers a frame through which to listen to the sounds that already surround us.

Crackle-canvas #1
Tom Verbruggen
Tom Verbruggen studied fine arts at the Academy St Joost in Breda, Netherlands.
During his studies, his interest in sound art became his primary focus.
Crackle-canvas is a painting that produces analog-generated sounds and contains a circuit board, speaker, knobs, switches, wood and canvas. Each canvas makes sounds individually but can be connected via cables (patched) to other crackle-canvasses. Once patched, the paintings begin to react with each other. Each patch creates a different sound and drawings of cables on the wall or in the space the paintings are presented.

untitled #275
Francisco López
Francisco López ist einer der renommiertesten Protagonisten im breiten Feld der Klangkunst und Experimentalmusik. Seine Erfahrungen in den Bereichen Klangkreation und Feldaufnahmen erstrecken sich über einen Zeitraum von dreißig Jahren, in denen er ein beeindruckendes, sehr persönliches und mit allen Konventionen brechendes Klanguniversum schuf, das auf einer intensiven auditiven Wahrnehmung der Welt basiert.
untitled #275 ist eine auf einem typischen Instrument des 19. Jahrhunderts basierende Klangarbeit, die Einflüsse aus dem 20. Jahrhundert aufweist und mit den technischen/ästhetischen Mitteln des 21. Jahrhunderts realisiert wurde. Die unkonventionelle Komposition für Klavier besteht aus zwei Sätzen:
(i) Erster Satz für mechanisch präpariertes Klavier, interpretiert von Pianist Reinier van Houdt;
(ii) Weiterentwicklung und Transformation des ersten Satzes in einem Studio mit immersiver Mehrkanal-Tonanlage, interpretiert von Francisco López.

Organ of Corti
Liminal
Liminal ist eine Kooperation zwischen dem Architekten Frances Crow und dem Klangkünstler und Komponisten David Prior.
Liminals *Organ of Corti* bezeichnet ein experimentelles Instrument, das Umweltgeräusche recycelt. Es erzeugt keine eigenen Klänge, sondern versucht die Aufmerksamkeit auf bereits vorhandene Geräusche zu lenken, indem es diese neu aufbereitet. Das nach dem Corti-Organ, dem Hörorgan im Innenohr, benannte Instrument verwendet die Technologie akustischer Kristalle, um in dem breiten Klangspektrum, das etwa im Straßenverkehr oder in fließendem Wasser vorhanden ist, bestimmte Frequenzen zu betonen und abzuschwächen.
Organ of Corti hinterfragt, ob wir in unserer klanggesättigten Welt noch mehr Lärm brauchen, und konfrontiert uns stattdessen mit einer Konstruktion, die uns aus den uns bereits umgebenden Klängen ein neues Hörerlebnis bereitet.

Crackle-canvas #1
Tom Verbruggen
Tom Verbruggen studierte Bildende Kunst an der Kunstakademie St. Joost in Breda. Sein Interesse für Klangkunst entwickelte sich bereits während seines Studiums und steht seither im Zentrum seiner künstlerischen

Aktivitäten. *Crackle-canvas* ist ein Bild, das analog generierte Sounds verbreitet und aus einer Platine, Lautsprechern, Drehreglern, Schaltern, Holzrahmen und Leinwand besteht. Jedes Bild produziert einen eigenen Sound, kann aber über (gepatchte) Kabel auch mit anderen Bildern verbunden werden. Sobald die Verbindung besteht, beginnen die Bilder aufeinander zu reagieren. Jede Rangierung erzeugt einen anderen Sound und eine andere Kabelzeichnung auf der Wand oder in dem Raum, in dem die Bilder präsentiert werden.

What does it matter how many lovers you have if none of them gives you the universe

Bjørn Erik Haugen

Bjørn Erik Haugen absolvierte 2007 die Kunsthochschule Oslo und arbeitet vorwiegend in den Bereichen Komposition, Sound- und Videoinstallation.

Diese audiovisuelle Installation basiert auf der Transkription von altem Filmmaterial für mechanisches Klavier. Der Film zeigt eine Vorlesung des französischen Psychoanalytikers Jacques Lacan. Die Reaktionen des Publikums während der Vorlesung werden von einem Gitarrenverstärker wiedergegeben. Die profunde und dabei humorvolle Arbeit verfolgt einen sehr konzeptuellen Kompositionsansatz. Lacan wird während des Vorlesung, in der er über die Sprache als Grundlage unseres Weltbezugs spricht, plötzlich von einem Studenten unterbrochen, der Mehl und Wasser auf seine Unterlagen schüttet. Der Störer ist ein von Guy Debord inspirierter Situationist, der seine Aktion als Gesellschaftsprotest versteht. Nachdem er aus dem Saal geführt wurde, beginnt Lacan die Ansichten des Protestlers über Menschheit und Gesellschaft, Revolution und Liebe in seinen Vortrag zu integrieren.

Diese interessante Klangkunstarbeit überzeugt auf vielen Ebenen und thematisiert sowohl Geschichte und Humor als auch Sprach- und Gesellschaftstheorien.

Benoît and the Mandelbrots

Juan A. Romero, Holger Ballweg, Patrick Borgeat, Matthias Schneiderbanger

Benoît and the Mandelbrots betrachten den Laptop als ihr wichtigstes Instrument und widmen sich vor allem dem Live-Coding: der Entwicklung von Software in Echtzeit. Sie verwenden die Programmiersprache selbst als expressive Schnittstelle zwischen Mensch und Maschine, um mit Klängen und Musik zu improvisieren. Klangkonzepte und -strukturen werden live als Quellcode formuliert und vom Computer interpretiert.

What does it matter how many lovers you have if none of them gives you the universe

Bjørn Erik Haugen

Bjørn Erik Haugen has an MA from the National Academy of Oslo and works with compositions, sound and video installation.

This audiovisual installation is a transcription for mechanical piano of vintage film footage of a lecture by the French psychoanalyst Jaques Lacan. A guitar amplifier scores the audience's responses to the lecture. Thoughtful and humorous, this work represents a conceptual approach to composition. Lacan's lecture talks about language as a foundation for understanding our surroundings and is abruptly disrupted by a student who sabotages the lecture notes with flour and water as a protest against society. The protester is a situationist, inspired by Debord, and after he is ejected from the lecture hall Lacan incorporates the protester's views about people and society, revolution and love into his lecture. This strong piece of sound art is relevant on many levels, such as history, humor and reflection on language and concepts.

Benoît and the Mandelbrots

Juan A. Romero, Holger Ballweg, Patrick Borgeat, Matthias Schneiderbanger

Benoît and the Mandelbrots see the laptop as their main instrument and are dedicated to the concept of live coding: the process of writing software in real-time. Benoît and the Mandelbrots use the programming language itself as an expressive interface between man and machine in order to improvise sound and music. Sonic conceptions and structures are expressed live as source code and interpreted by the computer. The laptop musicians are connected over a network that enables them to communicate on stage, share parameters such as harmonic progressions and synchronize their timing and on-screen projections. With the flexibility of live coding, the sounds are generated specifically to fit the room and the characteristics of the audience.

Forma II

Thomas Ankersmit, Valerio Tricoli

Forma II is the first collaborative output by Thomas Ankersmit, a musician and installation artist based in Berlin and Amsterdam, and Valerio

Tricoli, an acousmatic music composer, improviser and sound-installation artist.
Composed and recorded in Berlin in 2010, the music consists of four electro-acoustic pieces based largely on analog-synthesizer material and one long, swarm-like composition for multiple overdubbed saxophones. Additional sounds range from metal foil floating on ultrasonic sound-beams to mechanical clickers recorded in the abandoned radar domes at Teufelsberg outside Berlin. The raw materials have been extensively processed and reconstructed using analog tape and digital methods. The five pieces shift between sharply detailed blizzards of electronic interference to passages of delicate balance, between calm and turbulence, between stasis and rapid shape-shifting, between multiple virtual spaces and non-spaces.

Sonic Vista

Bruce Odland, Sam Auinger

Bruce Odland and Sam Auinger are sonic thinkers, composers, and sound artists, known for their large-scale, public-space sound installations, which transform city noise into harmony in real time, changing the sonic identity of public spaces around the world.
Sonic Vista is an installation set in a large urban sound space (Deutschherrnbrücke, a railroad bridge over the River Main). The installation helps the observer listen to the inner workings and complexity of the city and hear its patterns of sound as a whole in the moment. The urban sound sources are subtly transformed in real time with "tuning tubes" enhancing harmonic patterns that the human brain can read out as music, as rhythm. The ear and eye of the observer become engaged in noticing the city's sonic patterns and forming a new mental map of the sources of its vibrations. The effect is one of decoding new information, hearing the sound of your culture as a sophisticated whole organism for the very first time. It is the sound of us, our "hive", our cultural inputs and outputs heard as an advanced urban musical pattern.

Die Laptop-Musiker sind über ein Netzwerk miteinander verbunden, das ihnen ermöglicht, auf der Bühne zu kommunizieren, Parameter wie z.B. Harmonieprogressionen auszutauschen, ihr Timing zu synchronisieren und einzelne Schritte der Programmierung auf eine Leinwand zu projizieren. Aufgrund der Flexibilität des Live-Codings ist es möglich, die Klänge spezifisch an den jeweiligen Raum und das Publikum anzupassen.

Forma II

Thomas Ankersmit, Valerio Tricoli

Forma II ist das Ergebnis der ersten Zusammenarbeit des in Berlin und Amsterdam lebenden Musikers und Installationskünstlers Thomas Ankersmit mit Valerio Tricoli, einem akusmatischen Musikkomponisten, Improvisator und Klanginstallationskünstler.
Das 2010 in Berlin komponierte und aufgenommene Stück *Forma II* besteht aus vier elektroakustischen Stücken, die größtenteils auf analogem Synthesizermaterial beruhen, und einer langen schwarmähnlichen Komposition für mehrere hinzugemischte Saxophone. Das Spektrum der Klänge reicht darüber hinaus von auf Ultraschallbündeln schwebender Metallfolie bis hin zu mechanischen Klicks, die in den verlassenen Radarkuppeln in Teufelsberg bei Berlin aufgenommen wurden. Das Rohmaterial wurde aufwändig bearbeitet und unter Verwendung eines analogen Tonbands und digitaler Methoden rekonstruiert. Die fünf Stücke bewegen sich zwischen dem scharfen Rauschen elektronischer Interferenz bis hin zu Passagen von austarierter Balance zwischen Ruhe und Turbulenz, Stasis und rasantem Formwechsel, multiplen virtuellen Räumen und Nicht-Räumen.

Sonic Vista

Bruce Odland, Sam Auinger

Bruce Odland und Sam Auinger sind Klangkünstler, Klangphilosophen und Komponisten und für großformatige Soundinstallationen im öffentlichen Raum bekannt, bei denen Stadtlärm in Echtzeit in ein harmonisches Klangerlebnis verwandelt und damit die klangliche Identität öffentlicher Plätze auf der ganzen Welt verändert wird.

Sonic Vista ist eine Installation in einem großen urbanen Klangraum (Deutschherrnbrücke, Eisenbahnbrücke über den Main in Frankfurt), die dem Publikum ermöglicht, in das komplexe Innenleben der Stadt hineinzuhören und ihre Klangmuster im jeweiligen Augenblick in ihrer Gesamtheit wahrzunehmen. Die urbanen Klangquellen werden mit „Resonanzrohren" auf subtile Weise in Echtzeit transformiert und in harmonische Klänge verwandelt, die das menschliche Gehirn als Musik, als Rhythmus auslesen kann. Auge und Ohr des Betrachters werden angesprochen, nehmen die Klangmuster der Stadt wahr und entwerfen davon ausgehend einen neuen mentalen Stadtplan. Die Wirkung entspricht in etwa der Verarbeitung neuer Informationen, dem erstmaligen Hören des Klangs der eigenen Kultur als komplexen Organismus. Es ist der Sound von uns selbst, eines symphonischen „Bienenstocks", unseres kulturellen Inputs und Outputs, der als hoch entwickeltes urbanes Klangmuster zu hören ist.

Project Integration / Intervention into Tenryu City
Minkoku Hyakunen

Project Integration / Intervention into Tenryu City ist die erste offizielle Veröffentlichung von Minkoku Hyakunen (民国百年.) Wie aus dem Titel bereits hervorgeht, verwenden die Mitglieder von Minkoku Hyakunen die Geräusche der Stadt Taipeh als Klangmaterial, wobei sie teilweise einfach Feldaufnahmen machen, um die Geräuschkulisse der Stadt aufzuzeichnen, teilweise sich selbst als Akteure in das Narrativ einbringen und das sich entfaltende Geschehen mit Sarkasmus, Ironie und politischer Satire würzen. Die 16 Tracks entstanden bei diversen Events und an unterschiedlichen Schauplätzen, wobei kaum versucht wurde, zu verhehlen, dass es sich um Aufnahmen handelt, was diesem faszinierend kraftvollen und dabei manchmal überaus komischen Werk einen kantigen Realismus und Authentizität verleiht.

Project Integration / Intervention into Tenryu City
Minkoku Hyakunen

Project Integration/Intervention into Tenryu City is the first official release by Minkoku Hyakunen (民国百年). As the title implies, the members of MH take the sounds of Taipei City as their sound pallet, sometimes simply as a field recording to capture the city soundscape and sometimes, perhaps more uniquely, insert themselves as active players in the narrative, injecting sarcasm, irony and political satire into the unfolding events. There are 16 tracks collected from many events and places, with little or no attempt to conceal the fact that they are recording, which adds edgy realism and authenticity to the overall feel of this intriguingly powerful yet sometimes hilarious body of work.

Crystal Sounds of a Synchrotron

Jo Thomas

Crystal is a 38-minute sound work for 5.1 DVD and download that was composed to highlight the engaging sounds of Diamond Light Source.

It is composed directly from frequencies generated by the electron-storage ring, a particle accelerator. The work also uses binaural recording from locations inside Diamond's experimental hall, storage ring and beamlines. Writing this work, my imagination was sparked from the start and my aim was to write a work of substantial length that reflected both the actual content of the spectrum of the space and also the metaphorical content of the sounds.

The Diamond synchrotron is a rich, multi-spectral environment with a cacophony of sounds generated by machines that hiss pure nitrogen, pump air from vacuum chambers and cool high-powered magnets. There is never one time where any sound is exactly the same. It is a large, circular space, extremely reverberative, vibrating complex tones from the electromagnetic and mechanical interfaces that generate the electron beam, which travels at close to the speed of light. The actual physical space of the synchrotron seems to capture pure human intelligence, concentration and the ability to look beyond what is currently possible. It is light, futuristic and like nothing I have ever seen before.

Crystal dauert 38 Minuten und wurde für 5.1 DVD und als Download konzipiert und komponiert, um auf den faszinierenden Sound der Synchrotronstrahlungsquelle Diamond Light Source aufmerksam zu machen.

Die Klangarbeit *Crystal* wurde direkt aus den Frequenzen komponiert, die der Elektronenspeicherring, ein Teilchenbeschleuniger, generiert. Auch binaurale Tonaufnahmen von Plätzen in der Experimentierhalle, dem Speicherring und den Beamlines von Diamond Light Source wurden für das Stück verwendet. Die Arbeit an der Komposition hat meine Fantasie von Anfang an beflügelt; meine Ambition war es, ein Stück von einer gewissen Länge zu komponieren, das sowohl das gesamte tatsächliche Spektrum des Raums als auch den metaphorischen Gehalt der Klänge reflektiert.

Das Diamond Synchroton ist ein riesiges multispektrales Environment, in dem eine Kakophonie von Klängen von Maschinen erzeugt wird, die zischend reinen Stickstoff entweichen lassen, Luft aus Vakuumkammern pumpen und Hochenergie-Magneten kühlen. Die Klänge wiederholen sich nie. Die Anlage ist weitläufig, kreisförmig und hat einen extremen Nachhall. Darin vibrieren komplexe Töne aus den elektromagnetischen und mechanischen Schnittstellen, die den Elektronenstrahl erzeugen, der nahezu Lichtgeschwindigkeit erreicht. Der physische Raum des Synchrotrons scheint menschliche Intelligenz, Konzentration und die Fähigkeit, über die derzeitigen Möglichkeiten hinauszudenken, in sich zu bündeln. Er ist hell, futuristisch und mit nichts zuvor Gesehenem vergleichbar.

Die Klänge, die in dieser Arbeit zu hören sind, stammen von Elektronen, die in bestimmten Intervallen in den Partikelbeschleuniger injiziert werden. Diese Injektionen erfolgen alle zehn Minuten. Sie sind vorhersagbar und gleichsam allgegenwärtig. Ihr Klang ist körnig und trocken. Ich habe den Mikrotonalitäten in den Strömen der Elektroneninjektionen zugehört, wie sie nuancierte Mikromelodien entwickeln, die kommen und gehen – Atominjektionen nicht unähnlich. Am Ende des Stücks sind die Injektionen zur Gänze zu hören. Auch eine Auswahl binauraler Feldaufnahmen von Positionen im Synchrotron-Bereich wurden für die Arbeit verwendet.
Positionsklänge von Elektronenstrahlen, kompiliert von Jo Thomas und dem wissenschaftlichen Mitarbeiter Guenter Rhem.

What you hear in this work are the sounds of electron injections into the particle accelerator at certain times of the day. This happens every ten minutes; it is predicable and ever-present. The sonic content of the injections is grainy and dry. I listened to the micro-tonalities captured in the streams of injections developing detailed micro-melodies, which appear and disappear not unlike the atom injections. The injections are heard in full at the end of the work. I also took binaural field recordings from points in the synchrotron area and used a selection of these within the work. Electron-beam position sounds collected by Jo Thomas and Research Scientist Guenter Rhem.

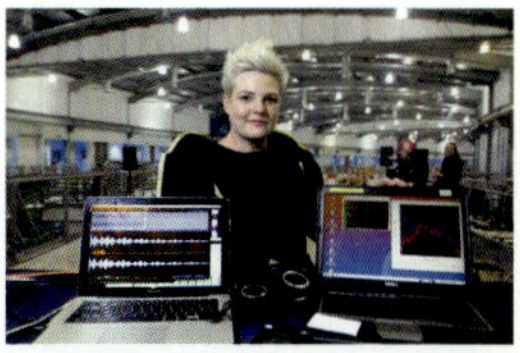

Jo Thomas (UK) is an electronic music artist living and working in London. Her debut solo LP, *Alpha*, was released by Entr'acte in 2010 and nominated for a Quartz 7 award in 2011. She performs her music on a regular basis. Working on multi-channel systems, her music repeatedly explores the polarities of failure and perfection, working with visual image, micro-sound, beats glitch and pure tone. New releases include a new solo CD by Entr'acte 2012 and her work with Asteroid Ensemble, by the label Electronic Musik 2012, and the *Active Crossover* compilation released on Cronica. Her music has been performed in venues such as the Round House, London, Cafe Oto, London, Basso, Berlin, Salon De Messian, Paris, Calarts, Los Angeles, ICA, London, New Federation Square, Melbourne, Electric Church, Berlin, Queen Elizabeth Hall, London, Resonance FM and BBC Radio Three.

Jo Thomas (UK) lebt und arbeitet als elektronische Komponistin in London. Ihre erste Solo-LP *Alpha* wurde 2010 von Entr'Act produziert und 2011 für den Quartz 7 nominiert. Sie arbeitet mit Mehrkanalsystemen und präsentiert ihre Musik bei regelmäßigen Auftritten. In ihrer Musik beschäftigt sie sich immer wieder mit der Spannung zwischen Perfektion und Scheitern und arbeitet dabei auch mit visuellen Bildern, Mikrosound, Störimpulsen und reinem Ton. Zu ihren Neuveröffentlichungen zählen eine Solo-CD bei Entr'acte 2012 und ihre Arbeit mit dem Asteroid Ensemble, veröffentlicht 2012 bei Electronic Musik, sowie die *Active Crossover*-Compilation, die bei Cronica erschien. Ihre Werke wurden weltweit aufgeführt und ausgestrahlt, u.a. im Round House (London), Cafe Oto (London), Basso Berlin, Salon De Messian (Paris), Calarts (Los Angeles), ICA London, New Federation Square (Melbourne), Electric Church (Berlin), der Queen Elizabeth Hall (London), Resonance FM und bei BBC Radio Three.

Scape-Sequencer

Xu Cheng

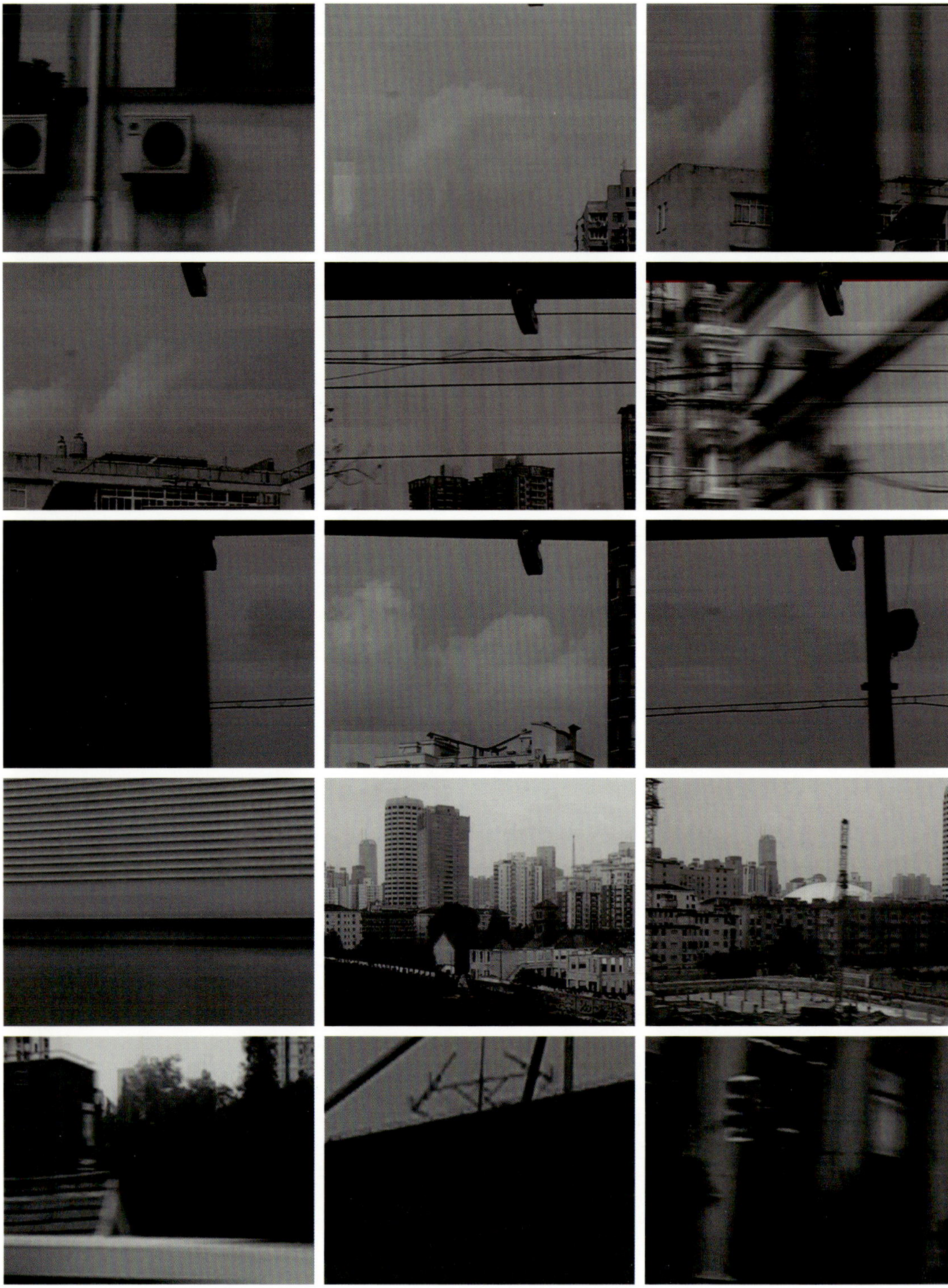

Scape-Sequencer (2010) ist ein audiovisuelles Werk für eine Live-Performance. Aufnahmen von Sinneseindrücken aus dem Alltag in Shanghai dienen als Ausgangsmaterial, das mithilfe von Software und Hardware-Controllern zu einem völlig neuen audiovisuellen Erlebnis remixt und synthetisiert wird.

Scape-Sequencer (2010) is an audiovisual work for live performance. It takes everyday sensory experiences in the city of Shanghai as its source material, which is then remixed and synthesized with software programming and hardware controllers into a brand-new audiovisual experience.

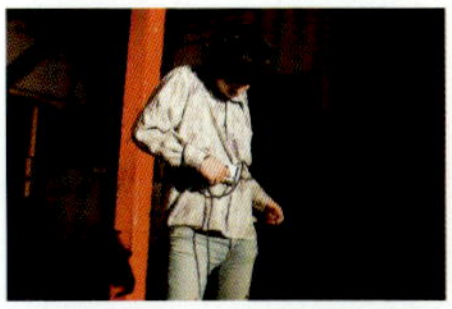

Xu Cheng (CN), born 1980 in Shanghai. Since 1999, Cheng has worked with different styles of sound and music, including concrete music, plunderphonics, electro-acoustic, harsh noise, ambient, and improvisation. In 2003, his works were selected in the first survey anthology of Chinese sound art *China–the Sonic Avant-Garde (Post-Concrete)*. In 2005, together with noise artist Junky, Cheng formed the NOIShanghai group to promote experimental music, which has since organized over 40 performances by sound artists and noise artist from around the world. In the same year, Cheng joined the world-renowned noise group Torturing Nurse, which has presented over 100 performances and 200 releases. In 2010, Cheng joined the free improvisation group Free Music Collective of Shanghai. **Xu Cheng** (CN), geboren 1980 in Shanghai, arbeitet seit 1999 mit unterschiedlichen Klangstilen und Musikrichtungen wie etwa Musique concrète, Plunderphonics, Elektroakustik, Harsh Noise, Ambient und Improvisation. 2003 wurden seine Arbeiten für die Doppel-CD *China – the Sonic Avant-Garde*, die erste Kompilation chinesischer Klangkunst, die beim Label Post-Concrete erschien, ausgewählt. 2005 gründete Xu Cheng mit dem Noise-Künstler Jnky die Gruppe NOIShanghai zur Förderung experimenteller Musik, die mittlerweile mehr als 40 Performances von Klang- und Noise-Künstlern aus der ganzen Welt organisierte. Im selben Jahr schloss er sich der weltbekannten Noise-Band Torturing Nurse an, die über 100 Auftritte und 200 Veröffentlichungen vorzuweisen hat. 2010 trat er der Improvisationsgruppe Free Music Collectiv of Shanghai bei.

#tweetscapes

Tarik Barri, Anselm Venezian Nehls

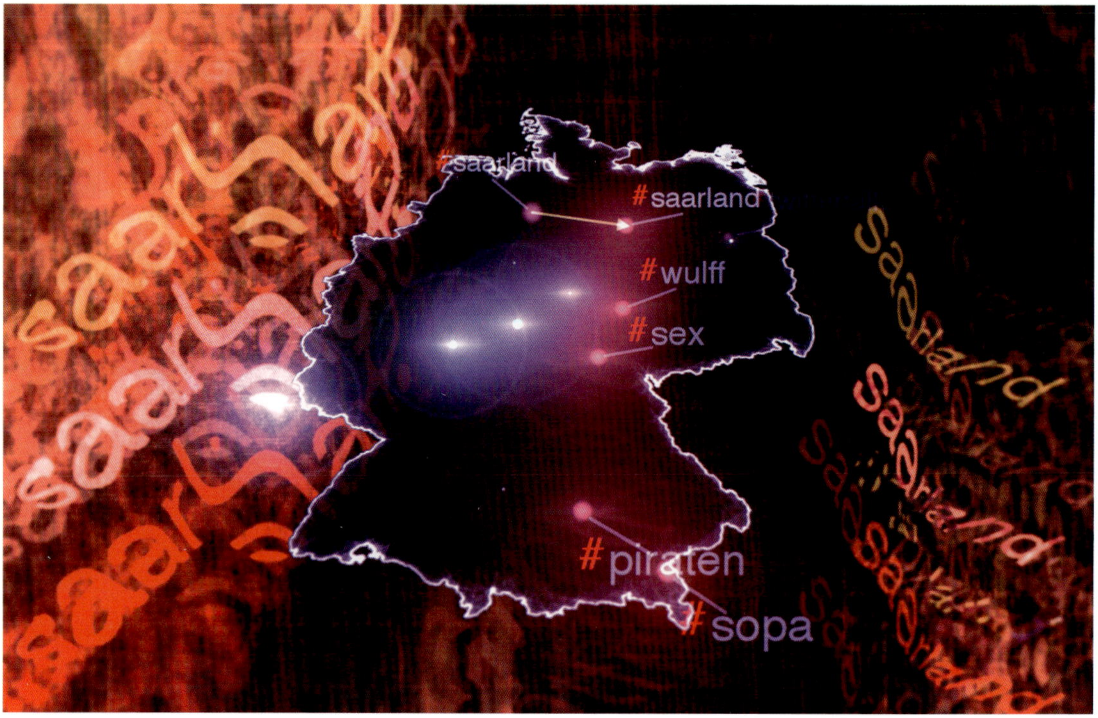

#tweetscapes instantly converts all German Twitter messages into abstract sounds as they are being sent. It is a real-time sonification of what is happening in the German Twitter-sphere, as well as an interactive composition, performed collectively by Germany's Twitter users.
#tweetscapes aims to add a sensual element to the development of discussion topics and the rhythm of the online dialog. Not only does this allow unique soundscapes to arise, but *#tweetscapes* shows the social network from a radically different perspective.
The Twitter messages are being sonified according to a fixed set of rules: tweets including a #hashtag (a thematic keyword), direct replies to another user, re-tweets (forwarded messages) and trending topics are each treated differently. For any possible topic of conversation, one individual, characteristic sound is created algorithmically, making it possible to conceive the development of the collective "multilogue" intuitively—and to sensually experience the overall mood of the Twitter-sphere at any given moment. Twitter

#tweetscapes verwandelt alle deutsprachigen Twitter-Nachrichten, sobald sie verschickt werden, in abstrakte Klänge. Es ist eine Echtzeit-Sonifikation der Vorgänge in der deutschen Twitter-Szene sowie eine interaktive Komposition, die kollektiv von Deutschlands Twitter-Nutzern performt wird. *#tweetscapes* möchte der Entwicklung von Themen und dem Rhythmus des Online-Dialogs eine sinnliche Komponente hinzufügen. Es lässt nicht nur einzigartige Klangwelten entstehen, sondern zeigt darüber hinaus das soziale Netzwerk aus einer völlig anderen Perspektive.
Die Tweets werden nach einem genau festgelegten Regelwerk vertont: Tweets mit einem #Hashtag (thematischen Stichwort), direkte Antworten auf einen anderen User, ReTweets (weitergeleitete Beiträge) und Trending Topics werden jeweils unterschiedlich behandelt. Für jedes potenzielle Thema wird algorithmisch ein eigener charakteristischer Sound kreiert, der es ermöglicht, die Entwicklung des kollektiven „Multilogs" intuitiv zu verstehen – und die Gesamtstimmung der Twitter-Szene zu jedem beliebigen Zeitpunkt mit den Sinnen zu erfahren. Twitter wird Ambience, der User Teil des Datenstroms.

#tweetscapes wurde ursprünglich 2011 im Auftrag von Deutschlandradio Kultur entwickelt und läuft regelmäßig in dessen Programm, wodurch deutsche Twitter-User live über das Radio das Kunstwerk interaktiv mitgestalten können. 2012 wurde das Format durch eine Visualisierung ergänzt und ist nun auf *http://tweetscapes.de* als audiovisueller 24/7-Live-Stream oder auch als audiovisuelle Surround-Installation *#tweetspace* zu sehen. In beiden Fällen kann das Publikum mittels Tweets per Handy oder auf dem Computer interaktiv mitwirken.

becomes an ambience, the user becomes part of the data stream.

#tweetscapes was originally developed on behalf of Deutschlandradio Kultur in 2011 and is being broadcast on its program regularly, allowing German Twitter users to interact with the artwork live on the radio. In 2012, it has been complemented by a visualization and takes the form of a 24/7 audiovisual live stream on *http://tweetscapes.de*, but also of an audiovisual surround installation called *#tweetspace*. Either way, the audience can use their mobile phones or computers to interact with the work through Twitter messages.

Anselm Venezian Nehls / HeavyListening: Idea, concept, sound, programming; Tarik Barri: Visualisation; Florian Eitel: Additional programming; Dr. Thomas Hermann: Scientific project support; Sam Auinger: Artistic project support; Marcus Gammel: Dramaturgy; Timm Knoerr: Artwork

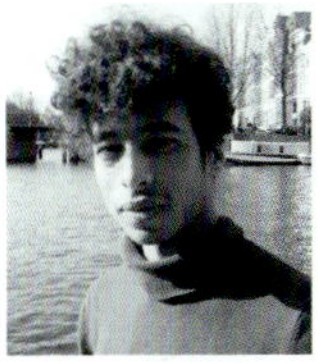

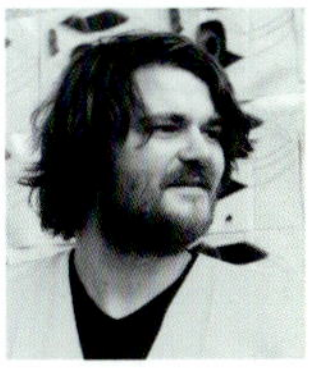

Tarik Barri (NL), born 1979, is an audiovisual composer and software developer. With tools such as Max/MSP, Java and SuperCollider he develops new applications for audiovisual performance, composition and data-representation. Using these tools, Barri aims to discover new synergies and aesthetics in the combination of image and sound. Barri has performed and displayed his works at Sonic Acts, Ars Electronica, Club Transmediale, TodaysArt, MIT Media Lab, EMPAC and many others. He was a guest lecturer at Berklee College of Music (Boston, US), the Berlin University of the Arts (DE) and the Hilversum School of Music and Technology (NL). **Anselm Venezian Nehls** (DE), born 1981, is a sound and media artist, musician, and co-founder of the HeavyListening label for sound art. He first received training as an audio engineer before studying popular music at Goldsmiths College, London. In 2012, he will receive his master's degree in sound studies from the Berlin University of the Arts, where he studied under Sam Auinger and Robert Henke, focusing on experimental sound design. Nehls' projects deal with a wide range of themes and techniques, but always aim at establishing strong connections between the realm of ideas and the physical world. **Tarik Barri** (NL), geboren 1979, ist audiovisueller Komponist und Softwareentwickler. Mit Tools wie Max/MSP, Java und SuperCollider entwickelte er neue Applikationen für audiovisuelle Performance, Komposition und Datenrepräsentation. Mithilfe dieser Tools möchte Tarik Barri neue Synergien und Ästhetiken in der Kombination von Bild und Klang entdecken. Er performte und präsentierte seine Arbeiten u.a. bei Festivals und in Kunst- und Medienzentren wie Sonic Acts, Ars Electronica, Club Transmediale, TodaysArt, MIT Media Lab, EMPAC etc. Tarik Barri war Gastdozent am Berklee College of Music (Boston), an der Universität der Künste (Berlin) und am Institut für Musiktechnologie (Hilversum, NL). **Anselm Venezian Nehls** (DE), geboren 1981, ist Klang- und Medienkünstler, Musiker und Mitbegründer des Labels für Klangkunst HeavyListening. Er absolvierte zunächst eine Ausbildung als Audioingenieur, bevor er Popmusik am Goldsmiths College in London studierte und den Masterstudiengang Sound Studies an der Universität der Künste Berlin bei Sam Auinger und Robert Henke mit dem Schwerpunkt experimentelle Klanggestaltung absolvierte. Nehls setzt sich in seinen Projekten mit unterschiedlichsten Themen und Techniken auseinander, strebt dabei aber immer nach starken Verbindungsgliedern zwischen der Welt der Ideen und der Welt der Erscheinungen.

Benoît and the Mandelbrots

Juan A. Romero, Holger Ballweg, Patrick Borgeat, Matthias Schneiderbanger

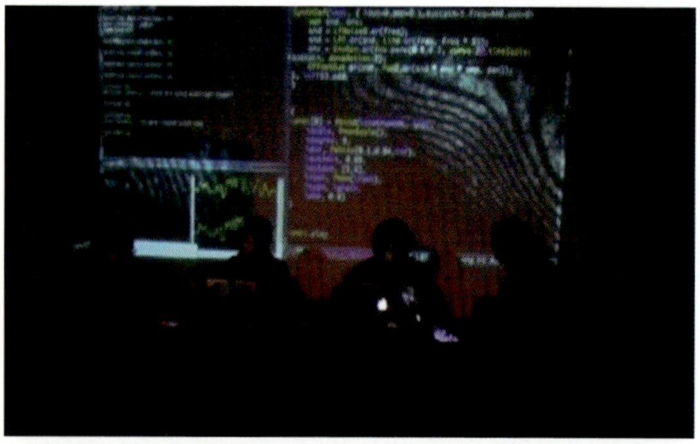

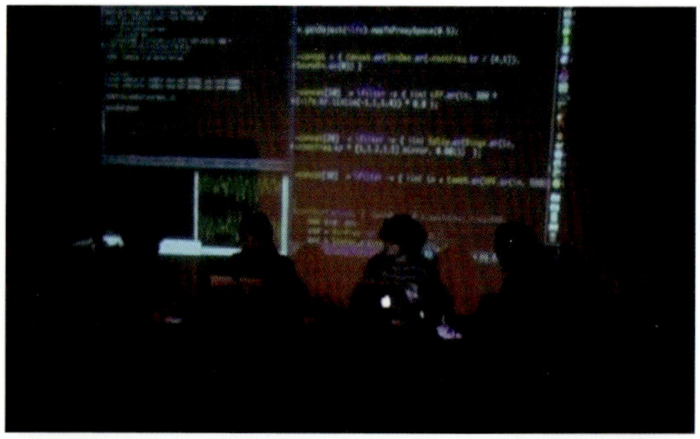

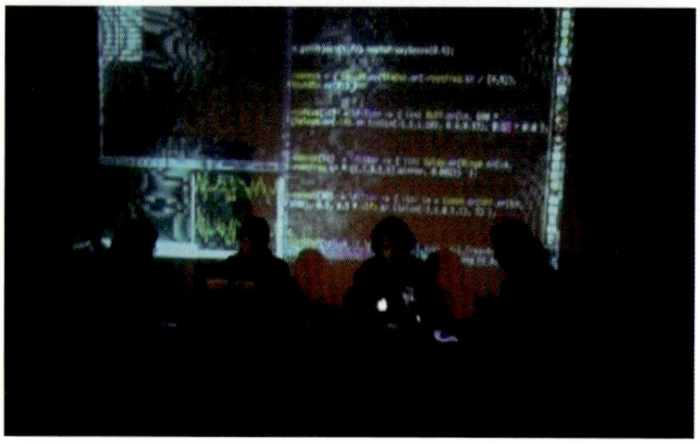

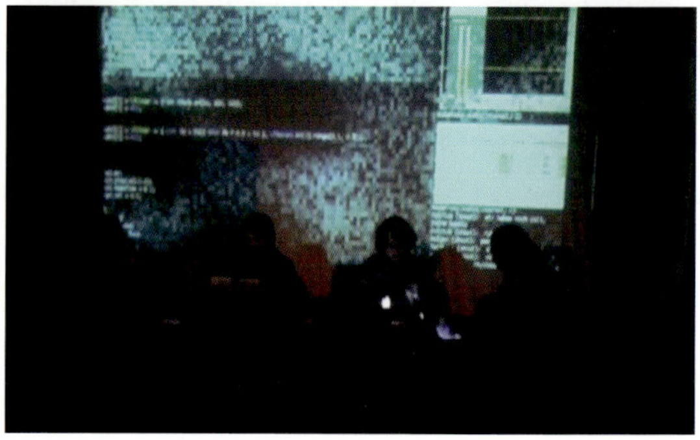

Benoît and the Mandelbrots betrachten den Laptop als ihr wichtigstes Instrument und widmen sich vor allem dem Live-Coding: der Programmierung musikalischer Prozesse in Echtzeit. Sie verwenden die Programmiersprache selbst als eine auf den ersten Blick zwar nicht intuitive, dafür aber expressive Schnittstelle zwischen Mensch und Maschine, um mit Klängen und Musik zu improvisieren. Klangkonzepte und -strukturen werden live als Quellcode formuliert und vom Computer interpretiert. Die Laptop-Musiker sind über ein Netzwerk miteinander verbunden, das ihnen ermöglicht, auf der Bühne zu kommunizieren, Parameter wie z. B. Harmonieprogressionen auszutauschen, ihr Timing zu synchronisieren und einzelne Schritte der Programmierung auf eine Leinwand zu projizieren.

Da jede Performance-Situation einzigartig und Improvisation das wesentliche Paradigma ist, führt die Gruppe keine „Werke" im klassischen Sinn auf, sondern betrachtet die Gesamtheit ihrer Performances und das ihnen zugrunde liegende Konzept als das eigentliche Werk, das mit jedem Auftritt eine Erweiterung erfährt. Die musikalischen Ergebnisse variieren – je nach Event, Publikum, Veranstaltungsort und Ablauf der kollektiven Improvisation – und erstrecken sich von Electronica und Ambient bis hin zu Experimentalmusik, Noise, Drone-Musik und Avantgarde.

Benoît and the Mandelbrots see the laptop as their main instrument; they are mainly dedicated to live coding, the process of writing software in real time. They use the programming language itself as an at first sight non-intuitive but simultaneously expressive interface between man and machine in order to improvise sound and music. Sonic conceptions and structures are expressed live as source code and interpreted by the computer. The laptop musicians are connected over the network to enable them to communicate on stage and share parameters, e.g. harmonic progressions, to synchronize their timing and project their screens on a dedicated machine.

As every performance setting is unique and improvisation is the main paradigm of the group, they do not perform "works" in a classic sense but consider their whole oeuvre and underlying concept as their work, which expands with every performance. The musical results vary from electronica and ambient to experimental, noise, drones and avant-garde depending on the event, audience, venue and course of the collective improvisation.

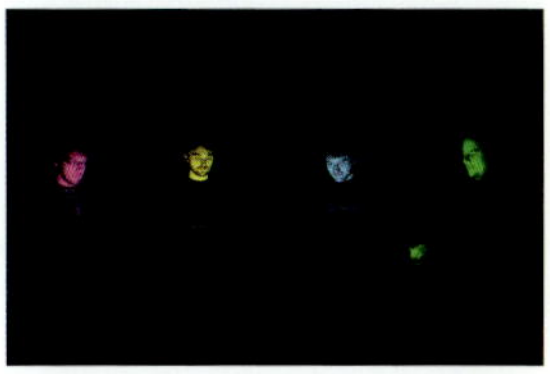

Benoît and the Mandelbrots (DE) was formed in winter 2009 by students of the IMWI (Institute for Musicology and Music Informatics) at the Karlsruhe University of Music: Holger Ballweg, Patrick Borgeat, Juan A. Romero, Matthias Schneiderbanger. Since then they have played in over 30 concerts in different locations and events, notably at Network Music Festival 2012 in Birmingham, Laptop Meets Musician Festival 2011 in Venice, next_generation 4.0 at ZKM Karlsruhe, SuperCollider Symposium 2010 in Berlin and LINKS Biennale für Neue Musik 2010 in Heidelberg.

Benoît and the Mandelbrots (DE) wurde im Winter 2009 von Studenten des IMWI (Institut für Musikwissenschaft und Musikinformatik) der Hochschule für Musik Karlsruhe gegründet und besteht aus Holger Ballweg, Patrick Borgeat, Juan A. Romero und Matthias Schneiderbanger. Seither bestritt das Ensemble über 30 Auftritte an unterschiedlichen Veranstaltungsorten und bei Festivals, wie etwa Network Music Festival 2012 in Birmingham, Laptop Meets Musician Festival 2011 in Venedig, next_generation 4.0 am ZKM Karlsruhe, SuperCollider Symposium 2010 in Berlin und LINKS Biennale für Neue Musik 2010 in Heidelberg.

BETWEEN | YOU | AND | ME

Anke Eckardt

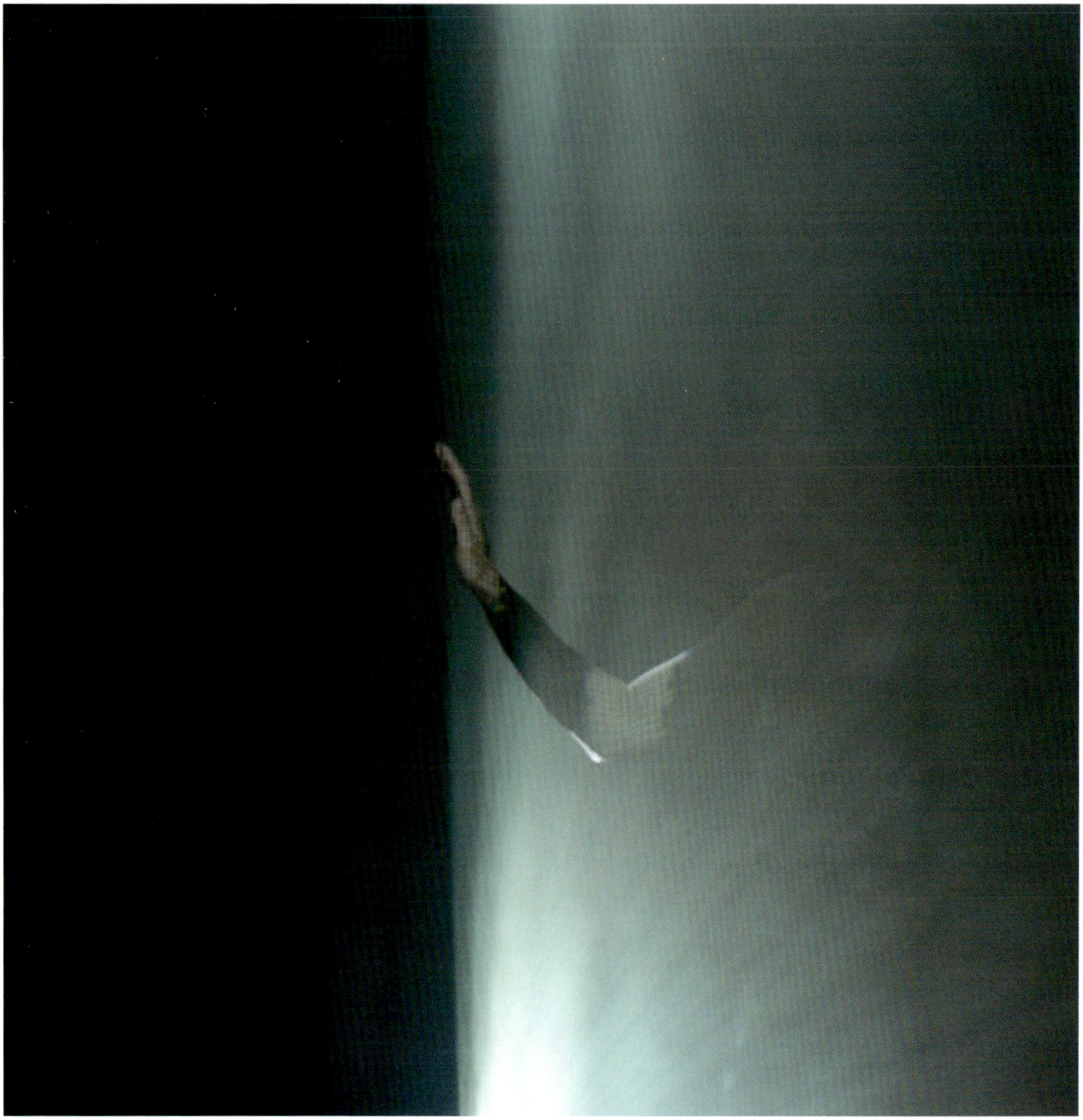

BETWEEN | YOU | AND | ME is a wall of sound and light. Like any other wall, it defines an architectural space, just it can be perceived only when the visitor comes close and interacts with it. Two thin membranes of light form a visible frame filled with sound. Extremely vectored hypersonic speakers

BETWEEN | YOU | AND | ME ist eine Wand von Sound und Licht. Wie jede andere Wand auch definiert sie einen architektonischen Raum, ist jedoch nur wahrzunehmen, wenn der Besucher sich ihr nähert und mit ihr interagiert. Zwei dünne Lichtmembranen bilden einen sichtbaren Rahmen, der mit Klang gefüllt ist. Über extrem gerichtete

Concept/Realization: Anke Eckardt; composition: Anke Eckardt & Henry Koch; programming: Yvan Volochine; technical support: Zolle. Thanks to: Peter Votava, Douglas Henderson; realized by means of The Artist-in-Residence grant of the Saxon State Ministry for Higher Education, Research and the Fine Arts 2011 which is awarded in cooperation with City of Dresden and co-funded by Culture Programme (2007–2013) in framework of European networking- and cooperation project ECAS – Networking Tomorrow's Art For An Unknown Future.

Lautsprecher sind Klangtexturen zerbrechenden Glases zu hören: eine Klangarchitektur innerhalb der Wand, bestehend aus sechs überlagerten, einzelnen Schallbündeln, deren Konstellation sich je nach der Position des Besuchers verändert. Aus einer gewissen Distanz betrachtet, löst sich die Wand auf: Transparenz und das Verhallen der Töne verweisen auf ihre Immaterialität.
Im Unterschied zu Stein- oder Betonwänden und zu den immateriellen Barrieren in der gesellschaftlichen oder politischen Realität kann die Abgrenzung hier überwunden werden. Die Installation lädt den Besucher ein, mit scheinbar zweidimensionalen Lichtmembranen zu spielen, sie mit dem ganzen Körper oder einzelnen Körperteilen zu überschreiten oder zu durchbrechen, zu beobachten, wie der Körper vom Licht zerschnitten wird und in die Wand eintaucht, wodurch eine veränderte Selbst- und Fremdwahrnehmung bewirkt wird.
Akustisch ist es eine Wand aus Glas. Das gesamte Klangmaterial wurde von der Künstlerin selbst aufgenommen. Mit einer Axt zerschlug sie systematisch Christbaumkugeln, Spiegel und den gesamten Gläserbestand eines aufgelassenen Restaurants. Mit dreidirektionalen Mikrophonen nahm sie das Zerbrechen, den Aufschlag und das Zersplittern des Glases auf und arrangierte die Klänge in einer Sechs-Kanal-Komposition.
Klang förmlich wie eine Skulptur zu modellieren, das ist die Grundidee, die Anke Eckardt zu ihrer Installation inspirierte. Die Hypersonic-Lautsprecher dieser Installation haben einen unnatürlichen Abstrahlwinkel von nur drei Grad und verwenden Ultraschall von 100 kHz als Trägerfrequenz für das Endsignal. Die Technologie wurde ursprünglich vom Militär für die psychologische Kriegsführung entwickelt. Die Polizei setzt sie weltweit zur Kontrolle von Menschenmengen ein, etwa 2012 bei den Demonstrationen in Senegal.

make the textures of broken glass audible: a sound architecture within the wall, comprising six juxtaposed single sound beams, whose arrangement changes depending on the visitor's position. Observed from a distance, the wall fades away: clear transparency and only faintly resonant tones attest to its non-existence.
Unlike walls of stone or concrete and intangible barriers of the social, national or political variety, the boundary in this installation can be overcome. The installation invites the visitor to play with seemingly two-dimensional membranes of light, to transgress them with his or her whole body or its individual parts, to observe their body being dissected by light, immersed in the walls, and thereby to perceive it as discrete from other bodies.
Acoustically, the wall consists of glass; all the sound material was recorded by the artist herself. She systematically cut Christmas tree balls with an axe, as well as mirrors and the complete stock of glasses from a former restaurant. Using three directional microphones, she recorded the breaking, fall and impact of the glass on the ground and arranged the sounds into a six-channel composition.
The inspiration behind Anke Eckardt's installation was to shape sound literally, as sculpture. The hypersonic speakers in this installation have an unnatural radiation angle of just three degrees and use ultrasound at 100 kHz as the frequency for the ultimate signal. The technology was originally developed by the military for psychological warfare. The police use it internationally as a means of crowd control, for example at demonstrations in Senegal in 2012.

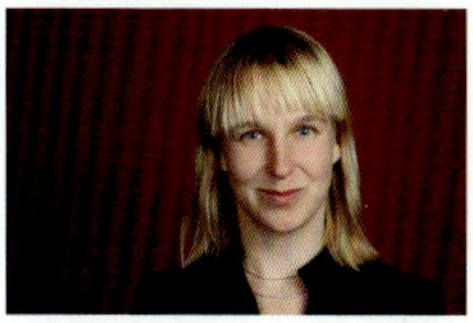

Anke Eckardt (DE), born in 1976, is a sound and media artist. Since 2008 her work has included sculptures, installations and a theoretical discourse on the topic of the phenomenology of sounds. For her sculptures and installations she uses sound (including ultrasound and infrasound) in combination with other media/materials such as moving light and water to build large-scale works of a rich metaphoric radiance. It is essential for Eckardt's work that the technically complex ensembles appear deceptively simple—in this way they can directly trigger the imagination of the audience. **Anke Eckardt** (DE), geboren 1976, ist Klang- und Medienkünstlerin. Ihr Werk seit 2008 umfasst Skulpturen, Installationen sowie einen theoretischen Diskurs zur Phänomenologie des Klangs. Für ihre Skulpturen und Installationen verwendet sie Klang (einschließlich Ultra- und Infraschall) in Kombination mit anderen Medien/Materialien wie bewegtes Licht und Wasser zur Konstruktion von großformatigen Arbeiten von starker metaphorischer Qualität. Wesentlich für Eckardts Arbeit ist, dass die technisch komplexen Ensembles täuschend einfach wirken – und so die Fantasie des Publikums am unmittelbarsten anregen.

Crackle-canvas #1

Tom Verbruggen

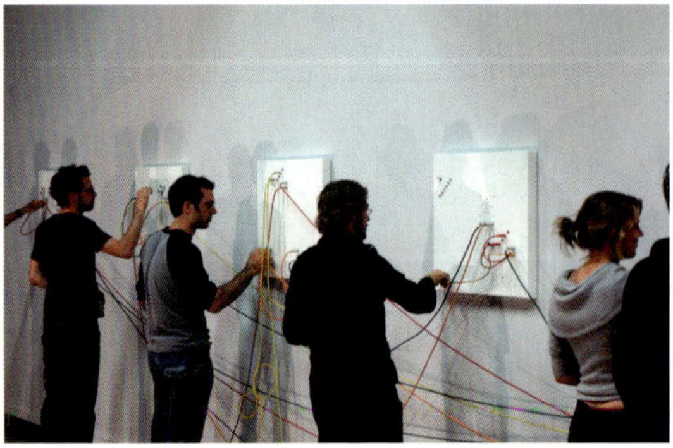

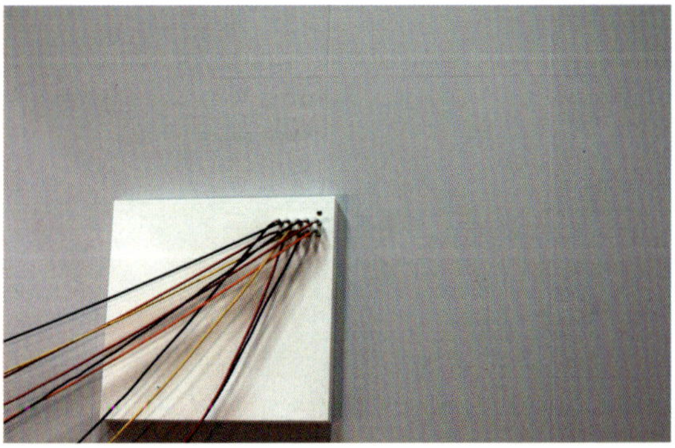

Crackle-canvas is a painting that produces sound. It contains a circuit board, speaker, knobs, switches, wood and canvas. Each canvas makes sounds by itself but can be connected via cables (patched) with other crackle-canvasses. This way the paintings start to react on each other. Each patch creates a different sound and drawing of cables on the wall or in the space the paintings are presented.
I present *Crackle-canvas #1* to the audience in a performance. In this performance I show the audience some of the many things *Crackle-canvas* can do. After this performance I invite the audience to play with *Crackle-canvas* themselves.

Als *Crackle-canvas* bezeichnet Tom Verbruggen ein Bild, das Sound erzeugt und aus einer Platine, Lautsprechern, Drehreglern, Schaltern, Holzrahmen und Leinwand besteht. Jedes Bild produziert einen eigenen Sound, kann aber über (gepatchte) Kabel auch mit anderen Bildern verbunden werden und auf diese reagieren. Jede Rangierung erzeugt einen anderen Sound und eine andere Kabelzeichnung auf der Wand oder in dem Raum, in dem die Bilder präsentiert werden.
Crackle-canvas #1 wird dem Publikum im Rahmen einer Performance präsentiert, in der einige der vielen Möglichkeiten aufgezeigt werden, die in der „knisternden Leinwand" stecken. Im Anschluss an die Performance hat das Publikum die Möglichkeit, selbst mit den Bildern zu spielen.

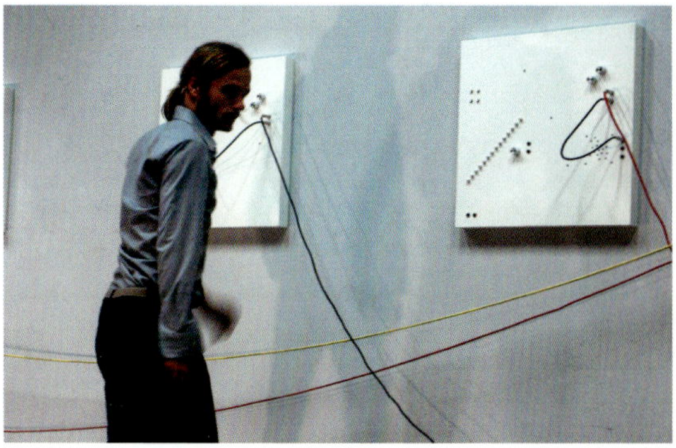

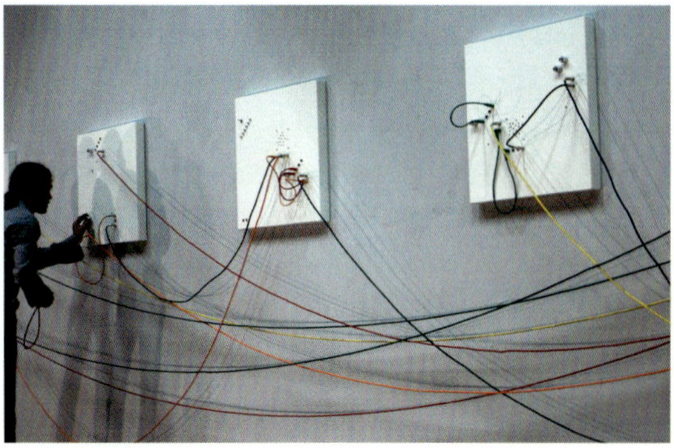

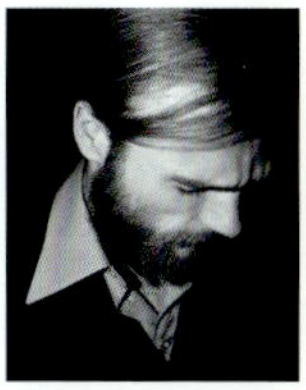

Tom Verbruggen (NL) studied fine arts at the St. Joost Art Academy in Breda (NL). During this study he became increasingly interested in sound, finally resulting in his *toktek* performance. Over the years, *toktek* has mastered the art of sampling anything that makes sound. After making only sound-art pieces and sound performances, he had the urge to make visual art again and started to experiment with and combine modern-day electronics and classical art forms such as sculpture and painting. Tom is interested in and fascinated by the contrast between tactile human gestures and the inhuman continuity of the machine. Natural materials such as wood and fabric vs. an electronic circuit. The past vs. the future. **Tom Verbruggen** (NL) studierte Bildende Kunst an der Kunstakademie St. Joost in Breda (NL). Bereits während des Studiums interessierte er sich zunehmend für klangliche Phänomene und entwickelte die *toktek*-Performance. Im Laufe der Jahre hat toktek alias Tom Verbruggen es zu einer Meisterschaft darin gebracht, alles, was Geräusche von sich gibt, für Samplings zu nutzen. Nachdem er sich eine Zeitlang nur mit Klangkunst und -Performance auseinandergesetzt hatte, zog es ihn wieder zur bildenden Kunst. Er begann zu experimentieren und kombinierte neueste Elektronik und klassische Kunstdisziplinen wie Skulptur und Malerei. Tom Verbruggen ist fasziniert vom Gegensatz zwischen dem menschlichen taktilen Empfinden und der unmenschlichen Kontinuität der Maschine. Natürliche Materialien wie Holz und Gewebe versus elektronischer Schaltkreis. Vergangenheit versus Zukunft.

Forma II

Thomas Ankersmit, Valerio Tricoli

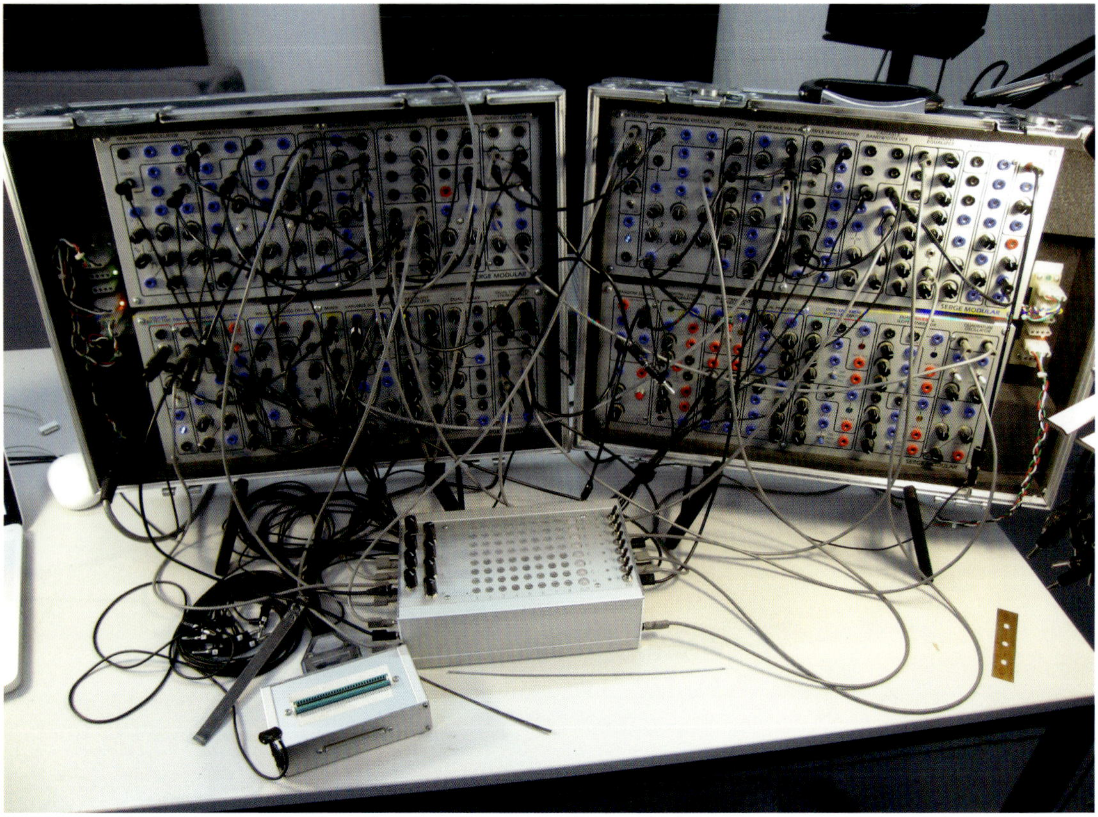

Composed and recorded in Berlin in 2010 *Forma II* consists of four electro-acoustic pieces based largely on analog-synthesizer material and one long-form, swarm-like composition for multiple overdubbed saxophones. Additional sounds range from metal foil floating on ultrasonic sound-beams to mechanical clickers recorded in the abandoned radar domes at Teufelsberg outside Berlin. The raw materials have been extensively processed and reconstructed using analog tape and digital methods. The five pieces shift between sharply detailed blizzards of electronic interference to passages of delicate balance, between calm and turbulence, between stasis and rapid shape-shifting, between multiple virtual spaces and non-spaces.

Das 2010 in Berlin komponierte und aufgenommene Werk *Forma II* besteht aus vier elektroakustischen Stücken, die größtenteils auf Klangmaterial von Analogsynthesizern beruhen, sowie einer langen, an Schwarmformationen erinnernden Komposition für mehrere Saxofon-Overdubs. Das Spektrum der sonstigen Klänge reicht von Metallfolien, die auf Ultraschall-Strahlbündeln schweben, bis hin zu mechanischen Klicks, die in den aufgelassenen Radarkuppeln in Teufelsberg bei Berlin aufgenommen wurden. Das Rohmaterial wurde aufwändig bearbeitet und mithilfe eines analogen Tonbands und digitaler Methoden neu arrangiert. Die fünf Stücke oszillieren zwischen den fein ziselierten Blizzards elektronischer Interferenzen und Passagen von austarierter Balance zwischen Ruhe und Turbulenz, Stillstand und rasantem Formwechsel, virtuellen Orten und Nicht-Orten.

http://www.thomasankersmit.net/
http://www.pan-act.com/

Die CD wurde von Rashad Becker im Studio Clunk in einer limitierten Auflage von 1.000 Stück gemastert. Sie ist in ein Digisleeve verpackt, das in einer PVC-Hülle mit ineinander verflochtenen geometrischen Siebdruckmustern, einer Illustration von Kathryn Politis und Bill Kouligas, steckt.
Forma II ist das Ergebnis der ersten Zusammenarbeit von Thomas Ankersmit und Valerio Tricoli, und Ankersmits zweite CD in voller Länge.

The CD was mastered by Rashad Becker at Clunk in a limited edition of 1000. It is packaged in a pro-press digisleeve jacket, itself inside a one-tone silk-screened PVC sleeve with interweaving geometric designs, with artwork by Kathryn Politis and Bill Kouligas.
Forma II is the first collaborative output by Thomas Ankersmit and Valerio Tricoli and is Ankersmit's second full-length CD.

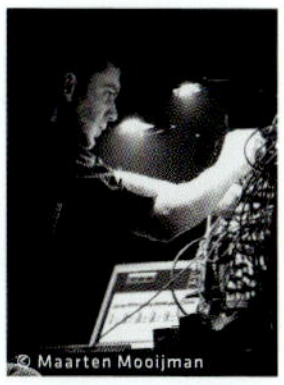
© Maarten Mooijman

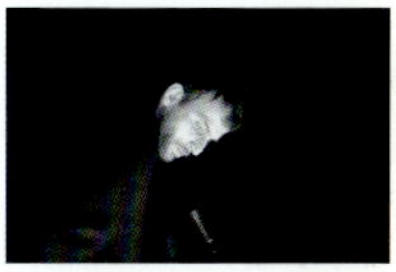

Thomas Ankersmit (NL), born in 1979, is a musician and installation artist based in Berlin and Amsterdam. His main instruments are the Serge analog modular synthesizer, computer and alto saxophone. Ankersmit regularly performs together with composer Phill Niblock, in duos with electro-acoustic artists Valerio Tricoli and Kevin Drumm, as well as in a trio with drummer and saxophonist Mats Gustafsson. He has also worked with Tony Conrad, Maryanne Amacher, Jim O'Rourke, Thomas Lehn and Jérôme Noetinger among others. **Valerio Tricoli** (IT) works as an acousmatic music composer, improviser, sound installation artist, producer, sound engineer and curator. His compositions span concrete music and conceptual sound forms. Tricoli plays live music with electronic instruments—most of them analog. He is one of the founders of the Bowindo label/collective and of ¾HadBeenEliminated, a daring synthesis between improvisation, electro-acoustic composition and avant-rock sensitivity. **Thomas Ankersmit** (NL), geboren 1979, lebt und arbeitet als Musiker und Installationskünstler in Berlin und Amsterdam. Seine Hauptinstrumente sind der analoge Serge Modular Synthesizer, Computer und Altsaxophon. Ankersmit tritt regelmäßig mit dem Komponisten Phill Niblock, als Duo mit den Elektroakustikkünstlern Valerio Tricoli und Kevin Drumm sowie als Trio mit dem Schlagzeuger und Saxofonisten Mats Gustafsson auf. Des Weiteren kooperierte er u.a. mit Tony Conrad, Maryanne Amacher, Jim O'Rourke, Thomas Lehn und Jérôme Noetinger. **Valerio Tricoli** (IT) ist als akusmatischer Musikkomponist, Improvisator und Klangkünstler, Produzent, Tonmeister und Kurator tätig. In seinen Kompositionen versucht er eine Verbindung zwischen Musique concrète und konzeptuellen klanglichen Formen. Tricoli spielt live meist mit analogen elektronischen Instrumenten. Er ist einer der Mitbegründer des Labels/Kollektivs Bwindo sowie von ¾HadBeenEliminated, einer gewagten Synthese von Improvisation, Elektroakustikkomposition und der Sensibilität des Avant-Rock.

I am thinking in a room, different from the one you are hearing in now

Samson Young

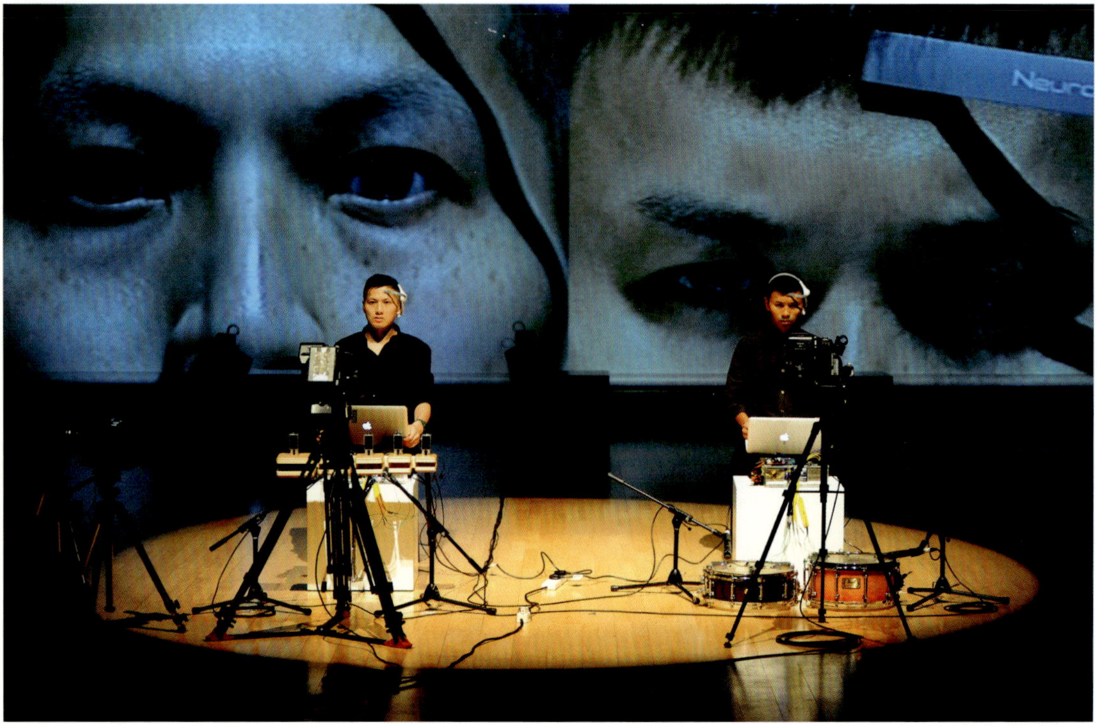

I am thinking in a room, different from the one you are hearing in now is a non-performance realized through sound.

The actors in this work are entirely immobile throughout the performance. While they sit still, brainwave sensors monitor their focus levels. Connected to the sensors are several solenoid motors, which are activated when the focus level is above a certain threshold. This level is pre-determined and scored into musical notation, which the actors attempt to "execute." The actors carry out focus and distraction at various points. While focus is a state of becoming and less predictable, actors can reliably induce distracted state by moving their eyeballs quickly, thus overloading the brain with visual-stimulation distractions.

There is tension between the performative setting of this work and the conditions of a "successful performance," which paradoxically relies on the actors' ability to ignore both the setting and

I am thinking in a room, different from the one you are hearing in now ist eine mithilfe perkussiver Klänge realisierte „Non-Performance".

Die Akteure verharren während der gesamten Performance völlig reglos. Während sie still dasitzen, wird ihr Konzentrationspegel von Gehirnwellensensoren überwacht. Mit diesen Sensoren sind mehrere Solenoidmotoren verbunden. Überschreitet der Konzentrationspegel eine gewisse Schwelle, werden die Motoren aktiviert. Der Konzentrationspegel ist vorbestimmt und wird in eine Notenschrift übertragen, die die Akteure umzusetzen versuchen. Sie performen in einem Spannungsfeld von Konzentration und Zerstreuung. Während der Prozess der Konzentration im Werden begriffen und daher weniger vorhersagbar ist, können die Akteure den Zustand der Zerstreuung zuverlässig selbst herbeiführen, indem sie die Augäpfel rasch bewegen und dadurch das Gehirn mit visuellen Ablenkungsreizen überfluten.

Es besteht eine Spannung zwischen dem performativen Setting dieser Arbeit und den Voraussetzungen einer

http://www.thismusicisfalse.com/?portfolio=2011-i-am-thinking-in-a-room-different-from-the-one-you-are-hearing-in-now-homage-to-alvin-lucier

„erfolgreichen Performance", die paradoxerweise auf der Fähigkeit der Akteure beruht, dieses Setting und auch die Präsenz des Publikums zu ignorieren. Der ständige Kampf zwischen Fokussierung der Aufmerksamkeit und gescheiterter Fokussierung, Absenz und Präsenz, Virtuosität und Kontrollverlust wird mithilfe perkussiver Klänge verstärkt. Darüber hinaus werden die Akteure abgelenkt, sobald sie sich der Aktivierung der Instrumente bewusst werden. Dies verursacht eine „Feedbackschleife" vom Gehirn zum Gehör und stellt das Scheitern der Akteure zur Schau.

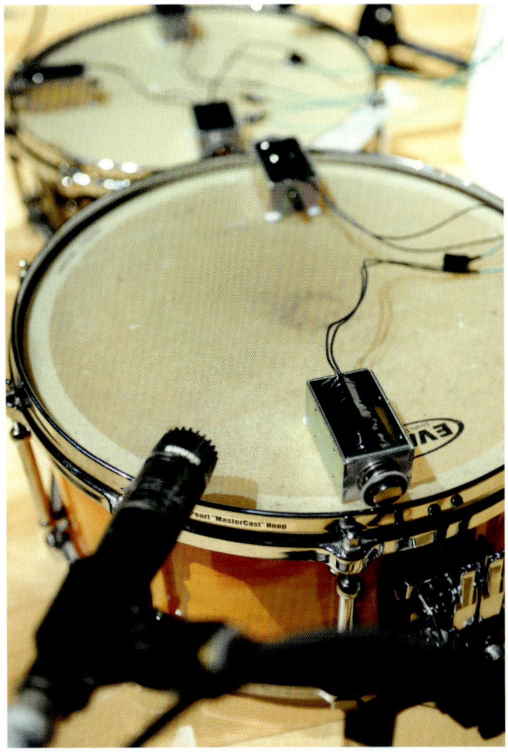

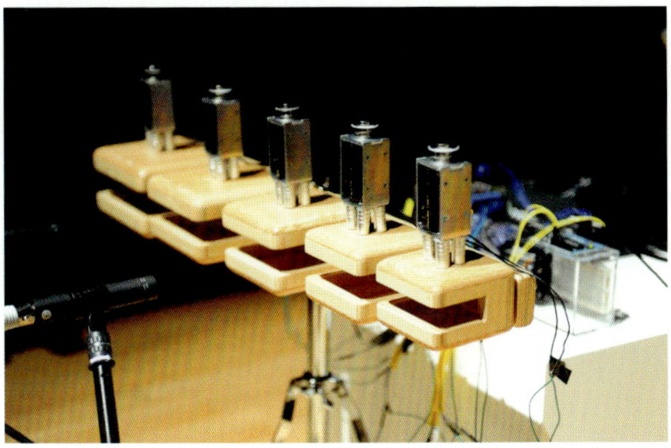

the presence of an audience. The constant struggle between focus and failure-to-focus, absence and presence, virtuosity and the loss of control is amplified through sound. Additionally, as soon as the actors become aware of the activation of the instruments they become distracted. This constitutes a mind-to-ear feedback loop and displays the actors' failure.

Samson Young (HK), born 1979, is a composer, sound artist and new-media artist. His works are fundamentally informed by an engagement with new cultural-technological paradigms, yet deeply grounded in the classical musical tradition. Young's creative output spans the widest possible range: from composition for orchestra and Game Boys, to amusement-ride-turned-sound-installation, to ensembles of iPads and iPhones, to multimedia music theatre. Young is currently a PhD fellow at Princeton University and an assistant professor in critical intermedia art at the School of Creative Media, City University of Hong Kong. His mentors include Chan Hing-yan and the electronic-music pioneer Paul Lanksy. **Samson Young** (HK), geboren 1979, ist Komponist, Klangkünstler und Medienkünstler. Seine Arbeiten sind im Wesentlichen von einer Auseinandersetzung mit neuen kulturtechnischen Paradigmen geprägt, dabei aber tief in der klassischen Musiktradition verwurzelt. Sein kreatives Schaffen umfasst ein sehr breites Spektrum: von Kompositionen für Orchester und Gameboys über mittels Münzkarussell funktionierende Soundinstallationen bis hin zu iPad- und IPhone-Ensembles und Multimedia-Musiktheater. Samson Young promoviert derzeit an der Princeton University und ist Assistenzprofessor für Critical Intermedia Art an der School of Creative Media der City University Hong Kong. Zu seinen Mentoren zählen Chan Hing-yan und der Pionier für elektronische Musik Paul Lanksy.

Minkoku Hyakunen: Project Integration / Intervention into Tenryu City

Dawang Huang, You-Sheng Zhang / Minkoku Hyakunen

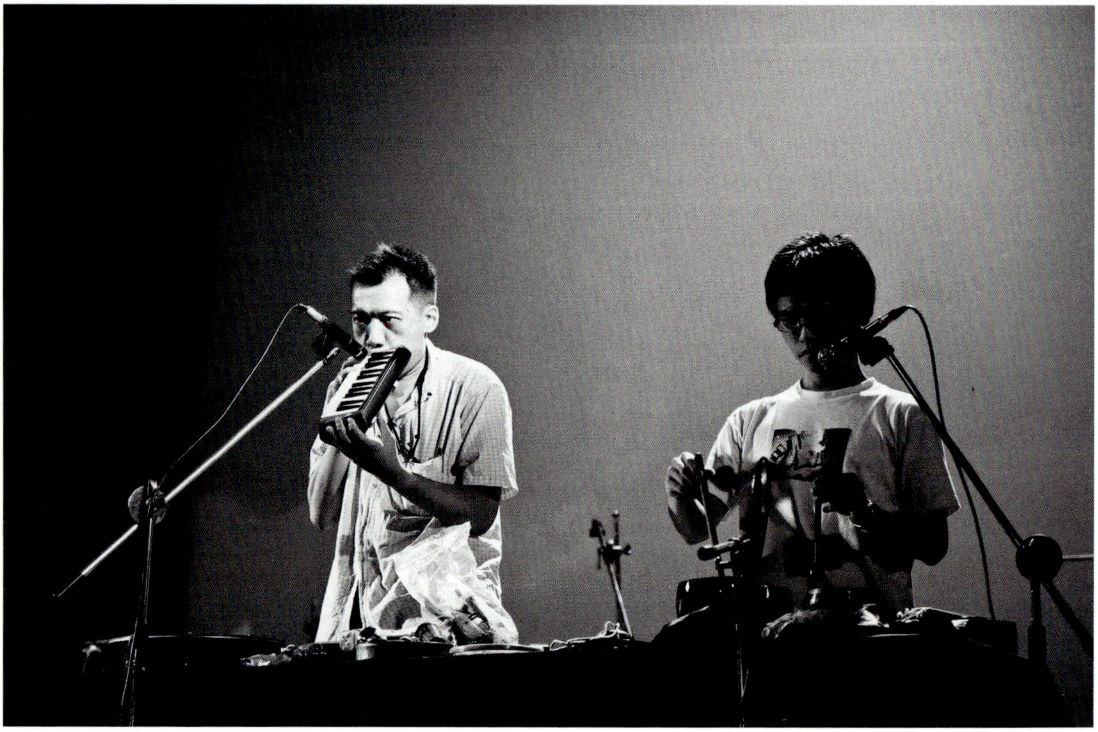

Photo: Etang Chen

This is the only official release of Minkoku Hyakunen (民国百年)—on an edition of 300 CDs. Its subtitle, *Project Integration / Intervention into Tenryu City*, means that the members of *Minkoku Hyakunen* take the sound of Taipei City as their "instruments." Sometimes they just did the field recording in order to catch the city soundscape. Sometimes they "performed" there and made themselves parts of the field and recorded the soundscape, which includes the sounds they make themselves. There are 16 tracks collected from many events and places, some of which Minkoku Hyakunen have edited. Naughty, noisy, and really interesting.

Artwork: Leo Wang. Released in 2011 by Kandala Records, Taiwan

Dies ist die einzige offizielle Veröffentlichung von Minkoku Hyakunen (民国百年) – in einer auf 300 Stück limitierten Auflage. Der Untertitel *Project Integration / Intervention into Tenryu City* weist darauf hin, dass die Mitglieder von Minkoku Hyakunen die Geräusche der Stadt Taipeh als „Instrumente" verwenden. Teils wurden einfach Feldaufnahmen gemacht, um die Geräuschkulisse der Stadt aufzuzeichnen, teils „performte" die Gruppe in der Stadt, wurde selbst Teil des Umfelds und nahm die Klanglandschaft, in die sie ihre eigenen Klänge setzte, auf. Die CD enthält 16 Tracks, die an unterschiedlichen Orten und Schauplätzen entstanden. Einige davon hat Minkoku Hyakunen zu Klangcollagen verdichtet: ungehörig, noisy und höchst interessant.

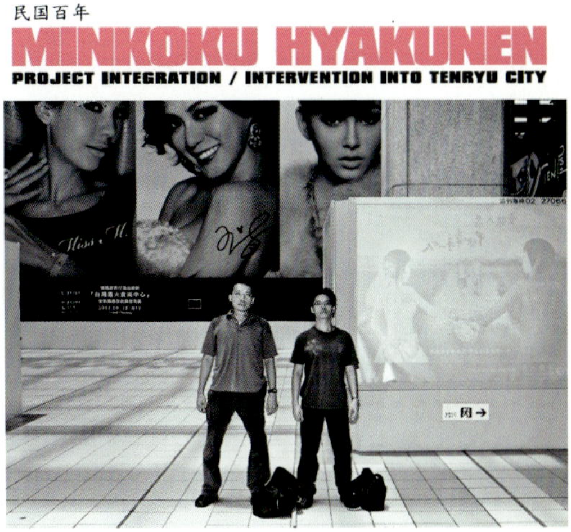

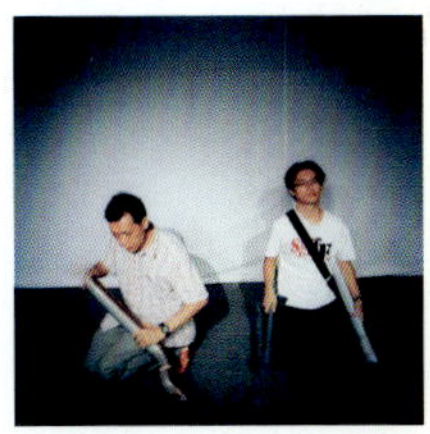

Zhang You-Sheng (TW) is a guitar / power-electronic noise artist. He reunited with multi-instrumentalist and singer **Huang Dawang** (aka Yingfan) in spring 2010, several years after some of Yingfan's impressive gigs. Both of them have their recorded works released on the Internet. Based on the common sense of revulsion for the "Centenary of Republic of China", an official, long-running celebration as propaganda much liked by dictatorships, on the last day of 2010 they formed Minkoku Hyakunen, which is the Japanese pronunciation of the "Centenary of Republic", played their final gig on December 9, 2011, and officially disbanded on the end of year. They use methods with political thoughts in live performance instead of talking about politics or relative keywords, and mostly play pieces without a stable tempo or happy melodies, making only stupid noise.

Zhang You-Sheng (TW) ist Gitarrist und Power-Electronic-Noise-Künstler. Im Frühling 2010 kam es zu einer erneuten Zusammenarbeit mit dem Multiinstrumentalisten und Sänger **Huang Dawang** (aka Yingfan). Beide Musiker veröffentlichten ihre Aufnahmen im Internet. Motiviert von ihrem gemeinsamen Unbehagen angesichts der pompösen offiziellen Feierlichkeiten – wie sie Diktaturen gerne zelebrieren – zur „Hundertjahrfeier der Republik China", gründeten sie am letzten Tag des Jahres 2010 die Band Minkoku Hyakunen (Japanisch für: „Hundert Jahre Republik"). Ihren letzten Auftritt gaben sie am 9. Dezember 2011, Ende des Jahres wurde die Band aufgelöst. Die beiden Musiker äußern sich nicht zu Politik etc., sondern lassen politische Ideen in ihre Live-Performances einfließen. Sie spielen meist Stücke ohne erkennbare Rhythmik und melodische Linie, Noise eben.

Organ of Corti

Liminal

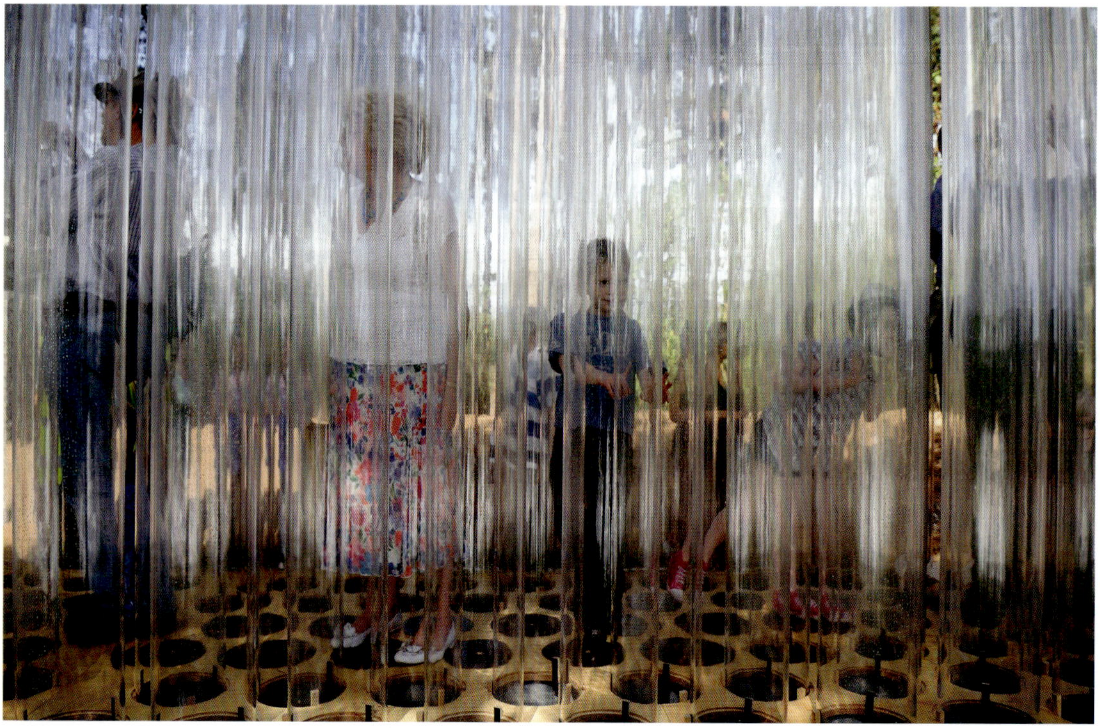

Organ of Corti is an experimental instrument that recycles noise from the environment. It does not make any sound of its own, but rather it attempts to draw our attention to the sounds already present by framing them in a new way.

Named after the organ of hearing in the inner ear, it uses the acoustic technology of sonic crystals to accentuate and attenuate frequencies within the broad range of sound present in road traffic or falling water.

By recycling surplus sounds from our environment, we hope to challenge expectations of what might constitute a piece of music by adding nothing to the existing soundscape but rather offering new ways of listening to what is already there. In a world saturated with sounds, the *Organ of Corti* questions whether we need any more noise, and instead it offers a frame through which to listen to the sounds that already surround us

In the summer of 2011 *Organ of Corti* toured England to four locations saturated in noise from road traffic or falling water. *Organ of Corti* recycles sound in the environment by filtering incoming sound waves through a lattice of four-meter-high

Organ of Corti bezeichnet ein experimentelles Instrument, das Umweltgeräusche recycelt. Es erzeugt keine eigenen Klänge, sondern versucht die Aufmerksamkeit auf bereits vorhandene Geräusche zu lenken, indem diese neu aufbereitet werden.

Das nach dem Corti-Organ, dem Hörorgan im Innenohr, benannte Instrument verwendet die Technologie akustischer Kristalle, um in dem breiten Klangspektrum, das etwa im Straßenverkehr oder in fließendem Wasser vorhanden ist, bestimmte Frequenzen zu betonen und abzuschwächen.

Durch die Wiederaufbereitung des Überangebots an Klängen in unserer Umgebung spielen wir mit den Erwartungen, was ein Musikstück ist, indem wir der vorhandenen Geräuschkulisse nichts hinzufügen, sondern lediglich neue Möglichkeiten bieten, bereits Vorhandenes zu hören. *Organ of Corti* hinterfragt, ob wir in unserer klanggesättigten Welt noch mehr Lärm brauchen und präsentiert stattdessen ein Instrument, das uns aus den uns bereits umgebenden Klängen ein neues Hörerlebnis bereitet.

Im Sommer 2011 wurde *Organ of Corti* an vier Orten in England installiert, wo starker Verkehrslärm herrscht oder Geräusche von Wasser zu hören sind. Der Sound

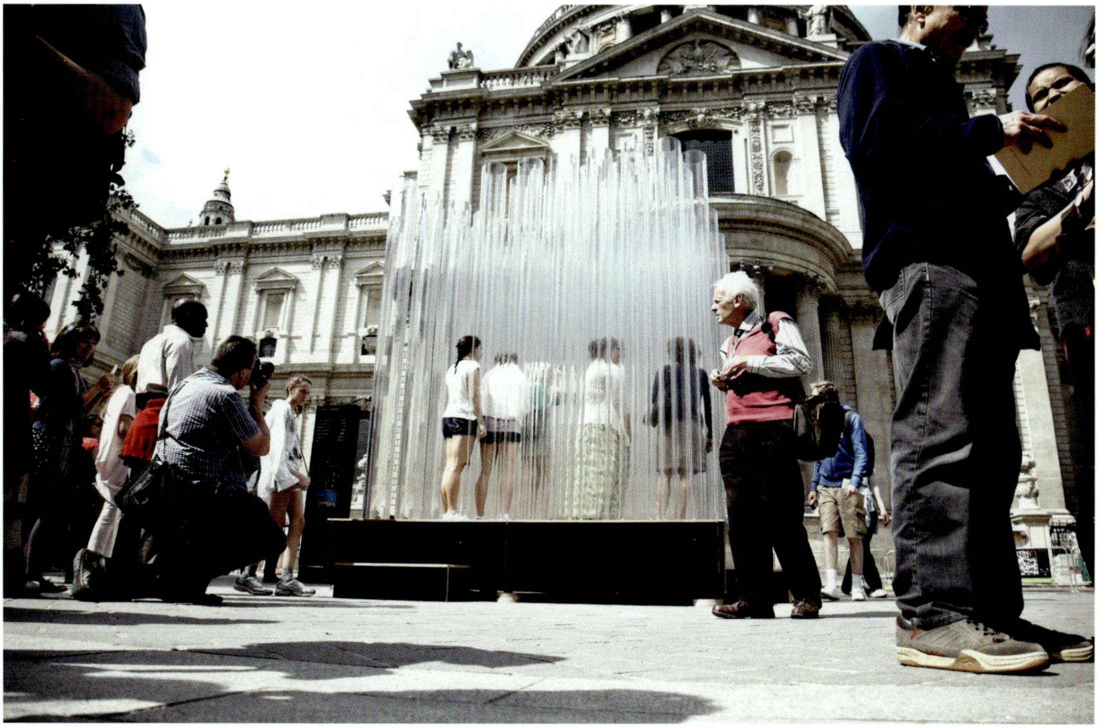

wurde vor Ort neu aufbereitet, indem ankommende Schallwellen durch ein Latticefilter aus vier Meter hohen Akrylzylindern, in denen akustische Kristalle eingebaut sind, gefiltert wurden. Je nach der Position des Zuhörers wurden durch die Konstruktion Bereiche des Frequenzspektrums abgeschwächt oder verstärkt, wodurch eine sich sukzessive verändernde Klangumgebung entstand, die zur Gänze auf der vor Ort bereits bestehenden Klangenergie beruhte.

acrylic cylinders, known as a "sonic crystal" array. Depending on a listener's position in relation to the array, the structure attenuated or accentuated areas of the frequency spectrum to create an evolving sound environment that relied entirely on the sound energy already present in the place in which it was installed.

Liminal (UK) is a partnership between architect Frances Crow and sound artist and composer David Prior. We began working together in 2003. Our work focuses on exploring the relationship between sound, listening and the environment. It encompasses site-specific interventions and sound walks, gallery installations, performances, research and consultancy as well as sound and music environments for exhibitions. David Prior is a composer and sound artist with a particular interest in the relationship between sound and space. Frances Crow is a qualified architect who has worked in practice since 1998. **Liminal** (UK) formierte sich 2003 als Kooperation zwischen dem Architekten Frances Crow und dem Klangkünstler und Komponisten David Prior. Im Zentrum ihrer Arbeit steht die Auseinandersetzung mit den Beziehungen zwischen Sound, Hören und Umgebung. Ihr Werk umfasst ortsspezifische Interventionen und Klangspaziergänge, Installationen in Galerien, Performances, Forschung und Beratung sowie Sound- und Musik-Environments für Ausstellungen. David Prior ist Komponist und Klangkünstler mit einem besonderen Interesse an den Beziehungen zwischen Klang und Raum. Frances Crow ist seit 1998 als Architekt tätig.

Sonic Vista

Sam Auinger, Bruce Odland

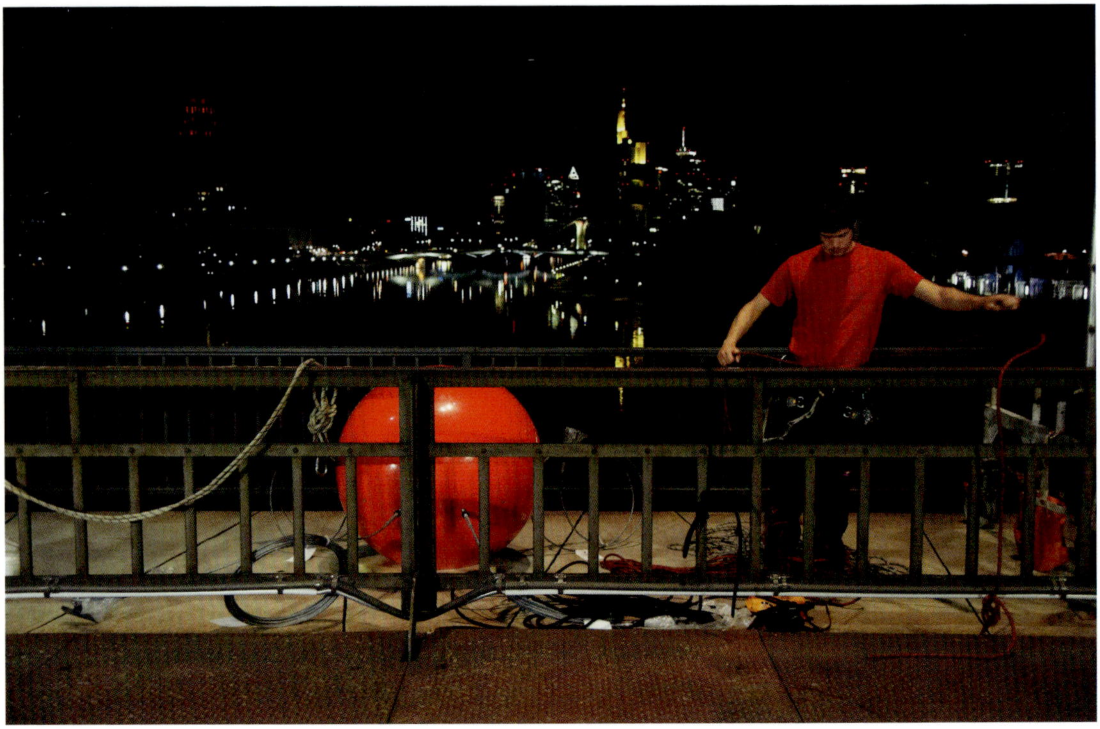

Photo: Stefan Cop

Sonic Vista is an installation in a large-scale urban sound space (Deutschherrnbrücke, a railway bridge over the River Main) that helps an observer listen into the inner workings and complexity of the city and hear its patterns of sound as a whole in the moment. The urban sound sources are subtly transformed in real time, with "tuning tubes" enhancing harmonic patterns that the human brain can read out as music, as rhythm. The ear

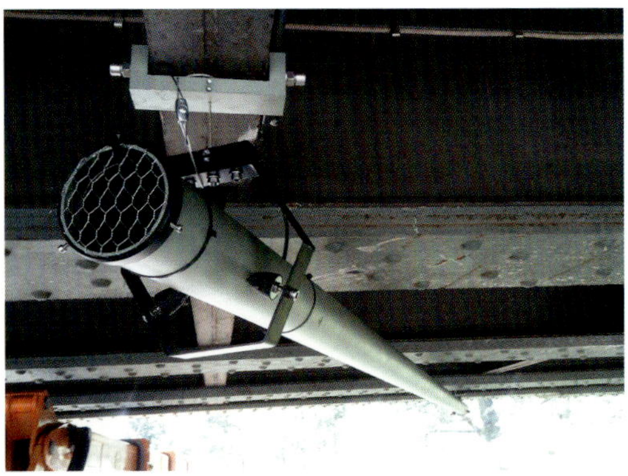

B tube Deutschherrnbrücke south, Photo: Werner Lorke

Sonic Vista ist eine Installation in einem großen urbanen Klangraum (Deutschherrnbrücke, Eisenbahnbrücke über den Main in Frankfurt), die dem Publikum ermöglicht, in das komplexe Innenleben der Stadt hineinzuhören und ihre Klangmuster im jeweiligen Augenblick in ihrer Gesamtheit wahrzunehmen. Die urbanen Klangquellen werden auf subtile Weise in Echtzeit mit „Resonanzrohren" transformiert und in harmonische Klänge verwandelt, die das menschliche Gehirn als Musik, als Rhythmus auslesen kann. Auge und Ohr des Betrachters werden angesprochen, nehmen die Klangmuster der Stadt wahr und entwerfen davon ausgehend einen neuen mentalen Stadtplan. Die Wirkung entspricht in etwa der Verarbeitung neuer Informationen, dem erstmaligen Hören des Klangs der eigenen Kultur als komplexen Organismus. Es ist der Sound von uns selbst, unseres kulturellen Inputs und Outputs, eines symphonischen „Bienenstocks", der als hoch entwickeltes urbanes Klangmuster zu hören ist. Die Möglichkeit, diesen Traum zu verwirklichen, ergab sich anlässlich des 20. Jubiläums des Frankfurter „Grüngürtels", durch die Unterstützung der Deutschen Bahn, der Stadt Frankfurt und der Europäischen Zentralbank. Die nördlichen und südlichen Teile des Grüngürtels sollen genau an diesem Standort mit seiner klassischen

„Postkarten“-Ansicht von Frankfurt miteinander verbunden werden. Um Besucher zu unserer *Sonic Vista* zu locken, konstruierten wir zwei große, kugelförmige Lautsprecher als visuelle Ikonen und Attraktoren. Diese Eyecatcher sind bereits aus großer Entfernung zu sehen. Sobald der Betrachter sich nähert, um die Objekte in Augenschein zu nehmen, bewegt er sich in einem dezenten Klangfeld – einer anderen Stimmung der Stadt, die harmonisch in Echtzeit verändert wird.

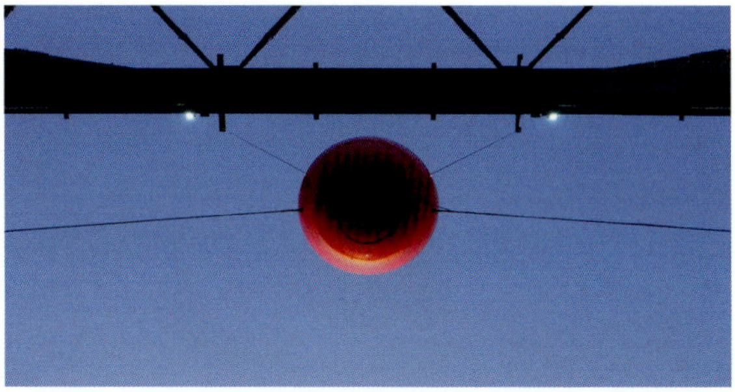

Red “Sphere Loudspeaker” playing fis tube (north), Photo: O+A

and eye of the observer become engaged in noticing the city's sonic patterns and forming a new mental map of the sources of its vibrations. The effect is one of decoding new information, hearing the sound of your culture as a sophisticated whole organism for the very first time. It is the sound of ourselves, our “hive,” our cultural inputs and outputs heard as an advanced urban-music pattern.
The opportunity to make this dream come true came through the 20th anniversary of Frankfurt's green belt, supported by the Deutsche Bahn, the City of Frankfurt and the European Central Bank. The north and south portions of the green belt are to be joined together at this very spot, with its classic “postcard” view of Frankfurt. To draw people to our *Sonic Vista* we create two large, bright spherical loudspeakers as visual icons and attractors, which can be seen from a long way away. But when people approach to investigate these objects they find a gentle field of sound—the city is harmonically altered, playing in real time.

Commissioned by: the City of Frankfurt am Main, Germany with the support of the European Central Bank. Grün-Gürtel project manager: Klaus Hoppe; technical realization: Werner Lorke

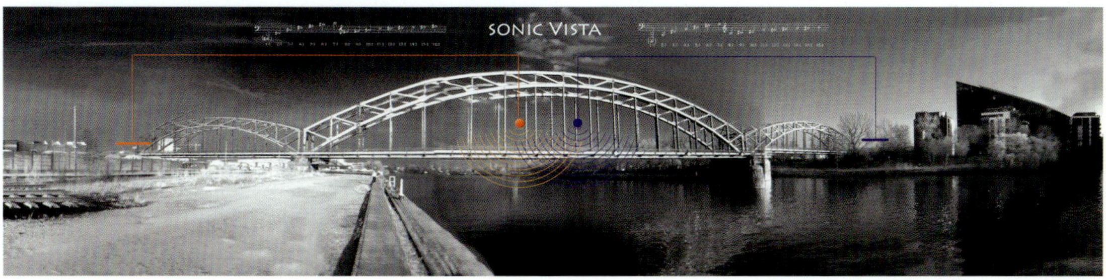

Photo: O+A

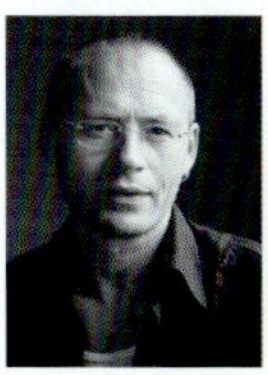

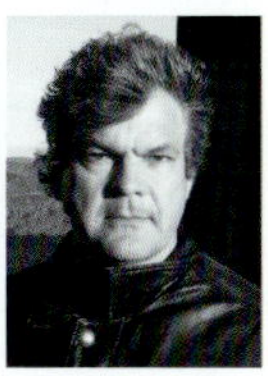

Sam Auinger (AT) and **Bruce Odland** (US) are sonic thinkers, composers, and sound-artists. They founded O+A in 1987. Their central theme is “hearing perspective.” Their work is known for large-scale, public-space sound installations that transform city noise into harmony in real time. In 2009 O+A started the *Sonic Commons* questioning the dominance of the visual culture in our perception of the world. *http://www.o-a.info* **Sam Auinger** (AT) und **Bruce Odland** (US) sind Klangkünstler, Klangphilosophen und Komponisten. 1987 gründeten sie O+A. Ihr zentrales Thema ist das „Denken mit den Ohren“. Auinger und Odland stehen für großformatige Soundinstallationen im öffentlichen Raum, die Stadtlärm in Echtzeit in ein harmonisches Klangerlebnis verwandeln. 2009 begannen O+A mit den *Sonic Commons*, die die Vorherrschaft des Visuellen in unserer Wahrnehmung der Welt hinterfragen. *http://www.o-a.info*

Terra Prosodia

Antje Vowinckel

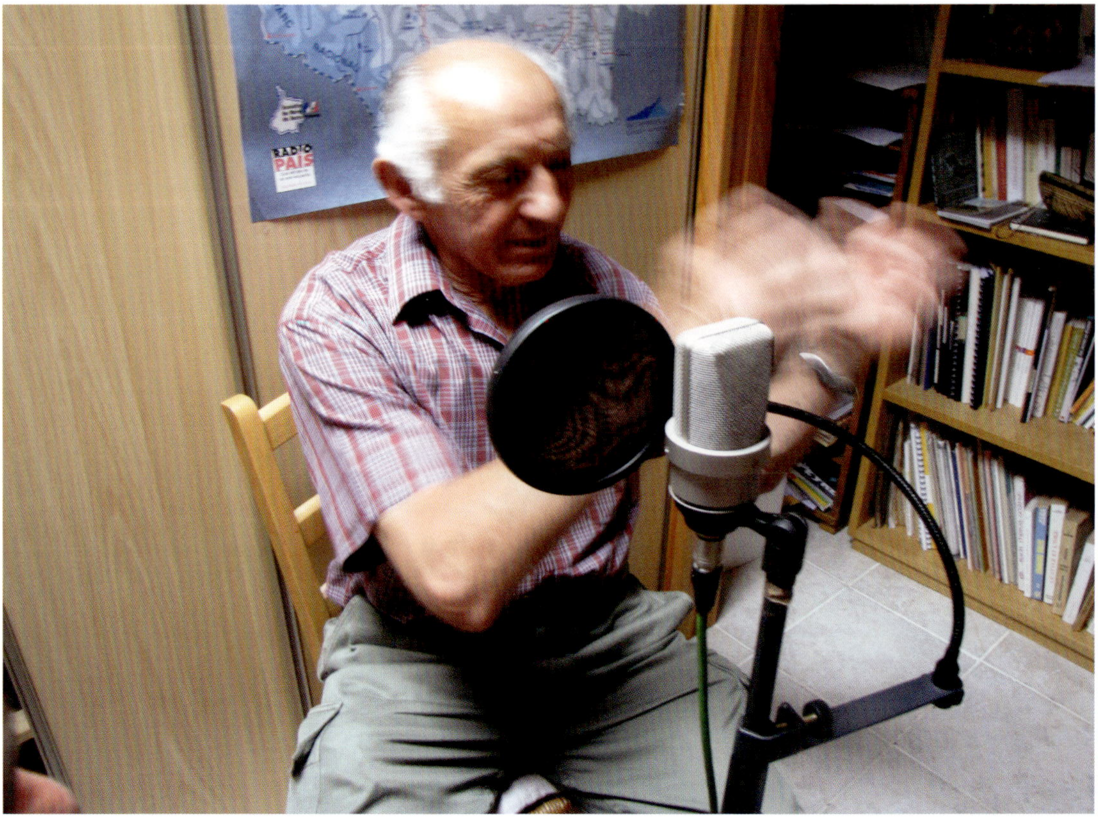

Dialect speaker: George Cadéac

Terra Prosodia is a radio composition based on prosodies of European dialects and minority languages that are in danger of extinction. The idea is to underline the richness and variety in melodies of spoken languages in Europe without using any folkloristic ornament.

The recordings were all made in 2011 in Gotland and Faro (Sweden), Lötschental and Tarrasp (Switzerland), Cavaillon and Tarbes (France) and Glasgow (Scotland). The dialects and languages are: Gutamal, Wallis-Dytsch, Rhaeto-Romanie, Provencal, Gascon and Scottish Gaelic. I visited the speakers where they live and asked them to tell me a personal story which is connected to the places where they live. However, it is intended and important that the majority of listeners do *not* understand the context.

For the seven parts of the composition in each case I used the whole story focusing on the melodies in the language. Using Melodyne software I exported

Terra Prosodia ist eine Radiokomposition, die auf den Prosodien, den rhythmischen und melodischen Aspekten, vom Verschwinden bedrohter europäischer Dialekte und Minderheitensprachen beruht. Die Idee dahinter ist, auf den Reichtum und die melodische Vielfalt europäischer Sprachen aufmerksam zu machen, ohne folkloristische Klischees zu bedienen.

Die Aufnahmen entstanden 2011 in Gotland und Faro (Schweden), Lötschental und Tarrasp (Schweiz), Cavaillon und Tarbes (Frankreich) sowie Glasgow (Schottland). Die verwendeten Dialekte und Sprachen sind Gutnisch, Walliserdeutsch, Rumantsch, Provenzalisch, Gaskonisch und Schottisch-Gälisch.

Ich habe die Sprechenden an ihrem jeweiligen Wohnort besucht und gebeten, mir eine Geschichte zu erzählen, die sie persönlich erlebt haben und die einen Bezug zu dem Ort hat, an dem sie leben. Ein wesentlicher und beabsichtigter Aspekt der Komposition ist, dass die Mehrheit der Zuhörer den erzählerischen Kontext nicht versteht.

Ich habe für die sieben Teile der Komposition jeweils die gesamte Erzählung verwendet, wobei der Fokus auf der Sprachmelodie lag. Mit der Software Melodyne wurde die gesprochene Sprache als MIDI-Datei exportiert. Diese Dateien dienten als Ausgangsmaterial für die melodische Gestaltung. Da MIDI-Dateien eine viel zu komplexe Sprachübertragung liefern, die eher an den Klang elektronischer Maschinen erinnert, habe ich einfachere, eingängigere und dynamischere Melodien ausgelesen und dann auf realen oder virtuellen Instrumenten gespielt. In einem Fall habe ich die Melodien gesummt. Manche dieser instrumentalen oder gesummten Melodien imitieren die Sprachmelodien, andere streben nach Unabhängigkeit wie die zweite Stimme in einer Fuge. Die Vereinfachung der Melodien entspricht der Reduktion von Komplexität in unserem normalen Hören. Die Ohren suchen – wie die Augen in einer Tropfsteinhöhle – immer nach erkennbaren Figuren und Motiven.

the spoken language as midi files, which I then used as a basis for melodic composition. As the midi files produce a much too complex translation of language, which sounds more like electronic machines, I extracted simpler, more recognizable and more dynamic melodies.

These were then either played by me on other instruments or by virtual instruments. In one case I hummed the melodies. These instrumental or hummed melodies sometimes imitate the language melodies and sometimes become independent, like a second voice in a fugue. The simplification of the melodies is related to the simplification of melodies in our normal hearing. Our ears are always searching for figures—like our eyes do in a cave of stalactites.

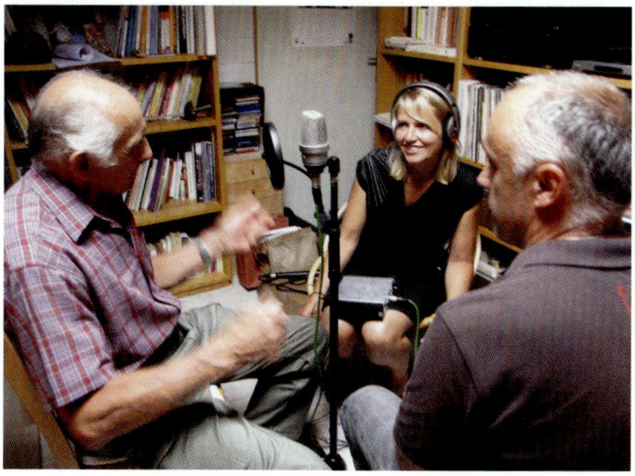

George Cadéac, Pascal Caumont, Antje Vowinckel

WDR – Studio Akustische Kunst 2011. Supported by Film- und Medienstiftung NRW. With: Ingvar Larsson, Ingrid Wahlgren (speaking Gutamal), Nesa Engler (speaking Rhaetoromanic), Remy Graillon (speaking Provencal), Georges "Jojo" Cadéac (speaking Gascon), Peter Meyer (speaking Wallis-Dytsch), Don Eoil (speaking Scottish-Gaelic)

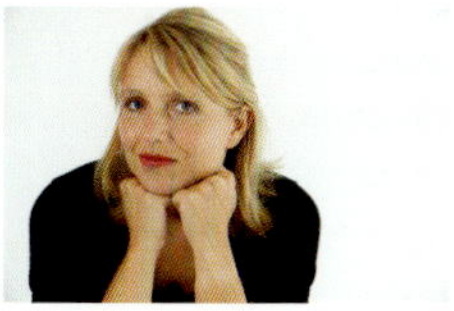

Antje Vowinckel (DE) is a composer, director and performer. She studied literature and music (flute/piano) and completed with a thesis on radio art. She creates radio plays and sound-art compositions for a variety of public radio stations such as WDR Studio Akustische Kunst, DRadio, SWR, BR, NDR. Her piece *Call Me Yesterday* has been broadcast in fifteen countries. Works have also been presented at various festivals, e.g. ZKM Karlsruhe, Biennale Bonn, Prix Italia, Festival Alicante, Prix Europa, Goethe-Institut Lisbon, Hammer Museum Los Angeles. In recent years, she has also created musical live performances, e.g. for organ and objects. **Antje Vowinckel** (DE) ist Komponistin, Regisseurin und Performerin. Sie studierte Literatur und Musik (Flöte/Klavier) und promovierte mit einer Dissertation über Radiokunst. Sie schreibt Hörspiele und Klangkunst-Kompositionen für zahlreiche öffentlicher Rundfunkstationen wie WDR Studio Akustische Kunst, DRadio, SWR, BR, NDR. Ihr Hörspiel *Call me yesterday* wurde in fünfzehn Ländern ausgestrahlt. Ihre Arbeiten wurden auch auf diversen Festivals präsentiert, z.B. ZKM Karlsruhe, Biennale Bonn, Prix Italia, Festival Alicante, Prix Europa, Goethe-Institut Lissabon, Hammer Museum Los Angeles. In den letzten Jahren hat sie auch Live-Musikperformances wie etwa *organ and objects* entwickelt.

untitled #275

Francisco López

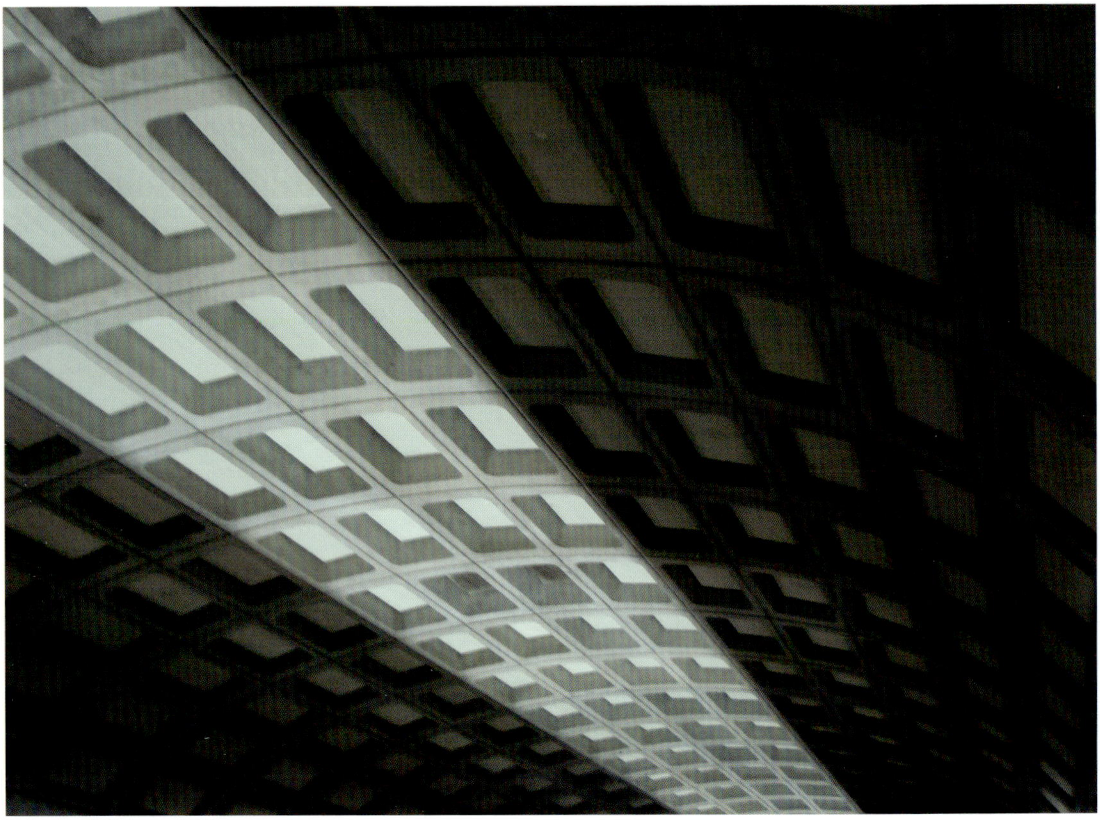

untitled #275 is an unorthodox piano composition in two parts:
(i) Movement 1, for mechanically-prepared piano, performed by pianist Reinier van Houdt, and (ii) evolutionary studio transformation of Movement 1 for immersive multi-channel sound system, performed by Francisco López.
untitled #275 is a sound work based on a paradigmatic instrument of the 19th century, with manipulations of the 20th century, and realized with the technology / aesthetic of the 21st century.

untitled #275 ist eine unkonventionelle Komposition für Klavier in zwei Sätzen:
(i) Erster Satz für mechanisch präpariertes Klavier, interpretiert von Pianist Reinier van Houdt;
(ii) Weiterentwicklung und Transformation des ersten Satzes in einem Studio mit immersiver Mehrkanal-Tonanlage, interpretiert von Francisco López.
untitled #275 ist eine auf einem typischen Instrument des 19. Jahrhunderts basierende Klangarbeit, die mit den technischen/ästhetischen Mitteln des 21. Jahrhunderts realisiert wurde.

Movement 1: Performed on mechanically-prepared piano by Reinier van Houdt. Movement 2: Created by evolutionary studio transformation of movement 1.
Composed and recorded at MuzyQ Studios and mobile messor (Amsterdam), August 2009 - February 2011. "Movement 1" recorded live in concert at De Toonzaal (s'Hertogenbosch) on February 10th 2011 by Kees van de Wiel / Concertzender. Released on CD by UnSounds (NL)

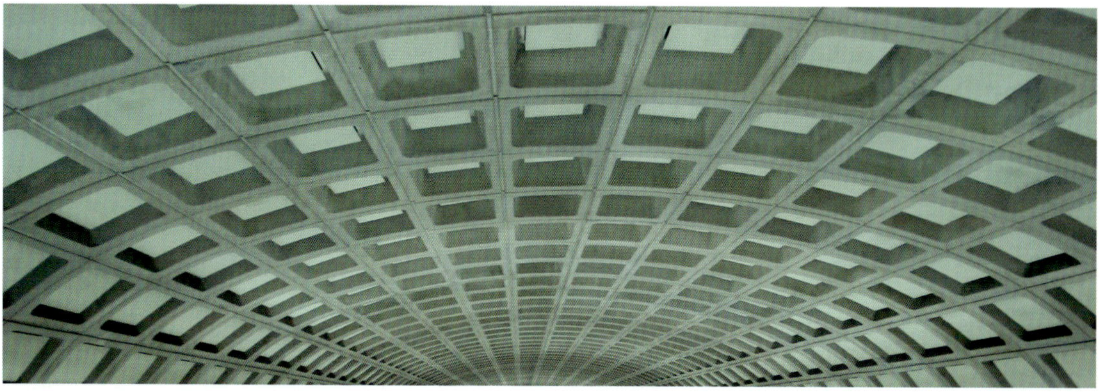

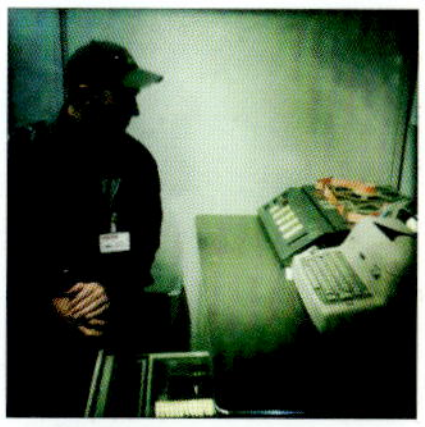

Francisco López (ES) is internationally recognized as one of the main figures on the stage of sound art and experimental music. His experience in the field of sound creation and work with environmental recordings covers a period of 30 years, during which he has developed an impressive sound universe that is completely personal and iconoclastic and based on profound listening to the world. He has performed hundreds of concerts, projects with field recordings and sound installations in 60 countries all over the world, including the main international museums, galleries and festivals, such as: PS1 Contemporary Art Center (New York), Museum of Modern Art (Paris), International Film Festival (Rotterdam), Festival des Arts (Brussels), Darwin Fringe (Darwin, Australia), Institute of Contemporary Art (London), Museum of Modern Art of Buenos Aires, Museum of Contemporary Art of Barcelona, Center of Contemporary Art (Kita-Kyushu, Japan), etc. His extensive catalog of sound pieces (with live and studio collaborations with more than 150 international artists) has been published by more than 250 recording companies all over the world. **Francisco López** (ES) ist international einer der renommiertesten Protagonisten der Klangkunst und Experimentalmusik. Seine Erfahrungen in den Bereichen Klangkreation und Feldaufnahmen erstrecken sich über einen Zeitraum von dreißig Jahren, in denen er ein beeindruckendes, sehr persönliches und mit allen Konventionen brechendes Klanguniversum schuf, das auf einer intensiven auditiven Wahrnehmung der Welt basiert. Er gab weltweit Hunderte Konzerte und realisierte Projekte mit Feldaufnahmen und Klanginstallationen in sechzig Ländern, in den wichtigsten internationalen Museen, Kunstgalerien und bei Festivals, wie PS1 Contemporary Art Center (New York), Museum of Modern Art (Paris), International Film Festival (Rotterdam), Festival des Arts (Brüssel), Darwin Fringe (Darwin, Australien), Institute of Contemporary Art (London), Museo de Arte Moderno de Buenos Aires, Museu d'Art Contemporani de Barcelona, Center of Contemporary Art (Kitakyushu, Japan) etc. Seine Klangkompositionen (darunter Live- und Studio-Kooperationen mit mehr als 150 internationalen Künstlern) wurde von über 250 Plattenfirmen weltweit veröffentlicht.

What does it matter how many lovers you have if none of them gives you the universe

Bjørn Erik Haugen

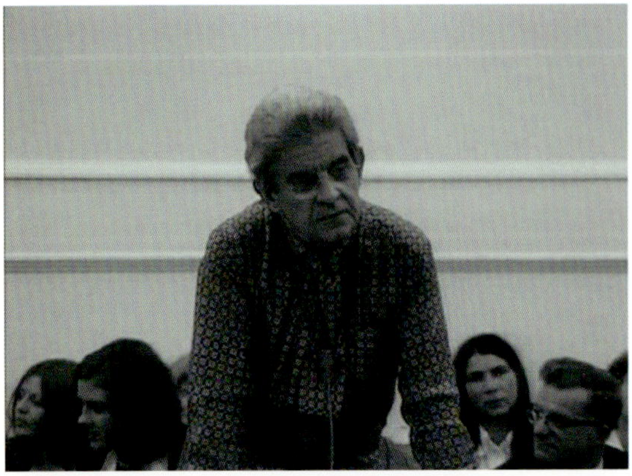

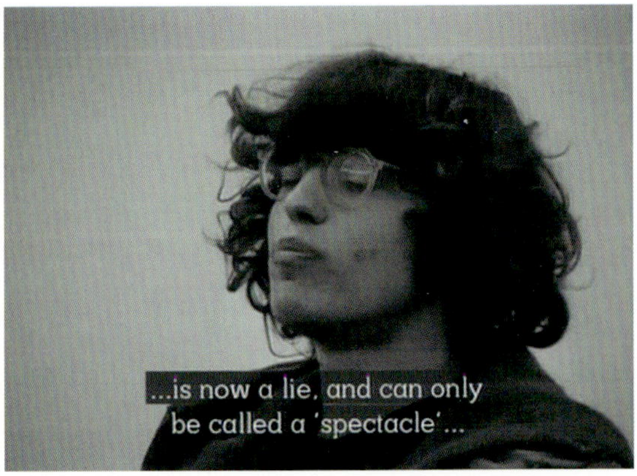

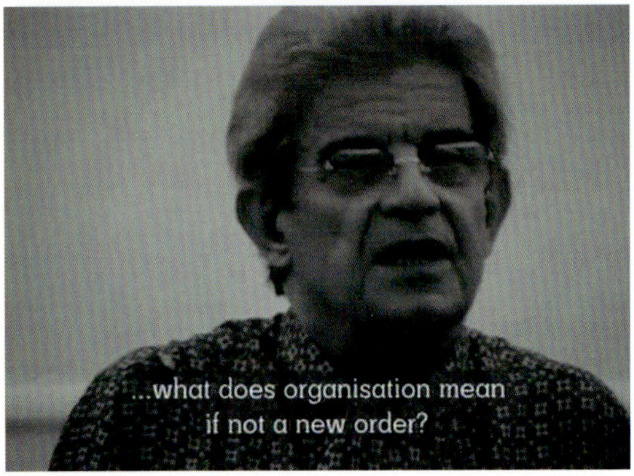

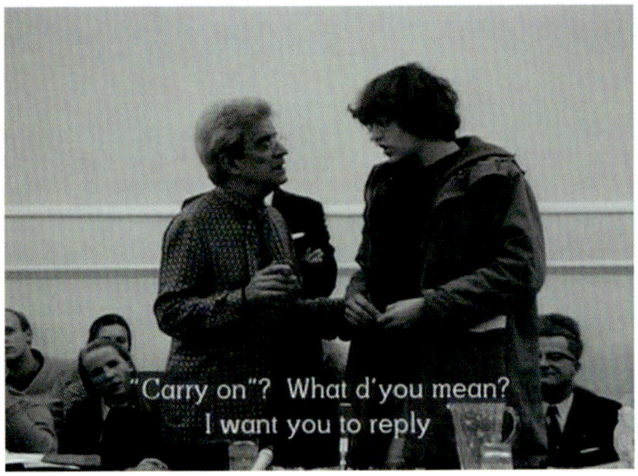

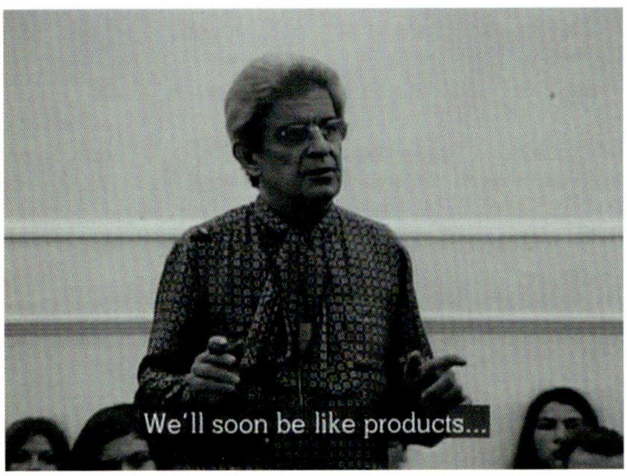

http://bjornerikhaugen.com/Websted/What_does_it_matter_how_many_lovers_you_have_if_none_of_them_gives_you_the_universe.html

Was zählt denn, wie viel Geliebte man hat, wenn keiner einem die Welt schenkt.
Jacques Lacan

Dieses Projekt basiert auf der Transkription einer Vorlesung des französischen Psychoanalytikers Jacques Lacan für mechanisches Klavier. Die Reaktionen des Publikums während der Vorlesung werden von einem Gitarrenverstärker wiedergegeben. Das Video der Vorlesung wird mit einem Videoprojektor projiziert.
Lacan wird während der Vorlesung, in dem er über die Sprache als Grundlage unseres Weltbezugs spricht, plötzlich von einem Studenten unterbrochen, der Mehl und Wasser auf seine Notizen schüttet. Damit wird Teil II des Stücks eingeleitet, in dem es um Gesellschaftsprotest geht. Der Student ist ein von Guy Debord inspirierter Situationist. Die beiden beginnen zu diskutieren, bis der Student plötzlich auf Lacan zugeht, seine Krawatte anschüttet und aus dem Saal geführt wird. Lacan beginnt nun über die Ansichten des Protestlers über Menschheit und Gesellschaft, Revolution und Liebe zu sprechen.
Sowohl Lacan als auch Debord spielen eine zentrale Rolle im Kunstdiskurs. In diesem Video prallen ihre gesellschaftlichen Ansichten aufeinander. Die Vorlesung fand 1971 statt. Das Happening ist stark vom Kontext, der Studentenrevolte in Frankreich in den späten Sechzigerjahren, geprägt, das Wort „Revolution" fällt häufig in dieser Diskussion.
Die Wahl des Klaviers als Instrument ist sowohl als Kritik als auch Hommage an Lacan und anderen postmodernen Denkern gedacht, die anfangs Theorien entwickelten, die unsere Welterfahrung revolutionierten und veränderten, bis sie schließlich als virtuose theoretische Performer endeten.

What does it matter how many lovers you have if none of them gives you the universe.
Jacques Lacan

This project is a transcription for mechanical piano of a lecture by the French psychoanalyst Jacques Lacan. The audience's response in the lecture is played through a guitar amplifier. The video of the lecture is screened with a video projector.
During the lecture where Lacan talks about the language as a foundation for our understanding of our surroundings, he is abruptly disrupted by a student who ruins his lecture notes with flour and water. This is part II of the piece: a protest against society. The student is a situationist, inspired by Debord. They start discussing before he ruins Lacan's tie and is thrown out of the lecture hall. Lacan then starts lecturing about the protester's views about people and society, about revolution and love.
Both Lacan and Debord are central to the art discourse. This is a meeting of their views upon society. This lecture took place in 1971. The happening is highly colored by the context, the student protests in France in the late sixties, and revolution as a frequently used word in discussion.
The choice of the piano is intended to be both a critique and a homage to Lacan and postmodern thinkers like him, as they first started with theories that revolutionized and transformed how we experience our world and later ended up as virtuous theoretical performers.

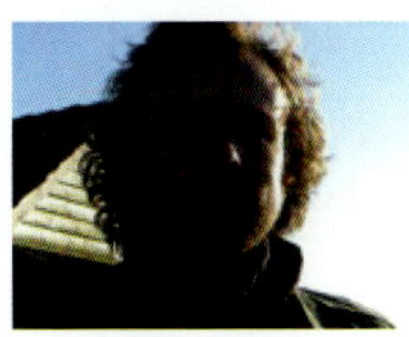

Bjørn Erik Haugen (NO), MA from the National Academy in Oslo 2007. He works mainly with compositions, sound and videoinstallation. He works from a conceptual platform where the idea to the work comes before the material, media or way of expression. He makes political works which have been shown on the annual national autumn exhibition in Norway, and have been screened in Vienna, Barcelona, Sweden, Germany, England and in the US. **Bjørn Erik Haugen** (NO) absolvierte 2007 die Kunsthochschule Oslo und arbeitet vorwiegend in den Bereichen Komposition, Sound- und Videoinstallation. „Ich arbeite auf einer konzeptuellen Ebene, auf der die Idee der Wahl von Material, Medium oder Ausdrucksmittel vorausgeht. Ich mache politische Projekte. Meine Arbeiten wurden auf der jährlich stattfindenden Herbstausstellung in Norwegen präsentiert und in Wien, Barcelona, Schweden, Deutschland, England und den USA gezeigt."

Years

Bartholomäus Traubeck

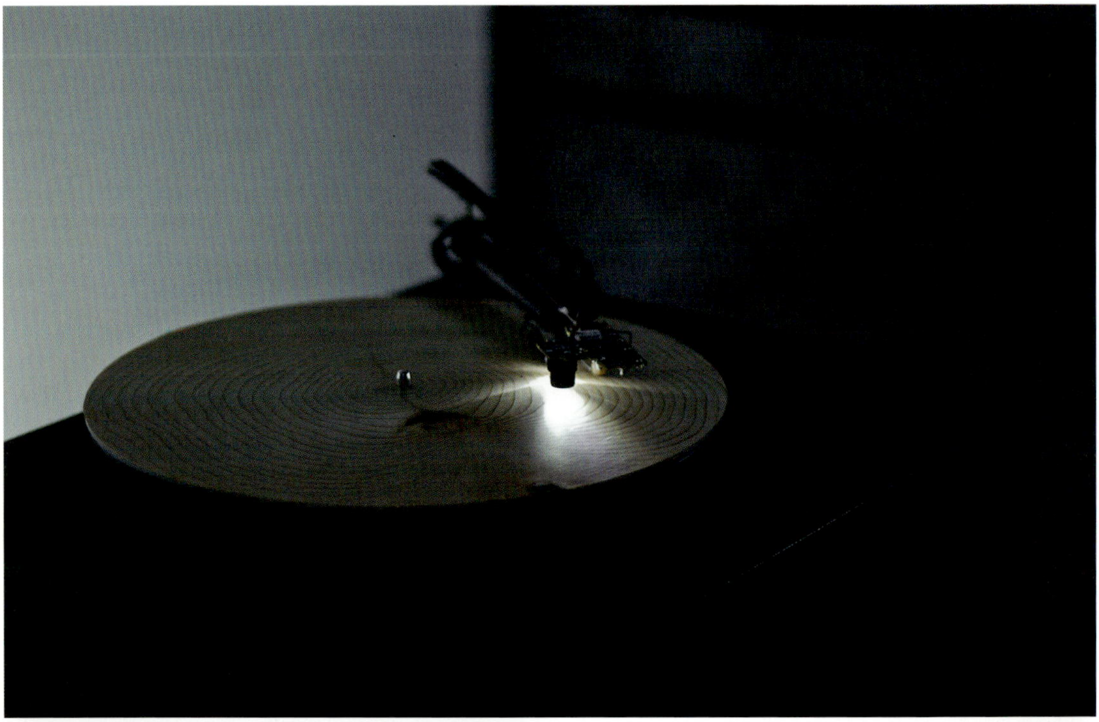

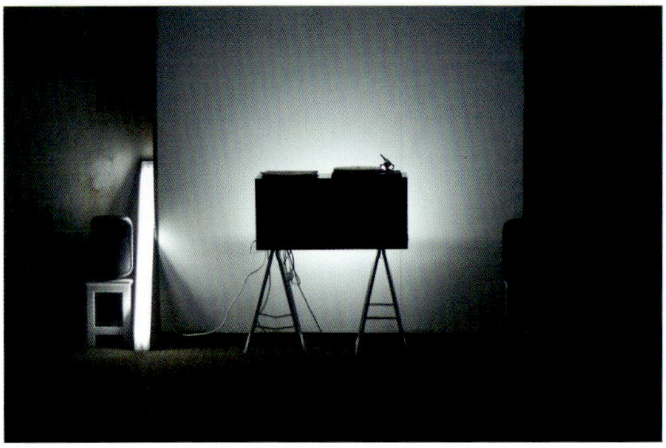

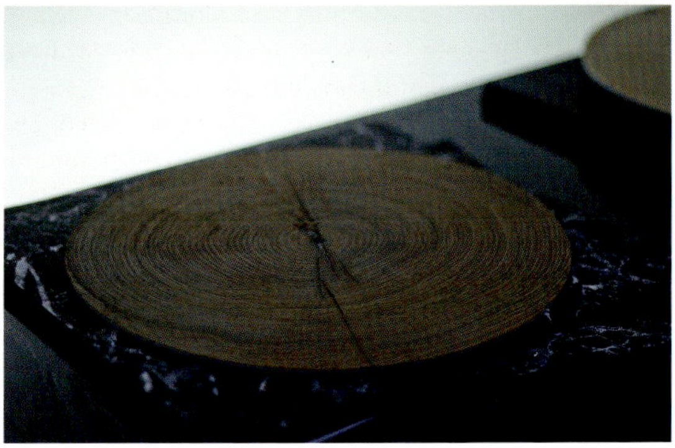

Years is a modified record player that reads a tree's year rings and outputs piano music. The tree's year rings are analyzed by a camera for their strength, thickness and rate of growth. This data serves as basis for a generative process that outputs piano music. It is mapped to a scale which is again defined by the overall appearance of the wood (ranging from dark to light and from strong texture to light texture). The foundation for the music is certainly found in the defined ruleset of

Die Installation *Years* besteht aus einem modifizierten Plattenspieler, der Holzscheiben abspielt und die Jahresringe eines Baumes in Klaviermusik überträgt. Die Nadel des Tonarms wurde durch eine Kamera ersetzt, die die Jahresringe ausliest und hinsichtlich Stärke, Dicke und Wachstum analysiert. Diese Daten dienen als Grundlage für ein generatives Verfahren, das Klaviermusik erklingen lässt. Die Daten werden auf einer Skala abgebildet, die wiederum von der äußeren Erscheinung des Holzes (die von dunkler zu heller und von starker zu schwacher

Maserung variiert) definiert wird. Grundlage der Musik ist zwar das festgelegte Regelwerk von Programmierung und Hardware-Konfiguration, durch die Variationen der von jedem Baum gewonnenen Daten kommt es jedoch zu sehr unterschiedlichen Interpretationen.

„Das Objekt ist sowohl materiell – eine interaktive Skulptur – als auch immateriell, da ein unbelebtes ‚Fossil' in die wohl abstrakteste aller Künste, die Musik, übertragen wird. Der Plattenspieler erfasst sowohl die präanaloge, seit Menschendenken bestehende natürliche Welt als auch die digitale Alchemie der Transkription visueller Daten in Klänge, wobei einem analogen Kultmedium als Brücke zwischen diesen zwei Welten Referenz erwiesen wird.
Der Mechanismus des Plattentellers ist vordergründig leicht durchschaubar: Seine regelmäßigen Drehungen sind die unmittelbare Grundlage der Musikwiedergabe, die in ihrer zeitlichen Ausdehnung der ästhetischen Erfahrung entspricht. [...] *Years* zeigt die Diskrepanz zwischen einem sich drehenden Plattenteller und den resultierenden Klängen auf, die sich so anhören, wie man es erwartet: nach einem von Menschenhand geschaffenen System, das entworfen wurde, um einem in der Natur vorkommenden Muster Sinn zu verleihen.
Ein Plattenteller zeigt und überwindet implizit die Disparität zwischen der Zeit als objektiver Quantität (Drehzahl der Aufnahme) und der erlebten Zeit (der inneren Zeitdimension der Musik), ungeachtet dessen, ob es sich bei der Aufnahme um eine Vinylschallplatte oder um eine Holzscheibe handelt. *Years* verstärkt diesen Effekt: Durch die Neuinterpretation der physischen Erscheinungsform der Jahresringe und des vertrauten Klangs des Klaviers vergrößert das Werk diese Diskrepanz, während es gleichzeitig die Beziehung zwischen dem Taktilen und dem Auditiven betont." (Ray Hu für *Core77*, 2012)

programming and the hardware setup, but the data acquired from each tree interprets this ruleset very differently.

"The design object is at once material—an interactive sculpture—and immaterial, interpreting an inanimate 'fossil' into arguably the most abstract art form: music. Thus, the record player spans the natural, pre-analog world of time immemorial and the digital alchemy of transcribing visual data into sound, duly referencing an iconic analog medium as the bridge between the two worlds.
Meanwhile, the turntable mechanism is an ostensibly transparent input device: its periodic revolution is the direct basis of the musical playback, which corresponds to the aesthetic experience as it extends across time. [...] *Years* reveals the disjuncture between a rotating disc and the coherent sounds that we hear for what it is: a man-made system designed to make sense of a naturally-occurring pattern.
Of course, a turntable implicitly reveals and transcends the disparity between time as an objective quantity (the RPM of the record) and lived time (the internal time of music), whether the 'recording' is a vinyl disc or a slice of wood. This is doubly true of *Years*: by recasting the physical appearance of the rings and the familiar sound of piano keys, the work amplifies this distance while underscoring the relationship between the tangible and the aural." (Ray Hu for *Core77*, 2012)

Actuator and drive technician: Karla Spiluttini (AT)

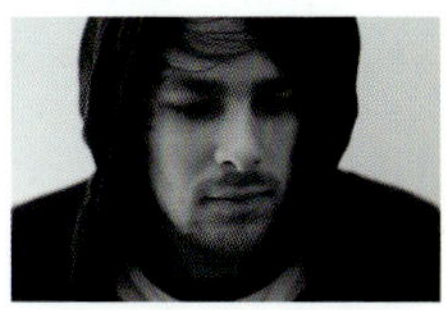

Bartholomäus Traubeck (DE), born 1987, is a media artist. He lives and works in Linz (AT) and in Rotterdam (NL). He has a BA in multimedia art (FH Salzburg) and a Master in Visual Communications, University of Arts Linz. Since 2012 he has been studying Networked Media at Piet Zwart Institute in Rotterdam. **Bartholomäus Traubeck** (DE), geboren 1987, lebt und arbeitet als Medienkünstler in Linz (AT) und Rotterdam (NL). Er studierte Multimediaart an der FH Salzburg Medienkultur und Kunsttheorie an der Kunstuniversität Linz. Seit 2012 absolviert er den Master-Studiengang Networked Media am Piet Zwart Institute in Rotterdam.

HYBRID ART

Meta/Media/Narrativity

Ursula Damm, Jens Hauser, Dietmar Offenhuber, Karin Ohlenschläger, Benjamin Weil

Launched in 2007, the category Hybrid Art is still young, yet it already has a tradition: in the face of the boundless diversity of media-technological, transdisciplinary and multi-discursive art practices, to explore the very "nature of the hybrid" itself each year. As a matter of course, artists increasingly seem to be claiming hybrids as their own—from the interlocking role of the artist-engineer and the epistemological investigation of the (natural) scientific production of knowledge, to politically motivated open-source strategies towards materials and their hybrids, such as "viewser" (visitor/user) or "prosumer" (professional/consumer). On the one hand, it makes sense that among the 472 projects submitted in this category, the jury encountered those that per se did not fit the definitions of the other existing categories. On the other hand, Hybrid Art simply continues the long series of efforts made since the 1960s to subsume the flow of new groundbreaking cultural work under terms such as inter-, trans- or multimedia. This also explains why, despite the media's shift and evolution, transhistorical clusters come to the fore: in this year's competition, for example, there is a strong presence of "helpless robots", projects on the topos of waste and recycling, or the hacking of digital black boxes, as well as on the tautological paradoxes of machines and the search for a non-technological alterity of human existence that enjoys manifesting itself in the form of pigs, slime mould or plants. Hence, from year to year, it is not surprising to find a growing number of art projects with bio-media that represent a contemporary form of producing "authenticity" using media and yet, in light of the ubiquity of everything technical, still enact referents of the "real". Though here the "real" turns out to be ever more elastic, nebulous and intangible; it comes into play as a meta-narrativity in overlapping levels, disciplines and genres. The genre of performance art is, however, also struggling with the burden of the theatrical and the dramatic—in fact, in the end, very few projects with a truly innovative potential came the jury's way. Nevertheless, nearly all the art projects that won awards may be understood as "performative", be it on the microscopic or macroscopic level—sometimes in extreme density, elsewhere in forms of hybrid storytelling that deliberately go beyond the usual coordinates of time and space.

Diese noch junge, erst seit 2007 bestehende Kategorie Hybrid Art hat bereits ihre Tradition: angesichts der ausufernden medientechnologischen, transdisziplinären und pluri-diskursiven Kunstpraxen Jahr für Jahr der „Natur des Hybriden" selbst nachzuspüren. Mehr und mehr scheinen Künstler das Hybride wie selbstverständlich für sich zu reklamieren – von der Rollenverschränkung des Künstler-Ingenieurs über die epistemologische Auseinandersetzung mit (natur-)wissenschaftlicher Wissensproduktion bis hin zu politisch motivierten materialen Open-Source-Strategien und ihren Hybriden wie „Viewser" (Visitor/User) oder „Prosumer" (Professional/Consumer). Einerseits leuchtet ein, dass die Jury in dieser Sparte unter den 472 Einsendungen auf Projekte stieß, die *per se* einfach den Definitionen der anderen etablierten Kategorien nicht entsprechen. Andererseits setzt Hybrid Art eine lange Reihe der seit den 1960er Jahren angestrengten Versuche fort, mit Begriffen wie „Inter-", „Trans-", oder „Multi-Media" den Fluss stets neu entstehender wegweisender Kulturakte zu fassen. Dies erklärt auch, dass trotz Medienwechsel und -evolution transhistorische Cluster zutage treten – im diesjährigen Wettbwerb z.B. die starke Präsenz „hilfloser Roboter", Projekte zum Topos Abfall und Recycling, das Knacken von „Black-Boxen" digitaler Technologien, tautologische Maschinen-Paradoxa, oder die Suche nach einer nicht-technologischen Alterität des Menschseins, die sich vorzugsweise in Gestalt von Schweinen, Schleimpilzen oder dem Pflanzlichen offenbart. So verwundert auch die jährlich ansteigende Anzahl von Kunstprojekten mit Biomedien nicht, welche eine zeitgenössische Form darstellen, mit Medien „Authentizität" zu produzieren und angesichts des allgegenwärtig Technischen dennoch Referenten des „Realen" zu inszenieren. Dieses „Reale" entpuppt sich allerdings als zunehmend elastisch, nebulös und ungreifbar; es tritt als Meta-Narrativität in überlappenden Ebenen, Disziplinen und Genres in Aktion. So scheint dann auch das Genre der *Performance Art* mit der Last des Theatralischen und Szenischen zu kämpfen – nur wenige Projekte mit wirklichem Innovationspotenzial gingen der Jury ins Netz. Dafür können dann aber fast alle prämierten Kunst-Projekte als performatif verstanden werden, sei es auf der mikroskopischen oder makroskopischen Ebene – manchmal in extremer Verdichtung, anderswo in Formen hybriden Geschichtenerzählens, die absichtlich die Grenzen gewohnter Zeit- und Raum-Koordinaten sprengen.

GOLDENE NICA

Bacterial Radio

Joe Davis

Die diesjährige Goldene Nica wird Joe Davis, Künstler und Forscher am Department of Biology des Massachusetts Institute of Technology und am Department of Genetics der Harvard Medical School, für seine sowohl technisch, poetisch als auch wissenschaftstheoretisch herausstechende Arbeit *Bacterial Radio* zuerkannt. Der Preis ist gleichzeitig als Würdigung einer mehrere Jahrzehnte langen Praxis eines Pioniers zu verstehen, der stets so unterschiedliche Felder wie Molekularbiologie, Bioinformatik, Laser, Raumfahrt, Telekommunikation etc. durch den roten Faden einer ebenso humorvollen wie kognitiv ausgereizten Konzeptkunst miteinander verbunden hat, und der von der jüngeren Generation als graue Eminenz biotechnologischer Kunstformen wahrgenommen wird. *Bacterial Radio* kann als retro-futuristisches Manifest gesehen werden. Es knüpft an frühere Projekte Davis' an, über Mikroorganismen mit außerirdischem Leben kommunikativ in Kontakt zu treten. Die Arbeit besteht aus gewachsenen elektrischen Schaltkreisen, die von genetisch modifizierten Bakterien hergestellt wurden. In Zusammenarbeit mit Ido Bachelet und Tara Gianoulis verwendet Joe Davis hier Bakterien, die leitfähige Platin- und Germanium-Verbindungen produzieren können. Dazu wurde eine Genvariante des Meerorange genannten Schwamms *Tethya aurantia* eingeschleust. Das eingebrachte Gen kodiert für ein spezielles Protein (Silicatein), das normalerweise für den Aufbau des Bio-Glas-Skeletts aus Siliziumoxid-Nadeln des Schwamms zuständig ist. Varianten dieses Gens befähigen Proteine, auch metallische Leiter und Halbleiter wie Germanium, Titandioxid, oder Platin anzureichern. Für *Bacterial Radio* hat Davis gentechnisch veränderte Bakterien mit nichtleitenden Metallsalzen in Verbindung gebracht, um so elektrisch leitende Schaltkreise für anachronistische Mittelwellen-Radios herzustellen. Mit der Verwendung des Proteins verweist der Künstler auf die weit verbreitete Verwendung von Silizium-basierten Produkten in der Telekommunikation. Gleichzeitig aber kommentiert er ironisch die Schaltkreis-Metapher in der heutigen Synthetischen Biologie, welche Ingenieursprinzipien auf die Biologie anwendet und „genetische Schaltkreise" als standardisierte biologische Bauteile entwirft. Umgekehrt wendet Davis seinerseits hier nun biologische Prinzipien auf das elektronische Ingenieurswesen an.

GOLDEN NICA

Bacterial Radio

Joe Davis

This year's Golden Nica goes to Joe Davis, artist and researcher at the Department of Biology at the Massachusetts Institute of Technology and the Department of Genetics at Harvard Medical School, for his outstanding technical, poetic as well as epistemologically grounded project: *Bacterial Radio*. With this prize, the jury also honors this pioneer—whom the younger generation sees as the gray eminence of bio-technological art forms—for his work over the past several decades. Through the central themes of his both humorous and cognitively challenging conceptual art, he has brought together such varied fields as, e.g., molecular biology, bioinformatics, laser technology, astronautics and telecommunication. *Bacterial Radio* may be seen as a retro-futuristic manifesto. It is related to Davis' earlier projects, which attempted to establish communication with extraterrestrial life via microorganisms. This work consists of grown electric circuits produced by genetically modified bacteria.

Here, in collaboration with Ido Bachelet and Tara Gianoulis, Joe Davis uses bacteria to produce conductive platinum and germanium connections. To do so, a gene was isolated from the orange puffball sponge (*Tethya aurantia*) and introduced into the bacteria. This gene encodes a special protein (silicatein) that is normally responsible for the development of the sponge's tiny glass skeleton, which is made up of silica needles (spicules). Variants of the gene enable proteins to enrich metallic conductors and semi-conductors, such as germanium, titanium dioxide and platinum. For *Bacterial Radio*, Davis has embedded genetically modified bacteria in non-conductive materials containing metal salts in order to produce electrically conductive circuits for anachronistic AM radios. By using this protein, the artist refers to the wide use of silicon-based products in the field of telecommunication. At the same time he ironically comments on the metaphor of the circuit in present-day synthetic biology, which applies the principles of engineering to biology and designs "genetic circuits" as standard biological parts. Davis reverses this logic by applying biological principles to electronic engineering.

AWARDS OF DISTINCTION

For the jury, both these projects reflect two strong trends in the field of hybrid art: new forms of storytelling and open-source DIY culture.

Moon Goose Analogue: Lunar Migration Bird Facility

Agnes Meyer-Brandis

The first award of distinction goes to *Moon Goose Analogue: Lunar Migration Bird Facility* by Agnes Meyer-Brandis, a multi-layered narrative, transspecies performance, film and installation. The project embodies many years of work and extreme commitment towards non-human otherness, interweaving fiction and artistically constructed scientific experiments. As starting point, the artist has chosen a tale written in the early 17th century by a British ecclesiast. It tells the story of an explorer bound for the moon in a chariot pulled by moon geese. The artist wonders what might have happened to this specific species today, and submits something to scientific methodology that can hardly be verified as actual fact. Though then, she creates facts by breeding and training a flock of geese. Hence, Agnes Meyer-Brandis raises the issue of whether the categorization of species is an arbitrary variable construed by scientists. The different parts of the project—*The Moon Goose Colony* breeding unit; *The Moon Analogue*, where the geese are trained for their moon landing; and *The Control Room*, which enables the visitor to enter into communication with the real geese—seek to question science itself as a meta-narrative and instance of storytelling rather than as an authority of absolute truth. In our world of elastic reality, where layers of mediated information tend to reshape our experiences, the jury acknowledges the intricate structure of this project as a reflection on how "reality" is being constantly bent and undergoing construction.

The Free Universal Construction Kit

Golan Levin, Shawn Sims

The second award of distinction, *The Free Universal Construction Kit* by Golan Levin and Shawn Sims, is conceived both as a practical solution to and a metaphor on interoperability between various brands of construction kits. It takes the devastatingly accurate logic of children as its starting point. Whereas toys are supposed to trigger

AUSZEICHNUNGEN

Die beiden Projekte spiegeln unseres Erachtens zwei auffällige Trends der Hybrid Art wider: neue Formen des Geschichtenerzählens und Open-Source- bzw. Do-it-yourself-Kultur.

Moon Goose Analogue: Lunar Migration Bird Facility

Agnes Meyer-Brandis

Die erste Auszeichnung geht an Agnes Meyer-Brandis' vielschichtige Erzählstruktur, Transspezies-Performance, Filmarbeit und Installation namens *Moon Goose Analogue: Lunar Migration Bird Facility*. Die Arbeit beinhaltet eine mehrjährige Auseinandersetzung mit und extreme Zuwendung zu einem nichtmenschlichen Anderen und verbindet Fiktion mit künstlerisch angelegten wissenschaftlichen Experimenten. Als Ausgangspunkt wählte die Künstlerin die Geschichte eines britischen Kirchenmanns aus dem frühen 17. Jahrhundert über einen Mondfahrer, der seine Reise in einem von Mondgänsen gezogenen Gefährt unternommen haben soll. Sie fragt sich, wie mit dieser Spezies heute verfahren würde, und unterwirft etwas schwerlich als Faktum zu Beweisendes einer strengen wissenschaftlichen Prüfung. Indem sie dann mit der Aufzucht und Ausbildung einer Gänseschar tatsächliche Fakten schafft, wirft Agnes Meyer-Brandis u.a. die Frage auf, inwiefern es sich bei dieser Spezies nicht um willkürliche wissenschaftliche Konstrukte handelt. Mit seinen verschiedenen Teilen – der Mondgans-Züchtung, der Mondnachbildung, in der die Gänse für die Mondlandung trainiert werden, und dem Kontrollraum, mit dessen Hilfe Ausstellungsbesucher mit den wirklichen Gänsen kommunizieren können – ergründet das Projekt die Wissenschaft selbst als Metanarrativ und einen Fall von Geschichtenerzählen statt als Hüterin einer absoluten Wahrheit. Die Jury sah in der komplexen Struktur des Projekts eine Reflexion auf die ständige Beugung und den permanenten Umbau der „Realität" in einer Welt, in der Erfahrung von unzähligen Schichten vermittelter Informationen überlagert und überformt wird.

The Free Universal Construction Kit

Golan Levin, Shawn Sims

Die zweite Auszeichnung ging mit *The Free Universal Construction Kit* von Golan Levin und Shawn Sims an ein Projekt, das sowohl als praktische Lösung wie auch als Metapher für die Interoperabilität zwischen verschiedenen Spielzeugbaukästen konzipiert ist. Ausgangspunkt bildet die umwerfend klare Logik von Kindern. Soll Spielzeug einerseits deren Fantasie beflügeln, so liegt den heftig ihre Marktanteile und Urheberrechte verteidigenden Marken andererseits kaum daran, die Kombinierbarkeit verschiedener Systeme zu fördern. Das *Free Universal Construction Kit* besteht aus einer Reihe von Bausteinen, die mit einem einfachen 3D-Drucker – wie dem online als Bausatz erhältlichen MakerBot-Modell – selbst hergestellt werden können. Jeder Baustein kann gratis als STL-Dokument (dem Standardformat für Stereolithografie) heruntergeladen werden. Das Projekt ist open source, d.h. jeder kann der Bausteinbibliothek neue Elemente hinzufügen und damit zur Flexibilität und Kompatibilität zwischen immer mehr Objekten und Systemen beitragen. Diese rasch wachsende Praxis weist auf die allmähliche Ersetzung von Massenproduktion und Massenkonsum durch einen effizienteren Do-it-yourself-Konsum voraus. Das *Free Universal Construction Kit*, dessen Name sich wohl dem darin enthaltenen Akronym verdankt, das als humoristische Beschreibung des Systemhackens gelesen werden kann, ist zugleich ein ausgezeichnetes Beispiel für Mediendesign.

ANERKENNUNGEN

Game Border
Jun Fujiki

Einer ähnlichen Logik folgt auch *Game Border*. Die von einem Team japanischer Künstler und Forscher unter der Leitung von Jun Fujiki entwickelte Arbeit besteht aus einer Reihe unterschiedlich großer Bildschirme, die, hintereinander an einer Wand angeordnet, eine panoramatische Landschaft ergeben. Die Bildschirme repräsentieren jeweils ein berühmtes Spiel oder eine Plattform mit einem meist proprietären Interface. Für diese wurden auf den Spielen beruhende Umgebungen und Charaktere programmiert, um ein Kontinuum zwischen den normalerweise inkompatiblen Welten herzustellen. Ziel des Spiels ist hier nicht das Erreichen immer höherer Levels, sondern das Durchstoßen der „Grenze" zwischen den einzelnen Welten, wodurch ein neues Narrativ oder eine Art *Cadavre Exquis* entsteht.

People Staring at Computers
Kyle McDonald

Unser Verhältnis zu technologischen Gadgets wird vom amerikanischen Künstler Kyle McDonald auf subversive Art und Weise thematisiert. McDonald installierte heimlich eine selbst entwickelte Software, die ein Bild auslöst, sobald ein Benutzer längere Zeit auf den Bildschirm blickt, auf den Demo-Geräten des New Yorker Apple Stores. Auf diese Weise sammelte er 3.000

children's imagination, the possibility of combining different systems is never encouraged by individual brands, who fiercely defend their market shares and copyright. The *Free Universal Construction Kit* consists of various elements produced by a low grade 3D printer—such as the MakerBot, available as a kit online—whose purpose is to enable interoperability between various brands of construction kits. Each element can be downloaded free of charge as an STL file (the standard for stereo lithography). The project is open source; anyone can add new parts to the library of components, thus contributing to a greater flexibility and compatibility between a growing number of objects and systems. This practice is developing rapidly and prefigures a world wherein mass production and consumption will gradually be replaced by a more efficient DIY mode of consuming. The *Free Universal Construction Kit*, which one can suspect has been given this name so as to generate an acronym that humorously comments on the act of hacking systems, is also an outstanding example of media design.

HONORARY MENTIONS

Game Border
Jun Fujiki

Along the same logic is *Game Border*, which was produced by a collective of Japanese researchers led by Jun Fujiki. It consists of a multitude of screens, each of a different size, lined up on a wall, so as to create a panoramic landscape. The artists have selected a number of famous games and platforms, which for the most part have proprietary interfaces. The programmers produced environments and characters inspired by those popular games, thus creating a continuum between games that are normally incompatible. Rather than reaching different levels in the same game, the player's goal is to skip through the "borders" between each game, creating a new narrative that evokes an "exquisite corpse" of sorts.

People Staring at Computers
Kyle McDonald

Our relationship to technological gadgets is explored in a subversive fashion by American artist Kyle McDonald in *People Staring at Computers*. McDonald secretly installed a software he had developed that triggered a photo as soon as a user stared for a while at the screen of a demo computer at an Apple Store in New York City. As a result, he was able to collect 3,000 portraits—they document how we stare spellbound at new gadgets, and explore surveillance infrastructures and the aesthetics of image recognition systems. At the same time, McDonald turns the salesroom of a company into a performance space... and this has its consequences, which he euphemistically describes as a "large-scale collaboration with Apple Inc. and the United States Secret Service".

Irrational Computing

Ralf Baecker

Ralf Baecker's installation *Irrational Computing* takes a microscopic look at the materials of the computer as a universal machine: here, crystals and minerals that serve as semiconductors display a number of sensually discernible properties. With this arrangement of the materials' analog effects as primitive form of a signal processor, Baecker uses the characteristics of crystals to reveal the boundaries of so-called universal information technology and of the digital culture that has evolved from computers. He presents electronics as a process that subjects the material aesthetics of minerals to an abstract process and thus to a reduction in complexity in order to, ultimately, represent complex effects again.

Protei

Protei

Protei is being developed by three collectives of researchers—Open_Sailing, randomwalks and Amorphica. They combine their different skills to produce a functioning prototype for a sailing robot that could form the basis for various ecological applications. These sailing drones have segmented hulls that should enable them to collect oil from the ocean's surface after accidental spills. Developed as an open hardware project, *Protei* has also sought financing through crowd funding. More than the final product, it is the process that makes *Protei* an interesting example of hybrid art.

Searching for the Ubiquitous Genetically Engineered Machine

ArtScienceBangalore

The project *Searching for the Ubiquitous Genetically Engineered Machine* by the student work

Porträts – Zeugnisse von unserem gebannten Blick auf neue Gadgets und gleichzeitig eine Auseinandersetzung mit Überwachungs-Infrastrukturen und der Ästhetik von Bilderkennungssystemen. Gleichzeitig macht McDonald den Verkaufsraum eines Konzerns zum Performance-Raum... nicht ohne Konsequenzen, die er euphemistisch als „großangelegte Kooperation mit der Firma Apple und dem US-Geheimdienst" umschreibt.

Irrational Computing

Ralf Baecker

Ralf Baeckers Installation *Irrational Computing* wirft einen mikroskopischen Blick auf das Material der universellen Maschine Computer: Kristalle und Mineralien, die als Halbleiter dienen, entfalten dabei ihre sinnlich wahrnehmbaren Eigenschaften. Baecker nutzt Eigenschaften der Kristalle, um mit dieser Anordnung analoger Effekte des Materials, als primitiver Form des Signalprozessors, die Begrenzungen der vermeintlich universellen Computer-Technologie sowie der auf dieser Maschine aufbauenden digitalen Kultur aufzuzeigen. Baecker stellt Elektronik als einen Prozess dar, der die materielle Ästhetik der Mineralien einem abstrakten Prozess und damit einer Komplexitätsreduktion unterwirft, um damit letztendlich wieder komplexe Effekte zu repräsentieren.

Protei

Protei

Protei ist ein Gemeinschaftsprojekt der Kunst / Forschungs-Kollektive Open_Sailing, randomwalks und Amorphica, die mit vereinten Kräften einen funktionsfähigen Prototypen eines Segelroboters als Basis für verschiedene ökologische Anwendungen entwickelt haben. Diese Segel-Drohnen mit segmentiertem Rumpf sollen in der Lage sein, Rohöl von der Meeresoberfläche zu absorbieren. *Protei* wird vorwiegend durch Crowdfunding finanziert. Mehr noch als das finale Produkt, ist es dieser gesamte Prozess, der *Protei* zu einem interessanten Beispiel der Kategorie Hybrid Art macht.

Searching for the Ubiquitous Genetically Engineered Machine

ArtScienceBangalore

Eine symbolisch-spekulative Open-Source-Anwendung ist auch das Projekt *Searching for the Ubiquitous Genetically Engineered Machine* der studentischen Arbeitsgruppe ArtScienceBangalore. Es handelt sich um ein einfaches Analyse-Werkzeug für Bauern, die damit der Präsenz gentechnisch modifizierter Organismen in den von ihnen bearbeiteten Böden nachspüren können sollen. Dazu nutzt ArtScienceBangalore einen *Hack* eines sogenannten *Biobrick*, so wie sie jährlich beim iGEM-Wettbewerb vorgestellt werden mit dem Ziel, eine offen zugängliche Bibliothek genetischer Bausteine zu erschaffen. Mit *Searching for the Ubiquitous Genetically Engineered Machine* antizipiert die Gruppe die Welt im Zeitalter der massenhaften Verbreitung derart genetisch veränderter Organismen.

The Great Work of the Metal Lover
Adam Brown
Extremophile Mikroorganismen, die unter extremen Umweltbedingungen überleben können, sind die Protagonisten in Adam Browns neo-alchemistischem Projekt *The Great Work of the Metal Lover*. Diese lösen das klassische Transmutations-Problem und stellen kristallines 24-karätiges Gold her, indem sie in einem Bioreaktor mit reduzierter Atmosphäre hohen Konzentrationen des giftigen Gold-Chlorids ausgesetzt werden und einen Biofilm ausbilden, der farblich dem mittelalterlichen Stein der Weisen entspricht. Der Biofilm wird dann zum Schmelzpunkt von Gold erhitzt, kleine Nuggets entstehen. Nicht Chemie, sondern Biotechnologie mit Einzellern bringt hier das Metall hervor, das mit dem Mythos ewiger Haltbarkeit assoziiert wird.

2.6g 329m/s
Jailia Essaidi
Der Name des Projekts bezieht sich auf den Leistungsstandard von schusssicheren Westen. 2,6 g und 329 m/s sind das maximale Gewicht und die maximale Geschwindigkeit einer .22 kalibrigen Gewehrkugel, vor der eine solche Weste schützen soll. Die israelische Bio-Künstlerin versucht menschlicher Haut diese Art von Unverwundbarkeit zu verleihen. Dabei experimentiert sie mit Spinnenseide, die von transgenen Ziegen produziert wird. Trotzdem oder gerade weil sie dieses Ziel nur ansatzweise erreichen konnte, schafft die Künstlerin eine komplexe Arbeit, die mit einfacher künstlerischer Sprache viele verschiedene Perspektiven anspricht – vom Traum der Unverwundbarkeit bis hin zu der von der politischen Realität in der Heimat der Künstlerin geprägten Idee von Sicherheit und der davon getriebenen militärischen Forschung.

The Body is a Big Place
Peta Clancy, Helen Pynor
Mit *The Body is a Big Place* präsentieren Peta Clancy und Helen Pynor eine Performance, bei der zwei aus dem Schlachthof bezogene Schweineherzen für 24 Stunden am Leben erhalten werden und so Aspekte der menschlichen Herztransplantation erlebbar machen. Die

group ArtScienceBangalore is also a symbolic and speculative open-source application. In this case we are dealing with a simple analysis tool for farmers, one with which they should be able to trace the presence of genetically-engineered organisms in the soil they are working. To do this, ArtScience-Bangalore hacks so-called BioBricks—such as annually presented at the iGEM Competition with the goal of creating a "registry of standard biological parts". With *Searching for the Ubiquitous Genetically Engineered Machine*, the group anticipates the world in the age of widespread dissemination of such genetically modified organisms.

The Great Work of the Metal Lover
Adam Brown
Extremophilic microorganisms that can survive under extreme environmental conditions are the protagonists in Adam Brown's neo-alchemist project *The Great Work of the Metal Lover*. They solve the classic problem of transmutation and produce crystalline 24-carat gold. This occurs by exposing them to high concentrations of toxic gold chloride in a bioreactor with reduced atmosphere. This causes them to develop a biofilm that resembles the medieval Philosopher's Stone in color. When the biofilm is heated up to the melting point of gold, tiny deposits of gold form. Here, instead of chemistry, biotechnology with unicellular organisms is used to produce the metal associated with the legend of longevity.

2.6g 329m/s
Jailia Essaidi
Jailia Essaidi's *2.6g 329m/s*: the project's name is a reference to the performance standard of bulletproof vests. 2.6 g and 329 m/s are the maximum weight and velocity of the .22 caliber rifle bullet which such a vest should protect you from. This Israeli bio-artist attempts to give human skin this same kind of invulnerability. She experiments with spider silk that has been produced by transgenic goats. Despite, or precisely because of, the fact that she has only been able to achieve this goal on a rudimentary level, the artist has created a complex work using simple artistic language that addresses many different perspectives—from the dream of invulnerability to the notion of safety, such as has been shaped by the political reality in the artist's homeland and the resulting military research on the topic.

The Body is a Big Place

Peta Clancy, Helen Pynor

With *The Body is a Big Place*, Peta Clancy and Helen Pynor present a performance in which two pig hearts obtained from a slaughterhouse are kept alive for 24 hours and enable viewers to experience aspects of the human heart transplant process. The apparatus is surrounded by a multiscreen video projection of an underwater performance that is being carried out by a group of swimmers who have themselves been recipients of organs. With this medical sculpture, the artists emphasize that death is a process that has a duration and not just an event that occurs in a single moment. The title refers to the great geographical and social distances often covered during organ transplants. The jury felt compelled by this investigation of a complex medical process that is very difficult to implement in the context of a gallery. The project uses a visual language that makes the human and social dimension of this procedure, which is invisible and difficult to grasp, viscerally understandable to the general public.

Un Réseau Translucide

Prue Lang

Prue Lang's *Un Réseau Translucide* is an "autonomous dance performance" in which the performers themselves produce the energy required for the technical systems on stage. In collaboration with Amanda Parkes from MIT Media Lab, the choreographer has developed special costumes that are able to convert the kinetic energy generated by the dancers' movements and store it in batteries that power the sound system. The performers nourish themselves on macaroons that they collect while dancing. They pedal a bike to generate electricity for the LED lighting grid. In this project, dance spaces—which normally exist in isolation—confront issues of ecological sustainability.

Maquila Región 4

Amor Muñoz

Named after Mexican textile and electronics factories along the US-American border, the performative intervention *Maquila Región 4* by Amor Muñoz is also about the role of art in light of technical production conditions. Muñoz hires day laborers, but pays the—higher—US minimum wage, for stitching electronic circuits and BiDi codes on

Apparatur ist umgeben von einer Multiscreen-Videoprojektion einer Unterwasser-Performance, aufgeführt von einer Gruppe von Schwimmern, die selbst Organempfänger sind. Mit ihrer medizinischen Skulptur zeigen die Künstlerinnen dass der Tod ein andauernder Prozess ist und kein einzelnes Ereignis. Der Titel bezieht sich auf die großen geographischen und sozialen Distanzen, die oft bei Organtransplantationen überbrückt werden. Die Jury überzeugte die Gegenüberstellung eines komplexen medizinischen Prozesses, der in einem Galeriekontext nur schwer umsetzbar ist, mit einer visuellen Sprache, welche die menschliche und soziale Dimension dieser für die Allgemeinheit unsichtbaren und schwer nachvollziehbaren medizinischen Prozedur nachvollziehbar macht.

Un Réseau Translucide

Prue Lang

Un Réseau Translucide von Prue Lang ist eine „autonome Tanzperformance", bei der die Akteure selbst die für die Bühnentechnik nötige Energie produzieren. Dazu entwickelte die Choreografin in Zusammenarbeit mit Amanda Parkes vom MIT Media Lab spezielle Kostüme, welche die von den Tänzern generierte kinetische Energie konvertieren und in Batterien speichern. Die Performer werden durch beim Tanzen aufgesammelte *Macarons* ernährt. Sie erstrampeln auf einem Fahrrad live den Strom für die LED-Bühnenbeleuchtung. Das Projekt konfrontiert die normalerweise isolierten Tanz-Räume mit Fragen der ökologischen Nachhaltigkeit.

Maquila Región 4

Amor Muñoz

Um die Rolle von Kunst angesichts technischer Produktionsbedingungen geht es auch in Amor Muñoz' performativem Projekt *Maquila Región 4*, benannt nach den mexikanischen Produktionsstätten entlang der US-amerikanischen Grenze, in denen vorwiegend Kleidung und Elektronik hergestellt wird. Muñoz heuert Tagelöhner an, zahlt aber den – höheren – amerikanischen Mindestlohn für den Job, mit leitenden Fäden elektronische Schaltungen und BiDi-Codes auf Textilien zu sticken. So wird gleichzeitig der Arbeitsprozess und der persönliche Hintergrund der Arbeitenden dokumentiert. Die Jury überzeugte die Mischung aus kritischem Kommentar zur von wachsender Informalisierung geprägten globalisierten Arbeitswelt mit einer fantasievollen Neuerfindung von traditioneller Handarbeit wie dem Sticken in einem High-Tech-Kontext.

50 Aktenkilometer: Ein begehbares Stasi-Hörspiel
Rimini Protokoll, Deutschlandradio Kultur
Das Projekt *50 Aktenkilometer: Ein begehbares Stasi-Hörspiel* der Gruppe Rimini Protokoll macht das Archiv der Staatssicherheit der vormaligen DDR am Ort des Geschehens selbst via GPS-Smartphone begehbar. In ihrem Beitrag zur Deutschlandradio-Hörspielreihe *Radioortung* schafft Rimini Protokoll eine Hybridtheaterform als doppelbödiges Spiel zwischen Observieren und Observiertwerden. In der Inszenierung von historischem Archivmaterial stellen die Künstler eine Parallele zu jenen Datenspuren her, die heute durch die Verwendung ortsbezogener digitaler Technologien generiert werden – Archive, deren Umfang ihr historisches Gegenstück bei weitem übertrifft.

Dream Water Wonderland
Hörner / Antlfinger
Der bereits in Vergessenheit geratene Schnelle Brüter Kalkar ist Ausgangspunkt für die Kunstinstallation *Dream Water Wonderland* von Ute Hörner und Mathias Antlfinger. Erst 1985 fertiggestellt, wegen sicherheitstechnischer und politischer Bedenken aber nie in Betrieb genommen, ist der Atommeiler Symbol der Altlasten der Hochtechnologie und wird – dekoriert mit einem Karusell – heute als Freizeitpark genutzt. Bei Hörner / Antlfinger wird er zur Kulisse für einen merkwürdigen Traum von einer technisch-biologischen Hybridkreatur, die sehr viel Energie verschlingt. Die Installation bildet ein absurdes Miniatur-Ensemble als Abbild einer zeitgenössischen Technikgeschichte.

textiles with conductive thread. In doing so, she documents both the work process and the workers' personal backgrounds. The jury was impressed by how the artist combined critical commentary on global work conditions, which are characterized by a growing informal sector, and a very imaginative reinvention of a traditional handicraft such as stitchery in a high-tech context.

50 Aktenkilometer: Ein begehbares Stasi-Hörspiel
Rimini Protokoll, Deutschlandradio Kultur
The project *50 Aktenkilometer: Ein begehbares Stasi-Hörspiel* by the group Rimini Protokoll allows participants, via GPS smartphone, to "enter" the archive of the GDR State Security (Stasi) at former sites of observation. In their contribution for a series of radio plays for mobile phones produced by Deutschlandradio Kultur and entitled *Radioortung*, Rimini Protokoll creates a hybrid form of theater as a double-edged interaction between observing and being observed. In enacting historical archive material, the artists establish parallels to the data track we leave when we use site-related digital technologies—and the volume of these archives greatly surpasses that of their historical counterpart.

Dream Water Wonderland
Hörner / Antlfinger
Kalkar, a nearly forgotten fast breeder reactor, was the starting point of the art installation *Dream Water Wonderland* by Ute Hörner and Mathias Antlfinger. Completed in 1985, the reactor never went into operation due to doubts about its safety and political concerns. Adorned with a carrousel and more, this reactor, which is a symbol of high-tech waste, is now being used as an amusement park. Hörner/Antlfinger make it the backdrop of a strange dream about a hybrid technical-biological creature that consumes incredible amounts of electricity. The installation forms an absurd miniature ensemble and is a reflection of the contemporary history of technology.

Bacterial Radio

Joe Davis

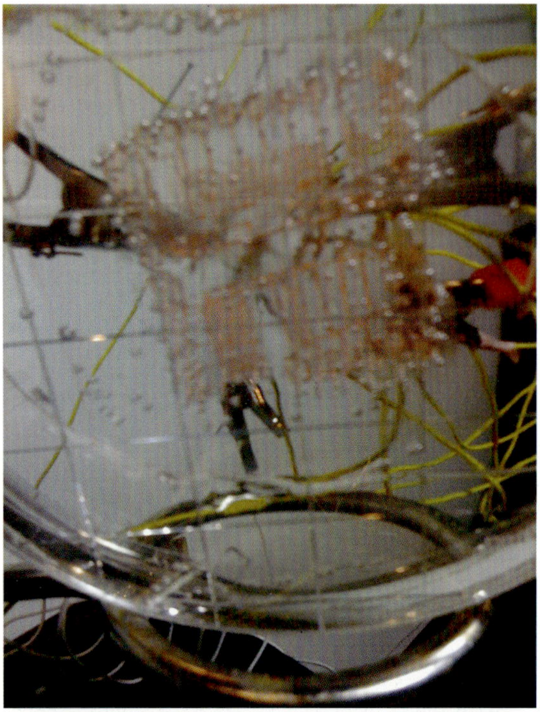

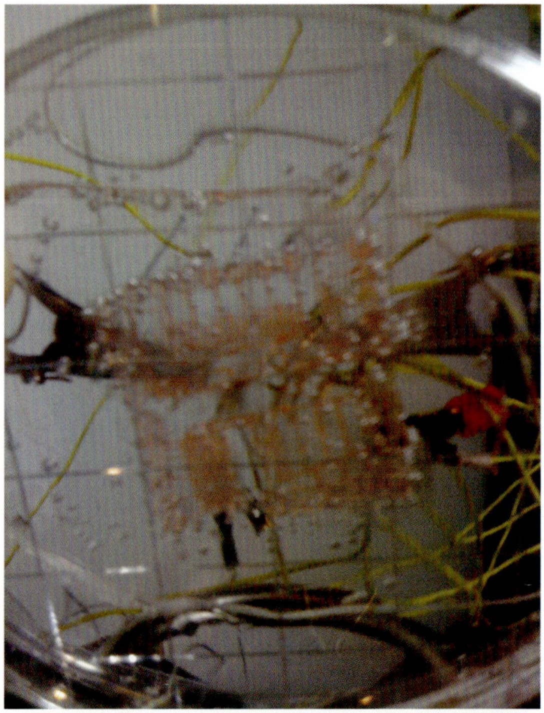

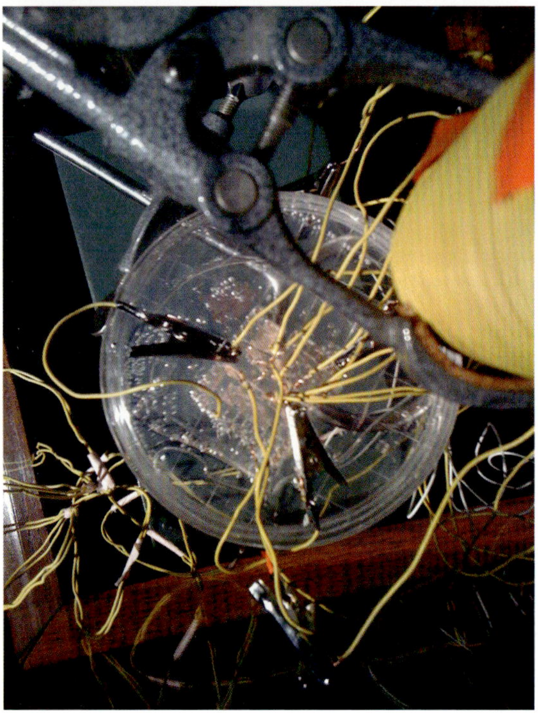

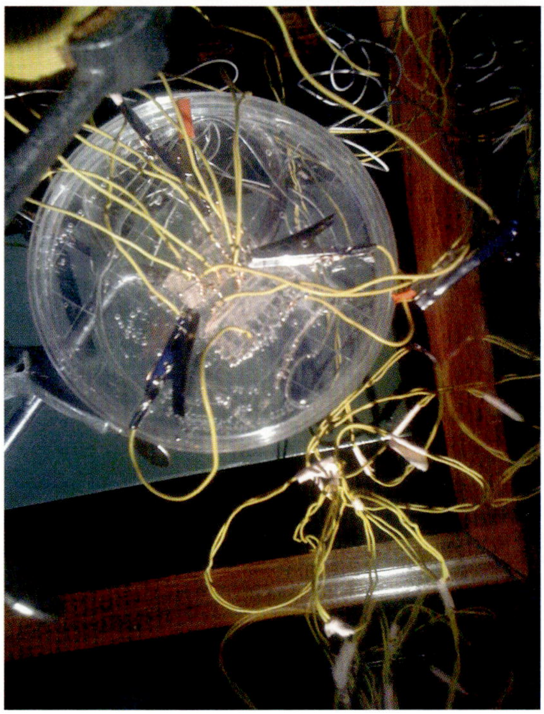

Es klingt nach Science-Fiction, ist es aber nicht. Auf dem Planeten Erde laufen seit Hunderten von Jahrmillionen in allerlei Arten von Fabriken hochkomplizierte Produktionsprozesse an richtiggehenden Fertigungsstraßen ab. Schon lange vor dem Auftreten des Menschen entwickelte die Natur biologische Techniken zur groß angelegten Fabrikation einer riesigen Vielfalt spezialisierter Materialien. *Homo sapiens* hat zahllose Grundstoffe durch Ausbeutung solcher natürlichen Fabriken gewonnen, einfach weil es ihm unmöglich war, vergleichbare Materialien ähnlich effizient selbst zu erzeugen. Bis heute werden biologisch gestützte Produktionsmethoden aber meist mit relativ geringem Verständnis für die ihnen zugrunde liegenden chemischen und molekularen Vorgänge eingesetzt.

In den letzten Jahrzehnten hat die Wissenschaft Licht in einige dieser Vorgänge gebracht. Da die Natur fast immer weit effizienter arbeitet als der Mensch, arbeitet die Forschung intensiv an verschiedenen biologischen Prozessen, die für menschliche Zwecke nutzbar gemacht werden können. Sie verspricht, viele der heute von der Schwerindustrie erledigten Aufgaben dereinst mit mikrobiellen Mitteln – und mit weniger Ressourcenverbrauch und Umweltbelastung – erledigen zu können. An dieser Schnittstelle von Biologie und Technik operiert auch das Projekt *Biological Radio*.

Ein Detektorradio ist ein einfacher Schwingkreis, der lediglich Induktivität, Kapazität und einen „Kristall" – einen mineralischen Halbleiter zur Umwandlung der empfangenen Radiosignale in elektrische Gleichstromsignale, die mit einem Kopfhörer in Schall aufgelöst werden können – benötigt. Ein solch einfacher Schaltkreis kommt ohne Batterien, Röhren oder Transistoren aus und arbeitet allein mit der Spannungsdifferenz zwischen Antenne und Erde.

Die Erfindung des Detektorradios fiel in die Spätzeit der industriellen Revolution. Die Technik gewann in der Folge rasch an Popularität, sodass Tausende begeisterter Radiobastler zur Verbesserung der Schaltkreise beitrugen. Diese ermöglichten eine kostenlose, fast mystische Verwandlung unsichtbarer Signale in Musik, Stimmen, Geschichten von fernen Orten und historischen Ereignissen. Und wiewohl Mittelwellensendungen inzwischen ganz andere Inhalte haben, so kann man doch auch heute noch mit einfachen Fertigbauteilen, natürlichen oder gefundenen Materialien ein Detektorradio bauen.

Die Geschichte des Detektorradios ist zugleich von herrlicher Unschuld und einer Art tragischen Ironie geprägt. Einerseits war das Detektorradio Ausdruck eines optimistischen Zeitgeistes: des Versprechens endlosen technischen Fortschritts und des Anbruchs eines Zeitalters,

It sounds like science fiction, but it is not. On planet Earth, sophisticated manufacturing processes with full-fledged assembly lines have been running in many different kinds of factories for hundreds of millions of years. Nature evolved biological techniques for large-scale production and manufacturing of a huge variety of specialized materials long before human beings ever existed. *Homo sapiens*, in turn, have historically exploited many such natural factories to obtain a long list of essential commodities simply because comparable materials could not otherwise be efficiently produced. Even today, biologically assisted methods of production are often put to use with relatively little understanding of the underlying chemical and molecular operations.

In recent decades, science has revealed details about some of these operations. Since nature is almost always much more efficient than human industry, researchers are focusing on various biological processes that can be put to work for humanity. The promise of this research is that microbial machinery will eventually carry out many operations now carried out by heavy industry, but with fewer resources and without environmental pollution. *Biological Radio* addresses this interface of biology and technology.

A crystal radio is a basic resonant circuit requiring only induction, capacitance and a radio "crystal," a mineral semiconductor used to convert received radio signals into DC electrical signals that can be resolved with headphones as sound. These simple circuits require no batteries, tubes or transistors and operate with only the difference in voltage between the antenna and the ground.

The invention of "wireless" coincided with the maturing *industrial revolution* of the late 19th century. Crystal radio technology rapidly gained popularity in the decades following its introduction and thousands of amateur radio enthusiasts contributed to the development of improved radio circuits. It was a cost-free, almost mystical conversion of invisible signals into music, voice and content about distant places and events in the unfolding march of history. Crystal sets can still be created with common off-the-shelf, natural and found materials, though the content of AM radio broadcasts has obviously changed.

The story of crystal radio contains both a sense of wonderful innocence and a kind of tragic irony. On one hand, crystal radio seemed to characterize the optimistic spirit of its age: the promise of unending technological progress and the onset of an industrial era that would relieve humanity of labor and tedium and open up unprecedented opportunities for leisure and learning. On the other hand, many social, environmental and economic impacts of that same industrial revolution have tended to interfere with those dreams.

At no point in history has humanity been more technologically advanced. Whole populations are probably far more educated now than at any point in the past. Yet, owing to parts of knowledge gone missing, the average person has never been more clueless about the technology that makes "quality of life" possible.

In a world of propriety and non-disclosure, methods and materials made inscrutable, potted circuits and secret formulae, advancement of knowledge has become largely subsidiary to business. Students of physics and chemistry learn by repeating classical experiments that inform them about how science and our understanding of the world have progressed step by step. Advancement of knowledge depends on these "in-between" steps of understanding. As a consequence of entrepreneurship and enterprise, many of these steps are effectively removed from the public domain, creating holes in the structure of knowledge. With the ongoing merger of academic research and the corporate world, we explicitly place our faith in corporations to solve many the world's problems. But in doing so, we can expect only those problems to be solved that can be solved at a profit. No one wants to sell you a radio that you can take apart and modify, much less tell you about one you can build yourself or one that will never require batteries.

Art is about opening up windows on the world, but you can't open a window on something you remain clueless about. The Vitruvian ideal, that artists must seek broad knowledge, is one of the layers of meaning embedded in the *Bacterial Radio* project.

In spring 2011, I created a flat circuit design that could be constructed in a Petri dish. This circuit was then cast in negative relief in PDMS (polydimethylsiloxane) gel. Cells and growth media were then applied to circuit impressions in the gel. The cells used were *E coli* modified with a gene for silicatein,[1] a ubiquitous protein native to many different marine organisms. These organisms use silicatein to polymerize silica from seawater in order to create glass endoskeletons and exoskeletons

das die Menschheit von Arbeit und Mühsal erlösen und ungeahnte Freizeit- und Lernmöglichkeiten eröffnen würde. Andererseits haben viele soziale, ökologische und wirtschaftliche Folgen der nämlichen industriellen Revolution diese Träume eher zum Platzen gebracht.

Technisch war die Menschheit noch nie in ihrer Geschichte so hoch entwickelt. Der Bildungsstand breiter Bevölkerungsteile ist heute größer denn je zuvor. Gleichzeitig aber war der durchschnittliche Bürger noch nie so ahnungslos in Bezug auf die unsere „Lebensqualität" ermöglichende Technologie.

In einer Welt des Privateigentums und der Geheimhaltung, der Verschleierung von Verfahren und Materialien, der integrierten Schaltkreise und geheimen Formeln ist die Erkenntnisgewinnung weitgehend dem Geschäft untergeordnet. Physik- und Chemiestudenten lernen durch die Wiederholung klassischer Experimente, wie sich unsere Wissenschaft und unser Weltverständnis Schritt um Schritt entwickelt haben. Diese Zwischenschritte sind eine Voraussetzung für die Gewinnung neuen Wissens. Privatunternehmen haben viele davon praktisch der Gemeinfreiheit entzogen und damit Lücken in die Struktur unseres Wissens gerissen. Mit der fortgesetzten Verflechtung von akademischer Forschung und Geschäftswelt legen wir die Lösung vieler Weltprobleme ausdrücklich in die Hände von Unternehmen. Damit dürfen wir aber nur die Lösung von Problemen erwarten, die auch einen Profit versprechen. Keine Firma wird ein zerleg- und modifizierbares Radio auf den Markt bringen oder gar das Wissen über eines verbreiten, das man selbst bauen kann und das noch dazu ohne Batterie auskommt.

Kunst hat mit dem Aufstoßen von Fenstern zur Welt zu tun, aber man kann kein Fenster zu etwas aufstoßen, worüber man im Dunkeln gelassen wird. Das Vitruv'sche Ideal vom Künstler, der nach möglichst breitem Wissen strebt, bildet eine der Bedeutungsschichten von *Bacterial Radio*.

Im Frühjahr 2011 entwickelte ich einen flachen, in eine Petrischale passenden Schaltkreis. Dieser wurde dann als Negativrelief in Polydimethylsiloxan-Gel gegossen. In die Einbuchtungen wurden Zellen und Nährmedien eingebracht. Bei den Zellen handelte es sich um *E. Coli*-Bakterien, die mit einem Gen zur Kodierung von Silicatein[1], einem bei vielen Meeresorganismen vorkommenden Protein, modifiziert worden waren. Mithilfe dieses Proteins polymerisieren diese Organismen Siliziumoxid aus Meerwasser, woraus sie dann ihre fantastische Vielfalt an Endo- und Exoglasskeletten schaffen. Das für *Bacterial Radio* verwendete Silicatein-Gen wurde aus dem Meeresschwamm *Tethya aurantia* isoliert.

Silicatein ist ein „promiskes" Protein; wird das Nährmedium statt mit Siliziumoxid mit Metallsalzen oder Halbleitern angereichert, polymerisiert es diese an seiner Stelle. So bekamen die beiden in *Bacterial Radio* verwendeten Bakterienkulturen ihre elektrischen Eigenschaften mitgeteilt. Die bakteriellen Bestandteile des Schaltkreises wurden schließlich im Polydimethylsiloxan-Gel fixiert und durch Kontaktstifte und Drähte miteinander und mit seinen externen Komponenten Antenne, Erde und Kopfhörer verbunden.

1 W. E. G. Muller, S. Engel, X. Wang, S. E. Wolf, W. Tremel, N. L. Thakur, A. Krasko, M. Divekar, H. C. Schroder, „Bioencapsulation of living bacteria (Escherichia coli) with poly(silicate) after transformation with silicatein-a gene", in: *Biomaterials* 29 (2008), S. 771–779.

in a fantastic variety of forms. The silicatein gene used in the Bacterial Radio experiments was isolated from the marine sponge *Tethya aurantia*. Silicatein is a promiscuous protein, so that if growth media is starved of silica and instead provided with metal salts or semiconductors, then the protein will try to polymerize those materials instead. In this way, electrical characteristics were imparted to the two respective cultures of bacteria used with *Bacterial Radio*. Bacteria were fixed and immobilized in the PDMS gel. Pins and wires were used to connect elements of the gel-embedded circuit to each other and to external components such as the antenna, the ground and headphones.

1 W. E. G. Muller, S. Engel, X. Wang, S. E. Wolf, W. Tremel, N. L. Thakur, A. Krasko,M. Divekar, H. C. Schroder, „Bioencapsulation of living bacteria (Escherichia coli) with poly(silicate) after transformation with silicatein-a gene", in: Biomaterials 29 (2008), S. 771–779.

Bacterial Radio molecular biology was carried out with Tara Gianoulis and Ido Bachelet at the Wyss Institute for Biologically Inspired Engineering and George Church's lab in the Department of Genetics at Harvard Medical School.

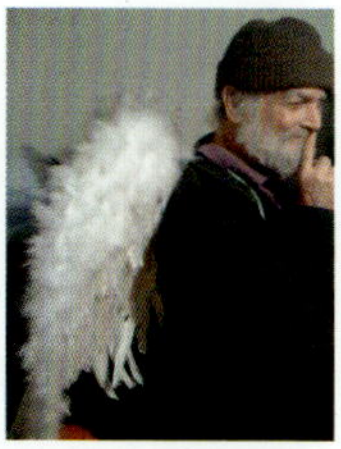

Joe Davis (US) is a research affiliate in the Department of Biology at MIT. He is an artist who has done extensive research in molecular biology and bioinformatics for the production of genetic databases and new biological art forms. He has also constructed sculptural installation pieces, laser teleoperator systems; and structural welding in mild steel. His teaching experience in the MIT graduate architecture program and in undergraduate painting and mixed media at the Rhode Island School of Design has informed his artistic practice. He has exhibited in the United States, Canada, and Europe.

Joe Davis (US) ist Forschungsmitglied am Department of Biology des MIT. Er ist ein Künstler, der umfangreiche Forschung in Molekularbiologie und Bioinformatik für die Entwicklung von genetischen Datenbanken und neuen biologischen Kunstformen betreibt. Er hat auch skulpturale Installationen und Laster-Teleoperator-Systeme konstruiert und mit Konstruktionsschweißung von Baustahl gearbeitet. Seine Unterrichtserfahrung am MIT Graduate Architecture Program und an der Rhode Island School of Design hat seine künstlerische Praxis mit beeinflusst. Seine Werke sind in den USA, Kanada und Europa gezeigt worden.

The Free Universal Construction Kit

Golan Levin, Shawn Sims

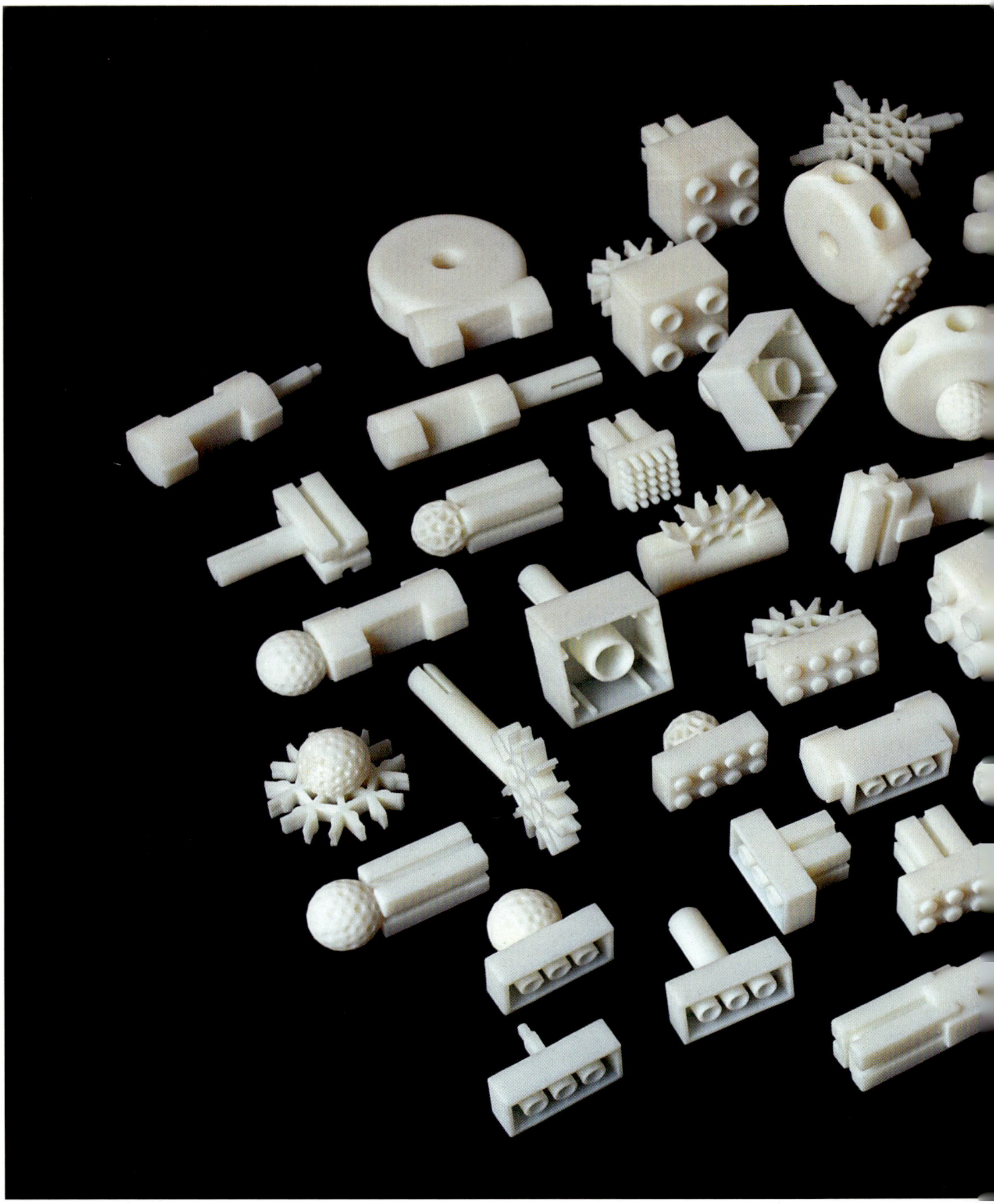

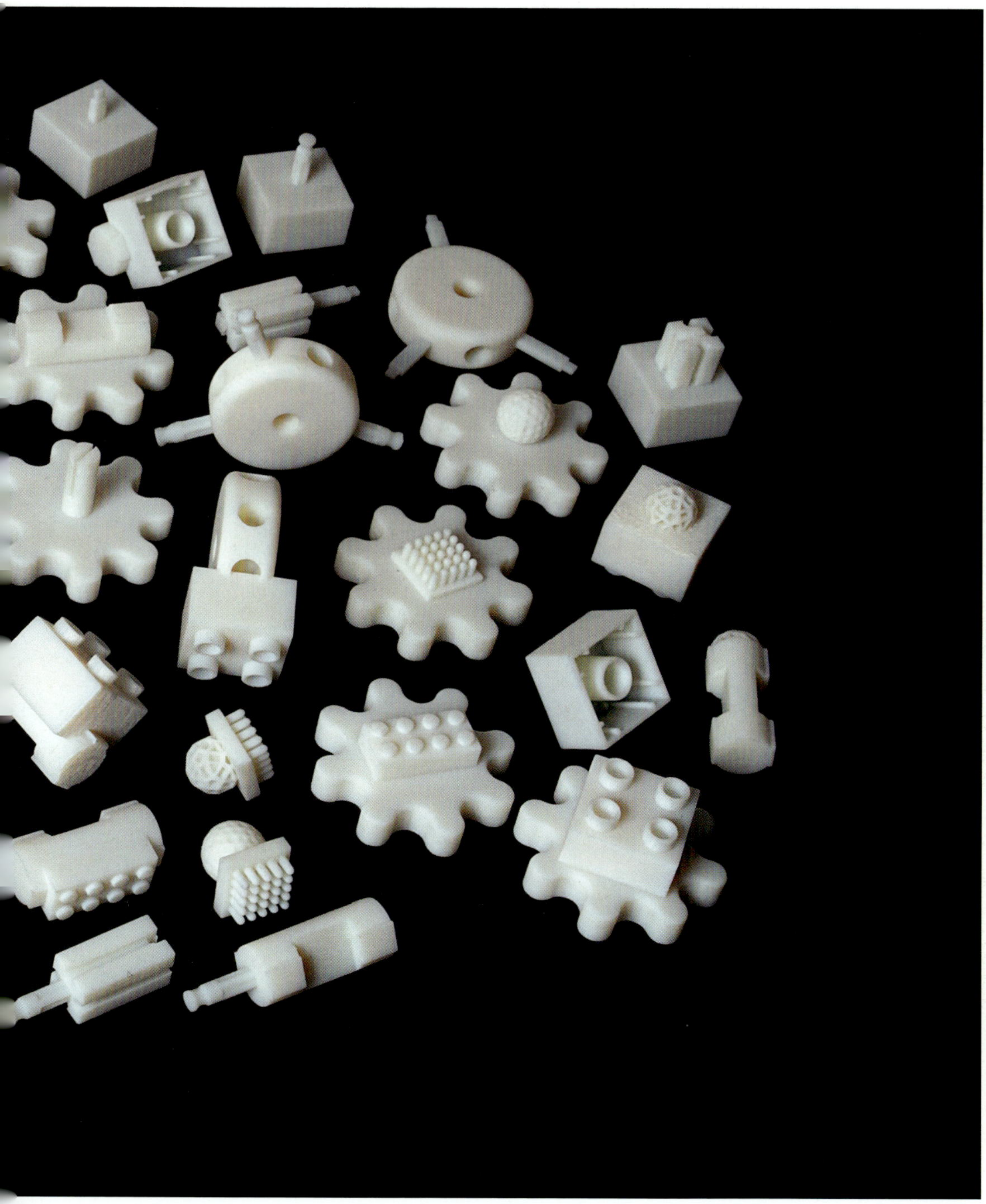

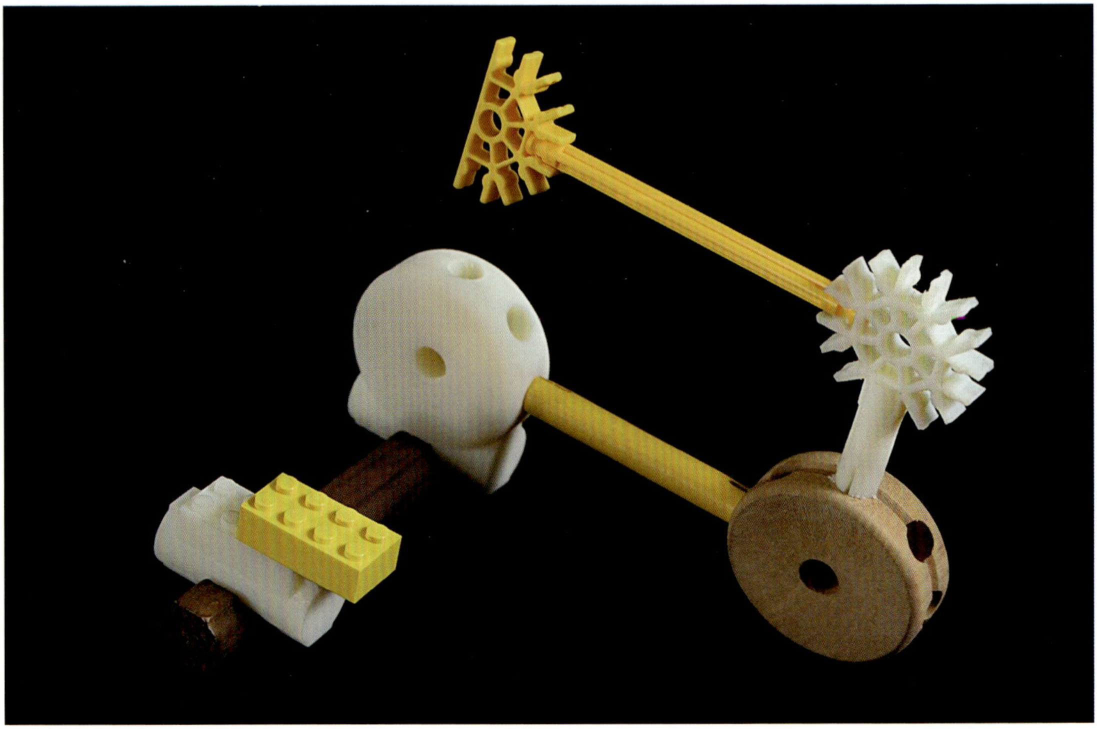

The Free Universal Construction Kit is a matrix of adapter bricks that enable complete interoperability between ten popular children's construction toys. By allowing any piece to join to any other, the kit encourages totally new forms of intercourse between otherwise closed systems. As with other grassroots interoperability remedies, the *Free Universal Construction Kit* uses proprietary protocols in order to provide a public service unmet, or unmeetable, by corporate interests. *The Free Universal Construction Kit* is not a product, but a provocation. It offers working adapters between Lego, Duplo, Fischertechnik, Gears! Gears! Gears!, K'Nex, Krinkles (Bristle Blocks), Lincoln Logs, Tinkertoys, Zome and Zoob—adapters that can be downloaded free from various sharing sites as a set of 3D models suitable for reproduction by personal manufacturing devices such as the Makerbot (an inexpensive, open-source 3D printer). In so doing, *The Free Universal Construction Kit* prompts consideration about intellectual property, open-source culture and reverse engineering as a mode of cultural practice.
Opening doors to new creative worlds is one major reason we created *The Free Universal Construction*

Das *Free Universal Construction Kit* ist eine Matrix aus Adapterstücken, die eine vollständige Interoperabilität zwischen zehn bekannten Spielzeugbaukästen herstellt. Da alle Bausteine miteinander verbunden werden können, ergeben sich vollkommen neue Formen des Austausches zwischen an sich geschlossenen Systemen. Wie auch andere Grassroot-Projekte zur Förderung von Interoperabilität nutzt das *Free Universal Construction Kit* proprietäre Protokolle zur Schaffung eines öffentlichen Angebots, das von kommerziellen Firmen nicht bedient wird – oder nicht bedient werden kann. *The Free Universal Construction Kit* ist kein Produkt, sondern eine Provokation. Es ist ein Satz funktionierender Adapterstücke zwischen Lego, Duplo, Fischertechnik, Gears! Gears! Gears!, K'Nex, Krinkles (Bristle Blocks), Lincoln Logs, Tinkertoys, Zome und Zoob. Die Adapterstücke können bei verschiedenen Internet-Tauschbörsen gratis in Form von 3D-Modellen heruntergeladen und mithilfe von persönlichen Fertigungsgeräten wie zum Beispiel Makerbot (einem kostengünstigen Open-Source-3D-Drucker) selbst hergestellt werden. Damit fördert das *Free Universal Construction Kit* auch die Reflexion über geistiges Eigentum, Open-Source-Kultur und Reverse Engineering als Kulturtechnik.

Das Erschließen neuer Gestaltungsmöglichkeiten war eines unserer Hauptmotive für die Schaffung des *Free Universal Construction Kit*. Zudem glauben wir, dass Kompetenz kein Wegwerfgut sein sollte; dass die hart erworbenen Fähigkeiten von Kindern im Umgang mit ihrem Spielzeug nicht jedes Jahr zu Weihnachten veralten sollten. Durch die Möglichkeit zur Verbindung verschiedener Spielzeugsysteme schafft das *Free Universal Construction Kit* auch neue Formen der „Vorwärtskompatibilität", die den Wert solcher Systeme über die gesamte Kindheit erhalten.

Wir hoffen, mit dem *Free Universal Construction Kit* zu zeigen, dass Reverse Engineering eine Bürgeraktivität sein kann: ein kreativer Prozess, bei dem jeder selbst die notwendigen Teile zur Überbrückung der Grenzen massenproduzierter kommerzieller Produkte entwickeln kann. Wir hoffen ferner, dass der Bausatz nicht nur dazu anregt, neue Gestaltungsideen umzusetzen, sondern auch unsere Beziehung zur materiellen Massenkultur – und den sich rasch entwickelnden Möglichkeiten für deren Anpassung an unsere Vorstellungskraft – zu überdenken.

The Free Universal Construction Kit umfasst knapp 80 Zweiweg-Adapter. Mit ihnen lässt sich jeder Baustein der unterstützten Spielzeugbaukästen (Lego, Tinkertoy, Fischertechnik usw.) mit jedem anderen verbinden. Die Dimensionen der verschiedenen Verbindungsstücke wurden mithilfe eines Messprojektors mit einer digitalen Auslesegenauigkeit von weniger als 2.54 Mikrometern nachgebaut. Durch diese Präzision ist gewährleistet, dass das *Free Universal Construction Kit* auch tatsächlich „funktioniert" und die Verbindungen zwischen den Adapterstücken und den kommerziellen Bauteilen gut greifen.

Der Bausteinsatz wurde von Golan Levin und Shawn Sims ersonnen und entwickelt und wird vom Free Art and Technology (F.A.T.) Lab und Synaptic Lab vertrieben. Die Entwicklung erfolgte mit Unterstützung des Frank-Ratchye Studio for Creative Inquiry an der Carnegie Mellon University. Das Projekt wird aus rechtlichen Gründen von Adapterz, LLC vertreten.

Kit. Another is that we believe expertise should not be disposable—and that children's hard-won creative fluency with their toys should not become obsolete each Christmas. By allowing different toy systems to work together, *The Free Universal Construction Kit* makes new forms of "forward compatibility" possible, extending the value of these systems across the life of a child.

In producing *The Free Universal Construction Kit*, we hope to demonstrate a model of reverse engineering as a civic activity: a creative process in which anyone can develop the necessary pieces to bridge the limitations presented by mass-produced commercial artifacts. We hope that the kit will not only prompt people to create new designs but, more importantly, to reflect on our relationship with material mass-culture—and the rapidly evolving ways in which we can better adapt it to our imaginations.

The Free Universal Construction Kit comprises nearly 80 two-way adapters. These allow each of the different construction toys (Lego, Tinkertoy, Fischertechnik etc.) to interface with any of the other supported systems. Prior to modeling, the dimensions of the various toy connectors were reverse-engineered with an optical comparator fitted with a digital read-out accurate to less than one ten-thousandth of an inch (0.0001in., or 2.54 microns). The resulting precision ensures that *The Free Universal Construction Kit* "actually works", enabling tight snap-fits between custom and commercial components.

The Kit was conceived and developed by Golan Levin and Shawn Sims, and released through the Free Art and Technology (F.A.T.) Lab and Synaptic Lab collectives. The Kit was developed with support from the Frank-Ratchye Studio for Creative Inquiry at Carnegie Mellon University and is represented, for legal purposes, by Adapterz, LLC.

The Free Art and Technology (F.A.T.) Lab (US) is an arts collective dedicated to enriching the public domain through the research and development of creative technologies and media, often at the intersection of open source and popular culture. **Golan Levin** has released works through F.A.T. Since 2010. Synaptic Lab (US), founded and directed by **Shawn Sims**, is a research and design group dedicated to the creation of new technologies [and/for/with] form. Sims is a graduate of the CMU Computational Design Lab, from which he received a Master's in Tangible Interaction Design. **Das Free Art and Technology (F.A.T.) Lab** (US) ist ein Kollektiv, das sich der Bereicherung der Public Domain durch die Erforschung und Entwicklung kreativer Technologien und Medien – meist an Schnittstelle von Open-Source- und Populärkultur – widmet. **Golan Levin** vertreibt seine Arbeiten seit 2010 über das F.A.T. Das von **Shawn Sims** gegründete und geleitete Synaptic Lab (US) ist eine Forschungs- und Designgruppe, die sich der Entwicklung neuer Technologien [und/für/mit] Form widmet. Sims studierte am CMU Computational Design Lab, wo er einen Master in Tangible Interaction Design machte.

Moon Goose Analogue: Lunar Migration Bird Facility

Agnes Meyer-Brandis

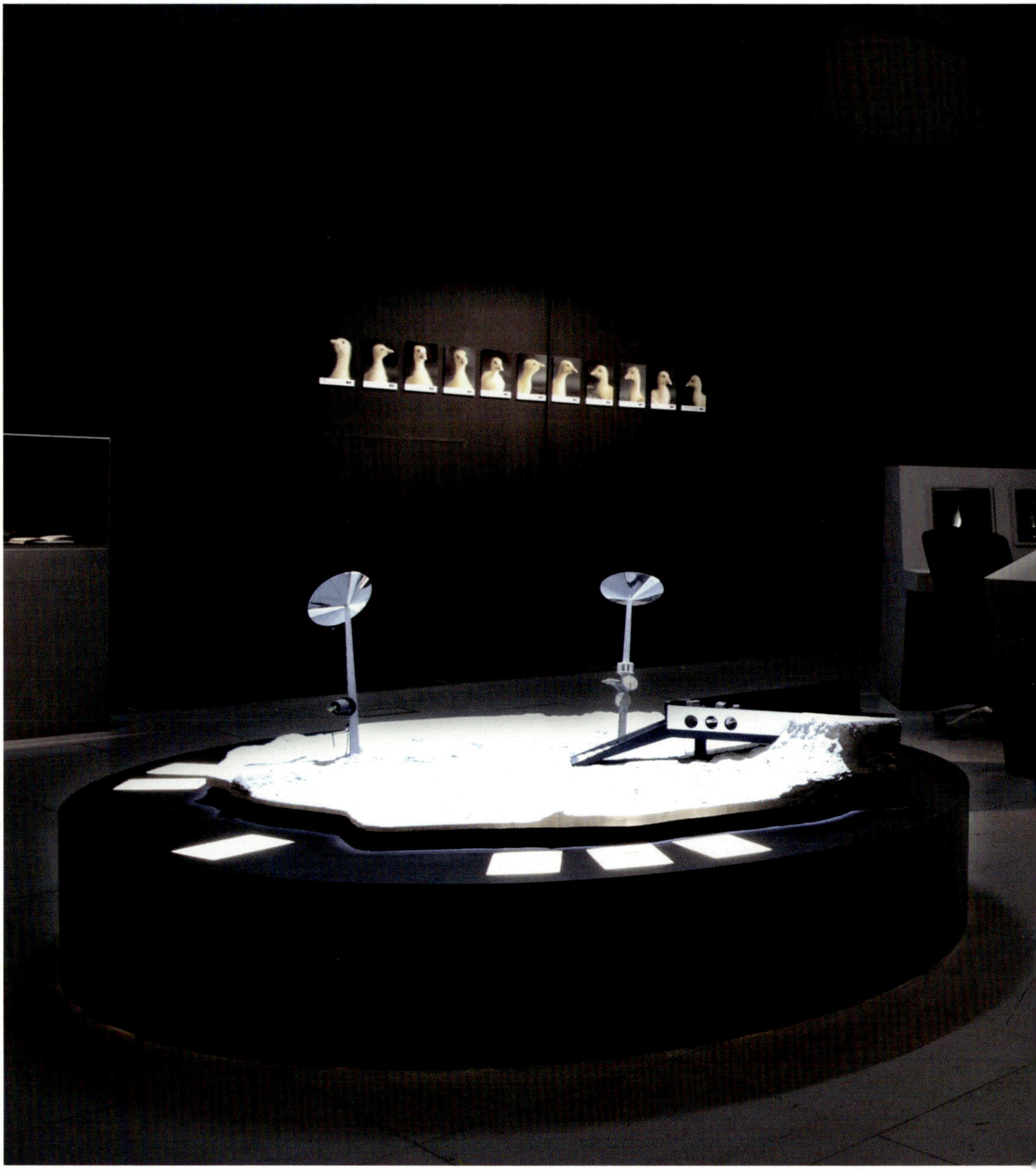

Agnes Meyer-Brandis's poetic-scientific investigations weave fact, imagination, storytelling and myth, past, present and future. In the project *Moon Goose Analogue: Lunar Migration Bird Facility* she develops an ongoing narrative based on *The Man in the Moone*, by Bishop

In ihren poetisch-wissenschaflichen Untersuchungen verwebt Agnes Meyer-Brandis Wirklichkeit und Erfindung, Geschichte und Mythos, Vergangenheit, Gegenwart und Zukunft. In *Moon Goose Analogue: Lunar Migration Bird Facility* entwickelt sie eine fortlaufende Erzählung, die an Bischof Francis Godwins Buch *The Man in the*

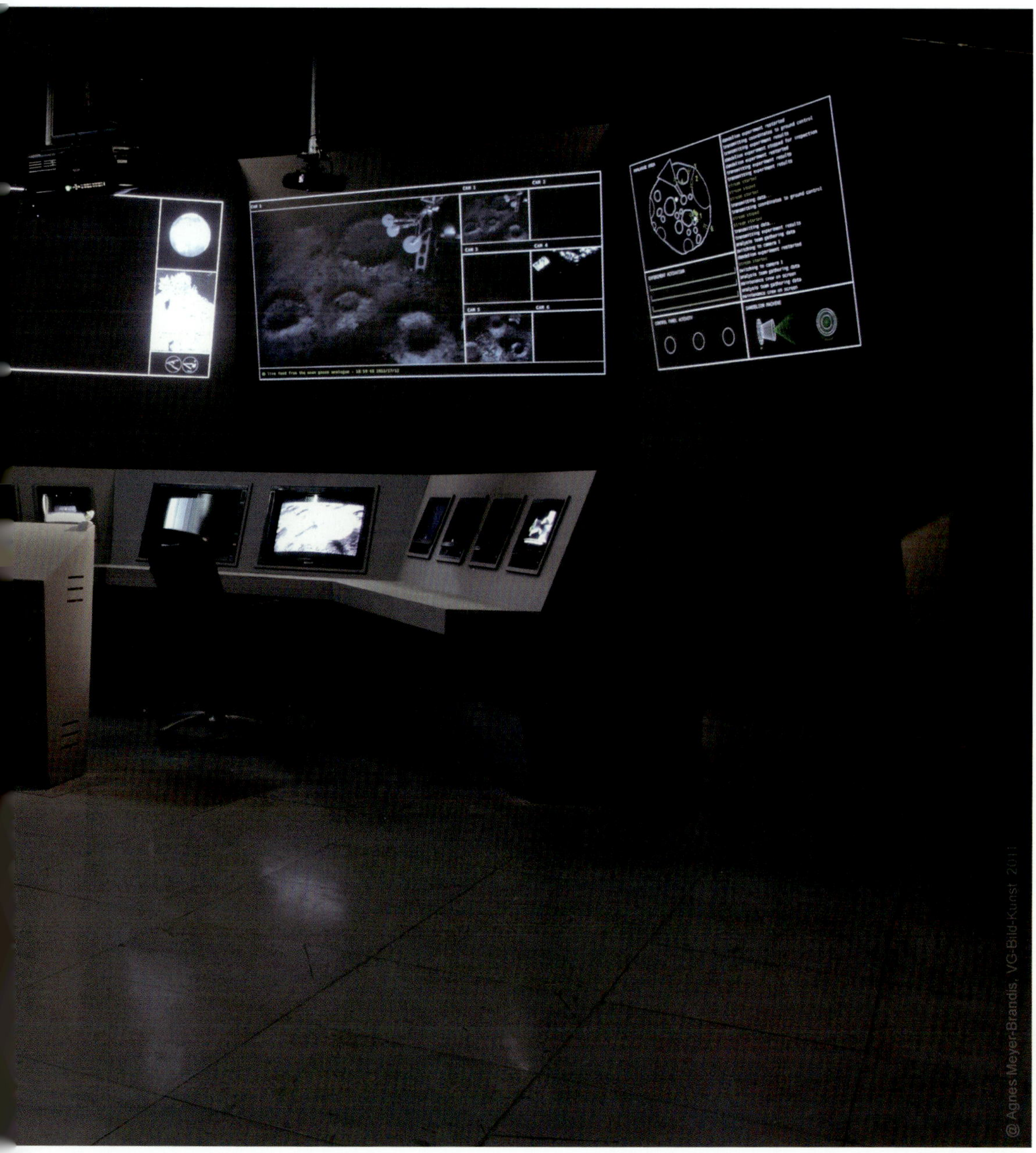

© Agnes Meyer-Brandis, VG-Bild-Kunst 2011

Moone (dt.: *Der fliegende Wandersmann nach dem Mond*) anknüpft, dessen Held eine Mondreise in einem von „Mondgänsen" gezogenen Gefährt unternimmt. Meyer-Brandis hat diese Vorstellung aktualisiert, indem sie elf Mondgänse großgezogen, ihnen Astronautennamen* gegeben, auf sich als Gänsemutter geprägt, mit

Francis Godwin, in which the protagonist flies to the moon in a chariot towed by "moon geese". Meyer-Brandis has actualized this concept by raising eleven moon geese, giving them astronauts' names,* imprinting them on herself as goose-mother, training them to fly and taking them on

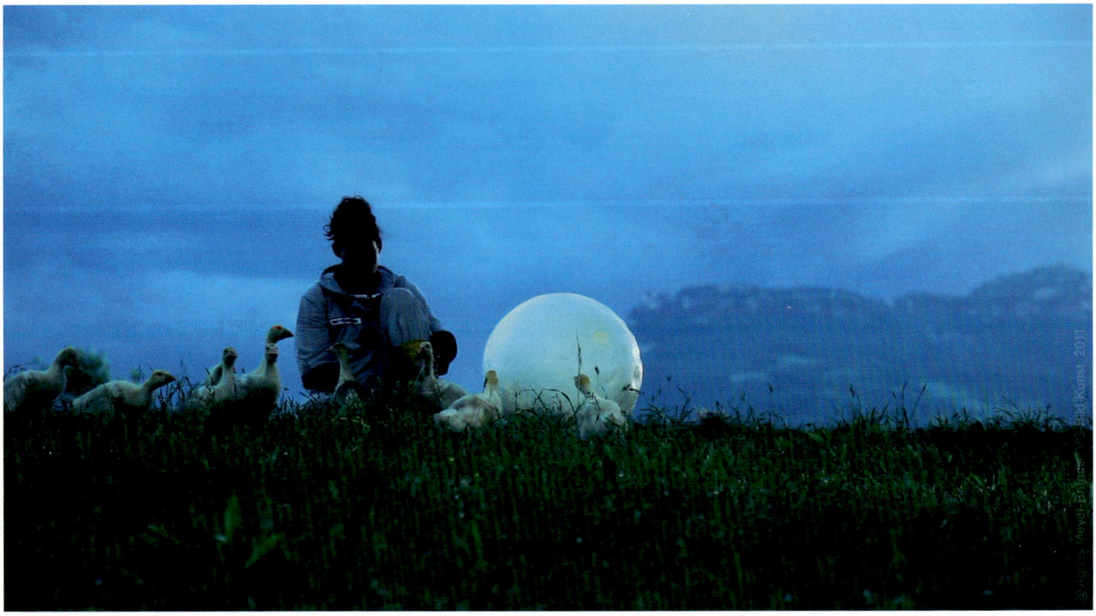

expeditions and housing them in a remote moon-analog habitat.

An analog is a rehearsal for living in space. At various remote facilities around the world astronauts are practicing for the psychological challenges humans can face living away from earth. Meyer-Brandis's remote analog habitat simulates the conditions of the moon and will be accessed and operated from Meyer-Brandis's control room installation within the gallery, where instructional videos, photographs and showcases of the goose eggshells and footprints will be displayed. The viewer can see and interact with the geese here in the control room in real time while the artist encourages you to explore the margins of reality, in that liminal space where scientific data becomes elegiac data.

Meyer-Brandis develops the contested history of Godwin's original fiction—posthumously and pseudonymously published in 1603 as the supposedly genuine account of the travels of Domingo Gonsales. She weaves a narrative that explores the observer's understanding of the fictitious and the factual, with a nod to notions of the believably absurd.

* Neil, Svetlana, Gonzales, Valentina, Friede, Juri, Buzz, Kaguya-Anousheh, Irena, Rakesh, Konstantin-Hermann

ihnen das Fliegen trainiert, Expeditionen unternommen und sie in einem Mond-„Analog", einem den Mond nachbildenden Lebensraum, untergebracht hat.

Ein „Analog" ist ein Trainingsgelände für das Leben im All. Astronauten bereiten sich an solchen über die Erde verteilten und doch weltentrückten Standorten auf die psychischen Herausforderungen vor, die den Menschen beim Leben außerhalb der Erde erwarten. Meyer-Brandis' Mond-„Analog" simuliert die lunaren Lebensbedingungen und wird von ihrer Kontrollrauminstallation in der Galerie aus gesteuert und dem Publikum zugänglich gemacht. Filme und Fotos sowie Vitrinen mit den Eierschalen und Fußabdrücken der Gänse komplettieren das Ausstellungsangebot. Die Besucher können vom Kontrollraum aus in Echtzeit mit den Gänsen interagieren und dabei die Grenzen der Realität ausloten: die Schwelle, an der wissenschaftliche Daten in elegische umschlagen.

Meyer-Brandis spinnt Godwins obskure Geschichte weiter, die 1603 – posthum und unter Pseudonym – als angeblich wahrer Reisebericht eines Domingo Gonsales erschien. Ihre Erzählung stellt – in einer ironischen Hommage an das Glaubhafte im Absurden und das Absurde im Geglaubten – unsere Auffassung von Wahrheit und Dichtung auf den Prüfstand.

* Neil, Svetlana, Gonzales, Valentina, Friede, Juri, Buzz, Kaguya-Anousheh, Irena, Rakesh, Konstantin-Hermann

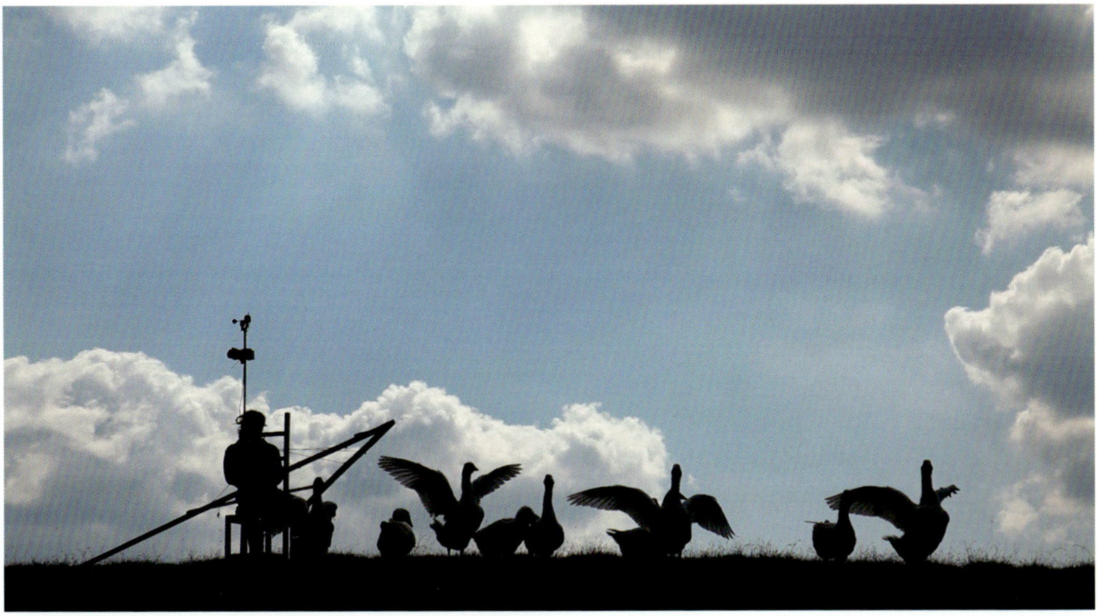

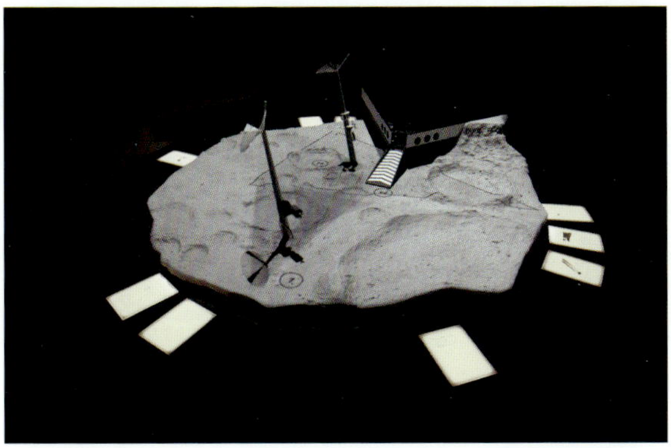

Moon Goose Analogue: Lunar Migration Bird Facility was commissioned by The Arts Catalyst and FACT Liverpool. Supported by the Arts Council England, in partnership with Pollinaria.

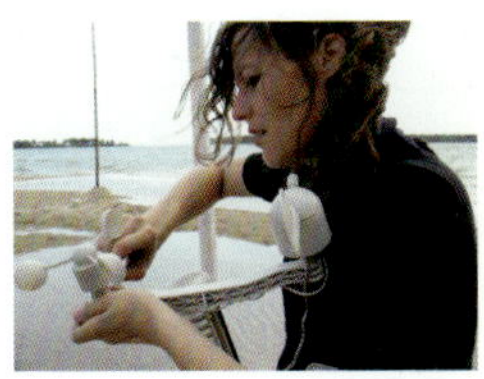

Agnes Meyer-Brandis (DE), born 1973, studied mineralogy for a year before transferring to the Art Academy in Maastricht, the Düsseldorf Art Academy and the Cologne Media Art Academy. Her background is in both sculpture and new media art. Exhibited worldwide, her work is at the experimental edge of art and science, exploring the zone between fact and fiction. Agnes Meyer-Brandis is the founder of the Forschungsfloß FFUR / Research Raft for Subterranean Reefology, a small institute whose chief aim is to explore and confirm subterranean phenomena and unknown life-forms. Since 2007 her focus of investigation has moved to a higher plane with its connected realities. *http://www.ffur.de*

Agnes Meyer-Brandis (DE), geboren 1973, studierte ein Jahr Mineralogie, ehe sie zunächst auf die Kunstakademie Maastricht, dann die Kunstakademie Düsseldorf und schließlich die Kunsthochschule für Medien in Köln wechselte. Ihr künstlerischer Hintergrund umfasst sowohl die Bildhauerei wie die Medienkunst. Ihre weltweit gezeigten Arbeiten bewegen sich an der Grenze von Kunst und Wissenschaft, wobei sie sich speziell für den Zwischenbereich zwischen Faktum und Fiktion interessiert. Agnes Meyer-Brandis ist die Gründerin von „FFUR / Forschungs Floß für unterirdische Riffologie“, eines kleinen Instituts zur Erforschung und Verifizierung unterirdischer Phänomene und unbekannter Lebensformen. Seit 2007 hat sie ihren Forschungsschwerpunkt in höhere Regionen verlegt. *http://www.ffur.de*

2.6g 329m/s

Jalila Essaïdi

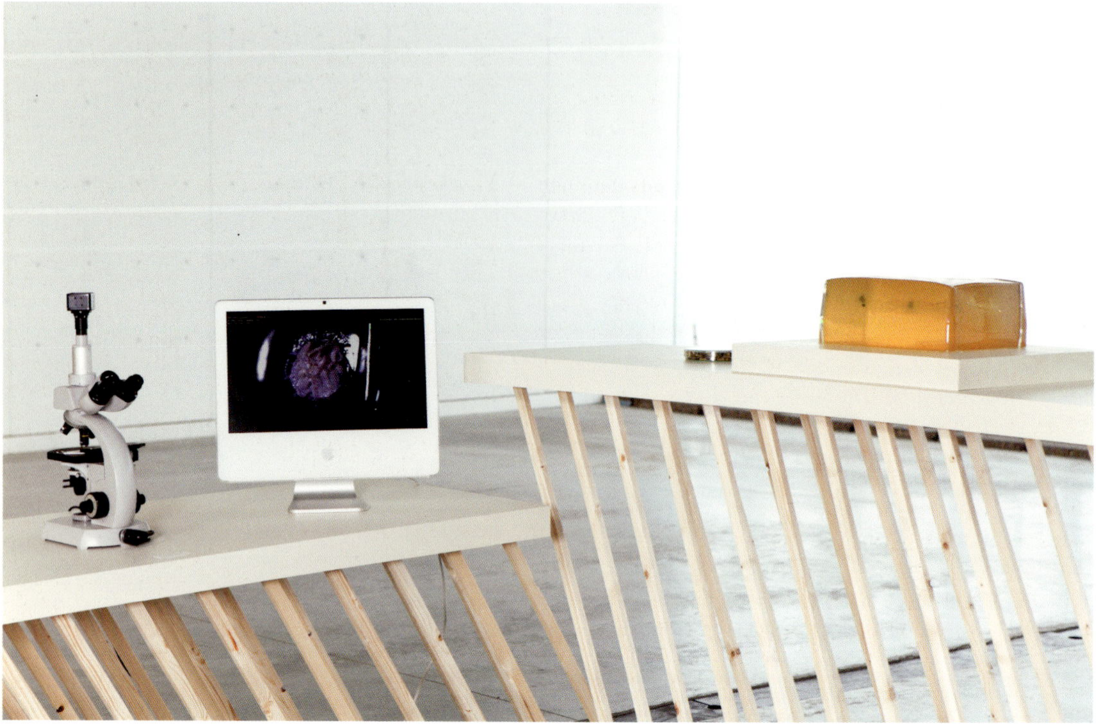

The name of this project, *2.6g 329m/s*, refers to the performance standard for bulletproof vests: exploring boundaries, by piercing barriers. 2.6g 329m/s are the maximum weight and velocity of a .22-calibre rifle bullet from which a Type 1 bulletproof vest should protect you.

Spider-silk thread is relatively much stronger than steel and can even be made by a living being. Woven, it would be capable of resisting the impact of a bullet, much like a bee hitting a spider's web. If human skin could produce this thread, would we be protected from bullets? Jalila Essaïdi takes the acid test: by implanting transgenic spider silk in human skin and letting a bullet do its work.

By using a bulletproof matrix of spider silk produced by transgenic goats in human skin, Essaïdi wants to explore the social, political, ethical and cultural issues surrounding safety in a world with access to new biotechnologies—issues that arise from the ancient human desire for invulnerability. It is legend that all of Achilles' body was invulnerable except his heel. Will we in the near future, due to biotechnology, no longer need to descend from a divine bloodline in order to posses traits like invulnerability?

Schon mit seinem Namen – dem Standardgrenzwert für kugelsichere Westen – verweist dieses Projekt auf das Ausloten von Grenzen und das Durchbrechen von Barrieren. 2.6g 329m/s steht für Gewicht und Geschwindigkeit einer Kleinkaliberpatrone, denen eine kugelsichere Weste vom Typ 1 standhalten muss.

Spinnenfäden sind vergleichsweise stärker als Stahl und werden noch dazu von einem Lebewesen erzeugt. Würden sie entsprechend verwoben, könnten sie dem Einschlag einer Kugel widerstehen, so wie ein Spinnennetz einer

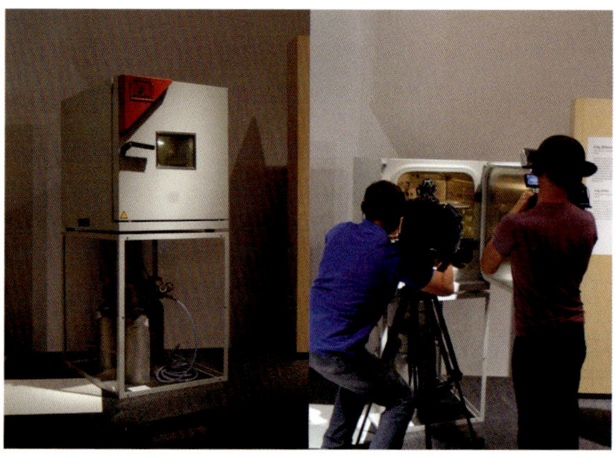

darauf landenden Biene. Wären wir vor Kugeln geschützt, wenn die menschliche Haut einen solchen Faden produzieren könnte? Jalila Essaïdi unterzieht diese Frage buchstäblich einer Feuerprobe, indem sie transgene Spinnenfäden in menschliche Haut einpflanzt und eine Kugel darauf abfeuert.

Am Beispiel einer kugelsicheren Matrix aus Spinnenfäden in einer von transgenen Ziegen erzeugten menschlichen Haut untersucht Essaïdi die sozialen, politischen, ethischen und kulturellen Fragen, die sich aus dem Zugang zu den neuen Biotechniken für das Thema Sicherheit ergeben – Fragen, die letztlich auf den uralten Wunsch nach Unverwundbarkeit zurückgehen. Der Legende nach verfügte ja Achilles bis auf seine Ferse über diese Eigenschaft. Werden wir dank der Biotechnologie schon in naher Zukunft auch ohne göttliche Abstammung unverwundbar sein?

Essaïdi zeigt mit ihrer Arbeit, dass Sicherheit im weitesten Sinn des Wortes etwas Relatives ist, wie schon der Begriff „kugelsicher" sagt. Die von ihr gezüchtete Haut konnte zwar einige verlangsamte Kugeln abfangen, bei voller Geschwindigkeit aber wurde sie durchschlagen. Gleichwohl ist das Experiment geglückt. Es hat Diskussionen über Ethik und Ästhetik, Nutzen und Notwendigkeit ausgelöst – und darüber, welche Form von Sicherheit überhaupt gesellschaftlich wünschenswert ist.

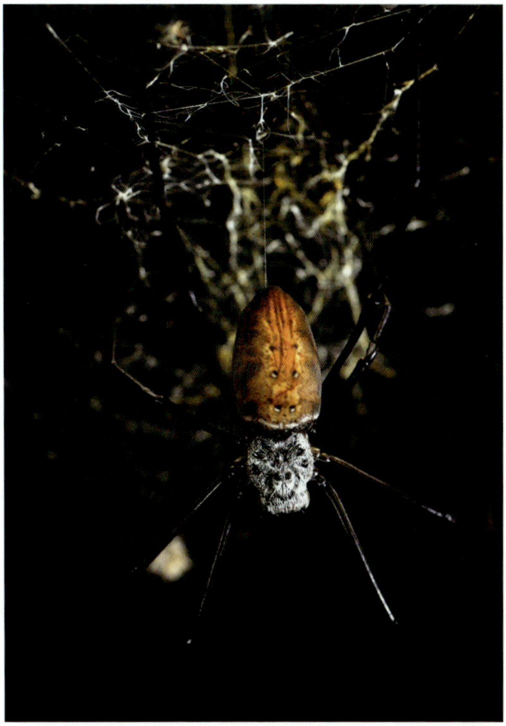

With this work Essaïdi wants to show that safety in its broadest sense is a relative concept, hence the term bulletproof. The work did stop some partly slowed bullets but not one at full speed. But even with the skin pierced by the bullet, the experiment is still a success. It leads to conversations about aesthetics and ethics, usefulness and necessity, and about which form of safety would benefit society.

2.6g 329m/s was made possible by the Designers & Artist 4 Genomics Award. The project suggests interesting materials research that goes beyond the expertise of Jalila Essaïdi and which utilizes the expertise of the Forensic Genomics Consortium, the Netherlands, Utah State University, Leiden University Medical Center, the Netherlands Forensic Institute and other institutions.

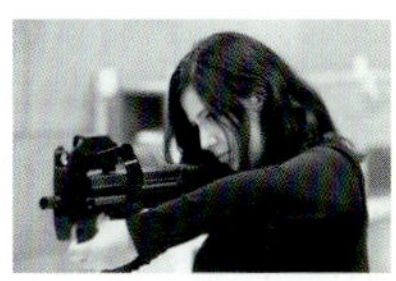

Jalila Essaïdi (NL), born in 1980, is a bio-artist who uses biology and the life sciences as an artistic medium. Her artwork is about the recognition of the transience of matter and a human desire to keep and hold. In her work, she embeds this desperate race against time by using living or organic matter that is capable of decay or the product of decay. Jalila earned her bachelor's in art at Fontys Hogescholen in 2009. She studied bio-art (honors) at Leiden University from 2008 to 2010, and is currently completing her master's in art at Alliantie Kunsten Fontys Zuyd. In 2011 she was a recipient of the Designers & Artists 4 Genomics Award. **Jalila Essaïdi** (NL), geboren 1980, ist eine Künstlerin, die im Medium Biologie und Life Sciences arbeitet. Im Zentrum ihrer Arbeiten steht die Vergänglichkeit der Materie und der menschliche Wunsch nach Dauer. Durch ihre Arbeit mit organischem Material, das dem Verfall preisgegeben oder selbst ein Zerfallsprodukt ist, integriert sie diesen verzweifelten Wettlauf gegen die Zeit in die eigene Arbeit. Jalila studierte Kunst an der Fontys Hogescholen (Bachelor, 2009) und Bio-Kunst (Honors) an der Universität Leiden. Derzeit macht sie gerade ihren Master an der Alliantie Kunsten Fontys Zuyd. 2011 erhielt sie den Designers & Artists 4 Genomics Award.

50 Aktenkilometer: Ein begehbares Stasi-Hörspiel

Rimini Protokoll, Deutschlandradio Kultur

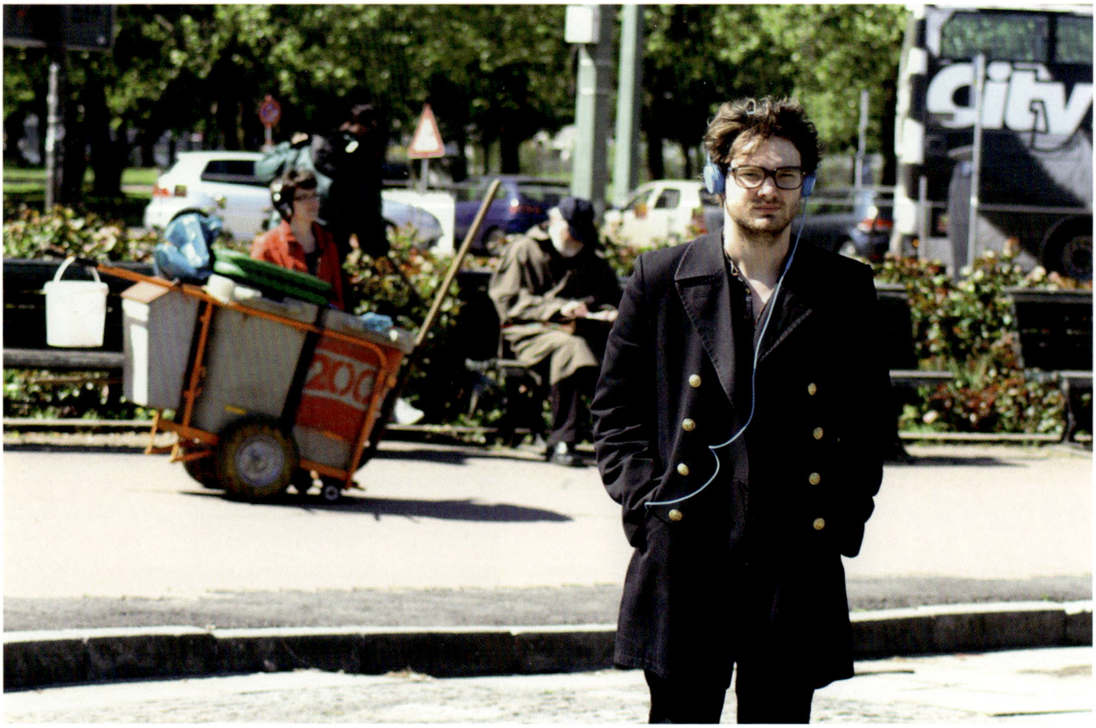

Radioortung–Radio Plays for Walkers is a newly developed series of radio plays for mobile phones, designed and produced by Deutschlandradio Kultur. These radio plays tell stories that are non-linear and linked to locations, as well as also reflecting the latest mobile technology, in order to create an awareness of the everyday, often hidden interventions into the listener's everyday life through localization, data collection and storage. The radio plays can be experienced within the city using the free, downloadable *Radioortung* app (Android) as well as online on the interactive map (dradio-ortung.de).

Radioortung – Hörspiele für Selbstläufer ist eine neue, von Deutschlandradio Kultur entwickelte und produzierte Hörspielreihe für Mobiltelefone. Die Hörspiele sind nichtlineare, standortbezogene Geschichten, die gleichzeitig die neueste Mobilfunktechnologie reflektieren, um beim Hörer ein Bewusstsein dafür zu schaffen, wie Lokalisierung, Datensammlung und -speicherung tagtäglich und meist versteckt in sein Leben eingreifen. Die Hörspiele können mittels einer herunterladbaren Android-basierten Gratis-App direkt im Stadtraum, aber auch online auf einer interaktiven Karte gehört werden.

Radioortung wollte ausdrücklich kein Format für weitere elektronische Schnitzeljagden oder ortsbezogene Romanadaptionen sein. Der Hörspielabteilung ging es vielmehr um eine künstlerische Auseinandersetzung mit den neuen Mobiltechnologien, bei der diese selbst zu einem Mitspieler in der jeweiligen Geschichte werden.
Das zweite Projekt in der Reihe *50 Aktenkilometer: Ein begehbares Stasi-Hörspiel* wurde vom Theaterkollektiv Rimini Protokoll realisiert. Über 50 Aktenkilometer stehen im Zentralarchiv der Bundesbehörde für Stasi-Unterlagen. Protokolle über Ereignisse, Zusammenkünfte, Gespräche. Aus diesem Material entwickelten Rimini Protokoll ein ortsspezifisches Hörspiel, bei dem sich einstige Überwachungsopfer am Schauplatz der Überwachung ihrer Akte annähern. An die hundert Menschen wurden befragt und vergegenwärtigen sich oder rekonstruieren am Mikrofon den jeweiligen Überwachungsvorgang. Wie hören sich Protokolle der Observation für den damals Observierten am Ort ihrer Aufnahme an und wie schnell wird man vom vorerst Unbeteiligten zum aktiven Mitspieler? Aber auch die Fußgänger und Online-Besucher müssen sich mit der Rolle der Überwachungsinstanz auseinandersetzen, wenn sie in der Stadt unterhalb der Stadt nach den Audioportalen suchen. Denn sie werden bei ihrem Gang durch dieses hörbare subjektive Archiv selbst beobachtet.

The idea behind *Radioortung* was explicitly not to recreate a geo-caching event or a location-based adaptation of a novel. Rather, the radio-drama department wanted to react artistically to the new mobile technologies in such a way that the technology itself becomes a player within the individual stories.
The second project in the *Radioortung* series, *50 Kilometres of Files: A Walk-In Stasi Radio Drama*, was produced by the Rimini Protokoll theatrical collective. More than 50 kilometers of files are stored in the central archives of the federal commission for the Stasi records. Protocols of actions, meetings, discussions. From this material, Rimini Protokoll developed a site-specific radio play, in which the subjects of former observations approach their files at the site of observation. About a hundred people were interviewed and recall or reconstruct observations on microphone. What do the observation protocols sound like at the site where they were recorded for those who were observed at the time, and how quickly can one switch from being uninvolved to becoming an active player? Dealing with the role of the surveillance authority is a matter for the strollers and online visitors themselves—in search of the audio portals in the city beneath the city. And while the listeners walked through this audible, highly subjective archive, they were being observed.

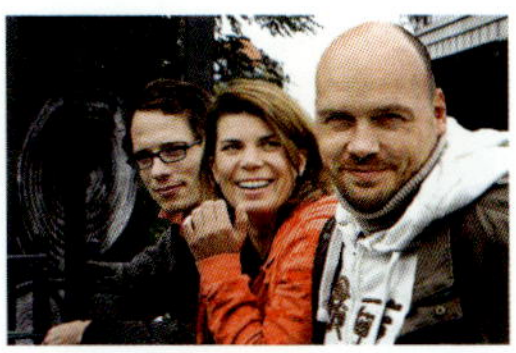

Rimini Protokoll (DE). Helgard Haug (1969), Stefan Kaegi (1972) and Daniel Wetzel (1969) work together (in various combinations) under the name of Rimini Protokoll. They are recognized as being among the leaders and creators of the theatre movement known as "Reality Trend" (Theater der Zeit), which has exerted a powerful influence on the alternative theatre scene. Each project begins with a concrete situation in a specific place and is then developed through an intense exploratory process. They have attracted international attention with their dramatic works, which take place in that colorful zone between reality and fiction. **Rimini Protokoll** (DE). Helgard Haug (1969), Stefan Kaegi (1972) und Daniel Wetzel (1969) arbeiten in unterschiedlichen Kombinationen unter dem Label Rimini Protokoll. Sie gelten als die „Protagonisten und Begründer eines neuen Reality Trends auf den Bühnen" (Theater der Zeit), der die junge Theaterszene geprägt hat. Alle ihre Projekte gehen von einer konkreten Situation an einem konkreten Ort aus und werden dann in einem intensiven Forschungsprozess erarbeitet. Mit ihren Theaterarbeiten, die in der bunten Zone zwischen Realität und Fiktion angesiedelt sind, haben sie international Aufmerksamkeit erregt.

Dream Water Wonderland

Hörner / Antlfinger

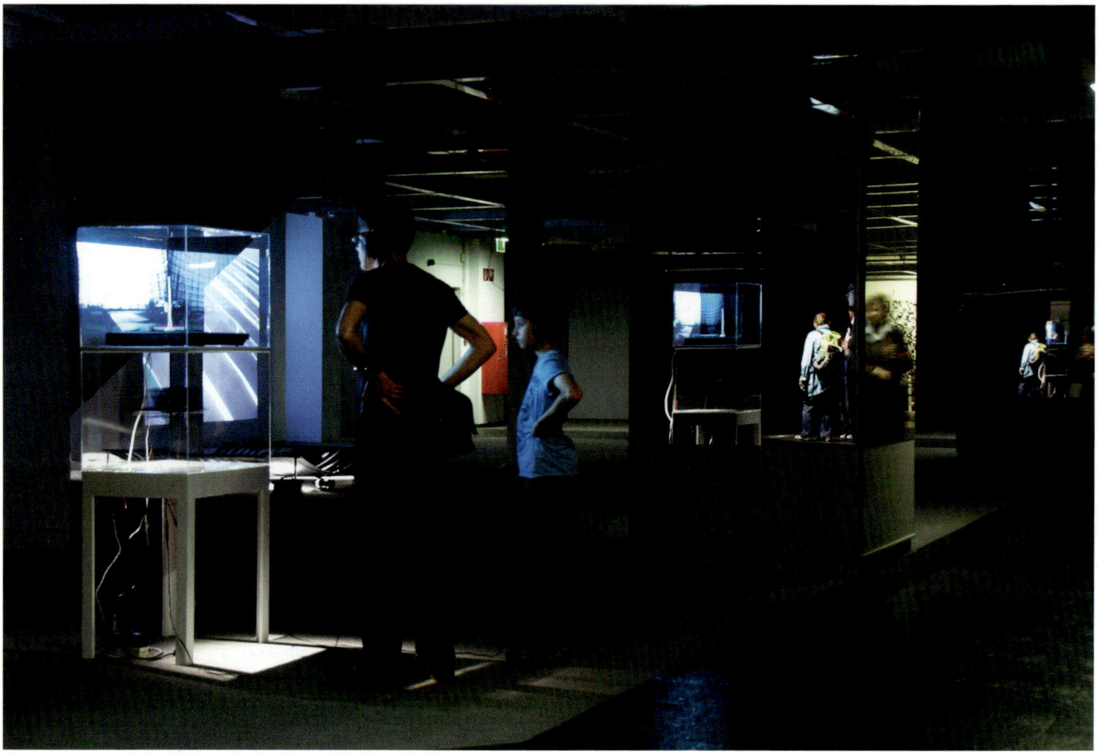

Since the advent of nuclear power in Germany, two sites have become synonymous with the end of a technological feasibility fantasy: the Kalkar fast-breeder reactor, which was never brought on line, and the Asse II atomic waste storage plant. *Dream Water Wonderland* transforms the legacy of the nuclear industry into a dream of half-life durations.
The installation consists of two Plexiglas cubes placed on top of each other. The upper level houses a futuristic record player from the 1970s. A crystalline tower rises from the center pin. Downwards, through the player itself, into the lower cube, a delicate, scale-model 3D print of the underground Asse II mine rotates like a radar beam.
The first sequence of the video projected on the rear panel shows the Kalkar cooling tower, which is now an amusement park. In the second sequence the camera flies inside the tower on a large carousel along the walls and over the edge of the tower into the sky. When the audience comes closer to the installation a sensor gives a signal to the record player, which then autonomously starts playing. The sound inside the cubes, an echolike

Seit Einführung der Atomenergie in Deutschland sind zwei Standorte zum Inbegriff für das Ende der technischen Machbarkeitsfantasie geworden: der schnelle Brüter in Kalkar, der nie im Betrieb genommen wurde, und das atomare Endlager Asse II. *Dream Water Wonderland* überführt das Erbe der Nuklearindustrie in einen Traum von Halbwertzeiten.
Die Installation besteht aus zwei übereinander stehenden Plexiglaskuben. Im oberen befindet sich ein futuristisch gestalteter Plattenspieler aus den 1970er Jahren, von dessen Zentrierstift ein kristallförmiger Turm aufragt. Im unteren dreht sich, angetrieben vom Plattenspieler, ein zarter maßstabgeteuer 3D-Druck der Mine Asse II wie ein Radarstrahl im Kreis.
Auf einer Videowand im Hintergrund ist zuerst eine Sequenz vom Kühlturm der mittlerweile zum Vergnügungspark umgewandelten Anlage in Kalkar zu sehen. In einer zweiten Sequenz fliegt dann die Kamera auf einem großen, innerhalb des Turms befindlichen Karussell zunächst die Wände entlang und dann über den Rand des Turms gen Himmel. Nähern sich Besucher der Installation, aktiviert ein Sensor den Plattenspieler, und die darauf liegende Traumplatte wird abgespielt. Der Ton in den Kuben,

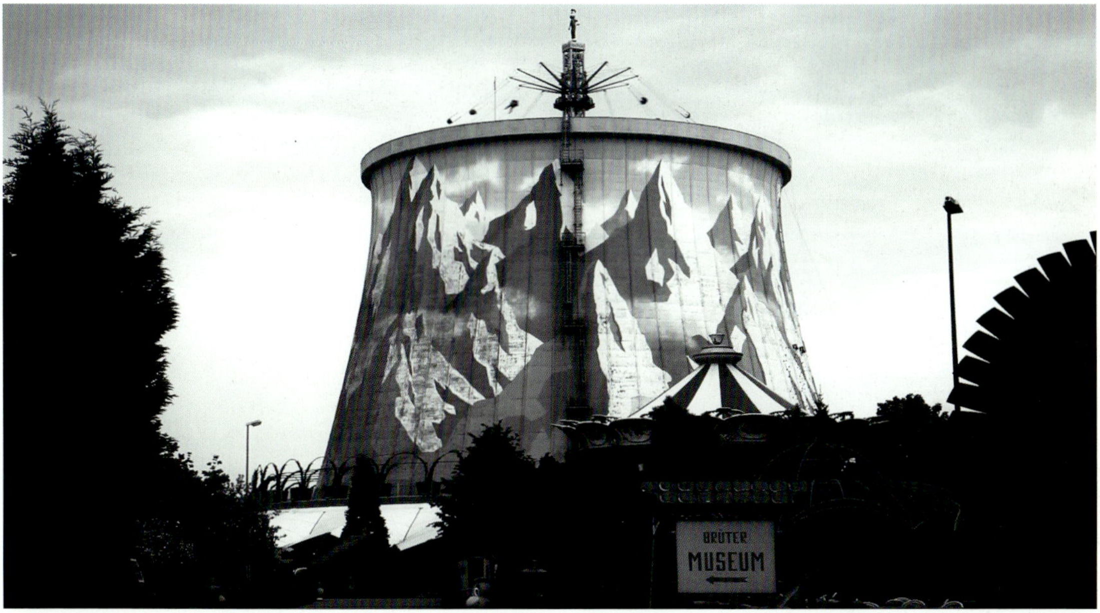

eine hallige „Atmo" aus dem Inneren des Kühlturms und eine Stimme von der auf dem Plattenspieler laufenden Platte, ist über davor hängende Kopfhörer mithörbar. Die Stimme erzählt einen Traum über ein eigenartiges, blaues, vogelartiges Wesen, das sich bei Familien einnistet und unglaubliche Mengen Strom verbraucht.

"Atmosound" of the tower and the dream record playing on the record player, can be heard on headphones hanging in front of the cubes. It tells a dream about a strange, birdlike, blue creature that is made to take up residence with families but which needs incredible amounts of electricity.

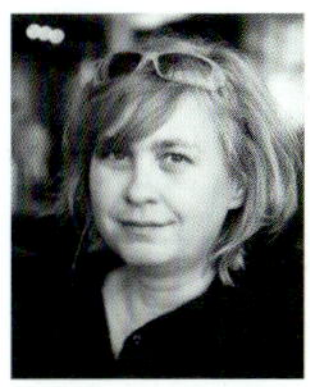
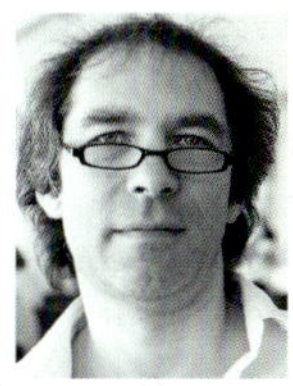

Ute Hoerner (DE), born 1964, studied sculpture at the Stuttgart Academy of Fine Arts with Prof. Inge Mahn and Prof. Alfred Hdrlicka. 1997-1999 XObject Space, Laboratory of Arts and New Media, Dusseldorf, 1998 festival director of Videonale 8 at the Bonner Kunstverein (together with Judith Ruzicka). 1999-2008, professor of media art at the Burg Giebichenstein University of Arts and Design, Halle. Since 2009, professor of media art at the Academy of Media Arts Cologne. **Mathias Antlfinger** (DE), born 1960, studied fine arts in teaching at the Stuttgart Academy of Fine Arts and mathematics at Stuttgart University. 1991-96, studies in sculpture and cybernetics at the Dusseldorf Academy of Fine Arts. 1999-2005, artistic member of staff, Media Art Department of Burg Giebichenstein, University of Arts and Design, Halle. Since 2009, professor of media art at the Academy of Media Arts Cologne. Hörner/Antlfinger have been an artist couple since the early 1990s. In their retro futuristic practice, they often combine ancient technologies of consciousness with new media and juxtapose personal visions with their collective counterpart.

Ute Hoerner (DE), geboren 1964, studierte Bildhauerei bei Inge Mahn und Alfred Hdrlicka an der Akademie der Bildenden Künste Stuttgart. 1997-1999 XObject Space, Labor für Kunst und neue Medien in Düsseldorf, 1998 Festivalleitung der Videonale 8 gemeinsam mit Judith Ruzicka. 1999-2008 Professorin für Kunst und Medien an der Burg Giebichenstein Hochschule für Kunst und Design, Halle. Seit 2009 Professorin für Medienkunst an der Kunsthochschule für Medien Köln. **Mathias Antlfinger** (DE), geboren 1960, studierte Kunsterziehung an der Akademie der bildenden Künste Stuttgart bei Sotirios Michou und Jürgen Brodwolf sowie Mathematik an der Universität Stuttgart. 1990-95 Studium freie Kunst und Kybernetik an der Kunstakademie Düsseldorf. 1999-2005 künstlerisch-wissenschaftlicher Mitarbeiter im Fachgebiet Kunst und Medien an der Burg Giebichenstein, Hochschule für Kunst und Design, Halle. Seit 2009 Professor für Medienkunst an der Kunsthochschule für Medien Köln. Hörner/Antlfinger arbeiten seit den frühen 1990er Jahren als Künstlerpaar. In ihrem retrofuturistischen Schaffen verbinden sie oft alte Bewusstseinstechnologien mit neuen Medien und persönliche Visionen mit ihren kollektiven Pendants.

Game Border

Jun Fujiki

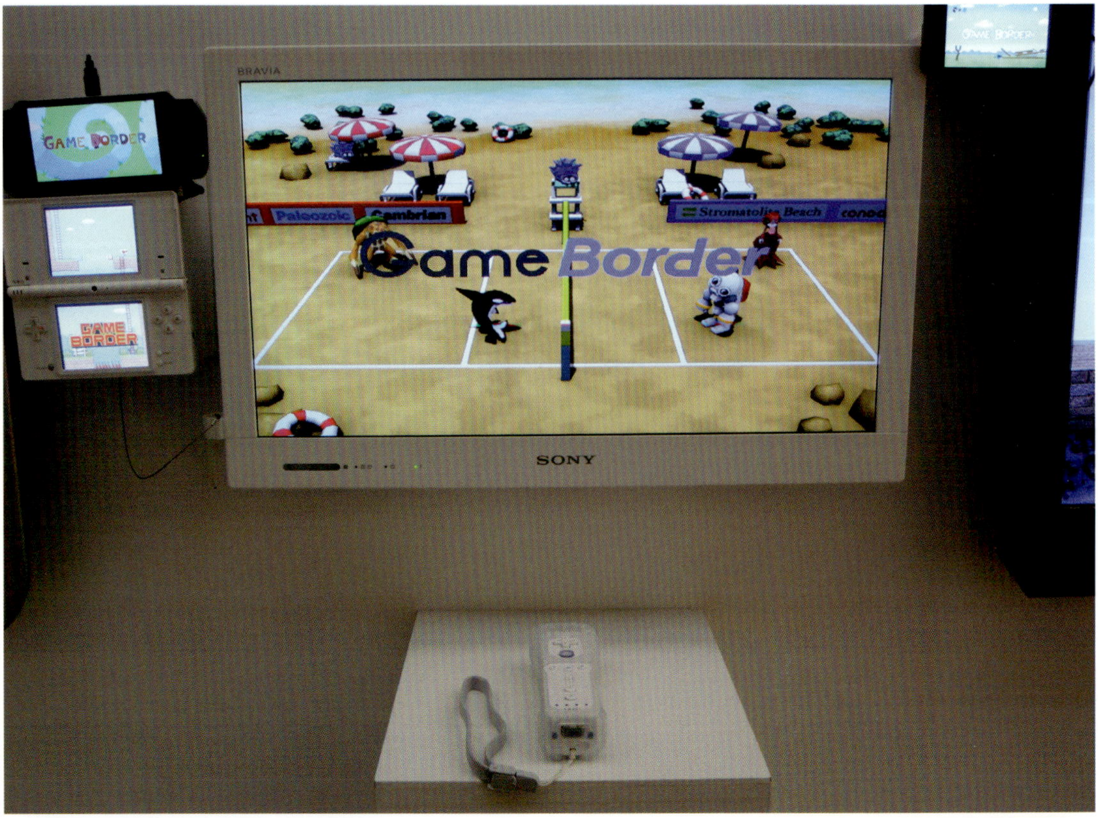

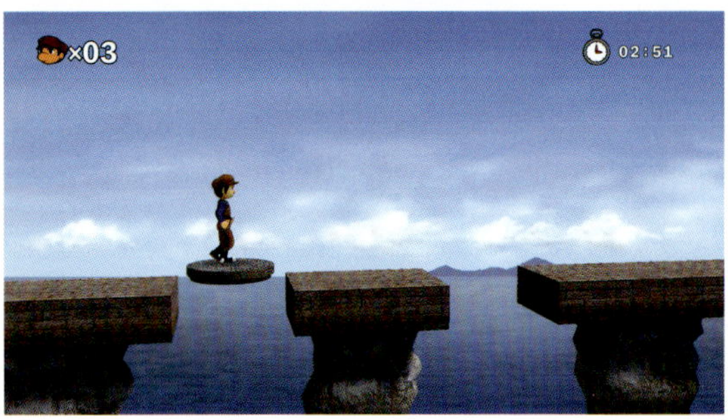

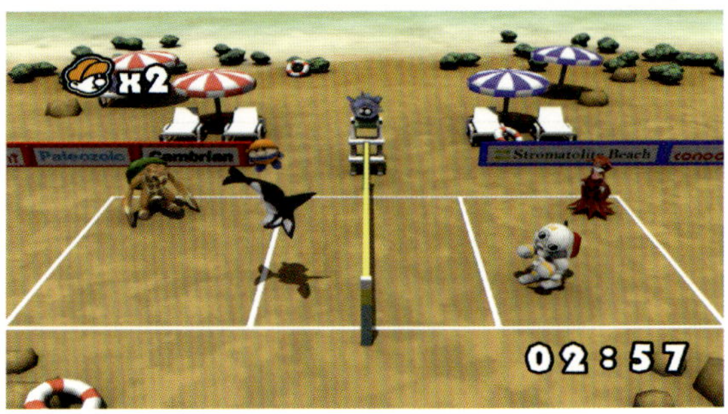

Co-produced with: A1, K, okuoku, Keisuke Ikeda, Tsutomu Ohya, Tomoyuki Suehisa, Keiko Segawa, Yusuke Tsuboi, Akiko Watanabe, Shoichi Isida, Cezan Iseda, Takuma Hayakawa, Tomoki Hayashida, Takeshi Okuya, Nobuyuki Mukai & Nao Yamawaki

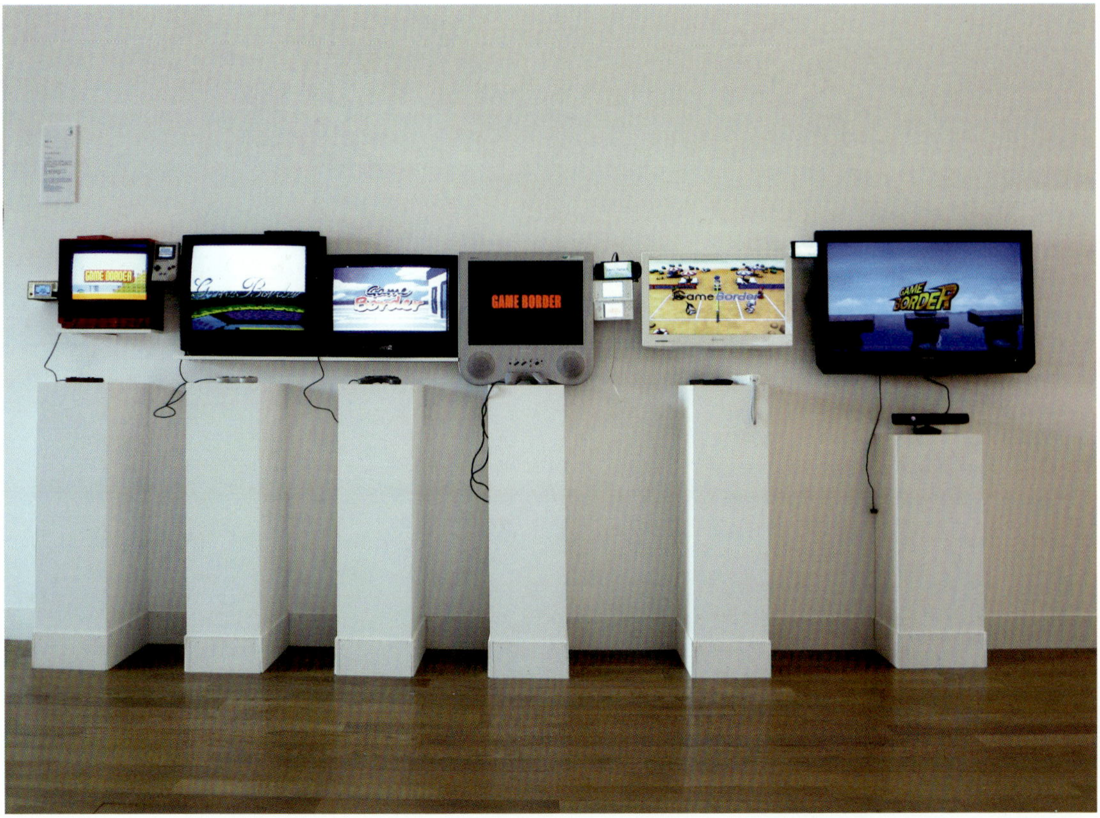

Game Border ist ein Spiel, das einem das Gefühl vermittelt, von einem Spielgerät zum nächsten springen und damit die Grenzen der Hardware überwinden zu können. Zudem fordert es den Spieler dazu heraus, die verschiedenen Spiele möglichst nahtlos miteinander zu verbinden. Wobei es nicht nur physische Grenzen zu überwinden gilt, sondern auch gesellschaftliche und solche der Wahrnehmung.

Game Border is a game that one can enjoy with the feeling of jumping from one game machine to another, transcending the borders of hardware. In addition, this is a challenge to connect the borders of various games seamlessly. The borders here are not limited to the physical, but include the borders of recognition and society.

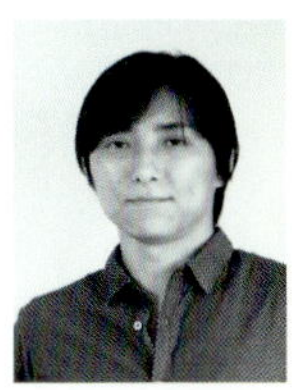

Jun Fujiki (JP), born in 1978, has a doctorate in design. He is a researcher for both the International Media Research Foundation and Presto (Precursory Research for Embryonic Science and Technology). He is looking for new relations between expression and principle and examining the laws of humans and of physics.
Jun Fujiki (JP), geboren 1978, promovierte in Design. Er arbeitet als Forscher für die International Media Research Foundation und für Presto (Precursory Research for Embryonic Science and Technology). Seine Arbeitsschwerpunkte sind neue Beziehungen zwischen Ausdruck und Prinzip sowie Gesetzmäßigkeiten von Mensch und Physik.

Irrational Computing

Ralf Baecker

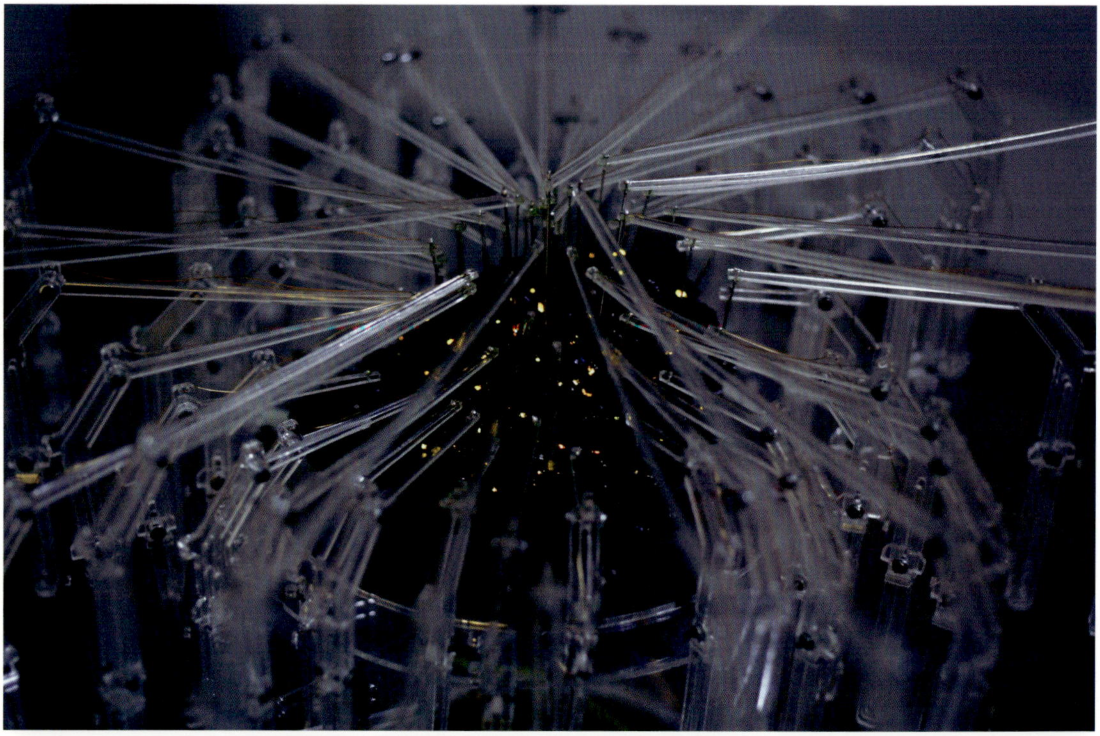

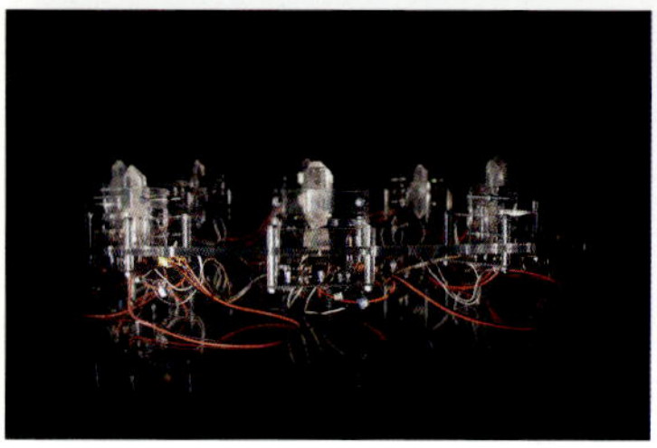

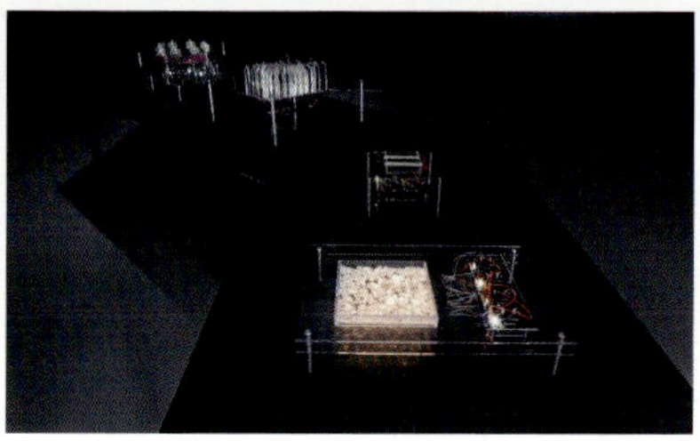

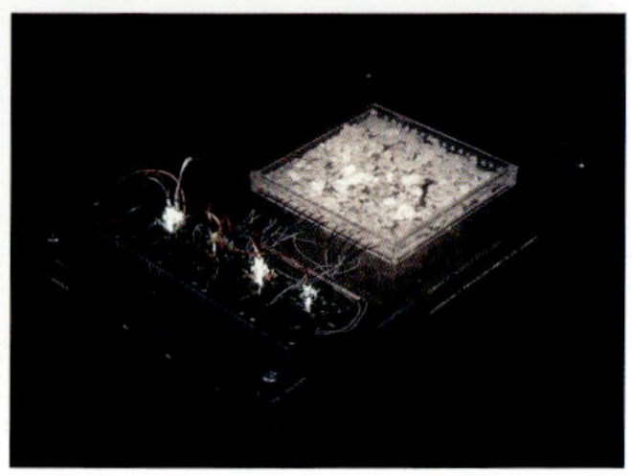

Irrational Computing investigates the material, aesthetics and potential of digital processes. The basic raw materials of our surrounding information technology are semiconductor crystals such as silicon, quartz or silicon carbide, which, thanks to today's advanced microtechnology and extremely sophisticated procedures, are processed into transistors or integrated circuits (IC), with the materiality of modern microprocessors having long since ceased to be graspable. The extreme miniaturization and the black-box set-up elude visual interpretation. The installation's circuit runs counter to the developments in information technology, representing the system in a dimension that is enlarged many times over.

Irrational Computing untersucht Material, Ästhetik und Potenzial digitaler Prozesse. Die uns umgebende Informationstechnologie besteht aus Halbleiterkristallen wie Silikon, Quarz oder Siliziumkarbid. Heute aber werden diese Materialien durch extrem aufwändige Verfahren zu Transistoren und integrierten Schaltkreisen verarbeitet, so dass sie bei modernen Mikroprozessoren praktisch überhaupt nicht mehr zu fassen sind. Die extreme Miniaturisierung und der Black-Box-Aufbau entziehen sich jeder visuellen Deutung. Der Schaltkreis von *Irrational Computing* stellt eine Gegenbewegung zu dieser Entwicklung dar und zeigt das System in einer Vergrößerung um ein Vielfaches.

Die Installation besteht aus fünf miteinander verbundenen Modulen, die die vielfältigen elektrischen und mechanischen Eigenschaften von Kristallen und

Mineralien nutzen und in ihrer Vernetzung eine Art primitiven makroskopischen Signalprozessor bilden. Die verwendeten Kristalle sind entweder direkt der Natur entnommen, aus industriellen Abfallprodukten gewonnen oder speziell für den Zweck gezüchtet worden. Ein Siliziumkarbidkristall wird an mehreren Punkten durch Elektroden zum Leuchten angeregt (LED), sodass eine Art Display entsteht, das von den durch die anderen Module erzeugten Datenströme angesprochen wird. Dabei wird der Kristallbrocken auch zum Klangerzeuger, da die elektrischen Impulse die Oberfläche des Kristalls verformen und ihn so zum Schwingen bringen. Über Lautsprecher werden diese mikroskopischen Schwingungen für das Publikum hörbar gemacht.
Digitale Systeme sind in ihrer Funktion logisch und rational konzipiert. Auf der ihnen zugrunde liegenden physikalischen bzw. elektrotechnischen Ebene (Kristalle mit Halbleitereigenschaften) beruhen sie jedoch auf quantenmechanischen, also statistischen, nicht genau vorhersagbaren Vorgängen. So gesehen stellt die moderne Computertechnik gewissermaßen ein gezähmtes oder domestiziertes Chaos dar. Genau dieses Paradoxon thematisiert Ralf Baecker, wenn er in dieser Arbeit das Material, aus dem das globale digitale Netzwerk entstanden ist, auf seine Ästhetik abklopft. *Irrational Computing* soll nicht „funktionieren" – es sucht nach der Poesie an der Grenze zwischen „Präzision" und „Chaos".

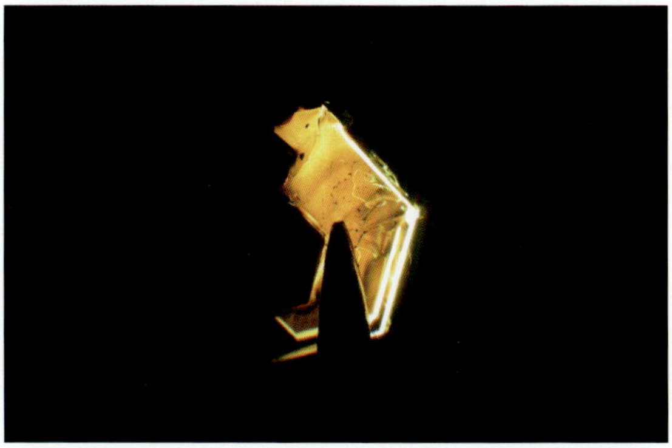

The installation consists of five interlinked modules that use the varied electrical and mechanical particularities and characteristics of crystals and minerals and, through their networking, form a kind of primitive macroscopic signal processor. The crystals used are either taken directly from nature, from industrial waste products or have been especially cultivated for the purpose. A silicon-carbide crystal, for example, is made to light up at numerous points with the help of electrodes (LED). A kind of display, which is targeted by the data flows generated by other modules, appears on the piece of crystal. At the same time, the crystal functions as a sound generator, since the electrical impulses change the surface of the crystal, causing it to vibrate. Loudspeakers make these microscopic reverberations audible for visitors.
The function of digital systems is conceived logically and rationally. The lowest physical or electrotechnical level (crystals with semiconductor properties), however, is based on quantum-mechanics, i.e. statistical or unpredictable processes. Modern computer technology has thus, so to speak, tamed and domesticated the chaotic. In his work, Ralf Baecker comments on this paradox by examining the aesthetics of the materials from which a global digital network has developed. *Irrational Computing* is not supposed to "function"—its aim is to search for the poetic elements on the border between "accuracy" and "chaos."

A production by Dock e.V. in cooperation with the Ernst Schering Foundation Berlin

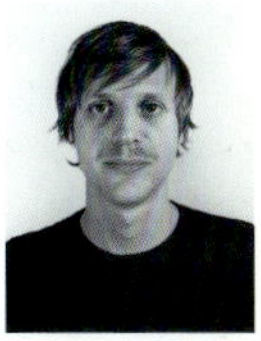

Ralf Baecker (DE); born 1977, studied computer science at the University of Cologne and media art at the Academy of Media Arts in Cologne (diploma 2007). 2007/2008, artistic staff at the Bauhaus University, Weimar. 2010/2011, teaching position at the University of the Arts Bremen. In his work Bäcker examines the relation of material and mind in the context of digital media. His installations and machines are critical investigations of our expectations of technology. **Ralf Baecker** (DE); geboren 1977, studierte Computerwissenschaft an der Universität Köln und Medienkunst an der Kunsthochschule für Medien Köln (Diplom 2007). 2007/2008, künstlerischer Mitarbeiter an der Bauhaus-Universität Weimar. 2010/2011 Dozent an der Hochschule für Künste Bremen. In seinen Arbeiten sondiert Baecker das Verhältnis von Geist und Materie im Kontext der digitalen Medien. Seine Installationen und Maschinen sind kritische Untersuchungen unserer Erwartungen gegenüber der Technik.

Maquila Región 4 (MR4)

Amor Muñoz

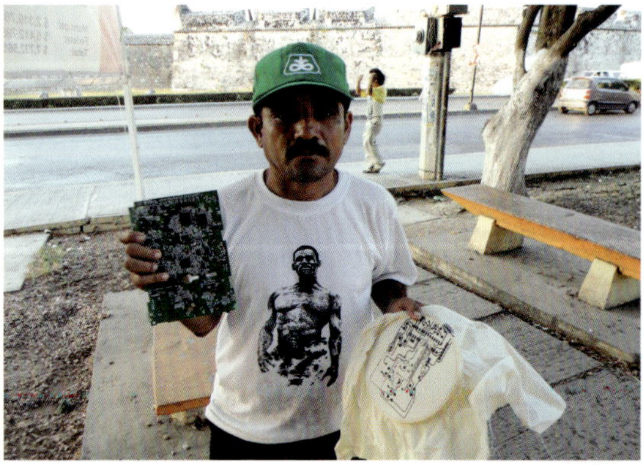

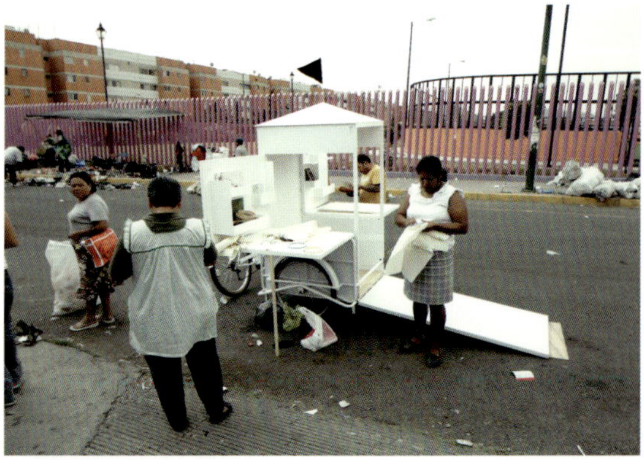

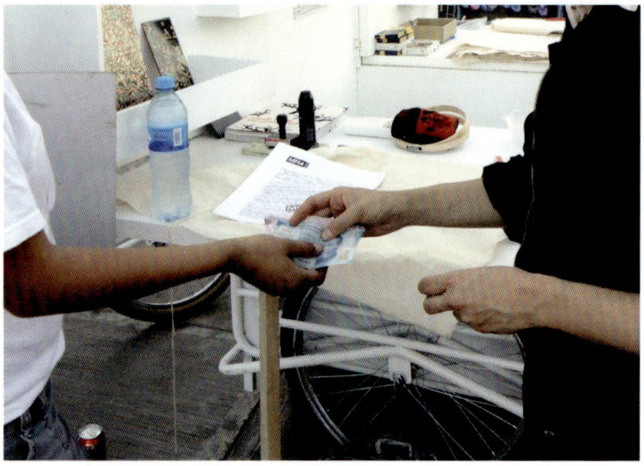

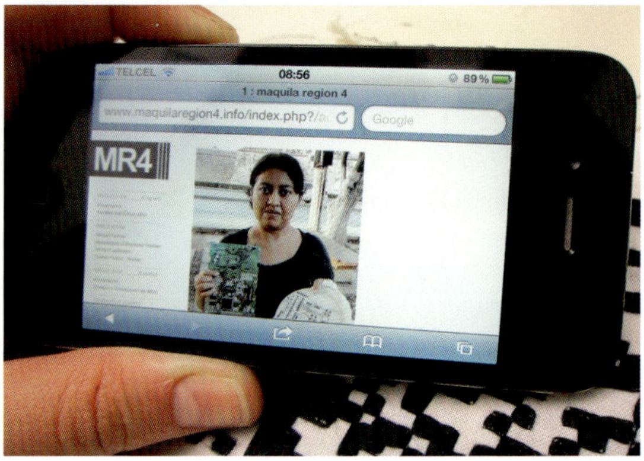

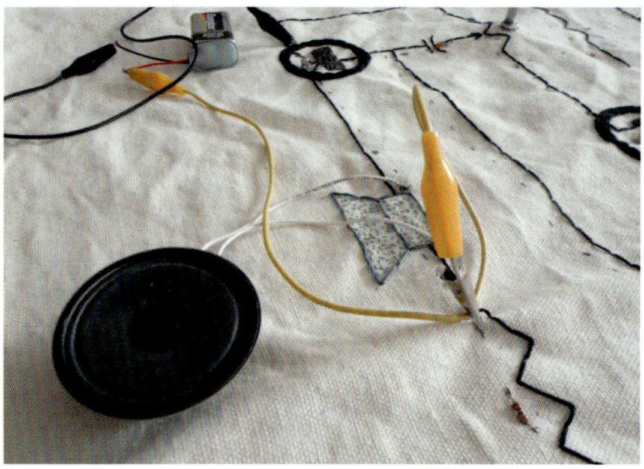

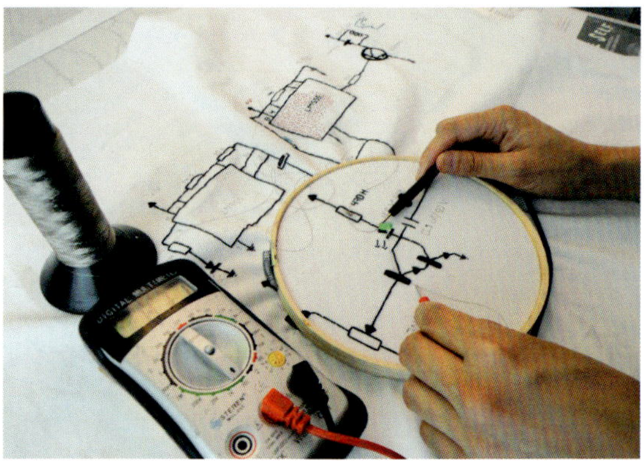

Maquila Región 4 (MR4) is a performative intervention in the labor landscape of marginal areas of Mexico. It is a mobile factory for the manufacture of electronic-textile artworks. This nomadic workshop travels to poor areas of Mexico offering the American minimum wage ($7.00 per hour,

Maquila Región 4 (MR4) ist ein performativer Eingriff in die Arbeitsverhältnisse mexikanischer Randgebiete. Es handelt sich um eine mobile Fertigungsstätte zur Herstellung elektronisch-textiler Kunstwerke. Die Wanderfabrik ist in armen Gegenden Mexikos unterwegs und stellt dort Arbeiter und Arbeiterinnen zum US-amerikanischen

Supported by: Secretaría de Cultura del Distrito Federal (MX); Secretaría de Cultura de Campeche (MX). Production Assistance: Luis Bolaños, Arcángel Constantini, Mar Fonoy Rivera, Carmita Pérez, Vanessa Regueiro, Leslie San Vicente, Norma Silva.

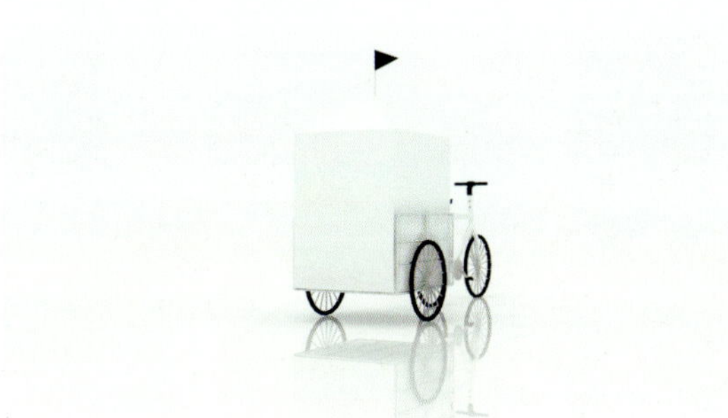

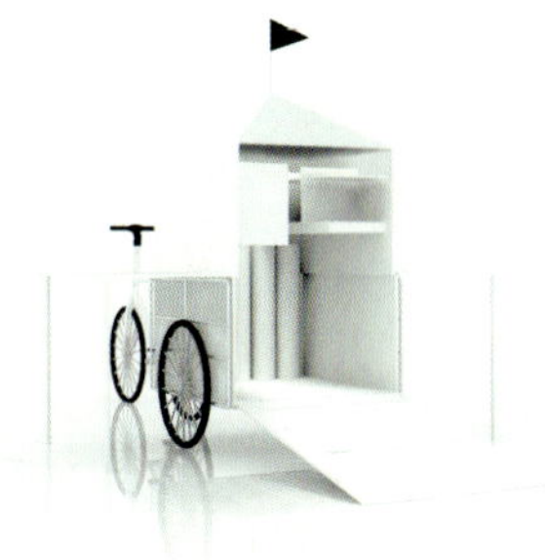

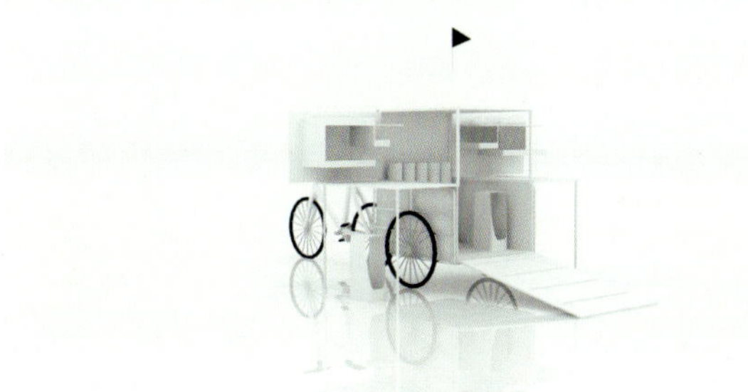

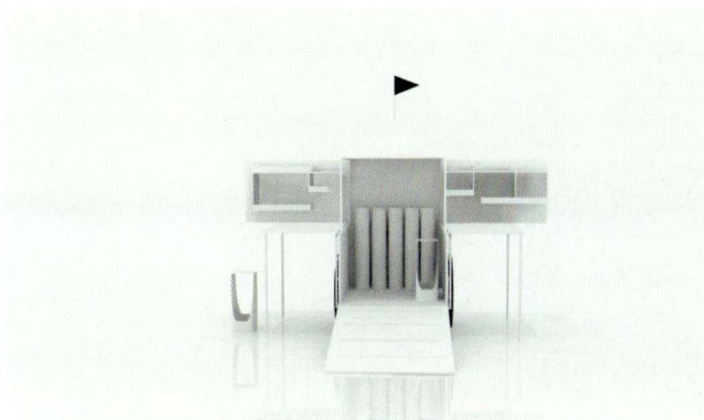

Mindestlohn ein (7 Dollar pro Stunde im Gegensatz zu den in Mexiko üblichen 60 Cent), um tatsächlich funktionierende elektronische Schaltpläne aus leitfähigem Garn sticken zu lassen. Bei den Schaltkreisen handelt es sich um Warnmelder mit verschiedenen Klingeltönen, die bei Aktivierung eines Annäherungssensors losgehen. Ist ein Stück fertiggestellt, stickt ihm sein Erzeuger einen einmaligen bidirektionalen (BiDi) Code ein (eine Art QR-Code). Wird dieser BiDi – in der Regel vom Käufer mit einem Smartphone – decodiert, erscheint eine Website mit der Produktionsgeschichte: Name des Arbeiters oder der Arbeiterin, Ort, Datum und Dauer der Herstellung, erhaltener Lohn, ein schematisches Diagramm sowie ein Raum für die Selbstdarstellung, in dem die jeweiligen Person zusätzliche Informationen über sich – Geschichten, Widmungen, Spenden, Videos und dergleichen – ablegen kann.

compared to $0.60 per hour in Mexico). People are hired to produce fully functional electronic circuits using conductive thread. The actual textile-schematic circuits produced are alarms which ring with different tones when a proximity sensor is activated. Once a piece is finished, the worker embroiders on it a unique bi-directional (BiDi) code (similar to a quick-response bar code). As the BiDi is decoded, typically by a consumer with a smart phone, a web page appears that shows the production history: name of the worker, location, date and duration of the work session, salary received, a schematic diagram and a "self-representation" section where the worker can add optional information on him or herself, stories, dedications, donations, videos or anything else.

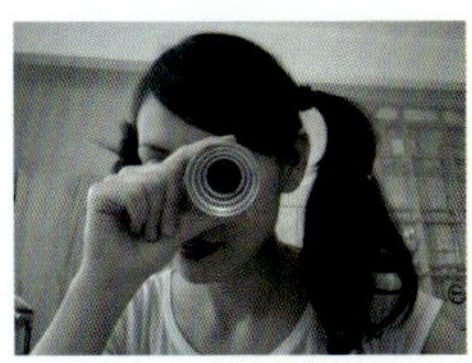

Amor Muñoz (MX) uses drawing, embroidery and electronic components in large-scale interactive pieces that juxtapose traditional handicrafts with technical diagrams and materials. Her work articulates an interest and exploration in art, design, illustration and electronic media, and is characterized by an interest in the interplay between material forms and social discourse. Muñoz has exhibited in museums and galleries around the world. **Amor Muñoz** (MX) arbeitet mit Zeichnung, Stickerei und elektronischen Bauteilen in groß angelegten interaktiven Projekten, die traditionelle Handwerkskunst mit technischen Bauplänen und Materialien verbinden. In ihren Arbeiten zeigt sich ein Interesse an Kunst, Design, Illustration und elektronischen Medien sowie an der Wechselbeziehung zwischen materiellen Formen und sozialem Diskurs. Muñoz hat weltweit in Museen und Galerien ausgestellt.

People Staring at Computers

Kyle McDonald

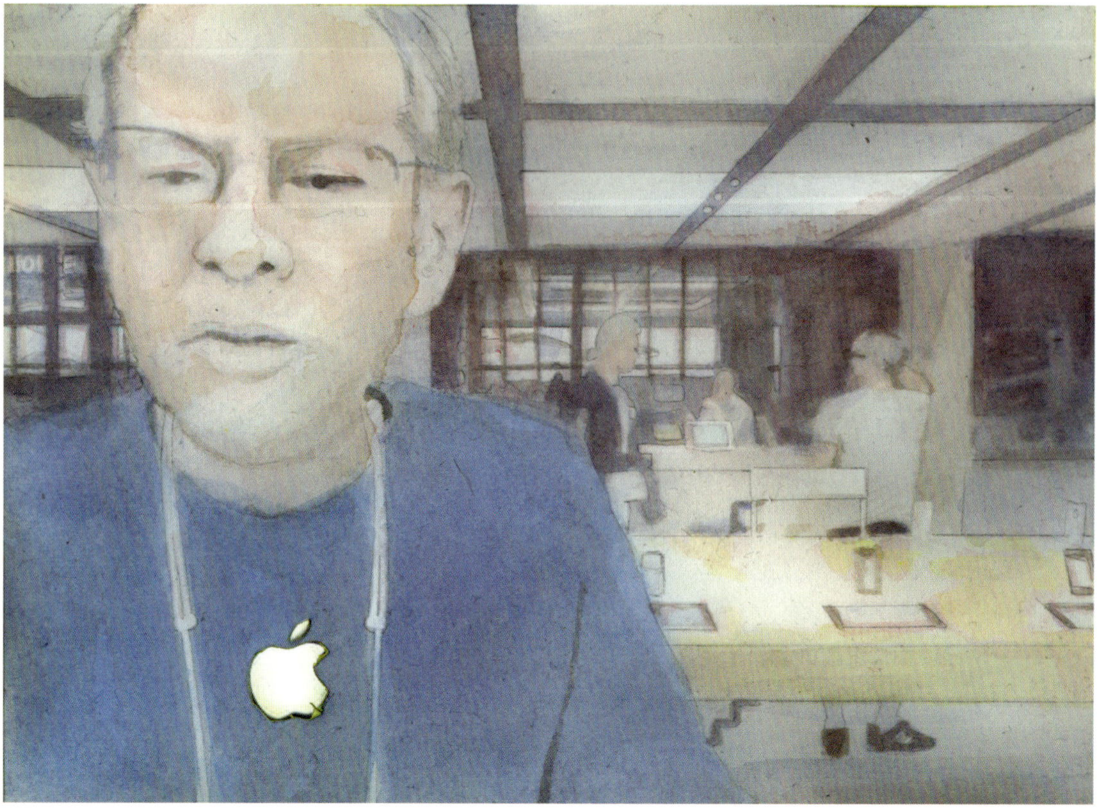

Watercolor by David Pierce

People Staring at Computers started as a photographic intervention exploring computer-mediated interaction and turned into a large-scale collaboration with Apple Inc. and the United States secret service, dealing with themes of privacy and surveillance. The work emerged from a brief "sousveillance" project that highlighted the empty expression people wear when using computers. In order to portray this expression more accurately and share it with others, the portraits of unsuspecting customers were captured at two Apple stores in New York. Custom software was installed manually on dozens of computers over several days, taking pictures once a minute and sending them back to a central server for exhibition online. On the final day the photos were exhibited simultaneously on all the computers at the Apple store at the site where they were taken.

Two days after the in-store exhibition, secret-service agents executed a search warrant, seizing the hardware used to create the work. Apple sent

People Staring at Computers begann als kleine fotografische Intervention zur Erforschung computervermittelter Interaktion und artete zu einer großen Kooperation mit der Firma Apple und dem US-Geheimdienst in Sachen Datenschutz und Überwachung aus. Die Arbeit ging aus einem „Sousveillance"-Projekt hervor, das den leeren Gesichtsausdruck von Menschen beim Umgang mit dem Computer dokumentieren sollte. Um diesen Ausdruck besser festhalten und mit anderen teilen zu können, wurden ahnungslose Kunden in zwei New Yorker Apple Stores porträtiert. Von Hand wurde auf einigen Dutzend Computern ein paar Tage lang eine eigens dafür geschriebene Software installiert, die jede Minute ein Bild schoss und es an einen zentralen Server schickte, um es online auszustellen. Am letzten Tag wurden die Fotos zugleich auf allen Computern des jeweiligen Apple Stores ausgestellt, in dem sie aufgenommen worden waren.

Zwei Tage nach der Ausstellung in den Apple Stores führten Geheimdienstleute eine Hausdurchsuchung durch und beschlagnahmten die gesamte für die Arbeit verwendete Hardware. Apple sandte Unterlassungsaufforderungen

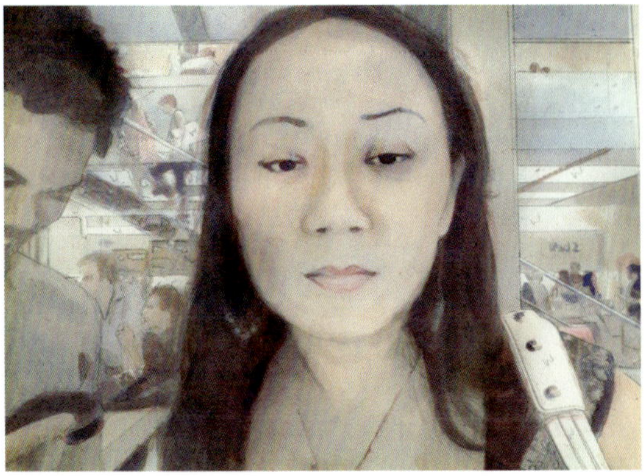

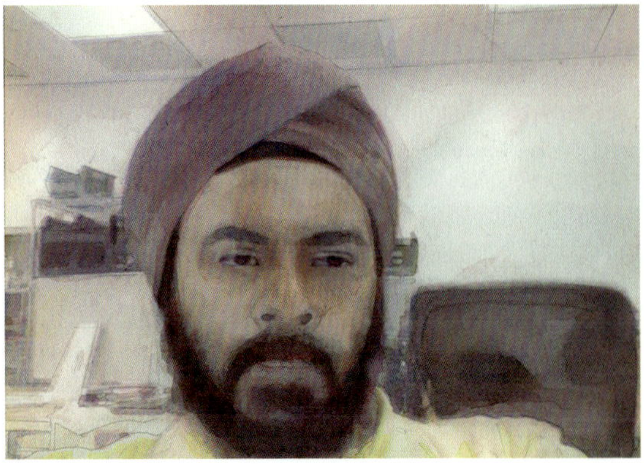

an alle Netzanbieter, die die Arbeit hosteten. Diese Kooperation beflügelte eine bereits in Gang befindliche Auseinandersetzung und hauchte der Arbeit neues Leben ein. Hunderte Kommentatoren im gesamten Netz beteiligten sich plötzlich daran. Sie diskutierten nicht nur über die Legalität des Werks, sondern auch darüber, was Kunst ist, schieden den öffentlichen vom privaten Raum und stritten über die Rolle der Überwachung in unserem Alltag. Aus einer fotografischen Intervention wurde eine Art Online-Happening.
Da die Fotografien selbst zu möglichen Unterlassungsaufforderungen durch Apple führen könnten, wird die Arbeit nun gemeinsam mit David Pierce fortgeführt, der die Bilder als Aquarelle umsetzt.

cease and desist requests to all web services hosting the work. This collaboration heightened the already present controversy, and the work found new life. Hundreds of commenters across the web joined in, not only discussing the work's legality but debating the definition of art itself, trying to distinguish public from private space and arguing about the role of surveillance in everyday life. The piece evolved from a photographic intervention into a sort of online happening.
Because the photos themselves may be subject to possible C&D requests from Apple, the work is now exhibited in collaboration with artist David Pierce, who has interpreted the images in watercolor.

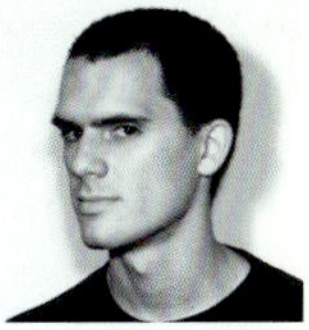

Kyle McDonald (US) is a media artist based in Brooklyn, New York. He works with sounds and codes, exploring translation, re-contextualization and similarity. With a background in philosophy and computer science, he strives to integrate intricate processes and structures with accessible, playful realizations that often have a do-it-yourself, open-source aesthetic. Kyle is a regular contributor to open-source arts-engineering initiatives such as openFrameworks, having developed a number of extensions that provide connectivity to powerful image processing and computer vision libraries. Kyle's camera-based artworks range from the hyper-formal to the tactical and interrogative. He recently completed the first Guest Research Project artist-in-residence program at the Yamaguchi Center for Arts and Media, Japan. **Kyle McDonald** (US) lebt als Medienkünstler in Brooklyn, New York. Er arbeitet mit Klängen und Codes, wobei er sich speziell für Übersetzung, Rekontextualisierung und Ähnlichkeit interessiert. Von der Philosophie und Computerwissenschaft kommend, versucht er komplexe Prozesse und Strukturen in einfache, spielerische Arbeiten umzusetzen, die häufig einen Do-It-Yourself- und Open-Source-Charakter besitzen. Kyle arbeitet regelmäßig an künstlerisch-technischen Open-Source-Initiativen wie openFrameworks mit, für die er eine Reihe von Erweiterungen entwickelt hat, die die Verbindung mit umfangreichen Bildverarbeitungs- und Computervisionsbibliotheken ermöglichen. Seine Kameraarbeiten reichen von hyperformalen bis zu taktischen und interrogativen Arbeiten. Er hat soeben das erste „Guest Research Project" im Rahmen des Artist-in-residence-Programms am Yamaguchi Center for Arts and Media in Japan abgeschlossen.

Protei
Protei

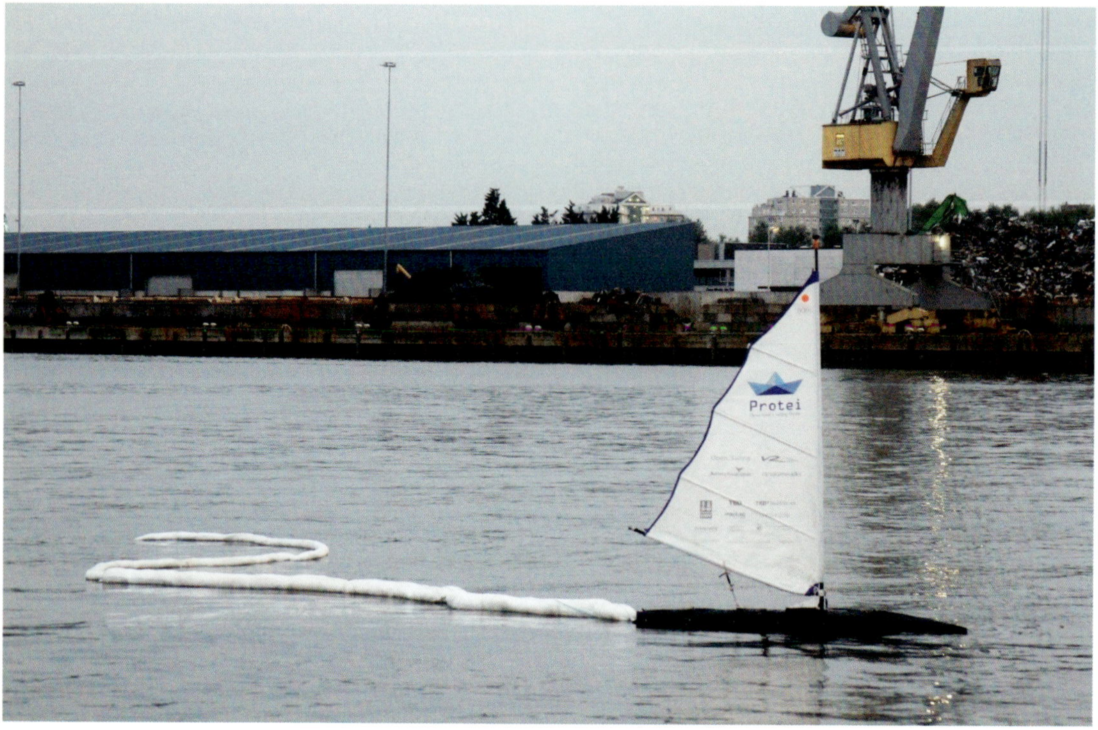

Protei is a fleet of pollution-collecting sailing drones. Initiated by senior TED fellow Cesar Harada it is a result of collaboration between artists, designers and scientists and as such it belongs to the intersection between fields. It is designed as a low-cost open-source oil-collecting device that semi-autonomously sails upwind, intercepting oil slicks going downwind. It is meant to be hurricane-ready, self-righting, inflatable, unbreakable, cheap and easy to manufacture for immediate response. It appropriates existing technologies so that it is possible to apply them quickly to address the crisis. The machine in development now is *Protei_Oil_Spill* for collecting oil spilled at sea, but being an open-source project other versions may be designed in the future for other purposes: *Protei* for the North Pacific plastic garbage patch, heavy

Protei ist eine Flotte von Segeldrohnen zur Bekämpfung der Meeresverschmutzung. Das von TED Senior Fellow Cesar Harada initiierte Projekt entspringt einer interdisziplinären Kooperation zwischen Künstlern, Designern und Wissenschaftlern. Ziel des Projekts ist die Entwicklung eines kostengünstigen Open-Source-Vehikels, das halbautonom gegen den Wind segelt und die *mit* dem Wind treibenden Ölschlieren einfängt. Es soll hurrikanfest, selbstaufrichtend, aufblasbar, unzerstörbar, billig und leicht herzustellen sein, damit es im Krisenfall rasch zum Einsatz gebracht werden kann. Aus demselben Grund arbeitet es auch mit bereits existierenden Technologien. Das aktuell in Entwicklung befindliche Vehikel *Protei_Oil_Spill* ist zur Bekämpfung der Folgen von Ölkatastrophen konzipiert, aber bei einem Open-Source-Projekt sind in Zukunft selbstverständlich auch *Protei*-Versionen für andere Zwecke denkbar: für den

Cesar Harada (FR/JP): Project Coordinator, TED Senior Fellow; Piem Wirtz (NL): Project Manager, V2_Institute for the Unstable Media; Sebastian Mullauer (DE): Industrial Product Designer; Kasia Molga (UK): Data Analyst and Visualization; Gabriella Levine (US): Hacker, Prototyper; Etienne Gernez (FR/NO): DNV Veritas Oslo

Produced by V2_Institute for the Unstable Media. Supported by Kickstarter, Kaag.

nordpazifischen Plastikmüllstrudel, für Schwermetalle in Küstenregionen, für Giftstoffe in urbanen Wasserstraßen usw.
Protei ist auf vielfältige Weise in Kunst (Schönheit ist unerlässlich), Design (brauchbare Dinge sind gut), Technik (sie definiert uns als Menschen) und den Wissenschaften verankert, die diese bahnbrechende Segeltechnologie gemeinsam entwickelt haben.
Protei wurde als Open Hardware entwickelt, und das nicht nur, weil das die ethischste, schnellste, billigste und vergnüglichste Methode ist, sondern auch weil auf diese Weise eine Gemeinschaft rund um die Technik entsteht, die darauf achtet, dass sie für den Dienst an der Umwelt eingesetzt wird.
Protei erhielt im Frühjahr 2011 großen Zuspruch auf Kickstarter und fand ein breites Medienecho (u.a. CNN, VICE TV, *Vogue Man Italy*, Good.is, Treehugger, *The Guardian*, FastCompany, *Fashioning Technology*, Motherboard TV, WWOZ New Orleans). Das Projekt gewann einen VIDA Art and Artificial Life Award der Fundación Telefónica (ES) und wurde u.a. auf dem Open Hardware Summit 2011 (NYC), auf der TED Konferenz 2011 (LA), bei den Wereldhavendagen (Rotterdam), TEDxMidAtlantic (Washington, DC), TEDxSeeds (Yokohama), TEDxBasquesCountry (FR) und TEDxSanDiego präsentiert.

metals in coastal areas, toxic substances in urbanized waterways etc.
Protei has multiple facets anchored in art (beauty is vital), design (commodity is good), engineering (technology defines us as human) and science as we came up with this ground-breaking sailing technology.
Protei has been developed as open hardware, not only because it is the most ethical, the fastest, cheapest and most fun way, but because it is building a community around the technology, ensuring our leadership to serve environmental purposes.
Protei gained huge support on Kickstarter during spring 2011 and media coverage (CNN, VICE TV, *Vogue Man Italy*, Good.is, Treehugger, *The Guardian*, FastCompany, *Fashioning Technology*, Motherboard TV, WWOZ New Orleans), and more. It won the Artificial Life Award der Fundación Telefónica (ES) and was presented at the 2011 Open Hardware Summit (NYC), TED2011 (LA), Wereldhavendagen (Rotterdam), TEDxMidAtlantic (Washington DC), TEDxSeeds (Yokohama), TEDx-BasquesCountry (FR) and TEDxSanDiego among many others.

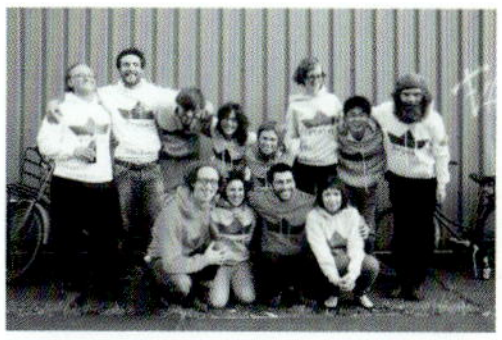

Protei (UK) was initiated by Goldsmiths University researcher and senior TED fellow Cesar Harada and is a result of collaboration between artists, designers, scientists, engineers and marine biologists. Brought together by common passion for the planet and oceans of this planet and its well being, we spent summer 2011 together in Rotterdam under the wings of the V2_ Institute for the Unstable Media working out the best technologies to make *Protei* happen.
Protei (UK) wurde von Cesar Harada, Forscher am Goldsmiths College und TED Senior Fellow, initiiert und ist das Ergebnis einer Zusammenarbeit von Künstlern, Wissenschaftlern, Technikern und Meeresbiologen. Verbunden durch das gemeinsame Engagement für den Planeten verbrachten wir den Sommer 2011 unter den Fittichen des V2_Institute for the Unstable Media in Rotterdam und erarbeiteten die besten Technologien für eine Verwirklichung von *Protei*.

Searching for the Ubiquitous Genetically Engineered Machine

ArtScienceBangalore

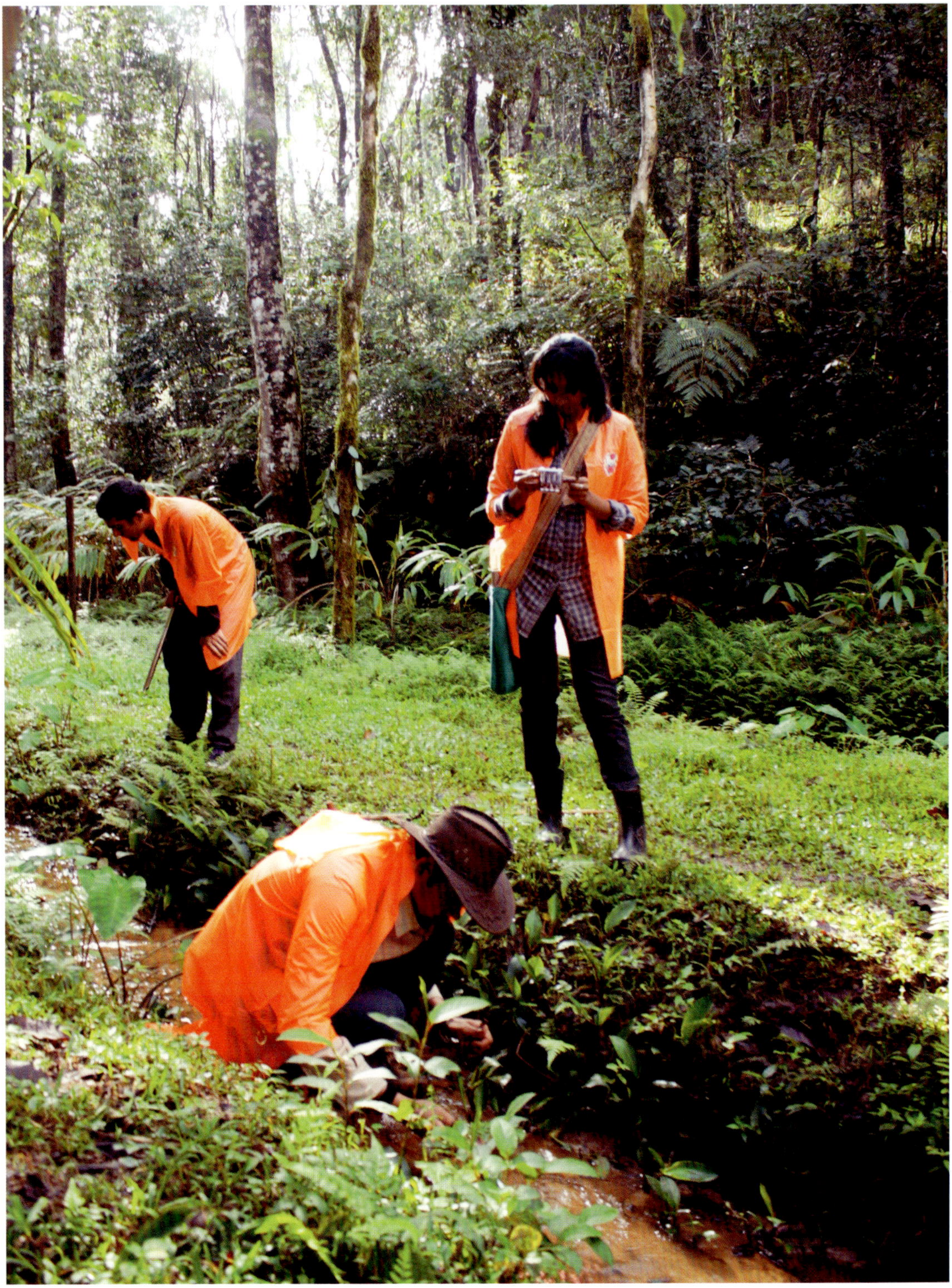

In der synthetischen Biologie werden BioBausteine als Abstraktion oder Template zur Herstellung standardisierter funktionaler Lebendteile eingesetzt. *Searching for the Ubiquitous Genetically Engineered Machine* zeigt eine alternative Anwendungsmöglichkeit des BioBausteins. Das Projekt verwendet BioBaustein-Primer als Primer für die Zufalls-PCR (Polymerase-Kettenreaktion) bei der Untersuchung von Bodenproben. Diese Zufalls-PCR liefert eine prägnante Signatur für die in den Proben vorhandene Biodiversität. Solche Bodenuntersuchungen dienen der Erkundung einer von nichtinstitutionellen Akteuren mit allgemein zugänglichen Mitteln betriebenen Bürgerwissenschaft und sie vermitteln einen Eindruck von einer „postnatürlichen" Welt, in der BioBausteine in unserer Umwelt landen und sich als Banden in einem Gel wiederfinden könnten. In einer Welt, in der BioBausteine zum allgemein akzeptierten Standard der synthetischen Biologie und solche technisch erzeugten Bioprodukte zu einem allgegenwärtigen Bestandteil unseres Lebens und unserer Umwelt geworden sind, werden die von uns gewonnenen Proben einmal als Messbasis für das Ausmaß des menschlichen Einflusses dienen können. Die Untersuchungen werden in einem maßgeschneiderten öffentlichen Forschungslabor durchgeführt, dessen Baupläne online zur Verfügung stehen. Dieses autonome öffentliche Labor kann als Template für Bürgerforschungslabore zur Durchführung biotechnischer oder anderweitiger „Experimente" dienen.

In synthetic biology the BioBrick has been used as an abstraction or template for creating standardized functional living parts. *Searching for the Ubiquitous Genetically Engineered Machine* is an alternate re-appropriation of the BioBrick by using existing BioBrick primers as random-PCR (polymerase chain-reaction) primers in investigating soil samples. This random PCR will provide a succinct signature of the biological diversity present in these samples. These investigations of soil lead us to ask questions about citizen's science "performed" by non-institutional actors using accessible tools as well as giving us a glimpse into the "post-natural world" where BioBricks may end up in our environment and may very well show up as bands in a gel. By imagining a world in which the BioBrick has become the accepted standard for synthetic biology, and where these engineered products are ubiquitous in our lives and environments, the samples we archive will serve as the baseline from which the subsequent extent of human influence can be measured. These investigations are carried out in a custom-built public research laboratory; the blueprints for making one are available online. These autonomous public laboratories can be used as template for creating a citizen's research lab with which one can carry out "experiments", biotechnological or otherwise.

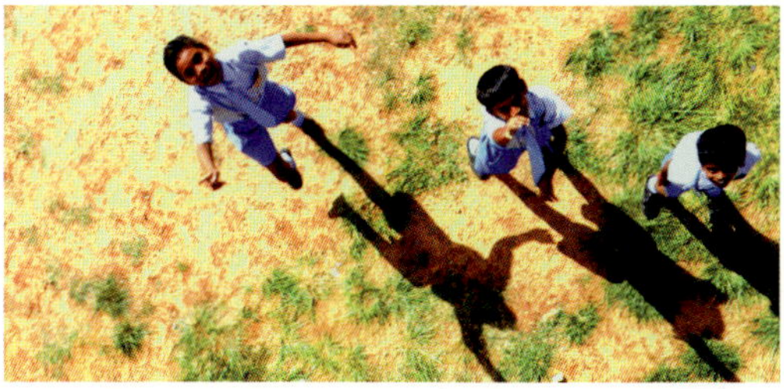

Supported by the National Center for Biological Sciences, Bangalore; Srishti School of Art, Design and Technology, Bangalore. Realized with the help of students from the Srishti School of Art, Design and Technology: Madhul Singh, Prakrithy Pradeep, Biswajith Manimaran, Achala Athreya, Akshaya Maria Thomas, Anvita Goenka, Biswajith Manimaran, Damyanti Choudhary, Durga Gawde, Manasa Thimmiya, Pranav Raman, Sidharta Guha Thakurta, Sohil Bhatia.

ArtScienceBangalore's (IN) work is at the intersection of art-science and pedagogy, creating spaces of dialog and interaction between artists, designers and scientists. Since 2009, the group has focused on building low-tech laboratories and low-cost equipment, making it easier for outsiders to explore the life-sciences. Their work has been awarded numerous prizes and recognition in both the arts and the science contexts. **ArtScienceBangalore** (IN) schafft am Schnittpunkt von Kunst, Wissenschaft und Bildung Räume für den Dialog und Austausch zwischen Künstlern, Designern und Wissenschaftlern. Die Gruppe entwickelt seit 2009 kostengünstige Lowtech-Labore und Laborgeräte, um Laien den Zugang zu den Biowissenschaften zu ermöglichen. Ihre Arbeit hat sowohl im Kunst- als auch im Wissenschaftskontext viel Anerkennung erfahren und wurde mit zahlreichen Preisen ausgezeichnet.

The Body is a Big Place

Peta Clancy, Helen Pynor

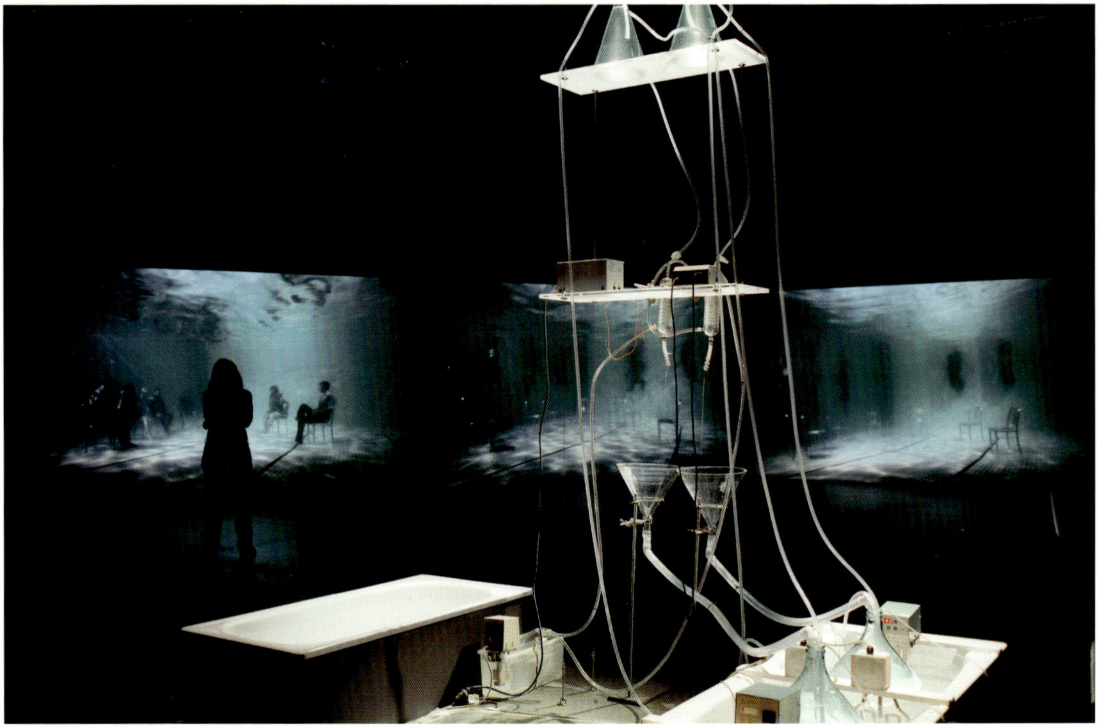

Peta Clancy and Helen Pynor. Performance Space, installation view. 5-channel video projection, heart perfusion device, single video screen, soundscape by Gail Priest. Collaborating cardiac physiologists: Professor John Headrick and Dr Jason Peart

The Body is a Big Place explores organ transplantation and the ambiguous thresholds between life and death, revealing the process of death as an extended durational moment, rather than an event that occurs at a single moment in time. This bio-art work is a large-scale immersive installation comprising a five-channel video projection, a fully functioning bio-sculptural heart-perfusion system, an undulating aqueous soundscape and a single-channel video work.

The Body is a Big Place re-enacted certain defining aspects of the human heart-transplant process. In two performances staged during the exhibition the heart perfusion device was used to reanimate a pair of fresh pig hearts to a beating state. Rather than sensationalizing these performative events, the artists sought to encourage empathic responses from viewers, activating the bodies of viewers by appealing to their somatic senses and fostering their identification with the hearts they were watching. This opened up the possibility of a deeper awareness and connection with viewers' own interiors.

The Body is a Big Place untersucht die Organtransplantation und die verschwommenen Grenzen zwischen Leben und Tod, die zeigen, dass das Sterben kein punktuelles Ereignis, sondern ein sich in die Länge ziehender Prozess ist. Das Biokunstwerk ist eine großräumige immersive Installation mit einer fünfkanaligen Videoprojektion, einer bioskulpturalen funktionstüchtigen Perfusionsapparatur für isolierte Herzen, einer auf- und abschwellenden Wasser-Klanglandschaft und einer einkanaligen Videoarbeit.

Die Installation vollzog bestimmte grundlegende Aspekte einer menschlichen Herzverpflanzung nach. Im Verlauf der Ausstellung waren zwei Performances angesetzt, bei denen mithilfe der Perfusionsapparatur zwei frische Schweineherzen zum Schlagen gebracht wurden. Das geschah nicht aus Sensationslust, sondern weil die Künstlerinnen bei den Betrachtern Empathiereaktionen auslösen wollten. Durch Aktivierung ihrer Körperempfindungen sollte die Identifikation mit den schlagenden Herzen verstärkt und der Bezug zum eigenen Körperinneren vertieft werden.

Die Arbeit war nur durch das Engagement der Melbourner Transplantations-Community möglich, deren Mitglieder

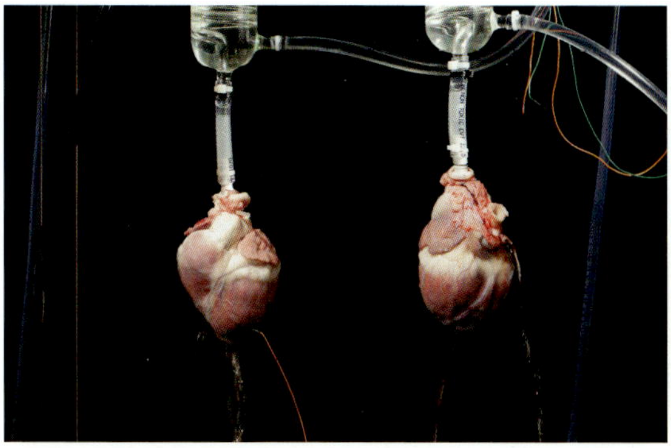

Still from live pig heart performance, 21 Nov, 2011, Performance Space. Sound by Gail Priest. Collaborating cardiac physiologists: Professor John Headrick and Dr Jason Peart. Photo: Geordie Cargill

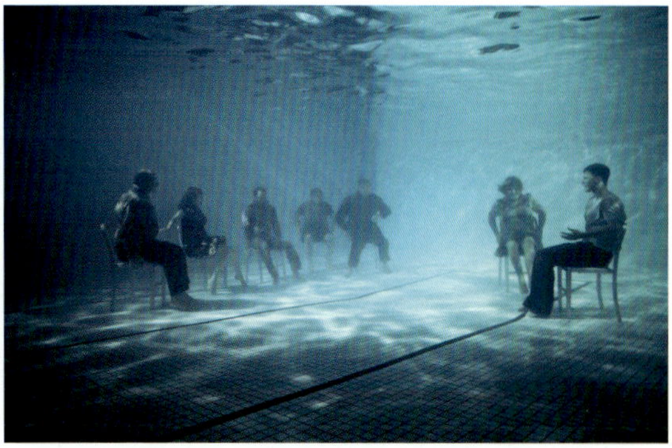

Performance Space, video still. Sound by Gail Priest. Collaborating cardiac physiologists: Professor John Headrick and Dr Jason Peart. Photo: Chris Hamilton

auch in den Unterwasser-Videosequenzen auftraten. Es sind Menschen, die als Organempfänger, Organspender oder Personen, die Organempfängern oder posthumen Spendern nahe stehen, extreme Erfahrungen gemacht haben.

Der Titel bezieht sich auf den Umstand, dass Körperteile im Zuge des Transplantationsprozesses oft große geografische, zeitliche und interpersonelle Distanzen überbrücken können. Das Projekt war mit Risiken und Ungewissheiten behaftet, welche die mit Organtransplantationen einhergehenden Unsicherheiten widerspiegelten. Kooperative intra- wie interdisziplinäre Forschungsanstrengungen von Medienkünstlern und Biowissenschaftlern waren ein prägendes Moment, wie die ganze Arbeit überhaupt erst durch die Großzügigkeit und den Vertrauensvorschuss aller Beteiligten entstehen konnte.

The work's realization depended on engagement with the organ transplant community in Melbourne, who were performers in the work's underwater video sequences. These were individuals who have gone through extraordinary experiences in the form of receiving, donating or standing closely by loved ones as they receive or posthumously donated human organs.

The work's title refers to the capacity for parts of the body to traverse vast geographic, temporal and interpersonal distances during organ transplantation processes. The project was underscored by risk and uncertainty, mirroring the uncertainties at the heart of organ transplantation itself. Collaborative research within and between the new media arts and life sciences, by artists and scientists, informed the work's development.

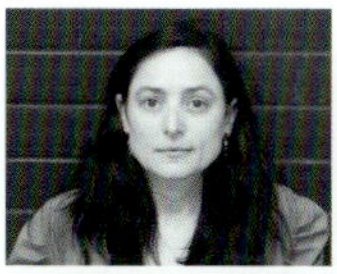

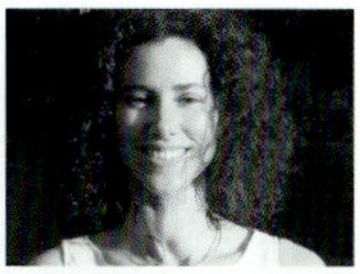

Peta Clancy (AU) has been exploring the intersections of art and medicine and of art and science for more than a decade. Clancy is a lecturer in the Fine Arts Department, Faculty of Art, Design & Architecture at Monash University, Melbourne, Australia, and was awarded the Dean's Excellence in Research by an Early Career Researcher Award in 2011. Clancy's practice includes installation, new media, video, performance, photography and sculpture. **Helen Pynor** (AU) originally trained as a biologist majoring in cell and molecular biology before training as an artist at Sydney College of the Arts, University of Sydney. She explores themes from the life sciences in her artistic practice, focusing on perceptions and experiences of the interior body and taboos surrounding the exploration of the body's interior. Pynor's practice includes installation, new media, video, performance, photography and sculpture. **Petra Clancy** (AU) arbeitet seit über einem Jahrzehnt an den Schnittpunkten von Kunst und Medizin bzw. Kunst und Wissenschaft. Clancy lehrt am Fine Arts Department der Faculty of Art, Design & Architecture an der Monash University in Melbourne, und erhielt 2011 den Dean's Excellence in Research by an Early Career Researcher Award. Clancys Schaffen umfasst Installationen, Medienkunst, Videoarbeiten, Performances, Fotografie und Plastik. **Helen Pynor** (AU) studierte ursprünglich Biologie mit Schwerpunkt Zell- und Molekularbiologie, ehe sie am Sidney College of Arts ein Kunststudium absolvierte. In ihren künstlerischen Arbeiten beschäftigt sie sich mit biowissenschaftlichen Fragen, insbesondere der Wahrnehmung und dem Erleben des Körperinneren und den Tabus, die in Bezug auf die Erforschung des Körperinneren bestehen. Pynors Schaffen umfasst Installationen, Medienkunst, Videoarbeiten, Performances, Fotografie und Plastik.

The Great Work of the Metal Lover

Adam Brown

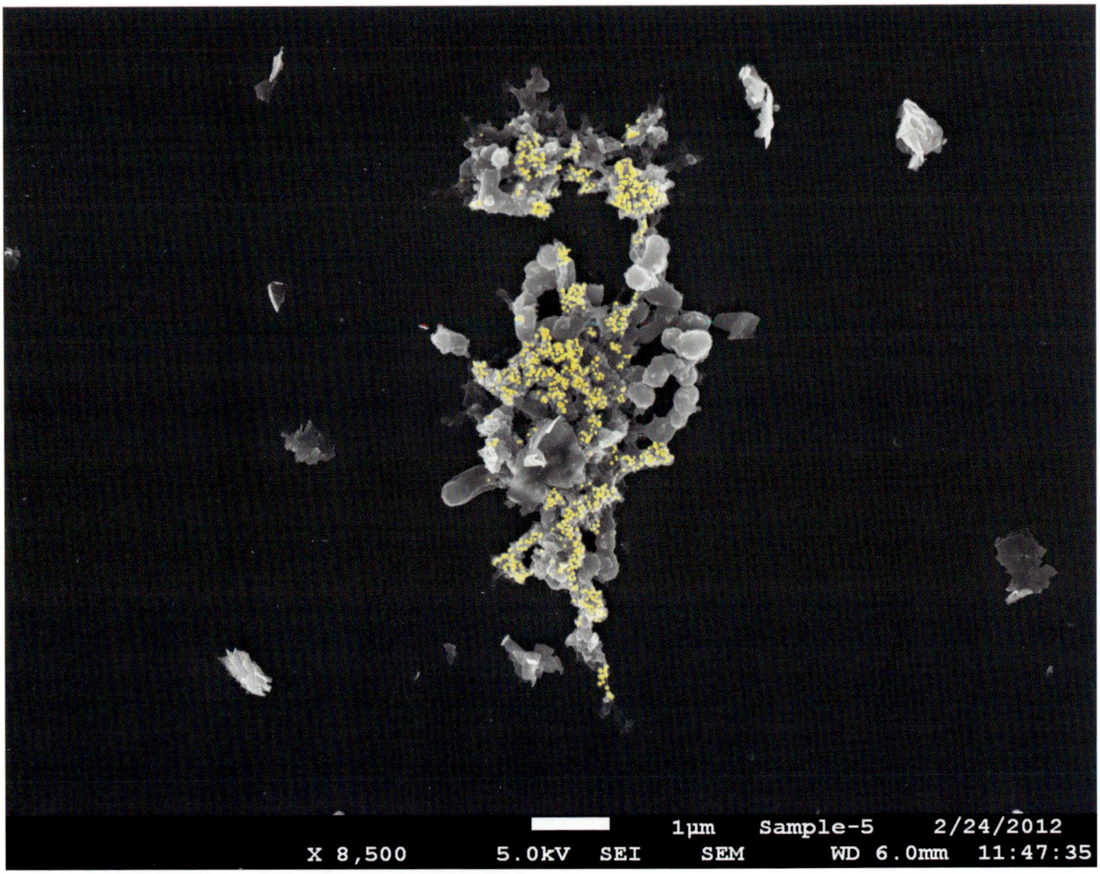

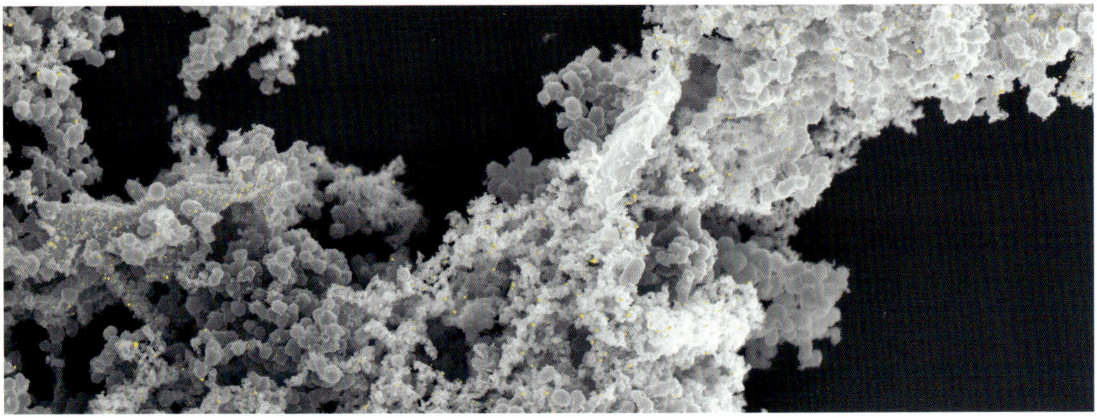

The Great Work of the Metal Lover is an artwork that sits at the intersection of art, science and alchemy, re-examining the problem of transmutation through the use of modern microbiological

The Great Work of the Metal Lover ist eine zwischen Kunst, Wissenschaft und Alchemie liegende Arbeit, die mit modernen mikrobiologischen Verfahren eine Neuinterpretation der Elementumwandlung versucht.

Dabei wird durch die Verbindung eines hochspezialisierten metalltoleranten extremophilen Bakteriums (*Cupriavidus metallidurans*) mit einer künstlichen, in einen maßgeschneiderten alchemistischen Bioreaktor eingeschlossenen Atmosphäre Gold erzeugt. Das extreme Minimal-Ökosystem im Bioreaktor zwingt die Bakterien, hochkonzentriertes giftiges AuCl4 (Goldchlorid) zu verstoffwechseln und so gelöstes Gold in 24K-Gold umzuwandeln.
The Great Work of the Metal Lover besteht aus zwei Teilen. Der erste Teil ist eine Installation der speziell entwickelten Laborapparatur, die sich aus dem gläsernen alchemistischen Bioreaktor, einer Gasverteileranlage und einem mit Kohlendioxid und Wasserstoff gefüllten Gasbehälter zusammensetzt, wobei der Prozess in Echtzeit von einem USB-Mikroskop mit Live-Videofeed dokumentiert wird.
Der zweite Teil besteht aus einer Reihe von mit einem Rasterelektronenmikroskop aufgenommenen Bildern, von denen mit modernster Technologie Digitalprints angefertigt werden. Darauf werden zunächst die von den Bakterien in einer Polysaccharidmatrix aus Zellaggregaten bzw. Biofilm erzeugten Goldlager identifiziert. Dann wird mithilfe alter Vergoldungstechniken 24-karatiges Blattgold auf einige Bereiche des Prints aufgebracht, an denen ein solches bakterielles Goldlager festgestellt wurde. Jeder Print enthält etwas von dem im Bioreaktor produzierten Gold.
Gold wird wie die Alchemie mit einem geheimen Wissen über die Erde, die Entstehung des Lebens und frühe Stoffwechselprozesse verbunden. *The Great Work of the Metal Lover* ist eine direkte Thematisierung des wissenschaftlichen Strebens, das Leben im postbiologischen Zeitalter nach unserem Willen zu formen, und fragt nach den ethischen und politischen Folgen dieses Versuchs, die Natur zu vervollkommnen.

practice. In this work, gold production is accomplished by the pairing of a highly specialized metallotolerant extremophilic bacterium (*Cupriavidus metallidurans*) and an engineered atmosphere contained within a customized alchemical bioreactor. The extreme, minimal ecosystem within the bioreactor forces the bacteria to metabolize high concentrations of toxic AuCl4 (gold chloride), turning soluble gold into usable 24K gold.
The Great Work of the Metal Lover exists in two parts. The first part is an installation consisting of custom laboratory equipment, including a glass alchemical bioreactor, a gas manifold and a gas tank filled with carbon dioxide and hydrogen. The process is all documented in real time by a USB microscope and a live video feed.
The second part of the work consists of a series of images made with a scanning electron microscope. Digital prints are made using modern technology. Gold deposits produced by the bacteria are identified within a polysaccharide matrix formed by cell aggregates or biofilms. Then, using ancient gold-illumination techniques, 24K gold leaf is selectively applied to regions of the print where a bacterial gold deposit has been identified. Each print contains some of the gold that was produced in the bioreactor.
Like alchemy, gold is imbued with secrets of the earth, origins of life and early metabolic processes. *The Great Work of the Metal Lover* speaks directly to the scientific preoccupation with trying to shape and bend biology to our will within the post-biological age, essentially questioning the ethical and political ramifications of attempting to perfect nature.

Supported by: Michigan State University Department of Art, Art History and Design, Michigan State Museum

Adam Brown (US) is an artist whose creative research incorporates art and science hybrids that include robotics, microbiology and emerging technologies. His works take the form of installations, interactive objects, videos, performances and photography. Brown is an associate professor of electronic art and intermedia in the Department of Art and Art History at Michigan State University. **Adam Brown** (US) ist ein Künstler, dessen kreative Forschung u.a. Kunst-Wissenschaft-Hybriden in Verbindung mit Robotik, Mikrobiologie und neu entstehenden Technologien umfasst. Seine Arbeiten nehmen die Form von Installationen, interaktiven Objekten, Videos, Performances und Fotografien an. Brown ist außerordentlicher Professor für elektronische Kunst und Intermedia am Department of Art and Art History an der Michigan State University.

Un Résau Translucide

Prue Lang

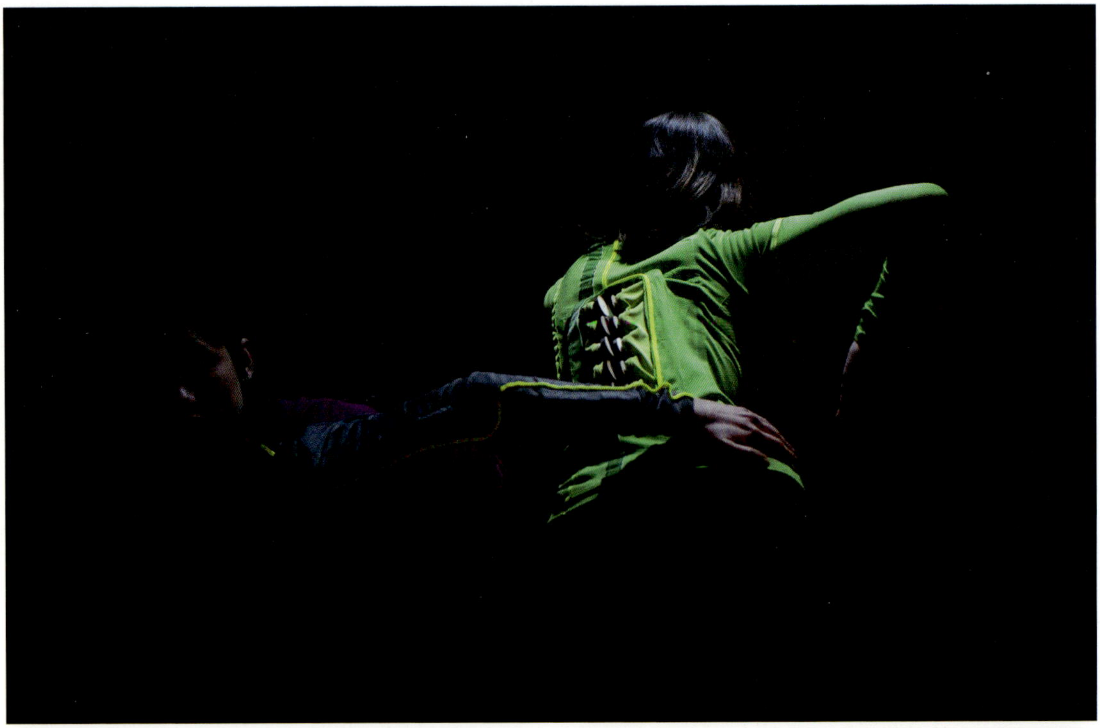

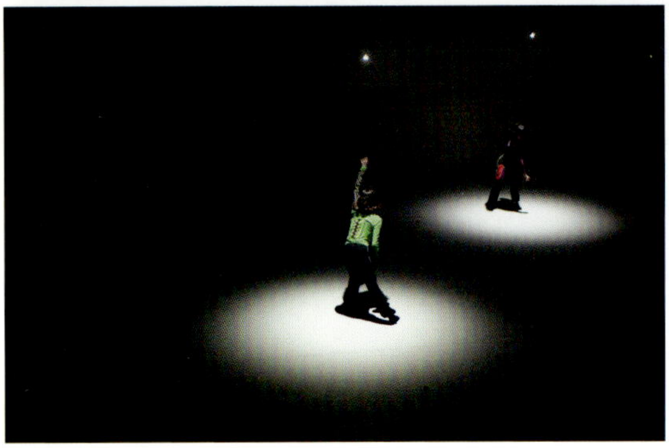

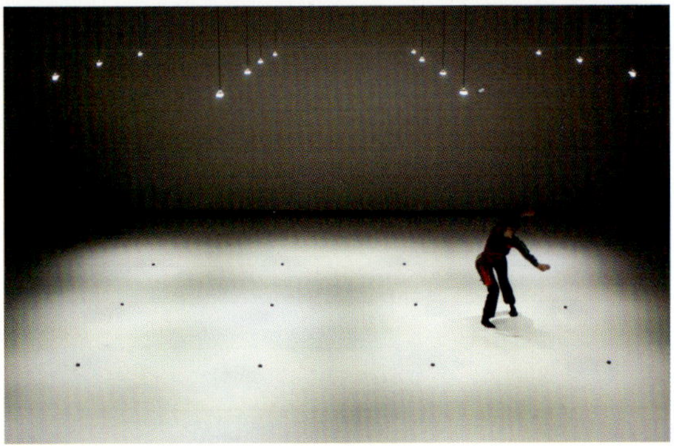

Photos: Hillary Goidell

Un Réseau Translucide is a work that poses the question "how do we make performances for the future?" Developing a choreographic system in which the performers also generate the electricity, the work examines the relationship between the body and its environment, while opening up a dialog on sustainable development in artistic practice. It re-thinks habitual modes of stage production by creating the first autonomous performance that runs 100 percent on its own energy.

Un Réseau Translucide ist ein Projekt, das der Frage nachgeht: „Wie sehen Aufführungen für die Zukunft aus"? Mittels eines choreografischen Systems, bei dem die Darsteller auch den für das Stück benötigten Strom erzeugen, untersucht es das Verhältnis von Körper und Umwelt und stößt einen Dialog über nachhaltige Entwicklung in der künstlerischen Praxis an. Mit dem ersten zu hundert Prozent energieautarken Bühnenstück werden gewohnte Formen der Theaterproduktion neu überdacht.

In Zusammenarbeit mit Amanda Parkes vom MIT Media Lab wurden „intelligente" Kostüme entwickelt, die es ermöglichen die Energie der Tänzer während der Aufführung zu ernten. Es entstanden Geräte, die die kinetische Energie der Tanzbewegungen in Strom umwandelten, der in kleinen, in die Kostüme eingebauten Batterien gespeichert wurde. Der Strom aus diesen Batterien speiste die Tonanlage, während das Raster aus energiesparenden lichtstarken LED-Leuchten von einem auf der Bühne stehenden, von den Tänzern betätigten Fahrrad versorgt wurde.

Die Arbeit untersucht das Verhältnis zwischen Körper und Umwelt mit einer Choreografie, in der die Darsteller essen, verbrauchen, erzeugen, reagieren, sich anpassen und produzieren. Nach jeder Aufführung gibt es eine öffentliche Diskussion über nachhaltige Entwicklung und die Frage einer möglichen Leitfunktion der Kunst für kreative Innovation.

Lang collaborated with Amanda Parkes from MIT Media Lab to invent "intelligent" costumes that could simultaneously harvest the dancers' energy during the performance. Technological devices were created to convert the kinetic energy generated by the dancers' movements into energy stored in small batteries sewn into their costumes. The energy from the batteries then powered the sound system, while a low-consumption high-luminosity LED lighting grid was hooked up to the dancers' onstage bicycle.

Developing a choreographic system in which the performers eat, expend, generate, respond, adapt and produce, the work examines the relationship between the body and its environment. Each performance is followed by a public discussion about sustainable development in artistic practice and the issue of "art leading technology" in order to innovate creatively.

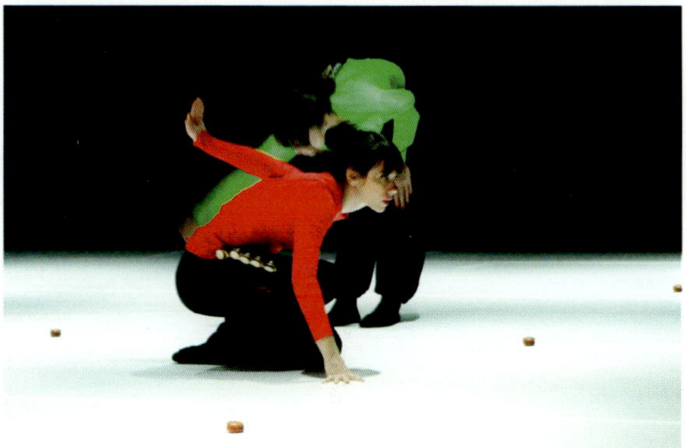

Photo: Nicolas Galinotti

Concept & direction: Prue Lang; Performance: Prue Lang, Vanessa Le Mat, Nina Vallon; Costume system: Amanda Parkes; Light system: Charles Goyard; Images: Hillary Goidell

Prue Lang (AU) works as an independent choreographer throughout Europe. She spent six years performing and choreographing for William Forsythe's Ballett Frankfurt. Her work includes installation, performance and interdisciplinary collaboration with a strong focus on exploring new formats for contemporary dance.

Prue Lang (AU) arbeitet als freie Choreografin in ganz Europa. Sie war sechs Jahre als Tänzerin und Choreografin in William Forsythes Ballett Frankfurt tätig. Sie arbeitet sowohl installativ als auch performativ sowie in interdisziplinären Kooperationen, mit einem besonderen Akzent auf der Entwicklung neuer Formate für den zeitgenössischen Tanz.

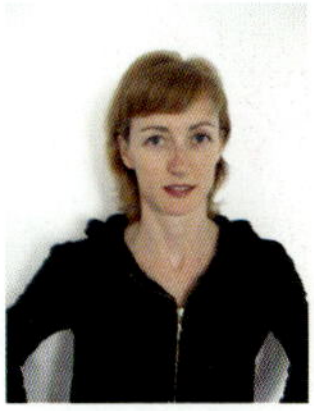

INTERACTIVE ART

Parallel Fictional Spaces / Fiktive Paralleluniversen

Ksenia Fedorova, Fiona Raby, Christa Sommerer, Junji Watanabe, Mariela Yeregui

This year selection was defined by a conscious move away from projects that justify themselves through technological or techno-political arguments to projects that take leaps into parallel fictional spaces, into the imagination, almost to the edges of absurdity. These private, self-constructed realities seem to be the only most really secure zones of freedom in the world of continuing political and economic instability. Artists suggest beginning with oneself, from the inside. Expressed artistically, personal dissatisfactions and irritations—either with financial and governmental systems or with priorities within culture itself—become sources of empowerment. This has long the core of art in general and interactive art in particular. Yet there is a noticeable shift: the gap between fictional and actual realities feels even bigger and more poignant; the desired destinations are either in the past (hence, vivid nostalgic motifs) or in the future. The individual authentic voice has to be more affective in order to be heard. The pungency of technological romanticism is that even in its idealistic mode (for instance, going beyond functionality) it desires real changes: "working" communities, translatability, harmonious relations across borders etc.

Are these fictions purely gratuitous? As demonstrated by the artists' work, they attempt to connect to responses that collectively can be recognized as not only deeply human but also empathetic. Individual stories become contextualized to expand our feeling of the other or so that others can share our experience. Political hierarchies become flattened and are critiqued. New types of language and devices to explore national and gender relations are invented to loosen the sense of boundaries, to re-evaluate communicative processes. Some artists have turned for answers to the Earth's ultimate resource—the wisdom of nature.

How do we hold on to this idealism and vision in the face of economic, political ecological crisis? What kind of contribution can we make? Would it be smart or irresponsible to give way to "complicated pleasure" (Martin Amis)? We live in complicated times full of dilemmas, and it becomes

Die diesjährige Wahl der Preisträger beruht auf einer bewussten Verschiebung von technisch oder technisch-politisch motivierten Projekten hin zu Projekten, die fast absurd anmutende Ausflüge in fiktive Paralleluniversen, ins Reich der Fantasie unternehmen. Diese privaten, selbst erschaffenen Welten erscheinen als die einzig gesicherten Freiheitszonen in einer von ständiger politischer und wirtschaftlicher Unsicherheit gekennzeichneten Welt. Persönliche Unmuts- und Frustrationsgefühle – sei es über das Finanzsystem, den Staat oder die Setzung von Prioritäten im Kulturbereich – werden in der künstlerischen Umsetzung zu einer Quelle der Selbstermächtigung. Zwar gilt das seit jeher sowohl für die Kunst im Allgemeinen als auch für die interaktive Kunst, doch hat es hier eine deutliche Veränderung gegeben: Die Kluft zwischen fiktiver und wirklicher Welt erscheint nun noch größer und einschneidender; die Wunschziele liegen nun entweder in der Vergangenheit (daher die ausgeprägten nostalgischen Motive) oder in der Zukunft. Die authentische Einzelstimme muss heute emotionaler sein, um gehört zu werden. Die Kraft dieser technologischen Romantik besteht darin, dass sie selbst in ihrer idealistischen Form (etwa wenn sie über die Funktionalität hinausgeht) *reale* Veränderungen anstrebt: „funktionierende" Gemeinschaften, Übersetzbarkeit, harmonische Beziehungen über Grenzen hinweg usw.

Sind diese Fiktionen ganz und gar willkürlich? Wie an den Arbeiten der Künstler zu sehen ist, suchen sie Anschluss an Empfindungen, die von jedermann als zutiefst menschlich und emphatisch erkannt werden kann. Individuelle Geschichten werden so kontextualisiert, dass sie unser Gefühle für andere erweitern oder andere an der eigenen Erfahrung teilhaben lassen. Politische Hierarchien werden kritisiert und abgeflacht, neue Sprachformen und Gerätetypen erfunden – ob zur Erforschung von Länder- und Geschlechterverhältnissen, zur Lockerung der Grenzwahrnehmung oder zur Neubewertung von Kommunikationsprozessen. Und einige Künstler suchen ihre Antworten sogar bei der ultimativen Ressource des Planeten: der Weisheit der Natur.

Wie sollen wir angesichts der ökonomischen, politischen und ökologischen Krise an Idealen und Visionen festhalten? Welchen Beitrag können wir leisten? Ist es klug oder eher unverantwortlich, sich dem „komplizierten Vergnügen" (Martin Amis) hinzugeben? Wir leben in schwierigen Zeiten voller Zwickmühlen, in denen es immer wichtiger wird, auch den zunehmend von Problemen erdrückten kommenden Generationen das Träumen zu gestatten.

GOLDENE NICA

Memopol-2

Timo Toots

Dieses Projekt des jungen estnischen Künstlers Timo Toots verbindet eine große komplexe Maschine mit einem Datenbanknetzwerk, aus dem bei Einführung einer Identitätskarte persönliche Daten des jeweiligen Nutzers oder der Nutzerin abgerufen werden. Dabei werden die unterschiedlichsten Daten über uns gesammelt: Arzneimittelverschreibungen, Schulzeugnisse und Steuererklärungen, Führerscheindaten usw. Der retrofuturistische Apparat stellt die aufgespürten Informationen auf bissige, witzig-respektlose Art und Weise auf einem düster und einschüchternd wirkenden Display dar. Ein Kontrollpult mit einem eingebauten Kartenlesegerät eröffnet den Zutritt zum persönlichen Gedächtnistunnel. Auf dem sich über drei Wände erstreckenden Display erscheinen die Datenreste der eigenen sozialen und persönlichen Entwicklung als kuriose Ansammlung von Einzelheiten und Verbindungen, die jeder selbst analysieren muss, die aber auch ein Bild der Kontrollgesellschaft und ihrer Funktionsweise zeichnen.

Das Projekt ist selbstreflexiv und hat deutlich parodistischen Charakter: Die riesigen grafischen Interfaces sind eine Überzeichnung der Kontrollapparaturen der 1960er und 1970er Jahre. Auch die Anklänge an Science-Fiction und den Kalten Krieg sind kein Zufall: Sie dienen mit ihrer bedrohlichen Atmosphäre aus Spielbegeisterung und Kriegsanspannung als Warnzeichen. Humor und kritische Distanz sind ein Schlüsselmoment der Installation. Sie machen sie zu einer Plattform für eine unbehaglich-anschauliche Umdeutung heutiger Überwachungs- und Kontrollmechanismen.

AUSZEICHNUNGEN

Solar Sinter Project

Markus Kayser

Ein Projekt, das seine Energie von der Sonne bezieht und an einem „Ort der Vollkommenheit" stattfindet. In einer

increasingly important that the coming generations burdened with accumulated problems are also allowed to dream.

GOLDEN NICA

Memopol-2

Timo Toots

This project by the young Estonian artist Timo Toots connects a large and intricate machine to a network database to retrieve visitors' personal information through their ID-cards. By collecting the traces we find ourselves in a continuous procedure of tracing multiple types of data: from prescription drugs to high-school exams, from tax reports to driving licenses etc. This retro-futuristic apparatus displays the information in a dark and intimidating as well as in a hilarious, irreverent and pungent way. A controller box containing the ID scanner allows the visitor to be connected to his/her own tunnel of memory. The three-wall display projects vestiges of social transitions and individual development as a social being, which is a curious bank of details and connections to analyze on your own, but in this case it becomes a distinct picture of how control societies work.

This project is not deprived of self-reflexivity and a clear sense of parody: hyperbolic graphic interfaces exacerbate the imagery of the control devices from 1960s and 70s. The combination of science-fictional and Cold War tints are not accidental in this environment either, they are warning signs creating an atmosphere of a ludic excitement and warfare tension. Humor and critical distance are among the key points in *Memopol-2* and build an uneasy and vivid platform to re-signify current mechanisms of surveillance and control.

AWARDS OF DISTINCTION

Solar Sinter Project

Markus Kayser

The energy source is the sun. The location is a place of "perfection", a desert, with a fabulous aluminum machine sparkling in the sunlight. It takes the surrounding raw material—sand—and slowly melts it as the sun beats down on the solar panels. A 3D form builds up very slowly, layer by layer—a bowl. The resolution is not particularly fine, but the process of transformation feels magical and inspirational.

The direct and immediate translation between energy, resource and finished product is the ultimate technological dream, an undistorted relation between man, nature and machine. It is a vision in a desert, almost a mirage, while the desert can be interpreted as an ideological desert that often lacks truly creative and constructive visions. It is almost too good to be true. It is exemplary of some fictional reality, alluding to our idealism and deeply human hope for a better world, for a technological, cultural and aesthetic union with our environment. The real function of this device is not to produce pots but to ignite beliefs.

It's a jungle in here

Isobel Knowles, Van Sowerwine with Matthew Gingold

This work presents an original take on interactive storytelling. Two visitors become part of a story about a victim and an attacker inside a train. The faces of the participants are keyed into whimsical-looking paper characters, and by seeing themselves the participants start to act out various stories that unfold inside the train. While the whole set-up looks cute and childish at the beginning, the stories start to become more and more aggressive and gruesome. Participants find themselves in the awkward situation of becoming voyeurs of their own actions and aggressions. Identification with the characters is preset, so there is no room for any loose interpretations or arbitrary associations (which in traditional filmmaking are imposed by the directorial authority). Through clever and fascinating storytelling, Knowles, Van Sowerwine and Gingold show us how a good story can draw us in, in the most direct and concrete meaning of the term.

Wüste glitzert eine fabelhafte Maschine aus Aluminium im Sonnenlicht. Sie nimmt das sie umgebende Rohmaterial – Sand – und bringt es mithilfe der auf Solarpaneele knallenden Sonne zum Schmelzen. In einer 3D-Form entsteht sehr langsam, Schicht um Schicht, eine Schale. Die Auflösung ist nicht gerade fein, aber der Umwandlungsprozess hat etwas Magisches, Beflügelndes.

Die unmittelbare Übertragung zwischen Energie, Rohstoff und Endprodukt ist der ultimative Traum der Technologie, eine ungetrübte Beziehung zwischen Mensch, Natur und Maschine. Es ist eine Wüstenvision, eine Art Fata Morgana, wobei die Wüste zugleich im übertragenen Sinn gelesen werden kann, als das Fehlen wahrhaft kreativer und konstruktiver Ideen. Die Vision ist fast zu gut, um wahr zu sein. Es ist ein Beispiel einer fiktiven Realität, die unseren Idealismus und unsere Hoffnung auf eine bessere Welt schürt, die technische, kulturelle und ästhetische Vereinigung mit unserer Umwelt. Die eigentliche Funktion dieser Maschine ist nicht das Produzieren von Gefäßen, sondern das Anfachen des Glaubens.

It's a jungle in here

Isobel Knowles, Van Sowerwine mit Matthew Gingold

Diese Arbeit ist ein origineller Versuch interaktiven Geschichtenerzählens. Zwei Teilnehmer werden in eine Opfer-Täter-Geschichte in einem Zug verwickelt. Ihre Gesichter werden in skurrile Papierfiguren einkopiert, sodass die Teilnehmer sich selbst eine Reihe von Situationen in dem Zug durchspielen sehen. Wirkt die ganze Installation auf den ersten Blick lieblich und harmlos, so werden die Geschichten zunehmend aggressiver und grausamer. Die Teilnehmer werden in die unangenehme Situation gebracht, dass sie Voyeure ihrer eigenen Handlungen und Aggressionen sind. Die Identifikation mit den Figuren ist vorgegeben und lässt keinen Platz für lose Interpretationen und freie Assoziationen (die im traditionellen Film durch die Regie unterstellt werden). Mit ihrer klugen und faszinierenden Erzählweise zeigen Knowles, Van Sowerwine und Gingold, wie uns eine gute Geschichte buchstäblich in sich hineinziehen kann.

ANERKENNUNGEN

Energy Parasites

Eric Paulos

Ökologische Fragen rücken zu Recht immer mehr ins Zentrum heutiger Kunstproduktion. Eric Paulos hat sich schon seine gesamte Karriere hindurch immer wieder mit Umweltfragen beschäftigt. Angesichts der leichten Durchschaubarkeit und der direkten Anwendbarkeit könnte man diese Parasiten als rein zweckorientiert ansehen (und sich fragen, ob nicht schon genug Ingenieure und Designer an Mechanismen der Energieerhaltung arbeiten). Doch hat die Idee eines Alltagsparasitismus und die Beschäftigung mit seinen elementaren Strukturen auch etwas überaus Künstlerisches und großen Witz. Beobachtung war immer schon das wichtigste Arbeitsmittel der Wissenschaft, und Anpassung an Umwelt und Naturgesetze ist ein Credo der Technologie. Oft aber schafft erst die Kunst die geistreichen Verknüpfungen, und genau diese plötzlichen Einsichten, diese kuriosen Entdeckungen verborgener Potenziale sind es, was wir als ästhetisch empfinden.

Osadok / Aftertaste

Kuda begut sobaki / Where Dogs Run

Die interaktive Videoinstallation des russischen Medienkunstkollektivs Where the Dogs Run konfrontiert den Betrachter mit etwas Unheimlichem, sich dem menschlichen Verstand Entziehenden. Langsam fallende Kartoffeln versetzen ihn oder sie in einen Zustand der Meditation, eine Offenheit für alles, ein Sich-Einlassen auf den Flow, eine unbestimmte Aufmerksamkeit. Das Bild einer Kartoffel ist etwas ganz und gar Alltägliches, dem in der russischen Kultur aber auch etwas Archetypisches und Mythologisches anhaftet. In einem Museumskontext wirkt es aus dem Zusammenhang gerissen, paradox, rätselhaft. Nicht jeder wird erkennen, dass die Künstler damit auf den russischen Kosmismus anspielen, eine esoterische Philosophie, die heute nur noch als nebulöser Rest, als vager Nachgeschmack existiert. Die Gruppe entfaltet ihre ironische Haltung, spielt mit der Erwartung und Verwirrung der Betrachter, setzt eine komplexe Dynamik des Bewusstseins für Stereotypen und Vorurteile, und der Wachsamkeit ihnen gegenüber, in Gang.

HONORARY MENTIONS

Energy Parasites

Eric Paulos

Ecological issues deservedly occupy increasingly central positions in today's art production. Eric Paulos has been addressing various environmental concerns consistently throughout his career. The easily recognized agency and direct applicability of this work may lead to a purely utilitarian reading of it (how many engineers and designers are already working on energy conservation devices and mechanisms?). Yet there is something intrinsically artistic and witty about the very idea of parasitism on everyday life and attention to its elemental structure. Observation has been the main tool of science, and adaptability to environment and natural laws is a credo of technology. But often it is art that introduces the insightful connections, and these moments of insight, the curious discoveries of hidden potentials, are aesthetic.

Osadok / Aftertaste

Kuda begut sobaki / Where Dogs Run

Interactive video installation by a Russian media art group Where the Dogs Run confronts the viewer with the experience of something uncanny, beyond human comprehension. The slowly falling potatoes produce a meditative disposition, an openness to anything, tuning in the flow, and attention. The image of a potato is very familiar, but in the context of Russian culture it is also archetypal and mythologized. Not very apt within a museum setting, it evokes a sense of incoherence, paradox, even mystery. Not everyone will recognize the artists' allusion to Russian cosmism in this image, an esoteric philosophy, nothing of which is left today apart from some nebulous residue, an aftertaste. The group builds its ironic attitude, playing with the viewers' expectations and bemusement, plunging them into the complex dynamics of awareness and vigilance towards stereotypes and preconceptions.

Occupy George

Andy Dao, Ivan Cash

This project was launched in conjunction with the Occupy Wall Street protests that began in New York City in 2011. Andy Dao and Ivan Cash made five info-graphics that indicate American economic disparity and stamped them on circulating one-dollar bills. As the Occupy Wall Street protests continued, the movement spread via the Internet. In addition to the political context of currency hacking, this project provokes a reflection on our limited recognition of the potential of money as a medium of exchange. The project catalyzes debates both on socio-political and media-specific issues. Pervasive, i.e. adjustable to any situation, money can be a medium for diverse range of interventions.

ADM8

RYBN

ADM8 (anti-data-mining) is an autonomous mechanism that allows investment and speculation on real financial markets. The algorithm of decision-making functions in accordance with various arbitrary external parameters, thus exemplifying principle of complex and often unfathomable causality within many real-life processes. Multiple data-flows interweave in an overpowering and eerie way. Being a purely abstract operating engine, the machine nevertheless allows us to relate to it as a subject able to deliver its personal story and perhaps even to express larger social concerns. It is an insider and our guide through the increasingly vast and alienating maze of financial apparatus.

LightType

François Chay, Léo Chéron

LightType is an installation generating words of tweets. When a message is tweeted on a certain topic, images of a cube made of LED bars are captured by a camera and then projected onto the wall. This cube can create all kinds of alphabetical characters by changing the positions of the lighting bars. The three-dimensional structure of the cube is once fragmented in terms of visual forms and

Occupy George

Andy Dao, Ivan Cash

Dieses Projekt entstand in Verbindung mit den Occupy-Wall-Street-Protesten, die 2011 in New York begonnen haben. Andy Dao und Ivan Cash entwarfen fünf Infografiken zur Illustration der wirtschaftlichen Ungleichheit in den USA und stempelten sie auf in Umlauf befindliche Ein-Dollar-Noten. Im Verlauf der Proteste weitete sich die Bewegung über das Internet aus. Abgesehen vom politischen Aspekt des Hackens einer Währung, verweist das Projekt auch darauf, wie eng unser Begriff von Geld als (Aus)Tauschmedium ist, wie es überhaupt zu Diskussionen über soziopolitische wie medienspezifische Fragen anregt. Als „pervasives", d. h. auf jede Situation anpassbares Medium eignet sich Geld für alle möglichen Interventionen.

ADM8

RYBN

ADM8 (anti-data-mining) ist eine autonome Maschine, die auf echten Finanzmärkten investiert und spekuliert. Der Entscheidungsfindungsalgorithmus ist an verschiedene willkürliche externe Parameter gekoppelt und stellt damit ein Beispiel für die komplexen und unergründlichen Kausalzusammenhänge in vielen Vorgängen des wirklichen Lebens dar. Eine Fülle an Datenströmen verschränkt sich in überwältigender und unheimlicher Weise. Trotz ihrer rein abstrakten Operationen können wir die Maschine auch als Subjekt begreifen, das eine persönliche Geschichte austrägt und vielleicht sogar ein größeres soziales Anliegen zum Ausdruck bringt. Als Insiderin führt sie uns durch das zunehmend unüberschaubare und entfremdete Labyrinth des Finanzapparats.

LightType

François Chay, Léo Chéron

LightType ist eine Installation, die Tweets typografisch umsetzt. Tweets zu einem bestimmten Thema aktivieren einen aus Leuchtröhren bestehenden Würfel, der, von einer Kamera aufgenommen, als Bild an die Wand projiziert wird. Der Würfel kann je nach Aktivierung der Röhren alle möglichen Zeichen erzeugen. Eine dreidimensionale Struktur wird zuerst visuell zerlegt und dann wieder zu lesbaren Sprachzeichen zusammengesetzt. Die Installation kreiert damit eine neue grafische Sprache.

Menstruation Machine – Takashi's Take
Sputniko!
Die japanisch-britische Künstlerin Sputniko! hat eine Maschine entwickelt, mit der selbst Männer eine Menstruation nachempfinden können. In einer zur Arbeit gehörigen Videodokumentation will ein fiktiver Junge namens Takahashi mithilfe der Maschine herausfinden, wie man sich als Mädchen wirklich fühlt. Ausgehend von dem Umstand, dass Technologien vom kulturellen Kontext ihrer Zeit abhängen, hinterfragt *Menstruation Machine* – gleichgültig, ob die Maschine nun rein konzeptuell ist oder nicht – die Rolle avancierter Technologien in Genderfragen. Das Besondere an der Methode der Künstlerin ist, dass sie mit der Thema der Monatsblutung die Geschlechterdifferenz nicht verringert, sondern verstärkt. Die Technologie wird hier zu einem Mittel, die Grenze zu überwinden.

Versus
David Letellier
Versus ist eine formvollendete kinetische Skulptur mit flüssigen, organischen Bewegungen und einer eigenen Klangwelt. Betreten Ausstellungsbesucher den Raum, stören sie die innere Logik des Systems, und die Skulptur versucht, den neuen Input zu verarbeiten. *Versus* erinnert an frühe kinetische Skulpturen aus den 1950er und 1960er Jahren, erweitert sie aber um eine subtile interaktive Komponente und treibt sie ästhetisch in neue Höhen.

fly tweet
David Bowen
Bei *fly tweet* werden lebende Fliegen in einer Acrylglaskugel mit einer Computertastatur gehalten. Bewegen sich die Fliegen über die Tastatur, wird das entsprechende Zeichen vom System getweetet. Mit der künstlerischen Übersetzung von Beliebigkeit und Geschwätzigkeit thematisiert die Installation die brennende Frage der Überkommunikation. *fly tweet* ist Teil einer Serie origineller und subtiler Arbeiten, in denen David Bowen Zufallsoperationen natürlicher Lebewesen in vernetzten telematischen Umgebungen erkundet.

Cross Coordinates (MX-US)
Iván Abreu
Dieses vielschichtige Projekt untersucht anhand einer Wasserwaage die Wahrnehmung von Grenzen und

reassembled into a word in a linguistic manner for reading. This installation successfully shows us a new type of graphic language.

Menstruation Machine—Takashi's Take
Sputniko!
The Japanese-British woman artist Sputniko! has designed a device that is aimed to provide an experience of menstruation even for a male user. The work is accompanied by a video documentary about a fictional boy called Takashi, who uses the device to get a real sense of what it feels like to be a girl. Starting from the point where technologies are essentially under the regulation of cultural contexts of the time, the *Menstruation Machine*, which may or may not be just conceptual, raises critical questions of the role of advanced technologies in gender issues. Yet her unique method is not to attenuate gender differences, exemplified by monthly bleeding, but rather to try to underscore them. Technology, then, is a means of transgressing these challenging borders.

Versus
David Letellier
Versus is a beautiful kinetic sculpture that moves fluidly and organically, creating original sounds. When visitors enter the room they interrupt the internal logic of the system and the sculpture tries to cope with the new input. *Versus* is reminiscent of early kinetic sculptures from the 1950s and 1960s; however, it adds a subtle new layer of interaction and pushes the aesthetic experience to another height.

fly tweet
David Bowen
fly tweet uses real flies inside an acrylic sphere that also contains a computer keyboard. When the real flies move over the keyboard, corresponding text characters are tweeted to the system. The installation addresses burning questions of excessive over-communication, by transforming randomness and chatter into an artistic medium. *fly tweet* is a work in a series of other original and subtle pieces in which David Bowen has been exploring

the idea of chance operations input produced by natural creatures located within networked and telematic environments.

Cross Coordinates (MX-US)

Iván Abreu

This multi-layered project takes a spirit-level as the focal point that makes it possible to question the notions of borders and the equilibrium between opposing parts. It is a delicate game where participants are supposed to balance a spirit-level, which would result in building communities through cooperation. The game has three dimensions: 1) the game across the real borders between Mexico and the US, 2) the game in the exhibition space, and 3) the game on a website. Various algorithms translate the balance values from the action with the electronically monitored real level or through the online participation and convert them into meters. The goal of participation is to overtake the length of the US/Mexico border (3,169,000m).

Löschen / DELETE

Marcello Mercado

This intriguing performance by Marcello Mercado displays a curious language to delete unwanted thoughts and to convert them to hieroglyphic signs. In order to cleanse language with no-language (or an enigmatic alternative language), a performer invites the audience to get rid of polluted thoughts through an unmanageable flow of cryptic signs. In a surreal attempt to eliminate bugs, overcome black holes and get rid of unwanted relics of language and invisible remnants of digital technologies, this piece turns thinking and erasing processes into part of the same action.

den Ausgleich zwischen gegnerischen Parteien. *Cross Coordinates* ist ein Spiel, bei dem die Teilnehmer eine Wasserwaage ins Gleichgewicht bringen sollen – als eine Form von Gemeinschaftsstiftung durch Kooperation. Das Spiel existiert in dreifacher Form: 1) als grenzüberschreitendes Spiel an der realen Grenze zwischen Mexiko und den USA, 2) als Spiel in einer Ausstellung und 3) als Internetspiel. Die beim Hantieren mit der elektronisch abgelesenen realen Wasserwaage oder bei der Teilnahme im Netz erzielten Gleichgewichtswerte werden durch verschiedene Algorithmen in Meter umgerechnet. Das Ziel besteht darin, die Länge der Grenze zwischen den USA und Mexiko (3.169.000 Meter) zu übertreffen.

Löschen / DELETE

Marcello Mercado

Diese faszinierende Performance von Marcello Mercado enthüllt eine seltsame Sprache zum Löschen unerwünschter Gedanken und deren Konvertierung in hieroglyphenartige Zeichen. Ein Performer fordert das Publikum auf, sich in einem haltlosen Strom kryptischer Zeichen seiner Gedankenverunreinigungen zu entledigen, um Sprache durch Nichtsprache (oder eine rätselhafte Alternativsprache) zu reinigen. In einem surrealen Versuch zur Beseitigung von Fehlern, Überwindung von schwarzen Flecken, Entsorgung von unerwünschten Sprachresten und unsichtbaren digitaltechnischen Rückständen wird in dieser Arbeit Denken und Löschen zu ein- und derselben Tätigkeit.

Ideogenetic Machine

Nova Jiang

Wie der Fantasie in einer visuell gesättigten Landschaft ständig recycelter Bilder auf die Sprünge helfen? Die *Ideogenetic Machine* generiert mit erlebnisorientierten Methoden spontane Geschichten. Betrachter werden live beim öffentlichen Performen aufgenommen und buchstäblich in eine Geschichte eingekapselt, indem ihre Aktionen angehalten und zu Strichzeichnungen in einem Comic umgewandelt werden. Sprechblasen antizipieren eine weitere improvisierte Erzählschicht. Für „Darsteller" wie umstehendes Publikum entsteht so eine intime Beziehung zu einer Geschichte, die es selbst zu vollenden gilt. Sie ist direkt und ungekünstelt, und es winkt zudem eine Belohnung: eine handfester Comic. Das performative Element dient nicht nur – wie im interaktiven Film – der Entfaltung der Geschichte, sondern fixiert überdies rein zeitliche Verhältnisse ein einem haptisch lesbaren Objekt.

MNM v091

Christian Graupner

MNM v091 ist ein gleichermaßen verschämter wie verführerischer Versuch über reine Fantasie und pure Lust: „Eine Ohrfeige für alle grundlosen Optimisten." Seine Triebkraft und Bestrebung ist gut mit der Frage beschrieben, „wie es jenseits des Klischees aussehen könnte". Wie im Bilderüberfluss der YouTube-Vimeo-Welt noch zu einem originellen zeitgenössischen visuellen Ausdruck gelangen? Die Frage nach dem Warum beantwortet Christian Graupner höchstvollendet: „Weil es POP ist ... verwirrend ... ready-made". Tatsächlich ist es verwirrend und verstörend, wie adäquat und frisch Pop-Art immer noch aussehen und welch schmerzliche Lust sie immer noch bereiten kann.

Ideogenetic Machine

Nova Jiang

How do we trigger and re-awaken the imagination in a visually saturated landscape of constantly recycled imagery? The *Ideogenetic Machine* uses experiential methods to generate spontaneous narratives. The viewer is captured "live" through their public performance and is literally encapsulated within a story, their actions frozen and turned into line drawings in a comic book. Speech bubbles appear in anticipation of another impromptu layer of story making. Both the "actor" and the audience share an empathetic relation to the story that *must* be completed. The connection is direct and without artifice, and there is a reward—the actual product of a graphic story. The performative element not only helps the story to unfold, as in interactive cinema, but it also fixes purely temporal relations in a tangible and readable object.

MNM v091

Christian Graupner

MNM v091 is a take on unadulterated imagination and pure pleasure. It is both shameful and alluring, "a punch in the face for all who are optimistic without reason." Its driving force and ambition is well described by the incisive question: "what to find beyond cliché?" In a YouTube-Vimeo world of visual excess, how do we find and create original contemporary visual expression? When asked why, Christian Graupner says quite perfectly: "It is POP ... it is confusing ... it is a readymade". It is indeed puzzling and disconcerting how adequate and fresh pop-art still looks and how painfully joyful it can still be.

Memopol-2
Timo Toots

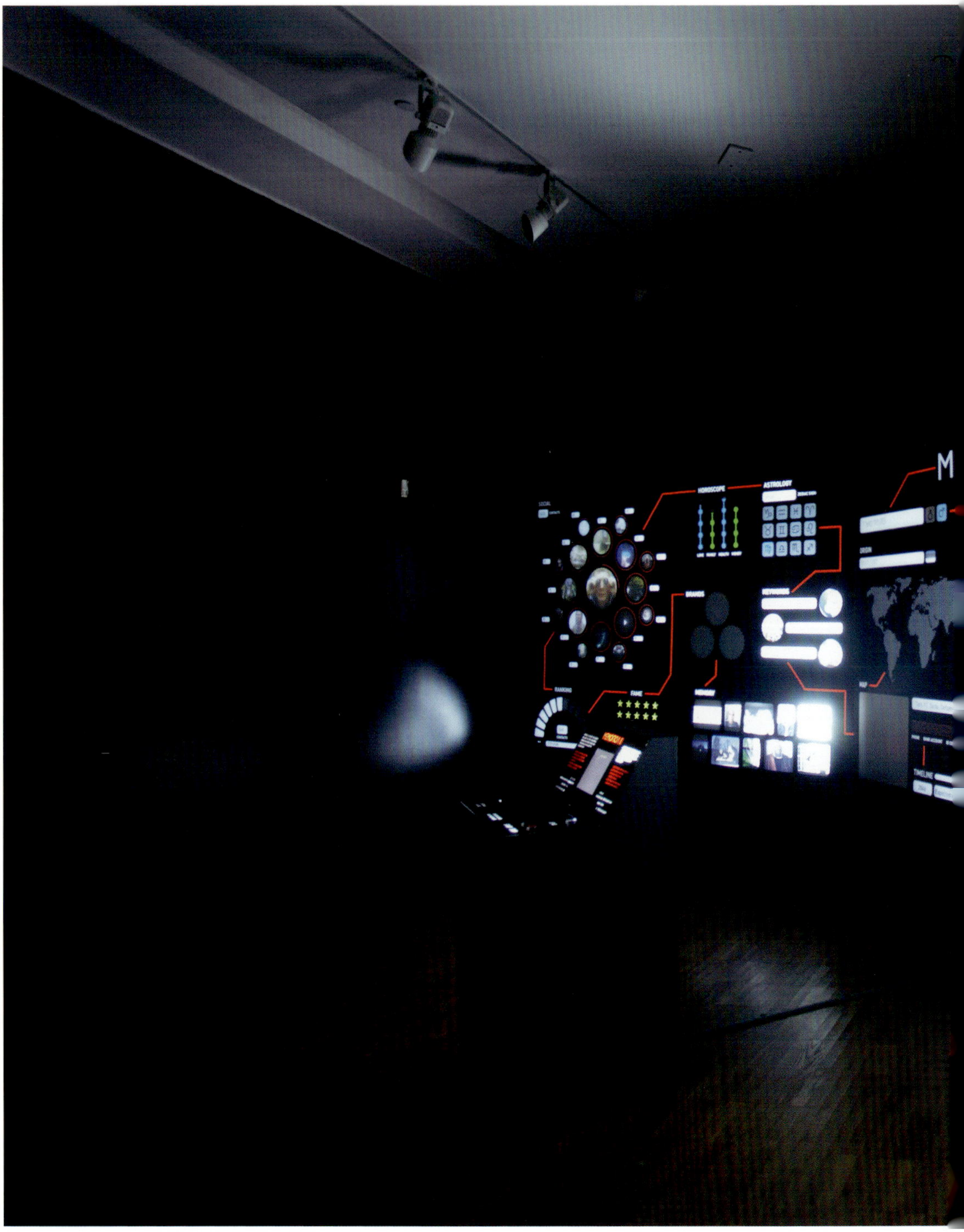

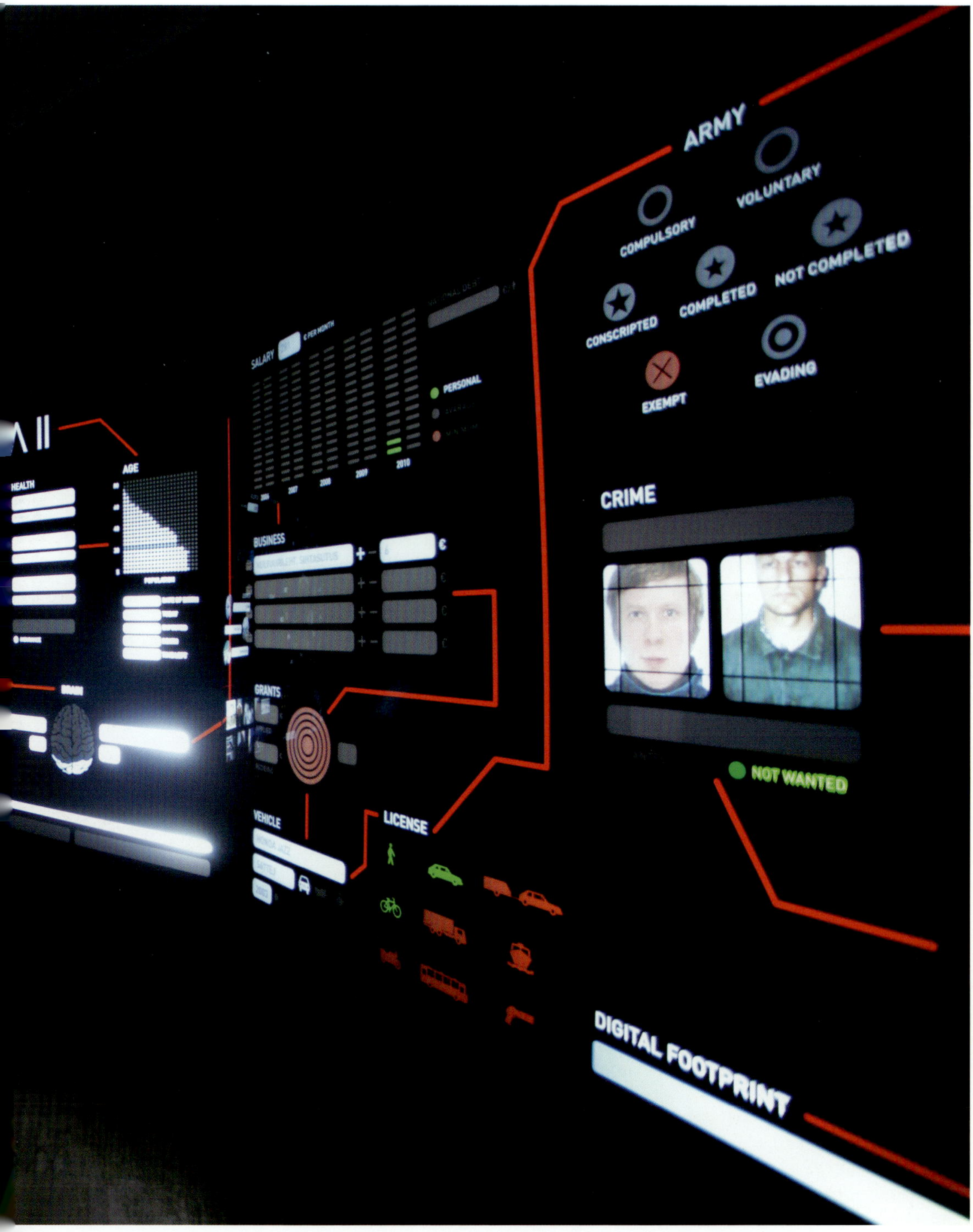
ARMY
VOLUNTARY
COMPULSORY
NOT COMPLETED
COMPLETED
CONSCRIPTED
EVADING
EXEMPT
SALARY
€ PER MONTH
PERSONAL
2006
2007
2008
2009
2010
AGE
HEALTH
BUSINESS
CRIME
NOT WANTED
GRANTS
BRAIN
VEHICLE
LICENSE
DIGITAL FOOTPRINT

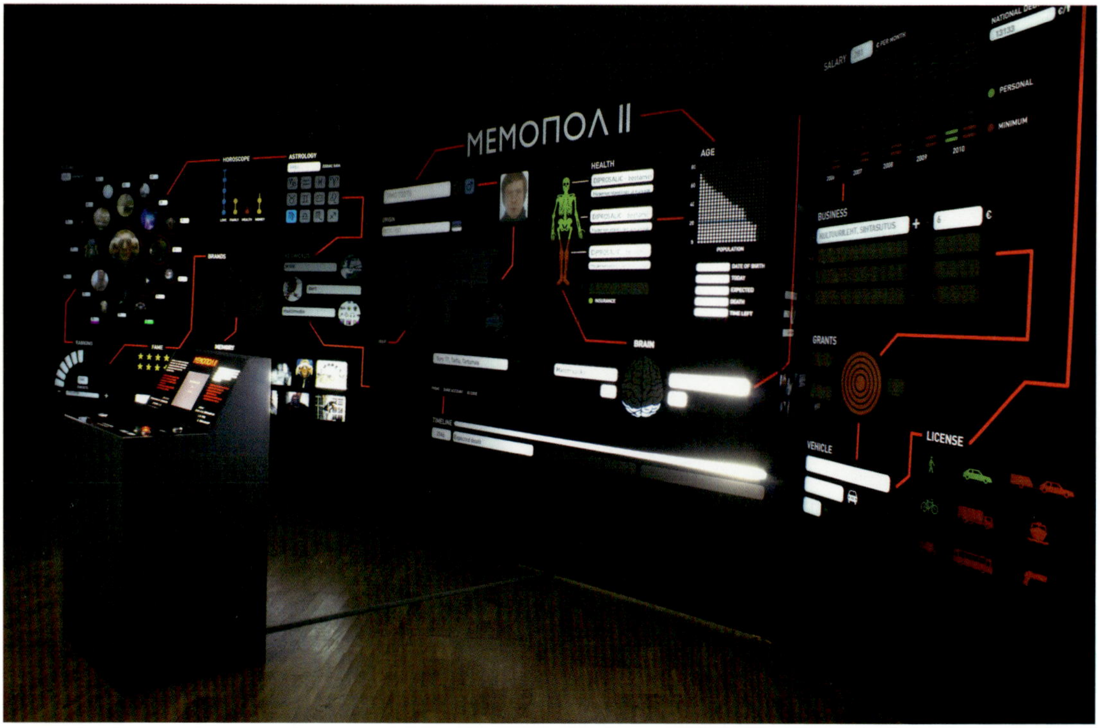

Memopol-2 is a social machine that maps the visitor's information field. When an identification document such as a national ID card or a passport is inserted into it, the machine starts collecting information about the visitor from (inter)national databases and the Internet. The data is then visualized on a large-scale custom display. People using the machine will be remembered by their names and portraits.

The Cyrillic spelling of the installation's name refers to George Orwell's concept of Big Brother from his dystopian novel *1984*. Over the past decades, technology has transformed the surveillance of society. When surfing the Internet, paying with an ATM card or using an ID card, people leave their digital traces everywhere. The Internet and social networks gather and provide a great deal of personal information, and a person's profile is no longer constituted by his or her physical being alone. Background checks through Internet search engines and social network sites have become routine. *Memopol-2* enables us to make a thorough background check on ourselves, mirroring our virtual image.

Memopol-2 ist eine soziale Maschine, die das Informationsfeld ihrer Nutzer kartografiert. Wird ein Identifikationsdokument wie zum Beispiel ein Personalausweis oder ein Pass eingeführt, beginnt die Maschine, Informationen über deren Inhaber aus nationalen wie internationalen Datenbanken und aus dem Internet zusammenzutragen. Diese werden dann auf einer großen, maßgeschneiderten Displayinstallation visualisiert. Nutzer der Maschine werden mit Namen und Porträt gespeichert.

Die kyrillische Schreibweise des Installationstitels ist eine Anspielung auf den Großen Bruder in George Orwells dystopischem Roman *1984*. Im Lauf der letzten Jahrzehnte hat die Technik die Überwachung der Gesellschaft tiefgreifend verändert. Bei jedem Surfen im Internet, jedem Bezahlen mit der Bankomat-Karte, jeder Benutzung eines Ausweises hinterlässt man eine digitale Spur. Internet und soziale Netzwerke sammeln und liefern eine Fülle persönlicher Informationen, und das Profil einer Person ist nicht mehr nur an deren physische Gegenwart gebunden. Die Hintergrundprüfung mithilfe von Suchmaschinen und sozialen Netzwerken ist längst zur Routine geworden. *Memopol-2* ermöglicht eine gründliche Prüfung des eigenen Hintergrunds, die unser virtuelles Abbild widerspiegelt.

Estland ist anderen Ländern bei der staatlichen Datenerhebung weit voraus. In Estland sind bereits seit zehn Jahren elektronische Personalausweise in Gebrauch und es existiert ein System, das alle staatlichen Datenbanken miteinander vernetzt. Mithilfe persönlicher Kartenlesegeräte sind diese Daten leicht abrufbar. Auf dem in einer hellgrünen, freundlichen, Vertrauen stiftenden Ästhetik gehaltenen Regierungsportal kann man die eigenen Daten – von Medikamentenverschreibungen bis zu den Schulnoten, von der Steuererklärung bis zum Führerschein – einsehen. *Memopol-2* ist eine Reaktion auf solche Entwicklungen und konterkariert ihre Ästhetik mit einem Erscheinungsbild, das übermächtig und böse, düster und Furcht einflößend ist: einer Rückprojektion zeitgenössischer Technik in retrofuturistische Zeiten. Die Mittel von *1984* stehen längst zur Verfügung. Die Frage ist, wie werden sie eingesetzt? In Friedenszeiten machen diese Mittel das Leben um vieles leichter. Aber was, wenn sich der politische Wind dreht?

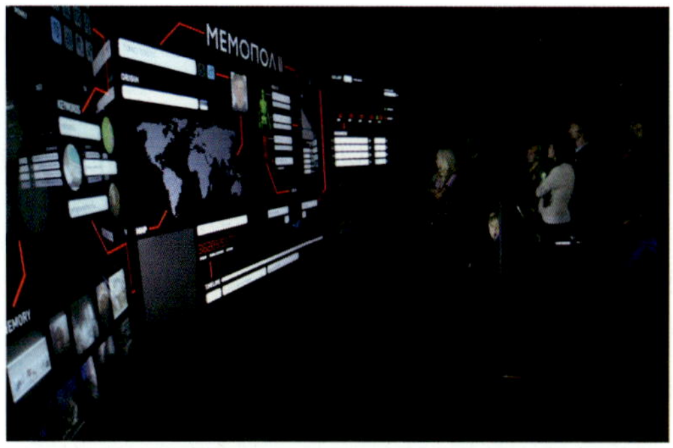

Estonia is well ahead of other countries in governmental data collecting. Estonia has used electronic ID cards for ten years and has built a system that interconnects all governmental databases. Personal ID-card readers provide a simple means of accessing the data. In the government portal, people can see their data, from prescription drugs to high-school exams, from tax reports to driving licenses. The online interface has light green, friendly and trustful aesthetics. *Memopol-2* is a reaction to these developments and uses contrasting aesthetics. It is big and evil, dark and scary. It projects present-day technology into retro-futuristic times. The tools of *1984* are already here, but the question is how do we use them. In peacetime these tools add a lot of comfort to everyday life, but what happens when the political winds change.

Idea, design, programming: Timo Toots; co-designer: Martin Rästa; co-programmer: Tanel Külaots; co-programmer: Arne Gödeke; sound design: Hendrik Kaljujärv, Karl Saks

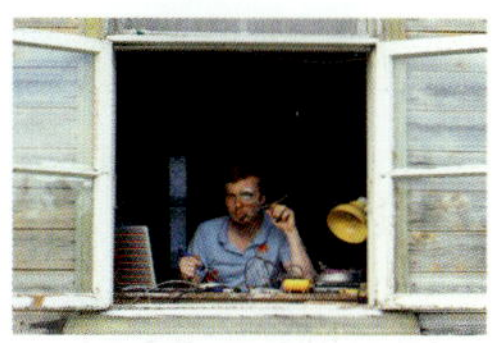

Timo Toots (EE), born 1982, studied computer science at the Tartu University but never graduated. Instead he studied photography at the Estonian Academy of Arts. Since 2005 he has created interactive art projects for group exhibitions in the Baltics, Finland, Russia and Germany. These mostly analyze, comment or reflect on developments in (information) society. He also likes working with projects to do with public space. His first solo exhibition was held in 2010 and was the start of the project presented here. His works are documented on his website *www.timo.ee*. **Timo Toots** (EE), geboren 1982, studierte zunächst Computerwissenschaft an der Universität Tartu und absolvierte danach ein Fotografiestudium an der Estnischen Kunstakademie. Seit 2005 realisiert er interaktive Kunstprojekte, die in Gruppenausstellungen im Baltikum, Finnland, Russland und Deutschland gezeigt wurden und Entwicklungen der (Informations)Gesellschaft analysieren, kommentieren oder reflektieren. Darüber hinaus arbeitet er auch an Projekten zum öffentlichen Raum. Bei seiner ersten Einzelausstellung 2010 wurde auch das hier vorgestellte Projekt aus der Taufe gehoben. Dokumentationen seiner Arbeiten finden sich auf seiner Website *www.timo.ee*.

It's a jungle in here

Isobel Knowles, Van Sowerwine with Matthew Gingold

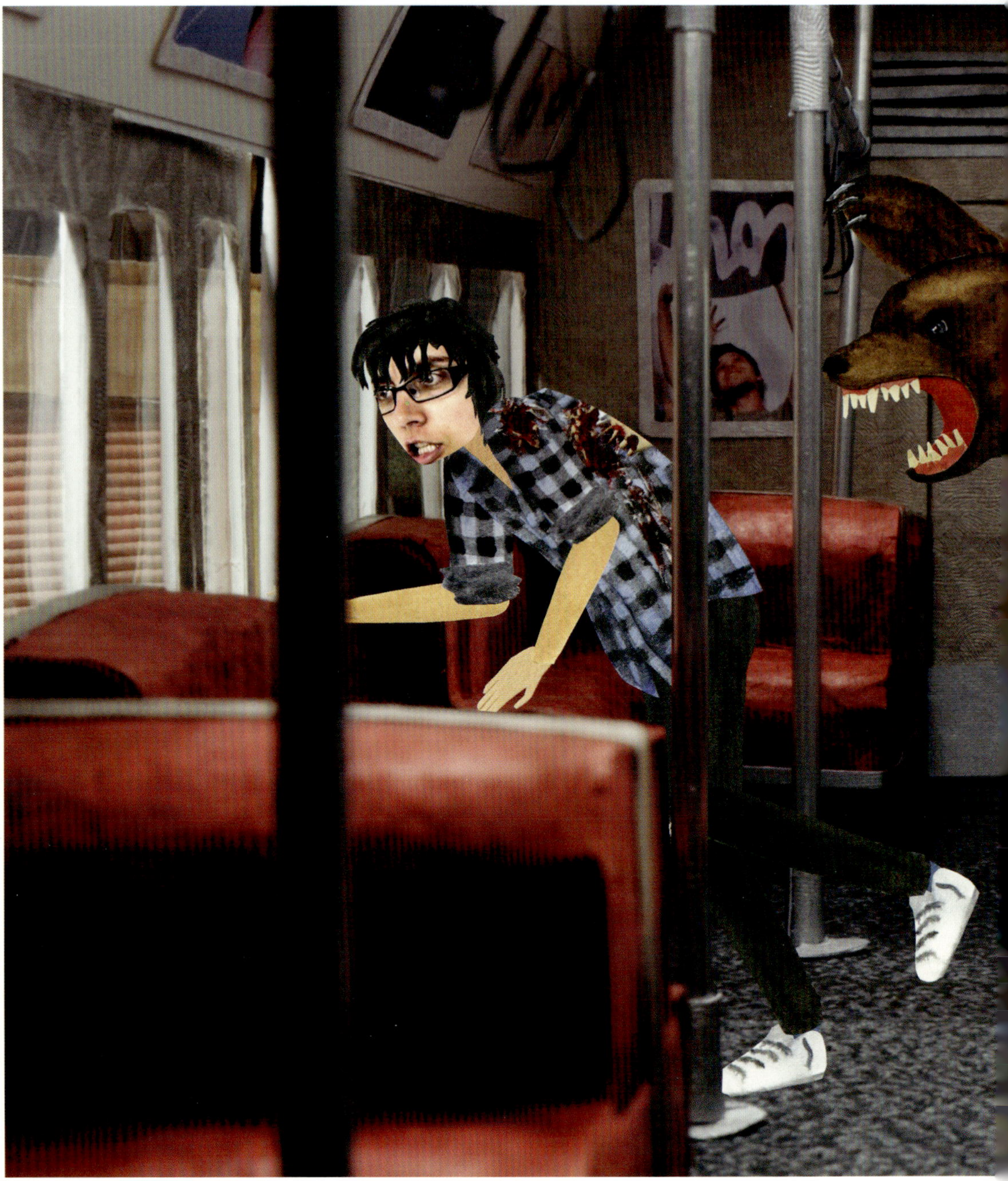

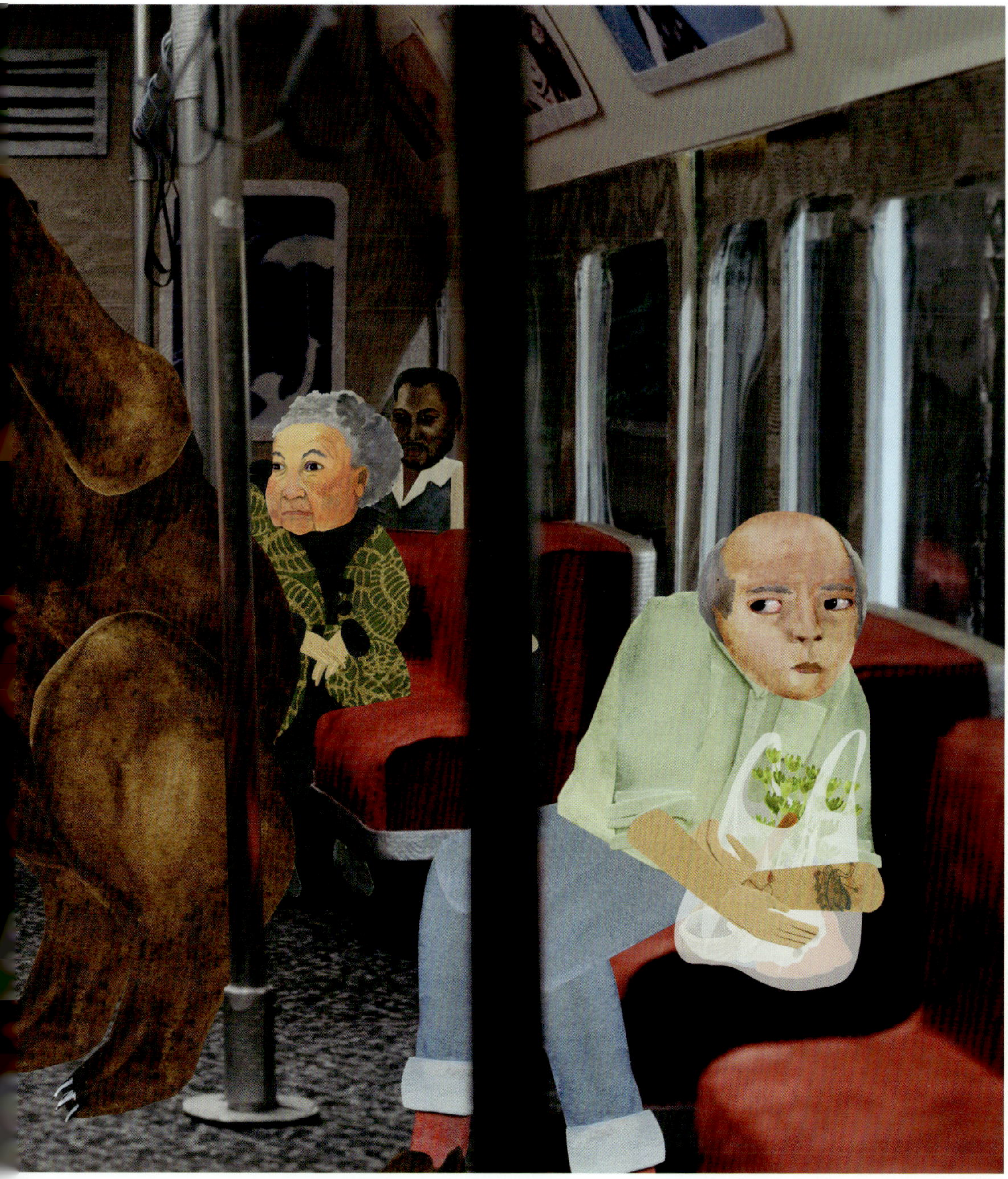

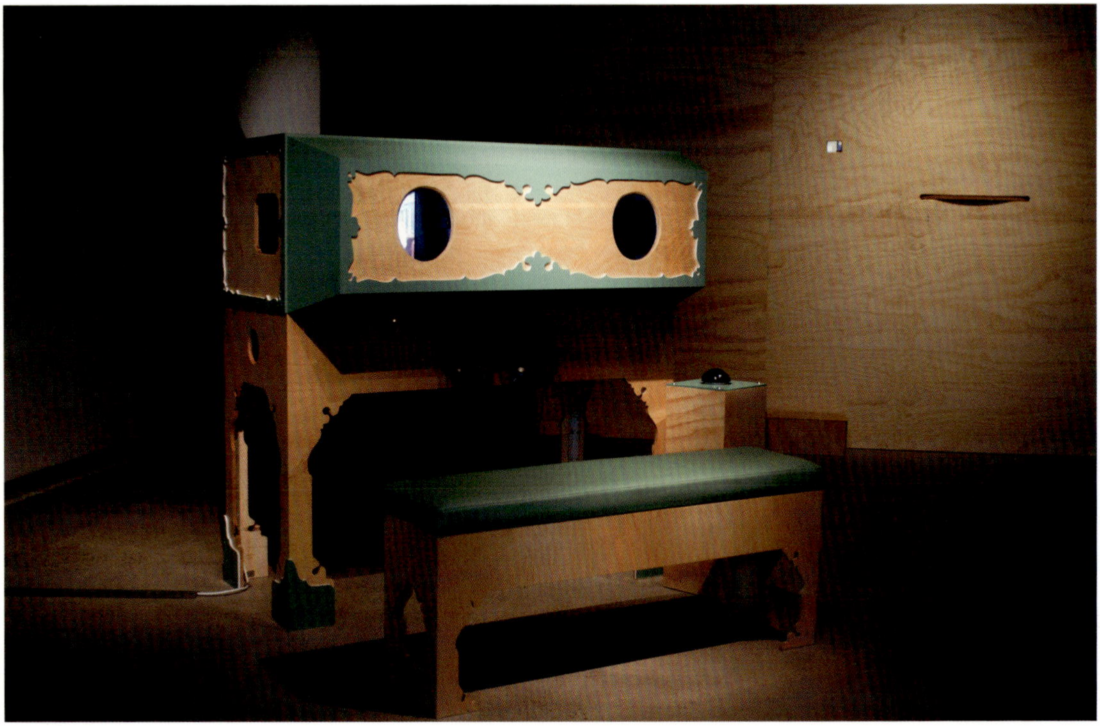

How would you react if someone started behaving inappropriately, or aggressively? Do you try to pretend it isn't happening, or protest and take action? This is the question posed by *It's a jungle in here*, an interactive installation that puts two people into a simulated environment and has them respond to a series of increasingly unsettling encounters.

Participants sit down at an ornate wooden booth and, donning headphones, place their heads in one of two portholes in the front panel. On a screen inside the cabinet they see a stop-motion animation of paper characters on a train, two of which have a live video-feed of the face of each participant from a webcam inside the cabinet.

Three stories unfold, one after the other. Each person is cast as victim or attacker. As the stories progress through user interaction they become more aggressive and tense. At the climax of each scenario the attacker transforms into an animal, cathartically venting our shared anxiety through the iconography of ancient fables.

Participants interact with the work using either a button or a microphone. The person playing the attacker presses a large button to continue their

Wie würden Sie reagieren, wenn sich jemand daneben benimmt oder aggressiv wird? Gehen Sie darüber hinweg, oder protestieren Sie und greifen Sie ein? Das ist die Frage, die die interaktive Installation *It's a jungle in here* aufwirft. Sie setzt zwei Personen einer simulierten Situation aus und lässt sie auf eine Reihe zunehmend verstörender Begegnungen reagieren.

Die Teilnehmer nehmen an einer verschnörkelten, hölzernen Schaubude Platz, setzen Kopfhörer auf und stecken ihre Köpfe durch zwei Löcher. Auf einem Bildschirm im Inneren der Bude sehen sie einen Stop-Motion-Trickfilm mit Papierfiguren, der in einem Vorstadtzug spielt. Zwei der Figuren tragen die mit einer Webcam aufgenommen Gesichter der beiden Teilnehmer.

Es werden drei verschiedene Geschichten erzählt, wobei die Rolle des Opfers bzw. Angreifers jeweils mit den beiden Personen besetzt wird. Im Verlauf der Geschichten wird die durch die User-Interaktion vorangetriebene Handlung immer aggressiver, bis sich der Angreifer schließlich in ein Tier verwandelt und sich die angestaute Angst in der Ikonografie alter Fabeln kathartisch entlädt.

Die Teilnehmer interagieren in dieser Installation mithilfe eines Druckknopfs bzw. eines Mikrofons. Die Person, die den Angreifer spielt, kann an bestimmten Stellen durch Betätigung des Druckknopfs die Handlung vorantreiben.

Die Person, die das Opfer spielt, kann durch Schreien ins Mikrophon ihren Protest zum Ausdruck bringen.
It's a jungle in here ergründet die Ausübung von Macht und ihren Einsatz zum Einschüchtern anderer, und zwar sowohl im wirklichen Leben wie auf dem Bildschirm. Die Arbeit untersucht das Verhältnis zwischen unserem realen Selbst und einer Bildschirm-Persona, die es uns ermöglicht, Macht auszuüben – und zu missbrauchen. Isoliertheit und Abgehobenheit der Bildschirm-Persona werden durchbrochen durch eine Interaktion mit der Filmhandlung, die zugleich eine mit dem lebenden, atmenden Wesen ist, das neben einem sitzt.
Teils Psychodrama, teils Multimediawunder, erkundet *It's a jungle in here* auf konfrontative Weise die fragilen Regeln unseres öffentlichen Lebens.

actions at various points. The person playing the victim can shout into a microphone to protest.
Ultimately, *It's a jungle in here* investigates the use of power and how it is exercised to intimidate others both in real life and on-screen. It explores the relationship between our real selves and an on-screen persona that allows us to use and abuse our power. *It's a jungle in here* disrupts the isolation and detachment of this on-screen self by creating an on-screen interaction that is simultaneously a physical interaction with a living, breathing person who is sitting right next to you.
Part psychodrama, part multimedia marvel, *It's a jungle in here* is a confronting tour of the fragile rules that organize our public lives.

This project has been assisted by the Australian Government through the Australia Council, its arts funding and advisory body.
Coding and interface electronics: Matthew Gingold; carpentry: Don Russell; soundtrack: Finn Robertson; additional coding: Oliver Marriott

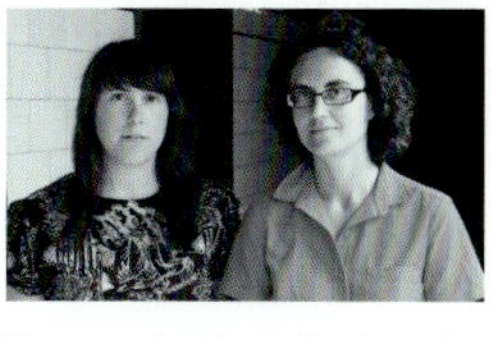

Isobel Knowles (AU) is an artist who works predominantly with animation. She incorporates it into installations, films, music videos, commercial work and anywhere else it might fit in. **Van Sowerwine** (AU), born 1975, is a new-media artist who works in the areas of animation, installations and interactives. Isobel and Van have collaborated on stop-motion animated films and interactive installations for many years. Their work has been exhibited nationally and internationally. **Isobel Knowles** (AU) ist eine Künstlerin, die vorwiegend im Bereich Animation arbeitet. Sie integriert diese in Installationen, Filme, Musikvideos, kommerzielle Arbeiten und wo immer sie sonst noch hinpassen mag. **Van Sowerwine** (AU), geboren 1975, ist eine Medienkünstlerin, die in den Bereichen Animation, Installation und Interaktion arbeitet. Isobel und Van arbeiten seit vielen Jahren gemeinsam an Stop-Motion-Animationen und interaktiven Installationen. Ihre Arbeiten wurden im In- und Ausland gezeigt.

Solar Sinter Project

Markus Kayser / Markus Kayser Studio

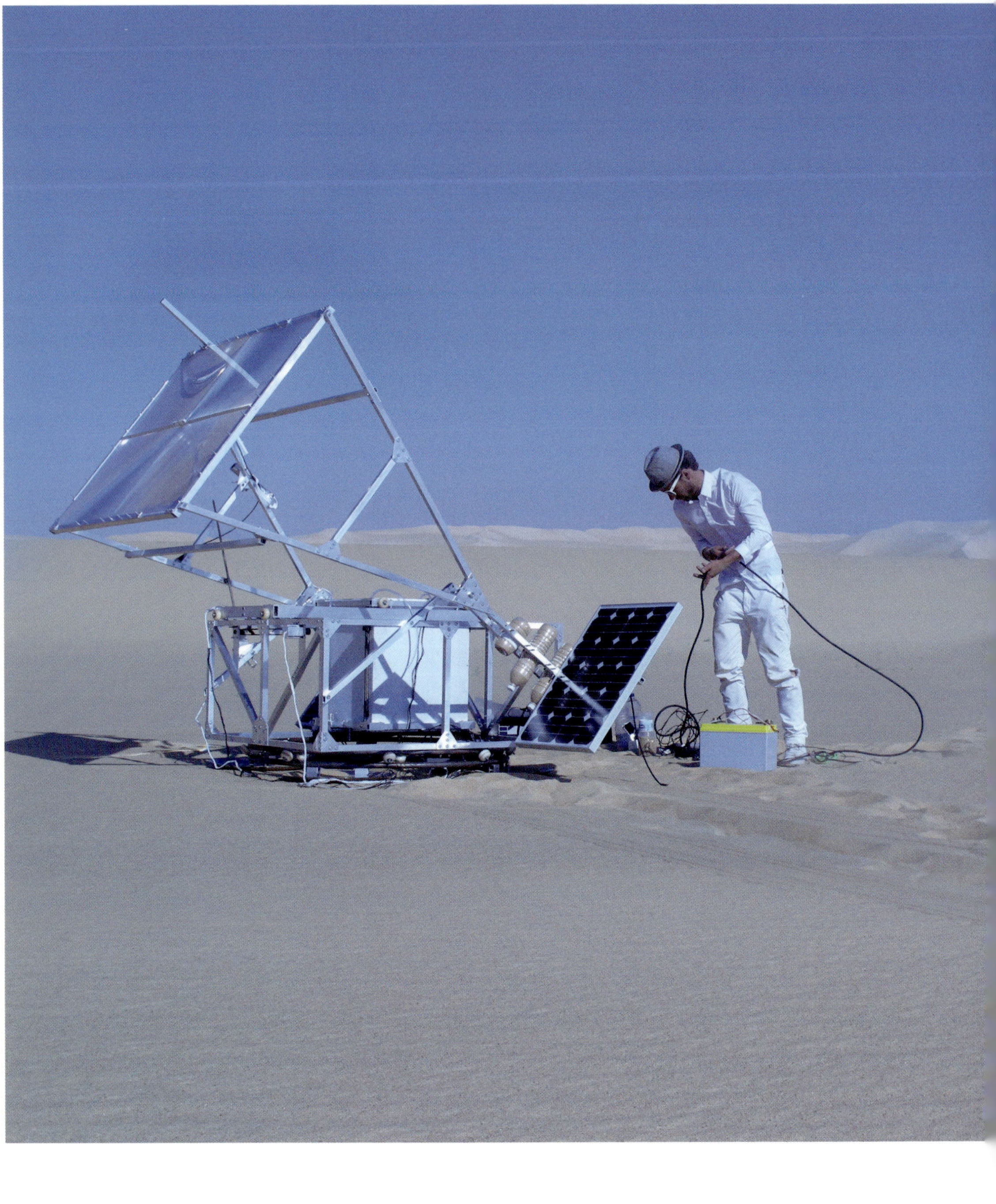

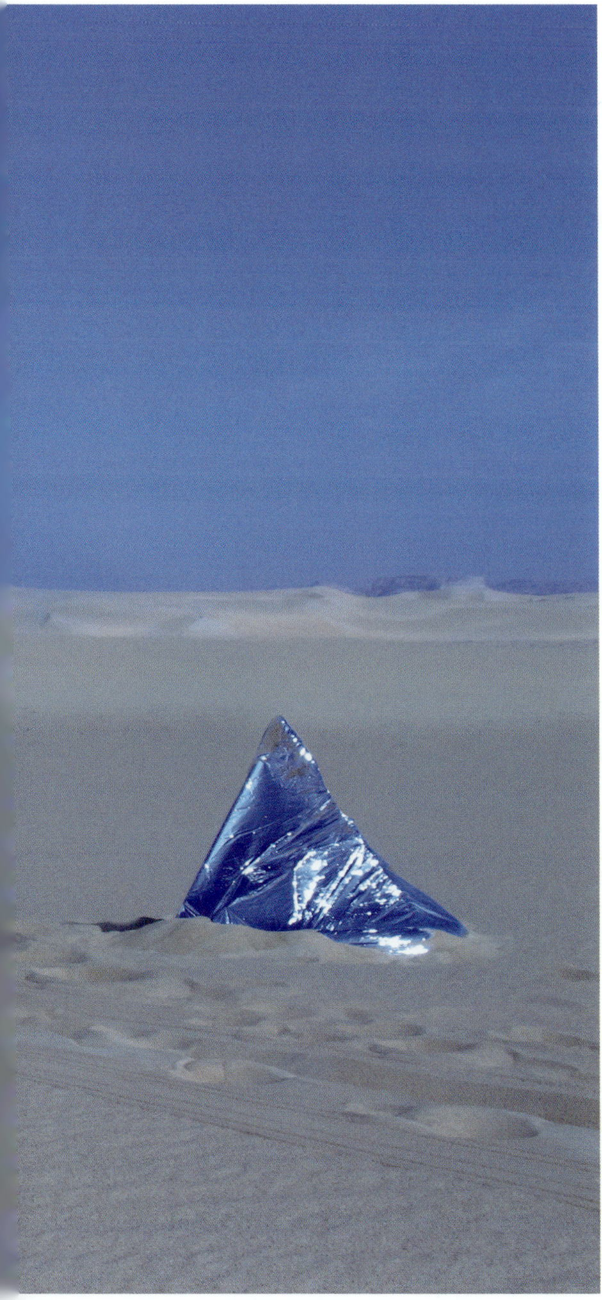

Solar Sinter in the Sahara Desert near Siwa, Egypt. Photo: Amos Field Reid

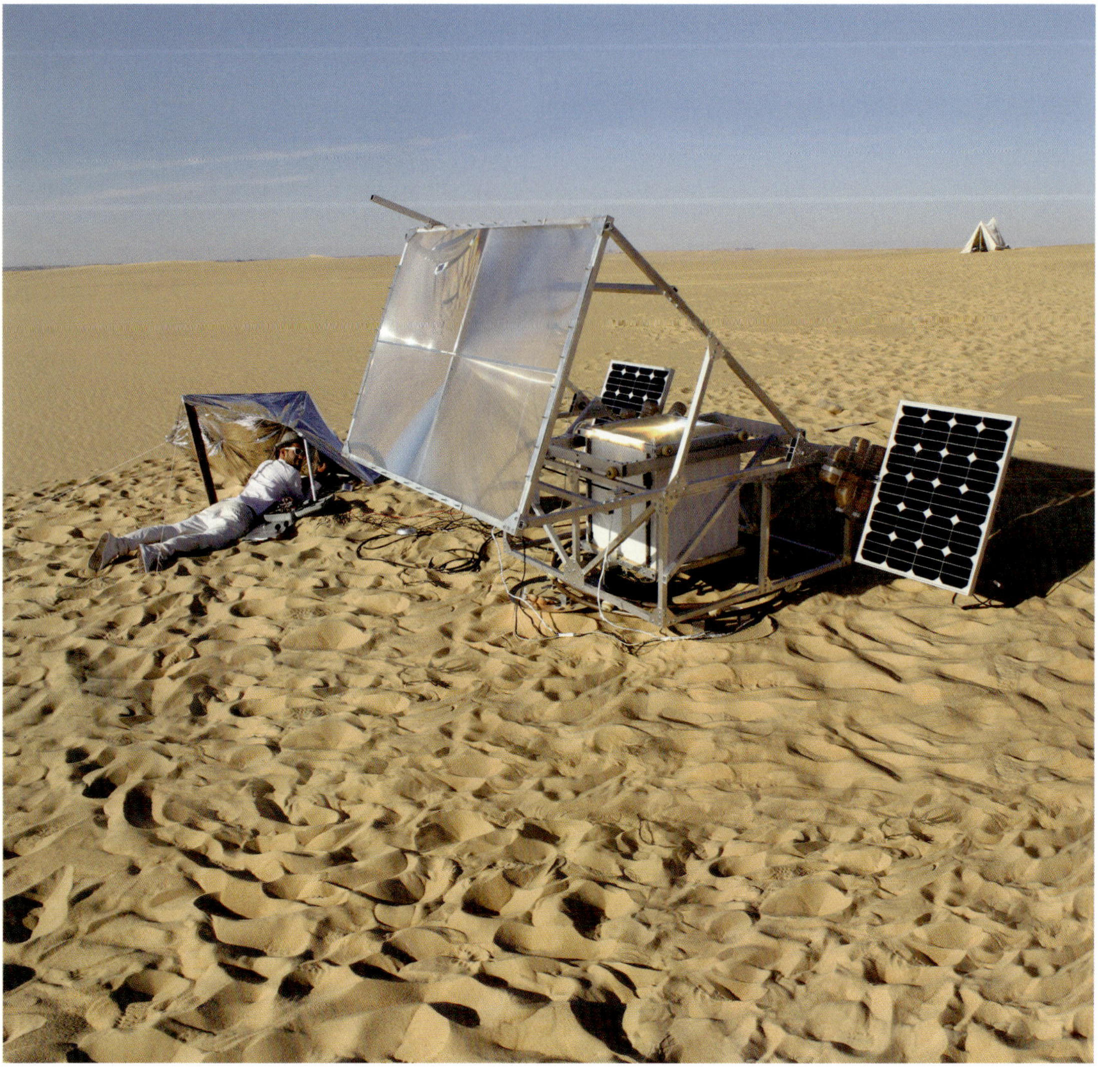

Solar Sinter in the Sahara Desert near Siwa, Egypt. Photo: Amos Field Reid

In einer Welt, in der Fragen der Energieerzeugung und Rohstoffknappheit eine immer größere Rolle spielen, erkundet dieses Projekt Fertigungsmöglichkeiten in der Wüste, wo es Energie und Material im Überfluss gibt.
In diesem Experiment werden Sonnenlicht und Sand als Rohenergie bzw. Rohmaterial für die Produktion von Glasobjekten mittels eines 3D-Druckverfahrens herangezogen, d.h. natürlich vorhandene Energie und natürlich vorhandenes Material mit avancierter Fertigungstechnik verbunden.
Das Solar-Sinter-Verfahren möchte Fragen über die Zukunft der Produktion aufwerfen und zum Träumen über die volle Nutzung des Produktionspotenzials unserer effizientesten Energiequelle – der Sonne – anregen. Das Experiment liefert keine endgültigen Antworten, sondern möchte eher einen Anstoß zu frischen Denkansätzen geben.

In a world increasingly concerned with questions of energy production and raw-material shortages, this project explores the potential of desert manufacturing, where energy and material are abundant.
In this experiment, sunlight and sand are used as raw energy and material to produce glass objects using a 3D printing process that combines natural energy and material with high-tech production technology.
Solar-sintering aims to raise questions about the future of manufacturing and triggers dreams of the full utilization of the production potential of the world's most efficient energy resource—the sun. While not providing definitive answers, this experiment aims to provide a point of departure for fresh thinking.

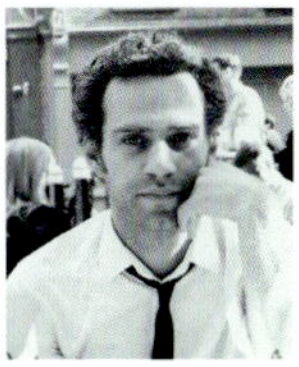

Markus Kayser (DE), born 1983. He studied 3D furniture and product design at London Metropolitan University from 2004 to 2008 and continued in 2009 with the study of product design at the Royal College of Art and gained his master's in 2011. Markus Kayser Studio was set up in London, UK, in 2011. The aim of the studio is to engage in discussion about opportunities in the production of design involving new as well as forgotten processes and technologies. The studio draws from science, art and engineering and aims to blur the gaps between seemingly separate fields. **Markus Kayser** (DE), geboren 1983, studierte von 2004 bis 2008 3D-Möbel- und Produktdesign an der London Metropolitan University, und ab 2009 Produktdesign am Royal College of Art, wo er 2011 mit einem Master abschloss. Im selben Jahr gründete er das Markus Kayser Studio in London. Ziel des Studios ist die Erkundung von Produktionsmöglichkeiten für Design mittels neuer und vergessener Prozesse und Technologien. Das Studio verbindet Wissenschaft, Kunst und Technik in einem Versuch, die Schranken zwischen vermeintlich getrennten Gebieten zu überwinden.

ADM8

RYBN

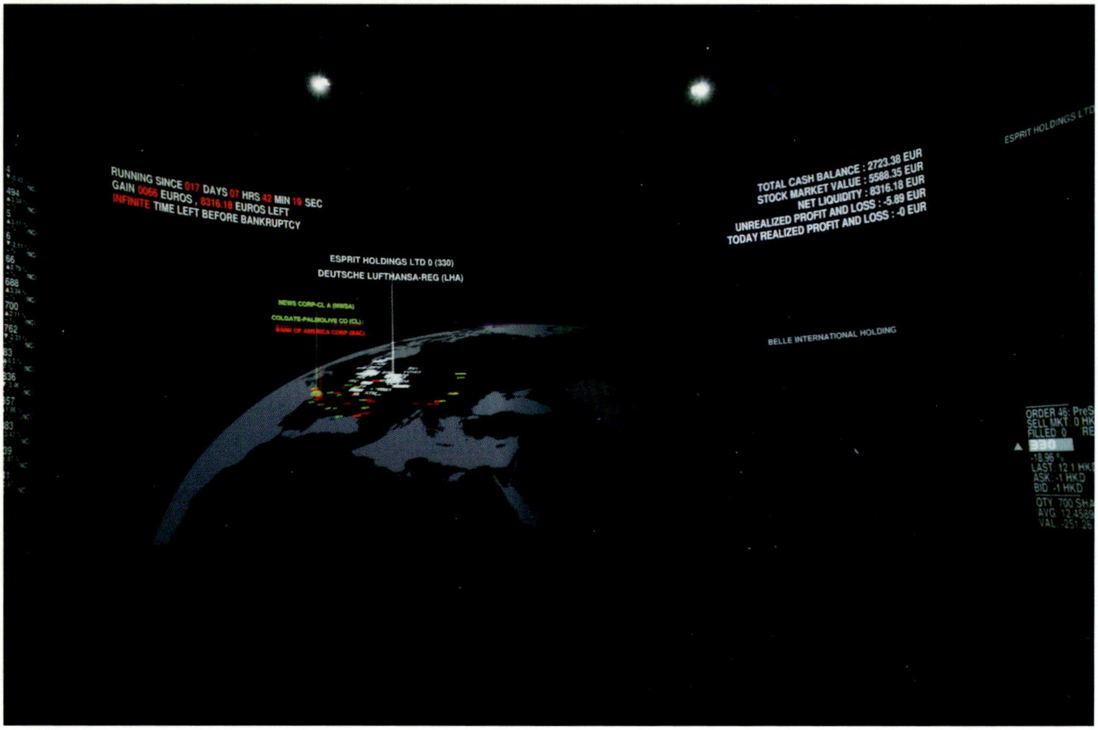

On May 6, 2010, around 2:40 p.m., the Dow Jones Industrial Average index fell about 900 points in less than twenty minutes. The loss was estimated at a trillion dollars. Following this event, all transactions made that day between 2:40 and 3 p.m. were canceled by joint agreement. This instantaneous stock market crash, which is now referred to as the "flash crash," was caused by miscalculations carried out by high-frequency trading robots operating on the markets. Despite its virtuality, this crash sheds light upon the actual architecture of finance: its particular temporality and scale that reaches far beyond human physical abilities and perceptions, where robots trigger thousands of orders every second and flood the market with millions of pieces of fake information to hide their true investments, a process called "quote stuffing."

Engaging finance in its most recent and complex developments, RYBN has undertaken the construction of its own trading bot, designed to invest and speculate on the financial markets. Using an online broker service to directly access the markets, this autonomous program can trigger

Am 6. Mai 2010 um 14:40 Uhr fiel der Dow-Jones-Index in weniger als 20 Minuten um 900 Punkte. Der Verlust wurde auf eine Billion Dollar geschätzt. Nach diesem Ereignis wurden sämtliche an diesem Tag zwischen 14:40 und 15:00 Uhr getätigte Transaktionen einvernehmlich annulliert. Dieser heute unter dem Namen „Flash Crash" bekannte Einbruch der US-Aktienmärkte wurde durch Fehlberechnungen des automatisierten Hochfrequenzhandels ausgelöst. Trotz seines virtuellen Charakters wirft dieser Börsencrash ein Licht auf die tatsächliche Architektur der Finanzwelt: ihre spezifische, die Fähigkeiten und das Wahrnehmungsvermögen des Menschen weit übersteigende Zeitlichkeit und Dimension, wenn etwa Roboter jede Sekunde Tausende von Orders platzieren und den Markt in einem als „quote stuffing" bezeichneten Prozess mit Millionen falscher Informationen überschwemmen, um die wahre Investitionsstrategie zu verbergen.

Um die Finanzwelt auf dem Feld ihrer neuesten und komplexesten Entwicklungen anzugreifen, hat RYBN einen eigenen Trading-Roboter zum Investieren und Spekulieren auf den Finanzmärkten konstruiert. Mithilfe eines Online-Brokerdienstes kann dieses autonome Programm direkt auf dem Markt Orders platzieren und Aktien ein- und verkaufen. Seine Entscheidungen fallen mithilfe eines internen algorithmischen Intelligenzsystems und können von einer Fülle externer freier Parameter beeinflusst werden. Mit seinem Entscheidungssystem kann das Programm bevorstehende Marktbewegungen voraussagen, indem es versucht, in den chaotischen Oszillationen des Finanzmarkts relevante, wirksame Muster zu erkennen und zu antizipieren. Die Aktivität des Roboters wird mit seinen Berechnungen und seiner Performance laufend beobachtet, aufgezeichnet und dynamisch visualisiert. Auf diese Weise entsteht ein Panoptikum an Informationen, das formal den Kontrollräumen in den Hinterzimmern der Börsenplätze gleicht. Im Gegensatz zur Black Box des algorithmischen Hochfrequenzhandels handelt es sich bei unserem Roboter allerdings um ein Open-Source-Programm.

orders as well as buy and sell stocks. Its decisions are taken with the help of an internal algorithmic intelligence system and can be influenced by a wide range of external, arbitrary parameters. The whole decision system allows the program to foresee the next moves in the markets while it tries to identify and anticipate the relevant and effective patterns within the financial chaotic oscillations. Along with its computations and performance, the robot's activity is monitored, recorded, and visualized within dynamic mapping. A panopticon of information unfolds that is formally similar to the control rooms of the stock exchanges' back offices. The whole program is designed and distributed in open-source format, in contrast to the black box of the algorithmic and high-frequency trading.

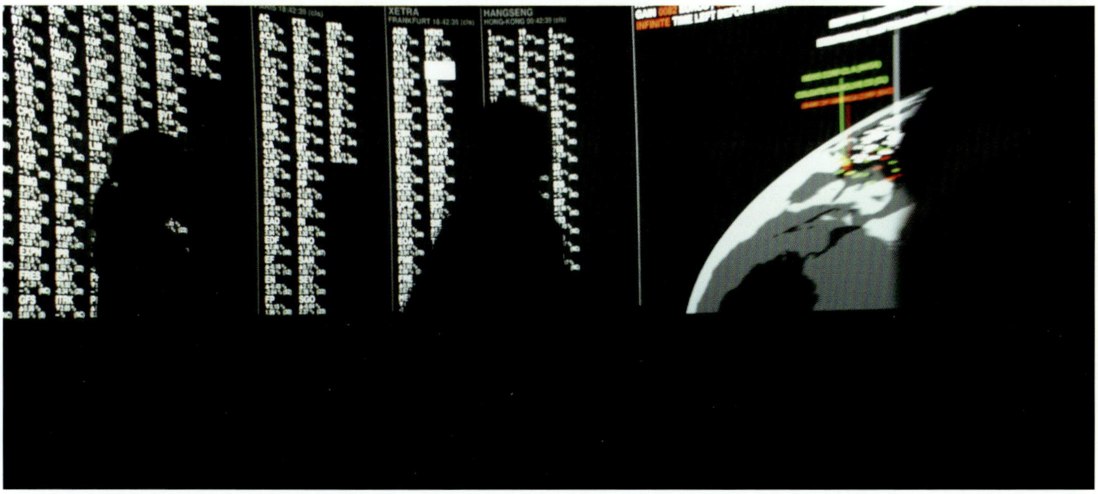

ADM8 was realized with the support of CNC/DICREAM, the French Ministry of Culture; ZKM, GAM / Institut für Bildmedien, Gaîté Lyrique / TAQ

RYBN (FR) is a multi-field artistic collective—Kévin Bartoli, Jean-Marie Boyer, Marika Dermineur, Bertrand Charles, Sylvain Le Beux—based in Paris (2000) and specializing in the realization of installations, performances and interfaces by referring to the codified systems of the artistic representation (painting, architecture, counter-cultures) as well as to human and physic phenomena (geopolitics, socio-economy, sensory perception and cognitive systems). Their axis of research is the construction of a "convergence semantics" via the coupling, diversion and perversion of writing and formalization tools connected with the technologies of communication, information and the sensory—webs, data flows, smell, surveillance, audiovisual, interaction, real time. **RYBN** (FR) ist ein seit 2000 existierendes, auf vielen Gebieten tätiges Pariser Künstlerkollektiv, bestehend aus Kévin Bartoli, Jean-Marie Boyer, Marika Dermineur, Bertrand Charles und Sylvain Le Beux. Seine Spezialität ist die Realisation von Installationen, Performances und Interfaces, die sich sowohl auf die kodifizierten Systeme künstlerischer Darstellung (Malerei, Architektur, Gegenkulturen) als auch auf menschliche und physische Phänomene (Geopolitik, Sozioökonomie, sinnliche Wahrnehmung und kognitive Systeme) beziehen. Arbeitsschwerpunkt ist die Schaffung einer „Konvergenzsemantik" durch Verknüpfung, Umlenkung und Verdrehung der mit den Kommunikations-, Informations- und Sinnestechnologien – Netzen, Datenströmen, Geruch, Überwachung, Audiovision, Interaktion, Echtzeit – verbundenen Schreib- und Formalisierungstools.

Cross Coordinates (MX-US)

Iván Abreu

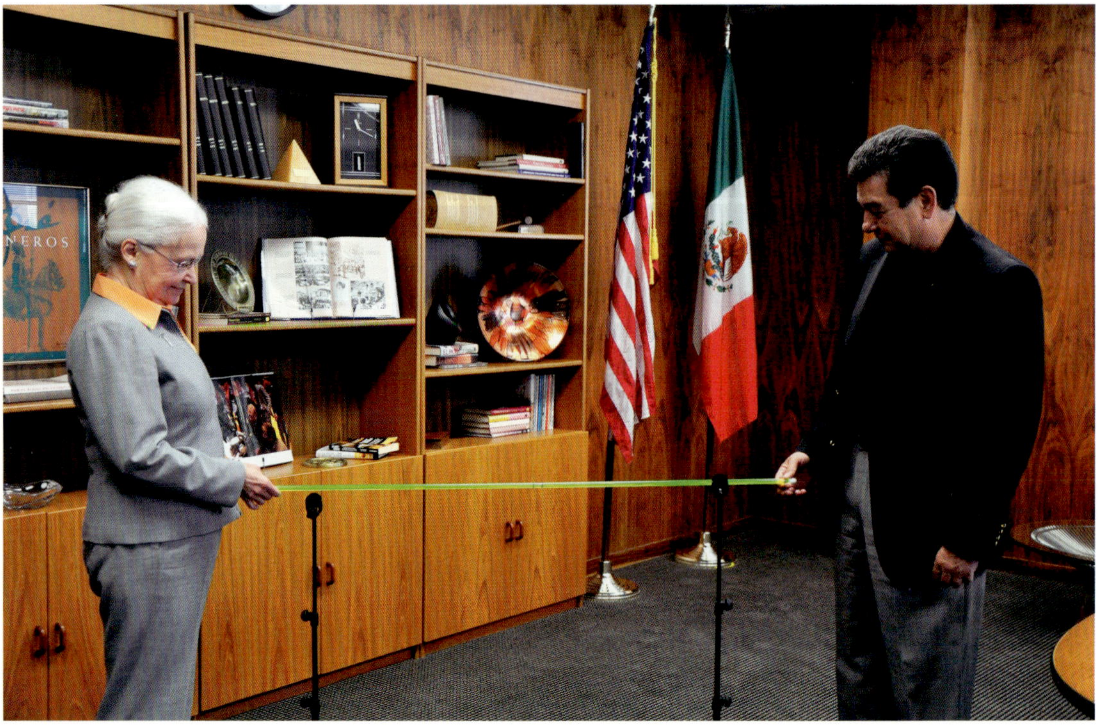

This bi-national project is about a delicate game with an uncommon dynamic. Two players win or two players lose a game with only one way of winning: to collaborate and balance with your opponent. During a month-long residency at the University of Texas at El Paso, the artist filmed scores of border residents as they played a game of cooperation by balancing a specially designed carpenter's spirit-level between them. The delicacy and difficulty of this task, and the goodwill and cooperation of the players, reflected the delicate balance of life on the border. During the four-month exhibition of the piece at the Rubin Center, gallery visitors played the same game using a different level, with an electronic device attached that detected balance and logged the face-to-face play time onto a data base and converted it to meters of cooperation. The goal of participation was to exceed the length of the US-Mexico border (3,169,000m). The final score at the gallery was 70,865 meters.

Afterwards, the project continued with a website application to keep up the goal of overtaking the length of the border. The website application adds meters under the following rules: 1) the time in the

Bei diesem binationalen Projekt handelt es sich um ein diffiziles Spiel mit einer ungewohnten Dynamik. Zwei Personen spielen ein Spiel, das sie nur auf eine Art gewinnen können: durch Zusammenarbeit und Ausgleich mit dem Gegner. Während eines einmonatigen Arbeitsaufenthalts an der University of Texas in El Paso filmte der Künstler zahllose Grenzanrainer dabei, wie sie eine speziell entwickelte Wasserwaage miteinander in die Waage brachten. Die Schwierigkeit dieser heiklen Aufgabe und die Kooperationsbereitschaft der Spieler spiegelt das fragile Gleichgewicht des Lebens an der Grenze wider. Während einer viermonatigen Ausstellung am Rubin Center spielten Besucher das Spiel mit einer anderen Wasserwaage, die mit einem elektronischen Gleichgewichtssensor ausgestattet war und die Spielzeit zweier Spieler in eine Datenbank übertrug und in „Kooperationsmeter" umrechnete. Ziel der Zusammenarbeit war es, die Länge der US-amerikanisch-mexikanischen Grenze (3.169.000 m) zu übertreffen. Das Endergebnis in der Ausstellung betrug 70.865 Meter.

Danach wurde das Projekt mit einer Webapplikation fortgeführt, um das gesteckte Ziel doch noch zu erreichen. Die Website akkumuliert Meter nach folgenden Regeln: 1) nach der auf der Site zugebrachten Zeit; 2)

nach der Beteiligung auf der Site – diese verdoppelt die akkumulierten Meter; und 3) nach der Anzahl der gleichzeitig zugreifenden Personen – die einen exponenziellen Anstieg der Meter bewirkt. Der Inhalt der Website ist eine offene Dokumentation auf der Grundlage eines 10:24 Minuten langen Videos, das durch Hinzufügen der eigenen Meinung verändert werden kann. Am 16. März 2011 wurden Leute zu einem Online-Meeting zusammengetrommelt, um das ursprüngliche Ziel des in der Ausstellung installierten Spiels zu erreichen. In einem Zeitraum von gut vier Stunden steigerten etwa 1.500 Teilnehmer den Spielstand auf 15 Millionen Meter, mehr als das Vierfache der Länge der US-amerikanisch-mexikanischen Grenze, und setzten damit ein gemeinschaftliches Zeichen für den Ausgleich und die Zusammenarbeit zwischen Städten, Ländern oder Ansichten.

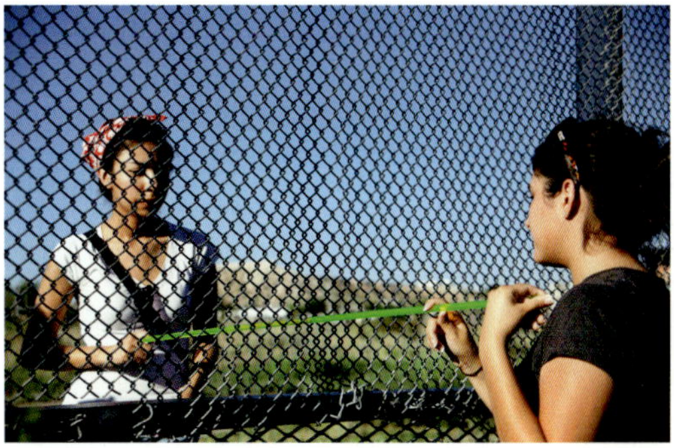

site accumulates meters, 2) sharing duplicates the meters accumulated during the visit, and 3) the number of simultaneously connected people accelerates the account in an exponential way. The website's content is an open documentation based on an online video of 10:24 min., which can be modified by publishing overlapping and synchronous opinions to the video. On March 16, 2011, people were summoned to an online meeting to achieve the initial goal of the game installed in the gallery. Over four hours, around 1,500 people raised the score to 15 million meters, over four times the length of the Mexico-US border, constructing a gesture in community to support the balance and the possibility of collaboration between two cities, countries or points of view.

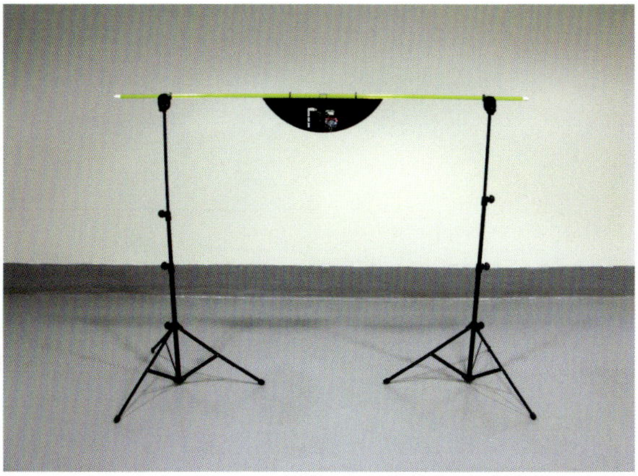

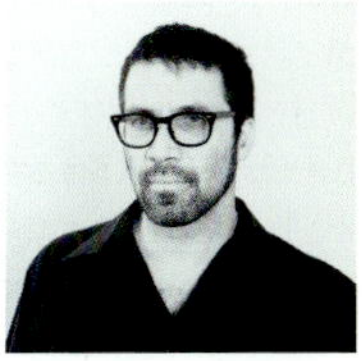

Iván Abreu (MX) is an artist and programmer who works and lives in Mexico City. His work integrates different processes of art, design and technology; by interlinking these disciplines he seeks to generate new tensions between the object, the space, the ideology or history of the place and language, to activate critical thinking and the desire of the possible. These strategies evade fiction or representation, presenting facts and relations with the public based on the truth value of the artistic gesture. He currently holds the grant awarded by the National System of Art Creators of the National Fund for Culture and the Arts of Mexico (FONCA) (2012–2014). **Iván Abreu** (MX) lebt und arbeitet als Künstler und Programmierer in Mexico City. In seiner Arbeit verbindet er verschiedene Prozesse aus Kunst, Design und Technologie mit dem Ziel, neue Spannungen zwischen dem Objekt, dem Raum, der Ideologie oder Geschichte eines Ortes oder einer Sprache zu erzeugen, kritisches Denken zu fördern und das Streben nach dem Machbaren zu beflügeln. Mit diesen Strategien gibt er Fakten und Publikumsbeziehungen, die auf der Wahrhaftigkeit der künstlerischen Geste beruhen, den Vorrang vor Fiktion und Repräsentation. Zurzeit ist er Stipendiat des Sistema Nacional de Creadores de Arte, einem Förderprogramm des Fondo Nacional para la Cultura y las Artes (FONCA).

Energy Parasites

Eric Paulos

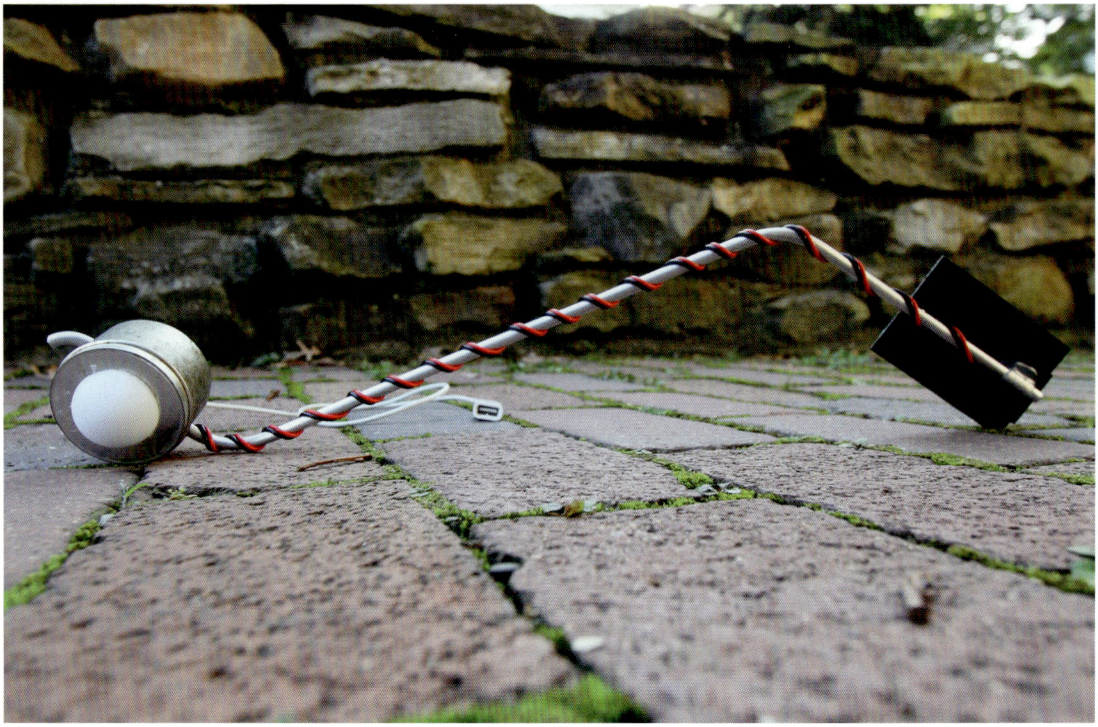

Headlight; Name: luxsap

Energy Parasites are handcrafted objects designed to opportunistically harvest small bits of energy across public landscapes. Agnostic to energy origin or ownership, these artifacts redirect their captured energy through a variety of means, including expressing it or storing it for later re-acquisition and usage. Central to this experience is the materiality of energy.

Energy Parasites foreground energy use and opportunities for re-use. They are both adversarial and helpful as they question concepts of energy ownership and opportunities for energy harvesting. Central to this is the reframing of energy as a material that can be infused and embedded with properties such as when, how, and the texture of the energy production. Can energy be sentimental, emotional, or uncomfortable?

Supported by: NSF, Heinz Endowments

Energy Parasites sind von Hand gefertigte Objekte zum opportunistischen Abzapfen kleiner Energiemengen an verschiedenen Stellen im öffentlichen Raum. Ohne sich für die Herkunft oder Eigentümerschaft der Energie zu interessieren, leiten diese Artefakte die gewonnene Energie auf verschiedene Weise um, drücken sie entweder aus oder speichern sie für den späteren Verbrauch. Das Wesentliche daran ist der materielle Aspekt der Energie.

Energy Parasites zeigen in erster Linie den Gebrauch und die Wiederverwendung von Energie. Zugleich schädlich und nützlich, stellen sie Auffassungen von der Eigentümerschaft von Energie und den Möglichkeiten der Energiegewinnung infrage. Zentraler Aspekt der Arbeit ist die Neufassung von Energie als Materie, etwas, das sich mit Eigenschaften wie dem Wann, Wo, Wie der Energieproduktion verbinden lässt. Kann Energie sentimental, emotional oder unbehaglich sein?

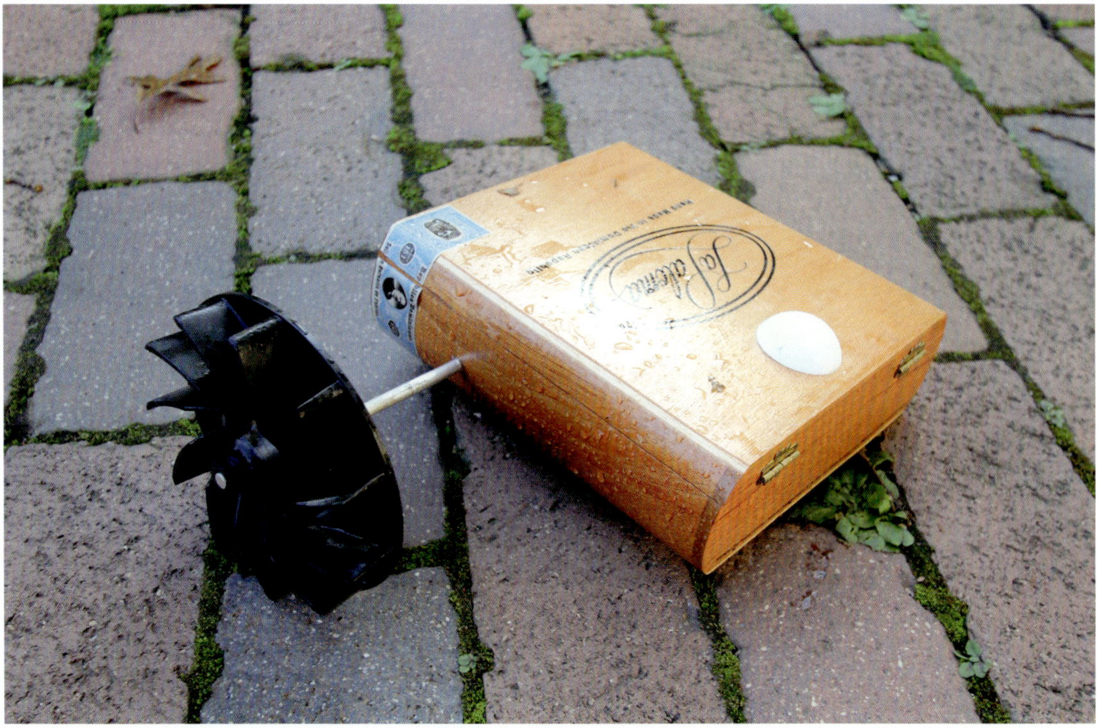

Gutter; Name: draindrain

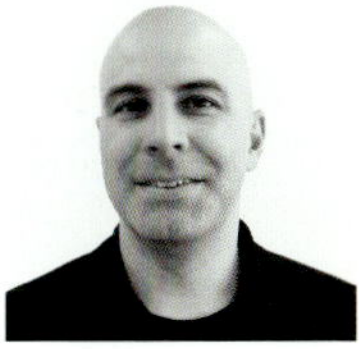

Eric Paulos (US) is the director of the Living Environments Labs and an Assistant Professor in the Center for New Media (BCNM) with a faculty appointment within the Electrical Engineering Computer Science Department at UC Berkeley. Previously, Eric held the Cooper-Siegel Associate Professor Chair in the School of Computer Science at Carnegie Mellon University. Eric is faculty within the Human-Computer Interaction Institute with courtesy faculty appointments in the Robotics Institute and in the Entertainment Technology Center. Previously he was a senior research scientist at Intel in Berkeley, California, where he founded the Urban Atmospheres research group. His areas of expertise span a deep body of research territory in urban computing, sustainability, green design, environmental awareness, social telepresence, robotics, physical computing, interaction design, persuasive technologies and intimate media. Eric received his PhD in electrical engineering and computer science from UC Berkeley, where he helped launch a new robotic industry by developing some of the first Internet tele-operated robots including space browsing helium-filled blimps and personal roving presence devices (ProPs). **Eric Paulos** (US) ist Leiter des Living Environments Lab und Assistant Professor am Berkeley Center for New Media. Er war Inhaber der außerordentlichen Cooper-Siegel-Professur an der Fakultät für Computerwissenschaft der Carnegie Mellon University. Er lehrt außerdem am Human-Computer Interaction Institute und ehrenamtlich am Robotikinstitut und am Center für Unterhaltungstechnologie. Zuvor war er leitender Forscher bei Intel in Berkeley, Kalifornien, wo er die Forschungsgruppe Urban Atmospheres gründete. Seine Expertise erstreckt sich auf ein weites Feld, das Gebiete wie Urban Computing, Nachhaltigkeit, grünes Design, Umweltbewusstsein, soziale Telepräsenz, Robotik, Physical Computing, Interaction Design, persuasive Technologien und personenbezogene Medien umfasst. Eric erwarb seinen PhD in Elektrotechnik und Computerwissenschaft an der UC Berkley, wo er auch die neue Roboterindustrie mit aus der Taufe hob, indem er einige der ersten über das Internet gesteuerten Roboter entwickelte, u.a. im Raum schwebende heliumgefüllte Ballone und PRoPs – personal roving presence devices.

fly tweet

David Bowen

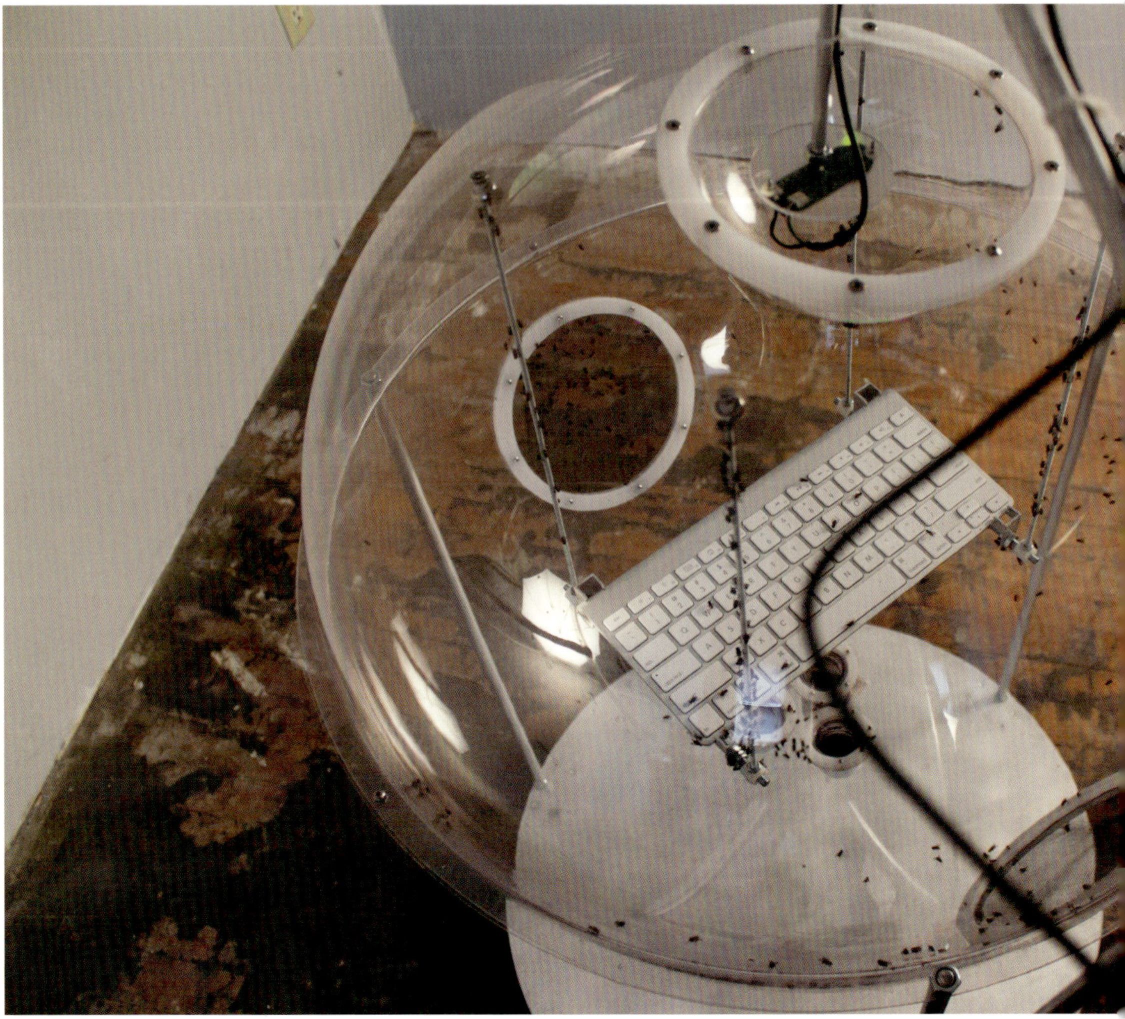

The *fly tweet* device sends Twitter messages based on the activities of a collection of houseflies. The flies live inside an acrylic sphere along with a computer keyboard. As they move and interact inside their home, they fly over the keys on the keyboard. These movements are collected in real time on video. As a particular key is triggered by the flies, the corresponding character is entered into a Twitter text box. When 140 characters are reached or the flies trigger the "enter" key, the message containing the accumulated characters is tweeted. Thus live Twitter messages are constantly sent in real time based on the simple movements of the community of houseflies. These continually

fly tweet sendet auf den Aktivitäten einer Hausfliegenkolonie beruhende Twitternachrichten. Die Fliegen leben in einer Acrylglaskugel, in der sich auch eine Computertastatur befindet. Eine Videokamera erfasst in Echtzeit, wann sich die Fliegen bei ihren Aktivitäten und Interaktionen in diesem Domizil über die Tastatur bewegen. Wird eine Taste überflogen oder berührt, wird das entsprechende Zeichen in ein Twitter-Textfeld eingetragen. Sind 140 Zeichen beisammen oder „betätigen" die Fliegen die Eingabetaste, wird die Nachricht mit der gesammelten Zeichenfolge abgeschickt. Auf diese Weise werden laufend Twitternachrichten abgesetzt, die auf den simplen Bewegungen einer Hausfliegenkolonie beruhen. Die akkumulierten Nachrichten erscheinen als Aufzeichnung

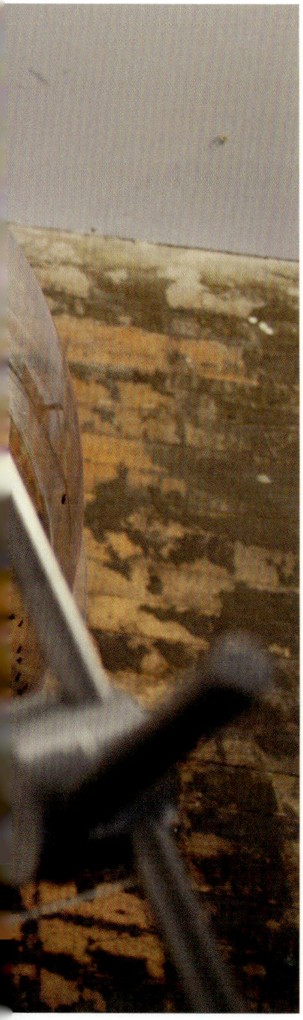

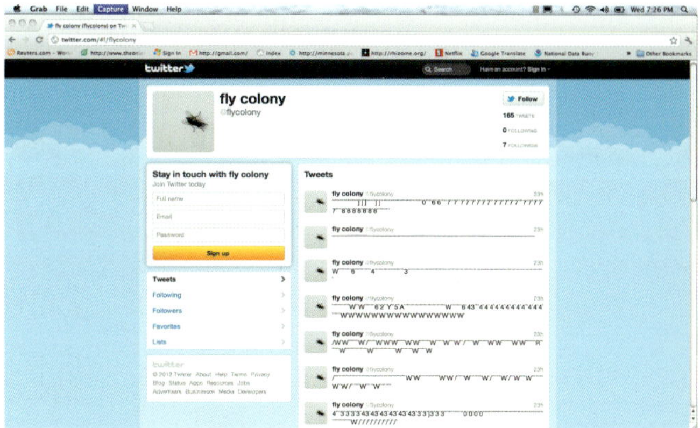

einer Zufallsaktivität im Raum der sozialen Medien und Netzwerke.

accumulating messages appear as records of random activity within the larger sphere of social media and networking.

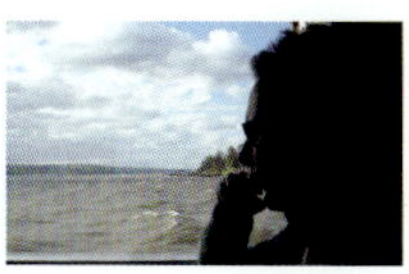

David Bowen (US) born in 1975, is a studio artist and educator whose work has been featured in numerous group and solo exhibitions nationally and internationally. Bowen's work is concerned with aesthetics that result from interactive, reactive and generative processes as they relate to intersections between natural and mechanical systems. He is currently Associate Professor of Sculpture and Physical Computing at the University of Minnesota, Duluth. **David Bowen** (US), geboren 1975, ist ein Künstler und Kunstpädagoge, dessen Arbeiten in zahlreichen Gruppen- und Einzelausstellungen im In- und Ausland gezeigt wurden. Er interessiert sich für eine Ästhetik, die sich aus interaktiven, reaktiven und generativen Prozessen an der Schnittstelle zwischen natürlichen und mechanischen Systemen ergibt. Er ist zurzeit außerordentlicher Professor für Bildhauerei und Physical Computing an der University of Minnesota in Duluth.

Ideogenetic Machine

Nova Jiang

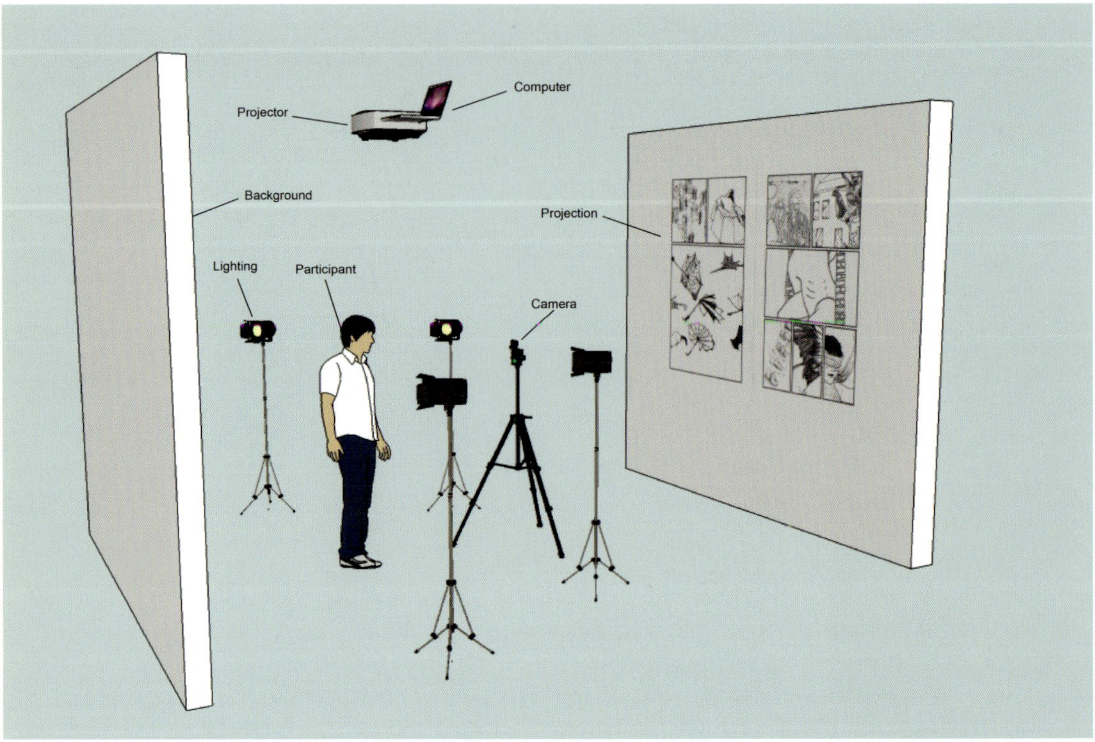

Ideogenetic Machine is an interactive installation that incorporates portraits of participants into an algorithmically generated comic book. A camera captures the portrait live while an algorithm transforms the photographic image into a "line drawing". Face recognition is used to insert code-generated blank speech bubbles into the narrative.

The software creates never-repeating compositions using a set of rules that approximate the compositional decisions made by a human comic-book author. The comic is projected live and consists of the algorithmically processed portraits as well as randomly chosen story elements from a database of drawings. The story elements are drawn by the artist, mostly illustrating speculative narratives based on current news and events. A participant can e-mail him or herself the finished comic as a PDF file. Participants are free to fill the blank speech bubbles with their own invented dialog at home.

Inspired by experimental narrative forms that use chance to aid the process of composition, such as the cut-up technique and Soviet montage theory, the project aims to generate unexpected narrative

Ideogenetic Machine ist eine interaktive Installation, die Porträts ihrer Teilnehmer in einen algorithmisch produzierten Comic-Strip einbaut. Der Algorithmus wandelt von einer Kamera live aufgenommene Fotoporträts in eine „Strichzeichnung" um. Mithilfe von Gesichtserkennung werden in die so entstehende Story automatisch leere Sprechblasen eingesetzt.

Nach einer Reihe von Regeln, die den Kompositionsentscheidungen eines menschlichen Comic-Zeichners nachempfunden sind, erzeugt die Software sich nie wiederholende Kompositionen. Der Comic wird live projiziert und besteht aus den algorithmisch bearbeiteten Porträts sowie narrativen Versatzstücken, die nach einem Zufallsverfahren aus einer Datenbank mit Zeichnungen entnommen werden. Diese Zeichnungen stammen von der Künstlerin und erzählen auf aktuellen Nachrichten und Ereignissen beruhende spekulative Geschichten. Die Teilnehmer können sich den fertigen Comic als PDF mailen und die leeren Sprechblasen zu Hause mit einem selbst erdachten Dialog füllen.

Inspiriert von experimentellen, den Zufall für den Kompositionsprozess nutzenden Erzählformen wie der Cut-up-Technik und der sowjetischen Montagetheorie versucht das Projekt durch die Kombination verschiedener Bilder

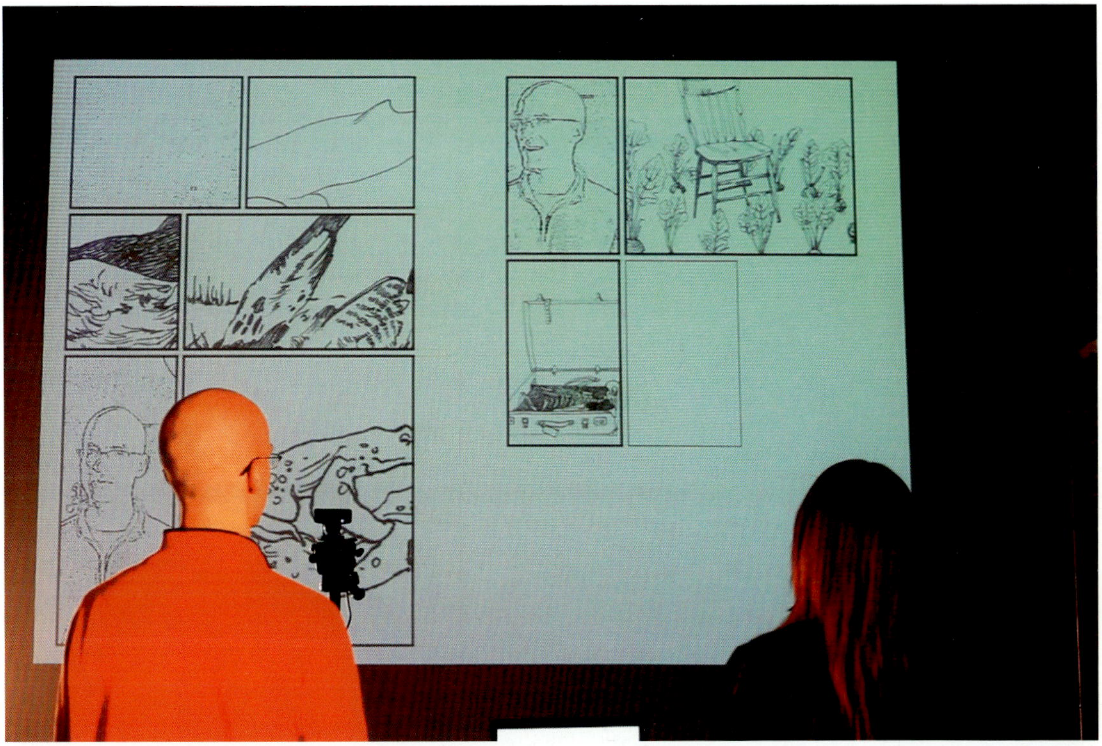

und unvorhersehbarer Publikumsaktionen ungeahnte narrative Möglichkeiten zu erschließen. Ein Computercode ermöglicht in diesem Projekt eine endlose Zusammenarbeit zwischen Künstler, Publikum und Zufallsoperationen.
Der Erfolg der *Ideogenetic Machine* ist vom kreativen Input des Publikums abhängig. Dieses ist aufgefordert, sich vor der Kamera darstellend zu betätigen und die Geschichte durch das Ausfüllen der leeren Sprechblasen zu vervollständigen.

possibilities through the juxtaposition of different images and unpredictable actions by the audience. In this project, computer code enables endless collaboration between the artist, the audience and the operation of chance.
The success of *Ideogenetic Machine* is dependent upon the creative contribution of the audience. They are encouraged to perform in front of the camera as well as completing the narrative by filling out the blank speech bubbles.

Supported by: Eyebeam Art and Technology Center

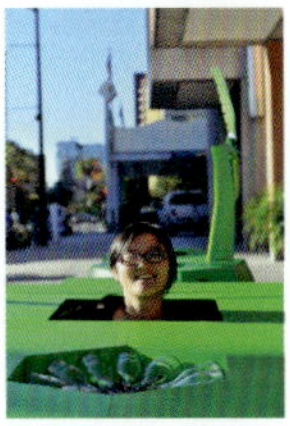

Nova Jiang (NZ), born 1985, is currently based in New York. She has an MFA from the Design Media Art Department, University of California, Los Angeles. She is the recipient of an Eyebeam Fellowship, a Skowhegan Fellowship, a Black Rock Arts Foundation Grant, a Sculpture Space Grant and a Wave Hill Van Lier Visual Artist Fellowship. She has exhibited at Sundance, 01SJ Biennial, MediaLab Prado, Sonar, Glow, TEDActive, Japan Media Arts Festival, Milan Public Design Festival and Transitio_MX. **Nova Jiang** (NZ) geboren 1985, lebt und arbeitet derzeit in New York. Sie hat einen MFA vom Design Media Art Department der University of California Los Angeles und erhielt u.a. folgende Stipendien und Förderungen: Eyebeam Fellowship, einer Skowhegan Fellowship, eines Black Rock Arts Foundation Grant, eines Sculpture Space Grant und einer Wave Hill Van Lier Visual Artist Fellowship. Ihre Arbeiten wurden beim Sundance Festival, bei der 01SJ Biennial, am MediaLab-Prado, bei Sónar, Glow und TEDActive, beim Japan Media Arts Festival und Milan Public Design Festival sowie bei der Transitio_MX gezeigt.

LightType

François Chay, Léo Chéron

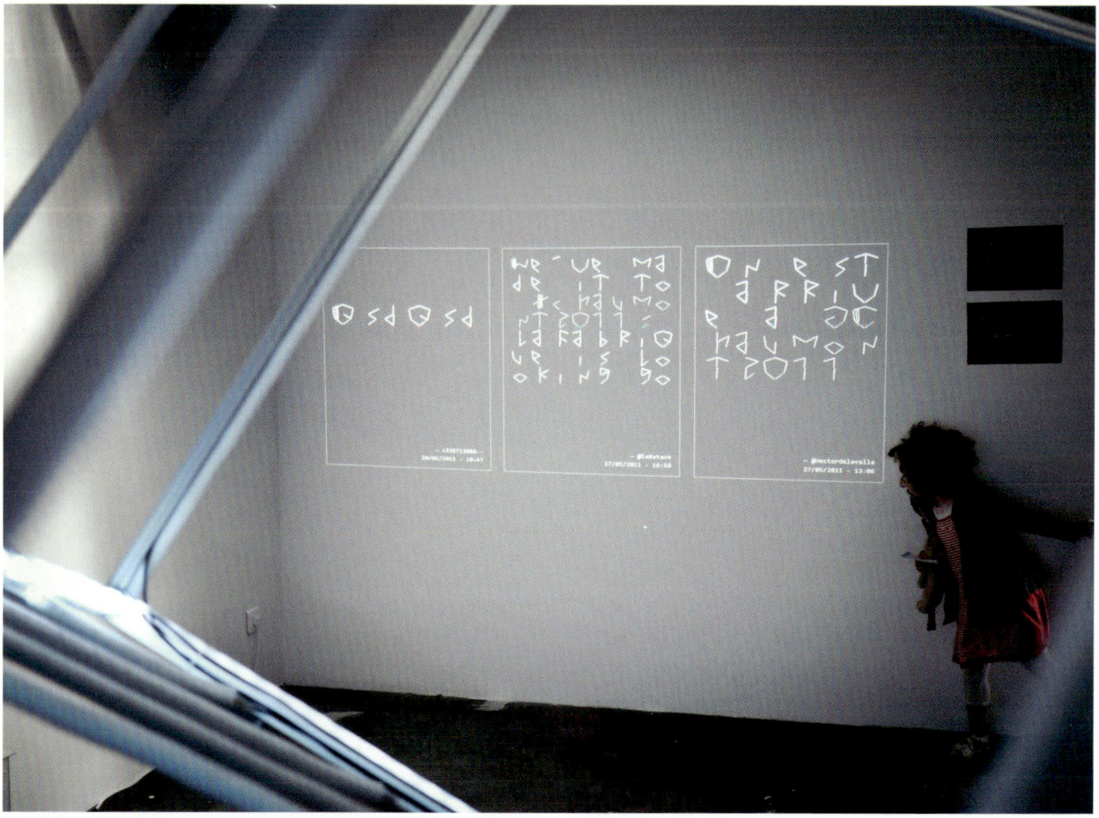

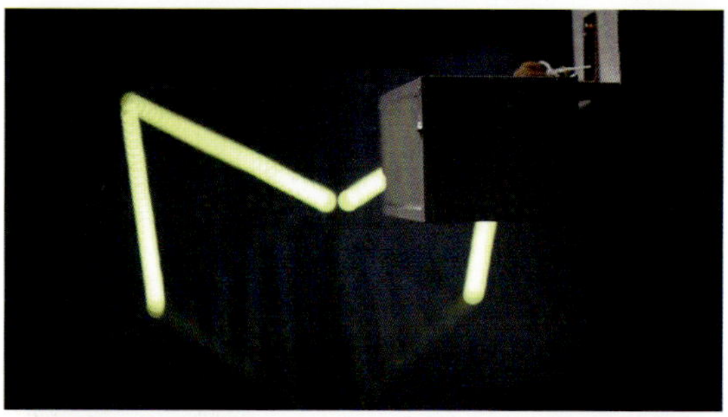

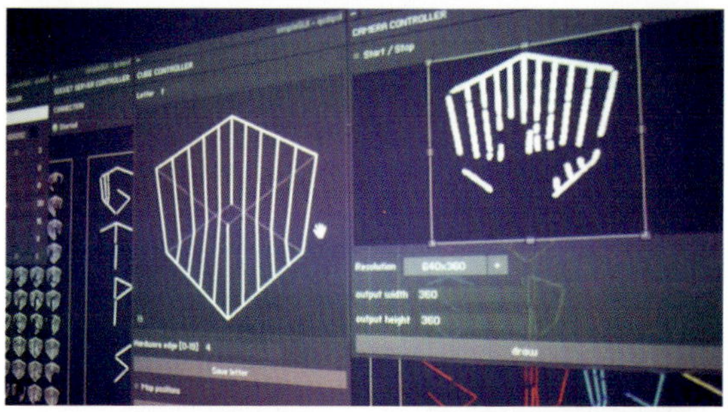

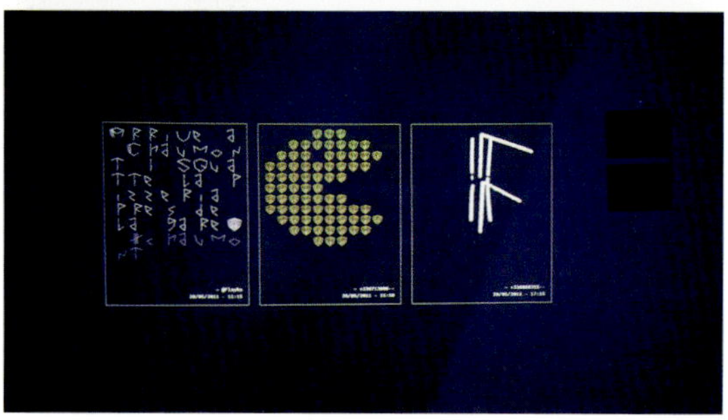

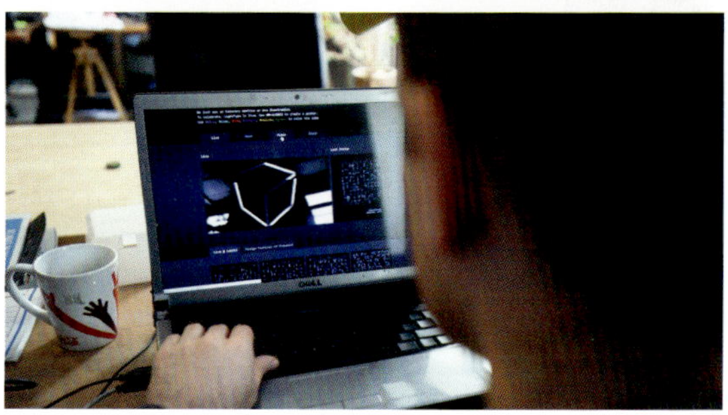

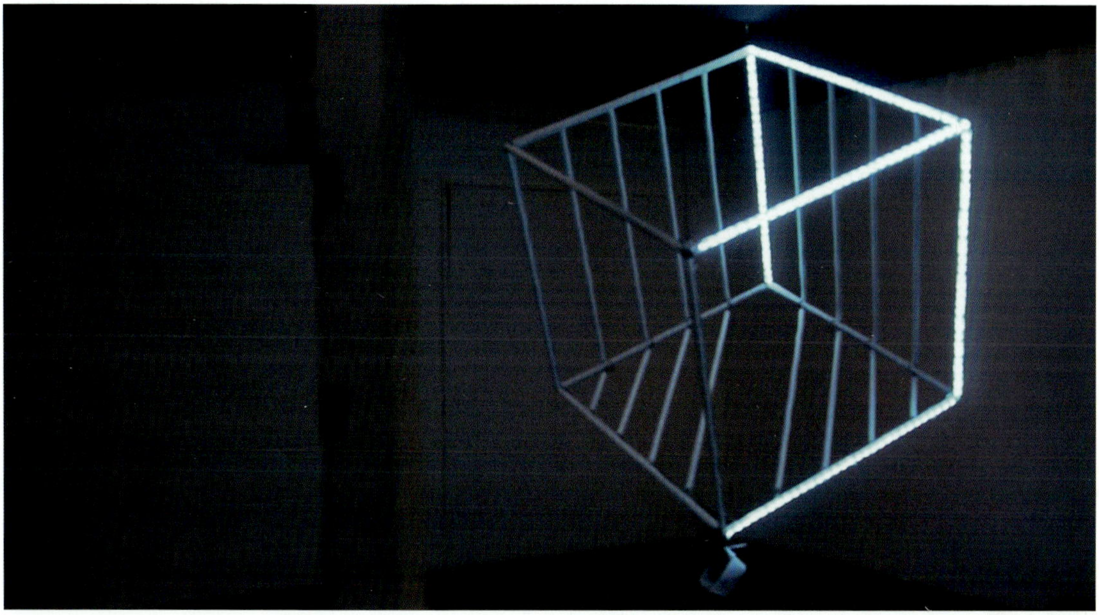

LightType ist eine Installation, die das Verhältnis von Druckgrafikdesign und Interaktivdesign untersucht. Ihr Hauptbestandteil ist ein Würfel aus LED-Leuchten. Je nach Aktivierung derselben entstehen Buchstaben, die die dreidimensionale Struktur in einen zweidimensionalen Leseraum verwandeln.
Die Installation holt sich Tweets zu bestimmten Themen. Der Würfel reagiert darauf und setzt die Nachrichten in Buchstaben und Wörter um. Von einer Webcam aufgenommen werden sie als virtuelle Poster an die Wand projiziert.

LightType is an installation questioning links between printed design and interactive design. Its main component is a cube made out of LEDs. Depending on which sides are on, we can create letters. The three-dimensional structure becomes a two-dimensional reading space.
The installation fetches tweets about a specified subject. When a message is tweeted, the structure reacts to it and creates each letter of each word. They are all captured on a webcam and the message is then projected on the wall to create a virtual poster.

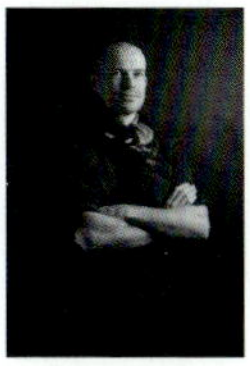

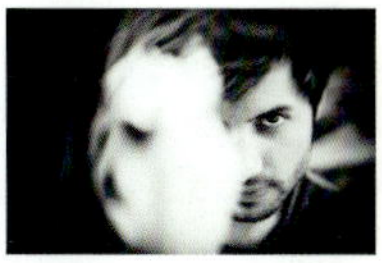

François Chay (FR) graduated from Les Gobelins (Paris) in 2009. He then went to Amsterdam to do an internship at the Roosje Klap graphic design and visual communications studio. He is now working in Paris, where he joined the Lab212 collective and works as a freelance graphic and interactive designer. **Léo Chéron** (FR) graduated from Les Gobelins (Paris) in 2009. He worked as an action-script developer in several of the most famous French interactive agencies Megalo(s), Uzik and Anonymous. His focus on creative coding gained him a considerable number of Favourite Website Awards. He is also involved in photography (CRCR) and part of the QSDQSD collective. **François Chay** (FR), Studium an der Les Gobelins in Paris. Nach dem Studienabschluss 2009 Praktikum bei Roosje Klap, einem Atelier für Grafikdesign und visuelle Kommunikation in Amsterdam. Mittlerweile arbeitet er wieder in Paris als Mitglied des Kollektivs Lab212 und als freischaffender Grafik- und Interaktivdesigner. **Léo Chéron** (FR), Studium an der Les Gobelins in Paris. Nach dem Studienabschluss 2009 Arbeit als Actionscript-Entwickler bei einigen der bekanntesten französischen Interaktivagenturen wie Megalo(s), Uzik und Anonymous. Sein kreativer Programmierstil brachte ihm eine Reihe von Favourite Website Awards ein. Außerdem arbeitet er als Fotograf (bei CRCR) und ist Mitglied des QSDQSD-Kollektivs.

Löschen / DELETE

Marcello Mercado

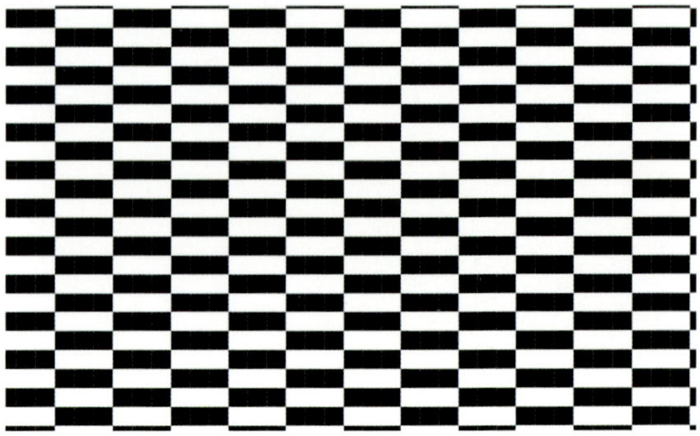

I have created a language to delete, to compact mental texts and graphics, to eliminate unwanted thoughts and make them personal hieroglyphics.
The performer is seated in front of the audience and simply starts writing on a laptop connected to a screen and stops when he or she cannot think/delete/write any more. The writing must be accompanied by an excessive and incoherent talkativeness. The performer invites the audience to participate and to delete/compact/maintain their own thoughts, keeping up an excessive and

Ich habe eine Löschsprache erfunden: eine Sprache zum Verdichten mentaler Texte und Bilder, zum Eliminieren unerwünschter Gedanken und deren Verwandlung in persönliche Hieroglyphen.
Der/die Performer/in wird vor das Publikum gesetzt und beginnt auf einem mit einem Projektor verbundenen Laptop zu schreiben, bis er/sie nicht mehr denken/löschen/schreiben kann. Das Schreiben muss mit einem überbordenden, zusammenhanglosen Gerede begleitet werden. Der/die Performer/in fordert das Publikum auf, mitzumachen und auch die eigenen Gedanken zu

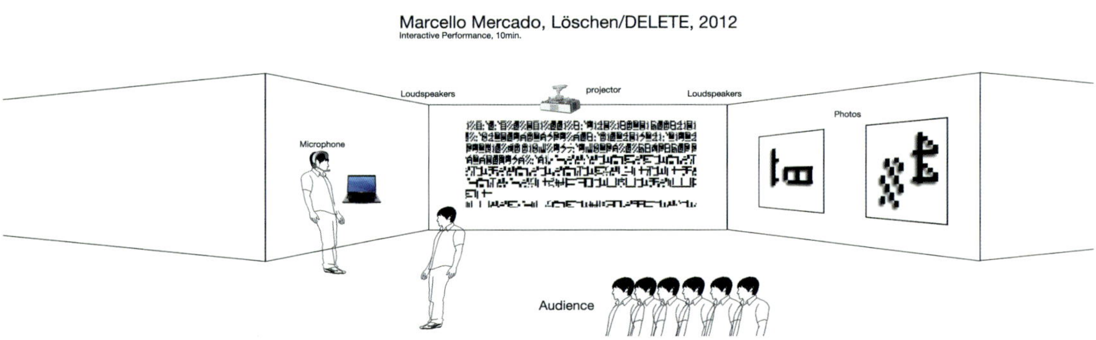

Concept and Typography: Marcello Mercado; programming, animation and editing: Marcello Mercado; music: Marcello Mercado.
Acknowledgements: Rainer Michels and Marcelo Santorelli

http://www.khm.de/~marcello
http://vimeo.com/36645107

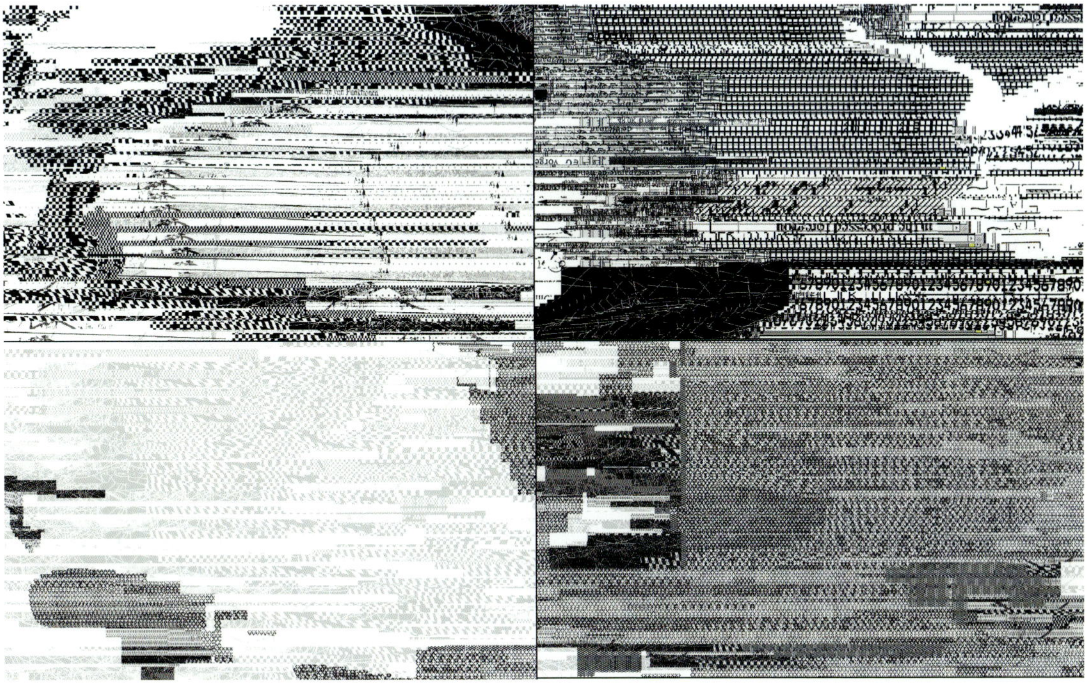

löschen/verdichten/bewahren, selbst einen exzessiven, unkontrollierbaren Wortstrom am Laufen zu halten.
Eine Löschsprache zu erfinden, die die Sprache zwischen Menschen und/oder Maschinen löscht: die Festplatten, Speicher, die Konvention des Alphabets, den Textlärm, den Abfall der Betriebssysteme, die Satellitendaten, die Online- und Offline-Identität, die selbst von Hämmern nicht zerstörbaren Algorithmenreste auf den Festplatten. Eine Sprache, die das Unlöschbare löscht.
Ein neues Alphabet zu schaffen und es zu kombinieren. Das Alphabet auszusprechen und das Gesagte gleichzeitig zu löschen. Die Möglichkeit der Sprache als schwarzes Loch. Denken und Löschen in einem, ohne dass ein Rest bleibt ... oder ein Alphabet.

uncontrollable flow of words. To create a language to delete: delete the language between humans and/or machines, hard drives, the memories, the alphabetic convention, textual noise, the "junk" operating systems, the satellite data, the identity online, the identity offline, the algorithmic remains on the hard drives that do not disappear under the hammer. A language to delete what is not possible to delete.
To generate a new alphabet, combine it and say it, thinking all the time of erasing what is being said, the possibility of a language as black hole. Thinking and erasing in one action that does not generate remains ... or alphabets.

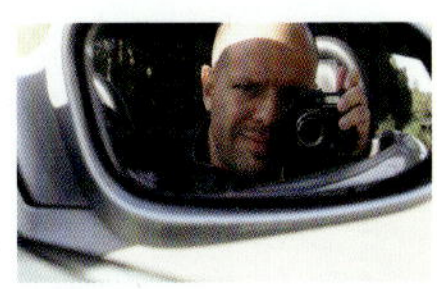

Marcello Mercado (DE), born in 1963, studied philosophy and humanities at the Universidad Nacional de Córdoba (RA) in the field of film and television. Fellowships: 1996 John D. and Catherine T. MacArthur Foundation, the Rockefeller Foundation and the Lampadia Foundation; 1999 at the Art University for Media, Cologne; 1993 Fundación Antorchas, Buenos Aires, Argentina. He works in an interdisciplinary way with painting, video, bio-art, objects, installations, sound art and net projects. **Marcello Mercado** (DE), geboren 1963, Studium der Philosophie und Geisteswissenschaften an der Universidad Nacional de Córdoba (RA) am Fachbereich Film und Fernsehen. Stipendien: 1996 John D. and Catherine T. MacArthur Foundation, Rockefeller Foundation und Lampadia Foundation; 1999 an der Kunsthochschule für Medien Köln; 1993 Fundación Antorchas, Buenos Aires, Argentina. Er arbeitet interdisziplinär mit Malerei, Video, Biokunst, Objekten, Installationen, Klangkunst und Netzprojekten.

Menstruation Machine—Takashi's Take

Sputniko!

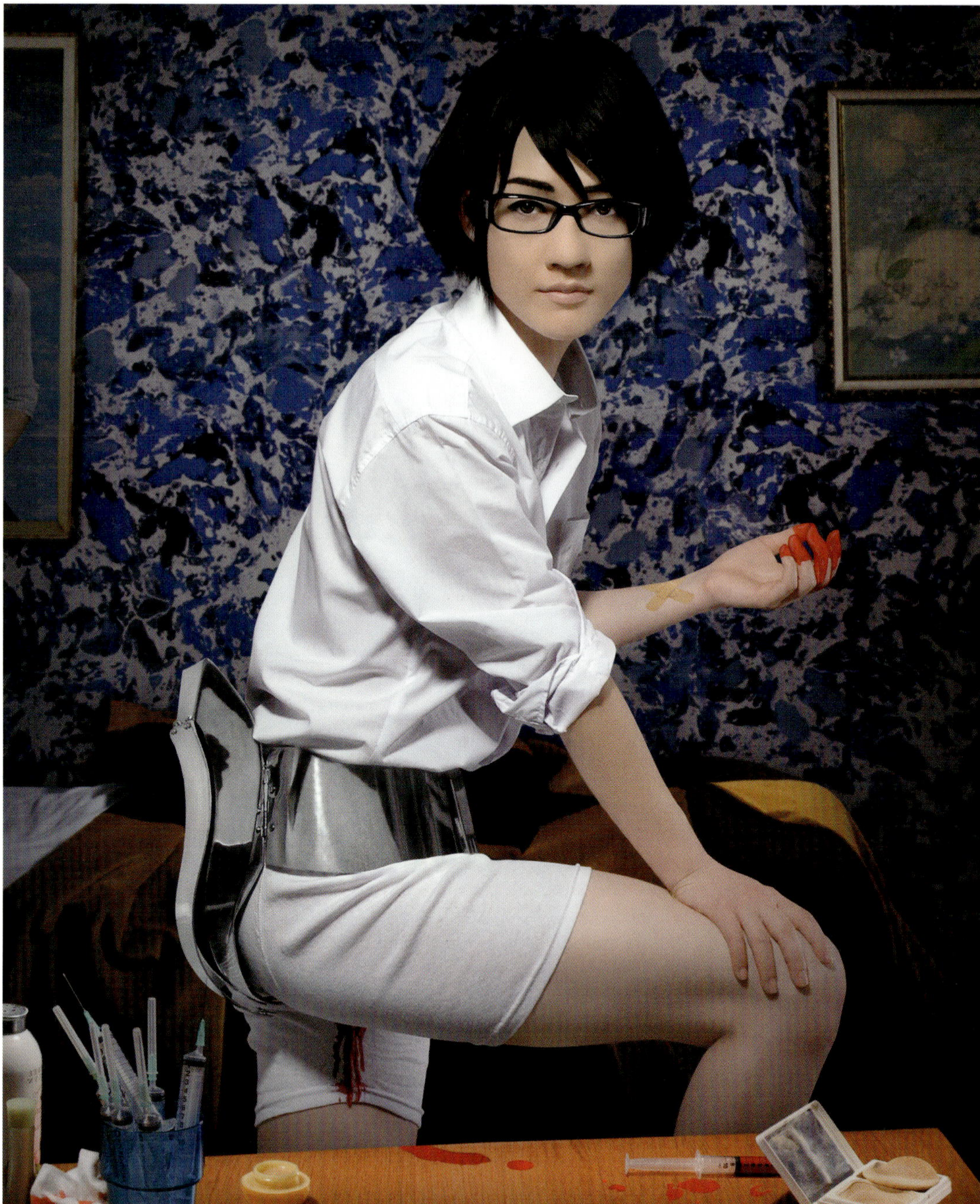

http://www.sputniko.com/?p=91600#

Wir schreiben das Jahr 2012, warum menstruieren Menschen eigentlich immer noch?
Für mich als Künstlerin war das eine wesentliche Frage, die ich unbedingt lösen wollte.
Bei der Markteinführung der Antibabypille in den 1960er Jahren wurde bewusst eine pillenfreie Woche pro Monat eingeplant, um Platz für die Menstruation zu lassen. Die Ärzte waren der Meinung, dass der Verlust der Periode für Frauen zu beunruhigend und unannehmbar sei. Seither sind 50 Jahre vergangen, in denen uns die Technologie noch viele andere Dinge beschert hat: Reisen ins All, Mobiltelefone, das Internet, Klone und gentechnisch veränderte Lebensmittel – aber Frauen bluten immer noch. Zwar wurden mittlerweile neue Pillen wie Lybrel und Seasonique entwickelt, die die Anzahl der Menstruationen auf vier pro Jahr oder gar keine reduzieren, aber sie werden nicht viel verwendet.
In Japan zum Beispiel brauchte das Gesundheitsministerium nur sechs Monate, um Viagra zuzulassen, während die Zulassung der Antibabypille (1999, drei Monate nach Viagra) mehr als neun Jahre dauerte. Es ist also klar, dass technologischer Fortschritt von den jeweiligen politischen, sozialen und kulturellen Verhältnissen abhängt.
Was bedeutet uns Menschen die Menstruation in biologischer, kultureller und historischer Hinsicht? Wer würde sich für eine Menstruation entscheiden? Und wie würde sie ablaufen?
Mit der *Menstruation Machine*, einem Mechanismus zur Abgabe von Blut und zur Stimulierung des Unterleibs, lässt sich der Schmerz und das Bluten einer fünftägigen Menstruation nachvollziehen.

It's 2012, so why are humans still menstruating?
As a female artist I had one intriguing question I wanted to solve.
When the contraceptive pill first became commercially available in the 1960s, it was deliberately designed to have one pill-free, menstruating week every month. This was because the doctors felt that female users would find having no periods too worrying and unacceptable. 50 years have passed since then, and modern technology has accomplished even more—space travel, mobile phones, the Internet, cloning and genetically modified food—but women are still bleeding. New pills such as Lybrel and Seasonique, which reduce the frequency of menstruation to none or four times a year have recently been developed, but they are not yet widely used.
For example, in Japan it only took the ministry of health six months to approve Viagra, but it took them more than nine years to approve the contraceptive pill in 1999 (which was approved three months after the approval of Viagra). It is quite clear that the advancement of technology can be heavily influenced by political, social and cultural backgrounds of the time.
So what does menstruation mean to humans, biologically, culturally and historically? Who might choose to have it, and how might they have it? *The Menstruation Machine*—fitted with a blood dispensing mechanism and electrodes simulating the lower abdomen—stimulates the pain and bleeding of a five-day menstruation process.

The machine was developed with research support from Professor Jan Brosens at the Department of Medicine, Imperial College London.

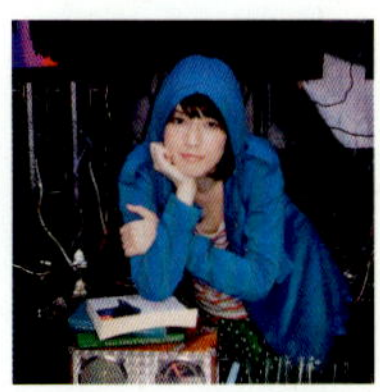

Sputniko! (UK/JP). Born to an English mother and a Japanese father, who are both mathematics professors, Sputniko! graduated high school early to study mathematics at Imperial College London. As she pursued her studies in science, she grew interested in arts, which allowed her science thinking to become more communicative and flexible, leading her to study for an MA at the Royal College of Art, London. Sputniko! creates machines, films and music exploring the intersections of technology, feminism and pop culture. Her narrative works are produced via research investigation with scientists and specialists to critically investigate a possible future of human and technology. **Sputniko!** (UK/JP) ist die Tochter einer englischen Mutter und eines japanischen Vaters, zweier Mathematikprofessoren. Nach einem vorzeitigen High-School-Abschluss studierte sie Mathematik am Imperial College in London. Im Lauf der Auseinandersetzung mit den Naturwissenschaften entwickelte sie ein immer stärkeres Interesse für Kunst, weil sie damit ihr wissenschaftliches Denken kommunikativer und flexibler gestalten konnte. So nahm sie schließlich ein MA-Studium am Royal College of Art auf. Sputniko! macht Maschinen, Filme und Musik an der Schnittstelle von Technologie, Feminismus und Popkultur. Ihre narrativen Arbeiten gründen auf Forschungen mit Wissenschaftlern und Fachleuten, die kritisch nach einer möglichen Zukunft von Mensch und Technik fragen.

MNM v091

Christian Graupner, feat. Ming Wei Poon & Mieko Suzuki

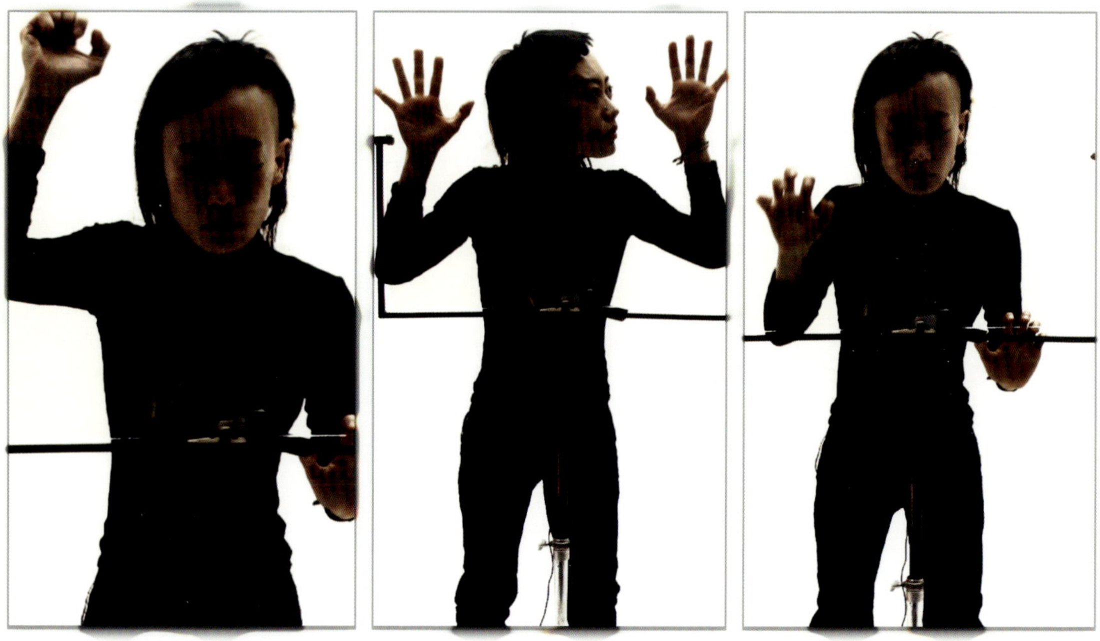

MNM v091 is a triple-channel audiovisual system of C. Graupner's HRP [Humatic Re-Performing] series. Humatic re-performance concepts and technologies allow visitors access to pre-recorded music and dance. The spectators are invited to control the flow of a pre-recorded activity. To do so, they are given easy-to-learn physical interfaces. They select their degree of involvement and can change their role from observer to player to co-performer

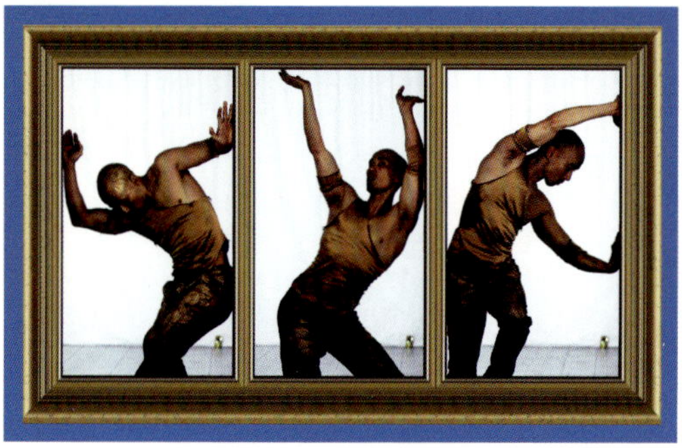

MNM v091 ist ein dreikanaliges audiovisuelles System aus C. Graupners Serie H.RP [Humatic Re-performing]. Humatic-Reperformance-Systeme sind Konzepte und Technologien, mit denen Ausstellungsbesucher auf Musik- und Tanzkonserven zugreifen und die aufgezeichnete Aktivität in ihrem Ablauf beeinflussen können. Zu diesem Zweck erhalten sie leicht erlernbare körperlich zu bedienende Interfaces. Sie können zwischen verschiedenen Involvierungsgraden wählen und ihre Rolle jederzeit vom Beobachter zum Spieler oder Mitspieler ändern – oder überhaupt die komplette Kontrolle über das System übernehmen und es wie ein Musikinstrument spielen.
MNM generiert automatisch ständig neue visuelle und musikalische Cluster, die durch die Bedienung von Druckknöpfen, Hebeln und einem Plattenteller beeinflusst und neu zusammengesetzt werden können ... wobei ein möglichst direkter (Körper)Kontakt zwischen Interface-Bediener/in und Videoperformer angestrebt wird.
MNM benutzt den Arm einer modifizierten japanischen Maneki Neko, einer Winkekatze. Das Triptychon mit seinem antiquarischen Goldrahmen ist eine Ohrfeige für

alle grundlosen Optimisten. Graupners wahnwitzige, radikale Arbeitmethoden resultieren in einem Balanceakt, der zwischen grenzwertiger Autistenmagie und Death-Metal-Spiralismus schwankt.
The *MNM*-Film ist als Triple-Helix organisiert. Die nichtlineare, flüssige Präsentation und der Echtzeit-Zugriff heben die Publikumsvorstellungen von vollendeter Bewegungs- und Klangkunst auf eine Ebene, auf der erahnbar wird, wie es jenseits des Klischees aussehen könnte. Komplexe Technologien und Konzepte stecken hinter kollabierenden Oberflächen, auf denen sich Unglücke permanent neu zusammensetzen und von menschlichem (Versagen) kontrolliert werden sollen.

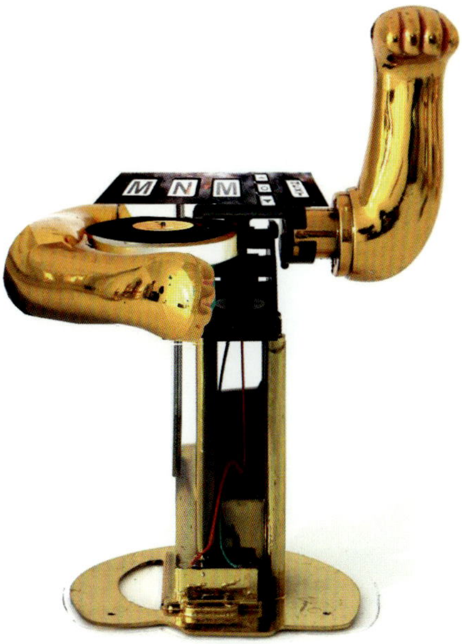

at any time, or can take over complete control of the system and play it as a musical instrument.
MNM autonomously generates always-new visual and musical clusters, which can be influenced and re-composed by operating push buttons, levers and a turn table interface ... targeting direct (body) contact between visitor and video-performer.
MNM employs the arm of a modified traditional Japanese mojo figure, Maneki Neko. The triptych in its antique golden frame is a punch in the face for anyone who is optimistic without reason. Graupner's radical, insane working methods result in a tightrope walk between cutting-edge autistic magic and death-metal spiralism.
The *MNM* film is organized in a triple helix. Nonlinear but non-abrupt presentation and real-time access boost the spectators' imagination of perfection in movement and sound art to a level where they might get an idea of what to find beyond cliché. Complex technologies and concepts are hidden behind collapsing surfaces showing permanently re-composing accidents to be controlled by human (failure).

Christian Graupner (DE): Humatic, concept & video, composer feat. Mieko Suzuki (JP): sound artist & performer: Ming Wei Poon (SG/DE): performer, dancer.
Collaborators: João Pais (PT): programmer & co composer; Nils Peters (DE): Humatic, software artist; Phuong Nguyen (DE): co choreographer; Alan Gleeson (IR): sound collaborator; Malte Steiner (DE): development partner; Ink Agop (JP): camera operator & team assistent; Itamar Zechvogel (DE): styling.

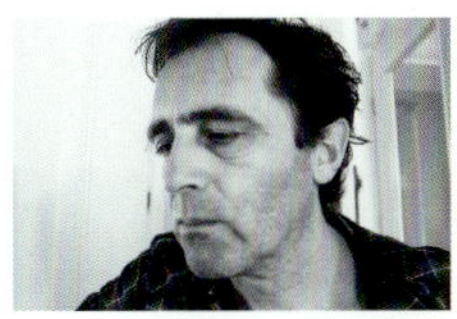

Christian Graupner (DE) is a composer, artist and the creator and developer of real-time media playback systems. His wide-ranging earlier works were made up of drawings, paintings and experimental electronic music, mostly published on records, CDs as well as in movies and radio plays under the pseudonym VOOV (Violation of Ordinary Values). In his recent works, he explores the practices and myths around pop and contemporary music and combines multi-channel video and sound with partly machine-partly user-controlled "humatic" interfaces and mechanisms. His recent sculptural / media work includes gambling machines and Asian mojo figures, feedback guitars and beatbox-like vocal and dance performances. **Christian Graupner** (DE) ist Komponist, Künstler und Erfinder-Entwickler von medialen Echtzeit-Wiedergabesystemen. Sein vielseitiges früheres Werk umfasst Zeichnungen, Gemälde und – unter dem Pseudonym VOOV (Violation of Ordinary Values) – hauptsächlich auf Platten und CDs, aber auch in Filmen und Hörspielen erschienene experimentelle Musik. In seinen neueren Arbeiten erkundet er Praktiken und Mythen des Pop und der zeitgenössischen Musik, indem er mehrkanalige Video- und Soundarbeiten mit teils maschinen-, teils userkontrollierten „humatischen" Interfaces und Mechanismen verbindet. Seine neueren skulptural-medialen Arbeiten beinhalten Spielautomaten und asiatische Mojo-Figuren, Feedback-Gitarren und beatboxartige Gesangs- und Tanzperformances.

Occupy George

Ivan Cash, Andy Dao

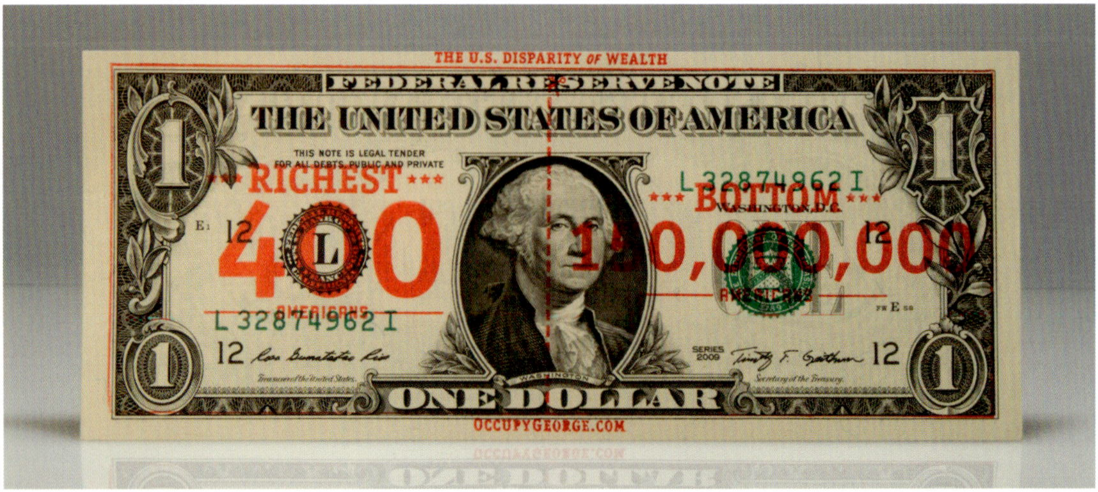

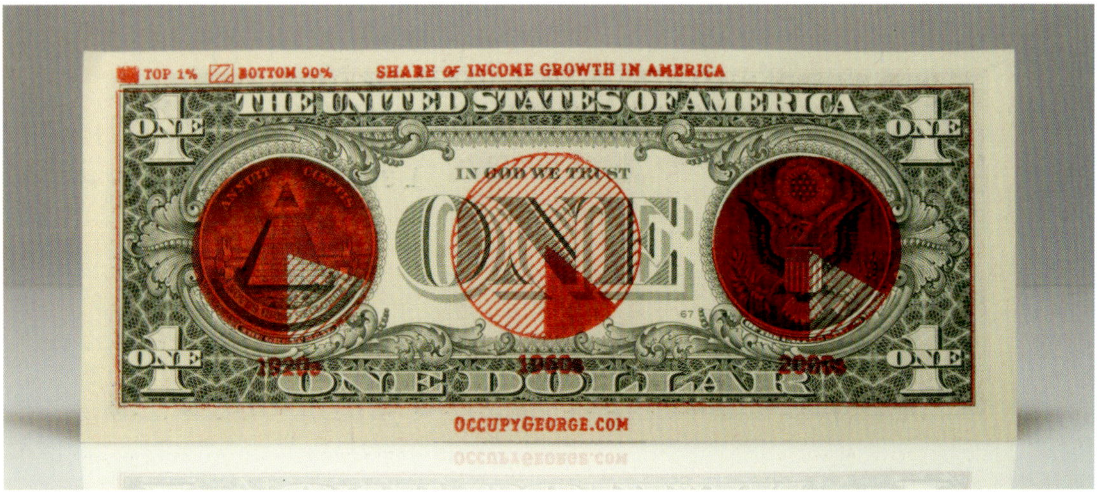

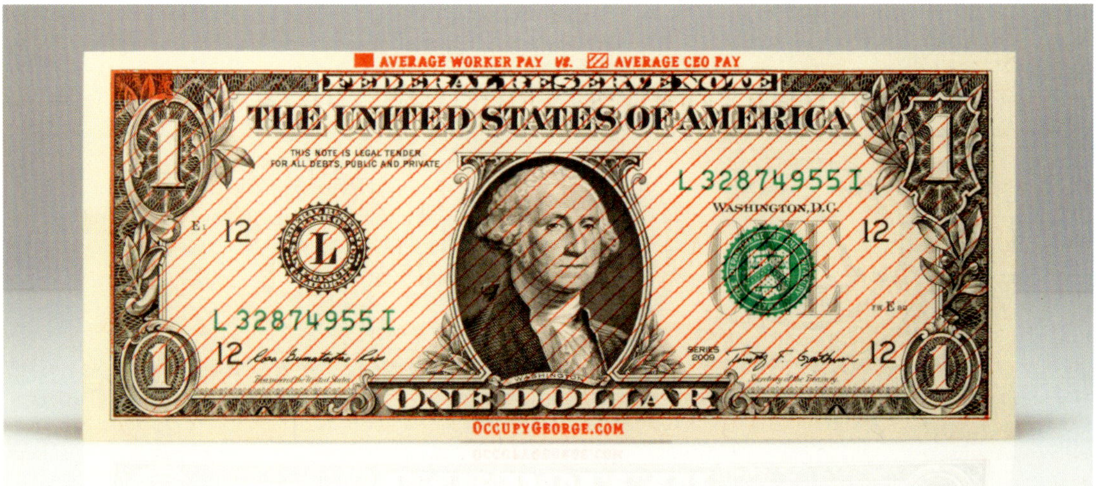

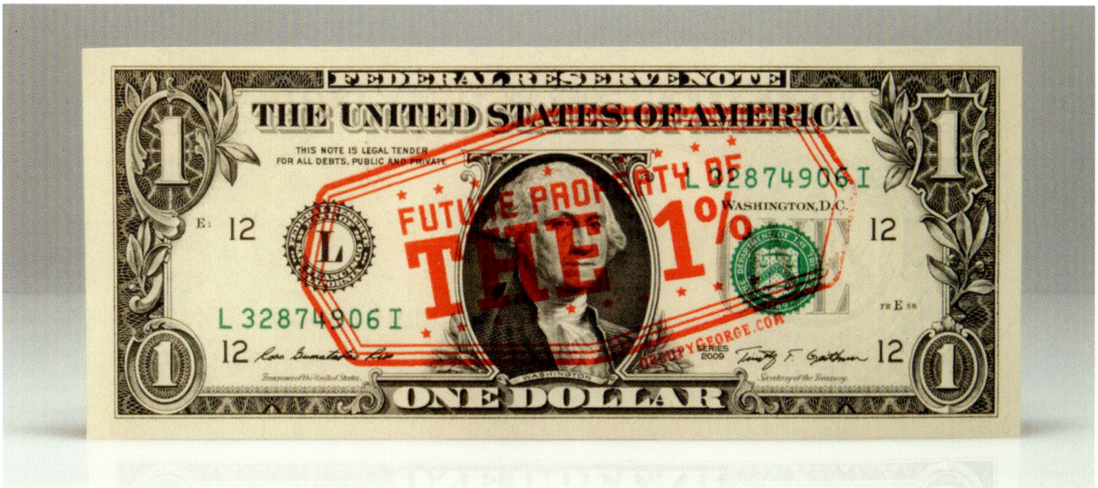

„Money talks – Geld spricht" – lautet eine Redensart in den USA. Aber nicht laut genug für die 99 Prozent. *Occupy George* bringt mit faktenbasierten Infografiken bestempelte Dollarnoten in Umlauf, um die Öffentlichkeit Schein für Schein über Amerikas horrende wirtschaftliche Ungleichheit zu informieren. Weil Geld Wissen Macht ist.

Money talks, but not loud enough for the 99%. By circulating dollar bills stamped with fact-based infographics, *Occupy George* informs the public of America's daunting economic disparity one bill at a time. Because money knowledge is power.

Web Development: Scott Blew

Ivan Cash (US) is a San-Francisco-based artist, designer and culture jammer who believes in creativity's power to engage people and radically change the way we see the world. Having developed a career in advertising while living in Cape Town, New York, San Francisco and Amsterdam, Cash continues commercial work on a freelance basis and loves creating independent projects that subvert pop culture and address themes of social activism. Cash is a big fan of street art, snail mail, mashups, meditation and writing in the third person. **Andy Dao** (US). I am fascinated by documentaries, stories from This American Life, and ones told by The Notorious B.I.G. I get my news from the Public Broadcasting Service and National Public Radio, which automatically makes me an elitist. I try to learn a lot about the world, meaning I'm a pest to cab drivers. In my past jobs I became a certified welder, scaled I-beams unreasonably high off the ground, tossed pizza dough, operated movie projectors, played basketball with ten year-olds for an entire summer, demolished said ten year-olds in Connect Four, set myself on fire (twice in the same day), smoked pot in walk-in freezers, flipped burgers and cleaned toilets after graduating from college. I can sincerely say, those are still the best times of my life. **Ivan Cash** (US) ist ein in San Francisco lebender Künstler, Designer und Culture Jammer, der daran glaubt, dass sich mit Kreativität Menschen bewegen und eine radikale Änderung unserer Weltsicht herbeiführen lässt. Nach einer Karriere in der Werbeindustrie, die ihn nach Kapstadt, New York, San Francisco und Amsterdam führte, arbeitet Cash mittlerweile als Freelancer und entwickelt vorzugsweise unabhängige, popsubversive und sozialaktivistische Projekte. Cash begeistert sich für Street Art, Schneckenpost, Mashups, Meditation und dem Verfassen von Texten in der dritten Person. **Andy Dao** (US). Ich liebe Dokumentationen, Storys, wie sie in der Radiosendung „This American Life" vorkommen oder wie sie The Notorious B.I.G. zu erzählen pflegte. Ich beziehe meine Nachrichten aus dem Public Broadcasting Service und dem National Public Radio, was mich wohl elitär erscheinen lässt. Ich versuche, so viel über die Welt zu erfahren, wie ich nur kann, weshalb ich Taxifahrern gehörig auf die Nerven gehe. In meiner bisherigen Berufslaufbahn wurde ich nach einem Collegeabschluss u. a. geprüfter Schweißer, hantierte in unvernünftigen Höhen mit Stahlträgern, schleuderte Pizzateig durch die Luft, bediente Filmprojektoren, spielte einen Sommer lang mit Zehnjährigen Basketball, vernichtete besagte Zehnjährige bei „Vier gewinnt", setzte mich an einem Tag zweimal in Brand, rauchte in Kühlhäusern Gras, briet Burger und putzte Toiletten – und kann ehrlich sagen, das waren immer noch die besten Zeiten meines Lebens.

Osadok / Aftertaste

Kuda begut sobaki / Where Dogs Run

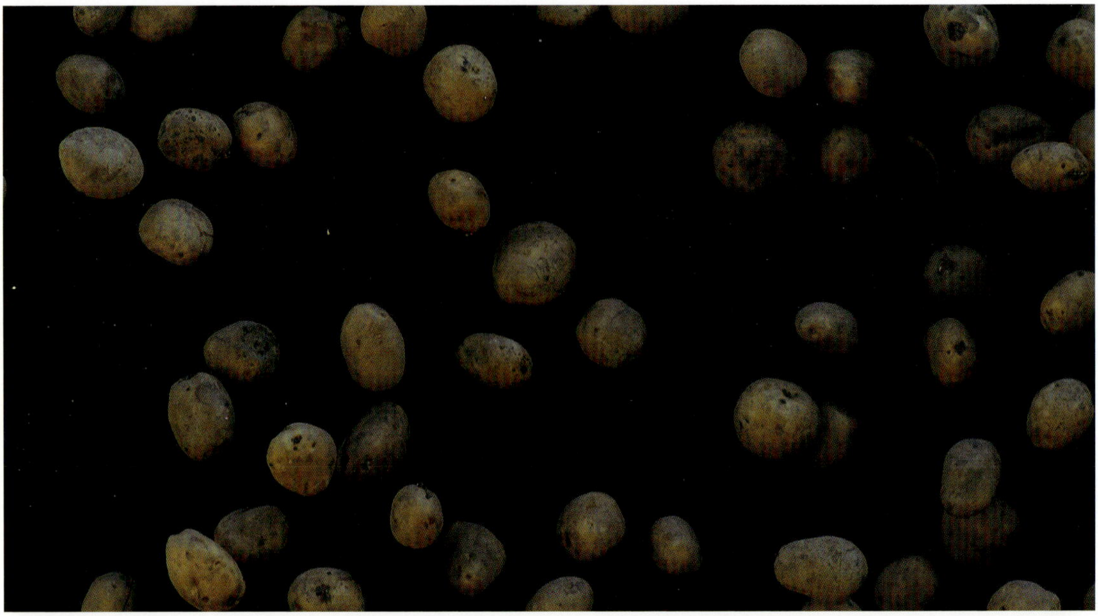

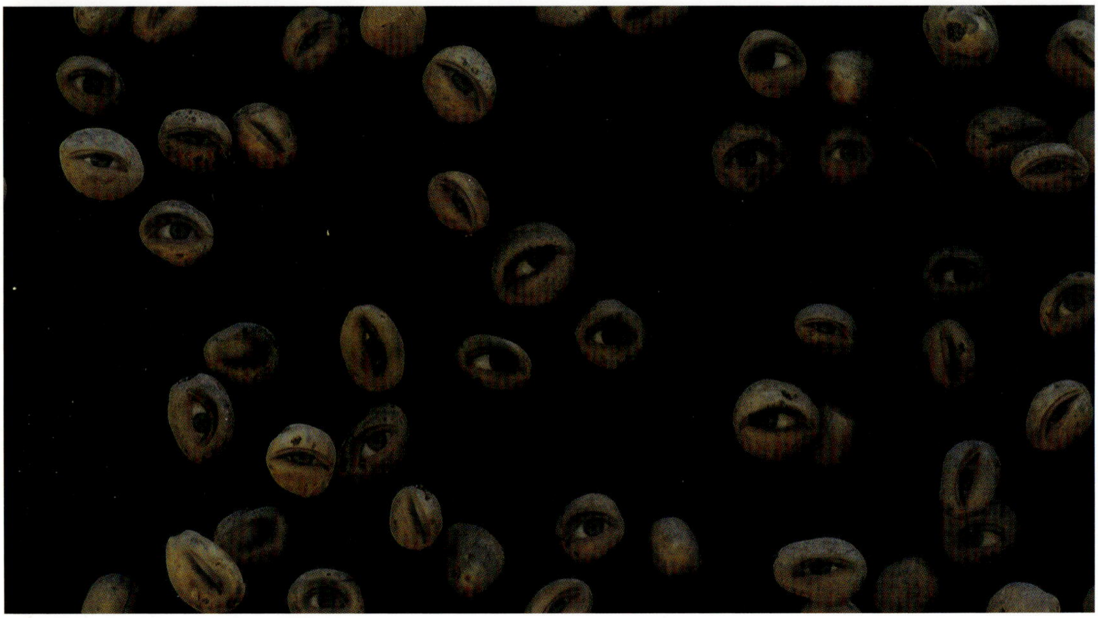

Die Installation *Osadok / Aftertaste* besteht aus einem Video mit langsam fallenden Kartoffeln. Hat der Betrachter lang genug darüber meditiert und schickt sich zum Weggehen an, passiert etwas Unerwartetes: Einige der Kartoffeln blicken die sich abwendende Person aus unheimlich echt wirkenden menschlichen Augen an. Der mit einer Hochgeschwindigkeitskamera (100 fps) aufgenommene Kartoffelregen ist supernaturalistisch, erinnert in seiner Zeitlupentechnik aber auch an die appetitlich-saftigen Tropfenkronen und üppig-lebendigen Texturen der Werbung.

Die Kartoffel, ein Archetyp russischer Alltagskultur, wirkt im Ausstellungskontext fremd: Aus dem Untergrund kommend, lebendig und leblos zugleich, hat sie etwas Unheimliches, Beunruhigendes. Der emotionalste Moment, der einen wie ein Wunder erschaudern lässt, ist aber der, in dem die Kartoffeln ihre menschlichen Augen öffnen (ebenfalls ein Archetyp – aber der eines spirituellen Kontakts). Wie ist ihr Blick zu deuten? Er ist mehr als ein visuelles Wortspiel, erscheint wie ein Aufruf zur Anteilnahme, der elementaren Anerkennung jener „anderen" atomaren, imaginären Welt, die in den Zwischenräumen des Alltags nistet.

Das russische Wort „Osadok" bedeutet nicht nur „Nachgeschmack", sondern auch „Bodensatz", „Ausfällung". Die Künstler spielen mit ihrer Arbeit auf eine mystische Bewegung der russischen Philosophie – den Kosmismus – an. Sie bilden aber nicht den Kosmismus selbst nach, sondern nur einen Nachgeschmack davon.

The *Osadok / Aftertaste* installation presents an image of slowly falling potatoes. When the viewer reaches the ultimate state of meditation and is ready to turn around to leave, he or she is confronted with something unexpected: some potatoes start gazing at the person leaving with very natural-looking eyes. Shot with a rapid camera (100 f/s), the potato flow appears quite naturalistic, while slow-motion techniques, with their appetizingly juicy splashes and luxuriant, breathing textures, reference advertising.

The potato may be considered here as an archetype of Russian everyday culture, yet in the museum space it is manifest as something alien: arising from the underground, at once alive and not alive, it is uncanny and alerting. The most affective moment, which gives the viewer a frisson of wonder, arises when the potatoes reveal their human eyes (again an archetype, in this case, of spiritual contact). How to interpret this gaze? Beyond a mere visual pun, it feels like a call for engagement, an elemental acceptance of that "other," atomic, imaginary world hidden in the interstices of the ordinary.

"Osadok" in Russian is not only "aftertaste," but also "residue" and "precipitation." One of the allusions the artists refer to is a mystical movement in Russian philosophy—Russian cosmism. But what is shown is not cosmism itself but only its "residue," "aftertaste."

Commissioned by the Ural branch of the National Center for Contemporary Art. Director: Alisa Prudnikova; curator: Svetlana Usoltseva

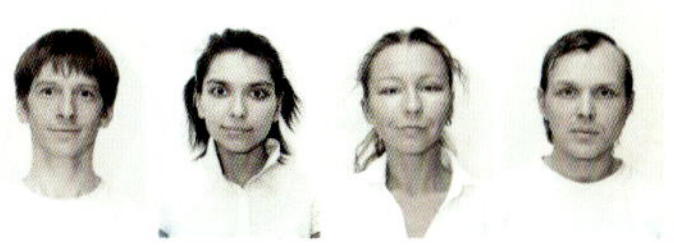

Kuda begut sobaki / Where Dogs Run (Olga Inozemtseva, Alexey Korzukhin, Vlad Bulatov, Natalia Grekhova) (RU) is one of the major art collectives in Russia. For over ten years it has been consistently extending the language of contemporary art into new technologies. That said, the artists are not so seduced by the far fringe of abundant technological possibilities that they lose the artistic image located at the center. **Kuda begut sobaki / Where Dogs Run** (Olga Inosemzeva, Alexei Korsuchin, Vlad Bulatov, Natalia Grechova) (RU) ist eines der wichtigsten russischen Künstlerkollektive. Seit mehr als zehn Jahren erweitert es die Sprache zeitgenössischer Kunst konsequent in den Bereich neuer Technologien. Die Gruppe lässt sich von den technologischen Möglichkeiten allerdings nicht dazu verführen, das eigentliche Bild aus den Augen verlieren.

Versus

David Letellier

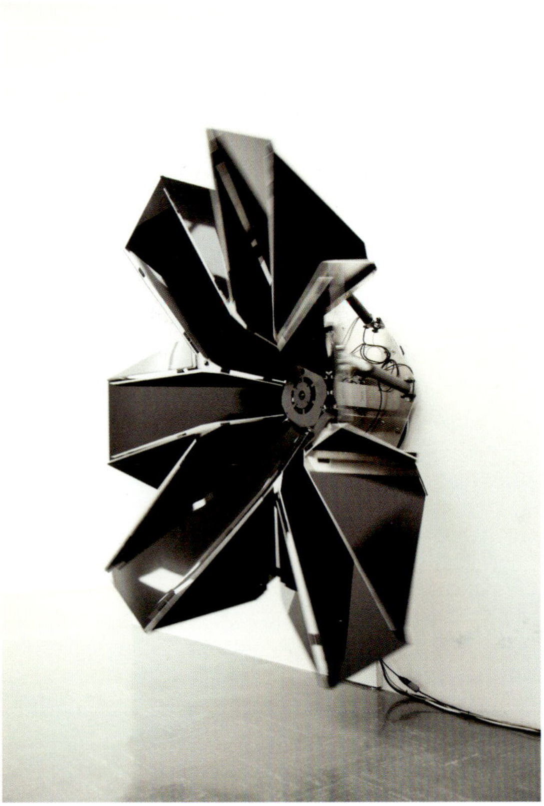

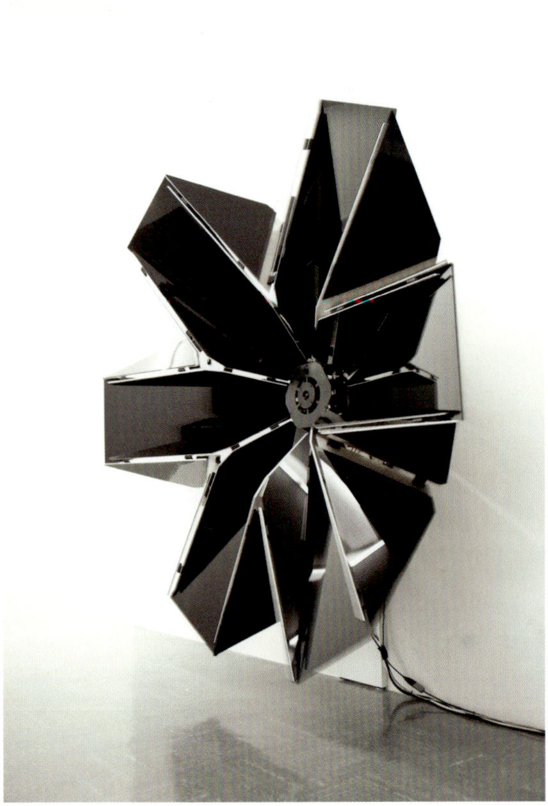

Versus is a sound installation consisting of two kinetic sculptures placed face to face. Each sculpture is made of 12 triangular panels, hinged and powered by six linear actuators, controlled by a specific program. At the center of each corolla, a loudspeaker and a microphone make it possible to play and record sounds.

At regular intervals each sculpture produces a sound, simultaneously recorded and analyzed by the opposite sculpture, which then moves according to the frequencies of this sound.

Like a feedback loop, it then plays back the recorded sound, with the errors and disturbances caused by the reverberating space and the visitors. By intervening in this conversation the viewers become actors, as they degrade the communication by their presence and the noises they produce. As the panels move back and forth at a pace determined by the environmental sound, they create a non-immediate interaction, where the

Versus ist eine Klanginstallation aus zwei einander gegenüber aufgebauten kinetischen Skulpturen. Jede davon besteht aus 12 dreieckigen mit Scharnieren verbundenen Paneelen, die von sechs computergesteuerten Linear-Aktuatoren in Bewegung versetzt werden. Im Zentrum der beiden blütenkelchförmigen Skulpturen befinden sich jeweils ein Lautsprecher und ein Mikrofon, die das Abspielen und Aufnehmen von Klängen ermöglichen.

In bestimmten Intervallen sendet jede der beiden Skulpturen einen Klang aus, der von der jeweils anderen Skulptur aufgezeichnet, analysiert und den eigenen Bewegungsmustern zugrunde gelegt wird. Der aufgezeichnete Klang wird, modifiziert durch die Raumresonanz und die Störungen der Ausstellungsbesucher, in einer Art Feedback-Schleife wieder zurückgespielt.

Indem sich die Zuschauer in diese Konversation einmischen, werden sie zu Akteuren, denn sie zersetzen die Kommunikation durch ihre Anwesenheit und den Lärm, den sie produzieren. Da die Faltbewegungen der Paneele vom Umgebungsklang abhängen, kommt es zu einer

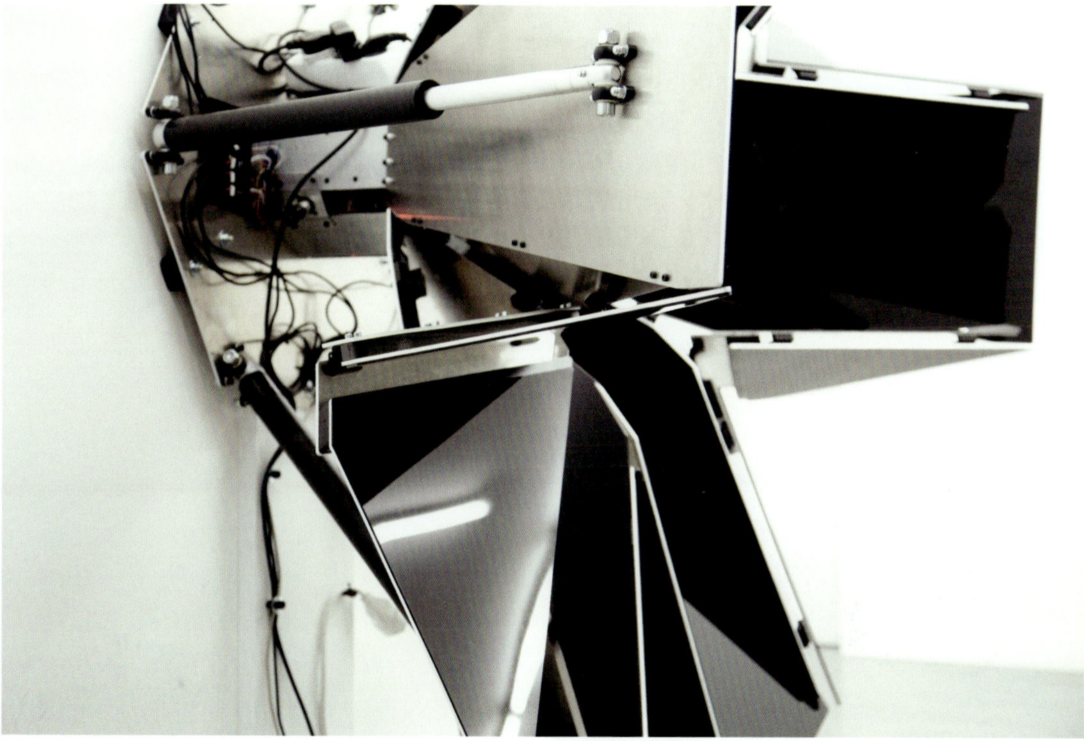

indirekten Interaktion, bei der die Unzulänglichkeiten der Reproduktion zu einem kreativen Faktor werden.
Der ursprünglich ausgesandte Klang wird ständig transformiert, sodass etwas vollkommen Neues und Unvorhersehbares entsteht. Die Speicherung vergangener Ereignisse hält immer nur so lange, bis sie reproduziert werden. Dann werden sie abgebaut, vergessen, durch den Augenblick ersetzt.

imperfections of reproduction become creative elements.
The original sound is continuously transformed and becomes something entirely new and unpredictable. The memory of past events is held for a moment, until it is reproduced, degraded, and then forgotten, replaced by the present.

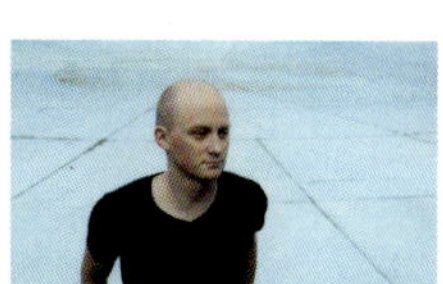

David Letellier (FR), born in 1978, lives and works in Berlin. He studied and graduated in architecture in Rennes and Berlin. His work focuses on the perception of sound and space, on the edge of architecture, sound and art. It ranges from audiovisual performances and sound installations to autonomous machines or conceptual drawings and can be defined as "an attempt to merge sound art and club culture." He releases music on the German Raster-Noton label under the pseudonym Kangding Ray. **David Letellier** (FR), geboren 1978, lebt und arbeitet in Berlin. Er studierte Architektur in Rennes und Berlin und arbeitet vor allem mit der Wahrnehmung von Klang und Raum am Schnittpunkt von Architektur, Musik und Kunst. Seine Arbeiten reichen von audiovisuellen Performances und Klanginstallationen bis zu autonomen Maschinen und konzeptuellen Zeichnungen und lassen sich als „Versuch einer Verschmelzung von Klangkunst und Club Culture" beschreiben. Beim deutschen Raster-Noton-Label veröffentlicht er Musik unter dem Namen Kangding Ray.

DIGITAL COMMUNITIES

A Hub of Creative Energy
Drehscheiben kreativer Energien

Wolfgang Blau, Peter Kuthan, Liu Yan, Leila Nachawati, Thomas Schildhauser

When introducing the Digital Communities award category for the first time in 2004, former juror Howard Rheingold wrote: "Digital communities can save lives, bridge differences and the digital divide, multiply knowledge, enable markets, revitalize democracy and provoke civic engagement but only if people seize the power that technology provides and wield it thoughtfully."

Online communities have been an integral part of the Internet from its earliest beginnings. It took the adoption of social networks on a mass scale, though, to make us understand that the net is primarily about community and not primarily about commerce or publishing. In fact, the most successful e-commerce and online-publishing companies in 2012 are those who see themselves as communities and have either built their own social platforms or are deeply integrated with the leading social networks of our time.

Today, with the rapid expansion of the Internet, of smartphones and social media, the role of the Internet as a driver of societal change is getting even larger than most of us were able or willing to imagine back in 2004, when this specific award category was first introduced.

A lot has been said and written about the supposed "Facebook Revolution" in the Arab world. While the term has been misleadingly giving more credit to the platform than to the people using it, it is certain that social networks have been crucial in enabling and fueling the uprising in the Arab world as well as the global spread of the Occupy movement.

In looking at the more than 177 award entries from 35 countries, the jury noticed an abundance of projects that are trying to find answers to the financial crisis and to the crisis of democratic representation. It is the intention of the jury to honor and to give credit to these movements, creators and collaborators who are searching for common ground and a modern definition of democracy and who provide tools and ideas for an engaged public that values creativity.

These were the criteria we have developed for assessing this year's entries:

Als die Kategorie Digital Communities 2004 zum ersten Mal durchgeführt wurde, schrieb der damalige Juror Howard Rheingold: „Digitale Gemeinschaften können Leben retten, Unterschiede und digitale Klüfte überbrücken, Wissen vermehren, Märkte erschließen, die Demokratie neu beleben und das Bürgerengagement fördern – aber nur, wenn Menschen die in der Technologie steckenden Potenziale nutzen und sie überlegt einsetzen."

Online-Communities waren seit Anfang an integraler Bestandteil des Internet. Aber erst als soziale Netzwerke ein Massenphänomen wurden, erkannten wir, dass es im Netz in erster Linie um Gemeinschaft und nicht ums Geschäft oder Publishing geht – ja, die heute erfolgreichsten e-Commerce und Online-Publishing-Firmen sind jene, die sich selbst als Community begreifen und entweder ihre eigenen sozialen Plattformen gebaut haben oder tief mit den wichtigsten sozialen Netzwerken verflochten sind.

Mit der schnellen Verbreitung von Smartphones und sozialen Medien gewinnt das Internet als Motor für sozialen Wandel noch größeren Einfluss, als die meisten von uns sich im Jahr 2004 – dem Geburtsjahr dieser Kategorie – wohl hätten vorstellen können.

Viel ist über die angebliche „Facebook-Revolution" in der arabischen Welt gesagt und geschrieben worden. Dieser Begriff könnte einem – irreführenderweise – glauben machen, die Plattform sei wichtiger als die Menschen, die sie nutzen, aber trotzdem steht fest, dass soziale Netzwerke eine entscheidende Rolle dabei gespielt haben, dass die Aufstände in den arabischen Ländern, aber auch die Occupy-Bewegung überhaupt entstehen und sich halten konnten.

Als wir in der Jury die 177 eingereichten Projekte aus 35 Ländern durchgingen, fiel uns auf, dass eine Menge Projekte versuchen, Antworten auf die Finanzkrise und die Krise der repräsentativen Demokratie zu finden. Die Jury möchte diese Bewegungen, ihre Initiatoren und Mitarbeiter anerkennen, die eine moderne Definition und eine gemeinsame Basis für Demokratie suchen und Instrumente und Ideen einer engagierten Öffentlichkeit zugänglich machen, die diese Form der Kreativität auch schätzt.

Wir haben folgende Kriterien für die Beurteilung der diesjährigen Einreichungen entwickelt:

1. Community: Ist die Community, die ein Projekt betreibt, lebendig und aktiv? Ist sie skalierbar oder gibt es technische oder konzeptuelle Faktoren, die ihr Wachstum begrenzen? Herrscht in dieser spezifischen Community ein angemessener Umgangston?
2. Zugänglichkeit: Kann jeder Zugang zu der Community erhalten?
3. Innovation: Wie innovativ ist dieses Projekt?
4. Nicht-kommerzieller Ansatz: Wir anerkennen den enormen Beitrag, den kommerzielle Communities zur Gesellschaft leisten. Aber wir entschieden, Preise nur an nicht-kommerzielle Projekte zu vergeben.
5. Technologie: Welche technische Qualität weist das Projekt auf? Wie geht es mit privaten Userdaten um? Ist es Plattform-unabhängig und für mobile Endgeräte optimiert?
6. Gesellschaftliche Wirkung: Welchen gesellschaftlichen Impact hat das Projekt? Wie sehr kann es sich in diese Richtung entwickeln?
7. Bedeutung des Preises: Welche Wirkung würde ein Preis des Prix Ars Electronica auf das Projekt haben? Und wie würde das auf den Prix selbst rückwirken?

Die Goldene Nica in der Kategorie Digital Communities geht an das Projekt *Syrian people know their way*. Auszeichnungen werden an die Projekte *Dark Glasses. Portrait* und *Apertus Open Source Cinema* vergeben.

GOLDENE NICA

The Syrian People Know Their Way

http://sha3b3aref.blogspot.com/;
https://www.facebook.com/Syrian.Intifada

Innerhalb weniger Monate gelang es einer Community syrischer KünstlerInnen und AktivistInnen, die mit digitalen Medien arbeiten und unterschiedlichen Background haben, herausragende Grafiken, Videos und Musik zu kreieren, die sich von der syrischen Revolution inspirieren ließen, aber umgekehrt diese auch wieder inspirieren. Diese jungen SyrerInnen wollen effektive Methoden des friedlichen zivilen Widerstands promoten, indem sie Kampagnen mit den Menschen vor Ort koordinieren und Bewusstsein für den Kampf des syrischen Volkes durch moderne Kunst und Technologie in einer für alle zugänglichen Art und Weise schaffen. Der Name *The Syrian People know their way* ist selbst schon eine

1. Community: Is the community of a project alive and active? Is the community scalable or are there technical or conceptual factors that will limit its growth? How civil is the tonality of interactions in this specific community?
2. Accessibility: Is the community openly and freely accessible?
3. Novelty: How novel or original is this project?
4. Non-Commercial Character: We acknowledge the enormous societal contributions of commercially run communities. However, we decided to give awards only to non-commercial projects.
5. Technology: What is the technical quality of this project? How does it treat private user data? Is its platform agnostic and ready for mobile devices?
6. Societal Impact: How much of a societal impact does this project have or how much of an impact might it develop?
7. Significance of the Award: What impact would a Prix Ars Electronica Award have on this project and how would it reflect on the Prix itself?

The Golden Nica in the Digital Communities category goes to the project *Syrian people know their way*. Awards of Distinction are given to the projects *Dark Glasses* and *Apertus Open Source Cinema*.

GOLDEN NICA

Syrian People Know Their Way

http://sha3b3aref.blogspot.com/;
https://www.facebook.com/Syrian.Intifada

In only a few months, this community of Syrian digital artists and activists from different backgrounds has managed to come up with outstanding pieces of graphic design, videos and music that aim both to gather and provide inspiration for the Syrian revolution. These young Syrians work on the promotion of effective methods of peaceful civil resistance, coordinating campaigns with Syrians on the ground and raising awareness of the Syrian struggle through modern art and technology in a simple straightforward way that is accessible to everyone. The name *The Syrian people know their way* is in itself a message of confirmation of the desire of the Syrian people to be independent and decide their own future. This slogan was later used in protests and political discourses, just as many of this community's creations.

AWARDS OF DISTINCTION

Dark Glasses. Portrait

http://ichenguangcheng.blogspot.com

Dark Glasses. Portrait is an online campaign to support Chen Guangcheng, a blind civil rights activist who was put under house-arrest by local authorities illegally and calling for his freedom. This campaign calls Chinese citizens and people around the world to express their concern and support for Chen Guangcheng. Every participant puts on a pair of dark glasses takes a portrait, writes a few words about his/her thoughts, and sends the picture to the campaign. The pictures form a silent picture wall at the campaign website, showing the participants' solidarity of standing together with Chen. This campaign has nearly 500 participants from all over the world, including seniors and children. It takes significant courage to take part in this project while being fully aware that the campaign is being monitored by Chinese authorities. *Darkglasses. Portrait* is a new form of an organized nonviolent micro-activism community in China against the abuse of government power and corruption. This project shows how to achieve political and social goals in a society where the citizens' awareness of human rights issues is still developing.

Apertus Open Source Cinema

http://www.apertus.org

Film-camera production has long been consigned to the realm of a select few high-end proprietary manufacturing corporations. Due to the expense involved in research, development and in low-volume, high-tech manufacturing, professional film cameras were reserved for only the most well funded clients. This represents the essence of a closed world. The goal of the *Apertus Open Source Cinema* project is to create a modular

Bestätigung des Wunsches des syrischen Volkes, endlich unabhängig zu sein und über seine Zukunft selbst entscheiden zu können. Dieser Slogan wurde später, wie viele andere Werke dieser Community, auch bei Protesten und im politischen Diskurs verwendet.

AUSZEICHNUNGEN

Dark Glasses. Portrait

http://ichenguangcheng.blogspot.com

Dark Glasses. Portrait ist eine Online-Kampagne zur Unterstützung von Chen Guangcheng, einem blinden Menschenrechtsaktivisten, der von lokalen Behörden illegalerweise unter Hausarrest gestellt wurde. Die Kampagne, die für Chens Befreiung eintritt, ruft alle chinesischen Bürger und Menschen aus der ganzen Welt auf, ihre Sorge und Unterstützung für Chen Guangcheng öffentlich kundzutun. Jeder Teilnehmer setzt Sonnenbrillen auf und macht ein Porträtfoto von sich, beschreibt seine Beweggründe und sendet das Bild an die Kampagne. Die Bilder ergeben eine stille Bilderwand auf der Webseite der Kampagne und stehen für die Solidarität der Teilnehmer mit Chen. An dieser Kampagne haben ungefähr 700 Personen aus der ganzen Welt teilgenommen, auch ältere Menschen und Kinder. Es zeugt von großer Zivilcourage, an diesem Projekt teilzunehmen, weil die Kampagne von den chinesischen Behörden genau verfolgt wird. *Dark Glasses. Portrait* ist eine neue Form des organisierten, gewaltfreien Mikro-Activismus in China, der sich gegen Machtmissbrauch und Korruption durch die Regierung stellt. Dieses Projekt zeigt, wie in einer Gesellschaft, in der das Bewusstsein der Bürger für Menschenrechtsfragen sich erst herausbildet, politische und gesellschaftliche Ziele verwirklicht werden können.

Apertus Open Source Cinema

http://www.apertus.org

Die Herstellung von Filmkameras war lange einigen wenigen proprietären High-End-Herstellern vorbehalten. Aufgrund der hohen Kosten für Forschung und Entwicklung und für High-Tech-Produktion in geringer Stückzahl waren professionelle Filmkameras zahlungskräftigen Kunden vorbehalten. Dies ist eine geschlossene Welt par excellence. Das Projekt *Apertus Open Source Cinema* will ein modulares Kamerasystem entwickeln, das aus verschiedenen Hardware- und Software-Modulen besteht. Dabei werden freie Software und offene Hardware genutzt, um ein Gerät zu bauen, das alle Funktionalitäten aufweist, die professionelle Filmemacher im Studio und outdoor brauchen. Das *Apertus*-Projekt begreift sich aber nicht nur als eine Hardware- und Software-Initiative. Es versucht, eine lebendige Plattform für Filmemacher, Creative Industries, Künstler und enthusiastische Amateure zu werden. Für die Jury ist dieses Projekt ein außergewöhnliches Beispiel für die sich herausbildende Open-Hardware-Bewegung und sie hofft, dass diese Bewegung auch Bereiche jenseits elektronischer Hardware erfassen wird und auch andere Industriezweige aufbrechen und erneuern wird, z. B. die Autoindustrie, deren Umweltschutzbestrebungen im Wesentlichen stagnieren.

ANERKENNUNGEN

XinCheJian

http://www.xinchejian.com

XinCheJian wurde von einer kleinen internationalen Gruppe von Geeks, Hackern und Open-Source-Befürwortern in Shanghai gestartet, die die Entwicklung von Physical-Computing-Projekten, die früher Ingenieuren vorbehalten waren, für den Durchschnittsuser zugänglich machten. Ihre Mission besteht darin, Physical Computing, Open-Source-Hardware und das Internet der Dinge zu promoten und zu unterstützen. Die Einrichtung und das Wachstum dieses ersten Hackerspaces in China hat eine DIY- und Maker-Bewegung in ganz China und Hongkong losgetreten. Das langfristige Ziel besteht darin, das Konzept und die Philosophie in ganz China zu verbreiten und die Gründung von Hackerspaces in allen Großstädten zu inspirieren. Innerhalb von zwei Jahren haben die Community und die Fans von *XinCheJian* fünf weitere Hackerspaces aufgebaut und 2012 den ersten Maker Carnival ermöglicht. Die Maker-Kultur ist eine wichtige Inspirationsquelle, wenn es darum geht, nachhaltiges Design und nachhaltige industrielle Herstellung in China zu fördern.

Safecast

http://safecast.org

Safecast ist ein globales Projekt, das Menschen Daten über die Umgebung, in der sie leben, zur Verfügung

camera system composed from several hardware and software modules. Free software and open hardware will be utilized to build a device sporting all the features required by professional filmmakers in both studio and outdoor environments. The *Apertus* project also sees itself as more than just a hardware and software initiative. It is attempting to become a burgeoning platform for filmmakers, creative industry professionals, artists and enthusiasts. The jury sees this project as an outstanding example of the emerging open-hardware movement and hopes that this movement will grow beyond electronic hardware and disrupt and renew other industries, such as the environmentally mostly stagnant automotive industry.

HONORARY MENTIONS

XinCheJian

http://www.xinchejian.com

XinCheJian was initially started small by a group of international geeks, hackers and open-source technocrats, who made the development of physical computing projects previously only achievable by engineers open to people of all backgrounds. Their mission is to support, create and promote physical computing, open-source hardware and the Internet of Things. The establishment and growth of this very first hackerspace in China has sparked a DIY and maker movement all over the country, including Hong Kong. Its long-term goal is to spread the concept and philosophy across China and inspire hackerspaces in every large city of China. Within two years, the community members and fans of *XinCheJian* have started five more hackerspaces all over China and made the first Maker's Carnival possible in 2012. Maker's culture is an important source of inspiration for bringing about a sustainable design and manufacturing industry in China.

Safecast

http://safecast.org

Safecast is a global project working to empower people with data, primarily by mapping radiation levels and building a sensor network, enabling people to both contribute and freely use the data collected. After the 3/11 earthquake and resulting nuclear situation at Fukushima Daiichi, it became clear that people wanted more data than what was made available by the Japanese government and the Tepco power company. Through joint efforts with partners such as International Medcom and Keio University, *Safecast* has been building a radiation-sensor network comprising static and mobile sensors actively deployed around Japan both in the exclusion zone around the reactor and elsewhere in the country.

Safecast supports the idea that more data freely available data is better. The goal of this project is not to single out any individual source of data as untrustworthy, but rather to contribute to the existing measurement data and make it more robust. Multiple sources of data are always better and more accurate when aggregated. While Japan and radiation is the primary focus of the moment, this work has made us aware of a need for more environmental data on a global level. The long-term work that *Safecast* engages in will address these needs.

Lorea

http://www.lorea.org

This hotbed of social networks responds to the growing need for freely federated and self-managed spaces. One of its most popular networks is N-1.cc, which became very popular with the May 15 movement, when many Spanish users started questioning privately owned online platforms and services such as Facebook as their tools for protest, campaigning and circulating information. *Lorea*, which means "flower" in Basque, provides netizens with social platforms created by the people for the people. The community has so far created ten online social networks and offers tools such as wikis, blogs, calendars, mail lists and microblogging services that aim to enable communication and collaborative work while giving people full control of their data.

stellen, und zwar in erster Linie, indem es Daten zur Strahlungsbelastung auf Karten verortet und ein Sensorennetzwerk aufbaut. Jeder kann zum Projekt beitragen und die gesammelten Daten frei nutzen. Nach dem Erdbeben vom 11. März 2011 und dem Nuklearunfall von Fukushima Daiichi wurde klar, dass die Bevölkerung mehr Daten wollte, als die japanische Regierung und die Betreiberfirma Tepco zugänglich machten. *Safecast* hat ein Netzwerk aus statischen und mobilen Strahlungssensoren aufgebaut, die aktiv in ganz Japan aufgestellt wurden, und zwar sowohl in der Sperrzone rund um den Reaktor als auch an anderen Orten im ganzen Land.

Der Grundsatz, der die Arbeit von *Safecast* bestimmt, lautet: Je mehr Daten – und zwar verfügbare Daten –, desto besser. *Safecast* will nicht eine einzelne Datenquelle als unzuverlässig etikettieren, sondern die bereits existierenden Messdaten ergänzen, um sie verlässlicher zu machen. Es ist immer besser, mit unterschiedlichen Datenquellen zu arbeiten, und die Ergebnisse sind genauer, sobald die verschiedenen Daten aggregiert werden.

Der Schwerpunkt des Projekts liegt zurzeit in Japan und auf Strahlungsdaten, aber da es einen Bedarf nach mehr umweltbezogenen Daten auf globaler Ebene gibt, will sich *Safecast* genau mit dieser Problematik beschäftigen.

Lorea

http://www.lorea.org

Diese „Brutstätte" für soziale Netzwerke reagiert auf das wachsende Bedürfnis für frei föderierte, in Eigenregie betriebene digitale Räume. Eines der populärsten Netzwerke ist *N-1.cc*, das im Zuge der Bewegung des 15. Mai sehr populär wurde. Damals begannen viele Spanier daran zu zweifeln, ob Online-Plattformen in Privatbesitz und Dienste wie Facebook das beste Werkzeug für den Protest, für Kampagnen und Informationsverteilung seien. *Lorea*, das im Baskischen „Blume" bedeutet, stellt den Netzbürgern soziale Plattformen zur Verfügung, die von Menschen für Menschen entwickelt wurden. Die Community hat bislang zehn soziale Online-Netzwerke erstellt und bietet Tools wie Wikis, Blogs, Kalender, Mailinglisten und Microblogging-Dienste an, die Kommunikation und kollaboratives Arbeiten ermöglichen und gleichzeitig voll Kontrolle über die eigenen Daten garantieren.

18 days in Egypt
http://www.18daysinegypt.com
2011 waren die Internet-User die treibende Kraft hinter den politischen Veränderungen im Mittleren Osten, in Nordafrika und anderen Teilen der Welt. Sie versuchten, Informations-Blackouts zu kompensieren, indem sie ihren eigenen Content produzierten und ihre eigene Geschichte mit den zur Verfügung stehenden Mitteln erzählten. Seit Beginn der Revolutionen haben die Ägypter ihre eigenen Aufstände und Mobilisierung in einem Kontext der Repression und staatskontrollierter Medien dokumentiert und kommentiert. *18 Days in Egypt* ist ein interaktives Dokumentationsprojekt, das aus dem Bedürfnis entstanden ist, die Geschichte der Revolution anhand jenes Materials zu archivieren, das während der 18 Tage jener Revolution, die den Beginn eines neuen Zeitalters in der Region markierte, produziert und geteilt wurde.

The Johnny Cash Project
http://www.thejohnnycashproject.com
Dieses Projekt zeigt die Macht und das Potenzial des Crowd-Creation-Prozesses. 250.000 Menschen steuerten ihre Werke zu *The Johnny Cash Project* bei. Es zeigt, wie die Möglichkeiten von Crowd-Creation und Voting ein nachhaltiges Kunstwerk schaffen können.

Young Africa Live
http://www.praekeltfoundation.org/young-africa-live.html
Dieses Projekt mit seinen vielen Community-bezogenen Funktionen ist ein gutes Beispiel für die Entwicklung eines Service speziell für junge Leute, das auf einer existierenden Infrastruktur für mobilen Access aufsetzt. Es ist dem Problem HIV/Aids gewidmet und zeigt, dass junge Menschen mit Funktionen wie Serious Gaming, mobilem Lernen, Quiz-Spielen und anderen Funktionen das nötige Rüstzeug in die Hand bekommen, um sich mit dieser Thematik auseinanderzusetzen.

Meine Abgeordneten
http://www.meineabgeordneten.at
Meine Abgeordneten ist gutes Beispiel für einen Ansatz, der Offene Demokratie und Transparenz via digitaler Communities fördert, denn es zeigt , dass man mit einem Community-basierten Ansatz relevante Informationen

18 days in Egypt
http://www.18daysinegypt.com
In 2011, netizens were at the heart of the political changes in the Middle East and North Africa and in the rest of the world. They tried to resist news and information blackouts by producing their own content, narrating their history in the first person with the tools at their disposal. Since the beginning of the revolution, Egyptians have been recording and narrating their own uprisings and mobilization within a context of repression and state-controlled media. *18 Days in Egypt* is an interactive documentary project that responds to the need for archiving and documenting the story of the revolution through the content shared by Egyptians during the 18 days of a revolution that marked a new period in the region.

The Johnny Cash Project
http://www.thejohnnycashproject.com
This project shows the power and potential of the crowd creation process. 250,000 people contributed artwork for the *Johnny Cash* video and it shows the possibilities of how crowd creation and voting can generate a sustainable art work.

Young Africa Live
http://www.praekeltfoundation.org/young-africa-live.html
With many community-related functions, this project is a good example of developing a service based on the existing infrastructure for mobile access, especially to young people. It addresses the very important topic of HIV/Aids and shows that young people could be enabled with functions such as serious gaming, mobile learning and quizzes among many other fruitful functions.

Meine Abgeordneten
http://www.meineabgeordneten.at
As a good example of an open-democracy and transparency approach via digital communities, *Meine Abgeordneten* helps to show how a community-based approach could bring relevant information about the independence of politicians to the public. There have been several contributions from

this area of increasing transparency of politicians. What distinguished *Meine Abgeordneten* from several other entries was the fact, that it is being crowd-funded via *respekt.net*.

Texting for Democracy

http://www.kubatana.net

Kubatana, an Zimbabwean NGO uses a variety of technologies to communicate with Zimbabweans and to foster electronic activism, particularly with the communication needs of marginalized communities in mind. *Texting for Democracy* is a project documenting SMS feedback, and is targeting groups without access to the Internet, but where the use of mobile phones is high. With an SMS membership of over 30,000 subscribers across the country, the project takes advantage of the immediacy and interactivity of SMS and mobile communications. An SMS survey is regularly used as a two-way communication tool, in which people share their feedback, observations, opinion and suggestions on timely topics such as the prevalence of political violence, the spread of typhoid cases or mixed reactions to planned door-to-door HIV testing. The feedback to bulk SMS is processed and cross-referenced with the database providing for localizsed and crowd- sourced information, which then enables the mapping of responses and the creation of visual displays.

iHub—Nairobi's Innovation Hub

http://ihub.co.ke

iHub is a fast-growing incubator space for Kenyan startups, investors and technologists providing an open space for the technology community in the area. Its focus is on young entrepreneurs, web and mobile- phone programmers, hackers, designers and researchers. It is an open community workspace, closely linked to popular concepts such aslike M-Pesa or the Ushahidi platform. African Digital Art's has launched their first event there, a website which has transformed the digital art space in Africa by giving thousands of artists a platform to showcase their work on. Other examples of companies started, or connections made, include mFarm (a mobile agricultural information

über die Unabhängigkeit von Politikern der Öffentlichkeit zur Verfügung stellen kann. Es hat etliche Einreichungen gegeben, die Politiker „transparenter" machen wollen. Was jedoch *Meine Abgeordneten* von ähnlichen Projekten unterscheidet, ist die Tatsache, dass es sich per Crowdfunding über die Plattform *respekt.net* finanziert.

Texting for Democracy

http://www.kubatana.net

Kubatana, eine NGO aus Zimbabwe, bedient sich unterschiedlichster Technologien, um mit der Bevölkerung zu kommunizieren und elektronischen Aktivismus zu fördern, wobei besonders auf die Bedürfnisse marginalisierter Bevölkerungsgruppen Rücksicht genommen wird. *Texting for Democracy* ist ein Projekt, das SMS-Feedback dokumentiert und sich vor allem an Randgruppen richtet, die zwar keinen Zugang zum Internet haben, aber einen intensiven Gebrauch von Mobiltelefonen machen.

Das Projekt hat 30.000 Abonnenten im ganzen Land und nutzt die Unmittelbarkeit und Interaktivität von SMS und mobiler Kommunikation. Es werden regelmäßig SMS-Befragungen durchgeführt, bei denen Menschen Feedback, Beobachtungen, Meinungen und Vorschläge zu aktuellen Themen teilen, z. B. zu politischer Gewalt, der Verbreitung von Typhus oder zu Plänen für mobile HIV-Tests. Das Feedback auf Massen-SMS wird mit einer Datenbank abgeglichen, die lokalisierte und via Crowdsourcing erhaltene Informationen enthält, die das Mappen der Antworten und eine Visualisierung der Daten ermöglicht.

iHub – Nairobi's Innovation Hub

http://ihub.co.ke

iHub ist ein schnell wachsender Inkubator for keniatische Start-ups, Investoren und Technologen und bietet einen offenen Raum für die Tech-Community der Region. *iHub* konzentriert sich auf die jungen Entrepreneure, Programmierer im Web- und Mobiltelefonbereich, Hacker, Designer und Researcher. Es ist ein offener Community-Workspace, der eng mit bekannten Initiativen wie M-Pesa oder Ushahidi verlinkt ist. Hier hat z. B. *African Digital Art* sein erstes Event abgehalten, eine Webseite, die die digitale Kunst in Afrika insofern transformiert hat, als sie Künstlern eine Plattform zur Präsentation bietet. Andere Unternehmen, die hier gestartet haben oder Networking betreiben, sind z. B. mFarm (ein mobiles Tool für landwirtschaftliche Informationen), Rupu (ein keniatischer Groupon-Klon) und Eatout.co.ke, das hier seine Investoren gefunden hat. Ermöglicht wird das durch ein Konzept offener Innovation und dementsprechender Software, wobei interne und externe bzw. Online- und Offline-Ressourcen in einer inspirierenden Umgebung kombiniert werden.

iStreet Lab

http://istreetlab.ning.com/

An eine der benachteiligsten gesellschaftlichen Gruppen - nämlich an in von Gewalt geprägten Stadtvierteln lebende Jugendliche zwischen 9 und 25 - wendet sich das Projekt *iStreeet Lab*, eine Initiative des Künstlers und Community-Entwicklers Mervin Jarman, die von einem Team von rund 20 Multimedia-Künstlern bereits an verschiedenen Orten umgesetzt wurde. Das *iStreet Lab* - ein „Mistkübel", der mit allem, was man für Multimedia-Produktionen braucht, ausgestattet ist - will diesen Jugendlichen mittels Technologie eine Stimme verleihen. Dabei geht das Konzept weit über eine Multimedia-Ausbildung hinaus: Im Rahmen des Projekts werden auch Beratung, Mentoring, Gewaltvorbeugung und Elternprogramme betrieben. Initiiert wurde das Projekt 2008 in Jamaika als Reaktion auf die steigende Kriminalität unter Jugendlichen. Inzwischen wurde es auch in Australien, Kanada und den USA durchgeführt und hat an die 400 Jugendliche erfasst.

Europe versus Facebook

http://europe-v-facebook.org/

Diese vom österreichischen Jus-Studenten Max Schrems initiierte Kampagne ist eine von vielen Einreichungen, die sich mit Fragen von Privacy und Datenschutz, vor allem im Zusammenhang mit sozialen Netzwerken, beschäftigen. *Europe versus Facebook* hat 22 Datenschutz-relevante Klagen beim Irischen Data Protection Commissioner (der für europäische Facebook-User zuständig ist) eingebracht und parallel dazu eine Anleitung veröffentlicht, wie man an seine FB-Daten herankommt. Inzwischen haben mehr als 40.000 User ein Ersuchen auf Herausgabe ihrer Daten gestellt. Grundsätzlich geht es der Initiative um mehr Transparenz, was die Verwendung personenbezogener Daten angeht. Zweitens um Opt-In statt Opt-Out, sprich jede/r UserIn soll sich nicht gegen die Veröffentlichung von Daten aussprechen müssen, sondern sich

tool), Rupu (a Groupon clone for Kenya) and investors found for Eatout.co.ke, among others. This is achieved through the concept and social software of oOpen iInnovation, which is the process of combining internal and external / online and offline resources in a very favourable and inspiring environment.

iStreet Lab

http://istreetlab.ning.com/

The *iStreet Lab* project, aimed at one of the most disadvantaged social groups—young people aged nine to 25 living in areas of cities marked by violence—is an initiative by the artist and community developer Mervin Jarman, which is carried out by a team of some 20 multimedia artists. *iStreet Lab*—a "trash can" equipped with everything needed for multimedia productions—aims to use technology to give young people a voice. This goes far beyond a concept of multimedia training: in the framework of the project, consulting, mentoring, violence avoidance and parenting are also carried out. The project was initiated in 2008 in Jamaica in reaction to the growing levels of criminality among young people. In the meantime it also been put in place in Australia, Canada and the US and has included some 400 young people.

Europe versus Facebook

http://europe-v-facebook.org/

Initiated by Max Schrem's Austrian law students, this campaign is one of the many submissions that deals with questions of privacy and data protection, above all inconnection with social networks. *Europe versus Facebook* submitted 22 data-protection complaints to the Irish Data Protection Commissioner (who is responsible for European Facebook users) and at the same time published instructions on how to access one's FB data. In the meantime more than 40,000 users have submitted requests for the release of their data.

The initiative confronts the world's largest social network with four primary demands: More transparency as far as the use of personal data is concerned; opt-in instead of opt-out, which means that users should not have to act to prevent publication of their data but rather give their permission for what would, by default, be prohibited; genuine control over the user's own data, which friends up to now have been able to reveal to Facebook up to now; and as well as data minimization in order to prevent the accumulation over time of enormous quantities of digital rubbish. Moreover, *Europe vs. Facebook* finds it unacceptable that the social network stores some certain data forever and stops withholds from users being able to delete itthe possibility of expunging them.

Crónicas de Heroes

http://www.cronicasdeheroes.mx

Crónicas de Heroes is a "positive thinking" campaign that documents examples of civil courage and cooperation in civil society—and among other places in Juárez, one of the most violent cities in the world. It gives people a place where they can mark small gestures of respect, of honesty and other positive contrbutions to society on a map and so make them public. *Crónicas de Heroes* is based on the *Hero Reports* campaign, a response to the "See Something, Say Something" campaign by the New York Metropolitan Transit Authority in reaction to 9/11, where suspicious activities were reported.

dafür entscheiden können. Drittens um echte Kontrolle über die eigenen Daten. Viertens Datensparsamkeit, um dem schier endlosen Datenmüll entgegenzuwirken, der sich über die Zeit ansammelt. Darüber hinaus stößt sich *Europe versus Facebook* daran, dass das soziale Netzwerk manche Daten für immer und ewig speichert – das Löschen dieser Daten ist den UserInnen unmöglich.

Crónicas de Heroes

http://www.cronicasdeheroes.mx

Crónicas de Heroes ist eine Kampagne „positiven Denkens", die Beispiele von Zivilcourage und Zusammenarbeit innerhalb der Zivilgesellschaft dokumentiert – und das u. a. auch in Juárez, einer der gewalttätigsten Städte der Welt. Es stellt den Bürgern einen Ort zur Verfügung, wo sie kleine Gesten des Respekts, der Ehrlichkeit und anderer positive Beiträge zur Gesellschaft auf einer Karte verorten und so publik machen können. *Crónicas de Heroes* basiert auf der der Kampagne *Hero Reports*, die eine Antwort auf die Kampagne „See Something, Say Something" der New Yorker Metropolitan Transit Authority als Reaktion auf 9/11 war und wo verdächtige Aktivitäten gemeldet wurden.

Abschließende Bemerkungen

Die Organisatoren und Juroren des Prix Ars Electronica bemühen sich mehr, als dies bei anderen Preisen der Fall ist, auch jenseits der florierenden und relativ gut finanzierten Online-Sphären Westeuropas und der USA zu blicken.

2012 gingen vier Preise an Digital-Communities-Projekte auf dem afrikanischen Kontinent. Afrika ist nach wie vor ein „dunkler Kontinent" auf der Karte der Internet-Connectivity, aber die Situation ändert sich: Ungefähr 140 Millionen Afrikaner sind nun online und 40 Millionen haben ein Facebook-Account.

In einem Kontinent, wo die Hälfte der Bevölkerung unter 15 Jahre und 70 Prozent unter 30 Jahre alt sind, werden Social Media ein wichtiger Entwicklungsfaktor. Afrikaner nutzen Social Media und sie sind stärker „connected" als je zuvor. 2012 gibt es in Afrika bereits 600 Millionen mobile Endgeräte mit Internet-Zugang. Aber die digitale Kluft besteht noch immer, und deswegen war es der Jury ein besonderes Anliegen, herausragende afrikanische Projekte, die eine Vision zur digitalen Inklusion verfolgen, oder die sich der Herausforderung stellen und eine Drehscheibe für kreative Energie, Networkung und Kollaboration bilden.

Closing Remarks

More than at any other award we know of, the organizers and jurors of the Prix Ars Electronica Award have always been efforting to look beyond the vibrant and comparatively well-funded online spheres of Western Europe and the United States of America.

For the year 2012, four awards went to digital community projects on the African continent.

Africa still is a "dark continent" on the map of Internet connectivity, but things are changing. About 140 million Africans are now online and 40 million are on Facebook. With half of the population aged under age 15 and with 70 percent of the population under the age of 30, social media is becoming an important feature in the continent's development path. Africans are using social media and they are connected more than ever before. In 2012, there are about 600 million connected mobile devices in Africa.

Against the backdrop of a continuing still existing digital divide in Africa, the jury wanted to give special emphasis to outstanding African projects with a vision of digital inclusion, to projects that who are challenging the odds and are providing for a hub of creative energy, networking and collaborations.

Syrian People Know Their Way

Syrian People Know Their Way is a community of young Syrian digital artists, designers, bloggers and activists who aim both to gather and provide inspiration for the Syrian struggle for freedom.

The project started as a Facebook page on Feb 26, 2011, to open the door for an analysis of Syria's situation and where it was heading, as we were able to see a change coming to Syria with the wider and bigger change hitting other countries in the area. We all had one goal: we all support democratic change, political discourse and the media of the revolution.

That was before the revolution started. Then, after the revolution in Syria officially started, other pages and organizations were working on getting the news out and sharing it on Facebook and Twitter. We felt that it was our duty to do something, to get more involved.

We thought one way of doing this would be to find a different way of transferring the news to and from the people, using all the available methods of media and working with activists on the ground, aiming to provide a political and theoretical view about daily events in Syria. We wanted to focus more on the human side of the revolution, the people, the Syrians, and wanted to provide the revolution with art that would be noticed and communicate the Syrian face to the world and to the Syrians themselves.

Syrian People Know Their Way ist eine Community junger syrischer Künstler, Designer, Blogger und Aktivisten, die Inspirationen aus dem syrischen Freiheitskampf sammeln und im Gegenzug den Menschen, die sich an diesem Kampf beteiligen, zugänglich machen.

Das Projekt begann am 26. Februar 2011 als Facebook-Seite, um eine Möglichkeit für die Analyse der syrischen Situation und deren Entwicklung zu schaffen. Angesichts der Veränderungen, die in anderen Ländern passierten, war uns schon damals klar, dass eine solche Veränderung auch auf Syrien zukommen würde. Wir alle hatten ein Ziel: die demokratische Veränderung, den politischen Diskurs und die Medien der Revolution zu unterstützen.

Das war, bevor die Revolution tatsächlich begann. Nach Beginn der Revolution gab es viele andere Webseiten und Organisationen, die Informationen zur Verfügung stellten und sie auf Facebook und Twitter teilten. Wir hatten das Gefühl, es sei unsere Pflicht, etwas zu unternehmen und uns stärker einzubringen.

Wir wollten neue Wege finden, Informationen unter die Leute zu bringen bzw. sie zu bündeln, indem wir alle verfügbaren Medien nutzten und mit Aktivisten vor Ort zusammenarbeiteten – immer mit dem Ziel, die täglichen Ereignisse in Syrien aus politischer und theoretischer Sicht zu betrachten. Wir wollten uns auf die menschliche Seite der Revolution konzentrieren, auf das Volk, die Syrer, und eine künstlerische Seite in die Revolution bringen, die Aufmerksamkeit erregen und das syrische Gesicht der Welt und dem syrischen Volk selbst kommunizieren würde.

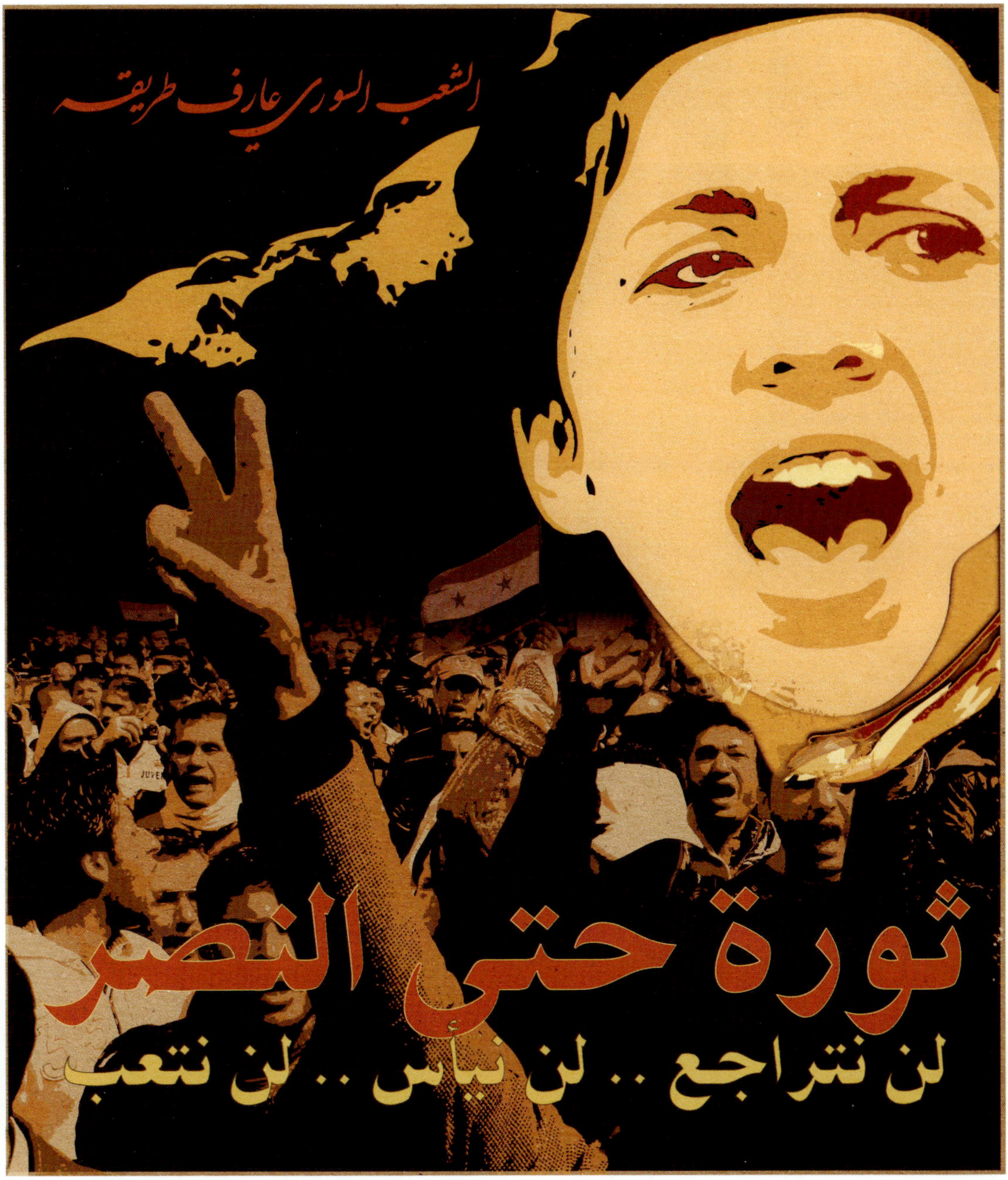

Revolution until Victory
We will not pull back ... we will not give up... we will not get tired

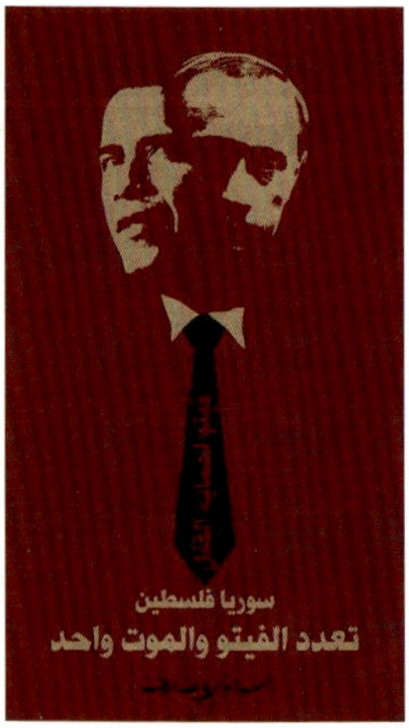

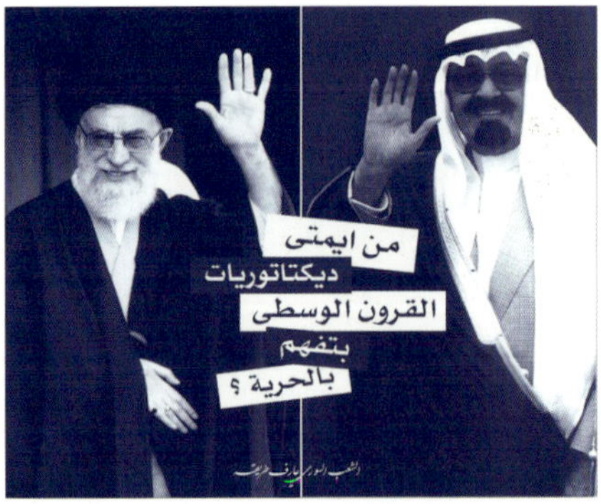

When were the middle age dictators aware of the freedom??!

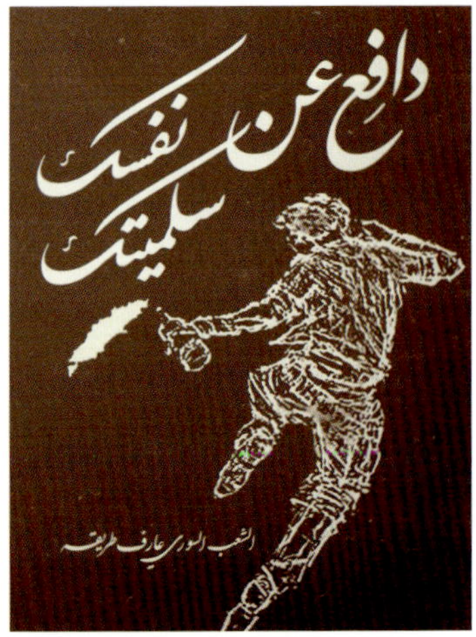

Syria and Palestine
different vetoes, same death

Defend yourself and your peaceful movement

We are doing this through modern art and technology in a simple, straightforward way that everyone can understand. Our work is inspired on the one hand by the activists on the ground and on the other hand by supporting them with practical ideas and theoretical thoughts of the everyday life that they are experiencing. We try to present our works of art in a way that makes it close to the street and away from the "art salon" type. To do so, we to use elements from Syrian folklore and language, formulating them in an open way that reflects the human heritage rather than using complex texts, simplifying the complex political concepts by formulating them in short phrases and in a popular manner or sometimes even in funny phrases. On the other hand, trying to keep a degree of depth and avoiding shallowness.

Our work is divided into various overlapping fields. For example some art pieces are based on the mixing idea; we take a well-known painting and merge it with Arabic calligraphy to show the humanistic dimension of the revolution, expressing elements that people in the streets concerned with, trying to reflect their voices. We also have work that uses art and beauty to provide the people with ways to peacefully re-evaluate, using history and

Wir tun dies durch moderne Kunst und Technologie, die wir auf sehr direkte und einfache Art und Weise nutzen, sodass unsere Botschaft für alle verständlich ist. Unsere Arbeit bezieht ihre Inspiration einerseits von den Aktivisten vor Ort, andererseits daraus, dass wir sie mit praktischen Ideen und theoretischen Überlegungen zum Alltag, den sie leben, versorgen. Wir versuchen, unsere künstlerischen Arbeiten auf eine Art und Weise zu präsentieren, die für die Menschen auf der Straße Sinn macht und nichts mit der Kunst der Kunstsalons zu tun hat. Deshalb verwenden wir auch vor allem Elemente aus der syrischen Folklore und Sprache, die wir in sehr offener Weise formulieren statt komplexe Texte zu veröffentlichen. Uns geht es darum, komplizierte politische Konzepte verständlich zu machen, indem wir sie in kurzen, populären, ja, manchmal auch witzigen Aussagen zusammenfassen. Andererseits versuchen wir aber auch, uns dabei eine gewisse Tiefe zu bewahren und nicht in hohle Phrasen abzugleiten.

Unsere Arbeit teilt sich in verschiedene einander überlappende Bereiche. Zum Beispiel basieren manche der künstlerischen Arbeiten auf der Idee des Mixing: Wir nehmen ein bekanntes Bild und verbinden es mit arabischer Kalligrafie, um die humanistische Seite der Revolution zu zeigen. So wollen wir Dinge ansprechen, die für die Menschen auf der Straße von Bedeutung sind, und auch ihre Stimme

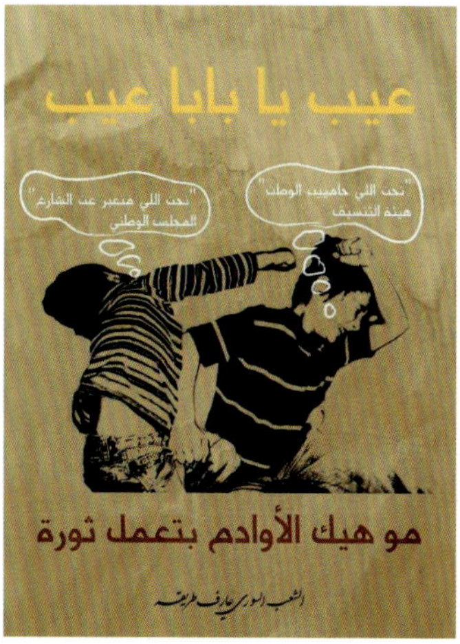

Father: *Shame on you kids.*
Kid 1 (Syrian National Council): *We represent the revolution.*
Kid 2 (National Coordination Body for Democratic Change): *We defend the homeland.*
Father: *Revolutions aren't made like this.*

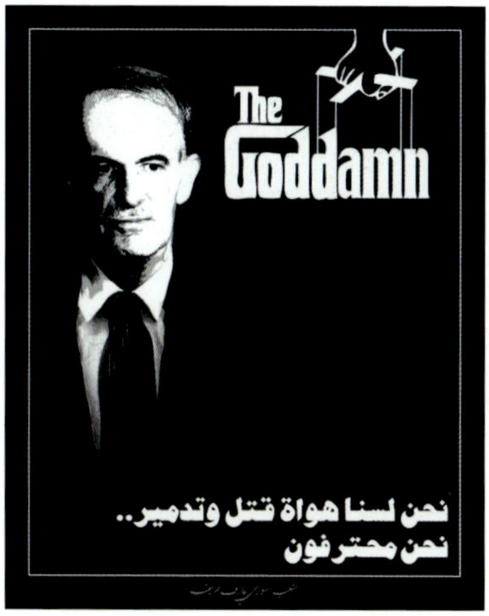

Killing and destroying are not our hobbies ...we are professional

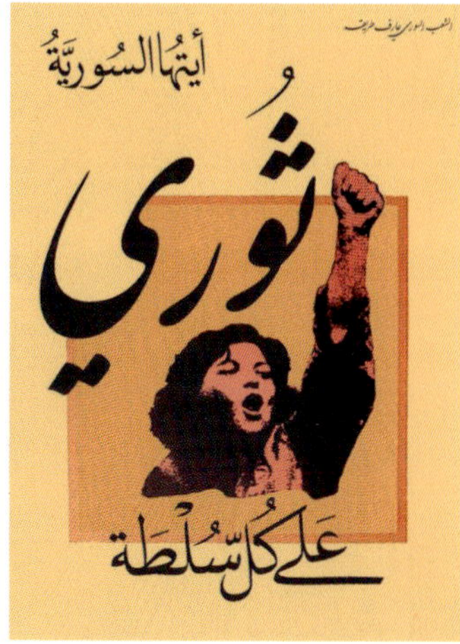

Oh Syrian women, rebel against all authorities

widerspiegeln. Einige unserer Projekte arbeiten bewusst mit Schönheit und Ästhetik, um die Menschen anzuregen, eine Situation aus einem Geist des Friedens heraus zu evaluieren und sich dabei auf die eigene Geschichte und Erfahrung zu stützen. Auf diese Weise versuchen wir zum Beispiel, dem syrischen Volk praktische Anregungen für den Kampf zu vermitteln und so eine gewaltfreie Haltung gegenüber dem Regime zu fördern.
Unsere Zielgruppe sind jene unentschiedenen Menschen, die noch nicht wissen, auf welcher Seite sie stehen. Wir möchten ihnen politische Vorstellungen und unterschiedliche Ideen über die Revolution in Bezug auf die politischen Ereignisse in Syrien vermitteln – und manchmal in der gesamten Region. Wir öffnen die Tür für Ideen und Reflexionen in und aus der ganzen Gesellschaft, sodass diese Gruppen sich nicht ausgeschlossen fühlen aus dem „zukünftigen Syrien", von dem wir träumen und für das wir kämpfen, mit unabhängigen Jugend-Medien, die ihren Stimmen in der Öffentlichkeit Gehör verschaffen, egal, welcher Richtung oder Kategorie sie angehören.

experience. An example of this work would be the art that depends on the aesthetic dimension to provide practical ideas to the Syrian people. Supporting them in the non-violent revolution (movement) against the regime.
We target the audience of the silent (neutral) people who have yet not decided to take sides, by offering them political views and different ideas about the revolution in relation to political events in Syria—and sometimes in the region. We open the door to more thoughts and ideas within (and from) the whole society and so these groups of people will not feel left out of the "future Syria" that we dream of and fight for, with an independent youth media that would be able to make their voices heard in public space regardless of what it is or in what category it fits.

Syrian People Know Their Way is a digital community of young Syrian digital artists, designers, bloggers and activists that aim to both gather and provide inspiration for the Syrian struggle for freedom. **Syrian People Know Their Way** ist eine Online-Community junger syrischer Künstler, Designer, Blogger und Aktivisten, die Inspirationen aus dem syrischen Freiheitskampf sammeln und im Gegenzug den Menschen, die sich an diesem Kampf beteiligen, zugänglich machen.

Apertus Open Source Cinema

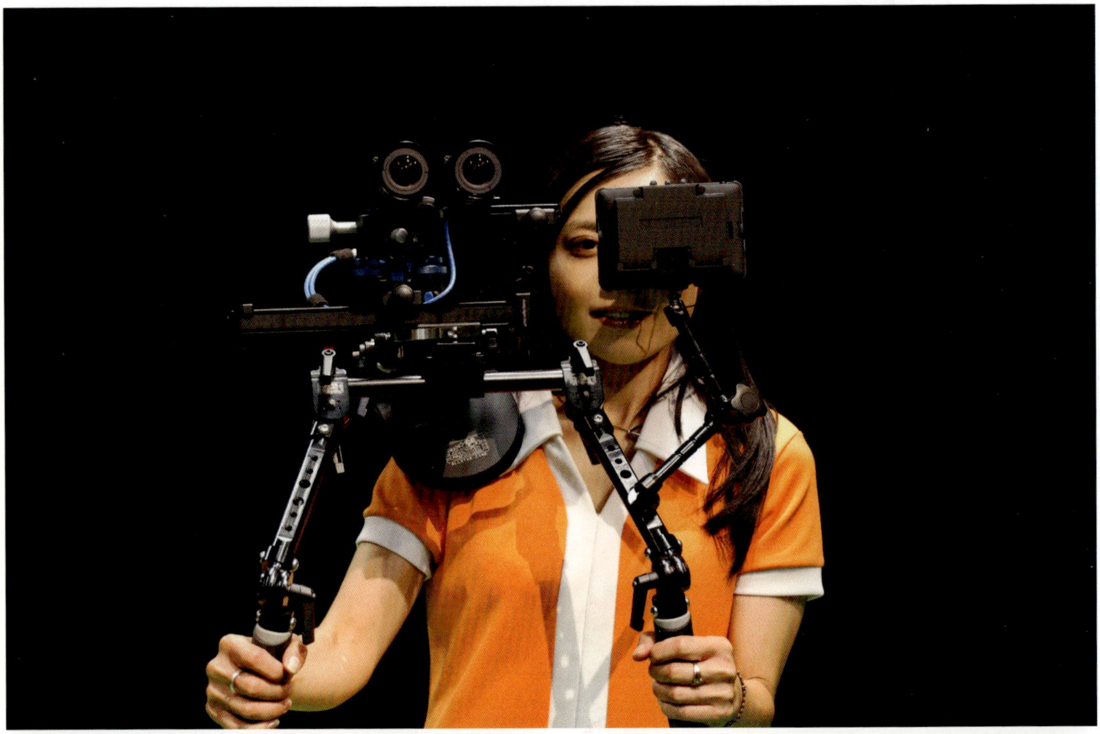

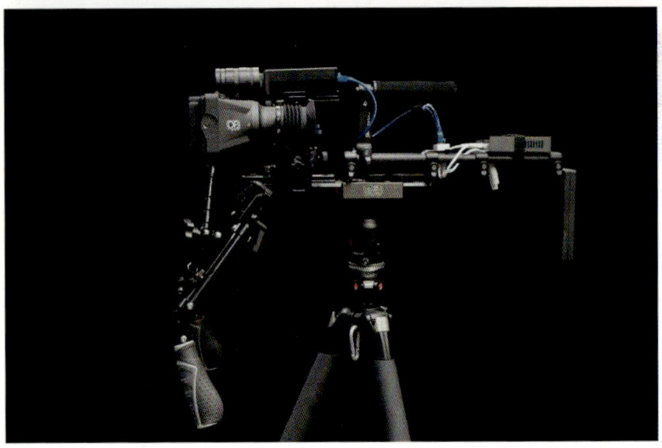

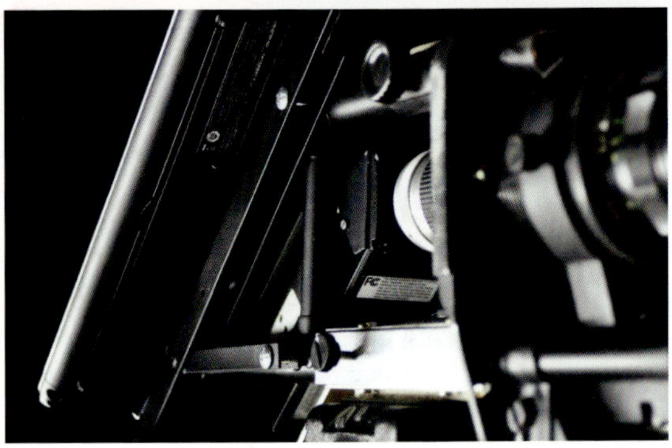

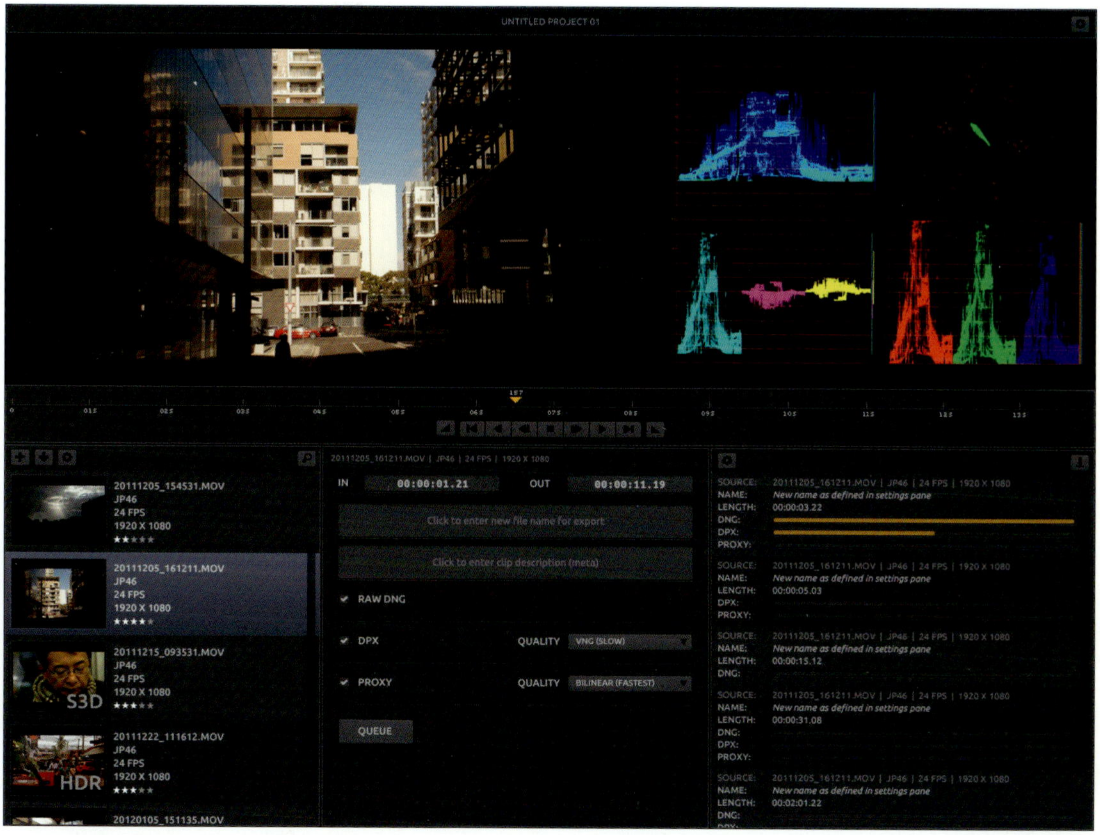

Das Projekt *Apertus Open Source Cinema* entwickelt ein modulares Kamerasystem, das aus etlichen Hard- und Softwaremodulen besteht. Dabei verwenden wir freie (FLOSS) Software und offene Hardware, um ein Gerät zu bauen, das alle Funktionalitäten aufweist, die professionelle Filmemacher sowohl im Studio als auch im Freien brauchen.

Das *Apertus*-Projekt ist seinem Verständnis nach mehr als eine Hardware/Software-Initiative. Es ist eine lebendige Plattform für Filmemacher, Leute aus der Kreativindustrie, Künstler und Liebhaber. *Apertus* ist gleichzeitig Community-Bewegung, Wissensforum und ein Ökosystem von Menschen die einander unterstützen und für Freiheit eintreten. Wir engagieren uns für freie Technologie, freie Information, freie Bildung, freies Wissen, freie Kultur, freie Kunst usw. Dazu gehört auch, dass wir alles, was wir entwickeln, der Öffentlichkeit zur Verfügung stellen und mit Lizenzen schützen, die Freiheit garantieren, wie dies von der Free Software Foundation definiert wird (GNU GPL, Creative Commons usw.).

The goal of the *Apertus Open Source Cinema* project is to create a modular camera system composed from several hardware and software modules. Free (FLOSS) software and open hardware are to be utilized to build a device sporting all the features required by professional filmmakers in both studio and outdoor environments. The *Apertus* project also sees itself as more than just a hardware/software initiative. It is a burgeoning platform for filmmakers, creative-industry professionals, artists and enthusiasts. *Apertus* is a community movement, a forum of knowledge, an ecosystem of people supporting each other also advocating freedom. We actively cultivate: free technology, free information, free education, free knowledge, free culture, free arts, etc. This requires that everything we create shall be released to the public and protected with licences that ensure freedom as defined by the FSF (GNU GPL, Creative Commons, etc.).

Film production has long been consigned to the realm of a select few, high-end proprietary manufacturing corporations. Due to the expense involved in research, development and low-volume, high-tech manufacturing, their products were reserved for only the most well-funded clients. This represents the essence of a closed world. Only in recent years have revolutionary changes taken place, with smaller companies creating innovative cameras and other tools at lower prices. However, their technological secrets are protected at all costs, and manufacturers have blocked access to the internal design of their products for fear of losing market share. This has resulted in vague or missing documentation, threats to void warranty—to prevent attempts at reverse engineering—and artificially crippled features. This leads to the paradoxical situation where the technology for filmmaking is now widely affordable at the expense of the loss of freedom to use these tools.

We at *Apertus* believe in open development and rely on fulfilling the four essential freedoms: freedom to access, use and study all knowledge; freedom to modify and change anything; freedom to redistribute all original knowledge; freedom to redistribute all modified and changed knowledge. In the beginning *Apertus* was just about building an open camera. As of 2012, it has become a much broader initiative. It now represents:

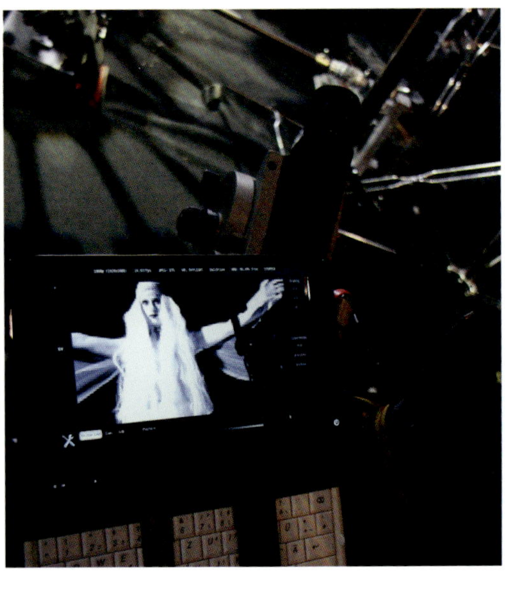

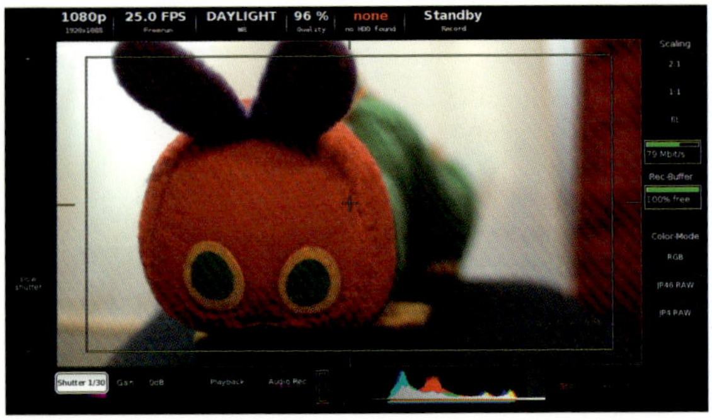

Die Filmproduktion galt lange als das Reich von ein paar auserwählten proprietären High-End-Herstellern. Dank des Geldes, das in Forschung, Entwicklung und Hightech-Herstellung in kleiner Stückzahl fließen, waren ihre Produkte nur den finanzstärksten Kunden vorbehalten. Dies ist eine geschlossene Welt par excellence. Erst in den letzten Jahren haben revolutionäre Veränderungen stattgefunden, und nun können auch kleinere Firmen innovative Kameras und andere Tools zu niedrigeren Preisen produzieren. Aber sie schützen ihre technologischen Geheimnisse um jeden Preis, und Hersteller blockieren den Zugang zum internen Design ihrer Produkte aus Angst, Marktanteile zu verlieren. Das hat dazu geführt, dass nur ungenaue oder überhaupt keine Dokumentationen existieren, und dass damit gedroht wird, Garantien für ungültig zu erklären – und zu künstlich beschnittenen Funktionalitäten. Das Ergebnis ist eine paradoxe Situation: Die Technologie fürs Filmemachen ist nun zwar verfügbar, aber nur dann, wenn die Freiheit, diese Tools zu nutzen, aufgegeben wird.

Bei *Apertus* glauben wir an offene Entwicklung und wollen in unserem Projekt vier wesentliche Freiheiten verwirklichen: Freiheit, Zugang zu sämtlichem Wissen zu haben, es zu nutzen und zu studieren; Freiheit, alles zu verändern und zu modifizieren; Freiheit, das ursprüngliche Wissen zu teilen; Freiheit, das Wissen über die Modifikationen und Veränderungen zu sharen. Am Beginn ging es bei *Apertus* lediglich darum, eine offene Kamera zu bauen. Im Jahr 2012 jedoch ist es bereits eine viel breitere Bewegung geworden. Nun steht das Projekt für:

- eine Bewegung, die die Idee, Wissen zu teilen und kollaborativ zu arbeiten, aktiv verbreitet;
- einen Pool von Filmemachern und Leuten aus den Kreativindustrien, die im professionellen Kinobereich und bei Kunstproduktionen zusammenarbeiten;
- eine Haltung, die Individuen ermuntert, einen aktiven Geist zu entwickeln und zu hinterfragen, worauf sie aufbauen, und der Gemeinschaft wieder etwas zurückgeben;
- eine Gruppe, die Wissen erarbeitet und publiziert, die Vorträge, Workshops und Events abhält;
- einen Pool von Entwicklern, die an freier Software und offener Hardware für Film und Postproduktion arbeiten.

- A movement actively spreading the idea of sharing knowledge and working together collaboratively
- A pool of filmmakers and creative-industry professionals collaborating on professional cinema and arts productions
- A missionary, encouraging individuals to develop an active mind, question what has come before them and give back to their respective communities
- A group that researches and publishes knowledge, gives talks, holds workshops and events
- A pool of developers working on free software and open hardware for film- and post-production.

Apertus Open Source Cinema. The core team currently consists of around 15 people. The membership forum currently has over 100 registered users. Anyone can join the community and engage in interaction/discussion or by contributing to the project. The entire community is very difficult to measure, but in combined social media we have a direct reach of around 1000 people.

Apertus Open Source Cinema. Das Kernteam besteht im Moment aus ungefähr 15 Personen. Das Mitgliederforum zählt über 100 registrierte User. Jeder kann der Community beitreten, an der Interaktion und Diskussion teilnehmen oder sich am Projekt beteiligen. Die gesamte Community ist größenmäßig schwer zu erfassen, aber wenn man alle Social Media einrechnet, erreichen wir ungefähr tausend Menschen.

Dark Glasses. Portrait

Hexie Farm

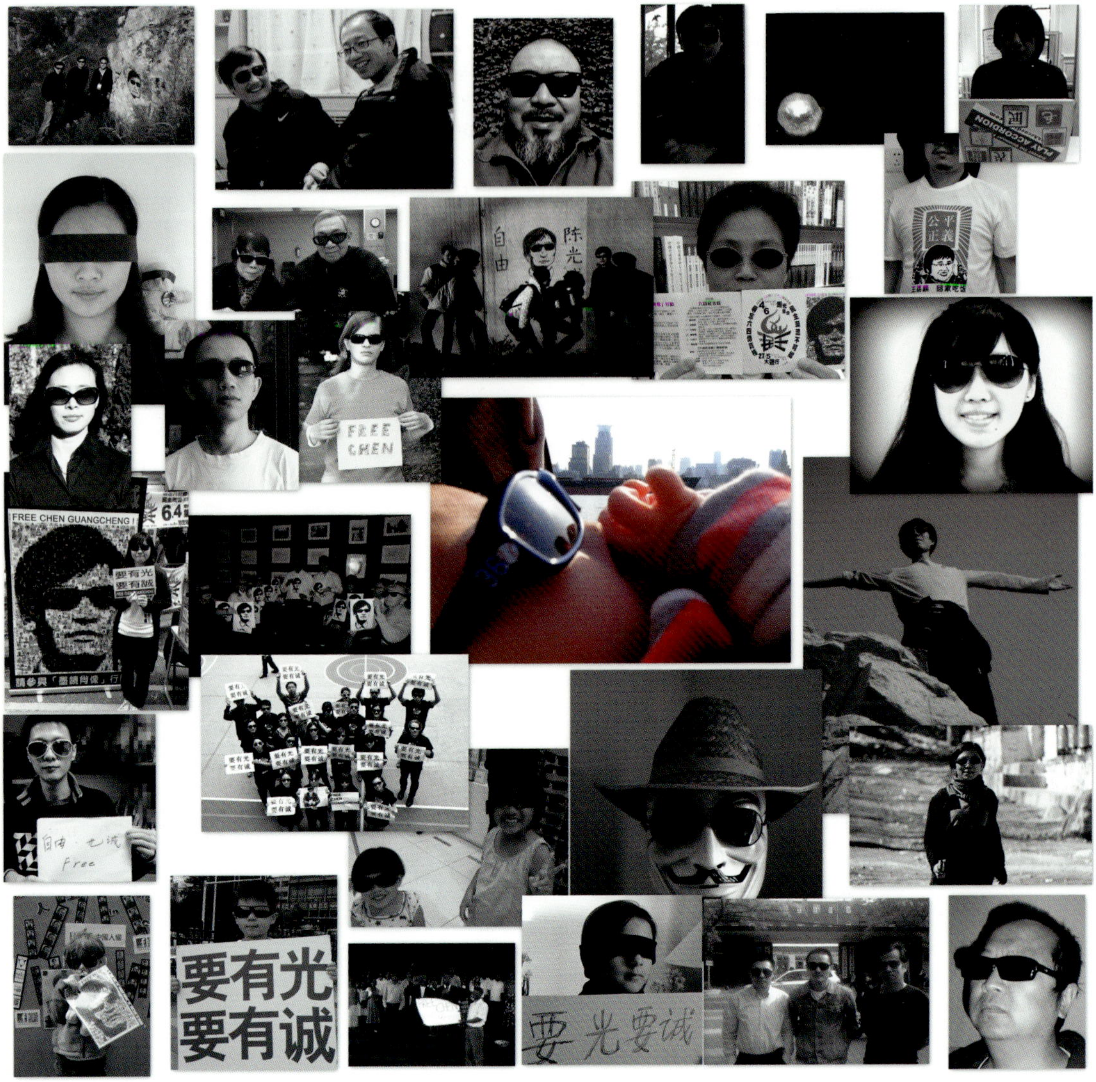

Dark Glasses. Portrait ist eine Online-Kampagne zur Unterstützung von Chen Guangcheng und ein Aufruf zu seiner Freilassung.
Chen Guangcheng ist ein blinder Bürgerrechtsaktivist. Er machte publik, dass Bewohner des Dorfes Lin Yi (Provinz Shandong) im Zuge der Durchsetzung der Ein-Kind-Politik Opfer von Gewalt seitens örtlicher Funktionäre wurden. Damit forderte er den Zorn der Behörden heraus und wurde wegen des erfundenen Vergehens „Beschädigung öffentlichen Eigentums und Störung des Verkehrs" zu einer Gefängnisstrafe verurteilt. Nach seiner Freilassung wurde Chen Guangcheng von der Regierung ohne Angabe von Gründen unter Hausarrest gestellt. Viele Unterstützer versuchten, Chen und seine Familie zu besuchen, aber sie wurden gewaltsam daran gehindert, beraubt, festgehalten und in manchen Fällen schwer misshandelt.
Chens zehn Jahre alter Sohn wurde gezwungen, bei Verwandten zu leben, um weiter in die Schule gehen zu können. Nicht einmal während des Neujahrsfestes war es ihm erlaubt, seine Familie zu sehen. Chens sechs Jahre alte Tochter Kesi kann nur unter strenger Überwachung die Schule besuchen: Ständig folgen ihr vier bis fünf „Leibwächter".
Am 20. April 2012 gelang es Chen Guangcheng aus dem Hausarrest zu fliehen. Am 23. April 2012 wurde er zuerst nach Beijing und dann von Freunden in die dortige amerikanische Botschaft gebracht. Nach Verhandlungen zwischen der chinesischen und amerikanischen Regierung wurde Chen Guangcheng ins Chaoyang-Spital in Beijing zur medizinischen Behandlung eingeliefert. Am 20. Mai 2012 flog er mit seiner Familie in die Vereinigten Staaten. Er lebt nun in New York.
Die Kampagne *Dark Glasses. Portrait* ruft chinesische Bürger und Menschen in der ganzen Welt auf, ihre Besorgnis und Unterstützung für Chen Guangcheng zum Ausdruck zu bringen. Jeder Teilnehmer setzt Sonnenbrillen

Dark Glasses. Portrait is an online campaign to support Chen Guangcheng and calling for his freedom.
Chen Guangcheng is a blind civil-rights activist. He exposed the violent treatment of villagers during local-government implementation of China's one-child policy in Linyi, Shandong province. This angered the authorities. He was sentenced to imprisonment for a fabricated crime of "damaging public property and disrupting traffic." After he was released, Chen GuangCheng was put under house arrest by the government for no reason. Many supporters attempted to visit Chen and his family, however they were turned away by force, threatened, robbed, detained and in some cases severely beaten.
Chen's ten-year-old son was forced to live with relatives in order to continue schooling. He was not even allowed to see his family on the Chinese New Year. Chen's six year old daughter, Kesi, attended school under strict supervision by four to five 'bodyguards' following her to all her classes.
On April 20, 2012, Chen Guangcheng escaped from house arrest. On April 23, 2012, he was driven to Beijing. Later, friends took him to the American Embassy. After negotiations between the Chinese and United States governments, Chen Guangcheng was sent to Beijing Chaoyang hospital for medical treatment. On May 19, 2012, he and his family flew to the United States. The family now lives in New York.
The *Dark Glasses. Portrait* campaign calls on Chinese citizens and people around the world to express their concern and support for Chen Guangcheng. Every participant puts on a pair of dark glasses (sunglasses / blindfold), takes a portrait, writes a

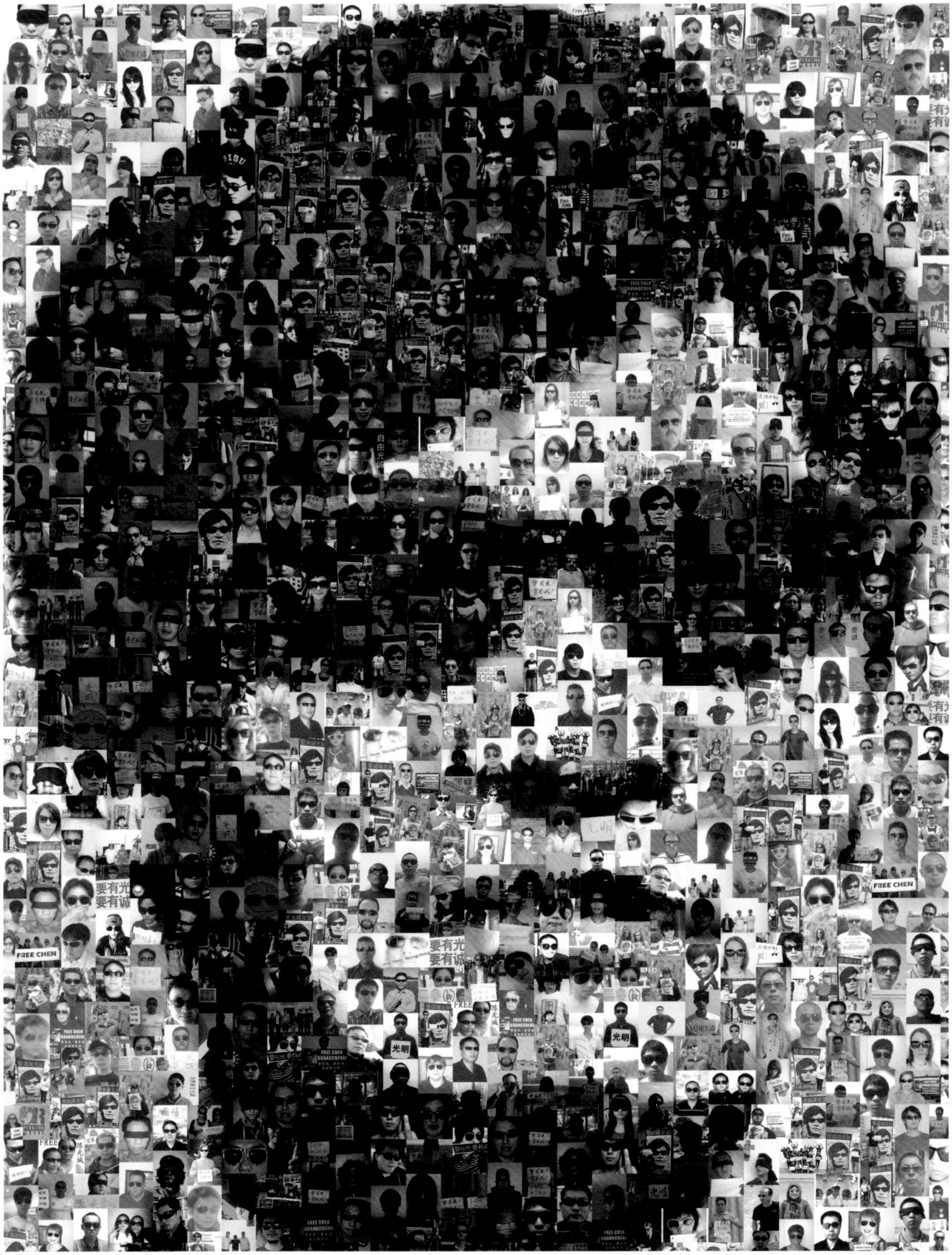
FREE CHEN
要有光
要有诚
光明
FREE CHEN
要有光
要有诚
光明

oder Augenbinden auf, macht ein Porträtfoto, schreibt ein paar persönliche Gedanken und sendet das Bild an die Kampagne. Diese Fotos bilden eine stumme Bilderwand (*http://ichenguangcheng.blogspot.com/*), um unsere Solidarität mit Chen zum Ausdruck zu bringen.

Diese Kampagne umfasst nun 636 Fotos von ungefähr 700 Teilnehmern. Die Menschen zeigen großen Mut, wenn sie teilnehmen, denn sie wissen, dass diese Kampagne von den chinesischen Behörden verfolgt wird. Das mosaikartige Poster wird von NGOs wie China Aids, Women's Rights without Frontiers, Front Line Defenders, Human Rights in China, The Alliance und Aktivisten in China verwendet. In den vergangenen Monaten fand es schnelle Verbreitung in China, Hongkong, Taiwan und den USA. Um ihre Unterstützung für Chen kundzutun, wurde es auf Fahnen, T-Shirts, Sticker und Poster gedruckt. Das Bild aus der Internet-Kampagne tauchte dadurch plötzlich in ganz verschiedenen Formen auf den Straßen auf. Es wurde auch in verschiedenen Medien veröffentlicht, z. B. RFA, China Real Time Report, ISunAffairs, China Files, Global Voices und anderen und wurde drei Mal bei den Hearings des US-Kongresses zu Chen Guangcheng erwähnt.

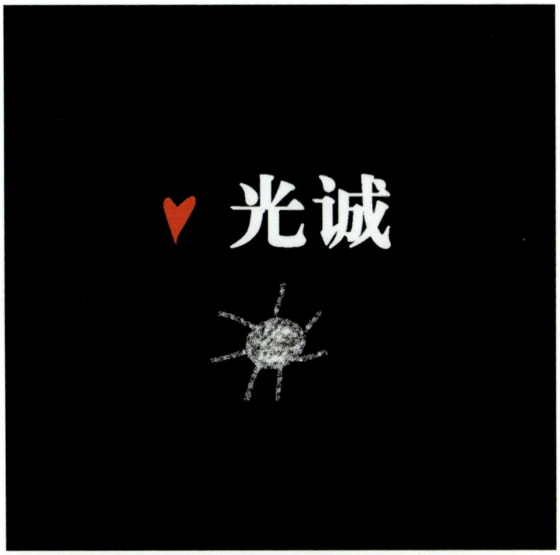

few words about their thoughts and sends the picture to the campaign. The pictures form a silent picture wall at *http://ichenguangcheng.blogspot.com/* to show our solidarity with Chen.

This campaign now has 636 photos and around 700 participants. People are showing great courage by participating even when they know that the campaign is monitored by the Chinese authorities. Mosaic posters of the photos are used by NGOs such as China Aids, Women's Rights without Frontiers, Front Line Defenders, Human Rights in China, The Alliance and activists in China.

In the past few months, the mosaic picture spread quickly in China, Hong Kong, Taiwan and America. To show their support for Mr. Chen, people printed the mosaic image on banners, T-shirts, stickers and posters. The image from the Internet campaign thus began to appear on the street in various forms. The mosaic picture also appeared in various media reports, including RFA, China Real Time Report, ISunAffairs, China Files, Global Voices, etc and was mentioned three times in the US congressional hearings on Chen Guangcheng.

Hexie Farm is a freelance editorial cartoonist and author of *Hexie Farm*. He publishes political cartoons anonymously on the Internet. *Hexie Farm* is a series of political cartoons, depicting dictatorship, censorship, and propaganda in contemporary China. It has been banned in mainland China since 2011. He is also a member of the Cartoon Movement. Some his work has appeared in Isunaffairs, China Digital Times, the Cartoon Movement, PRI, Foreign Policy, RFI, Trend, DE, the China Rights Forum and other media. **Hexie Farm** ist ein freiberuflicher Cartoonist und Autor von *Hexie Farm*. Er veröffentlicht politische Karikaturen, die Themen wie Diktatur, Zensur und Propaganda im heutigen China zum Inhalt haben. *Hexie Farm* ist seit 2011 in Festland-China geblockt. Er ist auch Mitglied des Cartoon Movement. Einige seiner Arbeiten wurden in Isunaffairs, China Digital Times, the Cartoon Movement, PRI, Foreign Policy, RFI, Trend, DE, im China Rights Forum und anderen Medien abgedruckt.

18 Days in Egypt

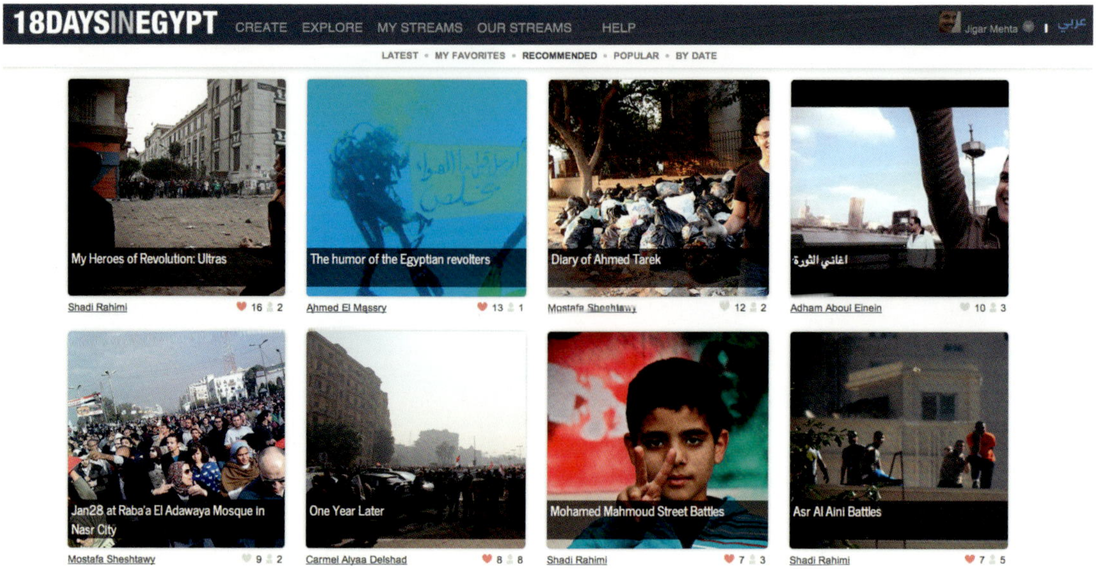

18 Days in Egypt is a collaborative documentary project to collect stories of the revolution and current events related to Egypt using social media fragments from tweets, to Facebook photos and posts, to Youtube videos, and photos. *18 Days In Egypt* aims to capture the events of the revolution in an interactive documentary website that everyone can access now and in the future. It empowers Egyptians to preserve the incredible social media they have created–their on-the-ground, eye-witness accounts–and to add their voice to a story that is incredibly important to the world and its quotient of human freedom in these early years of the 21st century.

In the 18 days of the uprising, Egyptians by the thousands did what previous revolutionaries could not do: they personally documented their revolution, as it unfolded, on thousands of personal devices. They not only witnessed history–they recorded it. *18 Days in Egypt* is an interactive documentary project that tells the story of the revolution, minute by minute, using these personal accounts. We want Egyptians to tell this story themselves, with their footage, their photos,

18 Days in Egypt ist ein kollaboratives dokumentarisches Projekt, das Geschichten über die Revolution und die aktuellen Ereignisse in Ägypten sammelt, wobei wir Social-Media-Fragmente wie Tweets, Facebook-Fotos und -Postings genauso wie Youtube-Videos und Fotos berücksichtigen. *18 Days In Egypt* will die Ereignisse der Revolution auf einer interaktiven Webseite dokumentieren, zu der jetzt und in Zukunft jeder Zugang hat. Dadurch wollen wir die Ägypter in die Lage versetzen, die unglaubliche Vielfalt an Social-Media-Beiträgen, die sie geschaffen haben – ihre Augenzeugenberichte –, bewahren und ihre Stimme in eine Geschichte einzubringen, die für die Welt sehr wichtig ist und einen Beitrag zur menschlichen Freiheit in diesen frühen Jahren des 21. Jahrhunderts darstellt.

In den 18 Tagen des Aufstandes taten die Ägypter, was frühere Revolutionäre nicht tun konnten: Sie selbst dokumentierten den Verlauf der Revolution über Tausende persönliche Devices. Sie waren also nicht nur Zeugen der Geschichte – sie zeichneten sie auch auf. *18 Days in Egypt* ist ein interaktives Dokumentationsprojekt, das die Geschichte der Revolution über diese Ebene der persönlichen Dokumentation Minute für Minute erzählt. Wir möchten, dass die Ägypter diese Geschichte

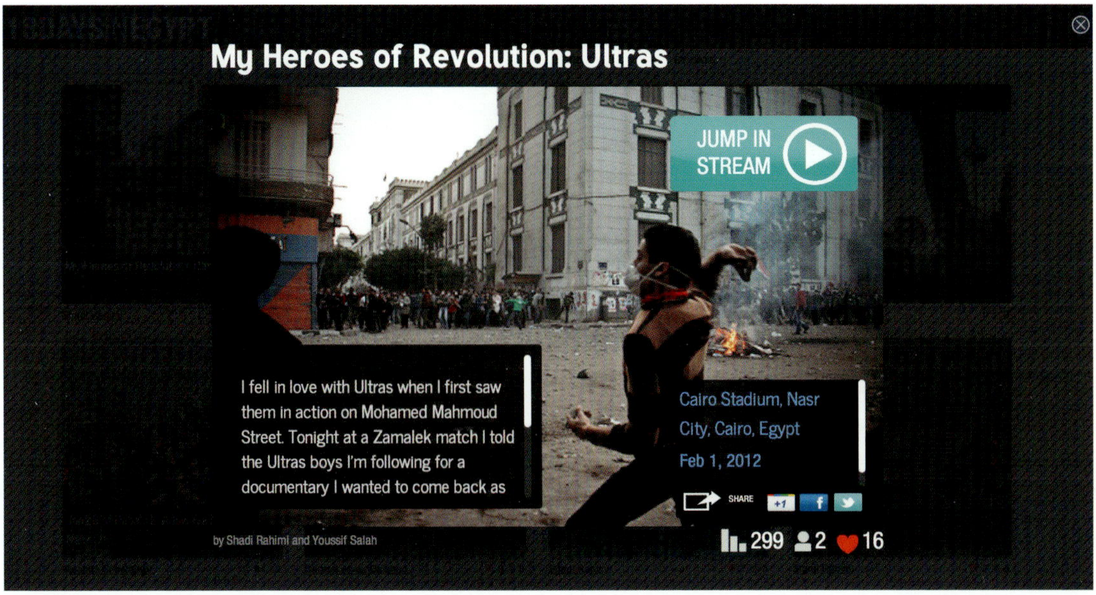

selbst erzählen, mit ihren Videos, Fotos, Emails, Texten, Tweets und Status-Updates, die während dieser 18 Tage generiert wurden.
Unser Team, das in Kairo und im Silicon Valley beheimatet ist, hat bereits begonnen, einen speziellen Social-Media-Space einzurichten, und Tausende von Medienfragmenten gesammelt und archiviert. Sobald sie alle erfasst sind, wird das Material mit den dazugehörigen Geschichten in einem zentralen durchsuchbaren Archiv auf unserer interaktiven Webseite *18DaysinEgypt.com* zugänglich gemacht.

their e-mails, their texts, their tweets and status updates—all created during the 18 days of the revolution.
Our team, based in Cairo and Silicon Valley, has already begun to create a unique social media space to gather and preserve thousands of media fragments from the revolution. Once sourced, the footage and associated stories will live in a searchable central archive on our interactive website *18 Days in Egypt*.

18 Days in Egypt consists of a team of technologists, journalists and designers. GroupStream is Yasmin Elayat, Jigar Mehta, Caroline Oh, Mohamed ElShinnawy and Emerge Technology. Yasmin Elayat (CEO and co-founder) is a creative technologist and interaction designer. Jigar Mehta (co-founder) is a video journalist previously with the *New York Times*, Caroline Oh (creative director) is a graphic and user-experience designer with a particular interest in film and narrative in design. Mohamed ElShinnawy, (technical lead) is a senior software engineer with a decade of experience. Our team also consists of six fellows, who are college-aged Egyptians with an interest in media, journalism and social justice. **18 Days in Egypt** besteht aus einem Team von Technologen, Journalisten und Designern. GroupStream besteht aus Yasmin Elayat, Jigar Mehta, Caroline Oh, Mohamed ElShinnawy und Emerge Technology. Yasmin Elayat (CEO und Mitgegründerin) ist eine kreative Technologin und Interaktionsdesignerin. Jigar Mehta (Mitbegründer) ist ein Video-Journalist, der früher bei *New York Times* arbeitete. Caroline Oh (Creative Director) ist eine Grafik- und UX-Designerin, die sich besonders für Film und Narration im Design interessiert. Mohamed ElShinnawy (technische Leitung) ist ein Software-Ingenieur mit mehr als zehn Jahren Erfahrung. Zum Team gehören auch sechs Fellows, die aufs College gehen und sich für Medien, Journalismus und soziale Gerechtigkeit interessieren.

Crónicas de Héroes

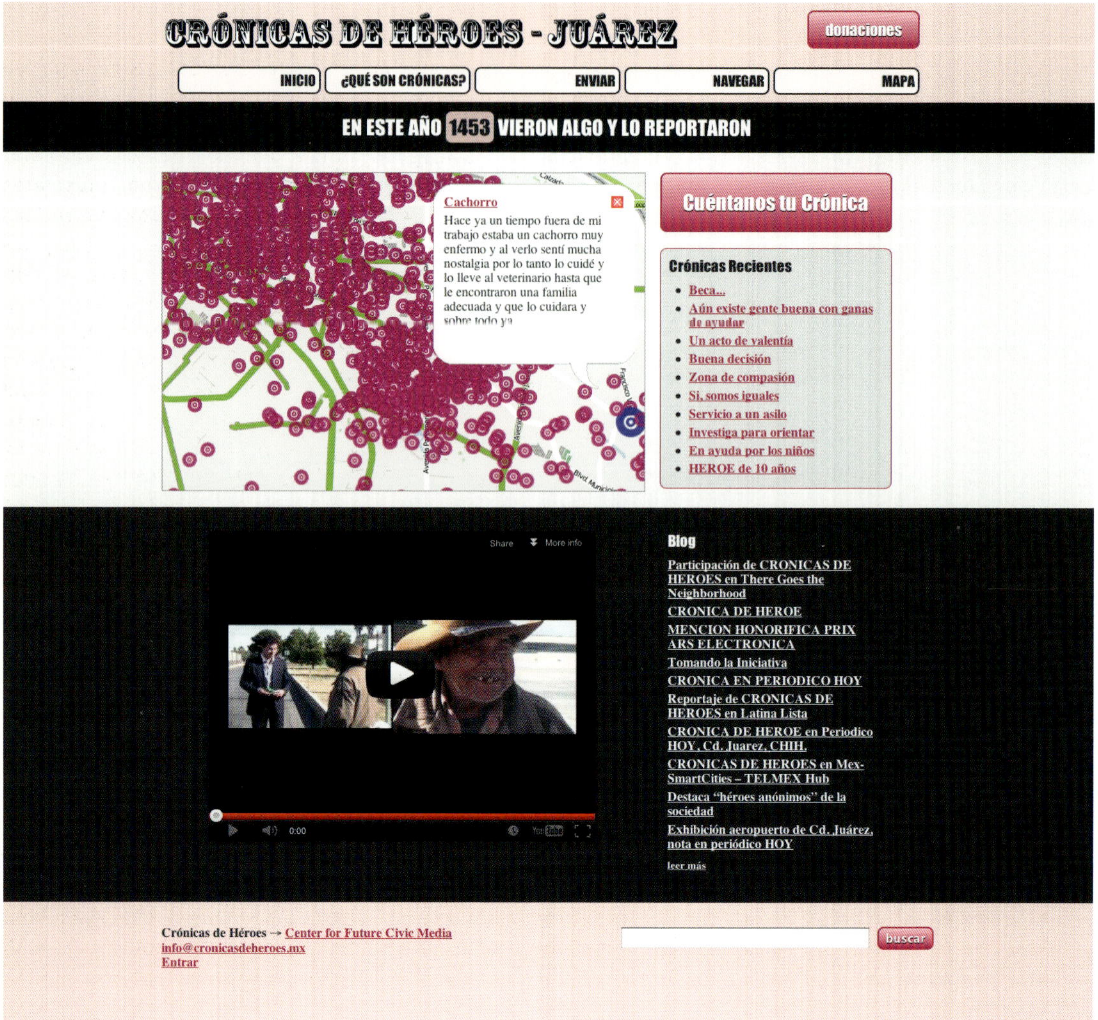

Crónicas de Héroes is a civic platform of positivism which through technology, art, education, direct insertion and other media focuses and promotes social values—responsibility, honesty, equality, respect, dignity, kindness, solidarity and cooperation. *Crónicas de Héroes* provides citizens with both online and offline tools to make public, carry out and share with other positive contributions to society.

Crónicas de Héroes ist eine Plattform für Bürgerengagement, die sich auf Berichte über positive Aktionen konzentriert und durch Technologie, Kunst, Bildung, direkte Beteiligung und andere Instrumente gesellschaftliche Werte fördern will: Verantwortung, Ehrlichkeit, Gleichheit, Respekt, Würde, Güte, Solidarität und Kooperation. *Crónicas de Héroes* gibt Bürgern Online- und Offline-Tools in die Hand, mit denen sie über positive Beiträge zur Gesellschaft berichten, selbst aktiv werden und dies mit anderen teilen können.

Seit dem Start von *Crónicas de Héroes* in Juárez, Mexico, im Dezember 2010 haben viele Zeitungen, Radio- und TV-Stationen über die mehr als 1.300 positiven Statements von Bürgern berichtet, die auf unserer Webseite dokumentiert sind.
http://juarez.cronicasdeheroes.mx. Das Mapping-Tool zeigt sowohl den Ort als auch die Dichte positiver Aktionen, die in dieser Stadt passieren. Die Gemeinde von Juárez hat sich dieser Initiative angeschlossen, weil sie darin ein Instrument sieht, öffentliche Aktivitäten zu fördern, die den Bürgern eine neue Form der Präsenz in der Stadt ermöglichen. Eines der Projekte sind z. B. kollektive Wandmalereien im öffentlichen Raum, die in Zusammenarbeit von Straßenkünstlern mit einer Gemeinschaft entstanden, die Graffiti an verschiedenen Orten der Stadt geschaffen hat und sich von positiven Berichten auf unserer Website inspirieren ließ.
Im Moment gibt es eine Version von *Crónicas de Héroes* für Monterrey, Mexico *(http://mty.cronicasdeheroes.mx/)* und Tijuana / San Diego, Kalifornien *(http://tj-sd.cronicasdeheroes.mx/)*, unsere erste grenzüberschreitende Plattform. *Crónicas de Héroes* will Menschen aller Altersstufen, jeden Geschlechts und wirtschaftlichen Status ansprechen, wobei alte und neue Medien sowie Methoden des Grassroot-Aktivismus zum Einsatz kommen.
Crónicas de Héroes wurde ursprünglich in New York nach den Ereignissen vom 11. September von Alyssa Wright, einer Studentin des Center for Civic Media / MIT Media Lab, als *Hero Reports* implementiert. Es war eine Reaktion auf die Kampagne „See Something, Say Something“ der NY Metropolitan Transit Authority, die sich auf Berichte über verdächtige Aktivitäten konzentrierte. Im Gegensatz dazu wollte *Hero Reports* die Bürger auffordern, über positive Ereignisse zu berichten, die eine konstruktive Veränderung in der Gesellschaft fördern können.

Since the launch of *Crónicas de Héroes* in Juarez, Mexico, in December 2010, many newspapers, radio stations and television outlets have picked up and written stories about the more than 1,300 positive citizens reports that have been logged and mapped on our website: *http://juarez.cronicasdeheroes.mx.* The mapping tool illustrates both the location and density of positive actions happening in this city. The Juárez community has embraced the initiative as a tool to establish public activities aimed at regaining a civic presence in the city, such as collective public paints in collaboration with street artists and the community who have created murals in different spaces around the city inspired by the positive reports on our site. Currently, *Crónicas de Héroes* is also being deployed in Monterrey, Mexico, *(http://mty.cronicasdeheroes.mx/)* and Tijuana/San Diego, CA *(http://tj-sd.cronicasdeheroes.mx/)*, our first binational platform.
Crónicas de Héroes aspires to reach and to influence a broad community of all ages, genders, and economic status in these communities, using new and old media as well as grassroots activism.
Crónicas de Héroes was originally established in New York after the 9/11 events as *Hero Reports*, a project carried out by Alyssa Wright, a student from the Center for Civic Media / MIT Media Lab. It was a reaction to the NY Metropolitan Transit Authority's "See Something, Say Something" campaign, which focused on reporting suspicious activity. In contrast, *Hero Reports* directed civic energy toward reporting positive activities that encourage constructive societal changes.

Crónicas de Héroes is led by Yesica Guerra and local advisory boards from the cities in which is implemented—Juarez, Monterrey, and Tijuana/San Diego. Yesica, a researcher in urban design with a master's degree in architecture and urbanism from MIT, devotes most of her research to border issues between Mexico and the United States. **Crónicas de Héroes** wird von Yesica Guerra gemeinsam mit lokalen Beratergremien aus den Städten, in denen das Projekt implementiert ist, betrieben: Juárez, Monterrey und Tijuana / San Diego. Yesica hat einen Master in Architektur und Stadtplanung des MIT und beschäftigt sich in ihrer Forschung mit der Problematik der Grenze zwischen Mexiko und den Vereinigten Staaten.

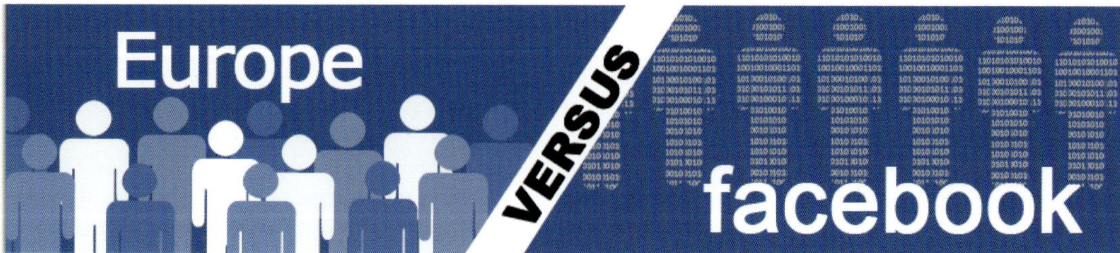

Start | Objectives | Legal Procedure | Data Pool | Get your Data! | MEDIA

Facebook's Data Pool

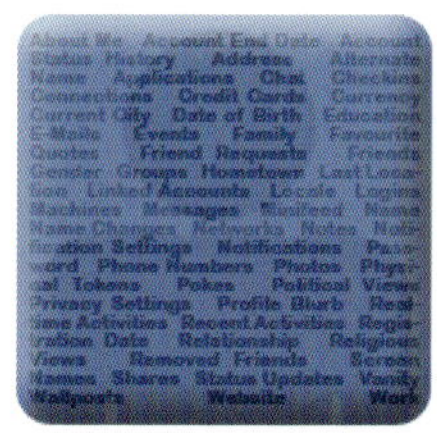

Introduction. Every person in the EU has the right to access all the data that a company is holding about him/her. You can find out how to access your facebook data on the page "your data...". After we got the first response by facebook it was clear to us that we had to publish this information online. By doing so, we want to make facebook more transparent and show every user which data facebook is holding about us.

There is more Data. Many groups of data are not included in this first set of data we got from facebook. For example data concerning the "like"-function, tracking on other webpages, face recognition, videos, postings on other users walls, indicators for the intensity of relationships, tags that werde removes and many more were (so far) not disclosed by facebook.

Index. These groups of data were disclosed by facebook (click for more details):

00. Target
00. Date Range
----
01. About Me
02. Account End Date
03. Account Status History
04. Address
05. Alternate Name
06. Applications
07. Chat
08. Checkins
09. Connections
10. Credit Cards
11. Currency
12. Current City
13. Date of Birth
14. Education
15. E-Mails
16. Events
17. Family
18. Favourite Quotes
19. Friend Requests
20. Friends
21. Gender
22. Groups
23. Hometown
24. Last Location
25. Linked Accounts
26. Locale
27. Logins
28. Machines
29. Messages
30. Minifeed
31. Name
32. Name Changes
33. Networks
34. Notes
35. Notification Settings
36. Notifications
37. Password
38. Phone Numbers
39. Photos
40. Physical Tokens
41. Pokes
42. Political Views
43. Privacy Settings
44. Profile Blurb
45. Realtime Activities
46. Recent Activities
47. Registration Date
48. Relationship
49. Religious Views
50. Removed Friends
51. Screen Names
52. Shares
53. Status Updates
54. Vanity
55. Wallposts
56. Website
57. Work

Note: Facebook is storing even more data categories. This is the (current) list of all data: PDF (485 KB)

Original Files. These are some excerpts and altered versions of the original files we got from facebook. Because of privacy concerns all personal information was edited out, some files were altered in order to make editing easier.

initials and userID	date	original file	blackened excerpt	blackened file
L.B. (747***)	2011-06-07	PDF (780 pages, 34 MB)		PDF (7,7 MB)
P.E. (129***)	2011-06-07	PDF (1.142 pages, 165 MB)	PDF (138 KB)	
M.S. (509***)	2011-06-09	PDF (18 pages, 56 KB)		PDF (95 KB)
M.S. (509***)	2011-07-11	PDF (1.222 pages, 496 MB)		PDF (11 MB)
"Removed" content that was still held by Facebook can be seen in this PDF file:				PDF (206 KB)

Alles begann, als Max Schrems, ein österreichischer Jus-Student, während seines Austauschsemesters an der Santa Clara University in den USA Mitglieder des Privacy-Teams von Facebook traf. Er war sehr erstaunt über deren „Neuinterpretation" der europäischen Gesetze zum Datenschutz und schrieb einen Artikel zu diesem Thema. Dafür bat er ein paar Freunde in Österreich, ein Auskunftsersuchen an Facebook Ireland Ltd., dem Vertragspartner aller Facebook-User außerhalb der USA und Kanada, zu stellen. Nachdem sie drei Datensätze mit bis zu 1.222 Seiten bekommen hatten, war klar, dass dies online gestellt werden müsste. Kurz darauf entdeckten sie, dass die Datensätze auch eine große Menge „gelöschter" Daten enthielten.

Unsere Studentengruppe stellte sich die Frage: „Warum tut niemand etwas dagegen?". Wir beschlossen also, das akademische Paper in 22 Klagen umzuformulieren und diese beim Irish Data Protection Commissioner (DPC) einzubringen, der für die Agenden von Facebook zuständig ist. Gleichzeitig veröffentlichten wir eine einfache Erklärung, wie man an seine Daten herankommt. Diese Erklärung verbreitete sich viral im Internet, Massenmedien verlinkten dorthin, und sie wurde von Blogs in der ganzen Welt kopiert. Bis Dezember 2011 haben laut Facebook 40.000 User ein derartiges Ersuchen eingebracht. Im Dezember 2011 veröffentlichte auch die irische DPC einen ersten Bericht, der von Facebook Ireland massive Änderungen verlangte. Es sind laut Auskunft von Facebook-Vertretern die tief greifendsten Privacy-Veränderungen, die Facebook je vornehmen musste.

Wir arbeiten im Moment daran, eine formelle Entscheidung zu erreichen. Gleichzeitig haben auch die Massenmedien und die Politik sich für diese Sache zu interessieren begonnen. Das machte es uns möglich, überall in der Welt zu erklären, welche Art von Daten Facebook sammelt und wie es sie nutzt. Sogar Viviane Reding (Kommissarin für Justiz, Grundrechte und Bürgerschaft der EU) zitierte unseren Fall, als sie ihren neuen Vorschlag für eine striktere europäische Datenschutzregelung präsentierte.

It all started when Max Schrems, an Austrian law student, met members of Facebook's privacy team during his exchange semester at Santa Clara University, California. After being stunned at their "reinterpretation" of European data-protection legislation, he wrote a paper on the issue. To do so he asked some friends in Austria to make an access request at Facebook Ireland, the contractor for all Facebook users outside of US and Canada. After receiving three data sets with up to 1,222 pages of data, it was clear that this ought to be published online. Later it was discovered that the data sets also included massive amounts of "deleted" data. The group of students again asked themselves why no one was doing anything about this. So they decided simply to transform the law-school paper into 22 complaints filed with the Irish Data Protection Commissioner (DPC), who is responsible for Facebook's operations. At the same time they published a simple explanation of how users could access their data, which soon became viral on the Internet and was linked to by the mass media and copied by blogs all around the world. According to Facebook, by December 2011, 40,000 users had made such a request. The Irish DPC published a first report in December 2011, demanding massive changes by Facebook Ireland. According to Facebook representatives these are among the most far-reaching changes on the privacy front that the company has ever had to undertake.

We are currently working on our goal to get a formal decision that will hopefully be much further reaching than this first report. At the same time the mass media as well as politics has picked up on the project. This enabled us to explain all around the world what data Facebook is gathering and how it uses it. Even Viviane Reding, (EU Justice Commissioner) quoted our case when presenting the new European proposal for stricter data-protection legislation.

Europe versus Facebook is more or less a scattered group of about ten students with one person (Max Schrems) taking the leading role. All complaints are in his name, since he is the group's only expert on data protection. He is supported by other members who help with press releases, corrections, the web page or by answering e-mails. The group is considering becoming a non-profit organization, especially as it will soon need to manage external funding (so far the only cost is a server). At the same time the complaints and legal action will ultimately have to go through an individual, which is currently Max Schrems. **Europe versus Facebook.** Wir sind eine lose Gruppe von ungefähr zehn Studenten, wobei Max Schrems die leitende Position innehat. Alle Klagen werden in seinem Namen geführt, da er der einzige Experte für Datenschutz innerhalb der Gruppe ist. Er wird von den anderen Mitgliedern unterstützt, die mit PR, Korrekturen, der Webseite oder beim Beantworten von E-Mails helfen. Wir überlegen, unsere Gruppe in eine Non-Profit-Organisation umzuwandeln, sobald wir mit Geldern von außen umgehen müssen (bislang fallen nur Kosten für den Server an). Gleichzeitig müssen die Klagen und rechtlichen Schritte aber von einer Person ausgehen, und das ist im Moment Max Schrems.

iHub – Nairobi's Innovation Hub

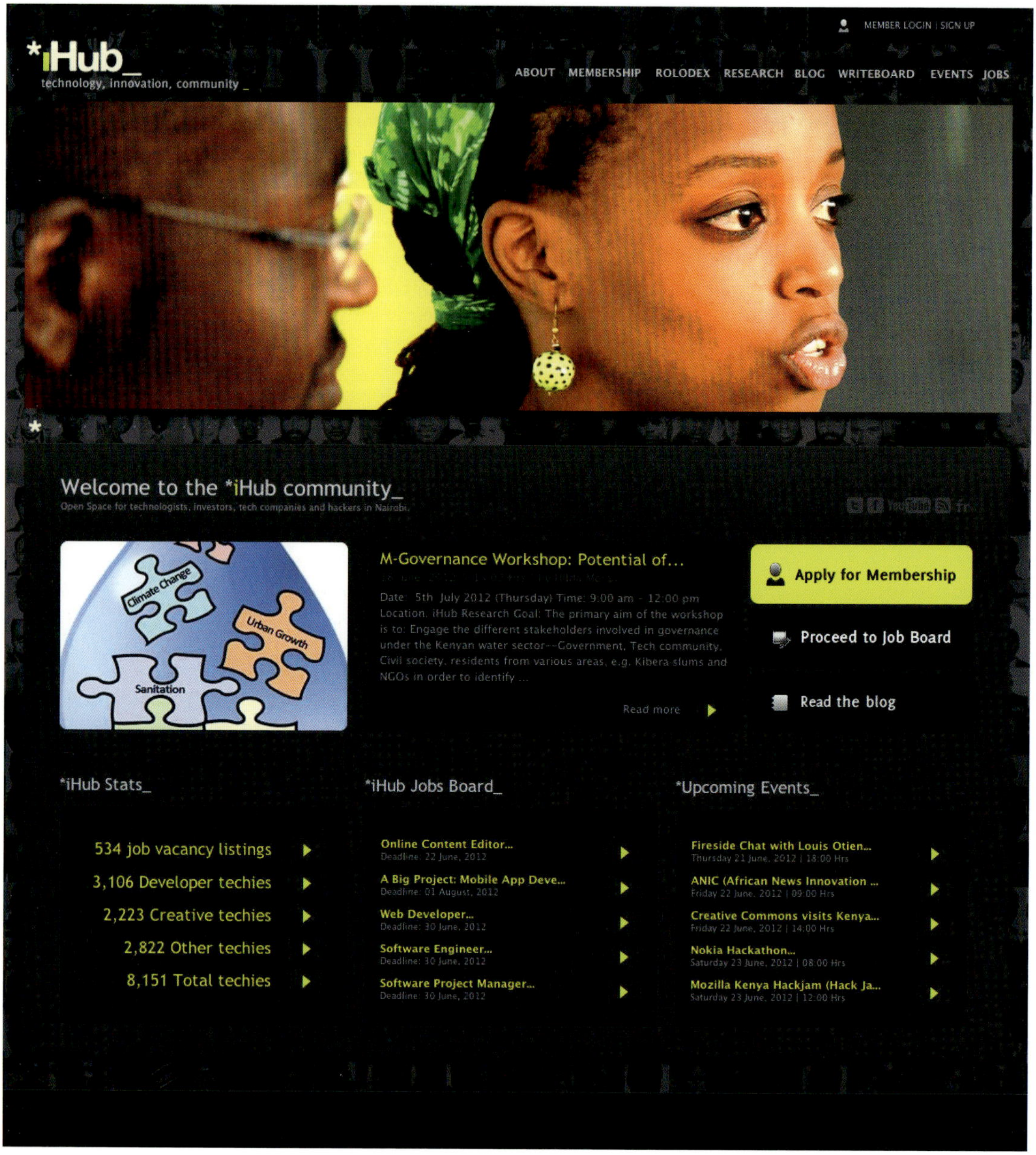

Kenia hat eine gut ausgebaute Telekommunikationsinfrastruktur und internationale Gateways von hoher Kapazität. Das Land hat auch bemerkenswerte Fortschritte bei der Formulierung und Umsetzung seiner ICT-Politik, inklusive messbarer Ergebnisse und Meilensteine, gemacht.
Parallel zu diesen politischen Maßnahmen und dem Ausbau der Infrastruktur verzeichnet das Land auch eine rasante Zunahme an Mobiltelefon- und Internet-Usern sowie Computerwissenschaftlern und IT-Studenten, die jedes Jahr an den privaten wie staatlichen Universitäten ihr Studium abschließen. All diese Faktoren scheinen drauf hinzudeuten, dass nicht nur für das aktuelle Wachstum des Landes ein großes ICT-Potenzial vorhanden ist, sondern auch für ein nachhaltiges Wachstum in der Zukunft.
Eine sehr lebendige digitale Community ist das im März 2010 eröffnete *iHub*. *iHub* hat mehr als 6.000 virtuelle Mitglieder, die via Web-Plattform miteinander in Kontakt stehen, 240 „grüne" Mitglieder, die den physischen Space nutzen, und neun „rote" Mitglieder, die für einen semi-permanenten Arbeitsplatz für 6 oder 12 Monate zahlen. *iHub* ist Netzwerk und Treffpunkt und hilft den keniatischen Innovatoren, ihre Ideen in die Praxis umzusetzen.
Dank *iHub* können sich Vertreter aus der Technologie-Community, der Industrie und den Universitäten sowie Investoren und Risikokapitalgeber treffen, Ideen austauschen und zusammenarbeiten. Das Zentrum ist das erste seiner Art in Afrika. Es sorgt dafür, dass Technologien nicht nur Ideen bleiben, sondern reale Produkte werden können. Der Schlüssel dazu ist offene Innovation – der Prozess, interne und externe Ideen sowie Zugänge zum Markt zu kombinieren, um neue Technologien zu entwickeln.

Kenya has set up a robust telecommunications infrastructure and high-capacity international gateways. The country has also made remarkable progress putting an ICT policy framework and implementation strategy in place, complete with measurable outcomes and time-frames.
In conjunction with this rapidly growing number of mobile and Internet users, supporting government policy and infrastructure, the number of computer science and IT students graduating each year continues to increase both in public and private universities. This seems to indicate great potential in ICT not only for current growth in the country but sustained future growth as well.
One quickly emerging digital community is *iHub*, which was opened in March 2010. *iHub* can boast of more than 6,000 virtual members, who interact via the web platform, 240 green members, who physically access the space, and nine red members, who pay for a semi-permanent desk space for a period of six to 12 months. *iHub* is a network and meeting place that enables Kenya's innovators to bring their ideas to fruition. Through *iHub*, the technology community, industry, academia, investors and venture capitalists can meet, share ideas and collaborate. The centre is the first of its kind to operate in Africa. It allows technologies to progress from the ideas stage to becoming real products and the key to its effectiveness is open innovation—the process of combining internal and external ideas, as well as internal and external paths to market, to advance the development of new technologies.

The **iHub** management team consists of passionate, hard-working people who genuinely care about the community because they are part of it. The management team exists to facilitate and support the community but the community themselves are the heart behind *iHub*. The iHub advisory board is made up of five people from the Nairobi tech community: Riyaz Bachani, Wananchi executive, now in charge of Wazi WiFi; Josiah Mugambi, co-founder of Skunkworks, works at Nokia Siemens; Rebeccah Wanjiku, technology reporter and founder of Fireside Communications; Conrad Akunga, blogger, co-founder of Mzalendo and highly respected software architect; Erik Hersman, technology blogger and co-founder of Ushahidi. Das **iHub**-Team besteht aus passionierten, hart arbeitenden Menschen, denen die Community ein Anliegen ist, weil sie selber Teil davon sind. Das Management-Team hat die Funktion, die Community zu unterstützen, aber das Herz von *iHub* ist die Community selbst. Das *iHub*-Beratergremium besteht aus fünf Personen aus der Tech-Community von Nairobi: Riyaz Bachani, Geschäftsführer von Wananchi, nun verantwortlich für Wazi WiFi; Josiah Mugambi, Mitbegründer von Skunkworks, der bei Nokia Siemens arbeitet; Rebeccah Wanjiku, Technologie-Journalistin und Gründerin von Fireside Communications; Conrad Akunga, Blogger und Mitbegründer von Mzalendo und angesehener Software-Architekt; Erik Hersman, Technologie-Blogger und Mitbegründer von Ushahidi.

iStreet Lab

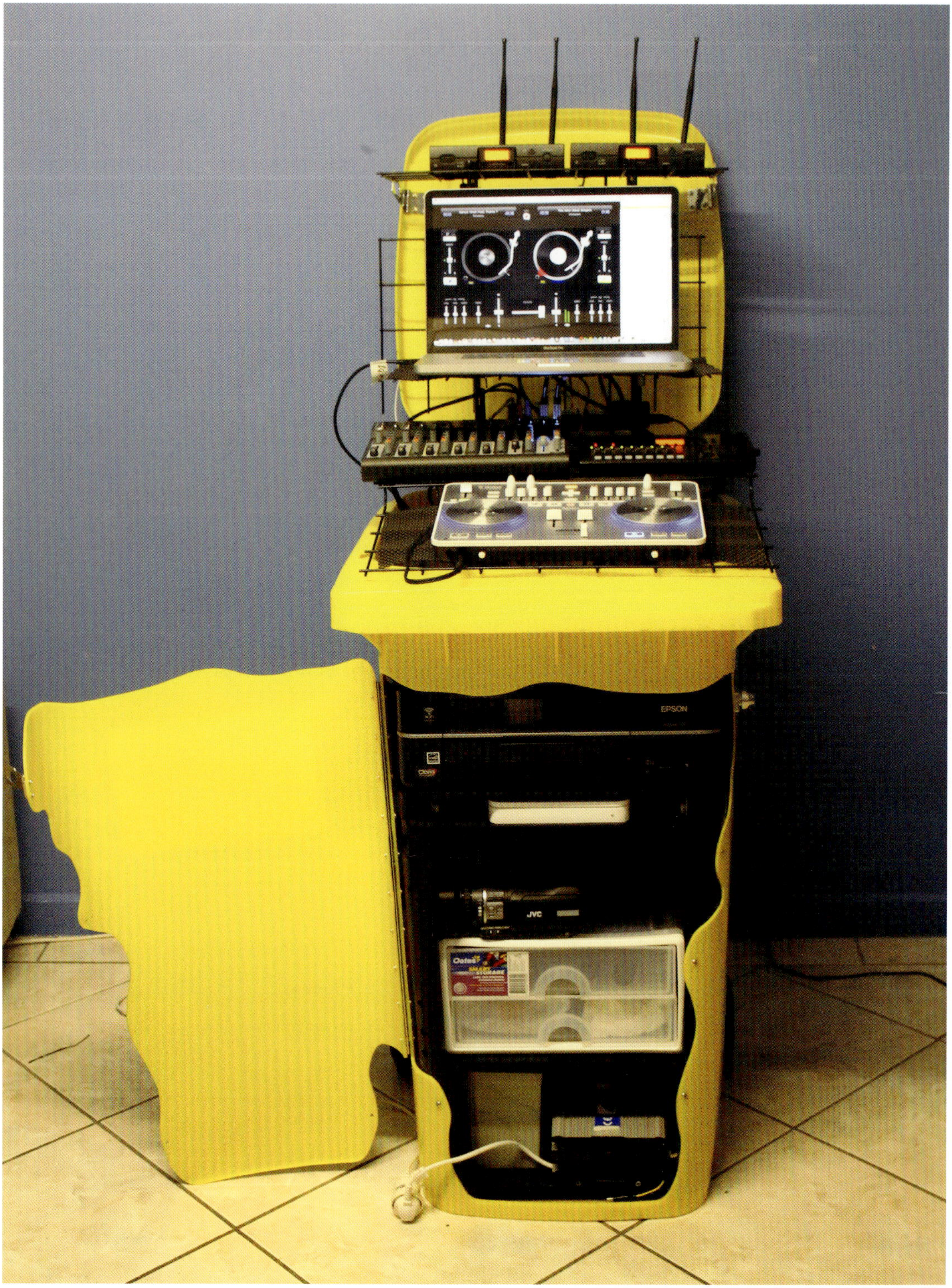

iStreet Lab ist eine Multimedia-Toolbox für die gemeinschaftliche Nutzung, die ausgegrenzten Gruppen Werkzeuge und Fertigkeiten vermitteln will, die notwendig sind, um die digitale Kluft zu überwinden. Das Lab ist ein 240-Liter-Abfalleimer auf Rädern, der alles für die Produktion von Musik, Video, digitalen Medien und Radio enthält und überall aufgestellt werden kann.
Wir sind der Überzeugung, dass selbst sozial dysfunktionale Menschen Wertvolles zur Entwicklung unserer Gemeinschaft und Gesellschaft beitragen können – und kreative Medien sind eine der besten Möglichkeiten, diese Produktivität zu fördern. Unser Projekt packt digitale Medientechnologie in einen Abfalleimer und bringt Technologie direkt zu den benachteiligten Jugendlichen, egal, wo sie sind: Straße, Jugendzentrum, Einkaufszentrum.
Das Ausbildungs- und Beschäftigungsprogramm, das rund um diese Technologie entwickelt wird, kann signifikante Erfolge verbuchen, wenn es darum geht, Jugendliche von Drogen, Alkohol und Gang-Gewalt wegzubringen und ihnen soziale Reintegration und eine geordnete Ausbildung zu ermöglichen. Wir verbinden aber die auf Integration und Ausbildung zielenden Elemente mit einer breiteren Perspektive, damit diese junge Leuten auch tatsächlich die Chance bekommen, sich selbst, ihre Gemeinschaft und die Welt zu verändern.
Das *iStreet*-Projekt zum Austausch von Skills zielt auf ausgegrenzte, schwer erreichbare junge Menschen und will den teilnehmenden Personen, Organisationen und Communities langfristigen Nutzen bringen und damit Transliteralität sowie ökonomische und soziale Entwicklung fördern. Alle Workshops sind für diese Zielgruppe konzipiert. Wir versuchen, die Vermittlung so zu gestalten, dass jede Interaktion einen Lernschritt darstellt, denn die Teilnehmer gestalten ihr Lernen selbst und bestimmen auch ihren Spielraum selbst.
Das Projekt wurde 2008 auf Jamaika als Reaktion auf die steigende Kriminalität und Gewalt in Palmers Cross Clarendon gestartet. 2010/11 wurde das Projekt erfolgreich in Queensland und New South Wales, Australien, mit Outreach-Workshops implementiert und kam auch in Kanada und UK zum Einsatz.

The *iStreet Lab* is a community multimedia tool box, designed to deliver marginalized communities with the tools and skill required to bridge the digital divide. The lab is a stand-alone, operate-anywhere, music/video/digital media production/broadcasting kit inside a 240-liter wheelie bin.
We believe that even the most socially dysfunctional among us have valuable contributions to make to the development of our community/society, and creative media is one of the best methods of bringing about this productivity. This unique project packs digital media technologies inside a wheelie bin to bring technology to the most marginalized and disadvantaged youth wherever they are.
The education and engagement programs built around this technology have had significant success in shifting the youth away from drugs, alcohol and gang violence, putting them on a path to mainstream education and social reintegration. We combined these elements of engaging and teaching with a global perspective to create opportunities for young people to change themselves, their communities and the world.
The *iStreet* skills-exchange project targets hard-to-reach and marginalized young people and will result in significant long-term outcome for individual participants, organizations and communities involved in the project and contribute to trans-literacy, economic and social development in these communities. All workshops are designed and implemented with this target group in mind. We are seeking to refine and design the delivery so there are lessons to be learned from each interaction as the participants themselves fashion their own learning and reinterpret their own margins.
The project was initiated in Jamaica in 2008 as a response to the rising levels of crime and violence in Palmers Cross Clarendon. In 2010/11 this method was successfully implemented in Queensland and New South Wales, Australia, with other outreach workshops and appearances in Canada and the UK.

iStreet Lab has been initiated by Mervin Jarman, a community art activist, and a founding member of the UK's Mongrel Collective (www.mongrel.org.uk) who in 2003 initiated *The Container Project* (www.container-project.net), a community media lab in a 40ft shipping container in rural Jamaica. The *iStreet Lab* core team is an extended group of some 20 multimedia artist and technology developers who act as facilitators on demand for the project. The project acts primarily as a sensitization process and has included over 400 young people worldwide. **iStreet Lab** wurde von Mervin Jarman initiiert, einem Community-Künstler-Aktivisten und Gründungsmitglied des Mongrel Collective (www.mongrel.org.uk), das 2003 *The Container Project* (www.containter-project.net) ins Leben rief, ein Community-MediaLab in einem 40-Fuß-Transportcontainer fürs ländliche Jamaika. Das Kernteam von *iStreet Lab* bildet eine Gruppe von ungefähr 20 Mulitmedia-Künstlern und Technologie-Entwicklern, die je nach Bedarf als Vermittler agieren. Das Projekt begreift sich in erster Linie als Sensibilisierungsprojekt und hat mit mehr als 400 jungen Menschen weltweit gearbeitet.

Lorea

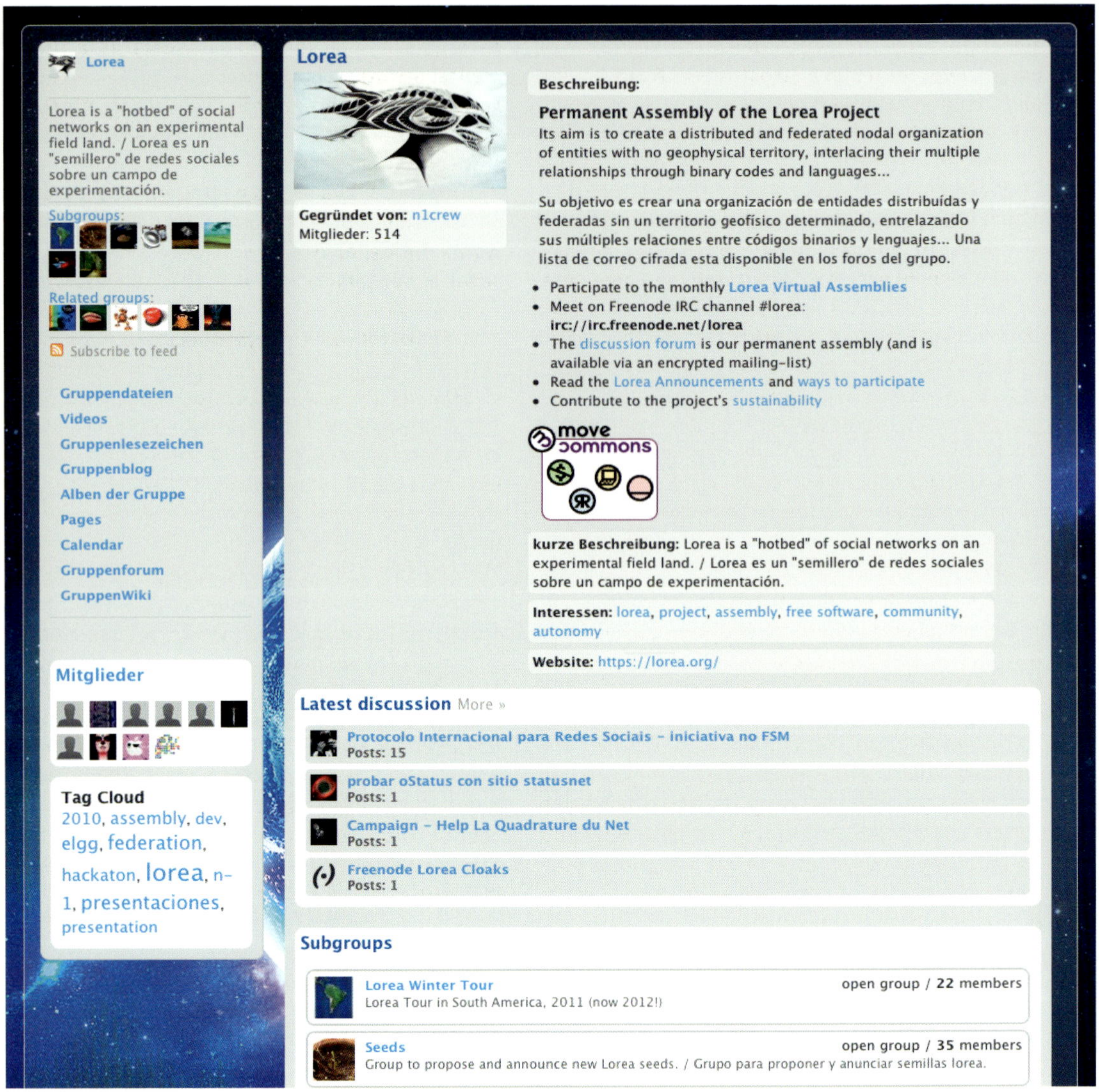

Lorea is a seedbed of free social networks linked by federation protocols that allow them to communicate. These networks run on software designed and built by and for non profits, members of the public and groups involved in social change. Lorea is not just software, but also a technical and political tool for the federated web, bringing back autonomy, freedom and total control over our data and our memory to the hands of the users of social networking sites themselves. The federation knocks down the walls of the panopticon

Lorea ist ein Entwicklungsbiotop für freie soziale Netzwerke, die durch Föderationsprotokolle verlinkt sind und so miteinander kommunizieren können. Diese Netzwerke basieren auf einer Software, die von und für Non-Profit-Organisationen und Gruppen, die sich dem sozialen Wandel verschreiben, entwickelt wird. *Lorea* ist aber nicht nur eine Software, sondern auch ein technisches und politisches Tool für das Federated Web, das den Usern von Social-Networking-Seiten wieder Autonomie, Freiheit und Kontrolle über ihre Daten und ihr Gedächtnis zurückgibt. Durch den föderierten Ansatz,

der die Netzwerkneutralität als fundamentales Architekturprinzip verteidigt, werden die von Unternehmen und politischen Interessen errichteten Mauern des 2.0-Panoptikums niedergerissen.
Lorea wird von einem informellen Kollektiv von Menschen betrieben, die sich für Sicherheit und Privacy im sozialen Web engagieren. Seit 2009 ist diese Entwickler-Community ständig gewachsen, und inzwischen gehören ihr Menschen an, die alle möglichen verschiedenen Netzwerke „bewohnen". Die Entwickler von *Lorea* sprechen nicht von Usern, sondern von „Bewohnern" eines transformativen Projekts: Einige Tausend Menschen nutzen nachweislich unsere Netzwerke, viele von ihnen sind in IT-Entwicklung, Serverbetrieb, Bug-Reporting, Dokumentation, Projektunterstützung und Verbreitung tätig.
Lorea lebt dank der Arbeit einer Community, die sich über eine Online-Version einer demokratischen Volksversammlung organisiert. Das Projekt basiert auf Zusammenarbeit und engagiert sich für freie Kultur und soziale Innovation. Es zielt auf die Zivilgesellschaft als Ganzes ab, d. h. auf Bürger, soziale Kollektive und Organisationen, die sich für sozialen Wandel einsetzen und deren Arbeit von Interaktion, Sharing, Veränderung und Lösungsorientiertheit bestimmt ist. Wir möchten all jene Menschen und Gruppen ansprechen, denen ihre Online-Identität, ihre Sicherheit und Privacy am Herzen liegt. Wir treten für das Recht auf freie Meinungsäußerung ein und für das Recht, Information und Wissen zu teilen, – und zwar innerhalb eines freien, neutralen sozialen Web. *Lorea* bietet eine Non-Profit-Alternative, die uns die Souveränität über die Welt der sozialen Netzwerke zurückgibt.

2.0 run by corporations and political interests, and defends the neutrality of networks as a fundamental architectural principle.
Lorea arises from an informal collective of people concerned about security and privacy issues on the social web. Since 2009 this developer community has grown and is now formed by virtually all kinds of people inhabiting various online networks. Hence, amongst Lorea developers we don't speak about service "users" but of "inhabitants" of a transformative project: several thousand people who knowingly use our networks, many of them active in IT development, server maintenance, error reporting and solving, documentation, project support and dissemination. Lorea survives daily via the work of a community which organises by means of an online version of a democratic people's assembly. It is based on mutual cooperation, promoting free culture and social innovation.
The project is aimed at civil society as a whole, i.e. citizens and social collectives and political change organisations that are motivated by the desire to interact, share, change things together, devise solutions. We seek to address all people and groups who value their online identities and their security and privacy. We value the right to freedom of expression, and the right to share information and knowledge and do so within a free and neutral social web. *Lorea* offers a non-profit alternative to regain our technological sovereignty in the world of social networks.

Lorea. The team was launched during the Hackmeeting, the annual gathering of hackers in Spain, in October 2009. At this meeting groups administering the *Lorea* based Arte Libre Digital (ALD) and the social network N-1 converged and decided to join forces to further develop free, secure, federated and self-managed social networks. Our technical team is composed of more or less 10 people but that number is variable. We have three people who are more concerned with documentation issues, translation, presentation and workshops. **Lorea**. Das Team fand im Oktober 2009 während des Hackmeetings zusammen, eines jährlichen Treffens spanischer Hacker. Dort haben sich die Gruppen, die die auf *Lorea* basierenden Netzwerke Arte Libre Digital (ALD) und N-1 betrieben, zusammengetan und beschlossen, gemeinsam freie, sichere, föderierte und selbst betriebene soziale Netzwerke weiterzuentwickeln. Unser technisches Team besteht aus ungefähr zehn Personen, aber die Anzahl variiert. Drei Personen kümmern sich in erster Linie um Dokumentation, Übersetzung, Präsentation und Workshops.

Meine Abgeordneten

IMPRESSUM & KONTAKT | REGISTRIERUNG | LOGIN

MEINE ABGEORDNETEN

HOME ABGEORDNETE NEWS PARLAMENTSREDEN OTS-AUSSENDUNGEN INFO SPENDEN

ein Projekt von Respekt.net INVESTIEREN IN DIE ZIVILGESELLSCHAFT und der 200 Investorinnen und Spenderinnen der Projektbörse www.respekt.net

SUCHE

"Meine Abgeordneten" finanziert sich ausschließlich über private Spenden.
Bitte unterstützen auch Sie unsere Arbeit!

Willkommen!

"Meine Abgeordneten" ist die erste Transparenzplattform, die öffentliche Daten zu allen österreichischen Nationalratsabgeordneten, Mitgliedern des Bundesrats, EU-Abgeordneten und Regierungsmitgliedern beinhaltet. Wir glauben, dass Transparenz in der Politik einen Wert an sich darstellt und zudem eine wichtige Vorbeugemaßnahme gegen Korruption ist. Die Plattform entstand aus einer privaten Initiative auf der Projektbörse www.respekt.net und wurde ohne öffentliche Fördergelder realisiert.

Social Media

Like 1.7k Send

Tweet 177

+1 71

Letzte Änderungen

Folgende Abgeordneten-Dossiers wurden zuletzt hinzugefügt oder geändert:

18.06.2012 Schennach, Stefan (SPÖ)
18.06.2012 Mühlberghuber, Edith (FPÖ)
18.06.2012 Marek, Christine (ÖVP)
18.06.2012 Königsberger-Ludwig, Ulrike (SPÖ)
18.06.2012 Hörl, Franz (ÖVP)

Alle Änderungen

MEDIACLAN

kolkhos.net

MAX KOSSATZ

Mit freundlicher Unterstützung durch:

D&B Decide with Confidence

CoreTEC

WISUR

foggensteiner

News

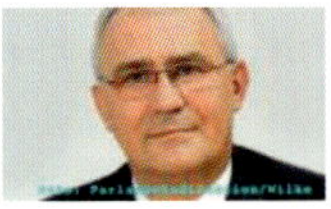

15.06.2012

MARTIN GRAF UND DER FC HELLAS-KAGRAN

derStandard.at berichtet am 15. Juni 2012 über die Auseinandersetzung zwischen der "Kronen Zeitung" und dem FC Hellas-Kagran. Hier einige Fakten als Hintergrund dazu:

Der 1. Obmann des FC Hellas-Kagran (ZVR 400076421), Werner Hammer, schreibt in einer

weiterlesen

Abgeordnete/r des Moments

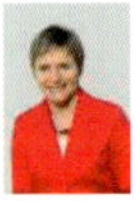

Bildquelle

Rosa Lohfeyer
SPÖ

Abgeordnete zum Nationalrat, Schriftführerin

Zum Dossier

Wussten Sie schon, dass …

die Wirtschaftskammer Österreich und das Institut für Bildung und Innovation (eine Organisation der Industriellen Vereinigung), österreichische EU-Abgeordnete durch bereitgestelltes Personal unterstützt? In der „Erklärung der finanziellen Interessen", geben Othmar Karas und Paul Rübig an, dass sie von beiden Organisationen Mitarbeiter gestellt bekommen, Richard Seeber wird personell von der Wirtschaftkammer Österreich unterstützt.

Parlamentsreden der letzten Sitzungen

2012-03-08 14:01:00
Wolfgang Zanger
Tagesordnungspunkt:
Erklärungen des Bundeskanzlers und des Vizekanzlers gemäß § 19 Absatz 2 der Geschäftsordnung des Nationalrates zum Stabilitätspaket 2012-2016

2012-03-08 13:56:00
Dorothea Schittenhelm
Tagesordnungspunkt:
Erklärungen des Bundeskanzlers und des Vizekanzlers gemäß § 19 Absatz 2 der Geschäftsordnung des Nationalrates zum Stabilitätspaket 2012-2016

2012-03-08 13:46:00
Robert Lugar
Tagesordnungspunkt:
Erklärungen des Bundeskanzlers und des Vizekanzlers gemäß § 19 Absatz 2 der Geschäftsordnung des Nationalrates zum Stabilitätspaket 2012-2016

2012-03-08 13:45:00
Gisela Wurm
Tagesordnungspunkt:
Erklärungen des Bundeskanzlers und des Vizekanzlers gemäß § 19 Absatz 2 der Geschäftsordnung des Nationalrates zum Stabilitätspaket 2012-2016

2012-03-08 13:41:00
Hermann Schultes
Tagesordnungspunkt:
Erklärungen des Bundeskanzlers und des Vizekanzlers gemäß § 19 Absatz 2 der Geschäftsordnung des Nationalrates zum Stabilitätspaket 2012-2016

Alle Reden

OTS-Aussendungen von/über politische VertreterInnen

2012-06-19 14:34:47
Freiheitlicher Parlamentsklub - FPÖ
FPÖ-Kickl: Erhöhung der Parteienfinanzierung zwischen Rot/Grün von Anfang an ausgepackelt

2012-06-19 14:21:38
SMA - Standort Marketing Agentur GmbH
Parndorf bekommt ein Einkaufszentrum - BILD

2012-06-19 14:13:11
Arbeiterkammer Wien
Aviso Morgen: AK/vida-Veranstaltung: Öffentlicher Verkehr hat Zukunft

2012-06-19 14:11:55
ÖVP Parlamentsklub
Cortolezis-Schlager gratuliert Boku-Rektor Martin Gerzabek zur Wiederwahl

2012-06-19 14:11:29
Bundespressedienst
AVISO: Pressekonferenz BK Faymann und VK Spindelegger

Alle OTS-Aussendungen

Meine Abgeordneten ist eine Online-Datenbank, die öffentliche Daten zu österreichischen Politikern beinhaltet („Dossiers"). Sie führt ihre Lebensläufe, frühere und aktuelle Nebentätigkeiten, Engagements in Unternehmen und NGOs sowie Mitgliedschaften in verschiedenen politisch relevanten Organisation an. Das Projekt enthält auch alle Parlamentsreden und Presseerklärungen, die nach definierten politischen Themen getagged werden können. Wenn man die Informationen aus dem Dossier mit dem tatsächlichen politischen Handeln eines Politikers kombiniert, können daraus Schlüsse auf mögliche Interessenskonflikte gezogen werden.
Meine Abgeordneten entstand auf Initiative des Präsidenten des Vereins Respekt.net, Martin Winkler, einer Plattform für gesellschaftspolitisches Engagement, die Menschen mit Ideen mit potenziellen UnterstützerInnen zusammenbringt. Mit der Projektbörse will Respekt.net vor allem Einzelpersonen und Gruppen helfen, ein lebendiges Forum für ihr Engagement zu finden, und Vorhaben fördern, mit denen BürgerInnen und Organisationen das private, wirtschaftliche und öffentliche Leben voranbringen.
Das Projekt kann in viele Richtungen ausgeweitet werden. Zur Zeit enthält es Materialien zu den österreichischen Nationalratsabgeordneten, Mitgliedern des Bundesrats, EU-Abgeordneten und Regierungsmitgliedern. Das Zielpublikum des Projekts sind in erster Linie Journalisten und Wissenschaftler, obwohl es seit seinem sehr erfolgreichen Start im November 2011 auch auf Interesse beim allgemeinen Publikum stößt.

Meine Abgeordneten (My Members of Parliament) is an online database of publicly available information ("dossiers"). on Austrian politicians It lists their CVs, past and present jobs, engagements in companies and NGOs as well as memberships in various politically relevant organizations. The project also lists all parliamentary speeches and press releases, which can be tagged according to pre-defined political topics. By combining the information from the dossier with the actual political agenda of a politician, conclusions on possible conflicts of interest can be drawn.
Meine Abgeordneten came into being at the initiative of the president of the Respekt.net association, Martin Winkler. It is a platform for socio-political involvement that brings people with ideas together with potential supporters. With the project exchange, Respekt.net aims above all to help individual people and groups to find a lively forum for their commitment and to support projects with which citizens and organizations promote private, economic and public life.
The project is expandable in every direction. Currently it lists the members of the Austrian parliament, the Austrian MEPs and members of the Council of Ministers.
The target audience of the project is primarily journalistic and academic, although it is already popular with the general public since its very successful launch in November 2011.

The **Meine Abgeordneten** platform is a private initiative of Respekt.net. The creation of the platform was funded by 200 individual donations from private donors. *Meine Abgeordneten* is strictly politically independent and exclusively committed to the creation of political transparency. **Meine Abgeordneten** ist eine private Initiative von Respekt.net. Die Entwicklung der Plattform wurde durch 200 private Spenden finanziert. *Meine Abgeordneten* ist politisch unabhängig und allein der Schaffung politischer Transparenz verpflichtet.

Safecast

SAFECAST

ABOUT MAPS FAQ SUBMIT DOWNLOAD DATA ENGLISH 日本語

Safecast is a global sensor network for collecting and sharing radiation measurements to empower people with data about their environments.

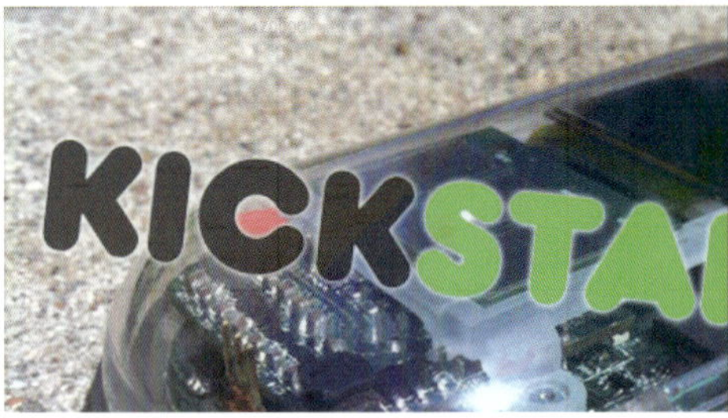

Safecast Geiger Counter Limited Edition!

Earlier this year we announced a new geiger counter, designed by bunnie that we were hoping would be in production soon. We're excited to announce two things – Firstly International Medcom is full steam ahead on a full production run of these devices that will be available later this year, and secondly we're releasing a [...]

1 2 3 4 5

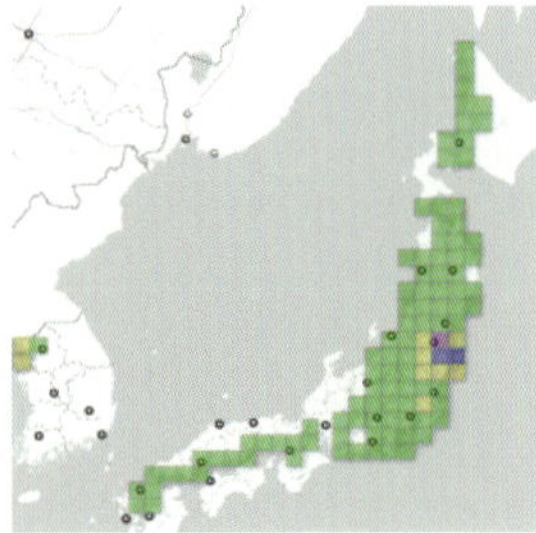

Gefällt mir 1.160 Personen gefällt das.

+1 +80 Recommend this on Google

Major Map Update!

June 16, 2012 22:59

Posted by sean on June 16, 2012 22:59

No Responses

Maps

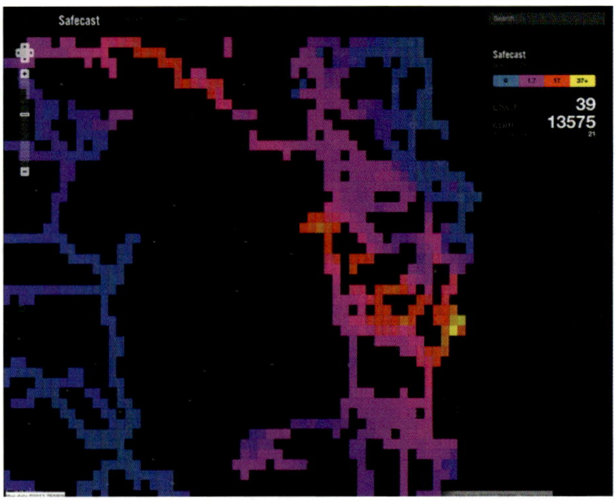

This update has been months in the making. Our visualization rock stars Samuel Luescher & Anthony DeVincenzi at the MIT Media Lab are primarily to thank for this, as well as Paul Campbell who has been diligently cranking away on our new database and API that manages all this data

We've collected and published over 3,000,000 measurements!

Interested in helping out? Please fill out this interest form and we'll get in touch soon!

Search

Safecast - Japan Radiation Monitoring

powered by globalgiving

Safecast Discussion List

Email:

Subscribe

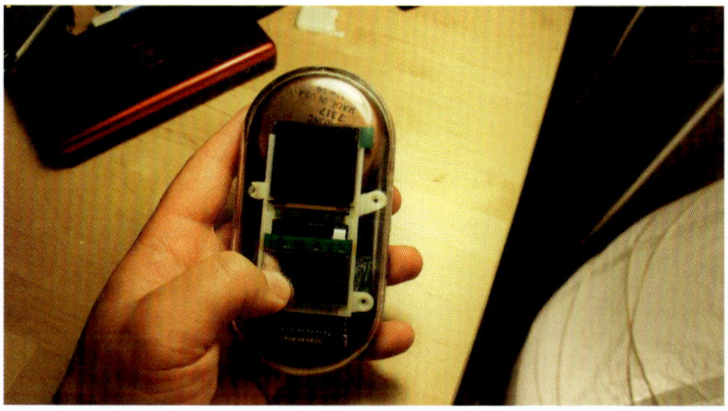

Safecast ist ein globales Projekt, das in den USA beheimatet ist, sich aber im Moment auf Japan konzentriert. Wir wollen Menschen Daten über die Umgebung, in der sie leben, zur Verfügung stellen, und zwar in erster Linie, indem wir Daten zur Strahlungsbelastung auf Karten verorten und ein Sensorennetzwerk aufbauen. Jeder kann zum Projekt beitragen und die gesammelten Daten frei nutzen.

Nach dem Erdbeben vom 11. März 2011 und dem Nuklearunfall von Fukushima Daiichi wurde klar, dass die Bevölkerung mehr Daten verlangte, als zugänglich waren. In Zusammenarbeit mit Partnern wie International Medcom oder Keio University hat *Safecast* ein Netzwerk aus statischen und mobilen Strahlungssensoren aufgebaut, die aktiv in ganz Japan aufgestellt wurden, und zwar sowohl in der Sperrzone rund um den Reaktor als auch an anderen Orten im ganzen Land.

Der Grundsatz, der die Arbeit von *Safecast* bestimmt, lautet: Je mehr Daten – und zwar verfügbare Daten –, desto besser. Wir wollen nicht eine einzelne Datenquelle als unzuverlässig etikettieren, sondern die bereits existierenden Messdaten ergänzen, um sie verlässlicher zu machen. Es ist immer besser, mit unterschiedlichen Datenquellen zu arbeiten, und die Ergebnisse sind genauer, sobald die verschiedenen Daten aggregiert werden.

In Japan liegt der Schwerpunkt im Moment auf Strahlungsdaten, aber im Zuge unserer Arbeit ist deutlich geworden, dass es einen Bedarf nach mehr umweltbezogenen Daten auf globaler Ebene gibt. Auf lange Sicht will sich *Safecast* genau mit dieser Problematik beschäftigen.

Safecast is a global project based in the US but currently focusing on outreach efforts in Japan. We are working to empower people with data about their environments, primarily by mapping radiation levels and building a sensor network, enabling people both to contribute and to freely use the data collected.

After the 3/11 earthquake and resulting nuclear situation at Fukushima Daiichi, it became clear that people wanted more data than was available. Through joint efforts with partners such as International Medcom and Keio University, *Safecast* has been building a radiation sensor network made up of static and mobile sensors actively deployed around Japan—both in the exclusion zone around the reactor and elsewhere in the country.

Safecast supports the idea that more data—freely available data—is better. Our goal is not to single out any individual source of data as untrustworthy, but rather to contribute to the existing measurement data and make it more robust. Multiple sources of data are always better and more accurate when aggregated.

While Japan and radiation is the primary focus of the moment, this work has made us aware of a need for more environmental data at a global level and the long-term work that *Safecast* engages in will address these needs.

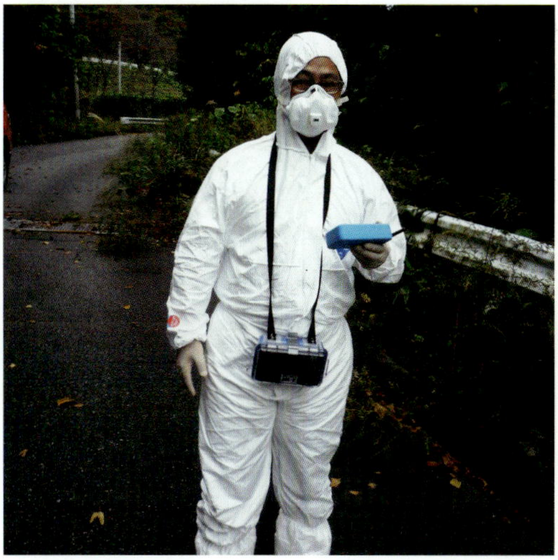

Safecast. While core operations are based out of the Tokyo hackerspace, our team includes members from around the world including, Joi Ito (Cambridge), Bunnie Huang (Singapore), Sean Bonner (Los Angeles), Pieter Franken (Tokyo) and Ray Ozzie (Seattle). **Safecast** operiert hauptsächlich vom Hackerspace Tokio aus, aber das Team umfasst Mitglieder aus der ganzen Welt: Joi Ito (Cambridge), Bunnie Huang (Singapore), Sean Bonner (Los Angeles), Pieter Franken (Tokyo) and Ray Ozzie (Seattle).

Texting for Democracy

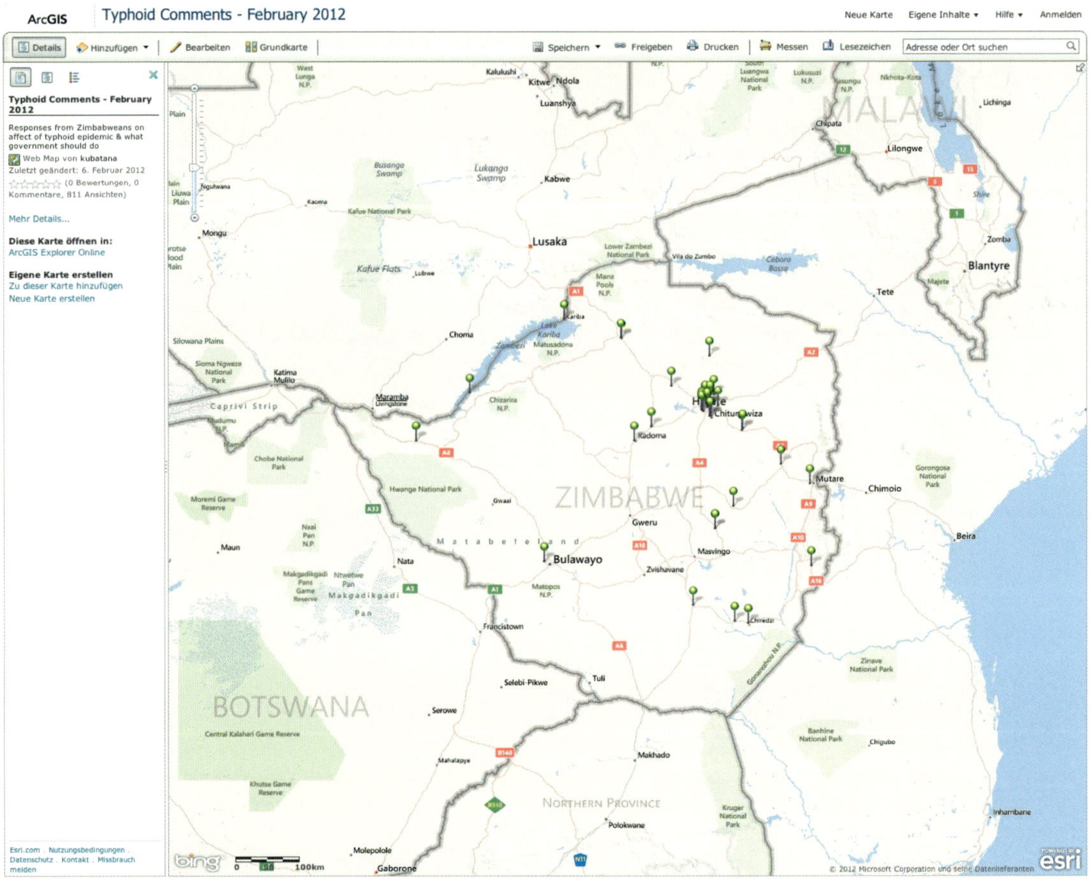

Kubatana uses e-mail, SMS and post to communicate with a wide and diverse network of Zimbabwean individuals and organizations. Our SMS membership of over 30,000 subscribers is distributed across the country, with a third based in Harare, a third in Zimbabwe's other cities and towns and a third in rural areas and growth points.

This reach makes us particularly able to take advantage of the immediacy and interactivity of SMS and mobile communications. Our SMS survey is regularly used as a two-way communication tool, in which people share their feedback, tips and suggestions with us, and through which we invite feedback, opinions and observations on timely and relevant topics.

Kubatana uses Clickatell's online bulk SMS service to send out text messages to our subscribers. The sender ID facility on Clickatell enables us to set the

Kubatana verwendet E-Mail, SMS und Postsendungen, um mit einem großen, diversen Netzwerk aus Einzelpersonen und Organisationen in Zimbabwe zu kommunizieren. Unser SMS-Pool umfasst mehr als 30.000 Mitglieder und ist über das ganze Land verstreut, wobei sich ein Drittel in Harare, ein Drittel in anderen Städten und ein Drittel in ländlichen Regionen befindet.

Dank dieses Netzwerkes können wir die Unmittelbarkeit und Interaktivität von SMS und mobiler Kommunikation besonders gut nutzen. Wir sehen unsere regelmäßigen SMS-Umfragen als ein Tool zur Zweiwegkommunikation, bei denen Menschen uns Feedback geben und Vorschläge machen und wodurch wir aktiv um Rückmeldung, Meinungen und Beobachtungen über aktuelle und relevante Themen bitten.

Kubatana nutzt den Massen-SMS-Dienst von Clickatell, um SMS-Botschaften an die Abonnenten zu verschicken. Die Sender-ID-Funktion von Clickatell erlaubt es uns, die Senderidentität, von der die Botschaften gesendet werden, selbst zu bestimmen. In unserem Fall ist es die Telefonnummer einer dedizierten SMS-Leitung in unserem Büro. *Kubatana* hat diesen Zweiweg-Feedbackkanal via SMS in der Vergangenheit mehrfach genutzt: um Meinungen und Informationen zu „crowdsourcen" und damit ein verlässlicheres Bild von lokalen und nationalen Ereignissen zu erhalten.

Zum Beispiel haben wir im Februar 2011 einen Anruf von einem vertrauenswürdigen Mitglied der Zivilgesellschaft bekommen, der von Gewalt im Zentrum von Harare berichtete. Wir versendeten eine Textbotschaft an unsere Abonnenten, in der wir sie von dieser Beobachtung informierten, sie zur Vorsicht mahnten und sie baten, ihre eigenen Beobachtungen zu berichten. Wir erhielten über 200 Antworten. Einige Abonnenten hielten sich gerade im Stadtzentrum auf, und manche berichteten von Gewalt in Harare, aber auch in anderen Orten. Dieses Feedback ermöglichte es uns, uns ein Bild von der Lage zu machen und auf unserem Community-Blog darüber zu berichten.

Am Beginn des Jahres 2012 traten in Harare und anderen Städten vermehrt Fälle von Typhus auf, und zwar in einem für Zimbabwe untypischen Ausmaß. Wir verschickten eine SMS an unsere Mitglieder und fragten sie, ob Typhus auch ihre Community betraf und was die Regierung ihrer Meinung nach unternehmen sollte. Wir erhielten ungefähr 200 Rückmeldungen. Wir verwendeten dann die Online-Mapping-Funktion von ArcGIS, um diese Kommentare zu verorten, die sich rund um Harare konzentrierten, aber auch auf andere Orte verteilt waren.

Kubatana hofft, durch die verstärkte Verwendung von Mapping- und Datenvisualisierungstechniken Informationen besser teilen und das Gefühl für Gemeinschaft innerhalb unserer Abonnenten weiter stärken zu können. Unserer Erfahrung nach sind die Ausdrucksmöglichkeiten für Menschen in Zimbabwe beschränkt und daher schätzen sie die Zweiwegkommunikation, die *Kubatana* auf seiner Plattform via E-Mail, SMS und anderen neuen und traditionellen Medien ermöglicht.

sender identity that the messages are sent from. In our case, this is the phone number of the dedicated SMS line at our office. *Kubatana* has used this two-way SMS feedback channel in a number of ways in the past year, to "crowd source" opinion and information and to help develop a broader picture of local and national events.

For example, in February 2011 we received a phone call from a trusted civil-society ally, informing us of violence in central Harare. We sent out a text message to our subscribers informing them of this report, advising them to be careful and asking them to submit their reports and observations. We received over 200 replies from subscribers, some of whom were in the city center at the time, and some of whom were using the opportunity to report on the violence they were experiencing in Harare and farther afield. This feedback enabled us to build a picture of events taking place and report on them on our community blog.

In early 2012, Harare and other cities were increasingly experiencing typhoid cases—at an extent atypical for Zimbabwe. We sent out a text message to our subscribers asking how typhoid had affected their communities and what they thought government should do. We received around 200 responses. We then used the free online mapping capacity on ArcGIS to plot these comments, which centered around Harare but were also distributed around the country.

Kubatana hopes increasingly to use mapping and data visualization techniques to share information from our subscribers and to create an even greater sense of community within our membership. In our experience, Zimbabweans have limited avenues through which to express themselves freely and therefore greatly value the two-way communications platform *Kubatana* provides through e-mail, SMS and other new and traditional media.

The Kubatana Trust of Zimbabwe aims to strengthen the use of e-mail and Internet strategies in Zimbabwean NGOs and civil society organizations. *Kubatana* makes human rights and civic education information accessible from a centralized, electronic source. Der **Kubatana Trust of Zimbabwe** will die Verwendung von E-Mail und Internet-Strategien unter zimbabwischen NGOs und Organisationen der Zivilgesellschaft stärken. *Kubatana* macht Informationen über Menschenrechte und politische Bildung über eine zentralisierte elektronische Quelle zugänglich.

The Johnny Cash Project

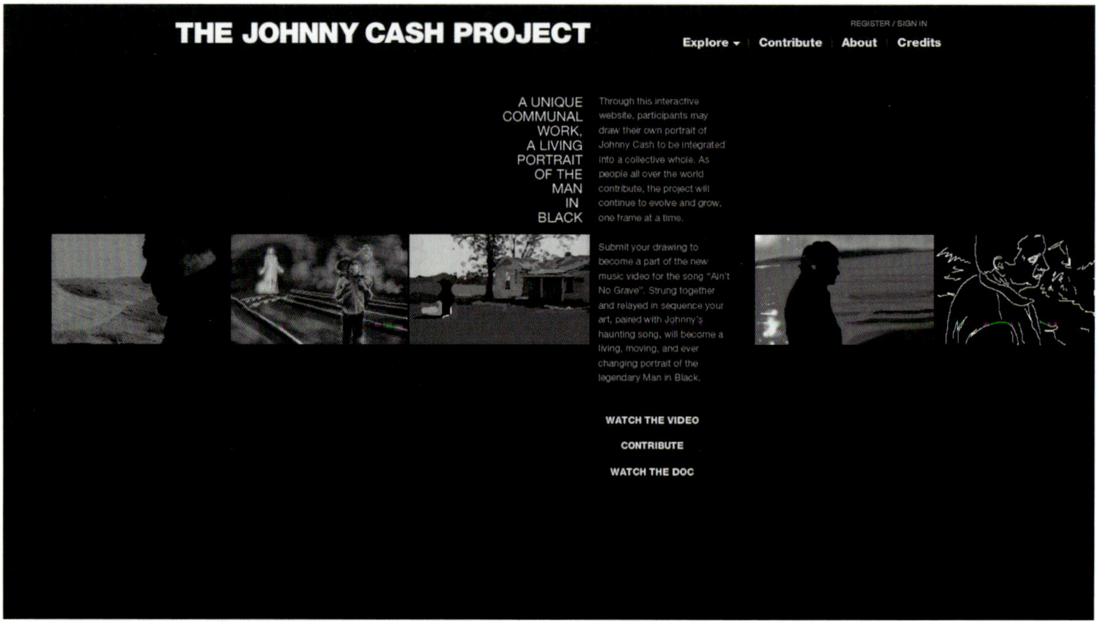

The Johnny Cash Project is a global collective public art project. Inspired by individually supplied frames of archival footage and through the use of a custom drawing tool, participants are invited to create and share their vision of the Man in Black. These unique and personal portraits are then strung together and played in sequence over the song "Ain't No Grave," creating a moving, ever-evolving homage to the musical icon. The result: an evolving, crowd-sourced animated music video, rising from a sea of one-of-a-kind portraits.

Das *The Johnny Cash Project* ist ein globales, kollektives öffentliches Kunstprojekt. Die Teilnehmer, die sich von individuell beigesteuerten Sequenzen von Archiv-Filmmaterial inspirieren lassen können, sind eingeladen, mit Hilfe eines speziell entwickelten Zeichen-Tools ihre persönliche Vision des „Man in Black" zu schaffen. Diese einzigartigen, persönlichen Porträts werden dann zusammengesetzt und zur Melodie des Songs „Ain't No Grave" nacheinander abgespielt, wobei ein Film entsteht, der sich ständig weiterentwickelt – eine Hommage an dieses musikalische Genie. Das Resultat ist ein sich ständig veränderndes, animiertes Musikvideo, das durch Crowdsourcing aus einer Unmenge von unverwechselbaren Porträts entstanden ist.

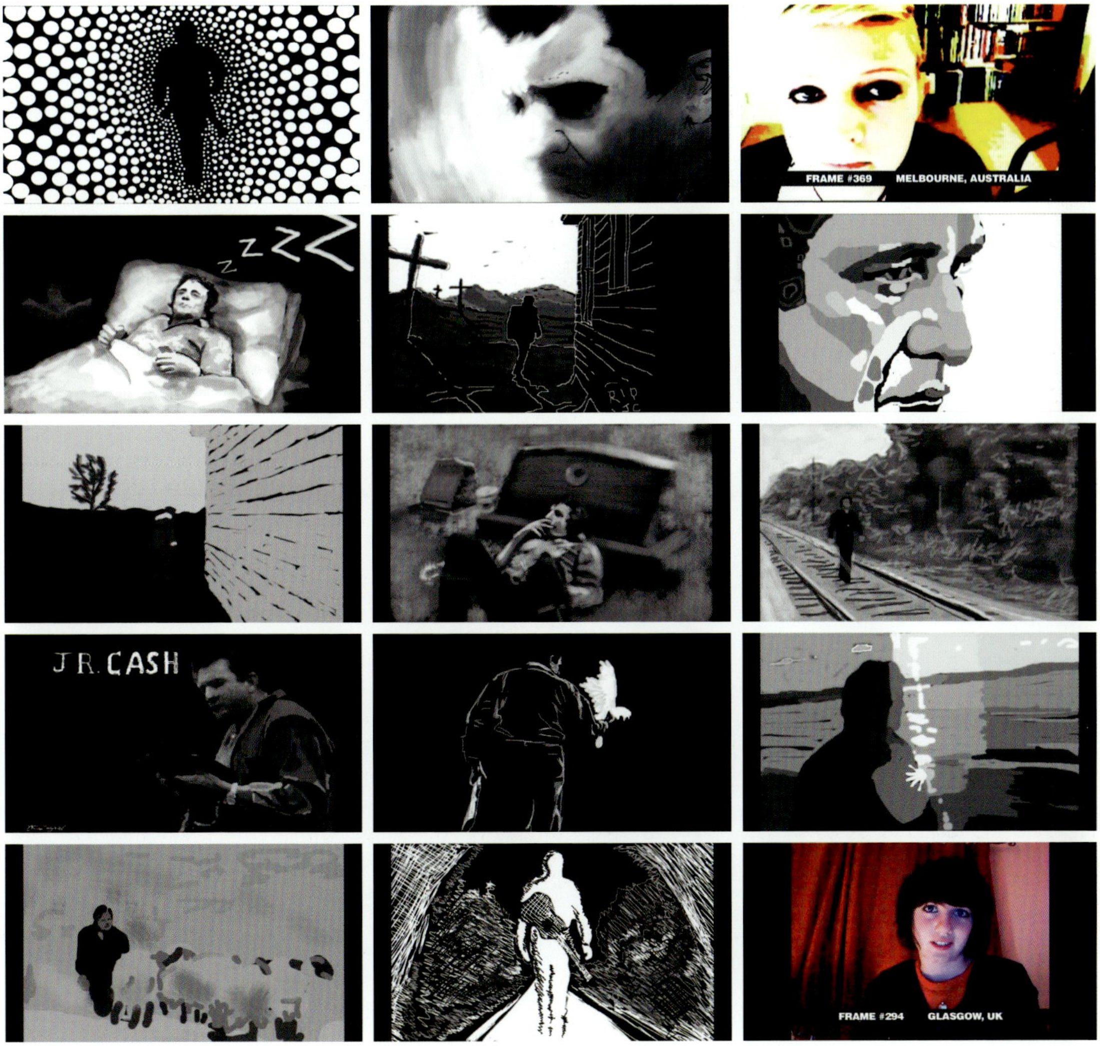

The Johnny Cash Project was conceived of and created by Chris Milk and Aaron Koblin. Aaron Koblin (US) is an artist and designer who works with data and digital technologies. Chris Milk (US) is an music video director and photographer. There have been more than a million users on the site, with hundreds of thousands of contributions. Participants include fans of Johnny Cash, passionate artists, illustrators and regular old Joes. The project is open to anyone who is interested in participating. Submissions are moderated to make sure they are not offensive but are otherwise accepted into the project. Das **Johnny Cash Project** wurde von Chris Milk und Aaron Koblin konzipiert und geschaffen. Aaron Koblin (US) ist ein Künstler und Designer, der mit Daten und digitalen Technologien arbeitet. Chris Milk (US) ist Regisseur von Musikvideos und Fotograf. Es haben mehr als eine Million User die Website besucht und hunderttausende Beiträge beigesteuert. Die Teilnehmer sind Fans von Johnny Cash, begeisterte Künstler, Illustratoren, aber auch Durchschnittsuser. Am Projekt kann jeder teilnehmen. Die Beiträge sind moderiert, damit keine anstößigen Inhalte verwendet werden, abgesehen davon ist aber jeder Beitrag willkommen.

XinCheJian: The First Hackerspace in China

新车间
[XINCHEJIAN]
Hackerspace in Shanghai

- ABOUT US | 有关我们
- EVENTS | 活动
- PROJECTS | 项目
- MEMBERSHIP | 会员制度
- MAKERS | 创客
- WORKSHOP | 工作坊
- TOOLS & KITS | 工具和套件
- CONTACT US | 联系我们
- LINKS | 连结
- LOGIN
- FEED

XinCheJian on Grand Design magazine

June 19th, 2012 § 0 comments § permalink

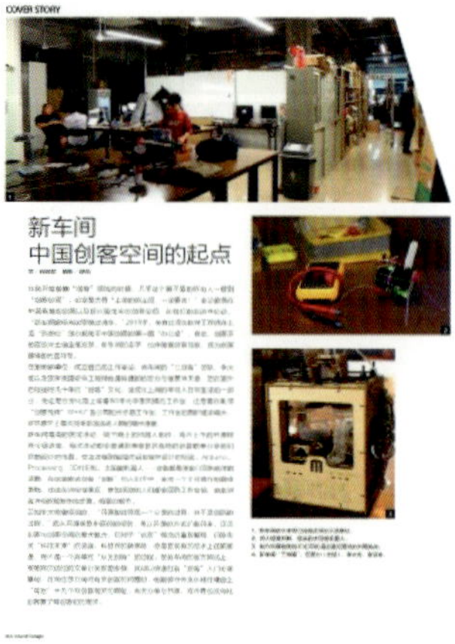
COVER STORY

新车间
中国创客空间的起点

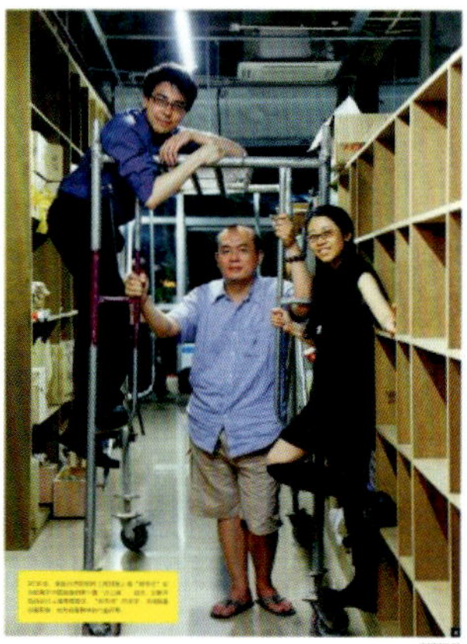

Web version

"odor of oregano" progress week 2 (20120618)

June 19th, 2012 § 0 comments § permalink

AFTER ANOTHER ONE WEEK, WE GOT PRETTY GOOD SEEDLING WITH strong roots; transplant was completed this evening with great support from Roger. More details will be shared on this Wednesday evening XCJ meetup; stay still and get your nose ready 😉

STATUS OF THE SPACE
Not available

LANGUAGE
English
中文

UPCOMING EVENTS
Shanghai Linux Users Group @ XCJ – 2012/06/23
Processing视觉编程入门课程 – 第五期 – 2012/06/24
机器车竞赛 – Roboracing Competition – 2012/06/30
Processing视觉编程入门课程 – 第五期 – 2012/07/01
Processing视觉编程入门课程 – 第六期 – 2012/07/15
Processing视觉编程入门课程 – 第六期 – 2012/07/22
Processing视觉编程入门课程 – 第六期 – 2012/07/29

RECENT POSTS
XinCheJian on Grand Design magazine
"odor of oregano" progress week 2 (20120618)
Aquaponic Update
"odor of oregano" progress week 1 (20120613)
Maker Portraits

SISTER HACKERSPACE
GOLD COAST TECHSPACE

ARCHIVES
June 2012
May 2012
April 2012
March 2012
February 2012
January 2012
December 2011
November 2011
October 2011
September 2011
August 2011
July 2011

XinCheJian ist der erste von vielen Hackerspaces in China und einer von Hunderten auf der ganzen Welt. Jeder Hackerspace ist eine autonome Einheit, aber alle teilen dieselbe Philosophie: Dinge bauen und Spaß dabei haben. Das Ziel von *XinCheJian* besteht darin, Physical Computing, Open-Source-Hardware und das „Internet der Dinge" zu unterstützen, zu fördern und selbst aktiv zu werden. Dazu organisiert *XinCheJian* Vorträge, Diskussionen, Projekte und Workshops, fördert Start-ups, organisiert Wettbewerbe und nimmt selbst an internationalen Wettbewerben teil.

Unser langfristiges Ziel ist es, das Konzept und die Philosophie der Hackerspaces in ganz China zu verbreiten und Gleichgesinnte zu inspirieren, Hackerspaces in jeder großen Stadt des Landes einzurichten. Wir tun dies, indem wir eine Community schaffen, die lose mit der globalen Community von Hackerspaces verbunden ist. In unserer Community herrschen Spaß, Kreativität, Teamarbeit, Problemlösung und Offenheit, und wir wollen Chinesen und Ausländern in China ein Lern- und Umwicklungsumfeld bieten.

Wir stehen in Kontakt mit Hackerspaces in anderen Ländern und nehmen an so ambitionierten Projekten wie der „Great Global Hackerspace Challenge" (Frühling 2011, einem internationalen Wettbewerb für alle Hackerspaces) und dem „100 Year Starship"-Projet (Herbst 2011) teil.

Unsere Community zieht Besucher und Projekte an und schafft so wertvolle Beziehungen zwischen Expats, der lokalen Community, Chinesen, die aus dem Ausland zurückkehren, und internationalen Besuchern. *XinCheJian* vermittelt neue Skills mittels Technologie, Projekten, innovativen Ideen und Kontakten in die Tech-Szene, wodurch sich wieder ganz neue Chancen auftun.

XinCheJian, the first of many hackerspaces in China, is one of the many hundreds of such spaces all around the world. Each hackerspace is an autonomous entity, but they all share the same philosophy of having fun building things.

XinCheJian mission is to support, create and promote physical computing, open-source hardware and the "Internet of Things." To achieve this, *XinCheJian* has talks, discussions, projects, start-ups promotion, workshops, competition organization and our own participation in international competitions.

Our long-term goal is to spread the concept and philosophy across China and inspire hackerspaces in every large city from east to west. We are doing this by creating a community loosely federated with the global community of hackerspaces across the world. The community favors fun, creativity, teamwork, problem-solving and openness to provide a learning and development opportunity to the Chinese people and foreigners in China.

We also maintain contact internationally with other hackerspaces, and we apply and participate in ambitious projects such as the Great Global Hackerspace Challenge (spring 2011; an international competition for all hackerspaces) and the 100 Year Starship project (fall 2011). Inside these projects we can build increasingly more complex cyber-electro-mechanical systems.

The community attracts visitors and projects, creating valuable connections between expats, local Chinese and returning Chinese and international visitors. *XinCheJian* generates new skill sets with technology, valuable projects, innovative ideas and contacts across the tech communities, which offer a whole new pool of opportunities.

XinCheJian was founded by Min Lin Hsieh, community manager, who has been contributing her financial, organizational, marketing skills and experience in helping engineering projects and clubs since her college days; David Li, foreman, who has a network of contacts in the local community, is respected for his technical achievements and knowledge of open hardware; and Ricky Ng-Adam, project generator, who has ambitious ideas, engineering experience, strategic planning, community-building and evangelistic skills. As of March 2012, twelve members joined the founding of *XinCheJian 2.0* with a 12-month pledge, sharing the responsibilities for funding *XinCheJian* allowing us to move into a new space and operate for another 12 months. **XinCheJian** wurde von Min Lin Hsieh, David Li und Ricky Ng-Adam gegründet. Min Lin Hsieh ist unsere Community-Managerin, die Erfahrung bei Finanzierung und Organisation sowie im Marketing einbringt, die sie bei der Arbeit für Engineering-Projekte und Klubs seit ihrer College-Zeit erworben hat. David Li ist unser „Chef", der in der lokalen Community extrem vernetzt und weithin anerkannt ist für seine Leistungen und sein Wissen im Bereich Open Hardware; Ricky, Projekt-Generator, hat ehrgeizige Ideen, Erfahrung in Engineering, strategischer Planung, Community-Building und das Talent, andere für Technologie zu begeistern. Per März 2012 hat *XinCheJian 2.0* zwölf Gründungsmitglieder, die sich für ein Jahr verpflichten und die Verantwortung für Mittelauftreibung teilen, sodass wir einen neuen Raum mieten und ein weiteres Jahr arbeiten können.

PRAEKELT FOUNDATION

HOME NEWS ABOUT US PRODUCTS PROJECTS PARTNERS CONTACT

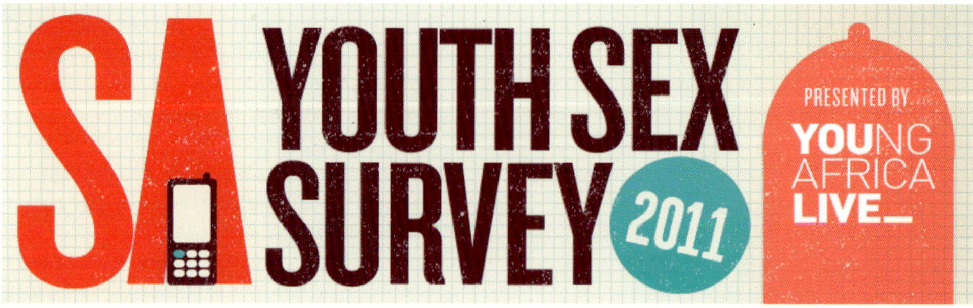

YoungAfricaLive Youth Sex Survey

08.06.2011

Oh yes they are! Results of groundbreaking YoungAfricaLive Youth Sex Survey released

Praekelt Foundation released the results of a groundbreaking Youth Sex Survey, conducted on its YoungAfricaLive mobile platform, that gives fascinating insight into the sexual behaviour and beliefs of South Africa's youth.

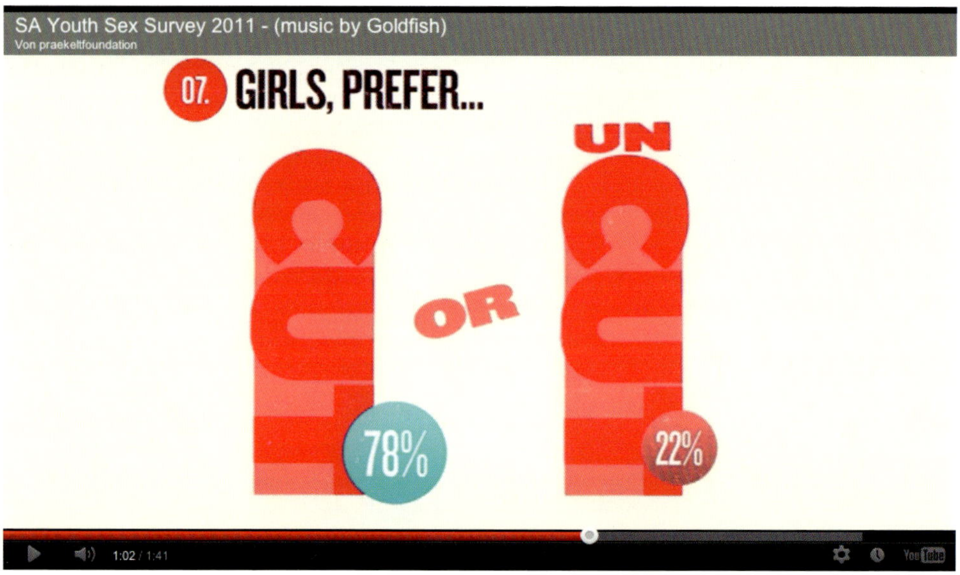

Based on over 50 revealing questions and over 138 954 frank responses, the YoungAfricaLive Youth Sex Survey reveals that whilst South Africa's youth are unquestionably sexually active (44%), they have strong views on the role of HIV/AIDS in sexual encounters, with a massive 81% equating 'not telling a sexual partner that you carry the virus' to outright murder.

In other findings, the survey showed that 66% of the responders identified themselves as less likely to have sex after they had been drinking with 33% admitting that they would be more likely to. The good news for national government's drive to use circumcision as part of an overall HIV prevention programme, a huge number of females - 78% - stated very clearly that they prefer their partner circumcised.

YoungAfricaLive (YAL) ist eine Plattform für Mobiltelefone, die lebensrettende Informationen über HIV/AIDS und sexuelle Gesundheit an junge Menschen kommunizieren will, und zwar auf eine Weise, die ansprechend, interaktiv und relevant ist.

Die Idee entstand, als uns bewusst wurde, dass in Südafrika, dem Land mit der weltweit größten HIV/AIDS-Pandemie, keines der großen Mobiltelefon-Portale Informationen über diese Krankheit anbietet – wo man sich testen lassen kann, wie man Safer Sex praktiziert und wie man vermeidet, angesteckt zu werden. Diese Lücke versucht *YoungAfricaLive* zu schließen.

YAL ist eine unterhaltungsorientierte, interaktive und provokante soziale Plattform, die Spaß macht. Hier können junge Menschen Themen diskutieren, die ihnen am Herzen liegen. Gleichzeitig werden über diese Plattform wichtige Informationen verbreitet und sexuelle Gesundheit gefördert.

YAL vermittelt nicht bloß Fakten und will junge Menschen auch nicht darüber „belehren", was sie zu tun und zu lassen haben, sondern will einen Raum schaffen, in dem junge Südafrikaner sich über heiße Themen, die ihren Alltag betreffen, austauschen können: Liebe, Sex, Beziehungen, Gender- und kulturelle Fragen, aber auch HIV/AIDS. Dieser Edutainment-Ansatz war extrem erfolgreich, denn unser Publikum hat nicht das Gefühl, belehrt zu werden, sondern kann sich in echte Diskussionen mit Gleichaltrigen einlassen und die Zeit genießen, die es auf diesem Portal verbringt.

Die wesentlichsten Ziele von *YoungAfricaLive* sind:
1) Informationen teilen und Erziehungsarbeit leisten;
2) Eine Diskussion in Gang bringen, und
3) HIV-Tests fördern und vermitteln, dass Safe-Sex-Praktiken etwas Normales sind.

YoungAfricaLive (YAL) is a mobile portal platform designed to communicate life-saving information about HIV/Aids and sexual health to young people in a way that is engaging, interactive and relevant.

The idea was originally sparked by the discovery that in a country with the biggest HIV/Aids pandemic in the world, none of South Africa's large mobile portals held a single piece of information about the pandemic—where to get tested, how to practice safe sex and how to avoid getting HIV/Aids. This gap created the opportunity for *YoungAfricaLive* to be born.

YAL is an entertainment-oriented, fun, interactive and provocative social platform that enables young people to discuss topics close to them while at the same time disseminating important information and promoting sexual health. It does not simply state the facts and "lecture" young people about the dos and don'ts, but rather creates a space where young South Africans can talk about hot topics that affect their daily lives: love, sex, relationships, gender and cultural issues, as well as HIV/Aids. This edutainment approach has been extremely successful as our young audience does not feel it is being lectured but is able to engage in discussions with peers and enjoy time spent on the portal.

The key goals of *YoungAfricaLive* are to:
1) Share information and educate:
2) Generate discussion, and
3) Promote HIV testing and normalize safe-sex practices

YoungAfricaLive. The core team carrying this project is a combination of writers, engineers and program managers. In each country, the team is made up of local content writers and/or bloggers, as well as content moderators. Centrally, the team is led by an overall content strategist, a lead engineer and a program manager. On 14 February 2012, *YoungAfricaLive* had 838,800 unique users. YAL users are African young people aged predominantly between 18 and 25. They are predominantly urban, but we also see a lot of rural users on the platform. **YoungAfricaLive**. Das Team hinter diesem Projekt ist eine Gruppe von Autoren, Ingenieuren und Programmmanagern. In jedem Land besteht das Team aus lokalen Content-Produzenten und/oder Bloggern sowie Content-Moderatoren. Das Kernteam wird von einem Content-Strategen, einem Lead-Ingenieur und einem Programmmanager geleitet. Am 24. Februar 2012 hatte *YoungAfricaLive* 838.000 individuelle Nutzer. Die User von YAL sind AfrikanerInnen zwischen 18 und 25. Die meisten leben in Städten, aber wir sehen auch eine Menge User aus dem ländlichen Raum auf unserer Plattform.

u19 – CREATE YOUR WORLD

Creating a Better World

Sirikit Amann, Robert Glashüttner, Martin Hollinetz, Martina Sochor, Markus Sucher

In 2012, the u19 category of the Prix Ars Electronica was expanded in content. In previous years its motto had been "freestyle computing", which meant that the works submitted had to be broadly related to computers or computer tools. Now u19 is open to life in its diversity and the world as a whole. "Create Your World" is the new motto. Somehow, as the years passed, it became increasingly absurd for us to feel we needed to make digital technologies appealing to children and young people—for ultimately they have grown up with them and, in fact, only know a non-digital, non-networked world through history books and the stories of older generations.

To accommodate these new and more open regulations, the u19 jury has also faced the challenge of having to rid itself of some old criteria. In the past, for instance, biological experiments and hand-drawn visions of the future might have been categorized as off-topic and relegated to the bottom for having been implemented without the computer. Thanks to CREATE YOUR WORLD, these projects may now receive the recognition they deserve. Already in u19's first year of reorientation, entries of this kind have won Awards of Distinction and Honorary Mentions.

Nevertheless, due to the u19's long tradition, the contents of submissions have not actually shifted all that greatly yet. Projects focusing on image processing as well as animations and videos still make up the bulk of the nearly 700 entries. Yet this makes sense, as the contents of the submitted videos have always been extremely diverse, and the exploration of digital tools occurs for the most part during production and postproduction at the computer. Once again, a number of remarkable video and animated works were submitted this year, ranging from a biting satire and critique of IT surveillance mechanisms (*ConnectIn(g)*),

Das Jahr 2012 markiert eine inhaltliche Erweiterung in der u19-Kategorie des Prix Ars Electronica. War das Motto jahrelang „freestyle computing" und damit eine Verpflichtung gegeben, dass die eingereichten Werke im weitesten Sinn mit Computern oder Computer-Werkzeugen zu tun haben müssen, ist u19 ab sofort für das komplette, pralle Leben und die ganze Welt geöffnet. „Create Your World" heißt nun das Motto. Irgendwie ist es mit der Zeit immer absurder geworden, Kindern und Jugendlichen den Umgang mit digitalen Techniken schmackhaft machen zu wollen – sie sind schließlich damit aufgewachsen und kennen eine nicht digitale, nicht vernetzte Welt ohnehin nur aus den Geschichtsbüchern und den Erzählungen der Altvorderen.

Entsprechend der neuen, offenen Richtlinien ist auch die u19-Jury vor der Herausforderung gestanden, einige alte Kriterien zu verwerfen. Wären früher biologische Experimente und mit Hand gezeichnete Zukunftsvisionen wegen des fehlenden Computereinsatzes möglicherweise noch als Themenverfehlungen weiter hinten angereiht worden, sind dies dank CREATE YOUR WORLD nun Projekte, die gebührend prämiert werden können und im ersten Jahr der neuen u19-Ausrichtung auch bereits mit Anerkennungen und Auszeichnungen versehen worden sind.

Wirklich stark verschoben haben sich die Einreichungen aufgrund der langjährigen Tradition von u19 allerdings noch nicht. Weiterhin machen digitale Bildbearbeitungen, Animationen und Videos den Großteil der knapp 700 Einreichungen aus. Das macht aber auch Sinn, denn die Inhalte der eingereichten Videos waren immer schon breit gestreut, und die Auseinandersetzung mit digitalen Tools erfolgt ohnehin bei der Produktion und Post-Produktion am Computer. Auch dieses Jahr wurden wieder einige bemerkenswerte Video- und Animations-Werke eingereicht, die von bissiger Satire und Kritik an IT-Überwachungsmechanismen (*ConnectIn(g)*) über einen kreativ inszenierten Beweis von gelungener Integrationspolitik bei Jugendlichen (*Bin Baum mit 2 Stämmen*)

bis hin zu komödiantisch aufbereiteten und aufwändig produzierten Science-Fiction-Geschichten (*Das Superhirn*) reichen. Manche Videos, wie das bereits genannte *Bin Baum mit 2 Stämmen*, das mit einer Auszeichnung prämiert wurde, haben in der Jury nach mehrmaligen Schauen ihre Magie immer mehr entfaltet. Dazu zählt auch das Video *handsome*, in dem nur Hände gezeigt werden, die miteinander in einen Dialog treten und so eindringlich klar machen, dass es keine Worte oder ausladende Gesten braucht, um zu kommunizieren, sich zu verstehen, emotionale Nähe herzustellen. Das positive Erstaunen über so auf den Punkt gebrachte Werke, die unser soziales Zusammenleben und damit die Grundlage unserer Gesellschaft zum Ausdruck bringen, hat nicht nur einmal Gänsehaut und manchmal sogar Tränen der Begeisterung bei den Jurymitgliedern hervorgerufen.
Software und Robotik sind zwei weitere Klassiker bei u19-Einreichungen, die auch in diesem Jahr nicht ausgeblieben sind. Besonders bemerkenswert hat die Jury das Programm *Riffgrabber* befunden, bei dem es in Grundzügen möglich ist, mit Gitarre in den Computer eingespielte Riffs in Gitarren-Tabs-Dateien umzuwandeln. Auch Computerspiele waren wieder mit von der Partie, wobei ein Game einen Teil der Jury besonders in ihren Bann gezogen hat und auch abseits der offiziellen Sitzungen intensiv gespielt wurde: *iTanky*, ein kleines Geschicklichkeitsspiel für iPhone und iPod Touch, nutzt sowohl die Bewegungssteuerung als auch den Touchscreen der tragbaren Apple-Geräte, um kleine Spielzeugpanzer durch eine virtuelle Landschaft zu steuern und durch taktisch geschickte Schüsse Gegner auszuschalten. Zwar bereitet dieses Game keine erhellende Zukunftsvision, macht aber sehr gut ersichtlich, wie gut niederschwellige interaktive Unterhaltung funktioniert und ein breites Publikum erreichen kann. Und wie viele Teenager können von sich schon behaupten, ihr eigenes Game in Apples AppStore verfügbar zu haben? Ebenfalls verspielt, aber vor allem technisch herausragend war das Projekt *Balancing Robot*, das von einem jungen Team entwickelt

and a creatively staged testimony of successful integration policies among young people (*Bin Baum mit 2 Stämmen*), to humorously enacted and elaborately produced science-fiction stories (*Das Superhirn*). Some videos, such as the just-mentioned *Bin Baum mit 2 Stämmen*, winner of the Award of Distinction, revealed their magic to the members of the jury a bit more each time they watched them. This includes the video *handsome*, in which viewers only see hands and how they enter into dialogue with each other. They make it compellingly clear that no words or grand gestures are needed to understand and communicate with others or to establish a sense of closeness. The jury was positively struck with amazement at these works that are so to the point and do such a good job of conveying our social lives together, and so express what is the very basis of our society. More than once the jury members got goosebumps and tears of joy came to their eyes.
Software and robotics projects are two other classics among u19 entries, and they were not missing this year either. The jury found the program *RiffGrabber* particularly noteworthy: it essentially allows users to convert riffs played on the guitar to the computer into guitar tab files. Computer games also played a role this year, and especially one game cast a spell on a number of the jury members, who then spent much of their time off from official sessions playing it intensively: a small game of skill for iPhone or iPod Touch, *iTanky* uses both the motion control and touch screen of portable Apple devices to maneuver little toy tanks around a virtual landscape and eliminate adversaries through clever shooting tactics. And although this game did not offer an illuminating scenario of the future, it reveals exceedingly well how wonderfully low-threshold interactive entertainment works and its ability to reach a wide audience.

Moreover, how many teenagers can claim that the game they created is available at the Apple App Store? Playful—though above all outstanding in its technology—is also the project *Balancing Robot* that was developed by a young team and took home the u14 non-cash prize. Here a small vehicle has been positioned on the rear wheel of a bike that moves back and forth. A clever control system that counteracts each movement as required ensures that the vehicle does not lose its balance. Less innovative, but potentially more popular as well as implemented to perfection is *Quadrocopter*—an aerial drone with four propellers, like those with a growing fanbase increasingly available as do-it-yourself kits.

An especially young team submitted their utterly charming ideas for the future. The *Zukunftswürfel* is a large, colorful, soft cloth cube created by a bright kindergarten project group. Each side of the cube has a transparent pocket into which a different colorfully drawn and painted notebook has been placed. These kindergarten kids have given free reign to their imaginations and hopes for the future. It was not long until it became evident to the jury that this project deserved a special award—this year's u10 non-cash prize.

The decision to award the Golden Nica to a specific project or not is always the last and most difficult item on the agenda at any Prix Ars Electronica jury session. It is particularly challenging to select a winner in the u19 category because many factors—age, gender, education, technical excellence, creativity, social relevance, etc.—are at play and need to be included in the decision. There was a long discussion about whether the remarkable *BioBookCover* project workshop should win or not. Much spoke in its favor: after all, this team has

worden ist und den u14-Sachpreis abgeräumt hat. Dabei steht ein kleines Fahrzeug auf einem sich hin und her bewegenden Hinterrad eines Fahrrads und wird von einer klugen Steuerung davon abgehalten, das Gleichgewicht zu verlieren indem es entsprechend der jeweiligen Bewegung gegensteuert. Weniger innovativ, dafür populärer und technisch astrein umgesetzt, ist der *Quadrocopter* – eine von vier Propellern angetriebene Flugdrohne, die immer öfter auch im Selbstbaukasten angeboten wird und über eine immer größer werdende Fan-Basis verfügt.

Ganz entzückende Zukunftsvisionen hat ein besonders junges Team eingereicht. Der *Zukunftswürfel* einer aufgeweckten Kindergarten-Projektgruppe ist ein großer, bunter, weicher Stoffwürfel. Er hat auf jeder Fläche ein eigenes, durchsichtiges Fach in dem ein jeweils unterschiedliches, bunt gezeichnetes und bemaltes Heft gesteckt ist. Die Kindergartenkinder haben hier ihrer Fantasie und ihren Hoffnungen über ihre Zukunft freien Lauf gelassen. Für die Jury war ziemlich schnell klar, dass dieses Projekt eine besondere Auszeichnung verdient – den diesjährigen u10-Sachpreis.

Die Entscheidung für (oder gegen) die Goldene Nica ist immer der letzte, aber auch schwierigste Schritt jeder Prix-Ars-Electronica-Jurysitzung. Bei u19 ist die Entscheidung besonders herausfordernd, weil hier viele Faktoren – Alter, Geschlecht, Ausbildung, technische Exzellenz, Kreativität, soziale Relevanz, usw. – in die Entscheidung miteinbezogen werden müssen. Es gab eine lange Diskussion, ob die bemerkenswerte Bastelstube von *BioBookCover* gewinnen sollte oder nicht. Vieles hat dafür gesprochen: Immerhin stellt hier eine mit Spezialrezepten vertraute Projektgruppe aus biologischen Bestandteilen selbst Plastik her! In Sachen ökologischer Nachhaltigkeit ist damit ein markantes Statement hinsichtlich CREATE YOUR WORLD gesetzt worden. Einzig die Tatsache, dass die Herstellung von Bioplastik kein komplettes Geheimnis mehr ist und

der Umstand, dass das biologisch abbaubare Plastik in ästhetischer Hinsicht noch optimierbar ist, waren Argumente gegen die Vergabe der Goldenen Nica.
Jene Frau, die die Goldene Nica in der Kategorie u19 dieses Jahr schließlich gewonnen hat, hat mit ihrem politischen Interesse und ihrem Mut die Jury so beeindruckt, dass diese zunächst ungläubig darüber war, ob das alles wirklich originär von der 18-jährigen Oberösterreicherin Agnes Aistleitner initiiert und umgesetzt worden war. Ein ausführliches Telefonat hat es dann bestätigt: Aistleitner ist auf eigene Faust nach Ägypten gereist, hat dort Menschen auf der Straße und ExpertInnen zum aktuellen Stand nach der Revolution im Zuge des Arabischen Frühlings befragt und daraus eine beeindruckende Videoreportage namens *state of revolution* gedreht. Mit so einer Goldenen Nica und 14 fantastischen Auszeichnungen und Anerkennungen in unterschiedlichen Unterkategorien ist der Auftakt für den Paradigmenwechsel von „freestyle computing" auf CREATE YOUR WORLD in bester Form gelungen und der Samen gelegt für von Kindern und Jugendlichen geschaffenen Zukunftsvisionen, die weit mehr sind, also bloße Hirngespinste oder realitätsfremde Sehnsüchte. Diese jungen Menschen leben im Hier und Jetzt, wollen ihre politische, wirtschaftliche und gesellschaftliche Gegenwart verbessern und lassen sich trotz einer komplizierten Welt nicht vom kreativen Ausleben ihrer Wünsche und Träume abhalten.

developed its own special recipe to produce plastic from organic ingredients! In terms of ecological sustainability, it makes a striking statement and fits the motto CREATE YOUR WORLD exceptionally well. Arguments against awarding the Golden Nica to this project were related to the fact that how to produce bioplastics is no longer really a secret and, aesthetically speaking, this biologically degradable plastic still needs to be optimized.
The young woman who ultimately won this year's Golden Nica in the u19 category impressed the jury with her political astuteness and courage so greatly that at first the jury could hardly believe 18-year-old Agnes Aistleitner from Upper Austria had actually initiated and implemented this project by herself. But then an extended phone call confirmed matters: she had travelled to Egypt on her own, interviewed people on the streets, as well as experts, on the state of affairs after the revolution known as Arab Spring. She filmed everything and put together an impressive video reportage entitled *state of revolution*, which also includes footage of her online research.
With this year's Golden Nica and fourteen fantastic Awards of Distinction and Honorary Mentions in diverse subcategories, the shift in paradigms from "freestyle computing" to CREATE YOUR WORLD has been kicked off successfully. Moreover, seeds have been sown for visions of the future that are much more than mere flights of fancy or wistful reveries, out of touch with reality. These children and young people live in the here and now and want to improve present-day political, economic and social conditions. Even though the world is extremely complicated, they do not allow themselves to be held back when it comes to living out their dreams and desires.

state of revolution

Agnes Aistleitner / HBLA für Künstlerische Gestaltung, Linz

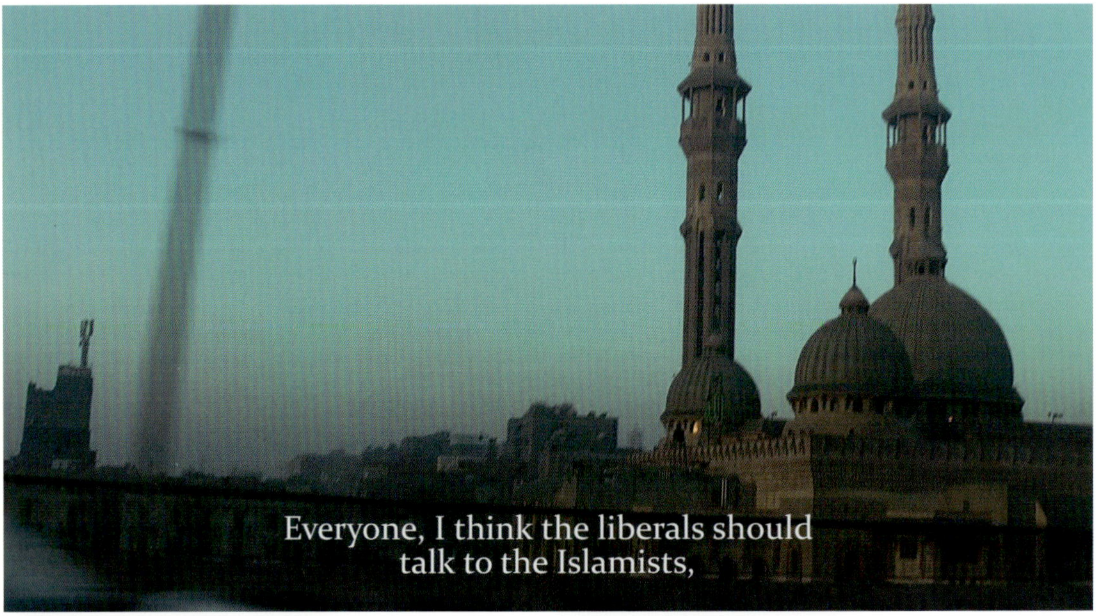

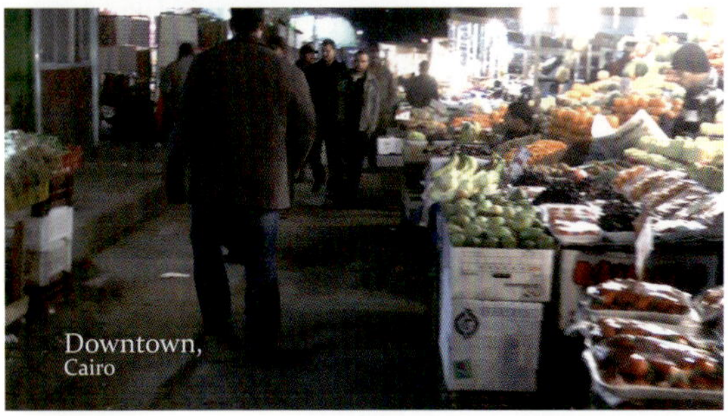

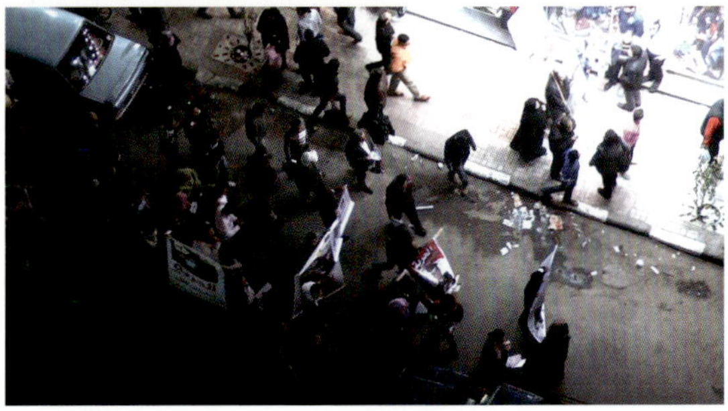

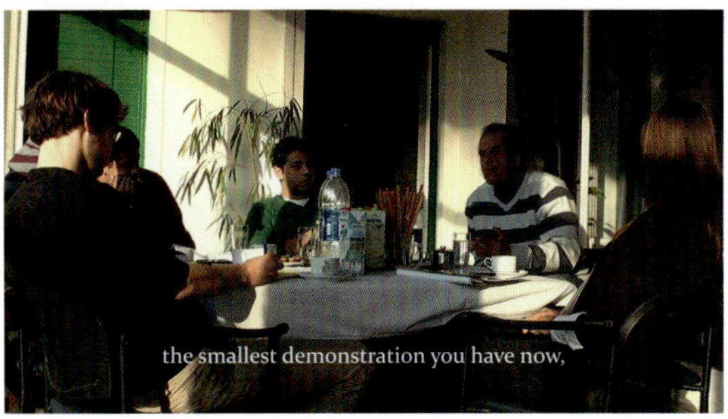

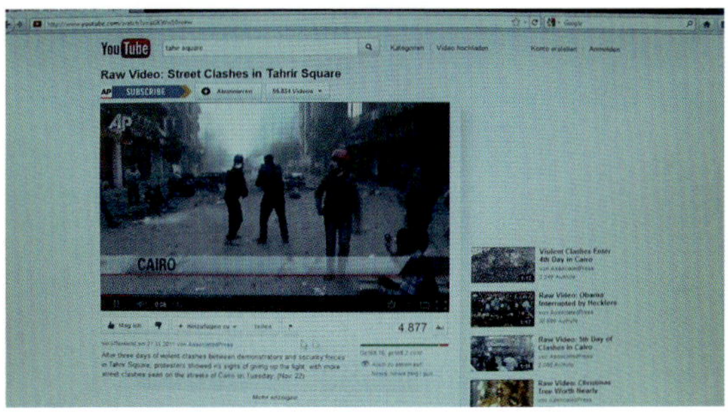

Im Jänner 2012, fast ein Jahr nach den größten Protesten in Ägypten, befinde ich mich auf einer Reise durch Kairo – auf den Spuren der Revolution. In einer Gesprächsrunde und in Begegnungen auf offener Straße versuche ich, Aspekte der politischen Ereignisse, des sogenannten „Arabischen Frühlings" in Ägypten, zu ermitteln.

Reale Konfrontation trifft auf Internet-Recherche

In meiner Videoarbeit ermittle ich Informationen zum Thema im Internet, diese Informationen treffen in meiner Arbeit auf den Realbezug.
Wie ist es wirklich? Der Rezipient meines Videos wird virtuell von der Observierung aus der Ferne zur Konfrontation vor Ort geführt.
In etwa 15 Minuten gebe ich Einblick in Eindrücke meiner Reise. Ich dokumentiere die Begegnung mit Studenten und einem Professor in einer Gesprächsrunde, in der über die Revolution gesprochen und philosophiert wird, aber auch die zufälligen Begegnungen auf der Straße, die einen Einblick in das facettenreiche Leben Kairos zeigen, werden festgehalten. Dazwischen stehen meine Recherchen am Computer, die mich als Beobachter aus der Ferne zeigen.
Ich gehe auf die Straße, um den Menschen zu begegnen: Ob durch die Märkte Kairos am Abend, auf der Straße oder am Tahrir-Platz, im Laufe des Videos treffe ich auf unterschiedliche Menschen, die unterschiedliche Meinungen zum Revolutionsgeschehen preisgeben.
In meiner Arbeit beleuchte ich verschiedene Aspekte des Geschehens und versuche, die Komplexität und Dynamik der Angelegenheit für den Betrachter zu verdeutlichen.

In January 2012, almost a year after the largest protests in Egypt, I found myself travelling around Cairo—seeking traces of the revolution. At a roundtable discussion and encounters on the street in Egypt I tried to identify different aspects of the political events of what is called the Arab Spring.

Real-life confrontation meets Internet research.

In my video I can be seen searching online for information on the subject. In my work, this information encounters real-life situations.
How are things really? Recipients of my video are taken virtually from observations made from afar to actual confrontations on site.
In about 15 minutes, I give viewers a few impressions of my journey. I document meeting students and a professor at a roundtable discussion during which they talk and philosophize about the revolution. I also record chance encounters on the street that give insight into the complexity of life in Cairo. In between, there is my research at the computer, which shows me as an observer from afar.
I go out into the streets to meet the people: whether I am wandering through Cairo's markets in the evening, along streets or around Tahrir Square, over the course of the video I meet different people who express a variety of opinions on the events of the revolution.
In my work, I illuminate different aspects of what happened and attempt to reveal the complexity and dynamics of the matter to the viewer.

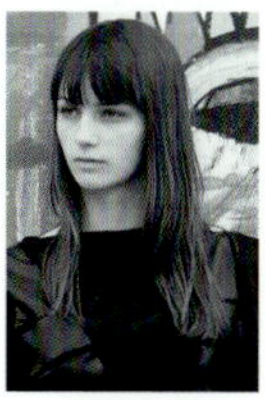

Agnes Aistleitner, born in 1993, began attending the HBLA for Artistic Design, a college preparatory school in Linz, in 2007 and graduated in June 2012. She spent a semester in Japan in 2010. Since 2009, she has completed a number of internships in the arts as well as fashion and public relations in Vienna, Los Angeles and New York. In 2012 she launched Globalcitizen, an organization that develops fashion, art and events. **Agnes Aistleitner**, geb. 1993, besuchte seit 2007 die HBLA für künstlerische Gestaltung in Linz, die sie im Juni 2012 abgeschlossen hat. 2010 verbrachte sie ein Auslandssemester in Japan. Seit 2009 hat sie zahlreiche Praktika im Kunst-, Mode- und PR-Bereich in Wien, Los Angeles und New York absolviert. Im Jahr 2012 gründet sie die Organisation „Globalcitizen", in deren Rahmen Mode, Kunst und Veranstaltungen entstehen.

BioBookCover
BG/BRG Stainach

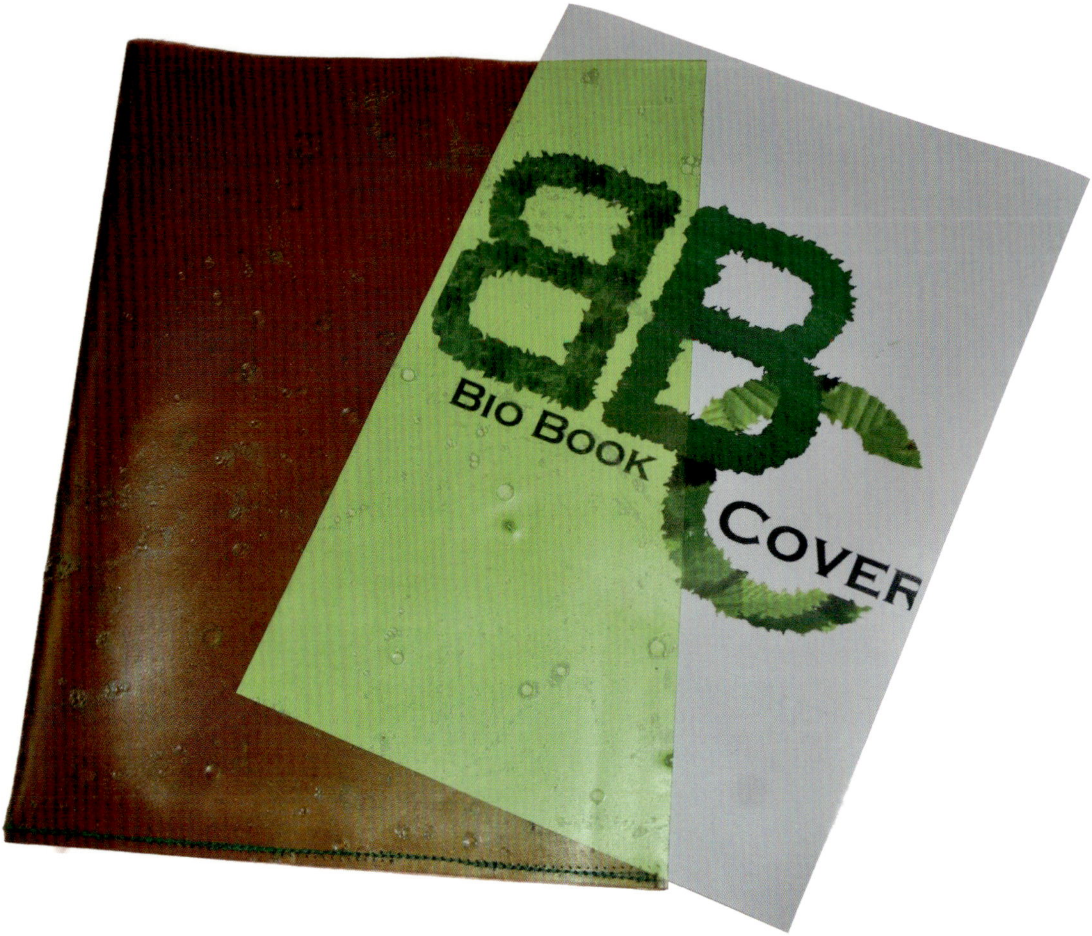

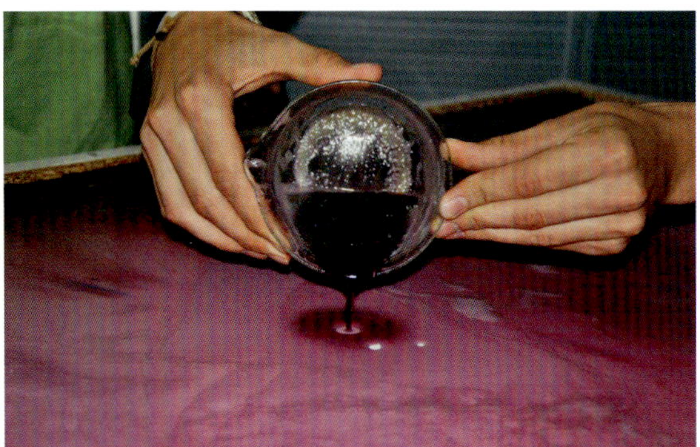

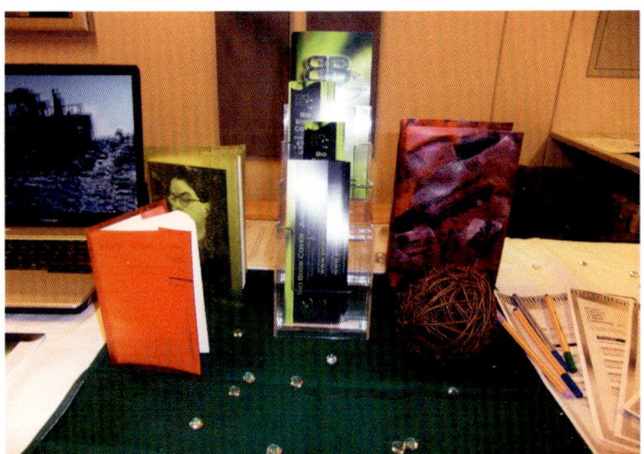

Gummibärchen statt Plastik. So lautet die Antwort unserer Projektgruppe „BioBookCover" auf das aktuelle Plastikproblem. Wir suchten nach einer umweltfreundlichen Alternative zu herkömmlichen Buch- und Heftumschlägen in unserer unmittelbaren Umgebung, der Schule, wo wir unglaubliche Müllberge aus Kunststoff orteten. Als Projektgruppe „BioBookCover" fanden wir eine gut verdauliche Lösung: Mit Unterstützung der Lehrer für Wirtschaft & Recht und Chemie entwickelten wir in einer langen Forschungs- und Entwicklungsphase eine innovative Antwort auf das Plastikproblem:
Wir produzieren und vermarkten bunte Buch- und Heftumschläge sowie die Schutzhülle „Cortex" aus kompostierbarem Bioplastik, hergestellt aus pflanzlichen Komponenten. Wie Gummibärchen bestehen auch die Öko-Hüllen aus Wasser, Kartoffelstärke, Gelatine und Lebensmittelfarben. Attraktive Designs in Veilchenfarben, Waldmeistergrün, Kirschrot oder Sonnengelb machen unsere Biocovers seit einiger Zeit zu einem Must-have für alle Bücherliebhaber, die unserer Umwelt etwas Gutes tun wollen.
Um unsere Idee weiter zu professionalisieren, erarbeiten wir derzeit ein unternehmerisches Konzept in Zusammenarbeit mit Innolab von Campus02 Graz. Unser erklärtes Ziel ist es, einen Unternehmenspartner in Österreich zu finden, um in die industrielle Fertigung unserer Biohüllen einsteigen zu können.

Jellybabies instead of plastic. That's our BioBookCover project group's answer to the global problem of plastic. We wanted to find an environmentally friendly alternative for the customary protective book and notebook covers in our immediate surroundings at school, where we had discovered unbelievable heaps of plastic rubbish. So we, the BioBookCover project group, tried to develop a good biodegradable solution. With the support of our teachers for business & law and chemistry, and in a long phase of research and development, we have found an innovative answer to the plastic problem:
We manufacture and market colorful covers for books and notebooks, as well as "Cortex" folders. These are all made of compostable bioplastic that has been produced entirely from vegetable ingredients. Like jellybabies, these ecological covers are made out of water, potato starch, gelatin and food coloring. Attractive designs in the colors of violet, woodruff green, cherry red or sunny yellow have made our bio covers a must-have for all book lovers who also want to do something good for the environment.
To pursue the idea on a more professional basis, we are now working on a business concept in cooperation with Innolab at Campus02 Graz. We have made it our goal to find a business partner in Austria as this would enable us to begin producing our organic covers industrially.

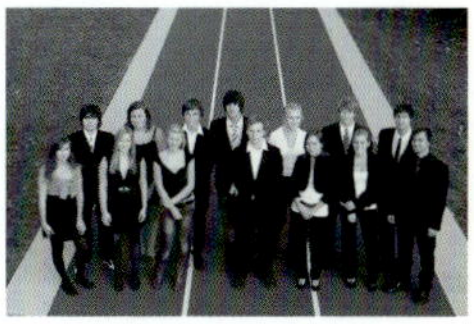

The BioBookCover project group: 14 students, specializing in business & law, from the 8B und 8C at the BG/BRG Stainach, a college preparatory school in Styria. **BioBookCover-Projektgruppe:** Die 14 SchülerInnen besuchen die 8B und 8C-Klasse des BG/BRG Stainach in der Steiermark mit dem Schwerpunkt Wirtschaft und Recht.

Bin Baum mit 2 Stämmen

Stephan Friedl, Asya Serimoglu, Anita Simic, Daniel Wieczorek, Lorena Zorkic / RadioPoly, PTS 3, Vienna

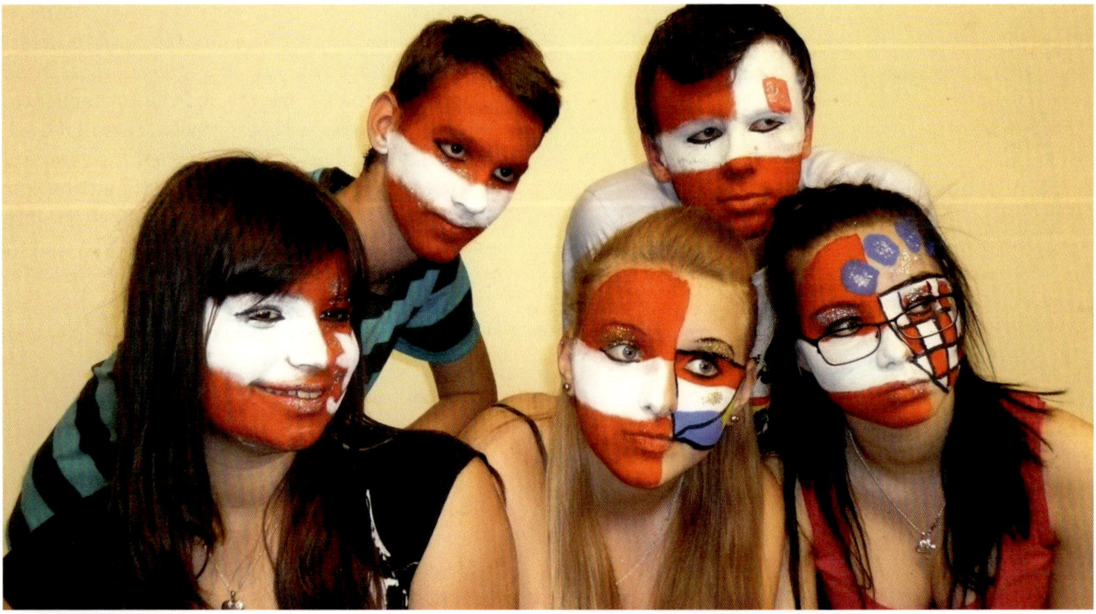

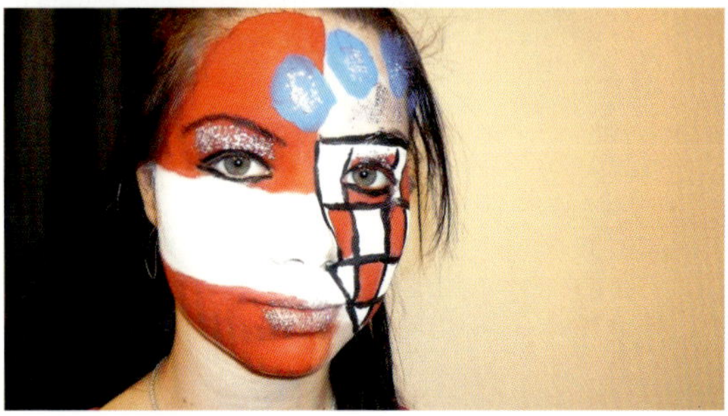

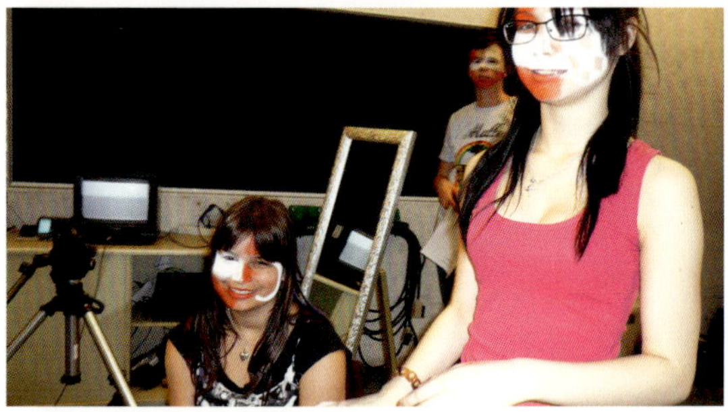

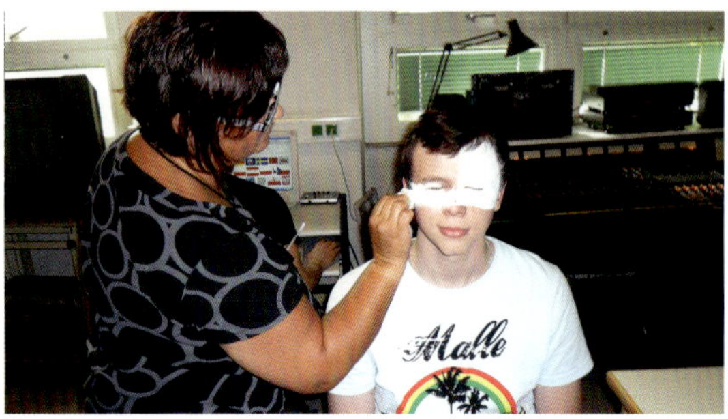

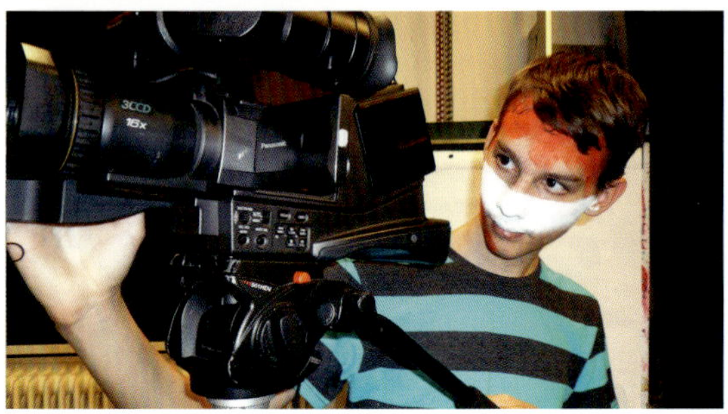

Bin Baum mit 2 Stämmen entstand nach intensiver Auseinandersetzung mit unserer Herkunft als Jugendliche mit nichtdeutscher Muttersprache im Rahmen einer Radiosendung von RadioPoly.
Ausgangspunkt war ein Interview, das unser Projektleiter, Helmut Hostnig, als Audiobrief aus Tetovo in Mazedonien mitgebracht hat, in dem sich zwei junge Albanerinnen, die lange Zeit in Österreich verbracht haben, darüber beklagen, dass sie sich in ihrer Heimat nicht mehr wirklich zu Hause fühlen. Das hat uns daran erinnert, dass auch in uns zwei Herzen schlagen: eines für das Land, aus dem wir oder unsere Eltern kommen, und das andere für Österreich, wo wir leben, zur Schule gehen und unsere Zukunft sehen.
Mit dem Videogedicht, dessen Bilder in knappen drei Stunden entstanden sind und das einen Text zur Grundlage hat, den uns der Projektleiter auf den Leib geschrieben und dann die Mutter von Asya ins Gesicht geschminkt hat, wollen wir aufzeigen, dass Integration trotz Migration gelingen kann, wenn unsere multikulturelle Herkunft nicht als Bedrohung, sondern als Bereicherung verstanden wird.
Wen ein detaillierteres Making-of dieser Gedichtvisualisierung interessiert, der sei auf unseren Blog verwiesen: *http://radiopoly.wordpress.com*

We—a group of young people whose mother tongue is not German—created *Bin Baum mit 2 Stämmen* (I'm a Tree with Two Trunks) after intensively exploring our origins and the consequences within the framework of a show at RadioPoly.
Our starting point was an interview that our project leader, Helmut Hostnig, had brought back in the form of an audio brief from Tetovo in Macedonia. In it two young Albanians, who had spent a great deal of time in Austria, complain that they don't really feel at home in their country of origin anymore. That reminded us that we also have two hearts beating in us: one for the country that we or our parents came from, and the other for Austria—the place where we live , go to school and see our future.
We filmed the images for our video poem in just under three hours. It is based on a text that our project leader wrote especially for us. Asya's mother then made up our faces to fit it all. With our video we want to show that, despite migration, integration can succeed, that is, if our multicultural backgrounds are not seen as a threat but as an enrichment.

RadioPoly is a pilot project of BMUKK (Austria's Ministry for Education, Arts and Culture) in cooperation with the Media Center Vienna and Meiselgasse Polytechnical School in Vienna's third district. Since 2010, project leader Helmut Hostnig and his teaching staff, Gabriela Pranieß and Florian Danheldem, have supervised the project with the aim of familiarizing young people with radio as a medium of communication. **RadioPoly** ist ein Pilotprojekt des BMUKK in Kooperation mit dem Medienzentrum Wien und der Polytechnischen Schule Meiselgasse im dritten Wiener Gemeindebezirk und wird seit 2010 vom Projektleiter, Helmut Hostnig, und seinen pädagogischen BetreuerInnen, Gabriela Pranieß und Florian Danhel, mit dem Anspruch geführt, Jugendliche mit Radio als einem Medium der Kommunikation vertraut zu machen.

Balancing Robot

Christian Grill, Magdalena Kranjec, Sonja Stankovic, Maximilian Tabelander, Sasa Vasiljkovic / NMS-Telfs-Dr.-Aloys-Weissenbach

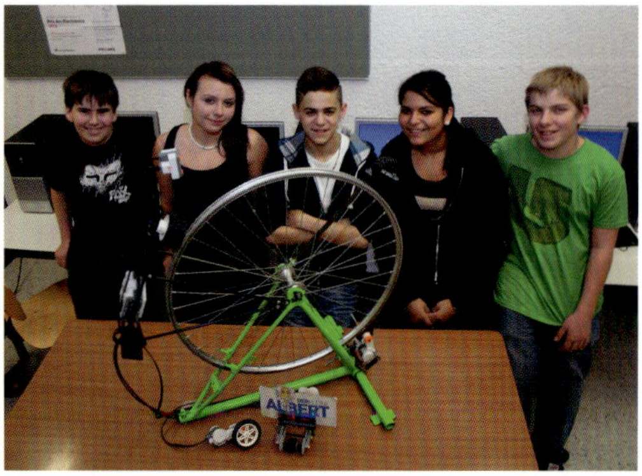

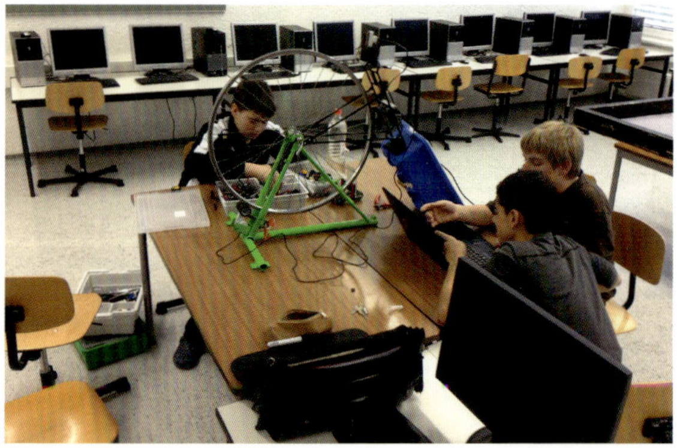

It all began with Sasa, when he found the back wheel of a bike. He immediately had the idea to design a project for the competition, and so asked Mr. Bellony, our teacher and expert on such matters, if he would have the time to work on a project with him. Mr. Bellony agreed to help and asked Sasa to find more students who wanted to participate. Sasa set out to do so, and before long Christian, Maximilian, Magdalena and Sonja joined the team. After thinking it over for quite a while, we came up with the idea of having our robot control a motor that would move the rim of the old bike wheel back and forth. On top of the rim, we decided to position a toy vehicle that was not supposed to roll off. Using the values measured by an ultrasound sensor and algorithms, the motor is made to rotate the wheel in such a way that the car doesn't fall off.

After the old wheel had been adapted to our purposes, we added a stop arm, an assortment of toy vehicles for the rim and some holders for the motor. Then we mounted the grey Lego motor and constructed a braking system that worked in both directions. Next we changed the program so that the motor did not always run at full power, which enabled its performance to be adjusted in accordance with the distance between the small vehicle and the sensor. In the end we turned our *Balancing Robot* into a game of skill that you can control by means of a small external steering wheel.

Begonnen hat alles mit Sasa, als dieser im EDV-Raum ein Hinterradteil entdeckte. Sofort kam es ihm in den Sinn, ein Projekt für u19 zu gestalten, und er fragte auch gleich unseren Herrn Fachlehrer Bellony, ob er Zeit hätte, bei dem Projekt mitzumachen. Herr Bellony sagte zu und beauftragte Sasa, noch Schüler zu suchen, die sich beteiligen wollen. Sasa machte sich auf die Suche und sofort waren Christian, Maximilian, Magdalena und Sonja dabei. Nach langem Überlegen kamen wir auf die Idee, dass unser Roboter einen Motor steuern könnte, der dann die Felge des alten Fahrradteils hin und her bewegt. Ganz oben auf der Felge sollte sich ein Fahrzeug befinden, das nicht herunterrollen darf. Über die Messwerte eines Ultraschallsensors und einer mathematischen Logik wird die Radfelge so mit dem Motor gedreht, dass das Fahrzeug nicht herunterfällt.

Nachdem das bestehende alte Rad für unsere Zwecke bearbeitet worden war, fügten wir einen Stopparm, verschiedene Felgenfahrzeuge und Motorhaltungen hinzu. Dann bauten wir den grauen Motor von Lego ein und errichteten beidseitige Stoppvorrichtungen. Als nächstes änderten wir das Programm so um, dass nicht immer die volle Energie am Motor ist, sondern die Motorleistung sich mit dem Abstand zwischen kleinem Wagen und Sensor ändert. Zum Schluss bauten wir den *Balancing Robot* auch noch zu einem Geschicklichkeitsspiel um, das man durch ein zusätzliches Lenkrad steuern kann.

The girls working on this project were all in the 4th form at the secondary school NMS-Telfs-Dr.-Aloys-Weissenbach and specializing in languages. The boys were all in the 4th form and specializing in biotechnology. Die an diesem Projekt beteiligten Mädchen besuchen die 4. Klasse der NMS-Telfs-Dr.-Aloys-Weissenbach mit dem Schwerpunkt „Sprache", die Buben gehen in die 4. Klasse mit dem Schwerpunkt „BioTeC".

Zukunftswürfel

Kindergarten Auwiesenstraße 60

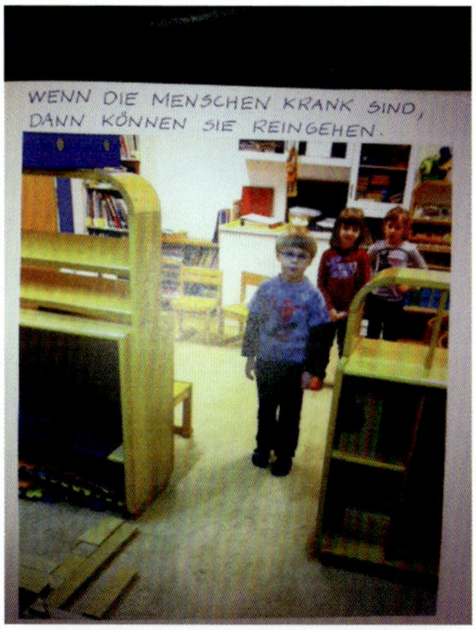

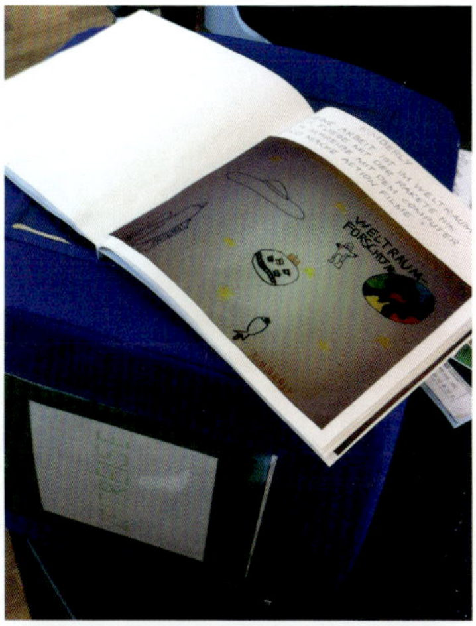

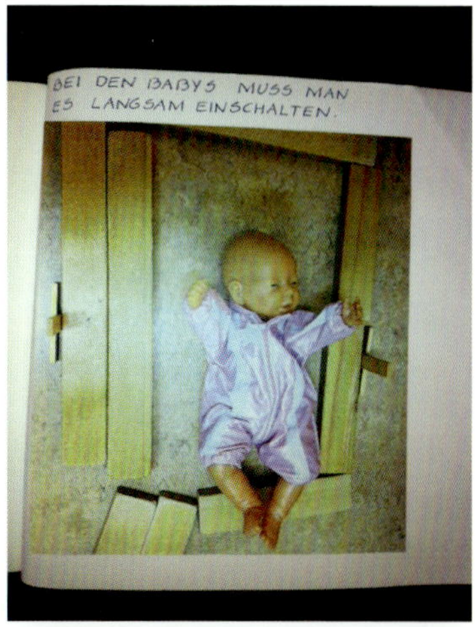

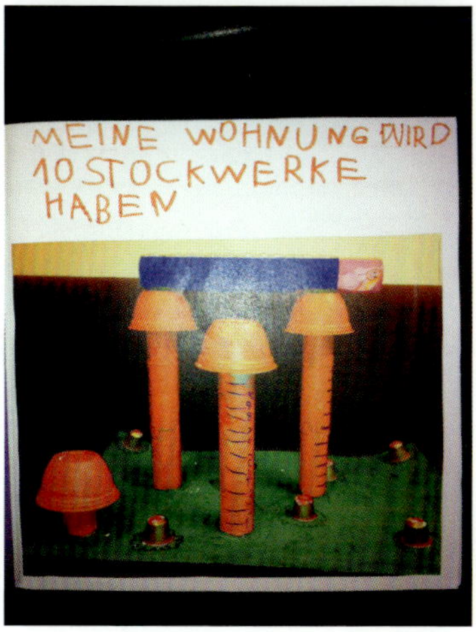

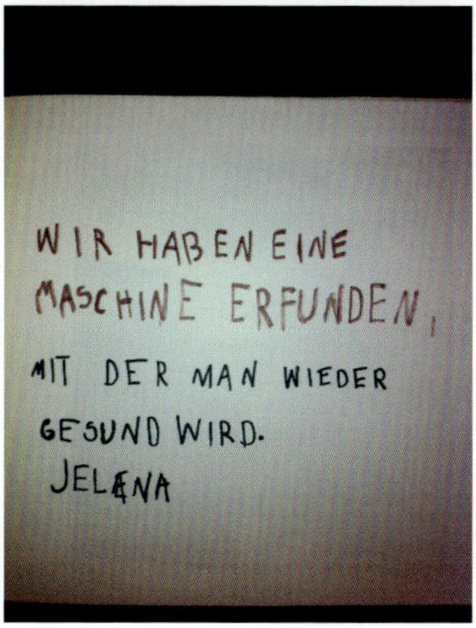

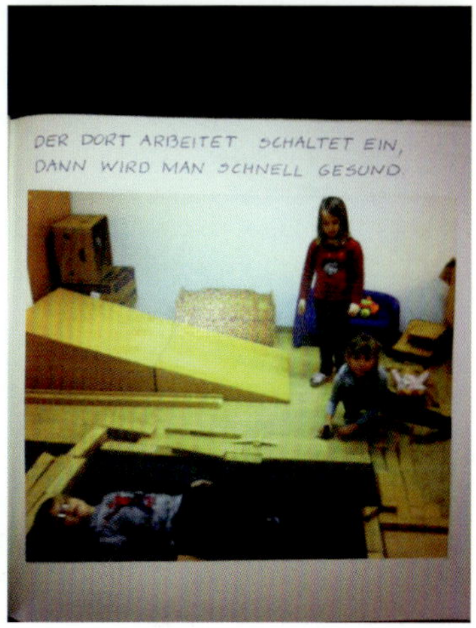

„Wir wollen berühmt werden!". Das war der große Wunsch der Schulanfänger, den sie im Rahmen einer Kinderkonferenz äußerten. Aus diesem Grund entschlossen wir uns für die Teilnahme am Projekt u19, bei welchem die Kinder eigene Zukunftsideen entwickeln und präsentieren können. In den letzten Wochen arbeiteten wir nun intensiv an der Entwicklung interessanter Ideen und Erfindungen. Daraus ergaben sich schlussendlich sechs Themenbereiche, die auf jede Seite des Würfels aufgeteilt wurden und in kleinen Heften anzusehen sind: gelb – Gesundheit; orange – Essen; blau – Arbeit; lila – Wohnung; grün – Zeitreise; rot – Zeitdauer.

"We want to be famous!" At a children's conference, we school beginners said this was our greatest wish. And so we decided to participate in the u19 competition, where kids can develop their own ideas for the future. We have worked intensively on developing interesting ideas. We ended up with six topics that we distributed around a cube, one on each side. We put together little notebooks on these topics that people can look at: yellow for health, orange for food, blue for work, purple for home, green for time travel and red for duration.

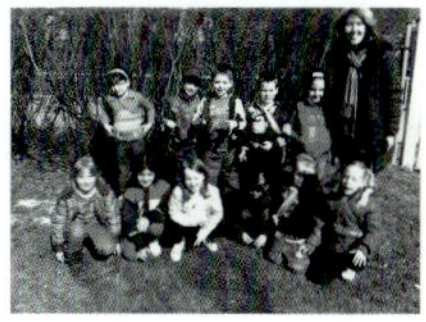

There are 18 school beginners from the Auwiesenstraße Kindergarten in Linz in our project group. Die Projektgruppe besteht aus 18 SchulanfängerInnen des Kindergartens Auwiesenstraße in Linz.

ConnectIn(g)

Dino Grgic, Magnus Reinstadler, Franz Reinstadler, Robin von Mendel / BORG Gastein

The project *ConnectIn(g)* was developed within two weeks. And although it is a school project, the contents were all created outside school. The animation *ConnectIn(g)* is an advertising spot for a fictional future product that allows you to control just about everything with your thoughts. In a relaxed manner, the spot deals with the pros and cons of such an invention. For instance, it criticizes data surveillance, which today already borders on the unacceptable. With the exaggerated example of an invention that would involve even greater amounts of data and more intimate details, we wanted to draw attention to the problem of being careless in the way we handle data. The characters, the texts and all the objects in the video were made with Autodesk Maya; the logos were produced with Adobe Illustrator and Adobe Photoshop. It was then edited with Adobe Premiere. Due to the enormous pressure of having to get everything done for the competition within two weeks alongside school, there are still a few errors in the video that we unfortunately didn't have time to correct.

Das Projekt *ConnectIn(g)* ist innerhalb von zwei Wochen entstanden. Obwohl es ein Schulprojekt ist, wurden im Grunde alle Inhalte außerhalb der Schulzeit erstellt. Die Animation *ConnectIn(g)* ist ein Werbespot für ein fiktives Zukunftsprodukt, welches einem ermöglicht, so gut wie alles per Gedanken zu steuern. Auf lockere Art und Weise soll sich der Werbespot mit dem Pro und Kontra einer solchen Erfindung beschäftigen. So wird zum Beispiel die Überwachung der Daten, die auch jetzt schon grenzwertige Bereiche erlangt hat, kritisiert. Anhand des übertriebenen Beispiels einer Erfindung, bei der weitaus mehr und intimere Daten anfallen, soll auf die Problematik eines leichtfertigen Umgangs mit Daten aufmerksam gemacht werden. Die Charaktere, die Texte, alle Gegenstände, die im Video vorkommen wurden mit Autodesk Maya erstellt, und die Logos wurden mit Adobe Illustrator und Adobe Photoshop erstellt. Mit Adobe Premiere wurde alles zusammengeschnitten. Auf Grund des hohen Zeitdrucks, innerhalb von zwei Wochen neben dem Schulalltag das Projekt rechtzeitig für den Wettbewerb fertig zu kriegen, sind noch ein paar Fehler in dem Video, die leider nicht mehr ausgebessert werden konnten.

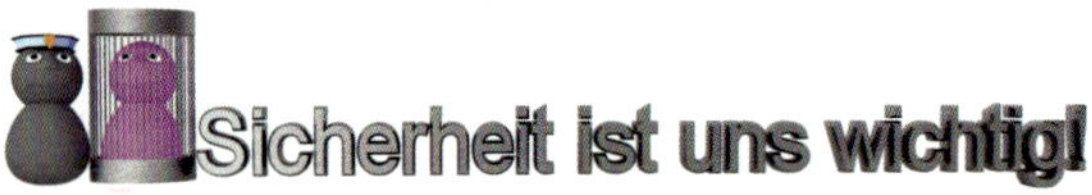

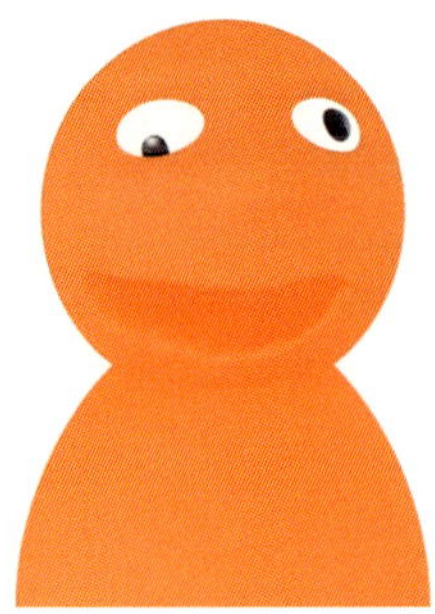

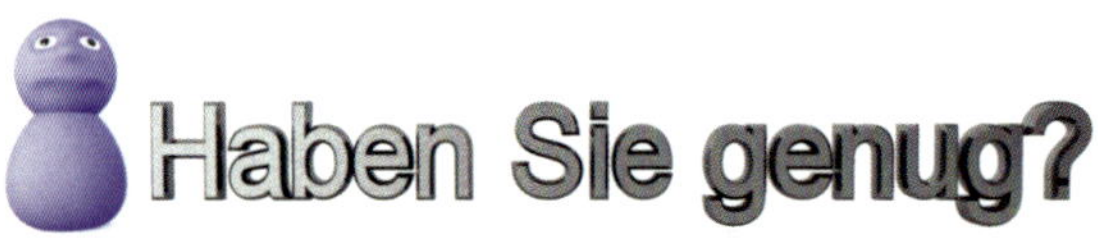

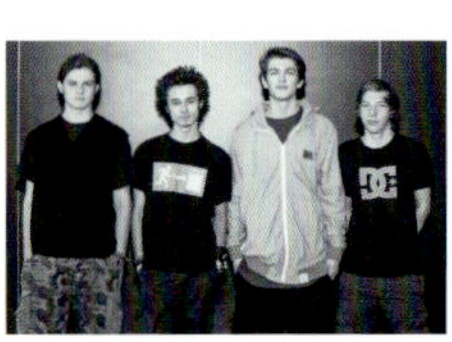

The four students—**Dino Grgic, Magnus Reinstadler, Franz Reinstadler and Robin von Mendel**—who worked on this project are in the 7th form of the Bundesoberstufenrealgymnasium Bad Hofgastein, a college preparatory school with an emphasis on the arts. Die vier Schüler **Dino Grgic, Magnus Reinstadler, Franz Reinstadler, Robin von Mendel** besuchen gemeinsam die 7. Klasse des Bundesoberstufenrealgymnasiums Bad Hofgastein mit musisch-kreativem Schwerpunkt.

Das Superhirn

BG Wasagasse

Die Idee zu einem gemeinsamen Filmprojekt mit Stefan Ludwig und der damaligen 3E entstand schon ein Schuljahr vor der tatsächlichen Realisierung. Stefan Ludwig hat als Filmemacher und Drehbuchautor schon viel mit Kindern und Jugendlichen gearbeitet. Wir überlegten uns einen Arbeitstitel und einen inhaltlichen Ausgangspunkt, der „Meine Stadt der Zukunft" war. Unser Ziel und die Aufgabenstellung an die SchülerInnen war es, einen Kurzfilm mit selbst gebauten Kulissen und realen Figuren zu machen.

Die SchülerInnen haben in Teams von 4 bis 5 Personen ihre Geschichte entwickelt, dazu die Hauptfigur und die Kulissen entworfen und gebaut. In vielen Gesprächen wurden die Geschichten gesammelt und zu einem Hauptgeschehen zusammengesetzt. So wurde aus den einzelnen unabhängigen Ideen eine zusammenhängende, einheitliche Story der ganzen Klasse, die in ein Drehbuch umgeschrieben wurde.

Die Kulissen wurden im Rahmen des BE-Unterrichtes dreidimensional gebaut und aufwändig gestaltet. An zwei langen Drehtagen wurden auf der Bühne des Festsaals der Schule die Kulissen abgefilmt und die Szenen vor einem Green-Screen gedreht, vertont und synchronisiert. Stefan Ludwig hat den Film abschließend geschnitten und die Endbearbeitung gemacht. Das fertige Filmprojekt bekam von der Klasse einstimmig den bezeichnenden Titel: *Das Superhirn.*

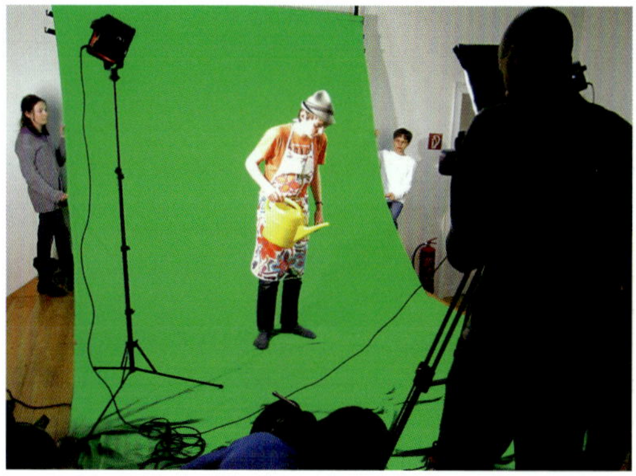

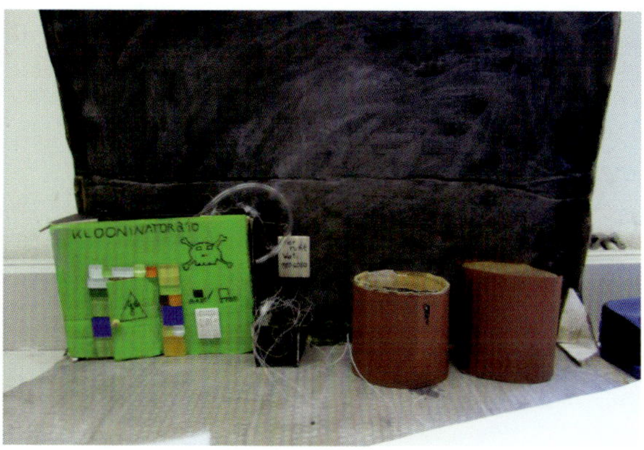

The students of the former 3E had the idea to do this film project with Stefan Ludwig a year before its actual realization. As a filmmaker and screenwriter, Stefan Ludwig was already very experienced in working with children and young people. We thought up a working title and figured out a starting point for the contents: "My City of the Future". The goal and our task was to make a short film with sets that we would build ourselves and real figures.

In teams of four to five people, the students developed stories and then worked on main figures and designed the scenery. In many discussions, the stories were collected and put together into a main plot. This meant that out of our many independent and individual ideas, a coherent story was developed for the whole class and turned into a screenplay.

The three-dimensional sets were constructed and elaborately decorated during our art lessons. On two long days of shooting, we filmed the sets on the stage of our school auditorium and then shot the scenes with the actors in front of a green screen. Afterwards we set it all to music and synchronized it. When we were done, Stefan Ludwig did the editing and post-production work. After finishing the project, it received its very telling title: *Das Superhirn* (The Superbrain).

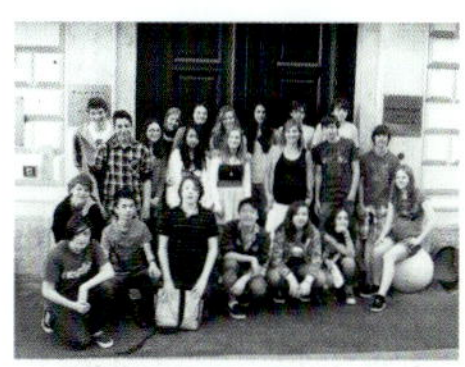

26 students from the **BG9** (Wasagymnasium), a college preparatory school in Vienna's ninth district, were in the 3E when they did this project. During their art classes, they realized the film project *Das Superhirn* under the supervision of filmmaker Stefan Ludwig and Marlis Cermak, and with funding from the parents' association and KulturKontakt Vienna. Die 26 SchülerInnen in Wien besuchten zum Projektdurchführungszeitraum die 3E des Wasagymnasiums in Wien 9. Im Rahmen des BE-Unterrichtes wurde mit der finanziellen Unterstützung des Elternvereins und Kultur Kontakt Wien das Filmprojekt *Das Superhirn* unter der Leitung des Filmemachers Stefan Ludwig und Marlis Cermak realisiert.

Flat Water Bottle / Evolution of Animation

Michael Schmidl

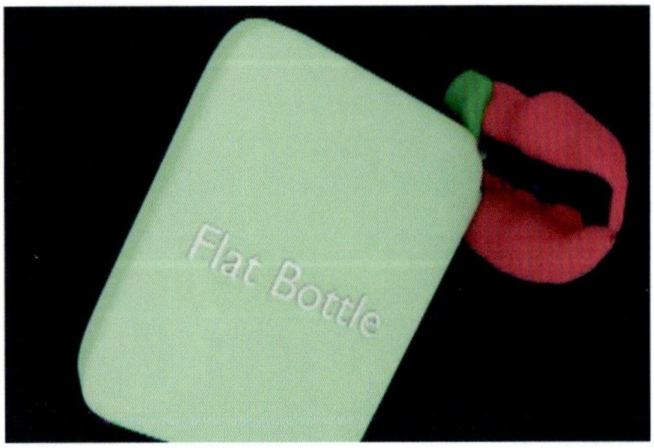

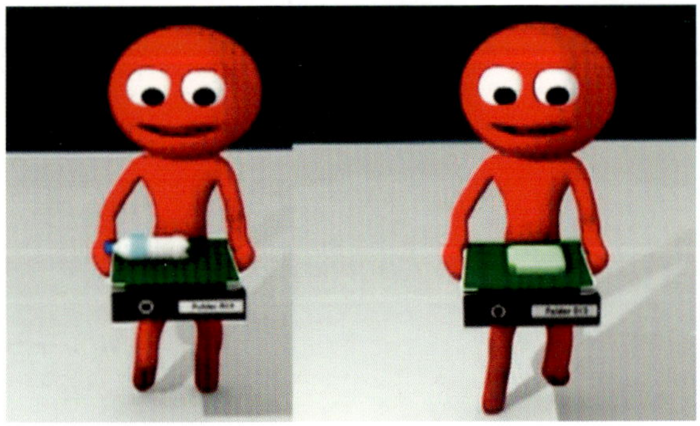

My advertising spot *Flat Water Bottle* revolves around presenting a flat plastic bottle. I produced the animation with Blender 3D and then did the editing and post-production work with Pinnacle Studio.
My film *Evolution of Animation* is about the history of animation and film. Over the course of the story you always see the same character—a simple stick figure with eyes. The film begins with a stop-motion animation that has been shot in black-and-white and in which the character always keeps walking on towards the right. After the figure disappears behind a wall, it reappears as a cartoon character. I drew this 2D animation (initially in black-and-white) first by hand and then used Toon Boom to animate and composite it. In this black-and-white 2D world, the figure continues walking until music suddenly comes out of a loud speaker—this represents the arrival of sound film. Next, as the figure walks on, a brush sweeps across the picture and suddenly everything is in color—symbolizing the beginnings of color film. The character continues on and then disappears behind a wall again. When it reappears, it is in a 3D world (I made the 3D section of the film with Blender 3D). Afterwards, the figure disappears behind a wall again. From this point on, the animation is in red/blue 3D (for which you need your own real 3D glasses). Then the figure hurls a pair of glasses at the camera and the picture goes black. At the end of the film, I made a bright white light appear—this stands for how technology is constantly being developed further.

In meinem Werbe-Film *Flat Water Bottle* geht es um die Präsentation einer flachen Plastikflasche. Die Animation habe ich in Blender 3D gemacht und anschließend im Programm Pinnacle Studio nachbearbeitet und zusammengeschnitten.
In meinem Film *Evolution of Animation* geht es um die Geschichte der Animation und des Films. Im Laufe der Geschichte kommt immer der gleiche Charakter vor – ein einfaches Strichmännchen mit Augen. Es beginnt mit einer Stop-Motion-Animation, die in schwarz-weiß aufgenommen ist, in dem der Charakter immer weiter nach rechts geht. Nachdem die Figur hinter einer Mauer verschwindet, kommt sie als Zeichentrick-Charakter wieder heraus. Die 2D-Animation (anfangs auch in schwarz-weiß) habe ich zuerst mit der Hand gezeichnet und dann in dem Programm Toon Boom Animate bearbeitet. In der schwarz-weißen 2D-Welt geht die Figur weiter, und plötzlich kommt aus einem Lautsprecher Musik – das soll für die Entstehung des Tonfilms stehen. Dann fährt ein Pinsel über das Bild, und plötzlich ist das Bild in Farbe, um die Entstehung des Farbfilms zu zeigen. Dann geht der Charakter weiter und verschwindet wieder hinter einer Wand. Als er hervorkommt, ist er in einer 3D-Welt (den 3D-Teil habe ich in Blender 3D gemacht). Anschließend verschwindet er wieder hinter einer Mauer, und danach ist die Animation in rot/blau 3D (mit echter 3D-Brille). Dann wirft die Figur eine Brille vor die Kamera, und das Bild wird schwarz. Am Schluss des Films habe ich ein weißes Licht erscheinen lassen, um zu zeigen, dass sich die Technik immer weiter entwickeln wird.

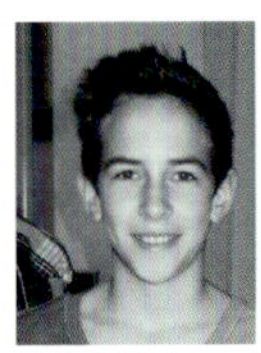

Michael Schmidl, born in 1998, is in the 8th form at a college preparatory school, the BRG 14 on the Linzerstraße in Vienna. He enjoys working on animations and films and would one day like to be an animation specialist or a film director. In 2010, he won the u14 non-cash prize for his animated film *Vom Himmel gefallen*. **Michael Schmidl**, geb. 1998, besucht zurzeit die 8. Schulstufe des BRG 14 Linzerstraße in Wien. Am liebsten arbeitet er an Animationen und Filmen und möchte später Animator oder Regisseur werden. 2010 hat er bereits mit seinem Film *Vom Himmel gefallen* den u14-Sachpreis bei u19 gewonnen.

Fragment Planet

Simon Stix

http://www.indiedb.com/games/fragment-planet

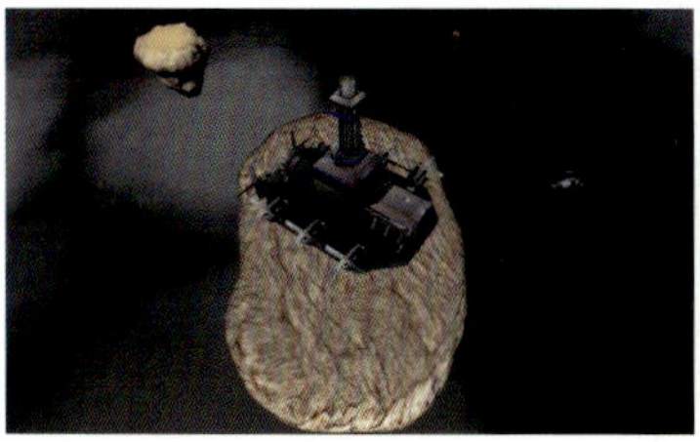
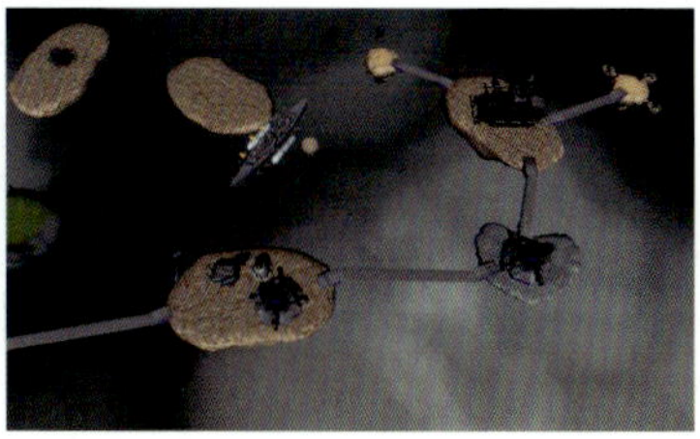
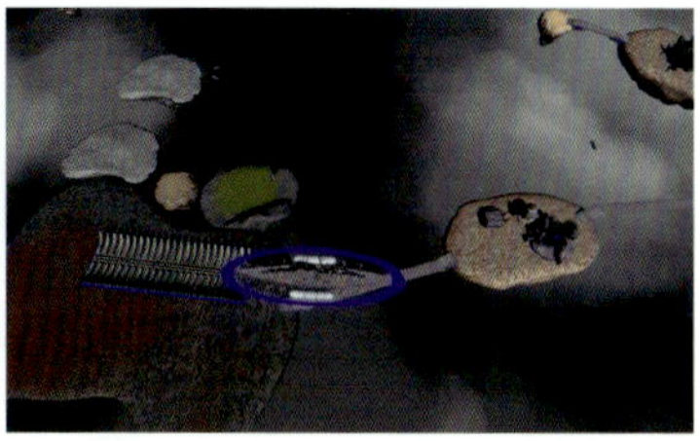

Fragment Planet ist ein Real-Time-Strategy-Game. Im Gegensatz zu den gängigen Strategiespielen habe ich das klassische Terrain durch fliegende Inseln ersetzt. Man kann entweder im Survival-Modus im Team gegen gegnerische Angriffswellen, oder im normalen Modus gegeneinander kämpfen. Ein Tutorial ist im Spiel integriert, allerdings ist es englisch, da ich das Spiel im Internet veröffentlichen möchte. Am Ende der Sommerferien 2011 habe ich mit der Entwicklung von *Fragment Planet* begonnen. Insgesamt habe ich fast 2.500 Stunden an dem Spiel gearbeitet.

Nachdem die Erde bei einem Experiment, auf der Suche nach einer neuen, unerschöpflichen Energiequelle, zerstört wurde, bekämpfen sich die Überlebenden, um fliegende Inseln zu erobern und so ihr eigenes Fortbestehen zu sichern. Mithilfe von zurückentwickelten Flugmaschinen, im Steampunk-Stil, erweitern sie ihre Basen und bauen Armeen, um den Vorstoß ihrer Kontrahenten zu verhindern. Die Wegwerfgesellschaft und das Verschwendertum vor der Katastrophe haben zur Vernichtung der gesamten Erde geführt. Die Überlebenden sind gezwungen, einen neuen naturverbundenen Lebensstil zu entwickeln, doch manchen fällt das schwerer als anderen. Im Laufe der zukünftigen Entwicklung werde ich zwei weitere Fraktionen einführen, wobei eine den alten Lebensstil vollständig weiterlebt und so ein Risiko für alle anderen darstellt. Noch mehr als heutzutage sind die letzten Menschen verpflichtet zu lernen, mit der Natur im Einklang zu leben.

Fragment Planet is a real-time strategy game. In contrast to the usual strategy games, I replaced the classic terrain with flying islands. You can either fight in survival mode in a team against waves of hostile attacks or in normal mode against each other. A tutorial is integrated into the game, though it's in English as I want to put the game on the Internet. At the end of summer vacation 2011, I began developing *Fragment Planet*. All in all, I have worked almost 2500 hours on the game.

After the Earth has been destroyed during an experiment looking for a new and inexhaustible source of energy, the survivors fight to conquer flying islands and so secure their own existence. With the aid of old-fashioned planes in steampunk style, the survivors expand their bases and build armies so as to hinder the advance of their opponents. Before the catastrophe, the throwaway society and its wastefulness had led to the destruction of the entire Earth. Survivors have been forced to develop a new lifestyle that is in touch with nature, though for some this is harder than for others. In the future when I develop this game further, I plan to introduce two more parties: the one will adhere totally to the old lifestyle and so pose a risk to the others. Even more so than today, these last human beings need to learn to live in harmony with nature.

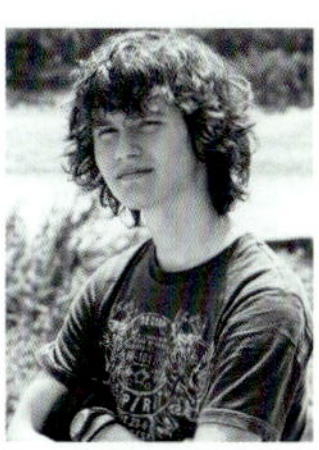

Simon Stix, born in 1994, is attending the BRG Fadingerstraße, a college preparatory school in Linz. Thanks to the project "Schüler/innen an die Unis", he was able to study computer science at the Johannes Kepler University for a semester in 2009. For years now, he has been exploring different computer-related fields in his free time, including programming, 3D modeling and the composing of soundtracks. These activities are his hobbies, alongside computer games, of course. Though in addition to being great pastimes, they are a source of inspiration for his work. **Simon Stix**, geb. 1994, besucht das BRG Fadingerstraße in Linz und hat 2009 ein Semester lang durch das Projekt „Schüler/innen an die Unis" an der Johannes Kepler Universität Informatik studiert. In seiner Freizeit setzt er sich seit Jahren mit vielen Bereichen am Computer auseinander, u. a. Programmieren, 3D Modellieren und Soundtrack komponieren. Seine Hobbies sind die oben genannten Aktivitäten und selbstverständlich Computerspielen, sowohl als Freizeitbeschäftigung, als auch als Inspirationsquelle für die eigene Arbeit.

handsome

Felix Brandstetter, Gregor Eckmayr, Valentina Heinisch, William Mikulaschek, Anna Neubauer, Killian Sochor / C.LOUD

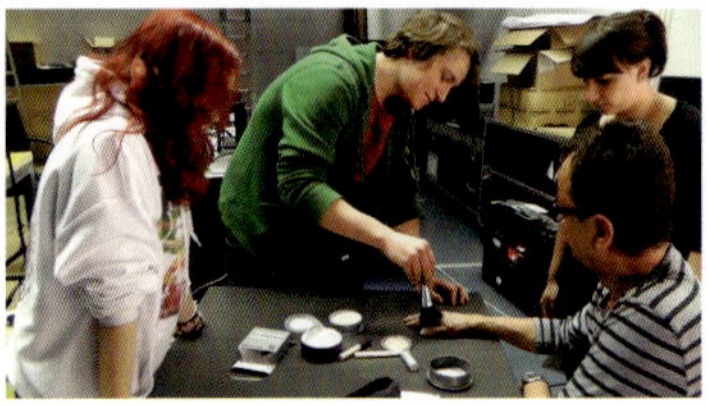

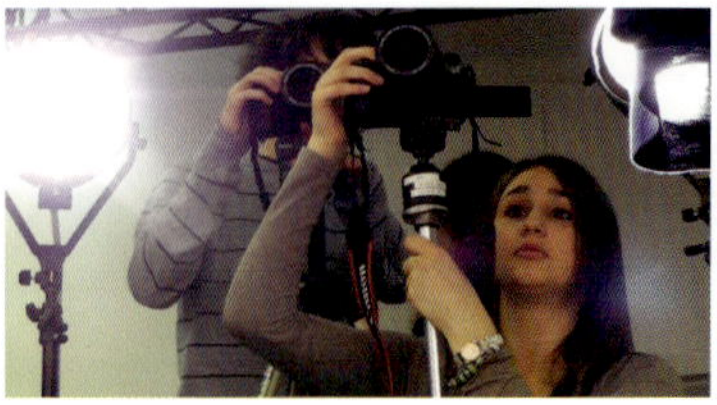

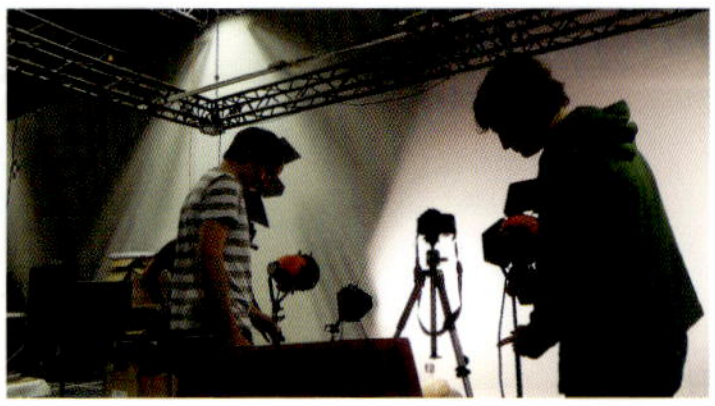

While working on the video project *handsome*, the young people involved in C.LOUD, a participatory media initiative, explored a number of topics intensively, including traditional gender roles, social conventions, cultural pluralism and nonverbal communication. In a 90-second video, they implemented the knowledge and insights they had gained from their reflections with the "helping hands" of grown-ups and children of different sexes, ages and origins. The motivation for this project came from questioning existing prejudices towards lovers who do not quite fit the norm. Evidently, same-sex couples, relationships between people from different ethnic backgrounds or with great differences in age are still not sufficiently accepted in our society—there's still a lack of tolerance. We quickly hit upon the idea of artistically realizing our idea by only portraying hands, though a more profound debate on the term "tolerance" revealed that for those who were affected by intolerance it had a negative connotation: tolerance merely means silently accepting certain circumstances; it does not mean equality and all that is positively associated with it. Before long the young people also came to the conclusion that the original topic of lovers was too narrow, and so expanded it to include a larger number of notions that can be expressed with hands. While making the video, the participating adults seemed rather baffled by the young people's technical and artistic competence.

Die Jugendlichen der Partizipations- und Medieninitiative C.LOUD setzten sich im Zuge des Videoprojektes *handsome* intensiv mit Themen wie traditionellen Geschlechterrollen, gesellschaftlichen Konventionen, kulturellem Pluralismus und nonverbaler Kommunikation auseinander. Die in diesem gedanklichen Prozess erarbeiteten Erkenntnisse und Einsichten setzten sie mit „helfenden Händen" Erwachsener und Kinder unterschiedlichen Geschlechts, Alters und unterschiedlicher Herkunft in einem 90-sekündigen Video um. Die Motivation für dieses Projekt gründete auf der Frage nach immer noch existierenden Vorurteilen gegenüber Liebespaaren, die nicht zu hundert Prozent der Norm entsprechen. So scheinen gleichgeschlechtliche Paare, Beziehungen zwischen Menschen unterschiedlicher Herkunft oder mit großem Altersunterschied in unserer Gesellschaft immer noch nicht hinreichend akzeptiert zu werden – was fehlt, ist Toleranz. Die Idee zur gestalterischen Umsetzung mit der ausschließlichen Abbildung von Händen war schnell gefunden, eine tiefergehende Auseinandersetzung mit dem Begriff „Toleranz" zeigte jedoch, dass dieser für von Intoleranz betroffene Gruppen mittlerweile negativ konnotiert war, da Toleranz lediglich das stillschweigende Hinnehmen gewisser Umstände meint und nicht die positiv assoziierte Gleichstellung. Weiters wurde das ursprüngliche Thema der Liebespaare von den Jugendlichen bald als zu eng gefasst empfunden und somit um eine Vielzahl von mit den Händen darstellbaren Ausdrücken erweitert. Bei der Produktion des Videos waren die beteiligten Erwachsenen angesichts der technischen und gestalterischen Kompetenz der Jugendlichen wohl am meisten verblüfft.

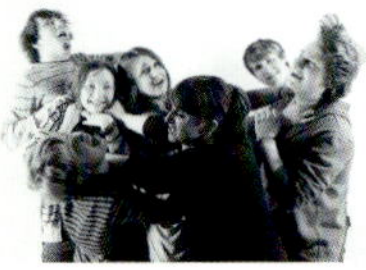

At **C.LOUD** young people produce their own media. Which medium they use is up to them: video, audio, blogs—anything goes when it come to expressing their opinions to others. For it is the objective of this initiative to show adults that young people have something to say and as members of society want to exercise their right to speak out. Bei **C.LOUD** produzieren Jugendliche ihre Medien selbst. Welches Medium dabei benutzt wird, ist ganz egal: Video, Audio, Blogs – alles ist recht um ihre Meinung nach außen zu tragen. Denn Ziel dieser Initiative ist es, Erwachsenen klar zu machen, dass Jugendliche etwas zu sagen haben und als Teil der Gesellschaft ihr Mitspracherecht wahrnehmen.

Impressive Titel (Paradise)

Laura Kaltenbrunner, Michaela Gehmayr

Der Trickfilm *Impressive Titel (Paradise)* soll die Suche nach der Freiheit und der eigenen Identität widerspiegeln. Der Wolf steht symbolisch für den Menschen, denn wie der Wolf ist der Mensch auch ein einsamer Jäger, der zwar die Gesellschaft der Artgenossen braucht, sich selbst aber trotzdem am nächsten ist. Auch der Wolf in dem Film strebt nach etwas, findet es im Leben aber nicht, und dann, als er dem Tode nahe ist, weiß er nicht, ob er denn überhaupt das finden will, was er gesucht hat. Ein Vogel begleitet ihn während seines Lebens – ein Zeichen für Freiheit.

Wie der Wolf im Film verliert auch der Mensch durch die Suche bedeutende Zeit, die ihm auch durch die immer größer werdenden Leistungsansprüche genommen wird. Das Erreichen des Durchschnitts und das Anpassen an das gesellschaftliche Mittelmaß erfordert viel Kraft, und andererseits geht dabei der Individualismus des Einzelnen verloren. In Zukunft sollte der Mensch etwas seines Kontrollbedürfnisses abgeben und sich auf das Hier und Jetzt besinnen, um sich selbst nicht zu verlieren.

Am Anfang standen verschiedene Überlegungen im Raum, wie der Film gemacht werden sollte, bis man sich schließlich darauf festlegte, die Skizzen per Hand zu zeichnen und am Computer mit dem Grafiktablett (Bamboo Pen & Touch) und dem Programm Gimp zu outlinen und zu kolorieren. Der Schnitt wurde mit Adobe Elements 3.0 gemacht. Der Ton wurde aus Gema- und AKM- freien Musikstücken gebastelt.

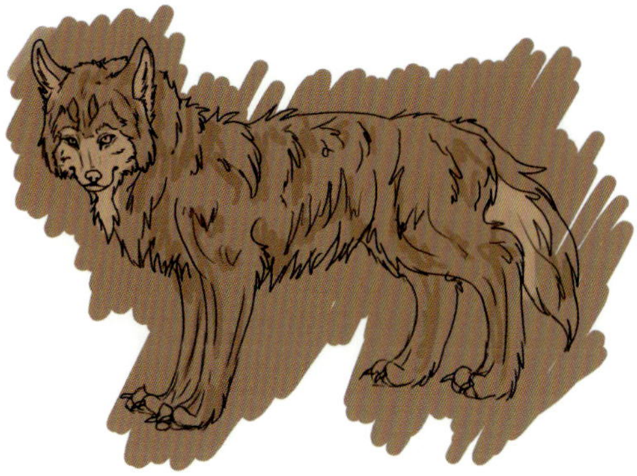

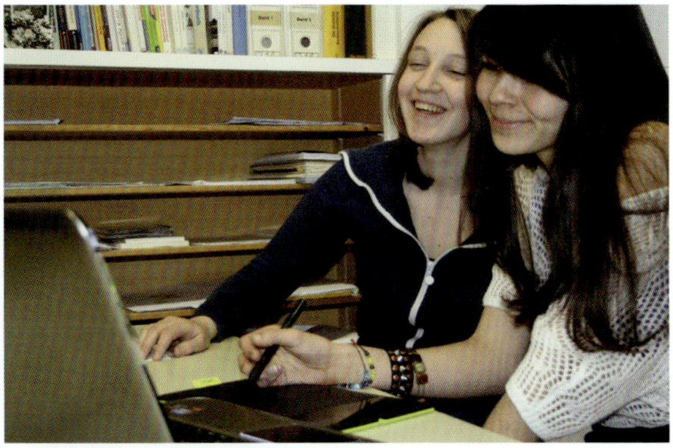

The animated film *Impressiv Titel (Paradise)* attempts to reflect on the search for freedom and identity. The wolf symbolizes the human being because, like us, he is a lonely hunter who needs the company of his species yet in the end feels closest to himself. The wolf in the film also strives to attain something, but he does not find it in life. As death nears, he no longer knows if he even wants to find what he has been searching for. Throughout his life, he has been accompanied by a bird—a sign of freedom.

Like the wolf in the film, humans waste significant amounts of time on searching and trying to live up to the mounting pressure to achieve. It takes a lot of energy to give even an average performance and to adapt to social norms. At the same time we tend to lose our individuality during this process. In the future, humans should to a certain extent let go of their need to control, and concentrate on the here and now so as not to lose themselves.

To start with, we considered a number of different ways to make the film. We then decided to draw the pictures by hand, and outline and color them on the computer using a graphics tablet (Bamboo Pen and Touch) and the program Gimp. We edited the film with Adobe Elements 3.0. The soundtrack was put together using music that was not registered with the GEMA (the German performance rights organization) and AKM (its Austrian equivalent).

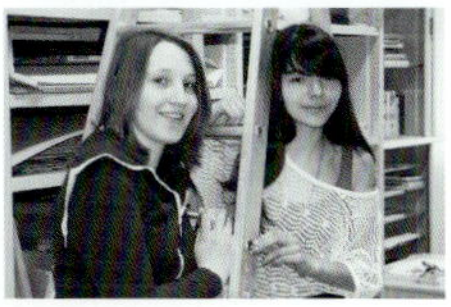

Michaela Gehmayr and **Laura Kaltenbrunner** are both students in the 5th form of a college preparatory school, the Realgymnasium am Benediktiner-Stift Lambach. Michaela Gehmayr is interested in psychology and philosophical topics. Laura is interested in art but also biology and, like Michaela, wants to study medicine. **Michaela Gehmayr** und **Laura Kaltenbrunner** besuchen derzeit die 5. Klasse des Realgymnasium am Benediktinerstift Lambach. Michaela Gehmayr interessiert sich für Psychologie und philosophische Themen. Laura interessiert sich für Kunst, aber auch für Biologie und möchte, wie Michaela, Medizin studieren.

iTanky
Felix Krause

http://itanky.com

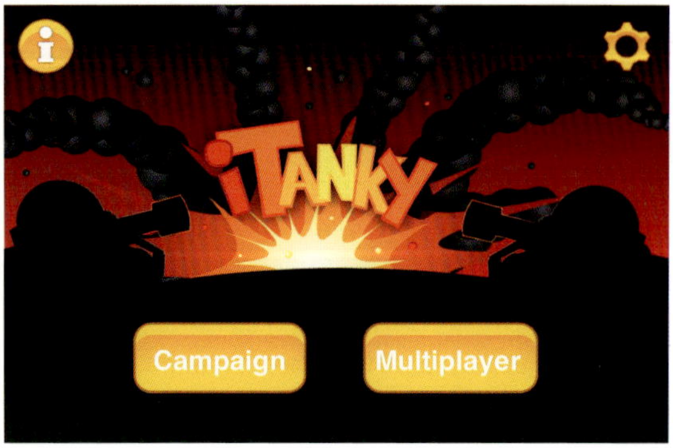

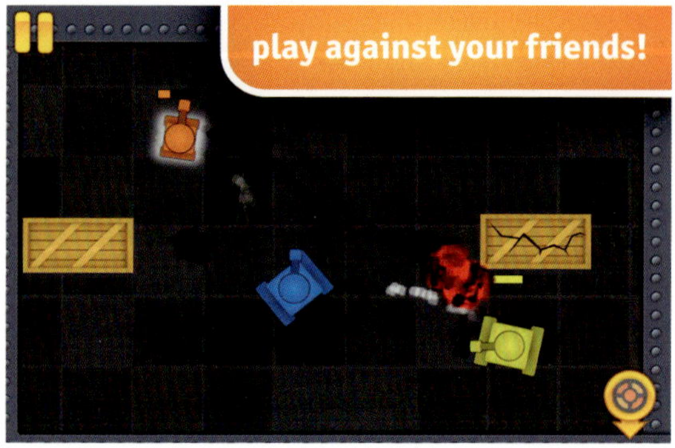

iTanky is a free two-dimensional tank game for your iPhone. There are many different levels, computer-operated tanks and a multiplayer mode with which to challenge friends. The goal of the game is to survive on the battlefield longer than anyone else and with as little damage as possible. First you choose a tank and then a map. During the game you try to collect items so you can get, for example, new weapons. In single-player mode, your opponents' tanks are computer-operated.
With the multiplayer mode, you can play against friends via Wi-Fi or Bluetooth. The next upgrade will offer many new functions, for instance, other weapons and items, as well as an online map editor for designing new levels.
I developed the entire physics engine and particle system by myself. For the maps, I programmed a level editor that can be used with any conventional browser. You can drag and drop the different map elements on the field and move them about. Then you can download the map onto your iPhone.

iTanky ist ein kostenloses, zweidimensionales Panzerspiel für das iPhone. Es gibt viele abwechslungsreiche Level, computergesteuerte Panzer und einen Mehrspielermodus, um Freunde herauszufordern. Das Ziel ist es, am Schlachtfeld am längsten zu überleben und möglichst wenig beschädigt zu werden. Zuerst wählt man einen Panzer und eine Karte aus. Während des Spiels kann man Items sammeln, um z. B. neue Waffen zu bekommen. Im Einzelspielermodus sind die gegnerischen Panzer computergesteuert.
Mit dem Mehrspielermodus kann man gegen Freunde per Wifi oder Bluetooth spielen. Viele weitere Funktionen werden im nächsten Upgrade geliefert, wie z. B. neue Waffen und Items, ein Online-Map-Editor, um neue Level zu gestalten.
Die komplette Physik-Engine und das Partikelsystem wurden von mir selbst entwickelt. Für die Karten habe ich einen Level-Editor programmiert, der in jedem gängigen Browser verwendet werden kann. Man kann die verschiedenen Kartenelemente per Drag&Drop in das Feld ziehen und verschieben und anschließend die Karte am iPhone herunterladen.

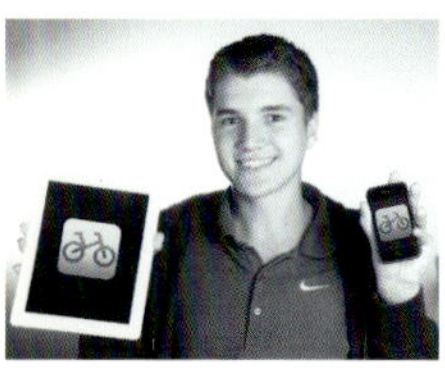

Felix Krause, born in 1994, attends the HTL Wiener Neustadt, a technical secondary school. He is interested in programming, robotics, tennis and golf. In 2010 he represented Austria in the Junior Soccer League at Robocup (the Robot World Cup) in Singapore. His professional goal is to become a developer in a start-up company in California. In 2011, he worked for three months at 6Wunderkinder on Wunderlist and Wunderkit, and received an Honorary Mention in u19 for his *Bikemap App*. In 2012 he won the European Botball Tournament with his team. **Felix Krause**, geb. 1994, besucht die HTL Wiener Neustadt, interessiert sich für Programmierung, Robotik, Tennis und Golf. 2010 hat er Österreich bei der Robocup Weltmeisterschaft in Singapur im Soccer Junior Wettbewerb vertreten. Sein Berufsziel ist Entwickler in einem kalifornischen Start-up Unternehmen zu werden. 2011 hat er für drei Monate bei 6Wunderkinder an Wunderlist und Wunderkit gearbeitet und für seine *Bikemap App* eine Anerkennung bei u19 gewonnen. 2012 gewann er mit seinem Team den europäischen Botball-Robotik-Wettbewerb.

Quadrocopter

http://quadrocopter.drseus.eu

Lukas Pfeifhofer, Tanja Roschanz / HTL Mössingerstraße

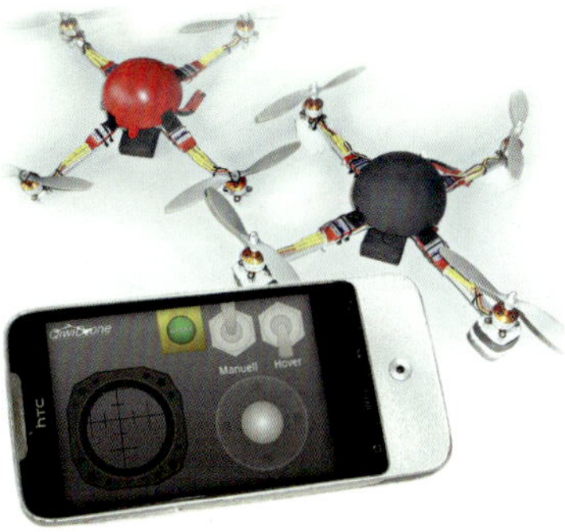

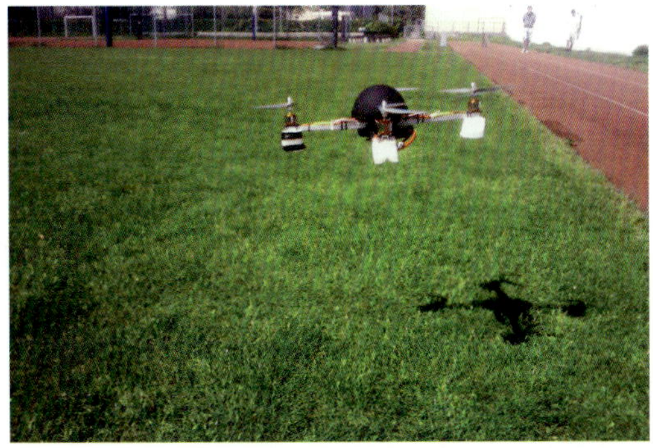

Ziel des Projektes war die Realisierung eines flugfähigen Roboters, der sich per Funktechnik manuell sowie computergesteuert in einem Raum bewegen kann. Bei den Robotern handelt es sich um mehrere auf dem AeroQuad-Projekt basierende Quadrocopter. Für uns war hier vor allem die Unabhängigkeit von Teilprodukten und deren Weiterentwicklungen wichtig, um ein stetiges Weiterentwickeln des Projektes sicherstellen zu können. Ein weiterer wichtiger Punkt für die Umsetzung dieses Bildungsprojekt ist die fast ausschließliche Verwendung von frei verfügbarer und veränderbarer Soft- und Hardware.
Der Flugroboter empfängt Steuerdaten von einer Steuereinheit und übermittelt dieser wiederum alle verfügbaren Sensorwerte. Die Kommunikation findet dabei über ein WLAN-Netz statt, um eine Steuerung ohne zusätzliche Elektronik zu ermöglichen. Für das manuelle Steuern des Quadrocopters steht dem Piloten eine Android-Applikation zur Verfügung, die dem Quadrocopter durch das Neigen des Androidgeräts und durch einen Touchscreen die Steuerbefehle übermittelt. Die empfangenen Sensorwerte werden wiederum mit der Android-Applikation ausgewertet und auf dem Gerät dargestellt.
Für das autonome Fliegen im Raum wird mittels Kameras und auf dem Roboter angebrachter Sensoren die Positionsbestimmung des Roboters bestimmt. Dadurch soll es möglich sein, einen Computer selbstständig Routen und Flugmanöver planen und ausführen zu lassen.

The goal of the project was to construct a robot that could fly and be moved about in a space manually or by computer using wireless technology. Based on the Quadrocopter of the AeroQuad Project, we built several robots during our project. For us the most important aspect was to ensure the independence of the individual components as products as well as their continued development, as this would also enable us to continue developing our project further. Another important aspect in implementing this educational project was our decision to use, almost exclusively, free software and hardware.
The flying robot receives navigational data to which it in turn transmits all available sensor values. Communication takes place via a WLAN network, which makes it possible to steer it without any additional electronic equipment. To manually steer the Quadrocopter, the pilot uses the Android application provided. The control commands are communicated by slanting the Android device and via a touch screen. The received sensor values are evaluated by the Android application and displayed on the device.
To enable the robot to move autonomously in space, its position is determined by cameras and sensors installed on the robot. This should make it possible for a computer to independently plan and execute routes and flight maneuvers.

Lukas Pfeifhofer and **Tanja Roschanz** are both in the graduating class at the HTL Mössingerstraße, a technical secondary school in Carinthia, and majoring in computer engineering. Lukas Pfeifhofer, born in 1993, is interested in software development and will begin studying computer engineering in autumn 2012. Tanja Roschanz, born in 1992, also plans to major in a technical field, though she wants to go in a different direction and study architecture. **Lukas Pfeifhofer** und **Tanja Roschanz** besuchen gemeinsam die Abschlussklasse der HTL Mössingerstraße in Kärnten mit dem Schwerpunkt Technische Informatik. Lukas Pfeifhofer, geb. 1993, interessiert sich für Softwareentwicklung und wird ab Herbst 2012 Technische Informatik studieren. Tanja Roschanz, geb. 1992, wird auch ein technisches Studium beginnen, jedoch in einer etwas anderen Richtung, der Architektur.

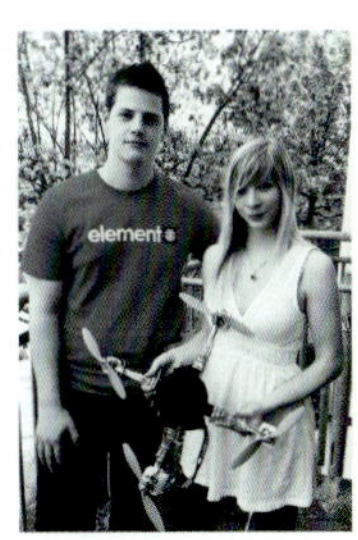

RiffGrabber

http://www.riffgrabber.at

Alin Kalam, Peter Paikl, Wolfgang Schneiderbauer, Manmeet Singh, Christian Sorko / HTL Ottakring

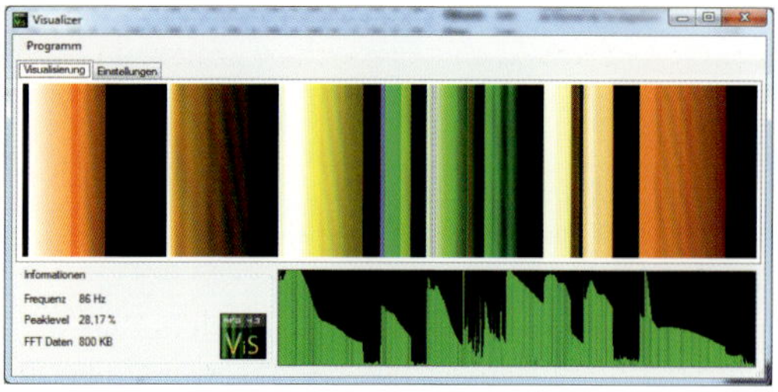

With our final year project *RiffGrabber*, our objective was to develop a software that could transcribe guitar riffs in real time. With it, the user can play a sequence of notes on a guitar that is connected to an audio interface on the computer (e.g., via microphone), or open and replay an audio file in the program. The sequence of notes is analyzed, identified and recorded by the program in real time. As this happens, the notes are written in tablature form (tabs). These tabs may then be stored on the computer as text documents and displayed again as needed.

In addition, we set up a website (*www.riffgrabber.at*) as a user administrator. It serves as a social network where users can upload, display, play, share and delete the tabs they have produced on their computers and/or download tabs by other users.

Furthermore, we developed several tools for analyzing sounds as well as other aids for guitarists. They are particularly helpful for self-taught beginners, and include a tuner, a synthesizer, a chord library and a metronome. These tools are available for Windows and as an Android app. While you play the guitar, the software enters the notes in real time on an XY graph. This makes it easier for the musician to identify the individual octaves (same notes in another—higher or lower—frequency range).

Since there are already a number of software programs for guitar on the market that focus on manual tab notation, the group had the idea of writing a software that would make it possible to automatically transcribe tabs in real time. The software is particularly practical for musicians who play in bands and have to jot down tabs on a daily basis.

Ziel der Diplomarbeit *RiffGrabber* war die Entwicklung einer Software, die Gitarrenriffs in Echtzeit transkribiert. Der User kann eine Tonfolge mit der an ein Audio-Interface angeschlossenen Gitarre am Computer (z. B. via Mikrofoneingang) einspielen oder eine Audiodatei im Programm öffnen und wiedergeben. Die Tonfolge wird in Echtzeit vom Programm analysiert, wiedererkannt und aufgezeichnet. Die Töne werden dabei in Form von Tabulaturen (Tabs) notiert. Diese Tabs können dann als Textdokument auf dem Computer gespeichert werden, um sie je nach Bedarf wieder anzeigen zu können.

Ergänzend wurde eine Website (*www.riffgrabber.at*) mit Benutzerverwaltung erstellt, die als Social Network fungiert, wo die User ihre am Computer erstellten Tabs hochladen, anzeigen, abspielen, freigeben, löschen und Tabs anderer User downloaden können. Des Weiteren wurden einige Tonanalyse- bzw. Hilfetools für Gitarristen entwickelt, die besonders für die autodidaktischen Anfänger sehr hilfreich sind: ein Stimmgerät, ein Synthesizer, eine Akkordbibliothek und ein Metronom. Diese Tools gibt es für Windows und als Android-App. Zusätzlich kann die Android-App Tabs anzeigen (mit Autoscrollen), freigeben und löschen.

Beim Gitarrespielen ordnet die Software die Noten in Echtzeit auf einem x-y-Notengraf so an, dass der Musiker leicht die einzelnen Oktaven (selbe Noten in anderen Frequenzbereichen, hoch/tief) erkennen kann.

Da es bereits einige Gitarrensoftware auf dem Markt gibt, die sich nur auf die manuelle Tabschreibung konzentrieren, hatte die Gruppe die Idee, eine Software zu schreiben, die eine automatische Tabschreibung in Echtzeit ermöglicht. Besonders Musikern, die in Bands spielen und sich zwangsläufig täglich mit der händischen Tabschreibung auseinandersetzen müssen, kommt die Software sehr entgegen.

Alin Kalam, Peter Paikl, Wolfgang Schneiderbauer, Manmeet Singh and Christian Sorko are in the 5th form of the HTBLA-Ottakring, a technical secondary school in Vienna. They are in the IT department and majoring in network engineering. **Alin Kalam, Peter Paikl, Wolfgang Schneiderbauer, Manmeet Singh und Christian Sorko** besuchen die 5. Klasse der HTBLA-Ottakring in Wien mit dem Schwerpunkt Netzwerktechnik in der Abteilung Informationstechnologie.

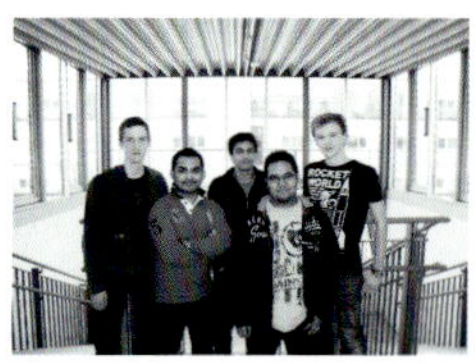

Weltrekord für eine bessere Welt

BG/BORG Kirchdorf

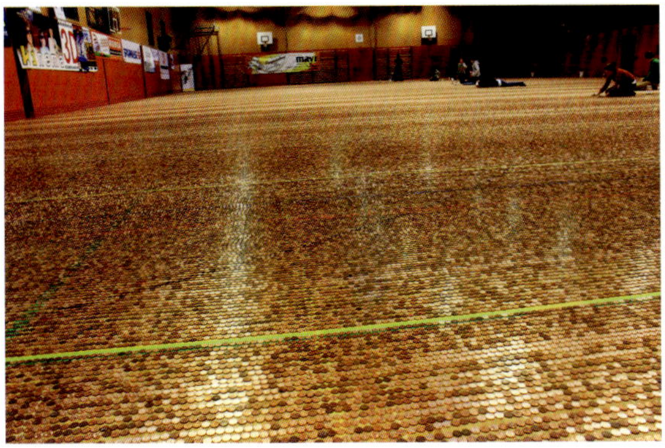

Soziales Engagement gehört in unserer Schule selbstverständlich dazu. Unser Weihnachtsprojekt 2011 war aber gleichzeitig der Versuch, einen bestehenden Weltrekord zu verbessern. Aus den gesammelten Spendengeldern sollte die längste Münzschlange der Welt, gelegt aus 1-Cent-Münzen, entstehen.

Ab Jänner 2011 waren wir mit dem Sammeln von Spendengeldern beschäftigt: im Familien- und Bekanntenkreis, durch Aufstellen von Spendendosen in Kaufhäusern, Betrieben und öffentlichen Einrichtungen, bei Gottesdiensten in den Heimatpfarren, durch verschiedene Aktionen (Karaokeabende, Kuchenbuffets, Ostereierfärben, Straßenmusik, Bastelarbeiten ...), Firmensponsoring. Parallel mussten die gesamten Spenden in 1-Cent-Münzen gewechselt werden.

In der Zeit von 5. bis 8. Dezember wurden die bis dahin gesammelten 4,5 Millionen 1-Cent-Münzen (entspricht 10,6 Tonnen) in der Stadthalle Kirchdorf und in den Turnsälen unserer Schule aufgelegt. Dabei arbeiteten zum Teil mehr als 200 SchülerInnen gleichzeitig. Es wurde streng darauf geachtet, dass die Münzen eine durchgehende Linie bilden und nebeneinander liegende Reihen sich nicht berühren. Am 9. Dezember wurde eine Münzschlangenlänge von rund 75,24 km notariell bestätigt. Damit war der aktuelle Weltrekord übertroffen.

Mit den nun zur Verfügung stehenden 45.000 Euro werden Projekte für Straßenkinder, Landlosenunterstützung, Wasserschutz, Familienförderung, behinderte Kinder in Brasilien, Bolivien und Kenia unterstützt. Mit einem Teil des Geldes wird aber auch sozial bedürftigen Menschen in Kirchdorf geholfen.

At our school, social engagement is the norm, of course. However, our Christmas project in 2011—*World Record for a Better World*—was also an attempt to beat an existing world record. We wanted to use the donation funds we had collected to make the longest line of one-cent coins in the world.

In January 2011 we began collecting donations. We did so among family and friends, with collection tins at department stores, businesses and public facilities, at church services in local parishes, at diverse events (karaoke evenings, cake stands, dyeing Easter eggs, making street music and handicrafts etc.); and through sponsoring by companies. Parallel to this, we had to change all these donations into one-cent coins.

Between December 5 and 8, we lined up the 4.5 million 1-cent coins we had collected (the equivalent of 10.6 tons) in the town hall of Kirchdorf and in our school gyms. This meant that at times more than 200 students were working simultaneously. Great care was taken to make sure that the coins formed a continuous line and that lines lying next to each other did not touch. On December 9, it was notarized: our line of coins was 75.24 kilometers long. We had broken the existing world record!

With the 45,000 euros at our disposal, we intend to support projects for street children, the landless and water protection, as well as assist families and disabled children in Brazil, Bolivia and Kenya. Part of the money will also be used to help those who are socially disadvantaged here in Kirchdorf.

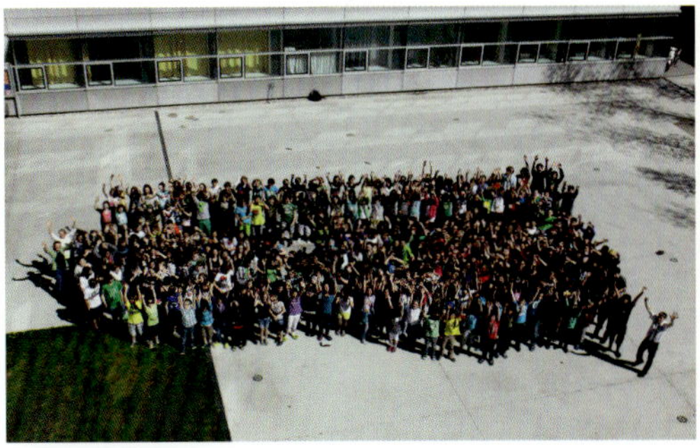

Approximately 850 students participated in the project. They were in the first to eighth forms of the Bundesrealgymnasium and Bundesoberstufenrealgymnasium, a college preparatory school in Kirchdorf on the Krems. Die rund 850 SchülerInnen, die an dem Projekt mitgewirkt haben, besuchen die ersten bis achten Klassen des Bundesrealgymnasiums und Bundesoberstufenrealgymnasiums in Kirchdorf an der Krems.

[the next idea]
voestalpine Art and Technology Grant

Beyond Market Value

Michael Doser, Horst Hörtner, Ela Kagel, Manfred Pietschmann, Gustav Pomberger, Michael Sterrer-Ebenführer

The 112 entries in [the next idea] voestalpine Art and Technology Grant category of this year's Prix Ars Electronica were from 31 nations. They were technological, scientific or artistic projects and displayed great diversity by dealing with such different fields as biotechnology, architecture, transport, communication, urban planning or energy production. The submissions addressed problems in society and presented some very interesting concepts for solutions, many of which were developed independently of their market value. The impressive number of participants from university facilities reveals that in its eighth year the competition has also found its way to the academic world.

The jury selected three projects: two of them revolve around Internet communication; the third, around architecture:

1. *qaul.net* by Christoph Wachter and Mathias Jud: The project implements an open communication principle for Wi-Fi-enabled devices that can form spontaneous networks—independently of commercial mobile phone providers, technical infrastructures and established online social platforms.
2. *Matopy* by Sam Jewell: This project uses language and sound effects to present the content and form of websites acoustically. This approach enables the visually impaired to use the Internet intuitively without needing Braille.
3. Designing *Zero Energy Building Components with Smart Thermobimetal* by Doris Sung: This project explores the development of façade components made out of thermo bimetal and nitinol wire that alter their form when they warm up in the sun. Without any external energy source, the system reacts automatically to strong solar radiation and in doing so shades the facade.

Die 112 Einreichungen in der Kategorie [the next idea] voestalpine Art and Technology Grant des diesjährigen Prix Ars Electronica kamen aus 31 Nationen. Sie wiesen eine große thematische Vielfalt auf und behandelten als technologische, wissenschaftliche oder künstlerische Projekte so unterschiedliche Bereiche wie Biotechnologie, Architektur, Transport, Kommunikation, Stadtplanung oder Energieproduktion. Die Beiträge adressierten gesellschaftliche Probleme und präsentierten durchwegs interessante Lösungskonzepte, auch unabhängig von ökonomischer Verwertbarkeit. Die beeindruckende Zahl von Teilnehmern aus universitären Einrichtungen zeigt, dass der Wettbewerb im achten Jahr auch in der internationalen akademischen Welt angekommen ist.

Die Jury selektierte drei Projekte, davon zwei aus dem Bereich Internetkommunikation und eines aus dem der Architektur:

1. *qaul.net* von Christoph Wachter und Mathias Jud: Das Projekt verfolgt ein offenes Kommunikationsprinzip für WiFi-fähige Endgeräte, die spontane Netzwerke bilden können – unabhängig von kommerziellen Mobilfunkanbietern, technischen Infrastrukturen und etablierten sozialen Plattformen im Internet.
2. *Matopy*: Das Projekt von Sam Jewell benutzt Sprache und Klangeffekte zur auditiven Darstellung von Webseiten in Form und Inhalt. Die Methode erlaubt sehbehinderten Menschen, das Internet ohne Einsatz von Braille-Schrift intuitiv zu nutzen.
3. *Designing Zero Energy Building Components with Smart Thermobimetal* von Doris Sung: Das Projekt behandelt die Entwicklung von Fassadenkomponenten aus Thermo-Bimetall und Nitinol-Draht, die bei Wärme durch Lichteinfall ihre Form verändern. Das System reagiert automatisch und ohne externe Energiequellen auf starke Sonneneinstrahlung und erreicht dadurch eine Beschattung von Fassaden.

[THE NEXT IDEA] VOESTALPINE ART AND TECHNOLOGY GRANT

The jury awards [the next idea] voestalpine art and technology grant to the project *qaul.net* for the following reasons:

Christoph Wachter and Mathias Jud's project enables independent access to an ad-hoc configurable communication network and this is the case even when a country or region is cut off from the Internet. *qaul.net* uses a mesh-routing protocol (OLSR) already employed by many other open-source networks. Yet often considerable technical

[THE NEXT IDEA] VOESTALPINE ART AND TECHNOLOGY GRANT

Die Jury hat den „the next idea voestalpine art and technology grant" an das Projekt *qaul.net* vergeben, und zwar aus folgenden Gründen:

Das Projekt Christoph Wachter und Mathias Jud ermöglicht den unabhängigen Zugang zu einem ad-hoc aufbaubaren Kommunikationsnetzwerk, das auch dann funktioniert, wenn Länder oder Regionen vom Internet abgeschnitten sind. *qaul.net* setzt auf ein Meshrouting-Protokoll (OLSR) auf, das bereits von vielen freien Netzwerken benutzt wird. Aber bei diesen Lösungen sind zum Teil erhebliche technische Voraussetzungen und Kenntnisse nötig. Die neue Methode beseitigt diese Zugangshürden. Jeder kann ohne technische Vorbereitung oder Kenntnisse Teilnehmer werden, die erforderliche Software wird bei Kontaktaufnahme automatisch zum Download angeboten. Im *qaul.net*-Netzwerk sind alle angeschlossenen Endgeräte gleichwertig, sie dienen sowohl als Sender wie als Empfänger und bilden gemeinsam die unhierarchische infrastrukturelle Basis des Netzes. *qaul.net* gleicht einem wachsenden Organismus, der sich bei Ausfall einzelner Zellen selbst repariert. Dadurch wird das Netz unabhängig von äußeren Einflüssen wie staatlicher Zensur oder Nutzungsbeschränkungen kommerzieller Kommunikationskanäle wie Facebook oder Twitter. Die Einreicher verbinden damit die Hoffnung, dass *qaul.net* zu einem wichtigen Kommunikationsinstrument für Demokratiebewegungen wird. Für das Urteil der Jury war entscheidend, dass *qaul.net* einen einfachen, unbeschränkbaren Zugang zu Netzressourcen, Information und freiem Dialog bietet.

ANERKENNUNGEN

Die Projekte *Designing Zero Energy Building Components with Smart Thermobimetal* und *Matopy* werden von der Jury durch Anerkennungen gewürdigt.

Designing Zero Energy Building Components with Smart Thermobimetal

Die Idee von Bimetall-Fassadenelementen bietet einen Lösungsansatz für das weltweite Problem der Gebäudeklimatisierung ohne Einsatz externer Energiequellen. Die Elemente bestehen aus einem „intelligenten" Material, das bei Wärme seine Form verändert. Besonders hervorzuheben ist die mit dem Einsatz verbundene eigene Ästhetik einer sich selbsttätig verändernden Gebäudehaut. Diese wird zu einer Art Membran, die je nach Witterung die Luft- und Lichtdurchlässigkeit steuert.

Matopy

Das Projekt von Sam Jewell stellt sich der Herausforderung, akustische Gestaltungselemente zu entwickeln, die in der Lage sind, die visuelle Welt des Internet gleichwertig in den auditiven Bereich zu übertragen. Dadurch bietet es sehbehinderten Menschen ungehinderten Zugang zum Internet. Die Jury würdigt insbesondere die Ambition des Einreichers, die damit verbundene Umwandlung von Webseiten zu automatisieren.

qualifications and knowledge are required to use these solutions. This new method eliminates such access barriers. Anyone can become a participant without technical preparation or skills; on establishing contact, automatic downloads provide the necessary software. With *qaul.net*, all the devices connected are equal, and function as both sender and receiver. Together they generate the network's basic non-hierarchical infrastructure. *qaul.net* is like a growing organism that in the case of a breakdown repairs individual cells itself. This makes the network independent from external influences such as state censorship or restrictions in use enforced by commercial communication channels such as Facebook or Twitter. Hence the entrants hope that *qaul.net* will become an important instrument of communication for pro-democracy movements. Ultimately, what was decisive for the jury was that *qaul.net* offers simple unrestricted access to network resources, information and open dialogue.

HONORARY MENTIONS

The jury award Honorary Mentions to the projects *Designing Zero Energy Building Components with Smart Thermobimetal* and *Matopy*.

Designing Zero Energy Building Components with Smart Thermobimetal

The idea of using bimetal façade elements is an attempt to solve the worldwide problem of needing to cool buildings without using external energy sources. The components are constructed of "intelligent" materials that change their form when they warm up. Remarkable here is the extraordinary aesthetic, which has resulted from using this building skin that adapts automatically. It becomes a kind of membrane that modifies itself depending on the weather and how much air and light permeates it.

Matopy

Sam Jewell's project takes on the challenge of developing acoustic design elements that are able to translate the visual world of the Internet effectively to the auditory world. In doing so his project offers the visually impaired unhindered access to the Internet. The jury would like to express its particular appreciation of this entrant's ambition to automate the conversion of websites involved in the process.

qaul.net—tools for the next revolution

Christoph Wachter, Mathias Jud

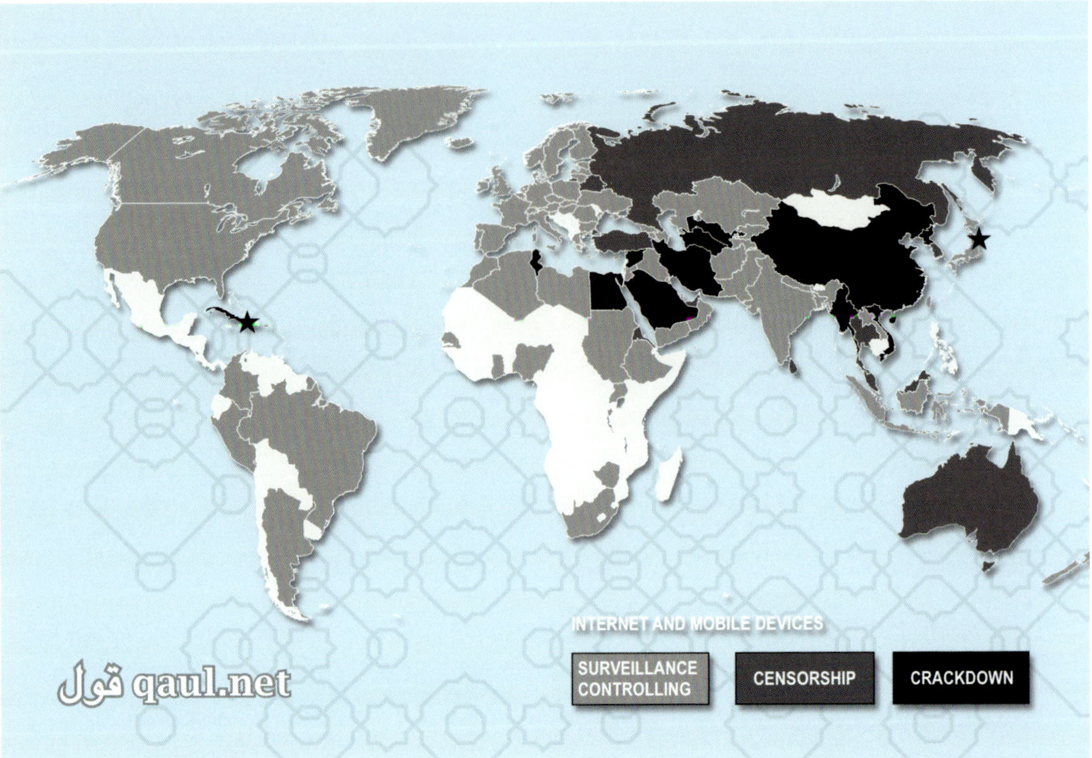

qaul.net implements a redundant open communication principle that directly allows Wi-Fi-enabled computers and mobile devices to form a spontaneous network. Chat and Twitter functions as well as movie streaming become accessible independently of the Internet and cellular networks. *qaul.net* spreads like a virus and an open source community may modify *qaul.net* as needed.

At times of communication blackouts in Egypt, Burma or Tibet and the large power outages often caused by natural disasters, *qaul.net* has taken on the challenge of critically investigating individual communication conditions while exploring new horizons together.

During the demonstrations in Egypt in January 2011, all Internet and mobile phone connections were shut down completely for six days. This blackout marked a caesura, as did other Internet crackdowns, such as those in Myanmar in 2007, Tibet in 2008, Iran and the Uighur territories in 2009 as well as in Libya in 2011. Also during the massive earthquakes in Haiti in 2010 and Japan in 2011, cellular antennas did not work and the remaining

qaul.net verwirklicht ein redundantes, offenes Kommunikationsprinzip, in dem WLAN-fähige Computer und Mobile-Devices direkt ein spontanes Netz bilden. Chat-, Twitterfunktionen und Filmstreaming werden unabhängig von Internet und Mobilfunk möglich. Wie ein Virus kann sich *qaul.net* verbreiten und eine Open-Source-Community kann *qaul.net* beliebig modifizieren.

In Zeiten der kommunikativen Blackouts in Ägypten, Burma oder Tibet und angesichts der großen Netzausfälle durch Naturkatastrophen wird *qaul.net* zur Herausforderung, die individuellen Kommunikationsbedingungen kritisch zu betrachten und gemeinsam neue Horizonte zu ergründen.

Während den Demonstrationen im Januar 2011 in Ägypten wurden alle Internetzugänge und der Mobilfunk für sechs Tage komplett abgeschaltet. Dieser Blackout markierte eine Zäsur wie andere Internet-Crackdowns auch, etwa in Myanmar 2007, im Tibet 2008, im Iran und im Uigurischen Autonomen Gebiet 2009 sowie in Libyen 2011. Auch bei den schweren Erdbeben in Haiti 2010 und in Japan 2011 gerieten Mobilfunkantennen außer Betrieb und die verbliebenen Netze waren überlastet, so dass die Menschen in Not keine Hilferufe aussenden konnten.

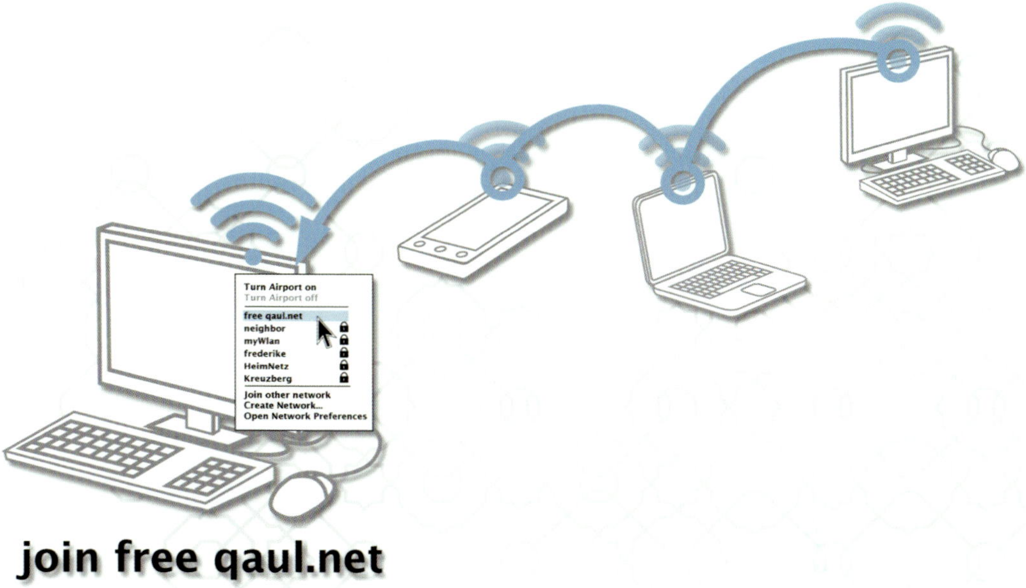

Die freie Vernetzung wurde immer wieder diskutiert. Auf OLSR (Open Link State Routing) basieren Mesh-Netzwerke wie *Funkfeuer*. Doch obwohl WLAN-Karten den Ad-Hoc-Modus zunehmend unterstützen, scheiterte eine Ausbreitung an der notwendigen Konfiguration und an fehlenden Standards. Das Sich-Vernetzen wird zur Pröbelei, der nebst dem wachsenden Angebot kommerzieller Anbieter und deren gezieltem Ausschalten der Konkurrenz faktisch keine Bedeutung mehr zukommt.

qaul.net implementiert OLSR, überträgt die Vernetzung direkt auf die WLAN-Geräte und kombiniert die Server- und Routersoftware mit den Applikationen. Netzwerk und Anwendung werden eins. Die Open-Source-Software steht unter der GPL (GNU Public License) zur freien Nutzung und zur Weiterentwicklung bereit.

WLAN-Router bilden heute ein dichtes Netz und könnten modifiziert gar bis zu 300 km überbrücken. Doch *qaul.net* soll nicht primär die Router, sondern direkt die einzelnen Computer und Mobil-Devices einbinden. Der Fokus liegt auf der Nachbarschaft und dem Kollaborativen. Das Netz wird damit ungleich dichter und spontane Netzwerke zwischen unterschiedlichsten Geräten sind jederzeit

networks became overloaded—this meant that people in distress could not call for help.

Free network connections for everyone have often been discussed. Mesh networks such as *Funkfeuer* are based on OLSR (Open Link State Routing). And although wireless cards increasingly support ad-hoc modes, they have failed to spread because of a lack of the necessary configurations and standards. Then self-networking becomes a matter of trial-and-error, which makes it—for all practical purposes—inconsequential next to the growing list of commercial providers and their systematic elimination of competitors.

qaul.net implements OLSR, transferring the network directly to wireless devices, and combines server and router software with applications. Network and operation become one. Open-source software are available under the terms of the GPL (GNU Public License) and so may be used free of charge as well as developed further.

Nowadays, Wi-Fi routers form a dense network and if modified properly even have a range of up to 300 kilometers. Yet *qaul.net* is not primarily

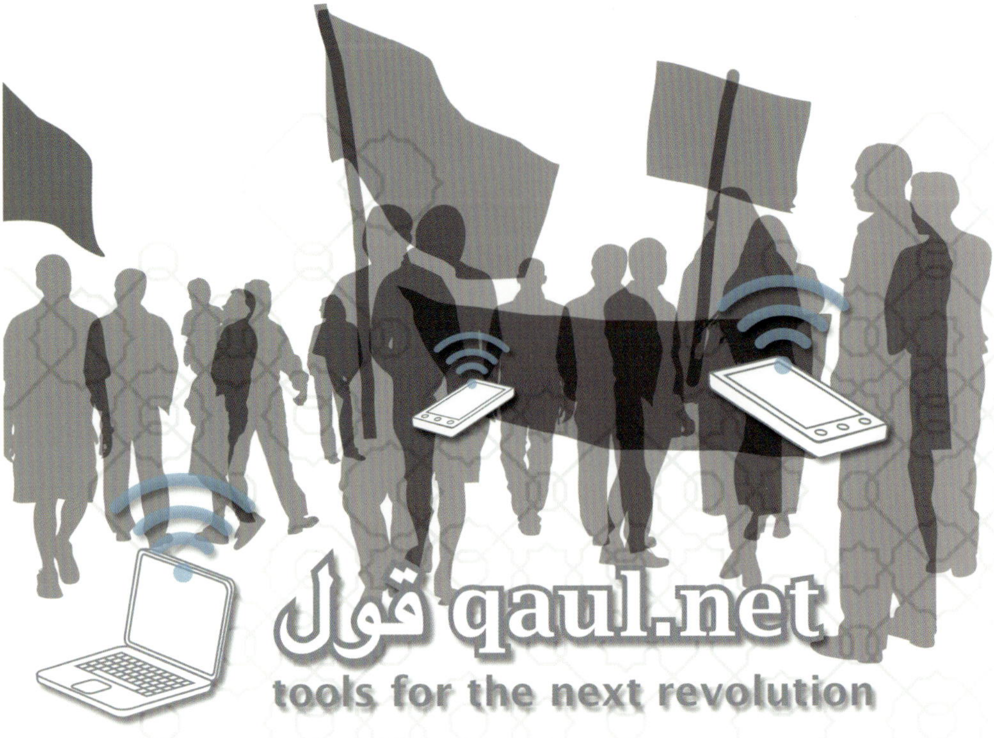

about connecting routers but individual computers and mobile devices. The focus is on the neighborhood and collaborating, and this results in much denser networks. Moreover, spontaneous networks between different devices may be established at any time. Network access is not central but passed on like a virus. When users gain Wi-Fi access with *qaul.net*, they can download and install the software directly via this connection. Anyone who has a Wi-Fi-enabled device can participate, expand an existing network or create their own.

In the digital age we are informed by communication conditions that are prerequisites of freedom of speech and information. *qaul.net* creates tools with which we can jointly probe general design options. This communication tool can bridge gaps in the infrastructure or spread spontaneously in the event of a power outage. And even when it is used just for fun, *qaul.net* sensitizes people to the infrastructure, conditions and dependencies—and offers an incentive to try new forms of networking.

The word "qaul" is Arabic and means statement, speech or word and is pronounced like the English

möglich. Auch der Zugang zum Netzwerk ist nicht zentral, sondern wandert wie ein Virus weiter. Wenn ein *qaul.net*-Access als WLAN-Zugang erscheint, kann die Software direkt über diese Verbindung heruntergeladen und installiert werden. Alle können mit ihren WLAN-fähigen Geräten partizipieren, das bestehende Netz vergrößern oder ein eigenes Netzwerk starten.

Im digitalen Zeitalter sind wir von Kommunikationsbedingungen geprägt, die unserer Informations- und Redefreiheit vorausgehen. *qaul.net* schafft Werkzeuge, um gemeinsam die generellen Gestaltungsoptionen zu sondieren. Das Kommunikationstool kann eine fehlende Infrastruktur überbrücken oder sich bei einem Netzausfall spontan ausbreiten. Doch auch als reine Spielerei sensibilisiert *qaul.net* für die Infrastruktur, die Bedingungen und Abhängigkeiten – und bietet Anreiz, neue Formen der Vernetzung auszuprobieren.

„Qaul" ist arabisch, heißt Aussage, Rede, Wort und wird wie das englische Wort „call" ausgesprochen. Die Maxime, weltweit und frei zu kommunizieren, kehrt *qaul.net* um und blickt stattdessen aus der Position des Hier und Jetzt, schaut in die Nachbarschaft und von da hinaus in die weite Welt. Als Hommage an die arabischen

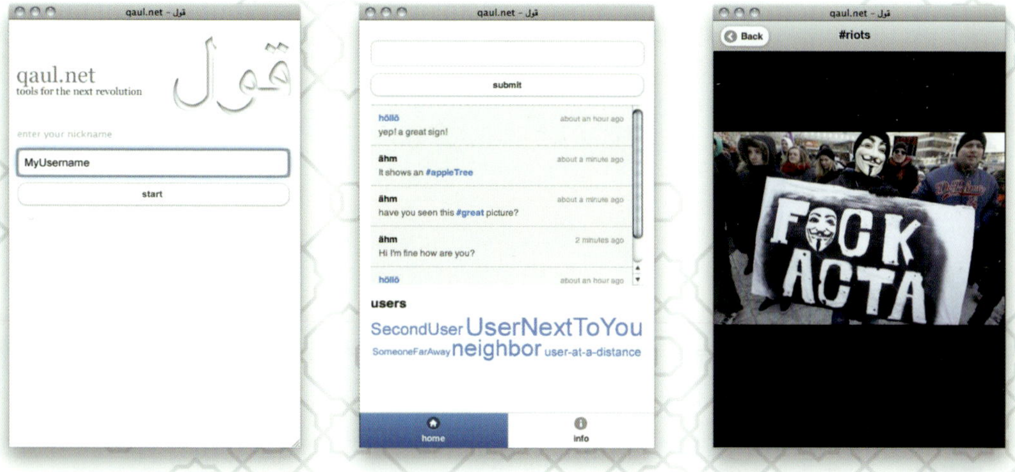

قول qaul.net tools for the next revolution

Aufständischen funktioniert das Projekt wie eine Gruppe von Aktivisten, die zusammenfindet und wagt, eigene Aktionspotenziale zu erproben, als Lichtblick gegenüber einer dominanten, scheinbar unverrückbaren Machtstruktur.

Supported by: Migros Kulturproduzent, Schweizerische Eidgenossenschaft, Bundesamt für Kultur BAK

word "call". *qaul.net* reverses the maxim of global and free communication, and—from the perspective of the here and now—looks out into the neighborhood and from there out into the big wide world. As a tribute to the Arab insurgents, this project works like a group of activists who have joined forces and so dare to test their own potential for action as a beacon against a dominant, seemingly immovable power structure.

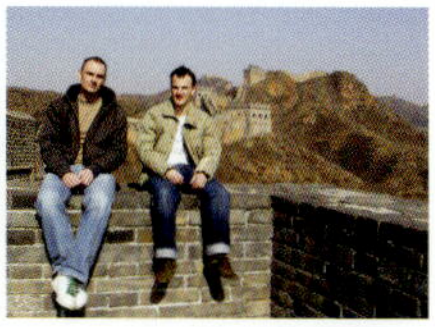

Christoph Wachter, Mathias Jud (CH) have worked together on participatory community projects since 2000. They have received awards from, e.g., Ars Electronica, Transmediale, the Saxon State Ministry for Science and the Arts, Swiss Federal Office of Culture, Migros Cultural Percentage, Canton of Zurich, CYNETART and EMARE. **Christoph Wachter, Mathias Jud** (CH) arbeiten seit 2000 gemeinsam an partizipatorischen Community-Projekten. Ihre Arbeiten wurden vielfach ausgezeichnet, u. a. von Ars Electronica, Transmediale, vom Ministerium für Wissenschaft und Kunst des Freistaats Sachsen, vom Schweizer Bundesamt für Kultur, Migros Kulturprozent, Kanton Zürich, Cynetart, EMARE.

Designing Zero-Energy Building Components with Smart Thermobimetal

Doris Sung / DOSU Studio Architecture and University of Southern California

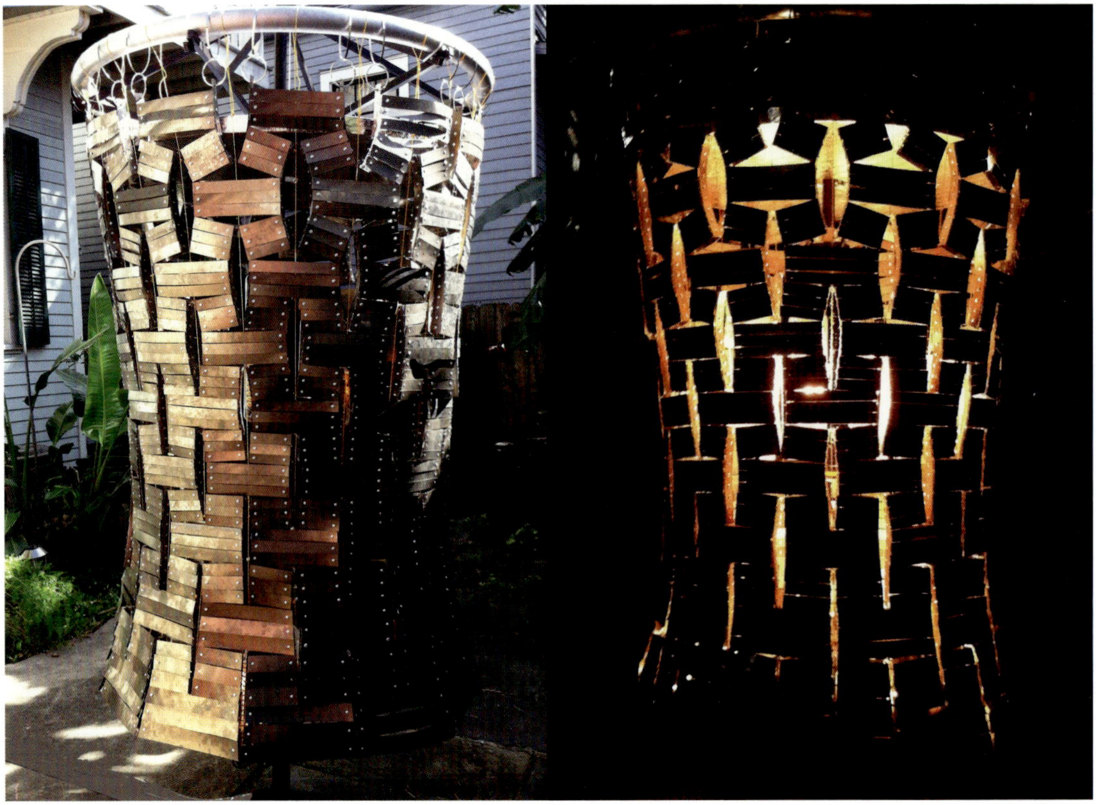

Challenging the traditional presumption that building skins are static and inanimate, this applied research project examines the replacement of this convention with one that posits the prosthetic layer between man and his environment as a responsive and active skin. Using sheet thermobimetals (TBM), a smart material that automatically curls when heated, and Nitinol, a wire material that shrinks when heated, building surfaces can self-ventilate and reduce its dependency on mechanical air conditioning. With today's digital technology and driving interest in sustainable design, this simple material can transcend its currently limited role as a mechanical device to a dynamic building surface material as well as expand the discourse of the performative architecture.

We want to develop two co-dependent systems in an effort to heightened performance of thermobimetal and Nitinol combinations: an interactive, hybrid system of the two dynamic materials

Entgegen der herkömmlichen Auffassung, eine Gebäudehülle sei etwas Starres und Unbelebtes, erkundet dieses angewandte Forschungsprojekt eine Möglichkeit, die prothetische Schicht zwischen Mensch und Umwelt durch eine von sich aus reagierende Haut zu ersetzen. Mithilfe von Bimetallblechen, einem intelligenten Material, das sich bei Hitze einrollt, und Nitinol, einem Drahtmaterial, das sich bei Hitze zusammenzieht, lassen sich selbstventilierende Gebäudeoberflächen herstellen und damit die Abhängigkeit von mechanischen Klimaanlagen verringern. Mit moderner Digitaltechnologie und nachhaltigem Design können diese einfachen Materialien über ihre beschränkte Rolle als mechanische Hilfsmittel hinaus zu einem dynamischen Fassadenmaterial weiterentwickelt und der Diskurs über performative Architektur um ein paar neue Aspekte ergänzt werden.

Wir wollen zwei sich gegenseitig stützende Systeme entwickeln, die dazu beitragen sollen, die Leistungsfähigkeit von Bimetal-Nitinol-Verbindungen zu steigern: eines interaktiven, hybriden Systems, bei dem die beiden dynamischen Materialien gleichzeitig aktiv sind, und

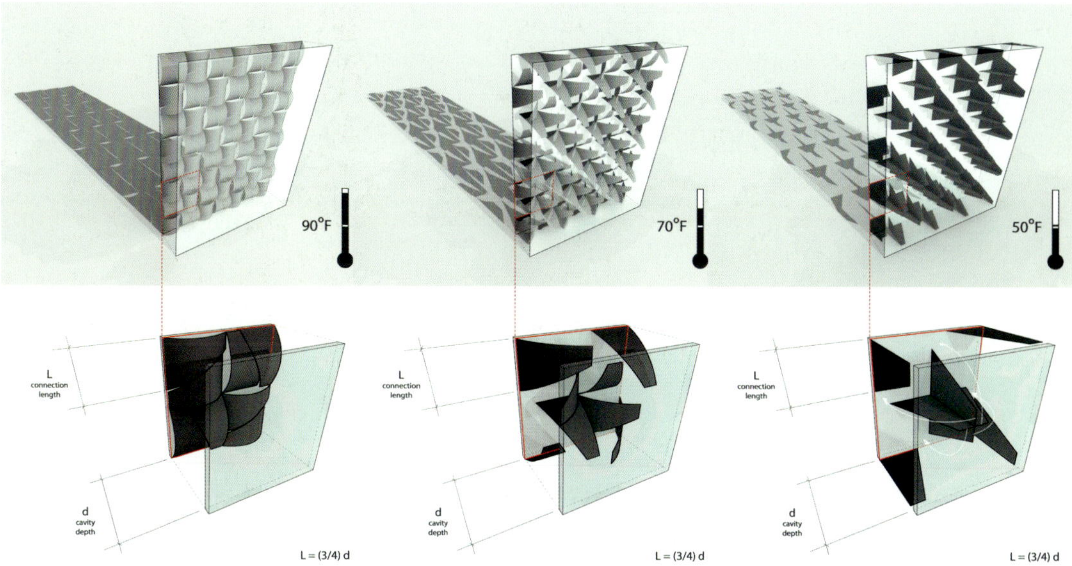

eines damit kompatiblen oszillierenden Systems, bei dem die Materialien abwechselnd aktiv sind. Die Ergebnisse der beiden Systeme sollen in die Entwicklung eines Vorhangfassadensystems aus Glasplatten und einer leicht installierbaren Sonnenschutzfolie für kommerzielle Anwendungen einfließen. Ihre optische Geometrie wird mithilfe von Struktur- und Performance-Modellen bestimmt, die auf komplexer digitaler Software beruhen. Dazu ist eine zweckspezifische Adaption von Standardsoftware – in einigen Fällen mittels Scripting – erforderlich. Die Verbindung dieser neuen Technologien mit traditionellen Systemen und Materialien ermöglicht die Entstehung von Formen, die sonst undenkbar wären.

operating simultaneously and a compatible system of oscillating performance where one material performs while the other remains static. The results of these two systems will be applied to a curtain wall glass panel system and to a bris-soleil surface intended for easy installation in commercial applications. With the use of complex digital softwares, structural and performance models will determine the optimal geometry. It is likely that these off-the-shelf softwares have to be custom altered to be useful to the process. In some cases, scripting will be method of choice. The combination of these new technologies with traditional systems and materials will produce forms that are otherwise impossible to imagine.

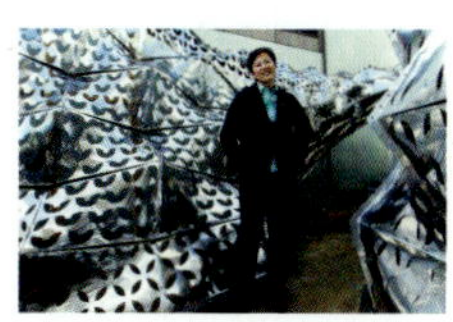

Doris Sung (US). After receiving her BA at Princeton University and M.Arch. at Columbia University, Doris Sung worked in various offices in cities across the US before arriving in Los Angeles in 2001. She developed her research focus while teaching at University of Southern California (USC), the Southern California Institute of Architecture (SCI-Arc), University of Colorado and the Catholic University of America. In 1999, she opened her office, dO|Su Studio Architecture, and soon received many AIA and ASID awards for her work. **Doris Sung** (US). Nach einem BA an der Princeton University und einem M.Arch. an der Columbia University arbeitete Doris Sung zunächst in einer Reihe von Architekturbüros in verschiedenen Städten der USA, ehe es sie 2001 schließlich nach Los Angeles verschlug. Ihr Forschungsschwerpunkt kristallisierte sich im Zuge ihrer Lehrtätigkeit an der University of Southern California (USC), dem Southern California Institute of Architecture (SCI-Arc), der University of Colorado und der Catholic University of America heraus. 1999 eröffnete sie ihr Büro dO|Su Studio Architecture und wurde für ihre Arbeit schon bald mit Preisen des American Institute of Architects und der American Society of Interior Designers ausgezeichnet.

Matopy

Sam Jewell

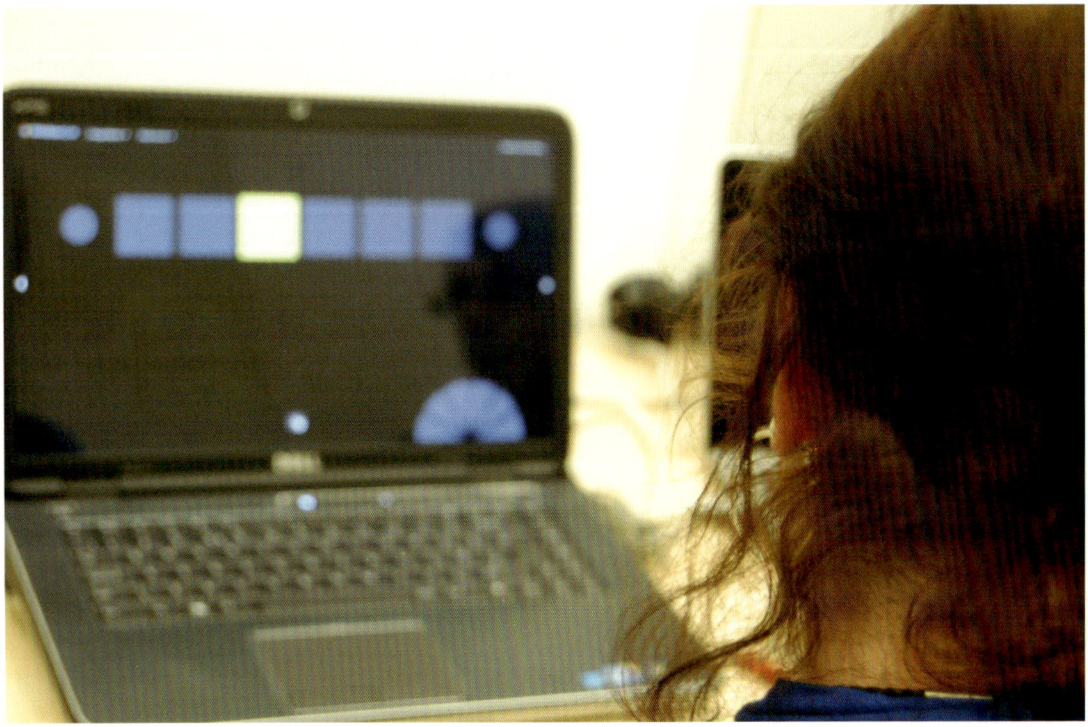

Matopy is changing the world by revolutionizing the way we interact with the web.
As babies we are listening all the time, and most people can speak by the age of three, but we only become competent at reading and writing when we reach seven or eight. *Matopy* will provide a more natural way of accessing any online content, which does not require a monitor, a keyboard or even a desk. In the not-too-distant future, the recipe you are following online will be read aloud to you by *Matopy* while your hands are covered in flour and egg.
It's time for the web to speak.
Matopy uses sound to present information in the way a graphic designer uses color, layout and style to convey information beyond the text of a page. We use audio cues, multiple voices and sound effects to convey context and add meaning to the textual content, giving a richer, deeper experience of the web. We are effectively embellishing the spoken word just as the graphic designer does to the written word.
For instance, headings would be spoken in a different voice to subheadings, and body text would be

Matopy wird unsere Interaktion mit dem Internet revolutionieren und damit die Welt verändern.
Als Babys hören wir immer nur zu, und die meisten von uns können mit drei Jahren sprechen. Lese- und Schreibfähigkeiten erwerben wir in der Regel erst im Alter von sieben oder acht. *Matopy* schafft eine natürlichere Zugriffsmöglichkeit auf Online-Inhalte – eine, die ohne Monitor, ohne Tastatur und sogar ohne Schreibtisch auskommt. In nicht allzu ferner Zukunft wird Ihnen *Matopy* das aufgerufene Rezept laut vorlesen, während Sie mit Eiern und Mehl hantieren.
Es ist höchste Zeit, dass das Internet sprechen lernt.
Matopy macht mit akustischen Elementen das, was Grafikdesign mit Farbe, Layout und Schriften machen. Wir reichern Textinhalte durch Audiosignale, unterschiedliche Stimmen und Soundeffekte mit kontextuellen und semantischen Zusatzinformationen an und steigern damit die Erlebbarkeit des Internet. Letzten Endes verschönern wir dabei auch das gesprochene Wort, so wie es das Grafikdesign mit dem geschriebenen tut.
Das geschieht zum Beispiel dadurch, dass Überschriften mit einer anderen Stimme gesprochen werden als Unter- oder Zwischenüberschriften, und der Haupttext mit wieder einer anderen (also etwa die Überschrift von

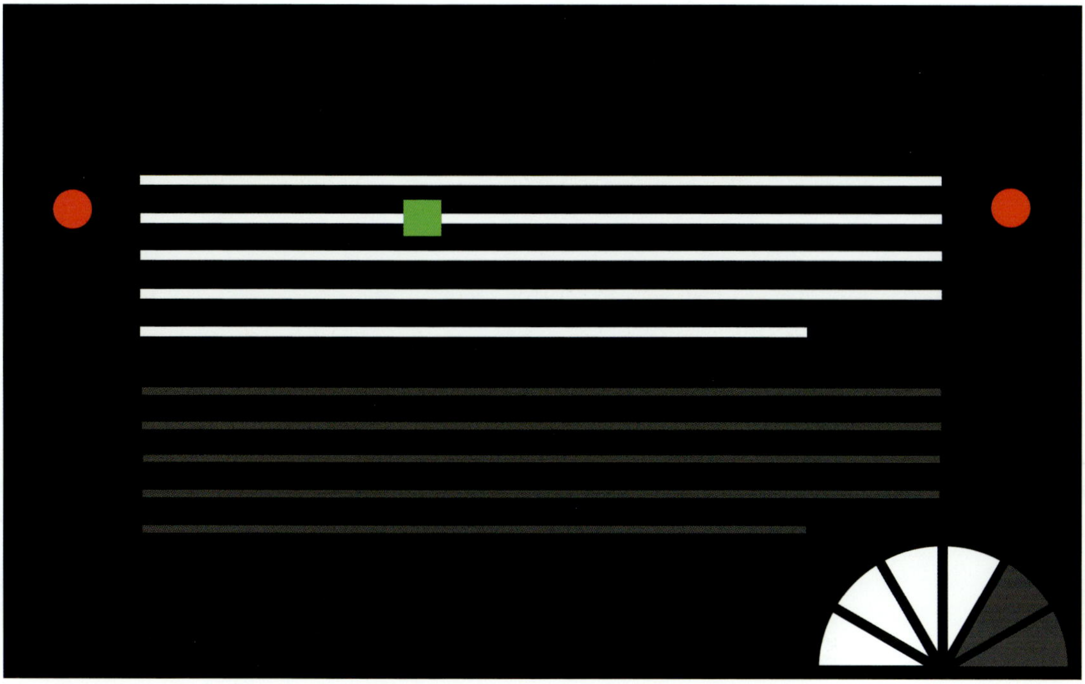

einer Frau, die Unterüberschrift von einem Mann und der Haupttext wieder von einer Frau). Links würden durch Soundeffekte oder durch Stimmveränderungen oder eine andere Hintergrundmusik kenntlich gemacht. Farbwechsel könnten auf ähnliche Art und Weise vermittelt werden.

Ziel ist die Entwicklung eines schönen, einnehmenden, vergnüglichen interaktiven Audioerlebnisses, das genauso vielfältig und individuell ist wie moderne visuelle Internetangebote. Langfristig schwebt uns die Möglichkeit einer ähnlichen Personalisierung von Audiowebsites vor, wie sie bei heutigen Blogs mithilfe von Stilvorlagen möglich ist. Größere Unternehmen werden sich ihre Corporate Identity mit ausgefeilten Soundtracks, Voiceover- und Audiointeraktionsdesigns maßschneidern lassen können.

spoken by a third voice (perhaps a woman for the heading, a man for the subheading and a second woman for the body text). Links would be implied by sound effects and potentially by changes to the tonal qualities of the voice or the background music. Color changes could be achieved in the same way.

The final result is to have a beautiful, absorbing, interactive and fun audio experience that is as rich and as individual as the visual experiences on the web today. In the long term we see people being able to personalize their audio sites just as they do today with themes for their blogs. Larger companies will be able to tailor their brands and their corporate identities with polished soundtracks, voiceovers and audio interaction.

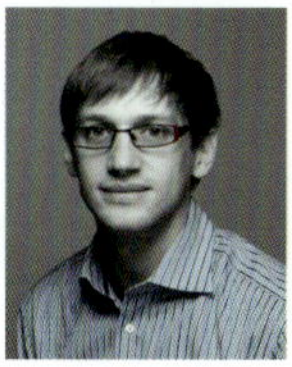

Sam Jewell (UK) is the ideator of *Matopy* and has a deep understanding of the visually impaired community. He has an MA and MEng from Cambridge and MIT and an MA and MSc in innovation design engineering, RCA.
Sam Jewell (UK) ist Gründer für *Matopy* und steht in enger Verbindung mit der Sehbehinderten-Community. Er hat einen Master of Art / Master of Engineering von der Universität Cambridge und vom MIT und einen Master of Art / Master of Science in Innovation Design Engineering vom Royal College of Art, London.

PRIX ARS ELECTRONICA COLLIDE@CERN RESIDENCY AWARD

Prix Ars Electronica Collide@CERN Residency Award

Michael Doser, Horst Hörtner, Ariane Koek, Gerfried Stocker

BACKGROUND

Prix Ars Electronica Collide@CERN Residency Award was launched in 2011 as an international competition for digital artists to win a residency at CERN, the world's largest particle physics laboratory, in Geneva. It was the first prize to be announced as part of the new Collide@CERN Residency Award initiated by the laboratory. The prize marked the beginning of a three-year science/arts cultural partnership and creative collaboration between CERN and Ars Electronica—which originated with CERN's cooperation with *ORIGIN*, the Ars Electronica Festival in 2011.

The aim of the Prix Ars Electronica Collide@CERN Residency Award is to take digital creativity to new dimensions by colliding the minds of scientists with the imaginations of artists. In this way, we seek to accelerate innovation across culture in the 21st century—creating new dimensions in digital arts, inspired by the ideas, engineering and science generated at CERN, and produced by the winning artist in collaboration with the transdisciplinary expertise of the FutureLab team at Ars Electronica.

The residency is structured in two stages—with an initial two months at CERN, where the winning artist has a dedicated inspiration partner to inspire him/her and his/her work. The second part is one month of collaborative residence with the Futurelab team and mentor at Ars Electronica Linz, to develop and make new work inspired by the CERN residency. From the first meeting between the artists, their CERN inspiration partner and Futurelab mentor, they participate in a dialog that will be a public blog of their creative process until the final work is produced and maybe beyond. In this way, the public will be able to join in the conversation.

The award was made following the jury meeting to assess 395 entries from over 40 countries around the world, after the seven-week open call was announced at the Ars Electronica Festival September 2011. The high quality of ideas and range of disciplines shows the strength of interest and focus on the importance of science and technology

HINTERGRÜNDE

Der Prix Ars Electronica Collide@CERN Residency Award wurde 2011 als internationaler Wettbewerb für digitale Kunst eingeführt, bei dem ein Forschungsaufenthalt am CERN, dem größten Forschungszentrum für Teilchenphysik in Genf, zu gewinnen ist. Es war der erste Preis, der im Rahmen des neuen, vom CERN initiierten Künstler-Residency-Programms Collide@CERN ausgeschrieben wurde. Der Preis bildete den Auftakt einer dreijährigen kulturellen Partnerschaft im Bereich Wissenschaft/Kunst und kreativen Zusammenarbeit zwischen CERN und Ars Electronica, die mit der Mitwirkung von CERN am Ars Electronica Festival 2011 mit dem Thema *ORIGIN* begann.

Ziel des Prix Ars Electronica Collide@CERN Residency Award ist es, der digitalen Kreativität neue Dimensionen zu eröffnen, indem man wissenschaftliches Denken und künstlerische Fantasie aufeinanderprallen lässt. Auf diese Weise wollen wir die innovative Entwicklungen in der Kultur des 21. Jahrhunderts beschleunigen – neue Möglichkeiten in der digitalen Kunst erschließen, die von den Ideen, der Wissenschaft und Technik am CERN inspiriert sind und vom Preisträger mit Unterstützung des interdisziplinären Futurelab-Teams der Ars Electronica realisiert werden.

Die Residency ist in zwei Abschnitte gegliedert. Zunächst verbringt der Preisträger zwei Monate am CERN, wo er von einem ihm eigens zugewiesenen Mentor betreut wird, der ihn bei seiner Arbeit inspirieren soll. Der zweite Abschnitt ist ein einmonatiger Aufenthalt bei der Ars Electronica in Linz, wo mit Unterstützung des Futurelab-Teams und eines Mentors eine neue Arbeit entwickelt und umgesetzt werden soll, die von der Residency am CERN inspiriert ist. Vom ersten Treffen an treten der Künstler, sein Partner vom CERN und sein Futurelab-Mentor in einen Dialog ein, der bis zur Fertigstellung der Arbeit und vielleicht darüber hinaus als Blog veröffentlicht wird, in dem der kreative Prozess beschrieben wird. Auf diese Weise kann die Öffentlichkeit die Auseinandersetzung mitverfolgen und kommentieren.

Der Preis wurde nach Bewertung der 395 Einreichungen aus mehr als 40 Ländern weltweit verliehen, die nach der beim Ars Electronica Festival im September 2011 verkündeten, siebenwöchigen Ausschreibung eingingen.

Die hohe Qualität der Ideen und das breite Spektrum der Disziplinen zeigt, wie stark das Interesse und wie groß der Stellenwert von Wissenschaft und Technologie als Inspirationsquelle im Kunstbereich heute ist. Die rege internationale Teilnahme sowie die künstlerische Qualität und inspirierende Kraft vieler Einreichungen sind ermutigende Indizien dafür, dass dieses Residency-Programm auf reges Interesse und eine zunehmende Begeisterung für wissenschaftliche Forschung stößt.
Die Einreichungen rekrutieren sich aus den verschiedensten Disziplinen: von experimenteller Klangkunst und Musik über Architektur, generative Kunst bis hin zu Social-Media-Projekten und New Design, das das Verhältnis des Menschen zu Wissenschaft und Technologie erforscht. In Anbetracht der hohen Beteiligung am Wettbewerb und der großen Bandbreite der eingereichten Ideen entschied die Jury, neben dem Hauptpreis auch Anerkennungen auszusprechen.

ANERKENNUNGEN

Die Gewinner der Anerkennungspreise wurden aufgrund ihres hohen Rankings im Bewertungsprozess ausgewählt, in dem nach folgenden Kriterien beurteilt wurde: Ästhetik, Originalität, innovativer Ansatz, Technik und Qualität der Präsentation sowie Interesse am CERN als Plattform wissenschaftlicher Auseinandersetzung. Die Anerkennungen des Prix Ars Electronica Collide@CERN Residency Award gehen an die Medienkünstlerin Nataša Teofilović (Serbien) für ihre Einreichung *O_O*, die internationale Musiktheater-Kooperation zwischen dem Komponisten Arnoud Noordegraaf (NL) und dem Schriftsteller Adrian Hornsby (UK) für ihre Einreichung *How I learned to love the particle* und den Vertreter generativer Kunst Eno Henze (DE) für sein Projekt *Das Gestell*.

GEWINNER DES RESIDENCY AWARD

Versuch unter Kreisen
Julius von Bismarck
Julius von Bismarck, dessen vielseitige und experimentelle künstlerische Praxis zunehmend international Beachtung findet, erhielt den Preis von der Jury für „seine

in our world as a source of inspiration across the art forms. The large international participation as well as the artistic quality and inspirational power of many of the submissions are encouraging indicators that this residency program is addressing the growth in interest in and excitement about science. The artistic fields ranged from experimental sound work and music, architecture and new design, sculpture, generative art and film to social-media projects and new design that explore how people relate to science and technology. In recognition of the high level of interest and participation in the competition, as well as the quality and range of ideas shown by the international artists, alongside the first prize, the jury decided to create an additional category of Honorary Mentions.

HONORARY MENTIONS

The Honorary Mentions were awarded due to their high ranking by the jury in the key criteria areas of aesthetics, originality, innovative approach, technique and quality of the presentation, and interest in the scientific ideas expressed by CERN. The Prix Ars Electronica Collide@CERN Residency Award Honorary Mentions are awarded to the new-media artist Nataša Teofilović (Serbia) for her proposal *O_O*, to the interdisciplinary music-theatre collaboration between composer Arnoud Noordegraaf (NL) and writer Adrian Hornsby (UK) for their proposal *How I learned to love the particle*, and to the generative artist Eno Henze (DE) for his project *Das Gestell*.

WINNER RESIDENCY AWARD

Versuch unter Kreisen
Julius von Bismarck
With a growing international reputation for his diverse and experimental artistic practice, Julius von Bismarck was given the award by the jury for "his proposal and work which manipulates and criticizes our notions of reality in unpredictable

ways, often with inventive use of video, objects and public interventions". His works are also characterized by his fascination with complex philosophical and scientific ideas. Furthermore, the jury were convinced by the caliber of his negotiation and engagement with the complex fields that surround particle physics and his use of them as a source of inspiration for his work. This was exemplified in his video testimonial, with its subtle use of a post-production technique—negative-echo—on his vocal track. Introducing himself he said: "I'm speaking to you through this video, with a negative echo, where I am explaining why I am going to be inspired by the residency at CERN." Von Bismarck's testimonial emphasized his mastery of media and his ability to assimilate and integrate scientific notions in often playful and meaningful ways.

The Creative Process
Prix Ars Electronica Collide@CERN Residency Award

The mission of the Collide@CERN residency program is to create a laboratory of the imagination—where the science, technology and engineering of the international particle physics laboratory are springboards of the imagination for the artist in residence. There are three key processes to enable this to happen, which keep the creative process in a dedicated balance and are directed by a creative producer experienced in creating new work with artists. First, matching the artist with a CERN inspiration partner—a term carefully chosen to reflect the equality between the arts and science, which is at the heart of the whole Collide@CERN program at the laboratory. This matching happened during Julius von Bismarck's three-day introduction seminars and tour of CERN in January 2012, two months prior to his residency, which began in March. During this three day visit, Julius met many leading scientists as well as visiting experiments, such as Atlas, the one of the largest particle detectors in the world, and Isolde, which houses other nuclear experiments and trans-science studies as well. During the three full days of seminars on everything from dark energy to luminosity and velocity,

Einreichung sowie seine Arbeit, die unsere Realitätsvorstellungen in unvorhersehbarer Weise manipuliert und kritisiert, oftmals unter einfallsreicher Verwendung von Video, Objekten und öffentlichen Interventionen". Seine Arbeiten sind auch von seiner Faszination für komplexe philosophische und wissenschaftliche Fragestellungen charakterisiert. Darüber konnte er die Jury durch seine Auseinandersetzung mit den komplexen Themenkreisen rund um Teilchenphysik überzeugen, die eine Quelle der Inspiration für sein Werk darstellt. Dies kam deutlich in seiner Videopräsentation zum Ausdruck, die er subtil nachbearbeitete, indem er zur Tonspur einen Vorhall hinzufügte. Er stellte sich darin mit folgenden Worten vor: „... Ich spreche zu Ihnen über dieses Video mit Vorhalleffekt, in dem ich erkläre, warum mich ein Aufenthalt am CERN inspiriert." Von Bismarcks Einreichung zeigte deutlich seinen souveränen Umgang mit Medien und seine Fähigkeit, wissenschaftliche Begriffe in oft spielerischer und bedeutungsvoller Weise zu übernehmen und zu integrieren.

Der kreative Prozess
Prix Ars Electronica Collide@CERN Residency Award

Aufgabe des Collide@CERN Residency-Programms ist es, ein Labor der Fantasie zu schaffen, in dem Wissenschaft, Technologie und Verfahrenstechnik des internationalen Forschungszentrums für Teilchenphysik Künstlern als Sprungbrett dienen und ihre Fantasie beflügeln.
Drei wesentliche Prozesse sind Voraussetzung, um diese Ambition zu verwirklichen und den kreativen Prozess in einer produktiven Balance zu halten. Sie werden von einem kreativen Leiter, der Erfahrung in der Entwicklung neuer Arbeiten mit Künstlern hat, begleitet. Zunächst wird ein sogenannter „Inspiration Partner", ein Mentor für den Künstler, vom CERN ausgesucht – wobei dieser Ausdruck sorgfältig gewählt wurde, um auf die Ebenbürtigkeit von Kunst und Wissenschaft zu verweisen, die ein zentrales Moment des gesamten Collide@CERN-Programms ist. Die Auswahl des Mentors erfolgte während des dreitägigen Einführungsseminars und der Besichtigung des CERN im Januar 2012, zwei Monate vor Beginn seiner Residency im März. Während dieses dreitägigen Besuchs begegnete der Künstler vielen namhaften Wissenschaftlern und bekam Einblick in Experimente, wie etwa das ATLAS-Experiment – ATLAS ist einer der

größten Teilchendetektoren der Welt – und ISOLDE, ein Programm, in dem Nuklearexperimente gemacht und transwissenschaftliche Studien betrieben werden. Während des dreitägigen Seminars mit einem dichten Programm, das von Dunkler Energie bis Luminosität und Geschwindigkeitsvektoren reichte, wurde rasch klar, dass der Experte für verborgene Welten und CERN-Theoretiker Dr. James Wells ein geeigneter Partner für den Künstler wäre. Beiden ist nicht nur eine intellektuelle Verspieltheit gemeinsam, sondern auch die Begeisterung für ein Denken, das über Paradigmen hinausgeht, und der Wunsch, es in die Praxis umzusetzen und Realität werden zu lassen. Zwei Monate lang trafen sie sich jede Woche entweder virtuell oder real, um Ideen zu erörtern, Erfahrungen auszutauschen, einander Ratschläge zu geben und zu unterstützen. Eines der unerwarteten Ergebnisse dieser Beziehung, das nicht vertraglich vereinbart war, ist, dass die beiden gemeinsam an einem künstlerischen Projekt arbeiten wollen. Man darf gespannt sein.

Der zweite wesentliche Prozess ist die zweimonatige kuratorische Begleitung der Künstler am Forschungszentrum. Jeder Künstler braucht unterschiedliche Impulse, hat andere Bedürfnisse und Ansätze, mit Ideen in der künstlerischen Praxis umzugehen, weshalb die zweimonatige Inspirationsphase umfassend kuratiert wurde. Julius von Bismarck ist ein Künstler, den Herausforderungen auf jeder Ebene – sei es technischer, wissenschaftlicher, künstlerischer und intellektueller Art – stimulieren. Deshalb wurde er in den ersten fünf Wochen jeden Tag mit einer der vielen Herausforderungen vertraut gemacht, die im CERN Teil der täglichen Arbeit sind – von der Präzision des Wasserstrahlschneidens und dem Ätzen von Mikrochips bis zu der Präzisionstechnik, eine sterile Nebelkammer zu konstruieren. Er hatte Essenseinladungen mit Wissenschaftlern aller Ebenen – u. a. auch mit einem jungen Wissenschaftler, der möglicherweise eine neue Entdeckung gemacht hatte, und Julius erzählte, wie es ist, wenn man mit 3.000 anderen Wissenschaftlern zusammenarbeitet. In den letzten drei Wochen hatte Julius mehr Zeit für sich zur Verfügung, um den diversen Anregungen und Ideen nachzugehen und sie weiterzuentwickeln.

Der dritte wesentliche Prozess im Rahmen von Collide@CERN ist die Auseinandersetzung mit der CERN-Community – der Artist-in-Residence setzt sich mit

it became quickly apparent that hidden-worlds specialist and CERN theorist Dr. James Wells was an appropriate match. Both Julius and James, as well as sharing an intellectual playfulness, have a mutual fascination with thinking beyond the paradigm and then putting these thoughts into practice by making them a reality. For two months, they met every week, either virtually or in person, to discuss ideas, share their experiences and give advice and support to each other. One of the unexpected outcomes of their relationship, which was not written into their contract, is that they are now committed to working on an art work together in the future. Watch this space!

The second crucial factor is the curation of the artist's two months at the laboratory. Every artist has different needs, different stimuli and ways of responding to ideas for their artistic practice, so the two months of inspiration were carefully curated. Julius is an artist who is stimulated by challenges on every level—technical, engineering, scientifically, artistically and intellectually. So for the first five weeks, each day he was introduced to one of the many of the challenges that CERN tackles as part of its everyday work—from the precision of cutting with water and acid-etching microchips to the precision engineering needed to create a sterile cloud chamber. He also had lunches with scientists at different levels of their careers—including a young scientist who had potentially made a new discovery and discussed with Julius how this works when one is working in collaboration with 3,000 other scientists. For the final three weeks, Julius had free time to follow up on and further explore any of the ideas he had encountered.

The third factor of Collide@CERN is the engagement with the CERN community—so the artist in residence engages with the science and the scientists in the spirit of equal exchange. Many residencies have the artist as the main focus, without making community engagement an official part of the residency, thus unwittingly creating distance and divisions. The Collide@CERN focuses on equal exchange and excellence, deliberately putting the artist and the scientists on the same level

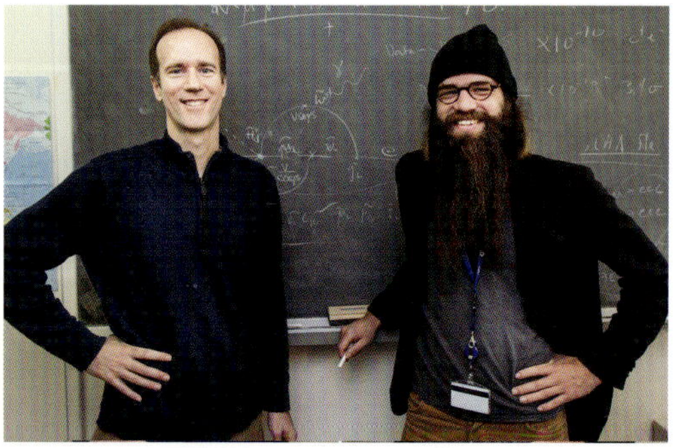

CERN inspration partners Dr. James Wells and Julius von Bismarck.
Photo: CERN

of mutual exchange in order to engender mutual respect and knowledge sharing. This is done not only on a personal level, with the dedicated inspiration partner, but also through the curation and open lectures at CERN's Globe of Science and Innovation at the beginning and end of the residency. Last but by no means least, the artist in residence is also asked to create a series of interventions in the CERN community.

One of Julius's intervention had over 20 scientists signing up to be plunged into the bowels of CERN and led through the dark into a space under the laboratories that they could not see and had never been to. In this environment, not knowing where they were or who/what was there, they were played a recording of Bertrand Russell discussing Plato's Cave and invited to share what they saw in the dark with the other voices in the space and discuss the nature of seeing. Another intervention was Julius's compressed re-enactment of his art school training in 90 minutes. As he said in the publicity for the event: "Everything is relative, and everyone is art."

With these seeds of inspiration and contacts sown during the two month residency at CERN, Julius was then ready to go to Ars Electronica's Futurelab to complete the development and production of one of the ideas he had started exploring. But many other ideas developed and blossomed at CERN—not just one—and as a Prix Ars Electronica Collide@CERN Residency Award prizewinner, Julius always has access to the laboratory, becoming part of the unique fellowship of other artists who will go on to win this prize, as well as the other awards in the Collide@CERN program.

(Text: Ariane Koek)

der Wissenschaft und den Wissenschaftlern in einer Atmosphäre kooperativen, gegenseitigen Austauschs auseinander. Bei vielen Residencies steht der Künstler im Mittelpunkt, Engagement für die Gemeinschaft ist kein offizieller Teil des Aufenthalts, wodurch ungewollt Distanz entsteht. Collide@CERN legt Wert auf gleichberechtigten Austausch und Exzellenz und stellt den Künstler und die Wissenschaftler im wechselseitigen Austausch bewusst auf dieselbe Ebene, um gegenseitigen Respekt und Wissenstransfer zu fördern. Dies gilt nicht nur für den Kontakt mit dem zugewiesenen Mentor auf einer persönlichen Ebene, sondern auch für die gesamte kuratorische Betreuung und die Vorträge in CERNs Globe of Science and Innovation zu Beginn und Ende des Aufenthalts. Nicht zuletzt wird der Artist-in-Residence auch gebeten, eine Reihe von Interventionen in der CERN-Community vorzunehmen.

Eine der Interventionen des Künstlers bestand darin, dass er zwanzig Wissenschaftler in das Innere des CERN-Gebäudes und im Dunkeln in einen Raum unter den Labors führte, den sie nicht sehen konnten und an dem sie noch nie waren. Ohne zu wissen, wo sie sich befanden und wer/was sonst noch vor Ort war, wurde ihnen in dieser Umgebung eine Aufnahme von Bertrand Russel vorgespielt, auf der er über Platos Höhlengleichnis sprach. Dann wurden sie aufgefordert, sich mit den anderen im Raum darüber auszutauschen, was sie im Dunkeln wahrnahmen bzw. das Wesen des Sehens zu diskutieren. Eine andere Intervention bestand in einer verdichteten Nachstellung seiner künstlerischen Ausbildung in 90 Minuten. Wie er vor der Öffentlichkeit sagte, die sich anlässlich des Events versammelte: „Alles ist relativ und jeder ist Kunst."

Mit diesen Keimen der Inspiration und den Kontakten, die während des zweimonatigen Aufenthalts am CERN entstanden, war Julius von Bismarck für das Futurelab der Ars Electronica gerüstet, wo eine der Ideen, an denen er zu arbeiten begonnen hatte, ausgearbeitet und realisiert werden sollte. Doch am CERN wurde nicht nur eine Idee entwickelt, viele reiften heran und wollen verwirklicht werden – als Gewinner des Prix Ars Electronica Collide@CERN Residency Award hat Julius von Bismarck jederzeit Zugang zum Labor, er ist Teil der einzigartigen Vereinigung von Künstlern, die diesen oder einen anderen Preis im Rahmen des Collide@CERN-Programms gewinnen werden.

(Text: Ariane Koek)

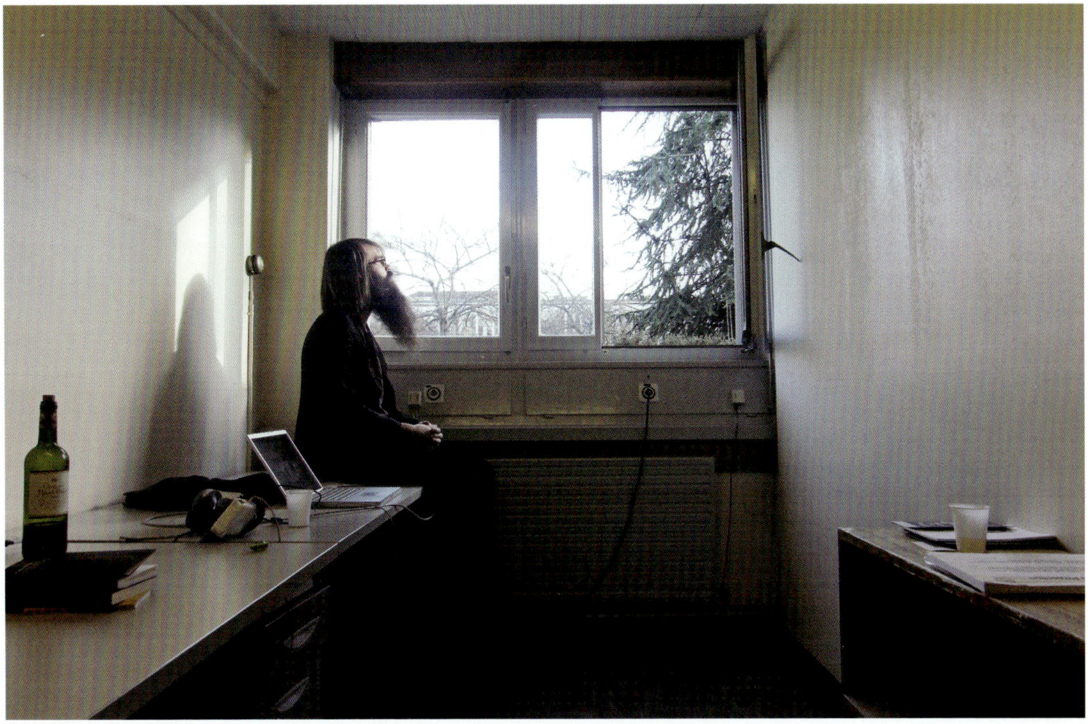

The window is open and there is someone sitting on a desk. He seems to be looking into the sun. On the desk there is also an almost empty bottle of red wine, a laptop and a few books. The rest of the office is almost empty. / Jemand sitzt vor dem geöffneten Fenster auf einem Schreibtisch. Er scheint in die Sonne zu schauen. Auf dem Schreibtisch neben ihm befinden sich eine fast leere Flasche Rotwein, ein Laptop und ein paar Bücher. Ansonsten ist das Büro fast leer.

ENTWICKLUNG DER IDEE

Versuch unter Kreisen

Julius von Bismarck

Betritt man den Raum, in dem der *Versuch unter Kreisen* installiert ist, bemerkt man zunächst nichts Ungewöhnliches, bis plötzlich etwas in Bewegung gerät. Alle Hängelampen beginnen langsam zu schwingen, als ob das Gebäude wie ein Schiff zu schwanken begänne. Die Lampen schwingen immer stärker und verwandeln die zuvor ruhige Atmosphäre in einen Raum voller Bewegung. Jedes Licht folgt einer bestimmten Choreografie, gemeinsam erzeugen die Lampen daher Harmonien, Dissonanzen, Interferenzen, Überlagerungsfrequenzen oder auch offenkundiges Chaos.

Die Installation lässt den ganzen Tag hindurch narrative Strukturen entstehen, präsentiert Choreografien, die von Pausen unterbrochen sind. Immer wenn die Lampen stillstehen, wird die Installation gleichsam unsichtbar,

IDEA DEVELOPMENT

Versuch unter Kreisen

Julius von Bismarck

When you enter the space where *Versuch unter Kreisen* [experiment under orbits] is installed you might not notice anything unusual until suddenly something moves. All the hanging lamps start swinging slowly, as if the building were see-sawing like a ship. The lamps start to oscillate, increasingly transforming the former calm atmosphere into a space full of motion. Every light follows a specific choreography, so that together the lamps form harmonies, dissonances, interferences, beat frequencies or apparent chaos.

The installation forms a narrative throughout the day, performing choreographies and pausing for different periods. Whenever the lamps stand still the installation becomes invisible, because the ordinary hanging lamps are perceived as an unquestioned part of the building. The work is composed not of the lamps themselves but of their composed movement.

Each of these oscillations is subtly stimulated by a fine pull on a thin string controlled by small motors connected to the lamp cable just under the ceiling.

The mathematically generated cyclical motion of the lamps is inspired by wave patterns that occur in nature on very small and large scales at which they usually remain invisible to the human eye. The examples Julius von Bismarck examined for this installation are the mathematical relationships between oscillating atoms in a crystal grid, the spins of sub-atomic particles and on a large scale the red shift of light caused by the expansion of the universe.

weil die gewöhnlichen Hängeleuchten als ein Teil des Gebäudes wahrgenommen werden, den man nicht hinterfragt. Nicht die Lampen machen diese Arbeit aus, sondern ihre kombinierte Bewegung.

Jede der Schwingungen wird durch einen feinen Zug in Gang gesetzt, der von kleinen Motoren gesteuert wird, die mit dem Kabel der Lampe unterhalb der Decke mit einer dünnen Kette verbunden sind.

Die mathematisch berechnete, zyklische Bewegung der Lampen ist von Wellenmustern inspiriert, die in der Natur in so kleinem und großem Maßstab auftreten, dass sie für das menschliche Auge im Allgemeinen nicht sichtbar sind. Beispiele, die Julius von Bismarck für diese Installation heranzog, sind die mathematischen Beziehungen zwischen schwingenden Atomen in einem Kristallgitter, die Spins subatomarer Teilchen und – in großen Maßstab – die Rotverschiebung des Lichts durch die Expansion des Universums.

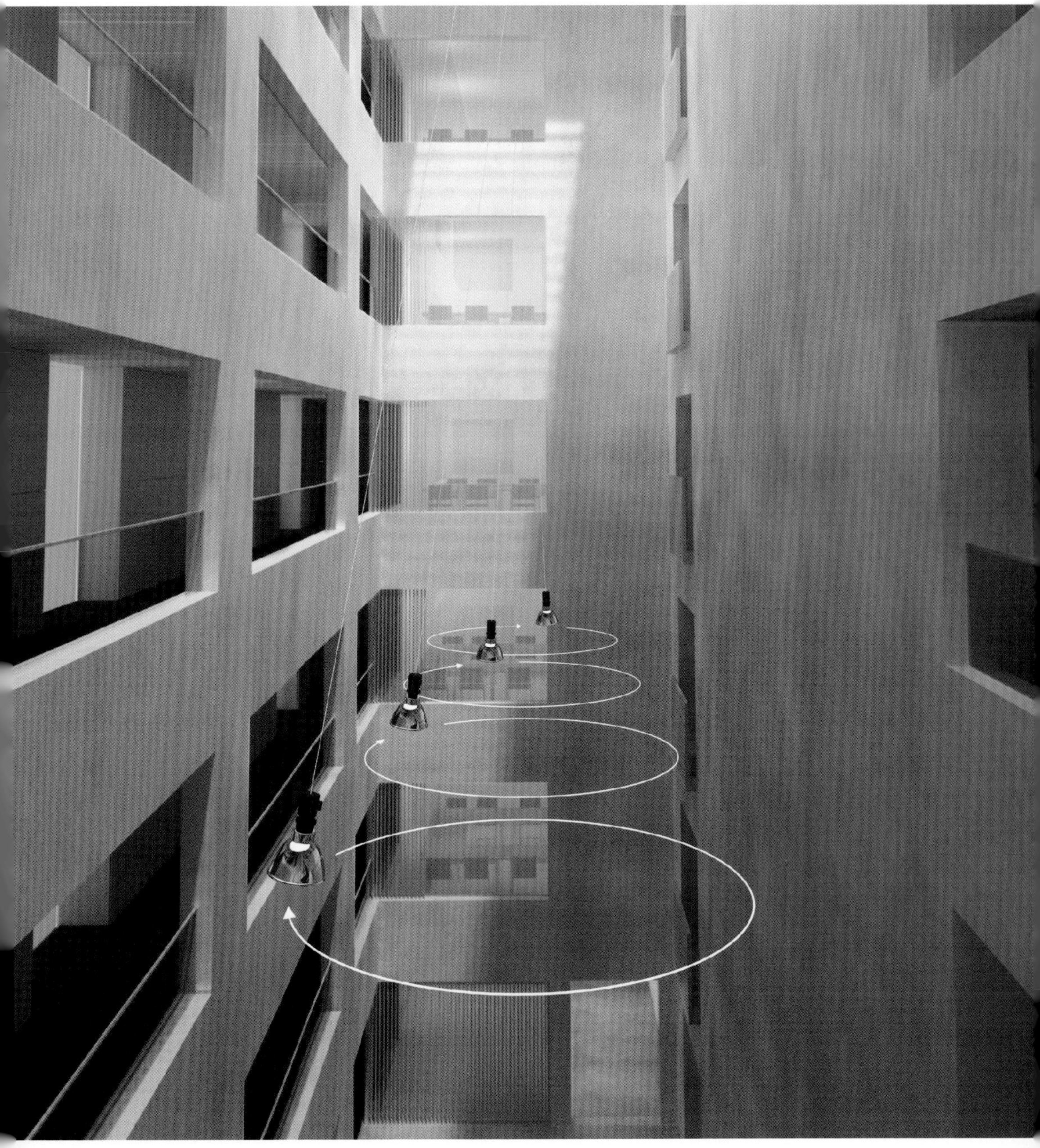

JURY

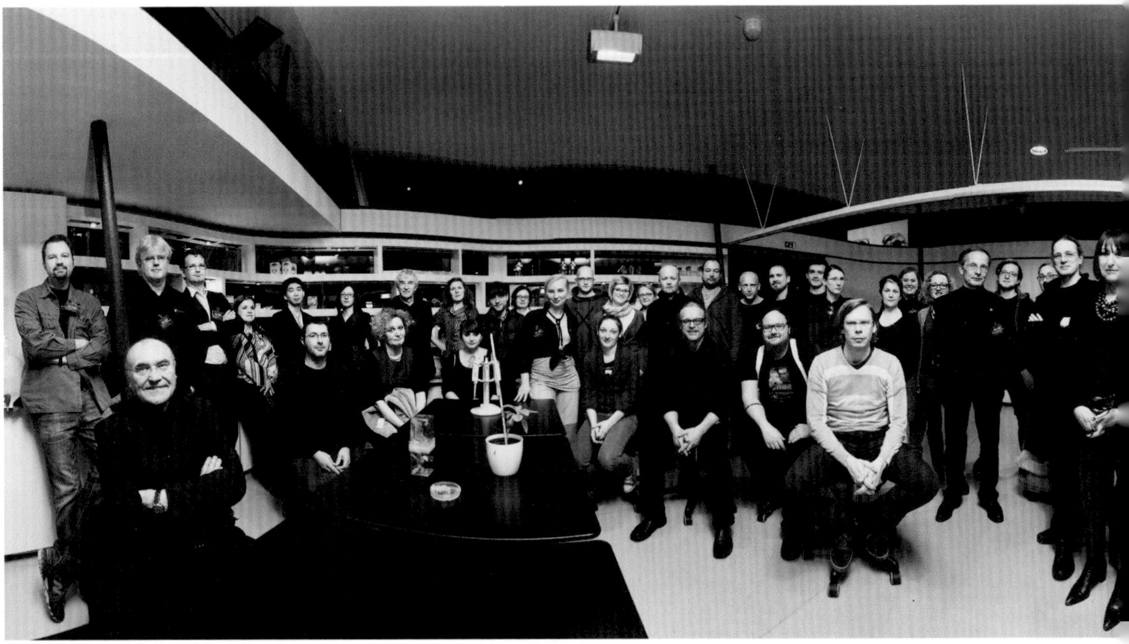

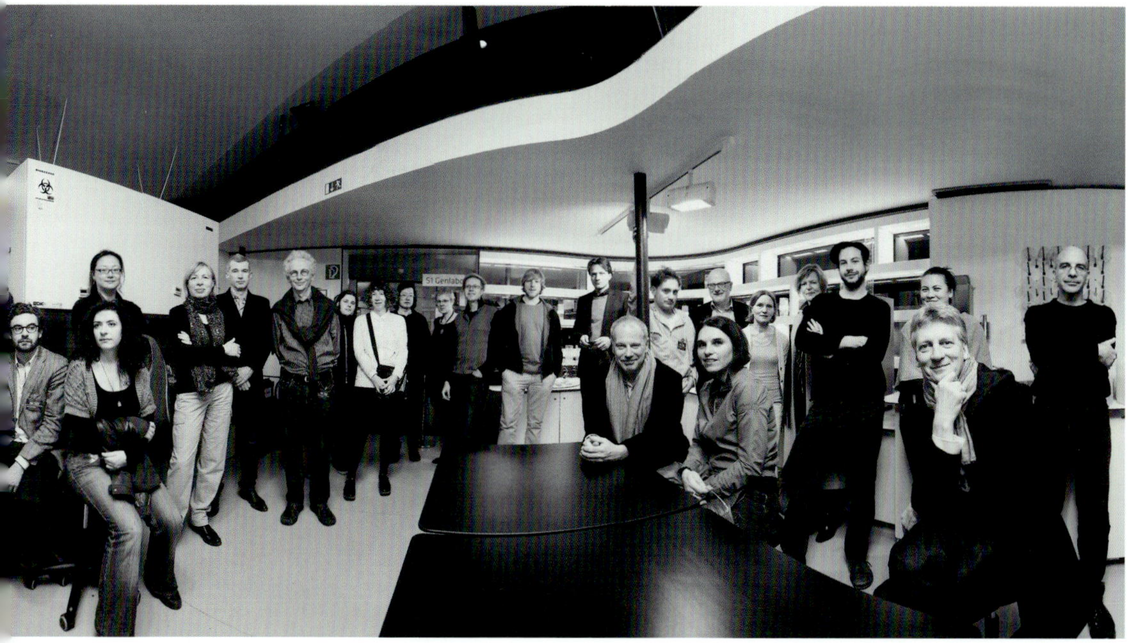

Computer Animation / Film / VFX
Paul Debevec, Isaac V. Kerlow, JP Lewis, Lorie Loeb, Boo Wong

Digital Musics & Sound Art
AGF, Christina Kubisch, Phil Mossman, Martin Supper, Dajuin Yao

Hybrid Art
Ursula Damm, Jens Hauser, Dietmar Offenhuber, Karin Ohlenschläger, Benjamin Weil

Interactive Art
Ksenia Fedorova, Fiona Raby, Christa Sommerer, Junji Watanabe, Mariela Yeregui

Digital Communities
Wolfgang Blau, Pether Kuthan, Liu Yan, Leila Nachawati, Thomas Schildhauer

u19 – CREATE YOUR WORLD
Sirikit Amann, Robert Glashüttner, Martin Hollinetz, Martina Sochor, Markus Sucher

[the next idea] voestalpine Art and Technology Grant
Michael Doser, Horst Hörtner, Ela Kagel, Manfred Pietschmann, Gustav Pomberger, Michael Sterrer-Ebenführer

Prix Ars Electronica Collide@CERN Residency Award
Michael Doser, Horst Hörtner, Ariane Koek, Gerfried Stocker

COMPUTER ANIMATION / FILM / VFX

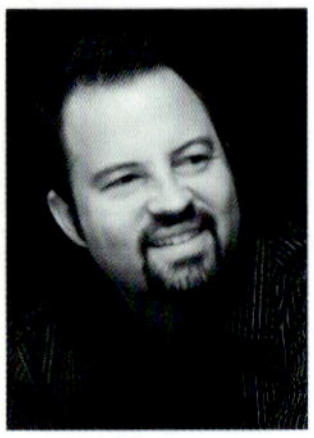

Paul Debevec (US) is a research professor at the University of Southern California and the Associate Director of Graphics Research at USC's Institute for Creative Technologies. His work has focused on image-based modeling and rendering techniques. He serves as the Vice-President of ACM Siggraph and recently received an Academy Award for his work on the Light Stage facial capture systems. The University of Southern California's Institute for Creative Technologies is a university-affiliated research center pursuing the next generation of virtual reality for training, education, and entertainment. *http://ict.usc.edu/~debevec*

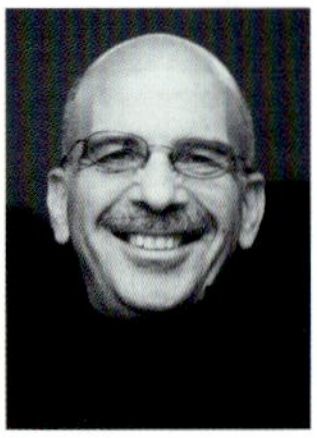

Isaac V. Kerlow (US) has a long career as a pioneer digital artist and independent filmmaker, and his work has been shown internationally. He is currently Artist-in-Residence at the Earth Observatory of Singapore and arrived on the island in 2005 as founding dean of the country's first professional art and film school. Isaac is also the author of several groundbreaking books, including *The Art of 3D Computer Animation and Effects*. His recent film *Mayon: The Volcano Princess* won the Best Concept Award at the United Nations Summit of Environmental Cinema in 2010.

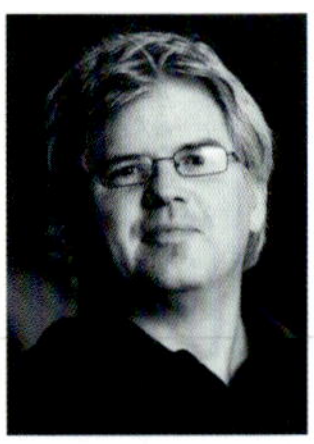

JP Lewis (US) is a research lead at Weta Digital and a part-time senior lecturer at Victoria University in Wellington (NZ). Lewis has software credits on several films, including *Avatar*, *The Matrix* sequels and *Forrest Gump*. Previously he has worked at academic and industrial research labs as well as in the film industry at companies including Industrial Light and Magic and Disney. His published algorithms have been incorporated in commercial software and adopted in the film industry. His current work involves applications of computer vision and machine-learning techniques to special effects.

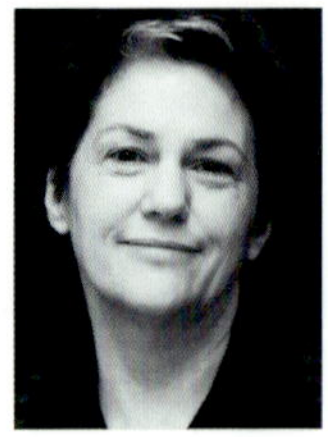

Lorie Loeb (US) is a professor in the computer science department at Dartmouth College, director of the digital arts program and President/co-founder of a start up (TellEmotion, Inc.). Lorie loves to build tools that synthesize art, science, technology and social activism to motivate changes in behavior or simply to make a story out of complex data. Before coming to Dartmouth, Lorie was Senior Research Scientist in the Computer Graphics Lab at Stanford University, where she worked with Chris Bregler as a founding member of the Movement Lab. She was a professor of film and animation production at NYU's Tisch School of the Arts and the Rhode Island School of Design.

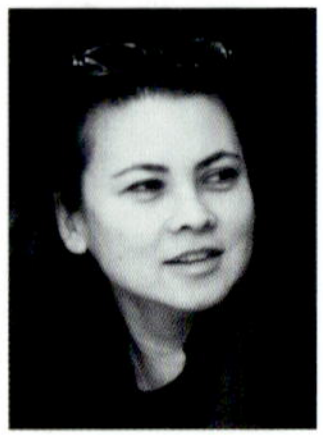

Boo Wong (US) is the Senior Producer of Design & Content at The Mill, with experience encompassing broadcast, film, web, games and print. She was Head of Production / Executive Producer at Psyop where she executive-produced Coca-Cola's multi-award-winning *Happiness Factory* among others. She was instrumental in spearheading Psyop's companywide pipeline and proprietary software tools. Boo has also produced animation, FX and graphics in long-form, most notably for Academy-Award-winning documentary *The Cove*, the Sundance Grand Jury prize-winner *And God Grew Tired of Us* and the Academy Award nominee *Murderball*. Boo has served on the board of directors for ACM Siggraph NYC.

DIGITAL MUSICS & SOUND ART

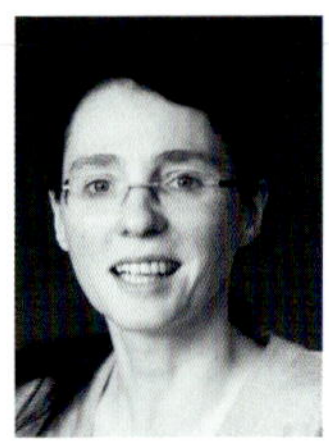

AGF (DE) is a digital songwriter, sound composer and poet. The focus of her work includes the relationship between language and sound, audiovisual live performance, digital communication, sound installations and commissions for movies and theater. Throughout her career, Greie has released 20 LPs and has been involved in numerous collaborations under aliases such as AGF/Delay (with Vladislav Delay), Greie Gut Fraktion (with Gudrun Gut) and The Lappetites (with Kaffe Matthews and Eliane Radigue) as well as many collaborations with the award-winning classical composer Craig Armstrong.

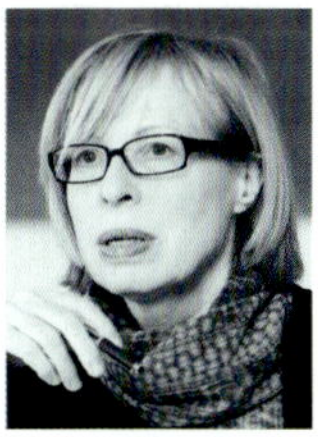

Christina Kubisch (DE) studied painting, music and electronics in Hamburg, Graz, Zürich and Milan. She made a name for herself in the 1970s with performances and video concerts, and since the early 80s with spatial sound installations, light spaces and works in public spaces. She has many electroacoustic compositions and radio productions to her credit. She has had guest professorships in Maastricht, Paris and Berlin, has been professor of audiovisual art at the HBK-University of Visual Arts Saarbrücken since 1994 and since 1997 a member of the Academy of the Arts, Berlin. She lives in Hoppegarten near Berlin. *www.christinakubisch.de*

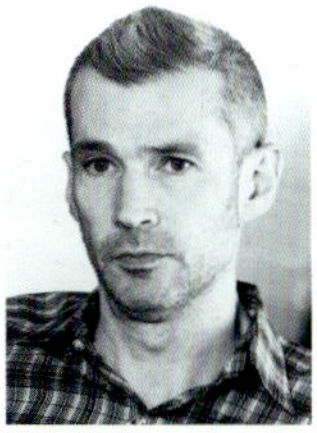

Phil Mossman (UK) is a veteran of groundbreaking music production who uniquely has recorded and toured with some of the most cutting-edge artists of the last 15 years while managing to create award-winning scores to pictures. In 2001, James Murphy invited Philip to join LCD Soundsystem. After five years with the band, Philip made the tough decision to quit touring but was recently invited to rejoin for the band's final shows at Terminal 5 and the now legendary and epic finale at Madison Square Gardens. In 2006, Philip accepted the position of Executive Producer at Amber New York, where he met fellow composer Will Bates. In 2010 Mossman and Bates launched their music duo Fall on Your Sword.

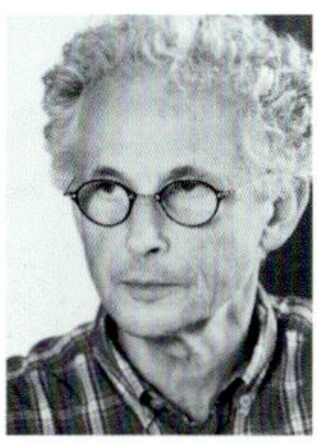

Martin Supper (DE) is professor of electroacoustic music and sound art at Berlin University of the Arts (UdK). He studied theoretical computer science, linguistics and musicology at the Technical University of Berlin, as well as computer music and electroacoustic music under Gottfried Michael Koenig. He has a post-graduate degree in computer science and a PhD in musicology. Since 1985, in charge of the UNI.K–UdK, Studio for Sound Art and Sound Research and since 2009 has been director of the Department of Sound Studies at the Central Institute for Continuing Education.

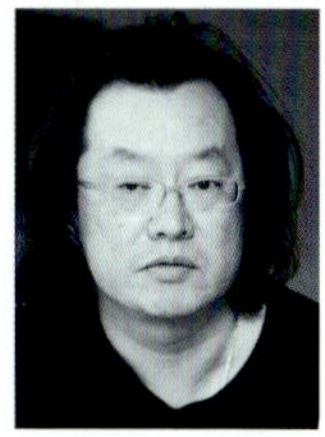

Dajuin Yao (US/TW) is a sound artist, producer, curator, radio host and art historian. Dajuin has created and promoted experimental music and sound art in China through concerts, radio shows, websites and teaching. He has curated international new-media performances in China, including Sounding Beijing 2003 and the opening concerts for the 2008 Shanghai eArts Festival. In 1997 Dajuin founded China Sound Unit, a pioneering phonography project, devoted to the documenting and recontextualizing of Chinese urban sound phenomena. He is currently director of the Open Media Lab at the China Academy of Art, Hangzhou. *www.dajuin.com*

HYBRID ART

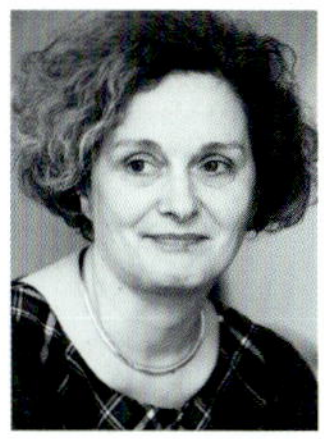

Ursula Damm (DE) has become known for her installations dealing with geometry and its social impact on public space. She has also developed numerous installation on the relationship between nature, science and civilization. She has had numerous solo and group exhibitions, and she has also participated in several international festivals. Since 2008 she has been the chair of Media Environments (Media Arts&Design) at the Media Faculty of the Bauhaus-University Weimar.

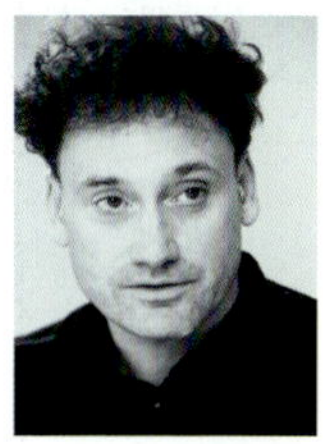

Jens Hauser (DE) is a Paris-based curator, author and arts and culture critic. With a background in media studies and science journalism, he focuses on the interactions between art and technology as well as on trans-genre and contextual aesthetics. He has curated exhibitions such as L'Art Biotech (Nantes, 2003), Still, Living (Perth, 2007), sk-interfaces (Liverpool, 2008, Luxembourg, 2009), the Article Biennale (Stavanger, 2008), Transbiotics (Riga 2010),Synth-ethic (Vienna, 2011) and Fingerprints... (Berlin, 2011, Munich, 2012).

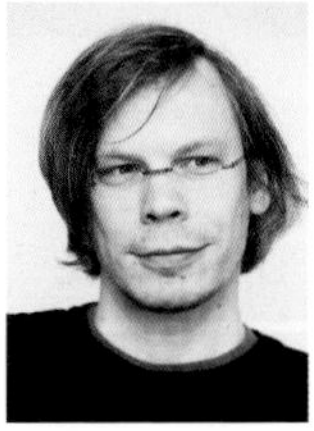

Dietmar Offenhuber (AT) has backgrounds in architecture, urban studies and digital media. He works on the spatial aspects of cognition, representation and behavior. Dietmar has degrees from the Technical University of Vienna and the MIT Media Lab. He was a key researcher in the Ars Electronica Futurelab and the Ludwig Boltzmann Institute for Media.Art.Research and taught in the Interface Cultures program as a professor at the Linz Art University. Currently he is researching his PhD dissertation in the Senseable City Lab at the Department for Urban Studies and Planning, MIT.

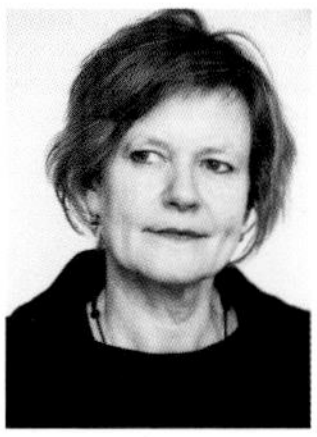

Karin Ohlenschläger (DE/ES) has been a critic and exhibition curator specializing in contemporary art and new media since 1985. She co-founded and co-directed MediaLab Madrid (2002-2006). She has directed various international initiatives, and her works have been shown worldwide. Karin Ohlenschläger teaches art, science and technology at the European University of Madrid and is the chairwoman of the Institute of Contemporary Art (IAC).

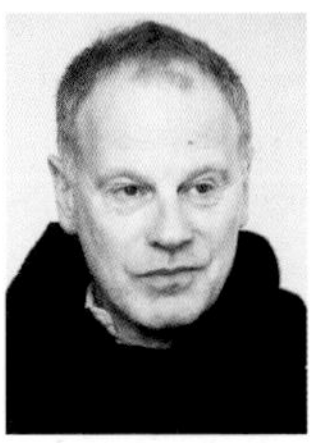

Benjamin Weil (FR) has been the artistic director at Laboral Centro de Arte y Creación Industrial (Gijón / ES) since 2009. He was curator of Media Arts at SFMOMA (2000-06) and executive director at Artists Space (2006-09). He curated Zones of Confluence (Villette Numérique festival, Paris, 2004) and was curatorial chair at Eyebeam Art & Technology Center in New York from 2003 to 2005. He has also been a visiting professor in the Visual Arts Department of IUAV (Università di Venezia) and from 2006 to 2011, he was the artistic director of H BOX, a video-commissioning program of the Fondation d'Entreprise Hermès.

INTERACTIVE ART

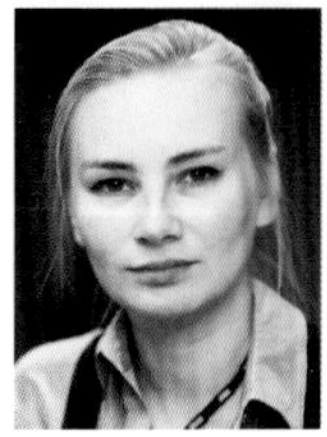

Ksenia Fedorova (RU) is a media art researcher and curator. She has been an initiator and curator of the Art-Science-Technology program at the National Center for Contemporary Arts (Ekaterinburg, RU) where she has curated a number of international exhibitions and events. She has taught classes on media art theory and history at the Ural State University and the Danube University, Krems (AT). She is a co-editor (with Nina Sosna) of the collection of articles on media theory. She is currently completing her PhD in Philosophy at the Ural Federal University (Ekaterinburg, RU) and is a PhD fellow at the Cultural Studies Graduate Group, University of California, Davis (US).

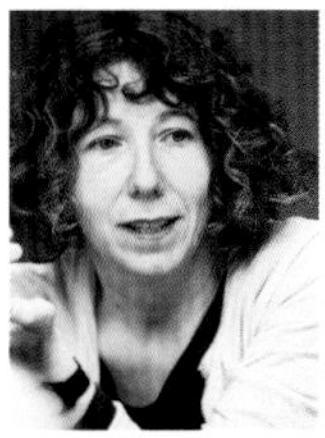

Fiona Raby (UK) is a partner in the design partnership Dunne & Raby, established in 1994. She is professor of industrial design at the University of Applied Arts in Vienna, and a reader in design interactions at the Royal College of Art in London. Dunne & Raby use design as a medium to stimulate discussion and debate amongst designers, industry and the public about the social, cultural and ethical implications of existing and emerging technologies. Their work has been exhibited at MoMA, the Pompidou Centre, and the Science Museum in London and is in the permanent collections of MoMA, V&A, FRAC and FNAC. They have published two books: *Design Noir: The Secret Life of Electronic Objects* and *Hertzian Tales*.

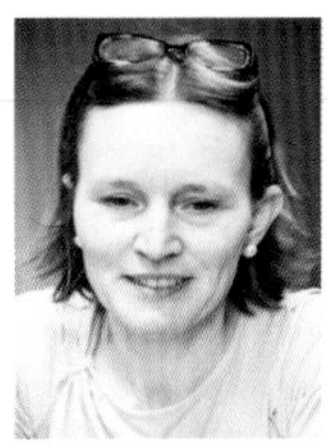

Christa Sommerer (AT) is professor and head of the Department for Interface Cultures at the Institute for Media at the University of Art and Design in Linz. She has been active as a media artist for 20 years, and together with Laurent Mignonneau she has received numerous awards. Their interactive art works have been shown in around 200 international exhibitions in museums and galleries. She has given many lectures and taught at several international universities in Asia and Europe. Together with Laurent Mignonneau she has published four books on interactive art.

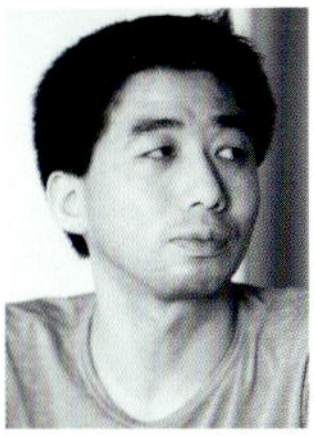

Junji Watanabe (JP) is a research specialist at NTT Communication Science Laboratories, with research focusing on perception and media technology. His studies have been published in major scientific journals in the field of neuroscience and interface technologies. He has also exhibited his works that demonstrated the influence of media technologies on perceptual experiences in technology showcases and science/art museums, such as in Siggraph and the Ars Electronica Center. He received a PhD in information science and technology at the University of Tokyo in 2005. For more information on his work see: *http://www.junji.org/*

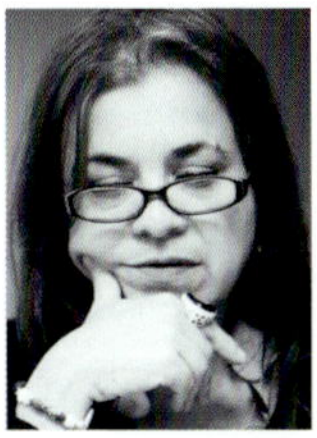

Mariela Yeregui (AR) is an electronic artist, and her works include interactive installations, video installations, net art, interventions in public spaces, video sculptures and robotic installations. Her works have been awarded prestigious prizes and exhibited at various festivals and exhibitions around the world. She has written several articles on the history and aesthetics of electronic art, the problems of robotic art and the transdisciplinary perspective in the interrelationship between art and technology.

DIGITAL COMMUNITIES

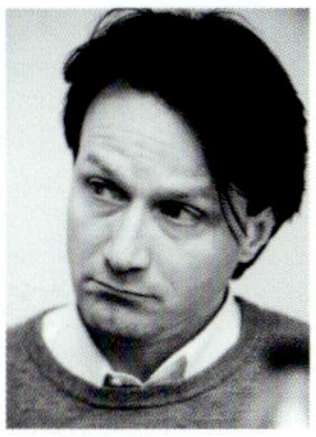

Wolfgang Blau (DE) was a radio newsanchor for Germany's National Public Broadcasting Corporation and a station voice for Germany's national television, ARD. From 1999 to late 2007, he worked in Silicon Valley and Washington DC as a freelance correspondent. In 1999, he developed *AudioWELT*, the first online-audio portal of a European newspaper. In 2008, he joined *Zeit Online* as editor-in-chief. In 2011, it won Germany's two most important awards for online journalism, the Grimme Online Award and two Lead Awards in Gold. Wolfgang Blau has recently been awarded Germany's Chief Editor of the Year 2011.

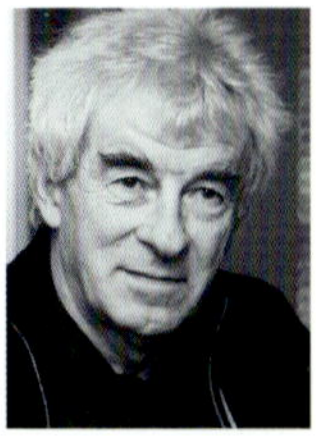

Pether Kuthan (AT), a sociologist, lived in Zimbabwe from 1989 until 1992, where he worked as a consultant in the field of cooperative development. After his return to Austria he worked as consultant for monitoring and evaluation for the Austrian foreign ministry and Austrian NGOs. Since 1993 he has initiated a number of cultural exchange projects between Austria and Africa. In 2001 he started *Tonga. Online*, which aims to provide the Tonga community with access to modern IT tools for education and cultural self representation. For some years Peter has been lecturing concepts and methods in international development cooperation at the University of Vienna.

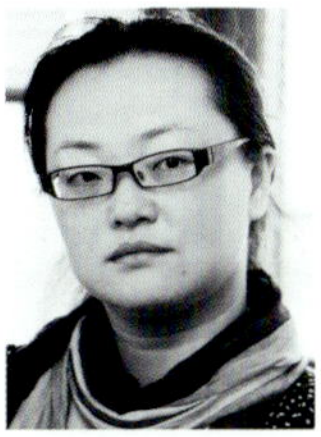

Liu Yan (NL/CN) is an advocate of cross-cultural and cross-discipline exchange, a social entrepreneur and a community organizer. She is the CEO and co-founder of Xindanwei, China's largest co-working community of 6,000 members and one of the leading creative centers in Shanghai. Liu Yan serves as an advisor, lecturer and mentor to students, entrepreneurs and startups on strategy, social innovation and social entrepreneurship. She regularly speaks at international conferences such as the Skoll World Forum, the Co-Working Europe Conference and TEDx. Liu Yan is a BMW foundation Young Global Leader and was named as "top female innovator" by Girl 2.0.

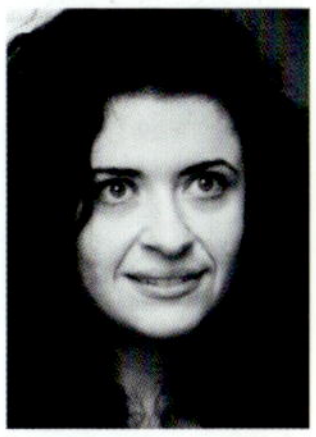

Leila Nachawati (ES) is a Spanish-Syrian blogger, communication strategist and human rights activist. She is an assistant professor of Communications at Carlos III University in Madrid and writes for several media outlets such as Periodismo Humano, Global Voices Online, Global Voices Advocacy and Al-Jazeera. She is also a board member of AERCO (Spanish Association of Social Media Managers). She has degrees in English studies, Arabic studies, and a master's degree in international cooperation.

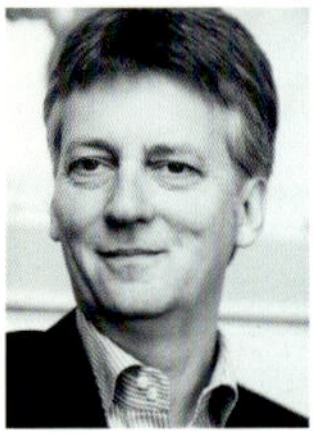

Thomas Schildhauer (DE) is professor of marketing at Berlin University of the Arts (UdK). He specializes in the field of electronic business. In 1999, he established the university's largest adjunct facility, the Institute of Electronic Business. He is also managing director of the UdK's College of Continuing Education. In these capacities, He is in charge of several masters' programs, including Leadership in Digital Communication, Sound Studies and Cultural Journalism. As director of the newly-established Alexander von Humboldt Institute for Internet and Society, Thomas Schildhauer pursues transdisciplinary research on Internet-enabled innovation.

u19 – CREATE YOUR WORLD

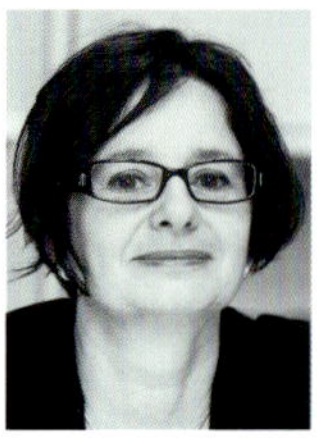

Sirikit Amann (AT) studied political science, theater and economics. Since the 80s, she has been involved primarily with cultural education in the context of new media on the national and international level. Since 2006 Sirikit Amann has been curating the Young Animations film program on behalf of Ars Electronica. In 2008, she took over the newly founded Department of Artistic and Cultural Mediation at the Austrian Federal Ministry of Education, Art and Culture.

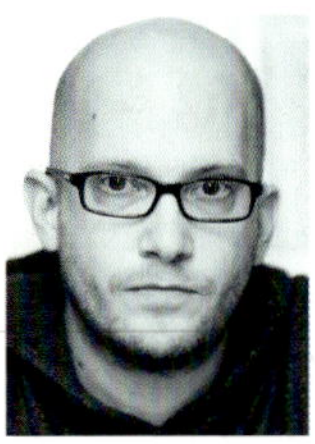

Robert Glashüttner (AT) is a journalist, writer, presenter and researcher with an emphasis on video-game culture and digital life. His main occupation is as a radio editor at Radio FM4 (part of the Austrian Broadcasting Corporation ORF), where he has been head of the IT, cyberculture and video-game department since March 2010. Robert also writes for online and print magazines and publishes articles in essayistic and scientific readers.

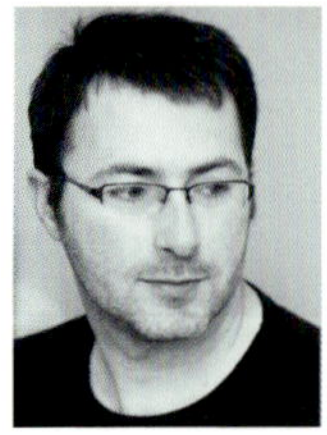

Martin Hollinetz (AT) is a social education worker and teacher, regional developer and passionate advocate of Digital Bohème. He has founded and mentored a series of business startups, projects and associations having to do with work, youth culture, IT and media. He set up Otelos (open-technology labs) in the Upper Austrian towns of Gmunden, Vöcklabruck and Kirchdorf. Their areas of emphasis are the creative economy, media, textile art, robotics and exhibition development for children aged ten and under.

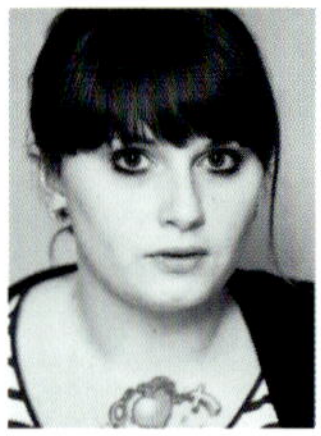

Martina Sochor (AT) was an independent contractor in the advertising industry until 2010, while discovering her true calling working with young people at the Kinderfreunde, Linz's children's advocacy organization. In the summer of 2011, she launched Umlaut M. to produce TV content designed expressly for young people. Since its inception, the organization's editorial staff have enjoyed ample opportunities to acquire impressive skills and use them to disseminate their views.

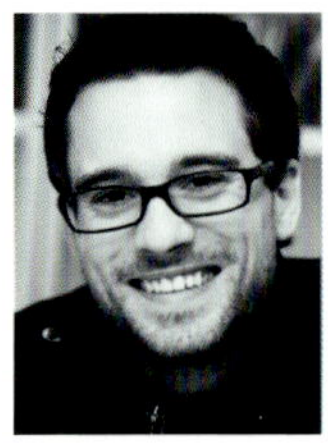

Markus Sucher (AT) works as a visual artist in a domain at the nexus of film, animation, graphics and art. His portfolio includes hundreds of individual and group projects in Austria, Germany, Qatar, the UAE and Bahrain. In 2005 his media art project *Rennacs Studies* took top honors in the Prix Ars Electronica's u19 category, which led to a series of exhibitions in Austria and abroad. Since 2006, he has concentrated on producing commercials and music videos, numerous illustrations, design concepts and feature films.

[the next idea] voestalpine Art and Technology Grant

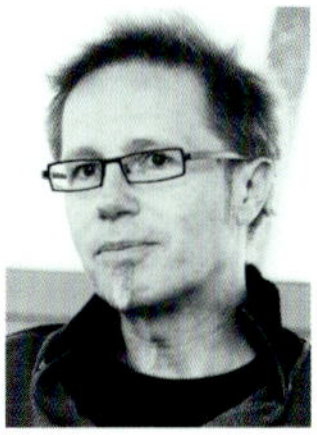

Michael Doser (AT/CH) has been working for CERN since 1991, where he is deputy department head of CERN's physics department. He has been working with antimatter since 1983, using it both as a tool and as an object of study, with the goal of understanding the first moments of the universe. In 2002, he was part of the team that made cold atoms of anti-hydrogen for the first time, and he currently leads the Aegis experiment to measure the effect of gravitation on antimatter. He is the author of more than 250 publications related to his work and to the Aegis experiment.

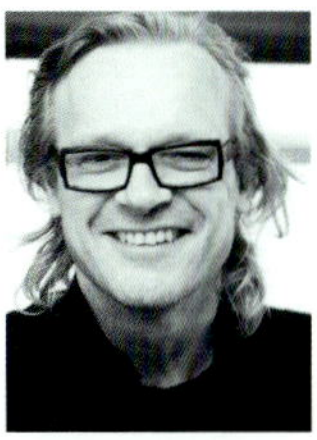

Horst Hörtner (AT) is a media artist and researcher. He is expert in the design of human-computer interaction and holds several patents in this field. Hörtner was a founding member of the Ars Electronica Futurelab in 1996 and since then has been directing this atelier/laboratory. He started to work in the field of media art in the 1980s and co-founded the media art group x-space in Graz, Austria, in 1990. Horst Hörtner works at the nexus of art and science and gives lectures and talks at numerous international conferences and universities.

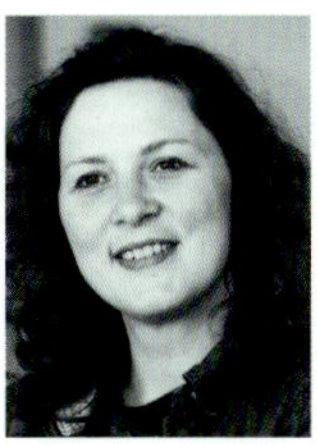

Ela Kagel (DE) is a freelance curator and producer. In 2010-11, she was a program curator at the Transmediale festival of art and digital culture. In 2011, she founded Supermarkt, Berlin's center for creative resources, and serves as its creative director. She initiated the Free Culture Incubator, which conducts various forms of research on the value and price of freelance creative work. Since 2005, she has also been a curator at Public Art Lab.

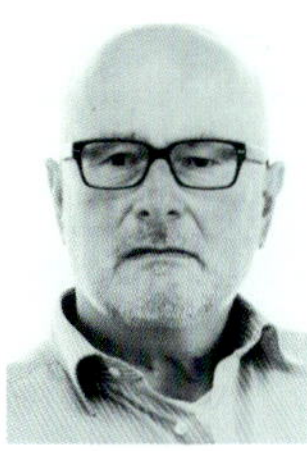

Manfred Pietschmann (DE) studied biology at the University of Hanover. After receiving his PhD in 1983, he worked as a freelance journalist. From 1992 to 1996 at Greenpeace Umweltschutzverlag, he was editor-in-chief of *Greenpeace Magazin* and *Greenpeace News*. Since November 2008, Manfred Pietschmann has been on the staff of the Heise Zeitschriften Verlag in Hanover as editor-in-chief of *Technology Review*, a monthly innovation magazine.

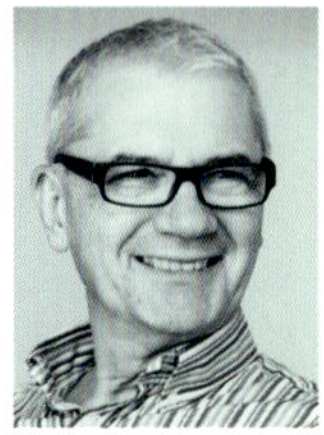

Gustav Pomberger (AT) is a full professor for software engineering and has been head of the Department of Business Informatics–Software Engineering at the Johannes Kepler University of Linz since 1987. In 1983 he was appointed professor of computer science at the University of Zurich. In 1987 he was simultaneously offered positions at ETH Zurich, the Technical University of Vienna and the Johannes Kepler University of Linz. From 1992 to 1999 he led the Christian Doppler Research Laboratory for Software Engineering. His basic research focuses on the design of high-quality software architectures and the systematic organization of software development processes. His applied research concentrates on the design of software architecture for augmented and virtual-reality-based embedded systems.

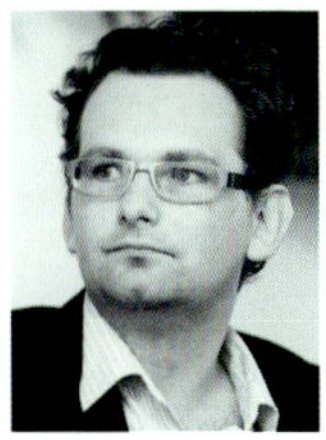

Michael Sterrer-Ebenführer (AT) is head of the sponsoring and special program, voestalpine AG.

Prix Ars Electronica collide@CERN Residency Award

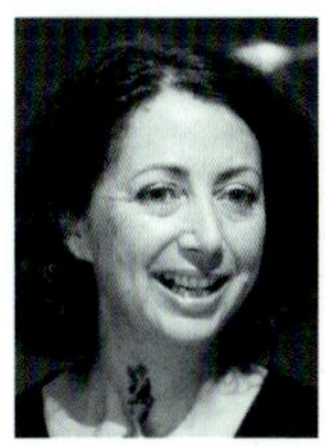

Ariane Koek (UK) is passionate about the power of the imagination and creativity across disciplines. She has worked extensively throughout the BBC as an award-winning producer in radio, and as director in television, going on to become CEO/Director of the Arvon Foundation for Creative Writing. Ariane was awarded a Clore Fellowship in 2009 for her work in culture, and she currently leads on International Arts at CERN, where she created their first cultural policy for engaging with the arts, including the Collide@CERN programme.

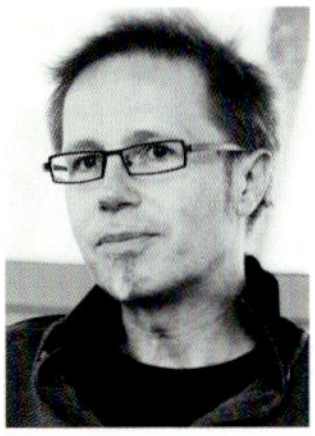

Michael Doser (AT/CH) has been working for CERN since 1991, where he is deputy department head of CERN's physics department. He has been working with antimatter since 1983, using it both as a tool and as an object of study, with the goal of understanding the first moments of the universe. In 2002, he was part of the team that made cold atoms of anti-hydrogen for the first time, and he currently leads the Aegis experiment to measure the effect of gravitation on antimatter. He is the author of more than 250 publications related to his work and to the Aegis experiment.

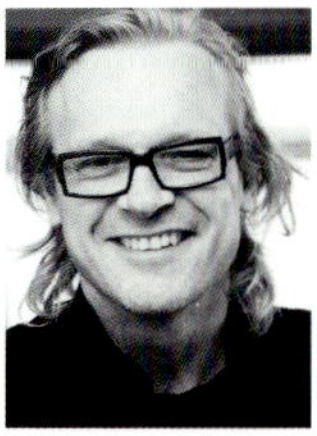

Horst Hörtner (AT) is a media artist and researcher. He is expert in the design of human-computer interaction and holds several patents in this field. Hörtner was a founding member of the Ars Electronica Futurelab in 1996 and since then has been directing this atelier/laboratory. He started to work in the field of media art in the 1980s and co-founded the media art group x-space in Graz, Austria, in 1990. Horst Hörtner works at the nexus of art and science and gives lectures and talks at numerous international conferences and universities.

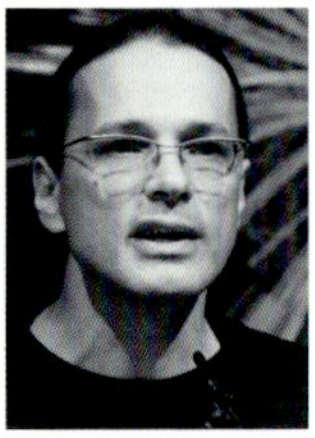

Gerfried Stocker (AT) is a media artist and telecommunications engineer. In 1991, he founded x-space, producing numerous installations and performances featuring elements of interaction, robotics and telecommunications. Since 1995 he has been artistic director of Ars Electronica. In 1995-96 he headed the crew of artists and technicians that developed the Ars Electronica Center's pioneering new exhibition strategies. He has been chiefly responsible for conceiving and implementing the series of international exhibitions that Ars Electronica has staged since 2004 and, beginning in 2005, for the planning and thematic repositioning of the new, expanded Ars Electronica Center.

Digital Communities 2012—Advisory Board

Christopher Adams (TW) is a publishing professional and free-culture advocate based in Taipei. He is a founding member of Sharism.org, and a member of the Creative Commons Network.

Heitor Alvelos (PT) is a cultural operator, designer, media culture researcher. He is professor of design / professor of new media at the Universidade do Porto.

Tim Causer (UK) is a research associate on University College London's Bentham Project, responsible for the crowd-sourced manuscript transcription project *Transcribe Bentham*.

Martijn de Waal (NL) is a writer and researcher. He co-founded The Mobile City conference and weblog. *http://www.themobilecity.nl/*

Peter Tomaž Dobrila (SI) is an IT engineer and a musician who focuses on the creative use of new technologies and was the founder of KIBLA and M3C. In 2011 he was adviser to the program Director at the Maribor 2012—European Capital of Culture.

Michael Eisenriegler (AT) has worked with online communities since he started Blackbox in 1992. He is CEO of Media-Clan and a lecturer for online media at Vienna University.

Wolfgang Gumpelmaier (AT) passionate web-user, trend-scout, online film and social-web marketer. Co-founder of *www.ununi.tv*.

Insulares / Divergentes Research (PE) is focused on an extensive case-study research on initiatives involved in Latin American social and cultural development supported by information technologies and new media. *http://www.insularesdivergentes.org/*.

Mike Jensen (ZA) is a South African independent consultant who co-founded Canada's first Internet service providers in 1987. Since 1990, he has worked in Africa, Asia and Latin America to provide advice on the development of national and international communications networks.

André Lemos (BR) is an associate professor at the Faculty of Communication at the University Federal da Bahia, Brazil.

Ronaldo Lemos (BR) is the director of the Center for Technology and Society (CTS) at the Fundação Getulio Vargas (FGV) Law School in Rio de Janeiro, and Project Lead for the Creative Commons in Brazil.

Andrés Monroy-Hernández (US) is a postdoctoral researcher at Microsoft Research and a fellow at the Berkman Center for Internet and Society at Harvard University. Previously, he was a doctoral student at the MIT Media Lab.

Marcus Neustetter (ZA), is a Johannesburg-based artist: *http://www.marcusneustetter.com*

Isaac Mao (CN) is one of China's best-known bloggers and former organizer of the Chinese Bloggers' Conference. He is also a software developer, a social-learning researcher, director of the Social Brain Foundation and sits on the advisory board of Global Voices.

An Xiao Mina (US) is an American artist and designer who makes new media art, focusing specifically on social media art.

Tiago Peixoto (BR) has worked for ten years as a practitioner and researcher in the field of ICT and participatory governance and is currently an open-government specialist with the ICT4Gov program of the World Bank Institute (WBI)'s Open Governance cluster.

Melinda Rackham (AU) is an Australian-based maker, curator and writer investigating the art forms emerging in networked and traditional technologies.

Ulrike Reinhard (DE) is a consultant, author, visionary, free spirit and passionate digital native rolled into one. Her belief in the Internet's ability to empower people and change our lives and worlds for the better drives all her work.

Clément Renaud (FR) investigates how online social practices are shaping a forthcoming economy of sharing. He has co-founded an independent research center, the Sharism Lab, with a community of Chinese bloggers and hackers.

Juliana Rotich (UG) is co-founder and Executive Director of Ushahidi. She is a technologist, African Futurist and a TED Senior Fellow. She often speaks at international conferences about tech and Africa.

David Sasaki (US) is principal of investments at Omidyar Networks and develops Omidyar Network's government transparency portfolio in Latin America, focusing on Brazil and Mexico.

Michael Stadler (AT) is a simulation specialist in the fields of engineering, architecture and biomedical engineering. He is a lecturer at the Joanneum University of Applied Sciences and at Graz University of Technology.

Moritz Stefaner (DE) works as a "truth and beauty operator" on the crossroads of data visualization, information aesthetics and user-interface design. His work balances analytical and aesthetic aspects in mapping abstract and complex phenomena. *http://moritz.stefaner.eu.*

Lei Yang (CN) is curator at the China Millennium Monument Museum of Digital Arts, Beijing, founder of the Notch Festival of live media and social innovation and founder of Radio Take10, a collective internet radio.

PARTICIPANTS

COMPUTER ANIMATION / FILM / VFX

Tharun Abraham GB
Przemyslaw Adamski PL
Manuel Casasola Merkle
AixSponza DE
emad Aleebrahim-Dehkordi FR
Whitney Alexander US
Patrick Altmaier DE
Alessandro Amaducci IT
Francesca Amati IT
Ismail Amr EG
Oliver Franklin Anderson US
Scott Andrew US
Jeanelize de Nys ZA
Christobal de Oliveira FR
Daniela de Paulis NL
Sarah Dean AU
Rafa Dengrá ES
Robert Derflinger AT
Jeff Desom LU
Celine Desrumaux GB
Alexei Dmitriev RU
Zhihuang Dong NL
Nathan Drabsch AU
Olivier Dressen BE
Nisha Duggal GB
Stefan Dumler DE
Gair Dunlop GB
Dvein Dvein ES
Michela Eccli IT
Gabor Ekes GB
Julius Endert DE
Toni Enström FI
Anna Margit Erber AT
Tomer Eshed DE
Thomas Esterer AT
Markus Feder DE
Simon Fiedler DE
Marius Fietzek DE
Andreas Nicolas Fischer DE
Stephen Fitzgerald US
Morghan Fortier CA
Daniel Franke DE
Joshua Frankel US
Frederic Frederic Dirickx BE
Yaniv Fridman MX
Iris Frisch DE
Jonathan Gales GB
Alison Gallego FR
Thomas Galler CH
Bettina Gandler AT
Guillermo García Carsí ES
Beatriz García Carsí ES
Damian Gascoigne GB
Emmanuel Gatera CA
Marie-Clémence Gauthier FR
Sharon Gazit IL
Alban Gily FR
Marcos Girado US
Clément Girard FR
Alex Glawion DE
Gustavo Godoy BR
Varun Gokhale IN
Elisa Gomes BR
Emil Goodman HU
Kevin Grady SE
Mihai Grecu FR
Laura Greil AT
Fabian Grodde DE
Florian Grolig DE
Elisabeth Gschaider AT
Aude Guibourt FR
David Guiraud FR
Juan Ha KR
Hannes Hagstrand SE
Stephan Hanf DE
Louise Harvey AU
iiMax Hattler GB
Barbara Helbich AT
Thomas Heller AT
Susann Maria Hempel DE
Dirk Henrotay BE
Marius Herzog DE
Josh Hetzler US
Oliver Hilbert NZ
Isamu Hirabayashi JP
Ryo Hirano JP
Wei-Ming Ho TW
Herwig Hoffmann DE
Karin Hofko NZ
Freya Holdsworth AT
Faith Holland US
Christian Holzer AT
Andreas Horvath DE
Mikko Hovi FI
Chien-Chieh Huang TW
Andrew Thomas Huang US
Shih-Chieh Hung TW
Kiron Hussain GB
Zach Hyer US
Eric Hynynen FI
Stephen Irwin GB
Jochen Isensee DE
Mitsu Isshiki GB
Yuichi Ito JP
Maciej Jackiewicz PL
Faiyaz Jafri US
Skirmanta Jakaite LT
Jules Janaud GB
Lars Jandel DE Sarah Janßen NL
Ruth Jarman GB
Katarzyna Jarzyna PL
Thomas Jaulin-Berge FR
Claire Jervert US
Sergio Jimenez ES
Andrew Ellis Johnson US
Slavka Jovanovic GB
William Joyce US
Jisuk Jung KR
Patrick Junghans NZ
Simon Käfer AT
Wolfram Kampffmeyer DE
Andreas Karaoulanis DE
Gunnar Karlsson IS
Kijek Katarzyna PL
Markos Kay GB
Herwig Kerschner AT
Katharina Keßler AT
Yi Hui Khoo SG
Hani Kichi AE
Sivan Kidron IL
Cedric Kiefer DE
Q-hyun (Gyuhyun) Kim US
Yongchan Kim US
Ji-Young Kim Choi KR
Miro Kirov US
Martinus Klemet EE
Jana Kluge FR
Jakub Knapik PL
Vladislav Knezevic HR
Nils Knoblich DE
Marcin Kobylecki PL
Sascha Koeth DE
Ilya Korobkov RU
Miroslav Kostic RS
Dirk Koy CH
Markus Kremsl AT
Daniel Kresmery HU
Veeramani Krishnan JP
Hayoun Kwon FR
Boris Labbé ES
David Labiano ES
Jan Lachauer DE
David Lai US
Victor Lakisov RU
Viktor Lakisov RU
Choon Khee Lam SG
Claudia Larcher AT
Stefan Larsson JP
Carlos Lascano ES
Colin Lawson GB
Simon Le Boggit GB
Raffael Leb AT
Henning M. Lederer DE
Hyejun Lee KP
Dana Lee KR
Mario Leichtfried AT
Juliane Leitner AT
Christian Lerch DE
DSK Lesta & Montero ES
Nicolas Liautaud FR
Darren Lim SG
Brooke Livingston US
Thorsten Löffler DE
Malo Loic FR
Francois Marie Loic BR
Adriaan Lokman FR
Carlos Lopez Estrada US
Accaries Loris AU
Anne Lucas FR
Abbey Luck US
Rimantas Lukavicius LT
Linus Lundin SE
Modesta Lupascu RO
Kristof Luyckx BE
Diran Lyons US
David Lyons US
Marianne Maderna AT
Nahomi Maki JP
Julia Malasok EE
Kevin Manach FR
Joni Männistö FI
Richard Mans NZ
Pristin Maribojoc PH
Ayme Marie FR
Elio Martusciello IT
Shintaro Matsushima JP
Kerstin Mayer DE
Moritz Mayerhofer DE
Martin Mayrhofer-Reinhartshuber AT
Neal McDonald US
Albert Merino ES
Alexander Miehle DE
Ninja Miori SE
Thomas Mohr NL
Marco Vinicio Morales Aburto MX
Robert Morgan GB
Klaus Morschheuser DE
Beeld Motion BR
Joao Martinho Moura PT
Jeremy Mourlam FR
Sophie Müller AT
Paul Mumford GB
David Muñoz ES
Valerio Murat IT
Pia Myrvold FR
Astrid Neumayr AT
Miles Nicholas AU
Tetsuka Niiyama JP

Günter Nikodim AT
Yoshiki Nishimura JP
Jonathan Nix AU
Alana O'Brien IE
Erick Oh US
Aiko Okamoto DE
Gérard Ollivier FR
Gabriel Orenstein US
Frédérique Ortega FR
Matthew Ostrowski US
Constantin Paeplow DE
Murat Pak TR
Michael Palmaers BE
Milos Paripovic BA
David Parker US
Eric Patrick US
Raoul Paulet GB
Tomas Pecha CZ
Miguel Angel Perez Alvarez MX
Ole Peters DE
Johannes Pfeifer AT
Andreas Pflanzl AT
Christian Pfohl FR
Agnieszka Piechnik PL
Ülo Pikkov EE
Kim Pimmel US
Libor Pixa CZ
Veljko Popovic HR
Josep Prim ES
Fabian Prudky AT
Casey Reas US
Diana Reichenbach US
Regina Reisinger AT
Martin Retter IT
Ben Richardson US
Lee Riley GB
Niklas Rissler SE
Ruairi Robinson US
Paola Rocchetti GB
Jilli Rose AU
Tal Rosner GB
Aaron Ross US
Rosto Rosto NL
Antoine Rouleau CA
Brian Routh GB
Georgie Roxby Smith AU
Marc Rühl DE
Petri Ruikka FI
Nina Sabnani IN
Laura Sahin AT
Andre Sales ZA
Roberto Santaguida CA
Rachelle Santelices PH
Cherelle Sappleton GB
Margarida Sardinha PT
Michael Sargent CA
Jaroslaw Sawko PL
Fabio Scacchioli IT
Francesco Scarponi IT
Sabrina Schmid GB
Eric Schockmel GB
Lukas Schrank GB
Bastiaan Schravendeel NL
Hans Schultheiss DE
Daniel Schwarz DE
Manfred Seifert DE
Dominique Sellitsch AT
Tsutomu Setomoto JP
Ann Seymour US
Gregory Sharp AU
Marianna Shek AU
Daihei Shibata JP
Kiwoun Shin GB
Tiffany Shlain US
Pu Shuai Cheng TW
Laura Sicouri FR
Piotr Sikora PL
Raoul Sinier FR
Mario Sixtus DE
Sebastian Skuhra DE
Susanne Slavick US
Studio Smack NL
Eva Sommeregger AT
Yongsub Song US
Antonio Sousa Dias FR
Anne Spalter US
Arthur Stammet LU
Jenny Steele GB
Karolina Stefansdottir IS
Mate Steinforth DE
Kim Stewart GB
Mark Stock US
Jennifer Stock US
Anja Struck DE
Robert Styblo AT
Axel Sucrow DE
Yuuki Suzuki JP
Sarolta Szabo FR
Tobias Szabo DE
Orion Tait US
Aaron Tam NZ
Philip Tan SG
David Tart DK
David Teng-Olsen US
Natasa Teofilovic RS
Soichi Terada JP
Josh Thorne SE
Jan Tiller DE
Tom Tlalim GB
Emile Tobenfeld US
tokyoplastic GB
Marielle Tollis FR
Paz Tornero ES
Bartholomäus Traubeck DE
Alessia Travaglini IT
Elena Tree DE
Shiu-Cheng Tsai TW
Hui-ching Tseng TW
Takahiro Tsushima JP
Natasha Turner NZ
Sebastian Ungrad DE
Anna Ursyn US
Martijn van Boven NL
Jerry Van de Beek US
Ajin Jospeh Vattamakkal SG
François Vautier FR
Tomas Vergara CL
Alex Verhaest NL
Evan Viera US
Eric Villeneuve CA
vismayasmax Animations IN
Milen Vitanov DE
Clara Voisin FR
Christian Volckman FR
Julien Vray FR
Drasko Vucevic CA
Patrick Wagesreiter AT
Markus Wagner AT
Tamas Waliczky HK
Claire Walka DE
Ian Walker GB
Martin Wallner DE
Markus Wambsganss DE
Shih-Ling Wang TW
Wei-Xiu Wang TW
Nicole Wegner DE
Judith Weidmann CH
Regina Welker DE
Adam Wells GB
Patricia Wells GB
Robert Whitworth GB
Andreas Widder AT
Susanne Wiegner DE
Manuel Wieser AT
Mihai Wilson CA
Halina Witek NL
Vera Wittkowsky AT
Philipp Wolf DE
Gergely Wootsch GB
Adrianne Wortzel US
Timo Wright FI
Chao Wu CN
Maïté Xia FR
Hikaru Yamakawa JP
Hui Ye AT
Yong Xiang Ivan Yew SG
Kazuya Yokoi JP
Davier Yoon SG
Jimmy Yuan AU
Daniel Zdunczyk PL
Maxim Zhestkov RU
Angelika Zieglerschick AT
Polina Zioga GR

DIGITAL MUSICS & SOUND ART

Francesco Abbrescia IT
Erfan Abdi Dezfouli NL
Tomomi Adachi DE
Ivan Afanasyev RU
Ryoko Akama JP
Masayuki Akamatsu JP
Lars Åkerlund SE
Efe Akmen DE
Said Alanís MX
Giulio Aldinucci IT
Ziad Alim BD
Jim Altieri US
Vasco Alves GB
Esther Alzate Romero DE
Oren Ambarchi AU
Jon Anderson US
Pablo Anglade AR
Thomas Ankersmit DE
Linda Antas US
Ted Apel US
Tatsuru Arai DE
David Arango Valencia CA
Kingsley Ash GB
Sam Auinger DE
Frauke Aulbert DE
Vasilis Avdelas GR
Miguel Azguime PT
Paula Azguime PT
Andrew Babcock US
Ain Bailey GB
Benton-C Bainbridge US
Andrej Bako GB
Alessio Ballerini IT
Holger Ballweg DE
Federico Barabino AR
Jacopo Barbaccia IT
Luca Barbeni IT
Joey Bargsten US
Dimitri Barnias GR
Justin Baroncea RO
Natasha Barrett NO
Tarik Barri NL
Karl Bartos DE
Constantin Basica DE
Fabio Battistetti IT
Mateusz Bednarz PL
Lilian Beidler CH
Andrea Belfi DE
Antonello Belgrano IT
Erich Berger FI
Nicolas Bernier CA
Belma Beslic-Gál AT
Emily Bezar US
Ranjit Bhatnagar US
Martin Bircher FI
Colin Black AU
Mercedes Blasco US
Per Bloland US
Philippe Bodino FR
Philippe Boisnard FR
Mark Bokowiec GB
Lea-Corinne Bolduc CA
Jason Bolte US
Lynn Book US
Sarah Boothroyd CA
Patrick Borgeat DE
Andrea Borghi IT
Andres Bosshard CH
Patricia Bosshard CH
Carlos Mariano Botto ES
Xavier Bourassa CA
Till Bovermann FI
Oliver Bown AU
Alex Braidwood US
Jens Brand DE
Tony Brennan AU
Yan Breuleux CA
James Brewster SE
Roman Bromboszcz PL
Eric Brotto GB
Etienne Brunet FR
Julius Bucsis US
James Bulley GB
Arturas Bumsteinas LT
Theo Burt GB
V Owen Bush US
Ariel Bustamante CL
Ronald Bustamante Medina CR
Diego Cáceres Ocampo CL
Marina Camargo BR
Anil Camci TR
Salvatore Carannante IT
Renata Carrasco CL
Thomas Carteron FR
Miguel Carvalhais PT
Io Casino ES
Philippe Cavaleri BE
Chin Ting Chan US
Richard Chartier US
Philippe Chatelain BE
Budhaditya Chattopadhyay DK
Mulian Chen CN
Chen Chenchen CN
Jean-Christophe Chenette CA
Hon Him Cheung HK
Alessio Chierico IT
Young-Shin Choi US
Joonyong Choi KR
Kyong Mee Choi US
Thanos Chrysakis GB
Jokūbas Čižikas LT
Eleanor Clare NO
Andrea Cohen FR
Giulio Colangelo IT
Ian J Cole GB
William Collins US
Olle Cornéer SE
Alan Courtis AR
Frances Crow GB
Elisabet Curbelo ES
Conor Curran GB
Paweł Cyrta PL
Werner Dafeldecker DE
Diego Dall Osto ES
Yannick Dauby TW
Xopher Davidson US
Michael Dawid DE
Ricardo de Armas AR
Stéphane de Gérando FR
Luca De Siena IT
Mario de Vega DE
Michel Décosterd CH
Louis-Philippe Demers SG
Adam Denton GB
Ruben Dhers DE
Francis Dhomont FR
Maria Catena Di Pasqua CH
Yorgos Diapoulis GR
Didi Didi Bruckmayr AT
Roberto Doati IT
Dyane Donck NL
Marco Donnarumma GB
Alex Dowling IE
Roger Doyle IE
John Driscoll US
Gabriel Dufour-Laperrière CA
Jorn Ebner DE
Anke Eckardt DE
Richard Eigner AT
Peter Eisold DE
Tessa Elieff AU
Lawrence English AU
Christopher Ennis GB
Matthias Erian DE
Juan Manuel Escalante MX
Hugo Espinosa CL
Peter Evans US
Ángel Faraldo NL
Thea Farhadian US
Dmytro Fedorenko UA
Daniel Feffs CL
Jaime Fennelly US
Vitor Joaquim Paredes Fernandes UA
Marcos Fernandes JP
José Miguel Fernández FR
Ambrose Field GB
Paolini Filippo IT
Vincenzo Fiorella IT
Jacqueline Fischer DE
Simona Fitcal DE
Christoph Flueler CH
Bill Fontana US
Georges Forget CA
Thomas Foster AT
Elin Franzen SE
Lee Fraser GB
Stefan Frauenberger AT
Fabiano Freitas BR
Heribert Friedl AT
Tatsuya Fujishiro JP
Larry Matthew Gaab US
Richard Gadd GB
Bojan Gagic HR
José Gallardo CO
T. A. Gambarotto CA
Bernhard Garnicnig AT
Amanda Ghassaei US
Daniele Ghisi ES
Roberto Giamberardino IT
Daniele Giannotta IT
Stelios Giannoulakis GR
Wolfgang Gil US
Matias Giuliani AR
Scarola Giuliano IT
Oleksandr Gladun UA
Robert Gligorov IT
Gilles Gobeil CA
Florian Goeschke DE
José Alberto Gomes PT
Kyriaki Goni GR
Gerard Gormley GB
Suguru Goto IT
sylvain Gourlay FR
Simon Grab CH
Giacomo Grassi IT
Ethan Greene US
Berit Greinke GB
Gaetan Gromer FR
Mario Guida IT
Paula Guimarães PT
Luc Gut CH
Martin Gut CH
Kip Haaheim US
Arnold Haberl AT
David Hahn US
Jürgen Hall DE
Alec Hall US
Lars Lundehave Hansen DE
Janko Hanushevsky DE

Jean Louis Hargous FR
Ben Harper GB
Louise Harris GB
Christian Hartard DE
Florian Hartlieb DE
Bjørn Erik Haugen NO
Christopher Haworth GB
Naoki Hayakawa JP
Lauren Hayes GB
Jens Hedman SE
Douglas Henderson DE
Matthew Herbert GB
Georg Herlitz SE
Ron Herrema GB
Jan Paul Herzer DE
Kathy Hinde GB
David Hindmarch GB
Hrvoje Hiršl HR
Geert-Jan Hobijn NL
Karl hochguertel MX
Jullian Hoff CA
Elizabeth Hoffman US
Peter Hölscher DE
Chulki Hong KR
Cat Hope AU
Kanta Horio JP
Bill Hsu US
Dawang Huang TW
Rupert Huber AT
John Hudak US
Thomas Huston US
Anna Maria Huszcza PL
Ryo Ikeshiro GB
Shintaro Imai JP
Daisuke Ishida DE
Yuichi Ito JP
Blonk Jaap NL
Arnaud Jacobs BE
Albert Jean-Michel FR
Daniel Jeffs CL
Geir Jenssen GB
Dana Jessen US
France Jobin CA
Daniel Jones GB
Per Jonsson SE
Charles Jowett US
Gary Joynes CA
Eunjin Jung KR GX
Jupitter-Larsen US
Ai Kamachi JP
Aleksandar Kanchev GB
Ejnar Kanding DK
Ji Youn Kang NL
Thanasis Kaproulias GR
Bugra Karabey TR

Orestis Karamanlis GR
Konstantinos Karathanasis US
Daniel Karlsson SE
Takuya Karusawa JP
John Kasiewicz US
Michiko Kawagoe JP
Masayuki Kawai JP
Leung Kei Cheuk HK
Eli Keszler US
Vadim Keylin RU
Mehdi Khansari CH
Sergey Khismatov RU
Peter Kiefer DE
Yuya Kikukawa JP
Hyung-Gyu Kim US
Taeyong Kim KR
Jenn Kirby IE
James Kirby DE
Jonathon Kirk US
Kenneth Kirschner US
Ahmet Kizilay TR
Stefan Klaverdal SE
Adrian Knight US
Yota Kobayashi CA
Andreas Kogler AT
Kenji Kojima US
Panayiotis Kokoras GR
Fani Konstantinidou NL
Pavel Kopecky CZ
Konrad Korabiewski IS
Anna Korsun DE
Tommi Koskinen FI
Sofia Koubli GR
Matthias Kranebitter AT
Gintas Kraptavicius LT
Briggan Krauss US
Max Kullmann DE
Visa Kuoppala GB
Ryoichi Kurokawa DE
György Kurtág Jr. FR
Yuni Kwon KR
Ingrid Ladurner DE
Esteban Lara CA
Leonhard Lass AT
Santiago Latorre GB
Sebastien Lavoie CA
Patrik Lechner AT
Youngji Lee KR
Mei-Yi Lee NL
Ray Lee GB
Dominik Leitner AT
Nolan Lem US
Miklós Lengyelfi II HU
Mario Lepera AT
Rita Leppiniemi FI

Kei Cheuk Leung HK
Hakan Lidbo SE
J Linton HK
Robert Lisek PL
Jung-Hua Liu TW
Owen Lloyd GB
Yun Ting Lo CN
Stephen Lomax GB
William Long JP
Simon Longo GB
Francisco López NL
Yair López MX
Apostolos Loufopoulos GR
Olivia Louvel GB
LOXOSconcept IT
Julio Lucio BR
Ignacy Łukasiewicz PL
Sergio Luque ES
Vangelis Lympouridis US
Eric Lyon GB
Daniel Maalman NL
Thessia Machado US
Zydrunas Maciulis LT
Thor Magnusson GB
Yutaka Makino DE
Stelios Manousakis US
Philip Mantione US
Matteo Marangoni NL
Damian Marhulets DE
Jeffrey Martin CN
Edgardo Hugo Martinez AR
Israel Martínez MX
András Márton HU
Jernej Marusic SI
Akita Masami JP
Omar Mashaal AU
Princess Maskara DE
Norbert Math AT
Silvia Matheus Matheus US
Robert Mathy AT
Berangere Maximin FR
Daniel Mayer AT
Thomas McConville IE
Damiano Meacci IT
Sonia Megias US
Markus Mehr DE
Augusto Meijer NL
Lvis Mejía DE
Joaquin Mendoza ES
Léonore Mercier FR
Martin Messier CA
Dan Michiu RO
Emmanuel Mieville FR
Andrei Mikhailau BY
Nanda Milbreta NL

Fabio Mina IT
Luca Mina IT
Nicola Monopoli IT
Andreas Monopolis GR
Bijan Moosavi GB
Hugo Morales Murguia NL
Scott Morrison AU
Michael Moser AT
Przemyslaw Moskal US
Ivan Mršić NZ
Paul Mumford GB
Valerio Murat IT
Natasha Musevic SI
Vlad Muzesky US
Wu Na CN
Yoichi Nagashima JP
Rie Nakajima GB
Hiroshi Nakamura JP
Takayuki Nakamura JP
Junji Nakaue JP
Steve Nalepa US
Anselm Venezian Nehls DE
Carsten Nicolai DE
Timothy Nohe US
Litten Nystrøm IS
Benjamin O'Brien US
Paul O'Donoghue IE
Linda O'Keeffe IE
Hideyuki Oda JP
Bruce Odland US
Mari Ohno JP
Junya Oikawa DE
Nozomi Okazaki JP
Hugo Olim PT
Michael Olson US
Kian-Peng Ong US
Zael Ortega Pérez MX
Federico Ortica IT
Ed Osborn US
Yasuhiro Otani JP
Felipe Otondo GB
Maciej Ozog PL
Ticiano Paludo BR
Maria Panayotova BG
Paolo Paolo Geminiani IT
Marianthi Papalexandri-
Alexandri DE
Shelley Parker GB
Bethan Parkes GB
Claudio Parodi IT
Chiara Passa IT
Marcela Pavia IT
Emilie Payeur CA
Maggi Payne US
Maria Paz SE

Sabrina Peña Young US
Pedro Pereira PT Armando Pérez Mántaras ES
Marc-Andre Perron CA
Mark Pilkington GB
Derek Piotr PL
Jörg Piringer AT
Sam Pluta US
Mark Polscher DE
Sandra Poppe DE
Eva Pöpplein DE
Gianluca Porcu IT
Sebastian Precht DE
Dyan Pritamo MX
Christian Proaño EC
Rostislav Prochovník CZ
Pierre Proske AU
Françoise Provencher CA
Roberto Pugliese IT
Rudi Punzo IT
Sandy Ralambondrainy FR
Philip Reeder GB
João Ricardo PT
Louie Rice GB
Greg Riddell AU
Robin Rimbaud GB
René Rissland DE
Dariusz Roberte AU
Andrew Roberts DE
Harry-Ed "d.d.rapids" Roland US
Jean-Michel Rolland FR
Neil Rolnick US
David Rolston US
Volker Rommel DE
Maik Ronz DE
Cristiano Rosa BR
Michael Rosas Cobian GB
Vanessa Rossetto US
Noam Rotem IL
Patrick Roudier FR
Donika Rudi BE
Michael Rüsenberg DE
Hanns Holger Rutz GB
Henrik Rylander SE
Hankil Ryu KR
Bistu Ryx ES
Martin Sadowski DE
Marcel Saegesser CH
Corrado Saija IT
Patrick Saint-Denis CA
Yiorgis Sakellariou LT
Sam Salem GB
Karl J. Salzmann AT
Dario Sanfilippo IT
André Santana BR
Janek Schaefer GB
Christian F. Schiller AT
Walter Schneider DE
Richard Schneider CZ
Marcel Schobel DE
Anna Schölß DE
Fabian Schöneich CH
Alexander Schubert DE
Bernd Schumann DE
Robert Schwarz AT
Ambrose Seddon GB
M Seligman HK
Alexander Senko RU
Gautier Serre FR
Gabriel Shalom DE
Gerriet Krishna Sharma AT
Kohshi Shimada JP
Kei Shiratori JP
Debashis Sinha CA
Stefanie Sixt DE
Wayne Slawson US
Scott Smallwood CA
Steven Snethkamp US
Timo Soppela FI
Alexander Spechtenhauser AT
Georgia Spiropoulos FR
Julius Stahl DE
Nikos Stavropoulos GB
David Stearn GB
Simon Steen-Andersen DE
Ralph Steinbrüchel CH
Gianni Stiletto AT
Jeroen Strijbos NL
Christiane Strothmann DE
Kathrin Stumreich AT
Jiří Suchánek CZ
Anggung Suherman ID
W. Mark Sutherland CA
Lewis Sykes GB
Nicholas Szczepanik US
Jagoda Szmytka DE
Andrea Taeggi NL
Akira Takaoka US
Talking Through a Slippa GB
Tristan Telander US
Aphra Tesla SI
Ranil the Panil LK
Benjamin Thigpen FR
Wilm Thoben DE
Jo Thomas GB
Sever Tipei US
Gaël Tissot FR
Manuel Torres MX
Bartholomäus Traubeck DE
Pierre Alexandre Tremblay GB
Valerio Tricoli DE
Michael Trommer CA
Ulrich Troyer AT
Ioannis Tsirikoglou NL
Roxanne Turcotte CA
Tetsuya Umeda JP
Basar Under TR
Yolanda Uriz Elizalde NL
Goran Uroich HR
Shiori Usui GB
Yukari Uto JP
Claudia X. Valdes US
Luis Valdivia AT
Stef van der Poel NL
Margriet van Eekelen NL
Evgeniy Vashchenko UA
Henry Vega NL
Esther Venrooy BE
Mario Verandi DE
Tom Verbruggen NL
Ben Vida US
Alejandro Viñao GB
Bodino Virginie FR
Tadej Vobovnik SI
Jean Voguet FR
Clemens von Reusner DE
Antje Vowinckel DE
Manfred Waffender DE
Eric Wahlforss DE
Yuk Bun Wan HK
Jing Wang US
Zhipeng Wang CN
Jing Wang US
Chris Watson GB
James Webb ZA
Pascale Weber FR
Georg Weckwerth AT
Ralf Wehowsky DE
Hannah Weinberger CH
Lee Weisert US
Andreas Weixler AT
Simon Whetham GB
Frances White US
Gareth Whittock GB
Lo Wie KR
Julie Wilson-Bokowiec GB
Kristina Wolfe US
Ryan Woodhall US
RD Wraggett CA
Mark Wright GB
James Wyness GB
Cheng Xu CN
Kyo Yanagi JP
Tetsuro Yasunaga JP
Donghoon Yi KR
Yi Yin CN
Kiyotaka Yoshimitsu JP
Masatsune Yoshio JP
Samson Young HK
Alla Zagaykevych UA
Kateryna Zavoloka UA
Emiliano Zelada GB
You-Sheng Zhang TW
Chris Ziegler CH
Zimoun Zimoun CH
Franz Zotter AT
Justyna Zubrycka PL

HYBRID ART

Rita A. G. Pedroso BR
Pedro Aibéo FI
Angelo Airò Farulla IT
Christa Amadea AT
Emanuel Andel AT
Jan-Erik Andersson FI
Filippo Andreatta IT
Mina Arko SI
Anando Arnold DE
Nur Akbar Arohfatullah ID
Philipp Artus DE
Nobuyoshi Asai JP
John Aslanidis AU
André Aspelmeier DE
Nicky Assmann NL
Marios Athanasiou GB
Sofian Audry CA
Kamila B.Richter DE
Ralf Baecker DE
Dean Bagar DE
Georgy Bagdasarov CZ
Selin Balci US
Sue Balint CA
René Bauer CH
Philippe Baylaucq CA
Kim Beck US
Philip Beesley CA
Cora Bellotto IT
Vicki Bennett GB
Alexander Berchert GB
Hans Bernhard AT
Todd Berreth US
Volker Bertelmann DE
Belma Beslic-Gal AT
Andy Best FI
Christa Biedermann AT
Michael Bielicky DE
Madeleen Bloemendaal NL
Martinka Bobrikova NO
Tom Bogaert JO
Marc Böhlen CA
Howard Boland GB
Balint Bolygo GB
David Bowen US
Harriet Bowman GB
Tega Brain AU
Jörg Brinkmann DE
Adam Brown US
H. Benjamin Brown US
Christof Brunner CH
Leonardo Budimlic Majnaric HR
Bastian Bügler DE
Piotr Bujak US
Helen Bullard GB
Andres Burbano US
Rob Burton GB
Dongsheng Cai JP
Marco Cantalupo CH
Ed Carter GB
Alexandra Caunes ES
Lynn Cazabon US
Khalil Charif Hussein Neto BR
Shu Lea Cheang FR
David Cheung CA
Nathalie Chikhi US
Fang Choi KR
Ka Fai Choy SG
Shing Tat Chung GB
Dave Ciaccio US
Laura Cinti GB
Peta Clancy AU
Ian Clothier NZ
Revital Cohen GB
James Bradford Cole JP
Peter d'Agostino US
Beatriz da Costa US
Donald Daedalus US
Constantinos Daldakis GR
Luisa Daniel CH
vishal k dar IN
Michaela Davies AU
Joe Davis US
Wally De Backer AU
Marloes de Valk NL
Laurent Debraux FR
Shawn Decker US
Caroline Delieutraz FR
Andrew Haik Demirjian US
Pascal Dombis FR
Karen Ann Donnachie AU
Kate Drazner US
Ben Dromey FI
France Dubois FR
Rainer Dunkel DE
Gabriel Dunne US
Barbara Dzierań PL
Koenraad Ecker BE
Enrique Radigales ES
Jalila Essaïdi NL
Helen Evans FR
Joaquín Fargas AR
Francesca Fini IT
Peter Fischer CH
Daniel Fischer DE
Karin Fisslthaler AT
Romina Flores AR
Anna Frants US
Andre Freyssen NL
Verena Friedrich DE
Martin Fröhlich CH
Jun Fujiki JP
Shiho Fukuhara JP
Bernhard Gal AT
Gyorgyi Galik CA
Fernanda Garcia Lopez GB
Charles Gershom GB
Oscar Gil Lorente NO
Carmen Gil Vrolijk CO
Alexandra Daisy Ginsberg GB
Matias Giuliani AR
Alexander Glandien AT
Claudia González CL
Daniel Goodbrey GB
Geoffrey Gordon US
Meg Grant NL
Dave Griffiths GB
Martin Groisman AR
Benjamin Grosser US
Björk Guðmundsdóttir US
Christian Gützer AT
David Hahlbrock DE
Nicholas Hanna CA
Brian Harris NZ
Ellie Harrison GB
Thomas Hawranke DE
Mateusz Herczka SE
Anja Hertenberger NL
Susanna Hertrich DE
Scott Hessels HK
Darsha Hewitt CA
Muhammad Hidayat ID
Sebastien Hildebrand FR
Linda Hilfling DK
Masami Hirabayashi JP
Ute Hoerner DE
Peter Holden DE
Tiffany Holmes US
Sue Ann Hong US
Beverley Hood GB
Martin Howse GB
Scottie Chih-chieh Huang TW
Wai Keung Hui HK
Albert Hwang US
Kim Hwang SG
Mio I-zawa JP
Makoto Iida JP
Irina Danilova US
Jorge Isaac NL
Motoi Ishibashi JP
Yuya Ito JP
Andreas Maria Jacobs NL
Mogens Jacobsen DK
Janez Janša SI
Chris Jeffs DE
Sion Jeong DE
Juana de Mar Jimenez Infante CO
Jeanne Jo US
Yevgeniya Kaganovich US
Boaz Kaizman DE
So Kanno JP
Junya Kataoka JP
Yuichiro Katsumoto SG
Mihalj Kekenj DE
Stephen Kelly CA
Adam Kelly CA
Haruma Kikuchi JP
Karl Kilian AT
Christoph Kilian DE
Yunchul Kim DE
Jae Yeop Kim GB
Hyun Ju Kim KR
Yong Hun Kim KR
Carole Kim US
Yong Hun Kim KR
Gal Kinan NL
Shachar Freddy Kislev IL
Sebastian Klemm DE
Joseph Knierzinger AT
Kensuke Koike JP
Stevan Kojic RS
Denys Kolokol PL
Pavel Kopriva CZ
Svenja Kratz AU
Nina Kurtela DE
Sebastian Kurth GB
Huckleberry Lain US
Prue Lang FR
Peter Lang DE
Robert Lawrence US
Julian Lee HK
Jae Min Lee KR
Sujin Lee KR
Suzie Léger AT
Bertrand Lembege FR
Joanie Lemercier GB
Mariano Leotta IT
Rita Leppiniemi FI
Golan Levin US
Gabriella Levine US
LIA AT
Nora Ligorano US
Robert Lisek PL
Nick Loewen US
Santiago Lozano CO
Felix Luque Sanchez BE
Nikola Lutz DE
Holger Mader DE
Kay Malek DE
Laura Malinverni ES

Daito Manabe JP
Aymeric Mansoux NL
Michael Markert DE
Ruth Maroto ES
Emanuele Martina IT
Reiner Maria Matysik DE
Brian May DE
Kelli McCluskey AU
Catherine McCurry US
Gennifer Meldrum CA
Sam Mendenhall US
Marcello Mercado DE
Agnes Meyer-Brandis DE
Marek Michalowski US
Daniel Miller US
Ricardo Miranda Zuniga US
Daichi Misawa AT
Shigenori Mochizuki JP
Hajoe Moderegger US
Luke Moloney CA
Fred Momotenko NL
Francesco Monico IT
Maurizio Montalti NL
Maria del Carmen Montoya US
Volker Morawe DE
Matthijs Munnik NL
Amor Munoz MX
Leila Nadir US
Takeshi Naemura JP
Hye Yeon Nam US
Reetta Neittaanmäki FI
Sofia Nelubina RU
Dennis Neuschaefer-Rube DE
Merja Nieminen FI
Sukebe Ningen NL
Michiko Nitta GB
Seb Noel GB
Adam Novota SK
Marcin Nowicki PL
Ricardo O'Nascimento NL
John O'Shea GB
Nika Oblak SI
Kilian Ochs DE
Marcela Okretič SI
Ilkka Olander FI
Julian Oliver DE
Kurt Olmstead US
Edna Orozco DE
Juan Orozco CO
Christian Oyarzún CL
Andres Padilla Domene MX
Baden Pailthorpe AU
Pablo Palacio ES
Manuel Palou US
Peter Palvén SE

Raquel Paricio ES
Matt Parker US
Kevin Patton US
Raphael Perret CH
Johannes Pfahler DE
Andres Pineros CO
Marco Pinter US
Fabrice Planquette FR
Helga Pogatschar DE
Sascha Pohflepp DE
Benjamin Pokropek AT
Jan Prošek CZ
Ivan Puig Domene MX
Merja Puustinen FI
Helen Pynor GB
Rafaël KR
Heather Raikes US
Kevin Raxworthy AU
Alexander Reben US
Marshall Reese US
Olaf Reinecke DE
Elke Reinhuber DE
Jacob Sikker Remin DK
Bruno Ribeiro FR
Antonio Riello AU
Claudia Robles Angel DE
Alona Rodeh IL
Muriel Romero ES
Henrique Roscoe BR
Philip Ross US
Lovro Rumiha HR
Maria Teresa Sanchez ES
Robert Saphin AT
Surabhi Saraf US
Eko Sato FR
Akiko Sato JP
Chihiro Sawamura JP
Paul Scerri US
Laura Schäffer DE
Alejandro Schianchi AR
Frauke Schmidt DE
Antoine Schmitt FR
Ulrike Schüchler DE
Roswitha Schuller AT
Domenico Sciajno IT
Bill Seaman US
Robert Seidel DE
Nuno Serrão PT
Yashas Shetty IN
Motoi Shimizu JP
Su Jeong Shin-Goldbach DE
Daichi Shirai JP
Andy Simionato AU
Mirko Sittek DE
Rasa Smite LV

Maja Smrekar SI
Scott Snibbe US
Bram Snijders NL
Ben Socrates GB
Oli Sorenson CA
Samuel St-Aubin CA
Nathaniel Stern US
Damian Stewart AT
Jens M. Stober DE
Axel Straschnoy FI
Jonáš Strouhal CZ
Alexander Stublic DE
Jari Suominen CZ
Beat Suter CH
Masaru Tabei JP
Misato Tachibana JP
Shohei Takei JP
Jun Takita FR
József Tasnádi HU
Justin Tyler Tate US
Hilde Teuchies BE
Carolien Teunisse NL
Stephan Thiel DE
Paul Thomas AU
Alison Thomson GB
Barry Threw US
Vyacheslav Tishin RU
Charlie Todd US
Georg Tremmel JP
Georg Tremmel JP
Agus Tri Budiarto ID
Diego Trujillo GB
Mayu Tsuzaka JP
Raewyn Turner NZ
Maki Ueda NL
Tomoyuki Ueno DE
Iheanyi Umez Eronini US
Åsa Unander-Scharin SE
Carl Unander-Scharin SE
Tatsuo Unemi JP
Leonie Urff NL
Andrey Ustinov DE
Edwin van der Heide NL
Jeroen van Loon NL
Rolando Vargas US
Sander Veenhof NL
Eric Vernhes FR
Bruno Vianna BR
Nils Völker DE
Addie Wagenknecht AT
Clea T. Waite US
Bill Washabaugh US
Brent Watanabe US
Kit Webster AU
Mirjam Weder CH

Moritz Wehrmann DE
Hermann Weizenegger DE
Marcelina Wellmer DE
Anna Werzowa AT
Jessica Westbrook US
Heike Wiermann DE
Paul Wiersbinski DE
Jennifer Willet CA
Luna Winter DE
McCrystle Wood US
Dominique Yakan Brand BE
Takahiro Yamaguchi JP
Pinar Yoldas US
Doo-Sung Yoo US
Hironori Yoshida NL
Garth Zeglin US
Danijel Zezelj US
Matthias Zimmermann CH
Michael Zöllner DE

INTERACTIVE ART

4 Gentlemen US
Ivan Abreu MX
Romy Achituv KR
Paul Adams CN
Denise Agassi BR
Jiyoung Ahn KR
Mert Akbal DE
Tetsuya Akimoto JP
Memo Akten GB
James Alliban GB
Marcio Ambrosio BR
Mouna Andraos CA
Andy Andy Meakin CA
Ciscar Ángeles ES
Pedro Ângelo PT
Naoya Aoki JP
Mariadele Arcuri SE
Diana Arellano DE
Ichiro Ariyama JP
Keith Armstrong AU
Bujdosó Attila HU
Balthazar Auxietre FR
Tahera Aziz GB
Péter Bajkó HU
Eduard Balaz RS
Dave Ball DE
Zsolt Balogh HU
Marion Bareil FR
Michele Barker AU
Brandon Barr US
Kevin Bartoli FR
Prokop Bartoníček CZ
Chris Basmajian US
Olivier Bau US
Katrin Beckmann DE
Alex Beim CA
Maria Maria Beltran CH
Peter Bennett GB
Gondouin Bertrand FR
Hagen Betzwieser DE
Svein Inge Bjørkhaug NO
Mark Bolotin AU
Julia Borovaya RU
Jonathan Brainin US
Ulrich Brandstätter AT
Martin Bravo US
Anrick Bregman GB
André Britz DE
Frederic Brodbeck NL
Carol Brown NZ
Jonah Brucker-Cohen US
Brian Brush US
Graham Budgett US
Dmitry Bulatov RU
Vivian Caccuri BR
Xinyuan Cai CN
Tyree Callahan US
Martin John Callanan GB
Rejane Cantoni BR
Micha Cardenas US
Lars Carlsson SE
Constanza Casas CL
Ivan Cash US
Dario Casillo IT
Alvaro Cassinelli JP
Juan Manuel Castro JP
Arturo Castro ES
Marianne Cauvard FR
Tsai-Jung Chan TW
François Chay FR
Jinsuk Che KR
Alexey Chebykin RU
I-Chun Chen TW
Léo Chéron FR
Matthieu Cherubini CH
Joanna Cheung US
Alon Chitayat IL
Hye-ryoung Choe KR
Min-jung Choe KR
Boram Choi KR
Wansup Choi KR
Jongwon Choi DE
Woosuk Choi KR
Shing Tat Chung GB
Emma Cianchi IT
Osvaldo Cibils IT
Matt Clark GB
Chris Clark GB
Bev Clark ZW
Christopher Coleman US
Jeff Conefry US
Jan Cordes DE
Sue Corke DE
Nuno Correia PT
Luc Courchesne CA
Lorne Covington US
Donald Craig US
Leonardo Crescenti BR
Robert Crouch US
Jeff Crouse US
Zoltan Csik-Kovacs HU
Stefano D'Alessio AT
Yan Da CN
Ed Dambik US
Andy Dao US
Christoph De Boeck BE
Marnix de Nijs NL
Frederik De Wilde BE
Simon Deeg DE
Amnon Dekel IL
Cyril Diagne FR
Lily Diaz FI
Vollenbroich Dirk DE
Alex Dodge US
Tai Doishita JP
Margaret Dolinsky US
Alfred Dong CN
Gilles Dubroca IT
Mikhail Dyachkov RU
Tobias Ebsen DK
Jeremy Eichenbaum US
Alexander Eichhorn NO
Kerstin Ergenzinger DE
Karlheinz Essl AT
Olle Essvik SE
Kristina Estell US
Titia Ex NL
Ana Carina Figueiredo PT
John Fillwalk US
Michael Flynn US
Paulo Fontes PT
Roch Forowicz PL
David Fried DE
Kazuyuki Fujita JP
Masahiko Furukata JP
Hiroyuki Futai JP
Ulrike Gabriel DE
Eran Gal-Or IL
Diana Garcia-Snyder US
Susanna Gartmayer AT
Benjamin Gaulon IE
Sachar Geiger IL
Paolo Ghezzi IT
Victoria Gibson CA
Lina Maria Giraldo US
Horst Gläsker DE
Tom Goijer NL
Josh Goldberg US
Patricio Gonzalez Vivo AR
Suguru Goto FR
Antoine Goudreault CA
Ivan Govorkov RU
Eberhard Graether AT
Jane Grant GB
Christian Graupner DE
Melanie Greußing AT
Rui Guerra NL
Byeongwon Ha US
Emanuel Haas AT
Spiros Hadjidjanos DE
Jury Hahn US
Andreas Haider AT
Harald Haraldsson IS
Toshiyuki Hashimoto JP
Toshiya Hayashi JP
Volker Helzle DE
Sanghun Heo KR
Yunsil Heo KR
Garnet Hertz US
Roland Heuger DE
Roland Heuger DE
Cees-Willem Hofstede NL
Michael Holzknecht AT
Akitoshi Honda DE
Toshiyuki Horie JP
Kodai Horita JP
Tamara Hridyayeva UA
Chun-Ko Hsieh TW
Hsin-Chien Huang TW
Wen-Hao Huang TW
Hsin-Chien Huang TW
Jae-suk Huh KR
Yi-Ping Hung TW
John Hunter GB
Kazutoshi Iida JP
Mao Imaizumi JP
Toshiyuki Inoko JP
kentaro inoue JP
Hiroshi Inukai JP
Daniel Iregui CA
Edith Isdal NO
Yuichi Itoh JP
Erik Jansen NL
Charlotte Jarvis GB
Ian Carlo Jaucian PH
So Yeong Jeon KR
Haru (Hyunkyung) Ji US
Nova Jiang US
Maria Johansson SE
Matthias John GB
Chris Jordan US
WU Juehui CN
Changgyun Jung KR
Christina Justiz US
Floris Kaayk NL
Hiroyuki Kajimoto JP
Vojtěch Kálecky CZ
Martin Kaltenbrunner AT
Heike Kaltenbrunner AT
Shinya Kamuro JP
Akihiko Kaneko JP
Eunsu Kang US
Laewoo Kang US
Sergey Kasich RU
Yoshimasa Kato JP
Una Kavanagh IE
Dmitry Kawarga RU
Markus Kayser GB
Friederike Kersten DE

Hiroyuki Kidokoro JP
Scott Kildall US
Minsu Kim GB
Youngeun Kim KR
Hyung gi Kim KR
Dong jo Kim KR
Sinae Kim KR
Sunyoung Kim KR
Masataka Kimura JP
Takashi Kimura JP
Darren Kirwan AT
László Kiss HU
Olga Kisseleva FR
Ralph Kistler ES
Ernesto Klar US
Mario Klingemann DE
Paul Klotz NL
Irena Knezevic US
Isobel Knowles AU
Sachiko Kodama JP
Pavlo Kodatenko UA
Rainer Kohlberger DE
Hideki Koike JP
Daniel Koniusz PL
Fevzi Konuk DE
Teemu Korpilahti FI
Alexey Korzukhin RU
Roee Kremer IL
Sam Kronick US
Linda Kronman AT
Gil Kuno US
Kalle Aldis Laar DE
Wan-Ying Lai TW
Jelena Lalić RS
Keith Lam HK
Miu Ling Lam US
Raphael Lang DE
Marold Langer-Philippsen DE
Béatrice Lartigue FR
Gregory Lasserre FR
Shawn Lawson US
Mirko Lazovic NL
Evelyn Lebis SE
Hyun Jin Lee KR
Dongseop Lee KR
Inmi Lee US
Jaejoong Lee KR
Min Hye Lee KR
Woncheoul Lee KR
Jinha Lee US
Zune Lee KR
Youna Lee KP
Yong Ju Lee US
David Letellier DE
Brett Levine US
Chung-Hung Lin TW
Shu-Kuang Lin US
Wen Liu AT
Néstor Lizalde Molinas ES
Jaime Alonso Lobato Cardoso MX
Matthias Lohscheidt DE
Raffaele Lopez IT
Colleen Ludwig US
He-Lin Luo TW
Andreas Lutz DE
Malcolm MacIver US
Ahmed Mahmoud EG
Dominik Mahnič SI
Yutaka Makino DE
Yasushi Matoba JP
Keiichi Matsuda GB
Takahiro Matsuo JP
Benoit Maubrey DE
Kyle McDonald US
Aurora Meccanica IT
Rodrigo Medeiros BR
Laleh Mehran US
Yiannis Melanitis GR
Mónica Mendes PT
Thatiane Mendes BR
Cristobal Mendoza US
Martina Menegon AT
Francesca Mereu ES
Eric Mesplé US
Lionel Michel DE
Seiko Mikami JP
Joshua Miller US
Mark Mitchell AU
Mark Mitchell AU
Friederike Mohr DE
Kasia Molga GB
Piers Morgan AU
Juliana Mori BR
Katherine Moriwaki US
Florian Mueller AU
Kazushi Mukaiyama JP
Geert Mul NL
Jane Mulfinger US
Raphaël Munoz CH
Anna Munster AU
Monica Mureddu ES
Roberto Musanti IT
Yuto Nakamura JP
Tsubasa Naruse JP
Albert Negredo ES
José Carlos Neves PT
Anne Niemetz NZ
Dimitri Nieuwenhuizen NL
Matti Niinimäki FI
Andrew Nip DK
Juco Nishiguchi JP
Valentina Nisi PT
Miao Niu US
Seung Seok Noh KR
Yann Novak US
Marlena Novak US
Julio Obelleiro US
Yoichi Ochiai JP
Masanori Ohwaki JP
Kärt Ojavee EE
Brendan Oliver GB
David Oppenheim IL
Luka Or IL
Ann Oren US
Orly IL
Michaela Ortner AT
Polly Oskam NL
Johannes P Osterhoff DE
Jifei Ou DE
Alexis Oyama US
Eszter Ozsvald US
Karen Palmer GB
Ricardo Palmieri BR
Artemiy Pankov RU
Zaven Paré BR
Jin Wan Park KR
Jin Hyung Park KP
Fred Paulino BR
Eric Paulos US
Ziyun Peng CN
David Peñuela US
Tommy Perman GB
Neal Peruffo IT
Jaakko Pesonen FI
Boris Petrovsky DE
Andreas Picker DE
Raphaël Pluvinage FR
Andrea Polli US
Wisut Ponnimit JP
Josefina Posch SE
Rehmi Post US
Matic Potočnik SI
Ivan Poupyrev US
Marco Pucci IT
Petr Pufler CZ
Tatiana Pushkareva DE
Qianwen Qu CN
Davide Quayola GB
Destieu Quentin FR
Niall Quinn GB
Kevin Ramseier CH
Morgan Rauscher CA
Tomas Rawski AR
Aaron Reed US
Alexander Reeder JP
Patrícia Reis PT
Mike Richison US
Stefan Riebel DE
Mónica Rikić ES
Justin Riley US
Julia Ringler DE
Michal Rinott IL
Christian Ristow US
Hector Rodriguez HK
Grzegorz Rogala PL
Gustavo Romano ES
Danielle Roney US
Dodi Rosadi ID
Stephanie Rothenberg US
Christopher Roush US
Federico Rueben GB
Nick Ryan GB
Sebastian Sadowski DE
Akiko Saito JP
Yana Sakellion US
Sho Sakurai JP
Carmen Salas GB
Ozge Samanci US
Kellee Santiago US
Toshiki Sato JP
Kumi Sato JP
Daniel Sauter US
Gordan Savičić AT
Thomas Scherzer NL
Marianne Schmidt DE
Sebastian Schmieg DE
Annelore Schneider GB
Armin Schnürer AT
Philipp Schoessler DE
Fabian Schulz DE
Stefan Schwabe DE
Kerry Segal CA
Jacob Sello DE
Angelo Semeraro IT
Carlos Sena Caires PT
Drew Seskunas US
Niamh Shaw IE
Noriko Shibano JP
Ryosuke Shibasaki JP
Shen-Guan Shih TW
Chihyoung Shim KR
Yae Dam Shin KP
Fumiki Shinohara JP
Jan M. Sieber DE
Rick Silva CA
Josh Silverman US
Alessio Silvestrin JP
Vygandas Simbelis SE
Michal Šimonfy SK
Matteo Sisti Sette ES

Sisyu JP
Chi Man Siu JP
Bengt Sjölén SE
Vadim Smakhtin RU
Karina Smigla-Bobinski DE
Eunsung Song KR
Tom Soya KE
Simon Spielmann DE
Andrew Spitz DK
Sputniko! JP
Theodore Spyropoulos GB
Stephen Spyropoulos GB
Nicholas Stedman CA
Malte Steiner DE
Liselott Stenfeldt DK
Nick Stevens NO
Pieter Steyaert BE
Michael Straus US
Eugene Strelkov RU
Christine Sugrue ES
Eiji Sumi US
Beat Suter CH
Yuri Suzuki GB
Hitoshi Taguchi JP
Koray Tahiroglu FI
Moto Takabatake GB
Nobuhiro Takahashi JP
Alejandro Tamayo CO
Piyatas Tantanapornchai US
Emilie Tappolet CH
Raquel Tasny Kogan BR
Berenice Terwey DE
The Product DE
Pierre Thirion FR
Neil Thomson GB
Ivan Thorley GB
Stefan Tiefengraber AT
Heidi Tikka FI
David Tinapple US
Hiroaki Tobita FR
Timo Toots EE
Mike Treanor US
Matthias Triendl AT
João Trindade PT
Marco Triverio IT
Tetsuya Tsukada JP
Christoph Überhuber AT
Jorge Luis Vaca Forero AR
Varun Vachhar CA
Willem van Engen NL
Allard van Hoorn NL
Thomas Van Oekelen NL
Thomas Van Ryckeghem BE
Lea van Steen BR
Nicolás Varchausky AR
Wijnand Veneberg NL
Pedro Veneroso BR
Marieke Verbiesen NO
Pieter Verhees NL
Teun Verkerk NL
Jean-Ambroise Vesac CA
Javier Villaroel ES
Amalia Violi IT
Jorick Vissers BE
Deepak Vohra CA
Petros Vrellis GR
Nineta Vretou GR
Matt Wade GB
Oliver Walker DE
Bruce Wall US
Annie Wan HK
Che-Wei Wang US
Martin Weber DE
Marian Weger AT
Rune Wehner DK
Stefan Weinzierl DE
Johannes Westendorp NL
Ellen Wetmore US
David Wicks US
Danielle Wilde AU
Matthias Wölfel DE
Matthias Wölfl DE
Chi Chuen Wong HK
Chung-yu Wong HK
Shi-Yen Wu TW
Ming-Chang Wu TW
Joseph Wu CA
Shumpei Yamakawa JP
Soo-in Yang KR
Xiying Yang US
Muharrem Yildirim US
Jay Alan Yim US
Sangjun Yoo US
Hideki Yoshimoto GB
Spencer Young US
liam young GB
Jeho Yun KR
Shahar Zaks US
Gabriel Zea AR
Ludwig Zeller CH
Alexis Zerroug JP
Dominik Zizka CZ

DIGITAL COMMUNITIES

18 Days in Egypt
http://www.18daysinegypt.com
24-hours.in
http://www.24-hours.in/tampere
52 weeks before it all ends
http://52pickupvideos.com/HTML/hogan_y2_grid.html
African Digital Art Network
http://africandigitalart.com
AISOS (The Birdbase)
http://www.aisos.at
And during that time, in Fukushima
http://synradio.fr/et-pendant-ce-temps-a-fukushima/
AntiMap http://theantimap.com
Apertus Open Source Cinema
http://www.apertus.org
AskBall
Augmented Window http://www.fenetre-augmentee.net
Bitcoin http://www.bitcoin-austria.at
#BKME http://bkme.org/
Black Women in Europe™ Social Network http://www.blackwomenineuropesocialnetwork.com
Bodyblog.com.pl http://bodyblog.pl
#bookcamping
http://bookcamping.cc/
Border Memorial: Frontera de los Muertos http://bordermemorial.wordpress.com/border-memorial-frontera-de-los-muertos/
Botaniq, Art conservation through the interactor's experience.
http://www.botaniq.org
Bunsella Bedtime Story
http://www.bunsella.com
Burning Rome http://www.jamez.it/project/burning-rome/
Camp Sambel
http://engagemedia.org
Change the Game Initiative
http://www.changethegame.org
Chequeado.com: a digital community for the quality of journalism
http://www.chequeado.com
China Digital Times' Grass-Mud Horse Lexicon
http://chinadigitaltimes.net/space/Grass-Mud_Horse_Lexicon
CitiVox http://nyc.citivox.com/
CityMedia
http://www.abstractmachine.net/blog/category/citymedia/
Cloud to the Ground, Connecting the Digital to Reality Through Micro-tasking
https://github.com/pgiraud/OSMTM
Common Ground News Service (CGNews) http://www.cgnews.org
Community Youth ICT Employment Initiative Ghana http://www.netsquared.org/projects/emfptech-ict-tools-ghana-and-beyound
Con Elmer ne combiniamo ... di tutti i colori
Coworking Manual http://xindanwei.com/lang/cn/service/about/
Creative Applications Network
http://www.creativeapplications.net
Cronicas de Heroes
http://www.cronicasdeheroes.mx
CrowdVoice.org – Tracking Voices of Protest http://www.crowdvoice.org
Dark Glasses.Portrait http://ichenguangcheng.blogspot.com
Das Autokratische Netzwerk http://www.das-autokratische-netzwerk.de
DasGehirn.info http://dasgehirn.info
Data Dealer http://www.datadealer.net/pressespiegel
Demoszene – Digitale Kultur in Echtzeit
Dérive App http://deriveapp.com/
Design For Change
http://www.dfcworld.com
Destructables.org
http://destructables.org/
Digitale Kultur e.V.
http://www.digitalekultur.org
europe-v-facebook.org
http://www.europe-v-facebook.org
Fantastic Futures
http://www.fantasticfutures.fm
Farfromhomepage – let content enter the stage
http://www.farfromhomepage.net
ForwardIT
http://www.forwardit.sa.gov.au
Frankfurt gestalten – Create Frankfurt
http://www.frankfurt-gestalten.de/
GarageLab http://garagelab.cc
Give Me Back My Broken Night
http://productofcircumstance.com/portfoliocpt/give-me-back-my-broken-night/
Giving
Global Voices

Global Yodel, travel through a local lens http://globalyodel.com
Glovico http://www.glovico.org
Goteo: open network for crowd-funding and collaboration around the Commons
http://www.goteo.org/?lang=en
Great Idea, Distance Learning in Afghanistan
http://afghanlearning.wordpress.com
Hack de Overheid
http://openstate.eu
HAXLR8R http://www.haxlr8r.com
Hello Sunday Morning http://www.hellosundaymorning.com
Hiroshima Archive
http://e.nagasaki.mapping.jp/p/japan-earthquake.html
HoopUp, a community-based art-educational tool http://hoopup.net
I am we_interactive image http://www.interactive-image.org/
iConnect-online
http://iconnect-online.org/
iHub – Nairobi's Innovation Hub
http://ihub.co.ke
[i-metro]: information commons
http://vimeo.com/user10460854
Insight Journalism.Net
http://www.insightjournalism.net
Interactive Watershed: Atlas of the San Miguel http://www.fourchambers.org/exploratorium/exploratorium_sfbay_opening.mov
"Invisible Airs" Database, Expenditure & Power
http://yoha.co.uk/invisible
iStreet Lab http://edgeqld.org.au/blog/2011/11/01/launching-the-lab/
Jaaga.in http://jaaga.in
Jaqi Aru: Promoting Our Mother Tongue Online
http://aym.globalvoicesonline.org
JeepneED Lab for the Philippines
http://www.jeepneed.org
Junk Jet http://junkjet.net
Kubatana.net – community activism in Zimbabwe
http://www.kubatana.net
Libre Bus http://librebus.org
Libre Graphics magazine
http://libregraphicsmag.com
Life http://www.vimeo.com/
floragreste
LifePrice
Like Bomb http://pixeldelay.com/portfolio/like-bomb/
Lilli – Linzer Linien – Öffis
https://market.android.com/details?id=at.linzag.linien
Liquid Democracy e.V.
http://liqd.net/
LiquidFeedback
http://liquidfeedback.org
littleBits http://www.littlebits.cc
Live Now http://www.welivenow.org
Lorea http://www.lorea.org
Made in Burkina http://issuu.com/relevant.studies/docs/made-in-burkina
Makesense http://we.makesense.org
Mamfakinch
http://www.mamfakinch.com
Matrixgrafiken
http://www.reto-schoelly.de
Meander
http://www.adeptprojects.co.uk
Meine Abgeordneten
http://www.meineabgeordneten.at/
Meipi | collaborative spaces
http://meipi.com
messages for our future: a Japanese tsunami mosaic http://www.secrettechnology.com/japan/
MetaReciclagem Network
http://rede.metareciclagem.org
MetroChange
http://blog.metrochange.org
Mideast Tunes: Music for Change
http://mideastunes.com
Mixed Reality Mirror Display
http://www.museumlab.eu/
Montségur Autorenforum
http://autorenforum.montsegur.de
My Dot Tour http://www.facebook.com/mydottour
Nerdy Day Trips
http://nerdydaytrips.com/
Newsgrape
http://www.newsgrape.com/
Noreint
http://norient.com/about/authors/
NSEAD network for sciences, engineering, arts and design
http://www.viz.tamu.edu/faculty/lurleen/main/NSEAD/
NT Mojo http://www.youtube.com/watch?v=jRmGACFJdJo&context=C3e3ea6cADOEgsToPDskK3PGYdweF895ZdWQZY1dLU
OCCCU – Occupy Currency
http://www.occcu.com
Occupy Wall Street http://occupy.net
Once Upon http://1x-upon.com/
OpenIDEO http://www.openideo.com/
Open Inspiration
http://www.OpenInspiration.com
Open Knowledge Foundation
http://okfn.org
P2P Gift Credit Cards – Gift Finance
http://www.p2pgiftcredit.com
PadiglioneInternet, The Internet Pavilion of the Venice Biennial
http://padiglioneinternet.com
pangbianr http://pangbianr.com/underground-b-sides-2/#en
PanSci-Science Citizen Network in Taiwan http://pansci.tw/
Pentametron
https://twitter.com/pentametron
Peripato Telematikos
http://www.peripato.net
Phone Story http://phonestory.org/
PirateBox
http://wiki.daviddarts.com/Press
PlainSite http://www.plainsite.org
Pontão de Cultura Digital juntaDados https://juntadados.org
Project Danube
http://versionvega.com/
Project Video Magazine European Capital of Culture http://www.european-capital-of-culture.eu/
Qomun http://en.qomun.com
Quakebook http://quakebook.org/
Queremos
http://www.queremos.com.br
Radia http://www.radia.fm
RE-DIGITAL
http://www.re-digital.org
Repetitionr.com
http://www.repetitionr.com
Respekt.net – die Projektbörse zur Erleichterung gesellschaftspolitischen Engagements
http://www.respekt.net
ROARMAG.org http://roarmag.org
Rootstrikers
http://www.rootstrikers.org
S2M http://www.s2m.to/
SAD Surveillance Awareness Database http://sadproject.tv
Safecast http://safecast.org
Sardine Manifest, the cruelty of the closed places
Sauti ya wakulima
http://sautiyawakulima.net
SecureSmartCam
http://www.witn.com/
Skype in the Classroom
http://education.skype.com/
Snail Mail My Email
http://snailmailmyemail.org
Social Aquaponics http://kijanigrows.com/oldmombasaroadfarm/ngokomi3.html
Solvyr http://solvyr.com
Stories of Chairs http://www.futureplaces.org/storiesofchairs/
Sunlight Foundation
http://influenceexplorer.com/
Syrian people know their way
http://sha3b3aref.blogspot.com/
TakeTheSquare.net http://globalrevolution.tv
teamLabHanger http://www.team-lab.net/portfolio/teamlabhanger/hanger-en.html
The Johnny Cash Project http://www.thejohnnycashproject.com/
The Postcard Collective
http://www.postcardcollective.org
The Public Laboratory for Open Technology and Science
http://spectralworkbench.org
The Social Artwork
http://www.socialartwork.org
The Vienna Experiment
http://www.theviennaexperiment.org
The Whole world is watching
http://w8r.com/the-whole-world-is-watching
Thimbl http://www.thimbl.net
Time and Place of Incident Time Notes
http://www.timenoteshouse.org/
Touch iPhone App
http://itunes.apple.com/gb/app/touch/id469617553?mt=8
Transparência Hacker
http://www.thacker.com.br
Tweet4Action.com
http://Tweet4Action.com
Universal Subtitles
http://www.universalsubtitles.org
Unlike Us: Understanding Social Media Monopolies and their Alternatives
http://networkcultures.org/unlikeus
ununi.tv – Unkonferenz am Unort

zur Unzeit http://www.ununi.tv/
urban bitLife
http://urbanbitlife.v3d.at/
Urban Spirits
http://www.urban-spirits.com
Verbeterdebuurt: Bringing civilians and local governments together
http://www.verbeterdebuurt.nl/
Visualizing.org http://www.visualizing.org/visualizations/visualizing-2011-video
webSYNradio http://www.facebook.com/profile.php?id=1694364385
whatchado – Everyone has a story to tell... http://www.whatchado.net
Wheelmap.org – Die Karte für rollstuhlgerechte Orte
http://wheelmap.org
Wiener Lerntafel
http://www.lerntafel.at
WikiHouse http://www.wikihouse.cc
Wikipedia Illustrated
http://wikipediaillustrated.org
Wlog http://www.walklog.org
www.scuolalodivecchio.it
http://www.scuolalodivecchio.it
XinCheJian
http://www.xinchejian.com
Yikon
YoungAfricaLive http://www.praekeltfoundation.org/young-africa-live.html
Youth Apartment Exchange Project
http://q.weibo.com/47534
Zaijietou Street Photography Collective http://zaijietou.com

[THE NEXT IDEA]

George Aguilar US
Martin Ankerl AT
Aikaterini Antouraki BE
Danielle Arets NL
Eric Baczuk US
Hans Baumann US
Pieke Bergmans NL
Tom Bieling DE
Peter Bijl DE
Nimish Biloria NL
Alex Cabunoc US
Virginia Carlocchia IT
Juan Carlos Carvajal Bermúdez AT
Jia Rey Chang NL
Kim Chow US
Hong-Yih Chu TW
Julien Combes FR
Ion Cuervas-Mons ES
Tjerk De Ridder NL
Tomas Diez ES
Roz Dimon US
Jan & Tim Edler DE
David Edwards FR
Ilya Firdman RU
Anaisa Franco BR
Oliver Franken DE
Paul Fredrickson US
Toly Genov US
Tsuneo Goda JP
Ulrike Gollner DE
Claudia González CL
Keith Green US
Adam Greenfield US
Darius Hajiani DE
Christoph Heindl AT
Fabian Hemmert DE
Kiyoshi Hoshino JP
Salvatore Iaconesi IT
Damjan Jagar SI
Sam Jewell GB
Tihomir Jolic HR
Mathias Jud DE
Gerrit Kaiser GB
Tai-Wei Kan TW
Minji Kang KR
Chris Kievid NL
Simon Kim US
Jirek Kocica SI
Thomas Kong US
Christoph Kopf AT
Roni Kordis SI
Sonja Maria Kröner DE
Ching Ling Lee GB
Michael Leister US
Todd Lester US
Yi-Chi Li TW
Areti Markopoulou ES
Timothy Marzullo US
Philipp Maul AT
Giacomo Miceli IT
Maria Michails US
Tarek Mokhtar EG
Leonel Moura PT
Owen Mundy US
Cora Neil US
Anna Neizvestnova RU
Rahul Nirmesh SG
Albert Yeboah Obeng GH
Forrest Oliphant FI
Michael Onyango KE
Soyoung Park DE
Joana Passi BR
Oriana Persico IT
Constanza Piña CL
Ziga Polc SI
Alex Posada ES
Matija Rijavec SI
Jeff Rowberg US
Steve Rowell US
Christoph Scholz DE
Vaibhav Somani IN
Robert Spaller US
Jennifer Stein US
Kristin Stransky Mallinger US
Dietmar Stuck Jun. AT
Doris Sung US
Anna Tereshkina RU
Graham Thompson GB
John Tylo AQ
Tomas Vivanco ES
Aleksandar Vojnovic SI
Ian Walker US
Tilo Westermann DE
Christoph Wiesmayr AT
Toshitsugu Yasaka JP
Chia Chi Yeh TW
Ji A You US
Ray Yun US

u19 – CREATE YOUR WORLD

Zejni Abdullahu
Marina Ackerl
Jannis Adamek
Peter Adorjan
Jakob Ahrer
Pia Aichmair
Christina Aigner
Agnes Aistleitner
Dan Akaczky
Yasin Aktas Lajla Alkic
Lisa Arminger
Leon Arslanovic
Semir Asceric
Alexander Au Yeong
Cornelia Auböck
Jana Augustin
Emil Avdic
Theresa Babos
Alen Bakal
Esra Bakir
Salih Bakirici
Sara Baltei
Dominic Bartl
Paula Marie Bauer
Christa Bauer
Stephan Julian Bauer
Thomas Bauer
Gerald Baumann
Selina Bayer
Marie Bechter
Valerie Berger
Verena Berger
Bianca Bichler
Lisa Bickel
Christoph Binder
Dominik Birngruber
Nadine Birngruber
Dominik Birngruber
Vanessa Bitter
David Blacher
Stanija Blagojevic
Johannes Sebastian Blatnik
Rebecca Bogeschdorfer
Lena Bohaumilitzky
Tanja Böhm
Daniela Böhm
Elisabeth Bossanyi
Nicole Brandecker
Patricia Brandecker
Anna Brandstetter
Felix Brandstetter
Johannes Brandstetter
Dominik Brandstetter
Julia Brauneis

Markus Breitenlacher
Kerstin Bruckner
Philipp Bruckner
Manuel Brunner
Martin Brunschmid
Nina Buchegger
Melanie Buchinger
Johann Buchriegler
Florian Bührle
Timea-Nicole Bukovszki
Elzbieta Burlita
Sophie Buxbaum
Hatice Cakici
Simon Casetti
Sabina Catic Cavarovic
Tereza Cavarovic
Iman Chasiew
Erol Cokovic
Karin Cui
Daniela Damian
Jelena Damjanovic
Sophie Danzer
Lukas Daxer
Bianca Decker
Georg Deinhammer
Maximilian Deisl
Bettina Denk
Lilian Derndler
Simon Deutsch
Andrea-Bianca Dhoubi
Kerstin Dirnberger
Claudia Diwold
Anna-Sophie Dock
Selina Viola
Doleschal Elisabeth
Maria Dopona
Markus Doppelhofer
Felicitas Doubrava
Gwanza Durglishvili
Julian Durstberger
Aron Ebner
Tanja Ebner
Michael Ecker
Benjamin Eckhart
Gregor Eckmayr
Christina Edegger
Juliana Eder
Claudia Eder
Alexander Ehwallner
Helene Eisenhofer
Josef Eisl
Akram El Kormany
Fatima El Morri
Ava Elahi
Constanze Englisch

Lisa Erhard
Manuel Esletzbichler
Stephanie Ettelt
Thomas Fabian
Elena Faderl
Sebastian Falk
Selina Fanninger
Alma Fetahovic
Carla Fink
Robert Fischer
Maximilian Fischer
Melanie Fitz
Stefanie Forster
Viktoria Forster
Christian Fösl
Sophie Freimüller
Miriam Freundlinger
Stephan Friedl
Judith Führer
Johanna Fürlinger
Katrin Ganglberger
Natalie Ganglberger
Christian Ganhör
Shereen Gassenbauer
Julia Gasser
Joseph Paul Gatterbauer
Maximilian Gattinger
Robert Gautsch
Alexander Gebeshuber
Sarah Gebetshuber
Michaela Gehmayr
Michael Geier
Valentin Gensthaler
Dennis Gercek
Julian Gleichweit
Xaver Goidinger
Konstantia Gölß
Carlos Gonzales-Martin
Kathrin Göschl
Julia Götz
Michelle Grabner-Haider
Patricia Graf
Georg Grasser
Johannes Greimeister
Kerstin Gressl
Dino Grgic
Nicole Griessler
Claudia Grießner
Christian Grill
Laura Grill
Alexandra Grögler
Maria Groiss
Michael Grömer
Maik Groß
Riccarda Grotte

Marcel Gruber
Jasmin Gruber
Michelle Gisela Grundböck
Tim Grünling
Valentina Grurl
Josef Gschneidtner
Lisa Gschwandegger
Bruno Gstötterer
Elisabeth Guggi
Maximilian Habl
Alexander Hackel
Lisa Hacker
Julia Hackl
Viktoria Hackl
Irma Hadziefendic
Johannes Hafner
Alexander Hagenauer
Maria Hageneder
Thomas Hahn
Christoph Haiderer
Julia Hallamayr
Kevin Haller
Aimon Hamdi
Jakob Hanner
Samuel Hanner
Michaela Hanslik
Naemi Haselauer
Nicole Haslehner
Tobias Haslinger
Matthias Haspl
Lukas Haubenhofer
Nina Haubenwallner
Marlene Hauser
Carina Hauser
Thomas Hauser
Sarah Häusle
Rene Hausleitner
Stefan Hausleitner
Endrit Havoili
Markus Heiderer
Johannes Heigl
Chiara Heilmann
Lisa Heinbach
Valentina Heinisch
Sonja Heinzl
Norbert Hemetsberger
Marie Hengsberger
Iris Hennebichler
Christian Henninger
Florian Hiden
Simone Hildenbrand
Cornelia Hinterberger
Simon Hinterwirth
Christoph Höbart
Sabrina Hödl

Julian Hofer
Christoph Hofer
Alexander Hofer
Caroline Hoffmann
Carmen Höfler
Dominik Höfling
Stefan Hofmeister
Marcel Höhl
Verena Hoislbauer
Rene Hölbling
Kristina Hold
Flora Nimue Hollinetz
Paul Holly
Daniel Holowaty
Nico Holzer
Marianne Hoppichler
Lena Horvath
Erik Hösel
Eriona Hoti
Niklas Hötzmannseder
Christina Hrdlicka
Jana Katharina Hummer
Adriatik Hyseni
Mathias Innerhofer
Serhar Irmak
Florian Jachs
Stefanie Jahoda
Jakob Janik
Johanna Janik
Matej Jaroslav
Maryam Jawadi
Lena Jelinek
Laura Joichl
Sebastian Juri
Sebastian Kaiser
Lisa Kaisermayr
Alin Kalam
Lena Kalinka
Laura Kaltenbrunner
Julia Kaltenegger
Ahmet Karadal
Eva Kargl
Rene Kaspar
Margarita Kaspar
Benjamin Kasper
Jakob Kastenhuber
Mira Sophia Salvia Kastinger
Martin Kaufmann
Pascal Kawasser
Julian Kiklin
Marcel Kilic
Jan Kiss
Ronny Kleidosty
Andrea Klein
Sabrina Klein

Christoph Kleinsasser
Emina Klicic
Andreas Klöbl
Michele Corina Kloiber
Tobias Kloihofer
Lara Köck
Florian Kögl
Harald Kogler
Robert Kogler
Anja Kogler
Nina Koller
Xhevahire Kolloni
Ines Kölndorfer
Yvonne Kolos
Matthias König
Eva-Maria Koppenberger
Ingrid Kozussek
Amin Kraiem
Magdalena Kranjec
Anja Lisa Kratzer
Tobias Krause
Felix Krause
Lena Krausler
Denise Kreuzriegler
Carina Kreuzriegler
Felix Kriegerl
Carina Kriesch
Thomas Kronsteiner
Sandra Maria Kropik
Neil Kubinger
Laurenz Kyral
Nadine Lackner
Jacqueline Lackner
Christina Lampl
Manuel Lang
Oskar Lang
Bianca Langthaler
Theresa Lechner
Daniela Lehmann
Monique Lehrbaumer
Roland Lemmerer
Stefan Lepperdinger
Daniela Lichtmannsperger
Christine Lindner
Claudia Linert
Julia Linert
Tamara Linhart
Selina Litschauer
Sonja Lorenz
Julia Ludwig
Oliver Lui
Melanie Lummerstorfer
Laurenz Mader
Felix Mader
Jonas Mader
Mohamed Mahrous
Verena Maier
Peter Maier
Gloria Maierhofer
Dominik Malinowski
Petra Mallin
Tamara Manojlovic
Vera Maringer
Patrick Marksteiner
Eva Martin
Julia Mathe
Vivian Matschiner
Carmen Mauerhofer Kapl
Max Marco Mayer
Nadine Mayerhofer
Angelika Mayr
Stefan Mazuheli
Philipp Meisl
Bea Meissner
Emma Meissner
Edvin Memic
Joyce Memic
Damir Mesic Metin
Meto Ögretmen
Denise Meyer
Paulo Meyer
William Mikulaschek
David Andrew Miller
Ashab Mintulaev
Katharina Mitter
Karoline Mödlhammer
Arthur Mohl
Antonio Moisa
Verena Mold
Gjaneta Morina
Riccardo Moser
Michael Mück
Helene Mühlehner
Benedikt Müllner
Alexandra Munteanu
Martin Naderer
Amelia Nestler
Anna Neubauer
Patrick Neulinger
Birgit Neumüller
Alexander Neuwirth
Nadja Niebauer
Michaela Niederhofer
Elisabeth Niederstetter
Sarah Nöckler
Caroline Maria Novak
Sarah Obermaier
Birgit Obermair
Kerstin Oberndorfinger
Dominik Öckhl
Marcel Oelzelt
Johanna Öhler
Raphaela Oßberger
Elias Oßberger
Sophie Osterberger
Claudia Ostermann
Sophie Pacher
Nadine Pachler
Peter Paikl
Maria Paschinger
Denise Paukner
Ursula Paumann
Melanie Paunovic
Daniela Pawelak
Markus Payer
Stefan Payer
Anna-Lena Peck
Sabine Pengelstorfer
Simon Penn
Sophia Penz
Sabrina Perkmann
Karin Pernicka
Maximilian Peter
Erich Peter Lukas Pfeifhofer
Jasmin Pflügl
Georg Pichler
Teresa Pichler
Matthias Pittrof
Tanja Pöll
Marko Popovic
Elisabeth Pöttler
Florentin Prammer
Laurenz Prammer
Lukas Prechtl
Marcel Prenn
Oliver Prexl
Anton Prinz
Bernadette Prinz
Fabian Prudky
Marco Prusa
Eva Puella
Maximilian Pulter
Anna Pumberger
Michalik Rakaczky
Steven Ramirez
Josef Ramsbacher
Sabine Ramskogler
Christina Rathberger
Alexander Ratzenböck
Daniela Reiff
Melanie Reingruber
Magnus Reinstadler
Franz Reinstadler
Simone Reiter
Lada Reiter
Anita Reithofer
Sarah Resch
Benjamin Resch
Michael Reschreiter
Anna-Maria Reschreiter
Christina Rettenwender
Sarah Rettmann
Stefan Reuter
Zohre Rezai
Thomas Rezar
Ukaj Rezarta
Pia Richter
Christopher John Roberts
Helena Röck
Daria Rodak
Florian Röder
Jonas Roither
Tanja Roschanz
David Rosenberger
Fabian Rosenkranz
Phillip Rössler
Martin Rovan
Stefanie Rumetshofer
Manuel Sackl
Büsra Saglam
Tobias Salzer
Bernhard Sampl
David Sandru
Anant Sangar
Ümit Sari
Alessandro Sasal
Valentina Savic
Julia Schauer
Bianca Schedlberger
Theresa Schedlberger
Christoph Scheffauer
Sarah Scherz
Fabian Schindler
Paul Schinnerl
Dominik Schipany
Eva Schitter
Thomas Schlager
Anna-Sophie Schlemmer
Julia Schmid
Moritz Schmid
Michael Schmidl
Lukas Schmidlehner
Sebastian Schmidt
Christoph Schneeweiss
Wolfgang Schneiderbauer
Matthias Schnöll
Christoph Schnöll
Corinna Schönbauer
Micha Emanuel Schoner
Katharina Schönhofer

Moriz Schröckenfuchs
Jennifer Schrotter
Sarah Schubert
Oliver Schürz
Maximilian Schuster
Sheena Schwaighofer
Tanja Schwamberger
Samuel Schwandl
Agnes Schwanzer
Patrick Schwarz
Moritz Schwarzl
Michael Schweighofer
Alexander Seemann
Hannah Seiwald
Asya Serimoglu
Lena Seufer-Wasserthal
Johanna Sexlinger
Omar Sharef
Lisa Sieberer
Sarah Sieberer
Stefan Christian Siedl
Felicia Sieghartsleitner
Anita Simic
Manmeet Singh
Philip Slapar
Alexander Karl Smekal
Killian Sochor
Iris Soliman
Carina Sölkner
Dominik Söllinger
Manuel Sonnleithner
Christian Sorko
Raphael Spies
Hans-Peter Spitzbart
Stephan Stadlmair
Sonja Stankovic
Patricia Stanoia
Martin Staudinger
Johannes Steindl
Ferdinand Steindl
Michelle Steindl
Eva Maria Steiner
Nina Steiner
Anna Mae Steinerberger
Thomas Steinkellner
Doris Steinmair
Jagsich Stella-Maria
Stefan Stifter
Markus Stifter
Stefan Stifter
Simon Stix
Theresa Stocker
Michael Stockhammer
Laura Stockinger
Philipp Stöllinger
Georg Stöllinger
Anna Catharina Stolz
Tobias Studnicka
Laura Stummer
Jennifer Stummerer
Michael Sturmaier
Hannes Styhler
Urzula Styrczula
Leon Sufajzl
Melanie Sujer
Lucas Sulzberger
Magdalena Sulzner
Sophie Sulzner
Joachim Sunzenauer
Tobias Süß
Christoph Süß
Andreas Süß
Daniela Süß
Zalán Szakács
Julian Szinicz
Maximilian Tabelander
David Taferner
Sinem Tanriverdi
Ahmed Tarboush
Thomas Taschauer
Selina Maria Terler
Therese Thalhammer
Sarah Thorwartl
Cynthia Thurner
Jasmin Titz
Anna Tomasiak
Sebastian Trinker
Anes Trto
Aleks Trujic
Patricia Ulbing
Katharina Ulbing
Jürgen Ulbrich
Markus Ullrich
Xaver Undeutsch
Elisa Unterholzer
Manuel Untermoser
Martin Uray
Melisa Uzunkaya
Flora Enrica Emanuela v Handel
Emma Elisabeth Giorgia v Handel
Sasa Vasiljkovic
Maria Venzl
Julia Vergianitis
Thomas Vetter
Dionysius Viehhauser
Theresa Vogl
Robin von Mendel
Daniela Vorläufer
Lukas Wagner
Kerstin Wagner
Hannah Wagner
Marcel Wagner
Martina Walchetseder
Kerstin Waldhör
Johanna Wallinger
Daniela Wallner
Jasmin Wally
Riccarda Wally
Melanie Warter
Franziska Weber
Daphne Weber
Lisa Wegscheider
Bianca Weibold
Manuel Weichselbaum
Florian Weichselbaum
Isabella Weichselbaum
Jasmin Weichselbaum
Sarah Weidinger
Susanne Weingrill
Alexandra Weinhauser
Julia Weinzettl
Alden Weiss
Laura Weiss
Max Weissenbacher
Kerstin Weixelbraun
Elisabeth-Sena Welker
Franziska Weymayer
Daniel Wieczorek
Georg Wiesenhofer
Kilian Wiesenhofer
Sonja Wilfing
Thomas Wimmer
Simon Wimmer
Saskia Wimmer
Thomas Wimmer
Andreas Winkler
Jan Winterauer
Jan Winterauer
Romed Wopfner
Xindy Wu
Clara Wutti
Nadine Yilmaz
Kimberly Zagler
Nol Zahiti
Anja Zauner
Sebastian Zehetbauer
Julia Zeinlinger
Thomas Zeiper
Carl Zeitlmann
Julian Zeller
Anja Zellhofer
Selina Zellhofer
Lydia Zimmermann
Dominik Zmek
Lorena Zorkic Rene Zorn

SCHOOLS / INSTITUTIONS

Amerlinggymnasium Wien
ASO Krems Krems
ASO Langenstein Langenstein
Berufsschule Rohrbach Rohrbach
BG/ GRG 23 Alterlaa Wien
BG/BRG Stainach Stainach
BG 9 Wasagasse Wien
BHAK Frauenkirchen Frauenkirchen
BHAK Hallein Hallein
BHAK Weiz Weiz
BORG Dreierschützengasse Graz
Borg Gastein Gastein
Borg Perg Perg
BRG 16 Wien
BRG Rosasgasse Wien
BRG/BORG Kirchdorf Kirchdorf
Europaschule Linz
GRG15 Wien
Gymnasium Schärding Schärding
HAK Bruck Bruck/Leitha
HLA für künstlerische Gestaltung Linz
HLA Herbststrasse Wien
HLFS Ursprung Salzburg
HLW Deutschlandsberg Deutschlandsberg
HLW-Steyr Steyr
Hort Mater Salvatoris Wien
HS Großpetersdorf Großpetersdorf
HS Munderfing Munderfing
HS Steinerkirchen Steinerkirchen
HS Zöbern Zöbern
HTBLuVA Salzburg Salzburg
HTBLuVA St. Pölten, Abteilung Informatik/EDVO St. Pölten
HTL Bregenz Bregenz
HTL Rennweg Wien
IRC Liebhartsgasse Wien
Kinderbüro Universität Wien Wien
Kindergarten Auwiesenstraße Linz
Komflex – Jugendbildungszentrum Wien Wien
Landesberufsschule für Tourismus Wien
MultiAugustinum St. Margarethen/Lungau
NMS Spittal / Drau Begabtenförderung Spittal/Drau
NMS Telfs – Dr. Aloys Weissenbach Telfs
NMS Zurndorf Zurndorf
NMS/HS Reichraming Reichraming
Pestalozzischule Vöcklabruck
Private Schule Elisabethinum Axams

PVS Campus Strebersdorf Wien
RG Lambach Lambach
Vienna International School Wien
VS Krems-Lerchenfeld Krems
VS 4 Mozartschule Linz
VS Asten Asten
VS Eggersdorf Eggersdorf
VS Landsteinergasse Wien
VS Langenzersdorf Langenzersdorf
VS Neußerling Neußerling
VS Pöllau Pöllau
Zentrum für Medienkompetenz Baden

PRIX ARS ELECTRONICA COLLIDE@CERN RESIDENCY AWARD

George Aguilar US
Alexander Andreou GB
Becs Andrews GB
Aikaterini Antouraki BE
Katerina Apostolska MK
Polyxeni Argyriou GR
Olga Ast US
Jason Aston US
Lina Aue Pogatschnigg GB
Orly Aviv IL
Benton Bainbridge US
Igor Baloste FR
Hayden Bannochie GB
Marian Bantjes CA
Carlos Baractho BR
Gonzalo Barahona DE
Lucy Barker GB
Tarik Barri DE
Leah Beeferman US
Amanda Belantara GB
Sarah Bell GB
Nelly Ben Hayoun GB
Adam Berg US
Julia Bezshtanko RU
Carrie Bodle US
Balint Bolygo GB
Ian Bowden GB
Øyvind Brandtsegg NO
David Brazier GB
Brooke Broussard US
Graham Budgett US
Sabine Bürger DE
Paul Bush GB
Bonnie Camplin GB
Daniel Canty CA
Teresa Carrasco DE
Shane Carrick US
Stephen Cartwright US
Claudio Osvaldo Catanese IT
Massimiliano Cerioni IT
Tom Chambers US
Daphne Christoforou GB
Matthew Cianfrani US
Alfredo Ciannameo NL
Milan Cirkovic RS
Ben Clarkson CA
Christopher Coleman US
Leonie Connellan AU
David Crooks ES
Craig Damrauer US
Eduardo Darino US
Xopher Davidson US
Christine Davis CA
Alfonso Ernesto de la Fuente Ruiz ES
Nick Demos US
Yorgos Diapoulis GR
Yuri Dokshitzer FR
Gearóid Dolan US
Maria Dolgopolova RU
Evelina Domnitch NL
Lee Donnelly GB
Nick Donovan GB
Abby Donovan US
Wendy Dubow Polins US
Alan Dunning CA
Nano Dust US
Jorn Ebner DE
Gilad Edelstein IL
Oleg Elagin RU
Archer Endrich GB
Patricia Enigl AT
Steven Erickson US
Charles Fambro US
Natalia Fedorova US
Jonathan Feldschuh US
José Miguel Fernández FR
Mikael Fernstrom IE
Michael Filimowicz CA
Davíð Brynjar Franzson US
Benjamin Fuhrman US
Shihe Gao FR
Olga Garaeva RU
Rodrigo Garcia Dutra GB
Dmitry Gelfand NL
Mohamed Ghazala EG
Victoria Gibson CA
Bertrand Gondouin FR
Tina Gonsalves AU
David Griffin CA
Alexey Grishankov UA
Jason Hall GB
Alexander Harding US
Louise Harris GB
Katharine Hawthorne US
Marika Hayashi JP
Siu Yun He HK
Robert Henke DE
Chris Henschke AU
Eno Henze DE
Anna Hill GB
Gerald Hochhauser AT
Robert Hodgin US
Carter Hodgkin US
Taylor Hokanson US
Rick Holland GB
Titus Hora CA
Alexander Horn US
Adrian Hornsby GB
Rupert Huber AT
Nick Hwang US
David Ibbett GB
Etan Ilfeld GB
Ryan Ingebritsen US
Pete Ippel US
Jake Ireland GB
Natalie Isenberg US
Takeshi Ishiguro JP
Setsuko Ishiguro JP
Jimmy Johnson US
Andrew Jones US
GX Jupitter-Larsen US
Eerees Katz-Bergmann IL
Oonagh Kearney GB
Graham Keddie GB
Solkin Keizer FR
Scott Kildall US
Carole Kim US
Mari Kimura US
Keith Kirchoff US
Olga Kisseleva FR
Sebastian Klemm GB
Ingrid Koenig CA
Joyce Beetuan Koh SG
Thomas Koner FR
Cindy Konits US
Miroslav Kostic RS
Marianna Kotsan UA
Marinos Koutsomichalis GR
Alex Kozhanov RU
Julia Krantz SE
Michael Krause DE
Laura Kriefman GB
Lauren Kronemyer AU
Anda Kryeziu CH
Aditi Kulkarni IN
Marold Langer-Philippsen DE
Jo Lawrence GB
Svein Lemarie FR
David Lettelier DE
Verneda Lights US
PerMagnus Lindborg SG
Robert Lisek PL
Jeannette Louie US
Lucy Lucy Pullen US
Clare Lymer IE
Dave Lynch GB
Lucinda Mackay GB
Chico MacMurtrie US
Francisco MacMurtrie US
Emmanuel Madan CA
Alireza Mahdizadeh Hakak NL
Walter Malaver CO
Scott Mallory Jr. US

Hektor Mamet FR
Rita Marcalo GB
Taras Mashtalir US
Ien Massey GB
Terrence Masson US
Antony Maubert FR
Simon Mckeown GB
Mollie McKinley US
Andrew McWilliams GB
Shane Mecklenburger US
Gawaine Meechan GB
Canner Mefe US
Andor Merks GB
Eric Michel FR
Takashi Mikami JP
Vesna Milanovic GB
Alève Mine CH
Oleg Molchan BY
Kasia Molga GB
Mauro Mombello IT
Pedro Morales VE
Shana Moulton US
Boz Mugabe IE
Tathagata Mukherjee IN
Tony Murray US
Richard Mutt TH
Julie Myers DE
Anna Naduda UA
Peggy Nelson US
Annabelle Ng MY
Kirsty Nichol GB
Predrag Nikolic RS
Kelly Nipper US
Jean-Paul Nogues FR
Robin Noorda NL
Philip Ntegidis GR
Matthew O'Donnell US
Daniel O'Donnell US
Brendan Oliver GB
Thomas Ollivier GB
Damian Ontiveros MX
Chiara Pa IT
Gautam Parwar IN
Mariya Pavlenko UA
Vesna Petresin Robert GB
Blaz Pirnat SI
Alexander Ponomarev RU
Mariagrazia Pontorno IT
Mariana Popescu NL
Julian Priest NZ
Rostislav Prochovník CZ
Paul Prudence GB
Yeung Pui Long HK
Viktor Pushkar UA
Renate Quehenberger AT
Hernan Quintana CO
Charles Raffety US
Rinat Rafikov RU
Martina Reinhart AT
Sol Rezza MX
Michael Rhoades US
Michael Ricciardi US
Maurice Rickard US
Kate Robinson GB
Nacho Rodriguez Bach MX
Hans-Joachim Roedelius AT
Tobias Rosenberger CN
Aaron Ross US
Tim Otto Roth DE
Mark Rowan-Hull GB
Andreas Samland DE
Marisol Sarabia Nogueda MX
Isabelle Sarrade FR
Jean Luc Sarrade FR
Tülay Schakir FI
Martin Scharfe DE
Christof Schlaeger DE
Ulrike Schüchler DE
Jeff Sell US
Anna Skotnikova (Shishkina) RU
Sarah Slifer Swift US
Gary Smaby US
Bram Snijders NL
Anastasia Zoi Souliotou GR
Travis LeRoy Southworth US
David Spriggs CA
Ben Steele US
Gerd Stern US
Lynden Stone AU
David Stout US
Debra Swack US
Peter Szely AT
Liam Taylor GB
Isobel Taylor GB
Sean Taylor IE
Nataša Teofilović RS
Hartwig Thim AT
Paul Thomas AU
Cal Thompson US
Jobina Tinnemans GB
Marco Trevisani PR
Halldor Ulfarsson IS
Allard van Hoorn NL
Hilton Vasey GB
Jose Vasquez EC
Sander Veenhof NL
Anatoliy Veretennikov RU
Iryna Vidava-Molchan BY
Roberto Vitalini CH
Jaap Vogel AU
Julius von Bismarck DE
Thomas Wagensommerer AT
Oliver Walsh GB
Craig Ward US
Haerri Weber CH
David Wells GB
Teresa Wennberg SE
Diana Wildschut NL
Christoph Witek AT
Halina Witek NL
Emmanuel Witzthum IL
Michael Womack US
Adrianne Wortzel US
Tim Wright GB
Mike Wyeld GB
James Wyness GB
Hideki Yoshimoto GB
Naama Yuria IL
Nadia Zaboura DE
Maria Zacharogianni GR
John Zaklikowski US

Ars Electronica 2012

Festival für Kunst, Technologie und Gesellschaft / Festival for Art, Technology and Society

Organization

Ars Electronica Linz GmbH

Managing Directors

Gerfried Stocker, Diethard Schwarzmair
Ars-Electronica-Straße 1, 4040 Linz, Austria
Tel: +4373272720
Fax: +4373272722
info@aec.at

Co-organizers

ORF Oberösterreich
General Director: Kurt Rammerstorfer

LIVA – Veranstaltungsgesellschaft m.b.H.
CEO: Wolfgang Winkler, Wolfgang Lehner

OK Offenes Kulturhaus im OÖ Kulturquartier
Artistic Director: Martin Sturm
Commercial Director: Gabriele Daghofer

Partners

Universität der Künste Berlin
afo – architekturforum oberösterreich
Lentos Kunstmuseum Linz
Mariendom Linz
Kunstuniversität Linz – Universität für künstlerische und industrielle Gestaltung
Landesgalerie Linz
Otelo – Offenes Technologielabor
BFI OÖ
Pädagogische Hochschule OÖ
Rotes Kreuz Oberösterreich
Youth Future Project e.V.
jugend innovativ – Austria Wirtschaftsservice GmbH
bm:ukk – Bundesministerium für Unterricht, Kunst und Kultur

Directors Ars Electronica: Gerfried Stocker, Christine Schöpf
Head of Festival: Martin Honzik
Technical Head: Karl Julian Schmidinger
Internal Organization: Veronika Christina Liebl

Production Team: Susanne Aichinger, Florian Bauböck, Katharina Edlmair, Ingrid Fischer-Schreiber, Rosi Grillmair, Oliver Haindl, Sarah Hellwagner, Barbara Hinterleitner, Simon Kopfberger, Christian Korherr, Tobias Michael Kösters, Romana Leopoldseder, Michael Lettner, Veronika Christina Liebl, Manuela Naveau, Kathrin Obernhumer, Emiko Ogawa, Maria Pfeifer, Roland Ploner, Georg Pühringer, Julia Rabeder, Miriam Schmeikal, Jutta Schmiederer, Florian Sedmak, Pia Stöffelbauer, Alice Strunkmann-Müller, Laura Welzenbach, Susi Windischbauer

Co-curators

u19 - CREATE YOUR WORLD: Susi Windischbauer
Theme Symposium: Ingrid Fischer-Schreiber, Adam Bly
Campus Exhibition: Sam Auinger, Georg Spehr
Pixelspaces: Horst Hörtner, Matthew Gardiner, Christopher Lindinger, Roland Haring, Roland Reiter
Interface Cultures Exhibition: Faculty: Christa Sommerer, Laurent Mignonneau, Martin Kaltenbrunner, Marlene Hochrieser, Michaela Ortner, Georg Russegger; Production: Ivan Petkov, Maša Jazbec; technical support: Alberto Boem; graphic design: Veronika Krenn, Vesela Mihaylova
Big Concert Night: Dennis Russell Davies, Wolfgang Winkler, Heribert Schröder
Deep Space Live: Dietmar Hager

Prix Ars Electronica 2012

Co-organizers

ORF Oberösterreich
General Director: Kurt Rammerstorfer

LIVA – Veranstaltungsgesellschaft m.b.H.
CEO: Wolfgang Winkler, Wolfgang Lehner

OK Offenes Kulturhaus im OÖ Kulturquartier
Artistic Director: Martin Sturm
Commercial Director: Gabriele Daghofer

Idea: Hannes Leopoldseder
Conception: Christine Schöpf, Gerfried Stocker
Coordination: Martin Honzik, Romana Leopoldseder, Barbara Hinterleitner
Technical Management: Karl Julian Schmidinger

Production Team: Susanne Aichinger, Bernhard Böhm, Viktor Delev, Christoph Einfalt, Ingrid Fischer-Schreiber, Sandra Gassner, Gregor Göttfert, Manuel Hartmann, Sarah Hellwagner, Barbara Hinterleitner, Romana Leopoldseder, Michael Lettner, Veronika Christina Liebl, Emiko Ogawa, Johannes Ramsl, Remo Rauscher, Theresa Schubert-Minski, Markus Wipplinger

Press: Christopher Sonnleitner, Robert Bauernhansl, Michael Kaczorowski

Marketing: Sina Balke-Juhn, Cornelia Erber, Isabella Grünauer, Martina Huber

Ars Electronica Archive: Martina Hechenberger, Nicole Höbart, Elvis Pavic, Heinz Sambs, Jutta Schmiederer, Theresa Schubert-Minski

Ars Electronica Linz GmbH

Ars Electronica Center: Andreas Bauer, Christoph Kremer, Renata Aigner, Viktoria Aistleitner, Lisa-Maria Arnreiter, Reinhard Bengesser, Tamara Böhm, Sarah Breinbauer, Blanka Denkmaier, Wolfgang Deutsch, Hans Peter Ecker, Johannes Egler, Karl Federspiel, Julia Felberbauer, Melinda File, Evelyn Fränzl, Andrea Fröhlich, Mitra Gazvini-Zateh, Christian Gerber, Elisabeth Gerhard-Mayrhofer, Fabian Geyerhofer, Tamara Geyerhofer, Nicole Grüneis, Ulrike Gschwandtner, Harald Haas, Gerid Maria Hager, Kathrin Haider, Birgit Hartinger, Florian Heiml, Martin Hieslmair, Thomas Hillinger, Denise Hinger, Gerold Hofstadler, Sri Rahayu Hofstadler, Philip Huemer, Elisabeth Innerwinkler, Thomas Jannke, Erika Jungreithmayr, Katharina Karrer, Elisabeth Kattner, David-Mathias Kemethofer, Daniel Kern, Herwig Kerschner, Viktoria Klepp, Thomas Kollmann, Michael Koller, Wolfgang König, Kristýna Krabatschová, Andreas Leeb, Sabine Leidlmair, Juliane Leitner, Dominic Lengauer, Anna Katharina Link, Kathrin Meyer, Clemens Mock, Horst Morocutti, Marc Mühlberger, Heinrich Niederhuber, Michaela Obermayer, Marlene Penn, Marius Petermandl, Svetlana Petrovic, Katharina Pilar, Armin Pils, Andreas Plakolm, Mathias Pöschko, Karl Hans Rois, Andreas Roth, Benjamin Perndl, Ulrike Rieseneder, Petra Saubolle-Hofmann, Alina Sauter, Birgitt Schäffer, Johann Schauer, Barbara Schmidt, Stefan Schwarzmair, Elio Seidl, Maria Seidl, Manfred Seifriedsberger, Lukas Steindl, Margarethe Stöttner-Breuer, Lioubov Studener, Johannes Stürzlinger, Istvan Szabo, Bhoomesh Tak, Kerstin Tak-Wakolbinger, Michael Thaler, Michael Trebo, Linda Vaňková, Thomas Viehböck, Florian Voggeneder, Karin Wabro, Florian Wanninger, Burak Yolcu, Sebastian Zach, Silvia Zainzinger

Ars Electronica Futurelab: Horst Hörtner, Christopher Lindinger, Roland Aigner, Tamer Aslan, Florian Berger, Sigrid Blauensteiner, Bernhard Böhm, Chris Bruckmayr, Cecile Bucher, Maria Eschlböck, Peter Freudling, Stefan Fuchs, Matthew Gardiner, My Trinh Gardiner, Imanol Gomez, Roland Haring, Yvonne Hauser, Christoph Hofbauer, Peter Holzkorn, Andreas Jalsovec, Martina Karrer, Petros Kataras, Fadil Kujundžić, Anna Lucia Kuthan, Martina Mara, Pascal Maresch, Johanna Maria Mathauer, Benjamin Mayr, Michael Mayr, Kathrin Agnes Meyer, Kristefan Minski, Stefan Mittlböck-Jungwirth-Fohringer, Harald Moser, Patrick Müller, Otto Naderer, Nicolas Naveau, Ali Nikrang, Hideaki Ogawa, Benjamin Olsen, Veronika Pauser, Dietmar Peter, Michael Platz, Andreas Pramböck, Gerald Priewasser, Erwin Reitböck, Roland Reiter, Vanessa Schauer, Roland Schmidt, Alexa Steinbrück, Markus Wipplinger, Claus Zweythurm

Ars Electronica Festival: Martin Honzik, Karl Julian Schmidinger, Susanne Aichinger, Florian Bauböck, Sarah Hellwagner, Barbara Hinterleitner, Romana Leopoldseder, Michael Lettner, Veronika Christina Liebl, Manuela Naveau, Emiko Ogawa, Jutta Schmiederer, Susi Windischbauer

Ars Electronica Management Services: Elisabeth Kapeller, Sina Balke-Juhn, Sebastian Bauböck, Robert Bauernhansl, Bettina Danninger, Florian Deutsch, Cornelia Erber, Michaela Frech, Bettina Gahleitner, Gerhard Grafinger, Michael Grausgruber, Isabella Grünauer, Andrea Hartl, Martina Hechenberger, Nicole Höbart, Gerald Hochhauser, Gerold Hofstadler, Martina Huber, Markus Jandl, Michael Kaczorowski, Heinz Klambauer, Martin Kneidinger, Stephan Kobler, Zulfija Magomedova, Peter J. Nitzschmann, Elvis Pavic, Heinz Sambs, Theresa Schubert-Minski, Christopher Sonnleitner, David Starzengruber, Julia Starzer, Daniel Weihrauch, Michaela Wimplinger

Ars Electronica Solutions: Bernd Albl, Michael Badics, Lukas Bischof, Youri Marko, Stephan Pointner, Gabriele Purdue

OK Offenes Kulturhaus im OÖ Kulturquartier

OK CyberArts Team
Artistic Director: Martin Sturm
Commercial Director: Gabriele Daghofer
Curator: Genoveva Rückert
Public Relations: Maria Falkinger
Technical Manager: Rainer Jessl
Production: Martina Rauschmayer, Aron Rynda
Technical Head: Markus Wallner

Production Team: Jarno Bachheimer, Attila Ferenczi, Alfred Fürholzer, Martin Haselsteiner, Bernhard Kitzmüller, Andreas Kurz, Daniel Mandel, Gerald Schreilechner, Andreas Steindl, André Tschinder, Tom Vens, Hans-Jörg Weidinger, Gerhard Wörnhörer, Simon Wilhelm

OK Team: Verena Atteneder, Johann Aufreiter, Erika Baldinger, Julia Brunner, Michael Dalpiaz, Walter Eckerstorfer, Max Fabian, Maria Falkinger, Michaela Fröhlich, Andrea Gintner, Manuela Gruber, Sabine Haunschmid, Evi Heininger, Robert Herbst, Maximilian Höglinger, Christa Höllhumer, Fritz Holzinger, Simon Lachner, Katharina Lackner, Elisabeth Lehner, Franz Minichberger, Walter Mühlböck, Wolfgang Nagl, Josef Pfarrhofer, Franz Pfifferling, Wilhelm Pichler, Angelika Pöschl, Franz Quirchtmayr, Brigitte Rosenthaler, Gerda Sailer, Markus Schiller, Ulrike Schimpl, Alexandra Schlager, Ulrike Seelmann, Renate Stummer

Brucknerhaus

Romana Gillesberger, Wolfgang Scheibner, Wolfgang Schützeneder, Ursula Kislinger

afo – architekturforum oberösterreich

Host: Gabriele Kaiser
Symposia Curators: Dietmar Offenhuber, Katja Schechtner

voestalpine Klangwolke 2012

Die voestalpine Klangwolke 2012 wird von tausenden Menschen gemeinsam gestaltet. Die Realisierung wird von Ars Electronica und Brucknerhaus geleitet.

Ars Electronica Linz GmbH

Managing Directors: Gerfried Stocker, Diethard Schwarzmair
Production Management: Martin Honzik, Horst Hörtner
Technical Management: Karl Julian Schmidinger
Production Team: Susanne Aichinger, Lisa Marie Arnreiter, Sina Balke-Juhn, Florian Bauböck, Andreas Bauer, Sigrid Blauensteiner, Florian Berger, Tamara Böhm, Christoph Bruckmayr, Hans Peter Ecker, Horst Eckl, Cornelia Erber, Stefan Fuchs, Matthew Gardiner, My Trin Gardiner, Ray Gardiner, Mitra Gazvini-Zadeh, Andreas Gruber, Isabella Grünauer, Gerid Maria Hager, Roland Haring, Yvonne Hauser, Hubert Havel, Barbara Heinzl, Sarah Hellwagner, Barbara Hinterleitner, Christoph Hofbauer, Martina Huber, Philip Huemer, Andreas Jalsovec, Michael Kaczorowski, Katharina Karrer, Harpreet Kaur, Simon Kopfberger, Christian Korherr, Tobias Michael Kösters, Christoph Kremer, Fadil Kujundžić, Juliane Leitner, Michael Lettner, Romana Leopoldseder, Veronika Christina Liebl, Martina Mara, Pascal Maresch, Michael Mayr, Kristefan Minski, Stefan Mittlböck-Jungwirth-Fohringer, Harald Moser, Patrick Müller, Otto Naderer, Manuela Naveau, Sarah Nokes, Kathrin Obernhumer, Ben Olsen, Emiko Ogawa, Hideaki Ogawa, Marco Palewitz, David Panhofer, Maria Pfeifer, Michael Platz, Mathias Pöschko, Andreas Pramböck, Gerald Priewasser, Georg Pühringer, Julia Rabeder, Erwin Reitböck, Roland Reiter, Vanessa Schauer, Miriam Schmeikal, Roland Schmidt, Maria Seidl, Martina Sochor, Christopher Sonnleitner, Alexa Steinböck, Pia Stöffelbauer, Alice Strunkmann-Müller, Thomas Viehböck, Joschi Viteka, Stefan Waschak, Laura Welzenbach, Susi Windischbauer, Markus Wipplinger, Burak Yolcu, Claus Zweythurm

LIVA – Veranstaltungsgesellschaft m.b.H.

CEO: Wolfgang Winkler, Wolfgang Lehner
Production Team: Romana Gillesberger, Daniela Haslecker, Günther Herzog, Ursula Kislinger, Bernhard Lang, Sabine Rößl, Wolfgang Scheibner, Wolfgang Schützeneder, Sandra Seitz, Claudia Werner, Hannelore Wojik

ORGANIZATION / VERANSTALTER

ARS ELECTRONICA

Ars Electronica Linz GmbH is a company of the city of Linz.
Ars Electronica Linz GmbH ist ein Unternehmen der Stadt Linz.

ORF OÖ
BRUCKNERHAUS
OK im oö kulturquartier

COOPERATION PARTNERS / KOOPERATIONSPARTNER

Universität der Künste Berlin
afo – architekturforum oberösterreich
Lentos Kunstmuseum Linz
Mariendom Linz
Kunstuniversität Linz – Universität für künstlerische und industrielle Gestaltung
Landesgalerie Linz
Otelo – Offenes Technologielabor
BFI OÖ
Pädagogische Hochschule OÖ
Rotes Kreuz Oberösterreich
Youth Future Project e.V.
jugend innovativ – Austria Wirtschaftsservice GmbH
bm:ukk – Bundesministerium für Unterricht, Kunst und Kultur
Seed Media Group

ARS ELECTRONICA RECEIVES SUPPORT FROM / ARS ELECTRONICA WIRD UNTERSTÜTZT VON:

Stadt Linz

Land Oberösterreich

Bundesministerium für Unterricht, Kunst und Kultur

Bundesministerium für Wissenschaft und Forschung

Bundesministerium für Wirtschaft, Familie und Jugend

impulse | evolve

Jugend Innovativ

Media Lt. Award

ARS ELECTRONICA RECEIVES SUPPORT FROM / ARS ELECTRONICA WIRD UNTERSTÜTZT VON:

voestalpine

bfi

Orange

Liwest

Mercedes-Benz

Linz AG

Sparkasse OÖ

Wirtschaftskammer OÖ

Ton + Bild

ÖBB

OÖ Nachrichten

Kronen Zeitung

Ö1

FM4

Felbermayr

Smurfit Kappa

Casinos Austria

Sony DADC

Technology Review

EU-Japan Fest Japan Commitee

Messe Linz

LIVA

NTS

Radio FRO

Trotec

Screenteam

Soundmasters

Banner Batterien

Soliday

Sampad

Additional Support: KulturKontakt Austria, Pöstlingberg Schlössl, Cubus

ORGANIZATION / VERANSTALTER

BRUCKNERHAUS

ARS ELECTRONICA

ORF OÖ

COOPERATION PARTNERS / KOOPERATIONSPARTNER

Heinz Biebl, Wartberg ob der Aist
Grießkogelschnalzer, Abtenau
Linzer Ruderverein Ister
EKRV Linz
Wassersportverein Ottensheim
Wasserskischule Kral
Sportvereinigung Urfahr 1912
ASKÖ Modellflugclub Linz
ASKÖ-Wassersportclub Linz
Freiwillige Feuerwehren aus den Bezirken Linz Stadt, Urfahr Umgebung, Linz Land, Freistadt, Perg, Steyr Land, Eferding, Wels Land, Rohrbach
Motor Yacht Club Nibelungen Linz
Papp Lab
Musikschule der Stadt Linz
Landesmusikschulen OÖ
Otelo – Offenes Technologielabor
RedSapata Tanzfabrik

voestalpine KLANGWOLKE RECEIVES SUPPORT FROM /
voestalpine KLANGWOLKE WIRD UNTERSTÜTZT VON:

MAIN SPONSOR / HAUPTSPONSOR

voestalpine
EINEN SCHRITT VORAUS.

TECHNOLOGY PARTNER / TECHNOLOGIEPARTNER

abatec group

Ascending Technologies

Conrad Electronic

Fanuc Robotics

HMS Mechatronik

LIWEST

Soundcloud

Ableton

Gifas-Electric

MEDIA PARTNER / MEDIENPARTNER

Kronen Zeitung

OÖ Nachrichten

Ö1

FM4

CyberArts 2012
International Compendium – Prix Ars Electronica

International Compendium - Prix Ars Electronica – Computer Animation / Film / VFX - Digital Musics & Sound Art – Hybrid Art – Interactive Art – Digital Communities – u19 – CREATE YOUR WORLD – [the next idea] voestalpine Art and Technology Grant – Prix Ars Electronica Collide@CERN Residency Award

Herausgeber / Editors: Hannes Leopoldseder, Christine Schöpf, Gerfried Stocker

Redaktion / Editing: Ingrid Fischer-Schreiber
Übersetzungen / Translations: Martina Bauer, Ingrid Fischer-Schreiber, Wilfried Prantner (Englisch–Deutsch / English–German), Catherine Kerkhoff-Saxon (Deutsch–Englisch / German–English)
Lektorat / Copyediting: Ingrid Fischer-Schreiber, Jutta Schmiederer, Dave Westacott

Grafische Gestaltung und Produktion / Graphic design and production: Norbert Artner, Mitarbeit / Assistance: Kathi Reidelshöfer
Schrift / Typeface: Klavika
Druck / Printed by: Gutenberg Werbering Gesellschaft m. b. H., Linz
Papier / Paper: BVS matt, 135 g/m^2, Galerie Vision, 285 g/m^2
Herstellung / Production: Gutenberg Werbering Gesellschaft m. b. H., Linz
Fotos / Photos: S. / pp. 118 - 121: Agnes Meyer-Brandis: Moon Goose Analogue: Lunar Migration Bird Facility, © VBK, Wien 2012; S. / pp. 288 –296: Norbert Artner; S. / pp. 295, 296: rubra

Erschienen im / Published by Hatje Cantz Verlag
Zeppelinstrasse 32
73760 Ostfildern
Deutschland / Germany
Tel. +49 711 4405-200
Fax +49 711 4405-220
www.hatjecantz.com

Informationen zu dieser oder zu anderen Ausstellungen finden Sie unter www.kq-daily.de / You can find information on this exhibition and many others at www.kq-daily.de.

Hatje Cantz books are available internationally at selected bookstores. For more information about our distribution partners please visit our homepage at www.hatjecantz.com.

ISBN 978-3-7757-3435-6

Printed in Austria

Umschlagabbildungen / Cover illustrations:
Thomas Caudron, Ingrid Menet, Laurent Mériaux, Clément Tissier / Supinfocom Valenciennes: L'ère bête; David Letellier: Versus; Hexie Farm: Dark Glasses. Portrait; Markus Kayser: Solar Sinter Project

PEFC
PEFC/06-39-27 **klimaneutral gedruckt** CP IKS-Nr.: 53401-1208-1004